"The Journey of the Owl"

~The Book of the Mind~

By: "Iron Owl"
(a.k.a. : Stephen W. Saska)

First Draft Copyright © 2004

* * * * *

This is the "Original" and "Unedited" version.
Uncut, uncensored, unexpurgated, uncompromised, unprecedented, and unparalleled…

* * *

First Edition

* * *

Abundantly and Intuitively
Illustrated
By:

~ *Kevin M. Rasel* ~
a.k.a. *"Raz"…*
("The Illustrious Illustrator")

* * *

Published in the U.S.A.
By:
The Iron Owl Liberation Press
P.O. Box 159
Cortland, Ohio 44410-0159 U. S. A.

First draft copyrighted © 2004 by: Stephen W. Saska (a.k.a. "Iron Owl")…
First printing in August., 2007…

Printed and bound in the U.S.A.
By:
"Iron Owl Liberation Press"

All Rights Reserved…

ATTENTION: Corporations, Universities, Colleges, Professional Organizations, Book Sellers, Independents, etc… Quantity discounts are available on bulk purchases of this book for retail sales or even gift purchases of six or more books, (plus shipping and handling)… Excerpts of this book can also be created for specific needs… For information, please contact:

Iron Owl Liberation Press
P.O. Box 159
Cortland, Oh., 44410-0159
U.S.A.

Or by e-mail, at:
IronOwl777@aol.com

ISBN 978-0-9796883-0-0

LCCN 2007933031

Printed in the U.S.A., and also in the U.K.

The caveat "Disclaimer"…

Although the Author/Publisher has made every effort to ensure the accuracy and completeness of information contained in this book, it still remains the personal viewpoint of the author, and despite the best of intentions, may contain errors, inaccuracies, omissions, inconsistencies, etc., for which the author can not assume responsibility, and the "reader" is requested and advised to verify the "Truth" of the information here presented… Also.., many situations regarding the Physical, Mental, Spiritual, and *Legal* well-being of the reader are addressed in this book, and the reader is further advised to consult with his "Professional" Medical Dr., Psychologist, Spiritual Advisor, Councilor, and "Whomever" may be pertinent to the situation, before acting on any information presented in this book… May God be with you on your own personal "Journey" through this book and through life…

* * *   * * *   * * *

Copyrighted © Material

It is to be understood that all preceding and subsequent materials, as well as those contained herein are copyrighted by the author. Also included in this copyright is the "Nom De Plume" (pen name): "Iron Owl"...

Copyright 2004 © by "Iron Owl"

All rights reserved. No part of this book may be reproduced in any form or by any means, including electronic or mechanical, including photocopying, recording, or by any information storage and retrieval system, without permission from the author.

Title: ***** "The Journey of the Owl" *****
Subtitle: ~ The Book of the Mind ~

~ CONTENTS ~
(with outlined overview)

(In an effort to facilitate the readers exploration through this book, and its vast diversity of subject matter, this (never done before) expanded version of "CONTENTS" has made the effort to consolidate, collate, reference, index, glossarize, appendecize, and combine these functions into a comprehensive *"locater study guide"*, to which the reader can refer, find, and "relate" this information into what will be seen as "the comprehensive whole" of *"The Great Mystic Faith in it's Entirety")*...

Hooo rah !

* * *   *   * * *

Forward.... Introduction; The Search for Truth

Book I.... The Legacy of the Owl... _____1

** To Know Thyself ** Solitude and cheap motels ** A Fifth Dimension ** The Vision of the Owl ** The Rite of Passage ** Chronology of Events ** Into the Absolute Void ** The Third Eye, of Insight ** The Sound of Silence ** The Form and Color of Sound ** The Transference of Consciousness ** The Divine Alphabet ** The Visitation of Satan ** The Fall from Grace ** The Redemption ** The Bodhisattva Vow ** The First of the "Superhuman Faculties" ** Beware the Dark Side **

Book II.... The Experience... _____14

** "Deja vu" again ** A Mystery not solved ** The Internal Strobe Light ** The Astonishment!! ** "Where is this Place"? ** The Soul Search ** The City of Gold ** The Astoundment! ** Of Divas and Behavioral Psychologists ** Of Cracker Crumbs and Universes ** Worlds within Worlds within Worlds and etc. ** The "Fifth Dimension" ** We are not alone! **

Book III.... Analysis of the Experience... _____21

** The Spoken Word; ..Evaporates! ** Evolution?; ..or Adaptive Modifications? ** Into the Microcosm ** Into the Macrocosm ** The "Missing Link", of Creation ** The Death of Existentialism **

**** Transforming Sunlight into Living Matter ** Sacred Geometry, and the Hand of Intelligence ** The Greatest Discovery of the 20th Century ** The Secret Clandestine Alchemical Laboratory ** Herbs of Mysterious Virtue **

**** Creativity; and the Lowly Skunk! ** The Question Never Asked ** From Whence Cometh this Knowledge? ** Genius; in a Butterfly's Wing! **

**** The Theory of De-evolution ** Adam; The Omega Man! ** The Zen Master, before there was a concept ** The Fall, into Self Consciousness ** Inbreeding, and Genetic Diseases ** The Tree of Life: The Microcosmic Mysteries, and the Macrocosmic Splendors ** The "Other" Tree; and Third Eye Blind ** Guilt, the World of Duality, and Naked Self Consciousness ** Good-by Methuselah **

**** *Quoting Myself;* (Experiences of the Soul) **

****The Unmistakable, Empirical, and Scientifically Conclusive **Fact** of Genetic Science: "Eve" was the Mother of the Human Race!!. ** But the Text Books.., Remain Unchanged! **

**** Obvious Contradictions to Evolutionary Theory ** A Fish!, with a Genius for Navigation, and Herculean Strength! ** There is **"Another Force"** at work, here! ** The Human Brain.., far in excess of any "Evolutionary" need **

**** The "Intellectual" Religion ** The New "Flat Earth" Society ** Their Basic Premise: "There is no God" ** Anything can be Rationalized ** The **Name** of the Religion of the Last Days ** To Which Religion do *You* Belong, Really? **

Book IV.... The Reality of the 5th Dimension... 33

** Where is this Place? ** Of Cracker Crumbs and Galaxies ** Dreams of Reality ** Buddha's Law ** The Deva Reality Consensus ** The Octave/Frequency/World/Universe/Dimension Spectrum; of Inner Space ** Eastern Vs. Western Schools of thought ** The Ancient Science ** Kundalini, and the Two Schools of thought ** The Noble Path, and the Super-Human Faculties ** The Clear Light, the Adept, and Concepts of Heaven ** The Temple of God ** The Chakras, and two more Schools of thought ** Buddhist Cosmology ** The Secret Holy Science ** Christians never go there! ** Why?? ** Intellectualism Vs. Intuition ** Personal Experiences **

**** Practical Techniques ** The Science of Transformation ** Divine Fishing **

Book V.... The Bardo... 43

** The Road Less Traveled ** Experience; the Substance of Knowledge ** Navigating the Bardo ** The Five Rules to be Observed ** Remember Your Purpose ** The After Death State **

**** Memorable Experiences ** Unmerited Favor ** Communion! ** What is it with Christ?? ** The Ladder of Knowledge ** The Threshold ** The Sin of Presumption ** On the Brink of the Abyss ** Encounter with a Demon ** Sabotaged!., by Government Interference ** The Grace of God ** Psychic Dreams **

**** "The Dark Night of the Soul" ** Forbidden Knowledge ** Sojourn through the Corridors of Hell ** Sentence carried out; to the last jot and tittle ** Abysmal Terror ** The Dilemma/Quandary ** Escape: to India **

Book VI.... Wanderings Through the Sangsara... 60

** Journey to India ** The School of Yoga ** The Question of Reincarnation ** The Combined Multiple Approach ** The Science of Alchemy ** Initiation.., One glimpse of *"IT"* in the Tavern, *Caught!* ** They Lied to me! **

**** Drugs of Virtue.., Drugs of Vice ** The War on Drugs ** The Bizarre sequence of events ** The Enormous Cost, of a losing strategy! ** The Army of Darkness ** A Police State! ** Willing Victims

** What to do?., What to do?. ** The Iron Owl Perspective ** A Solution to the Problem? ** The Cure for Heroin Addiction! ** The Violations of Life, Liberty, the Pursuit of Happiness, and Religious Freedom.., *by the Supreme Court* ** Natural Law, and Constitutional Law ** Ending the War, the Income Tax, and the National Debt! ** Where do *You* Draw the Line? ** The Ultimate High! **

**** Saving the Black Rhino, from Extinction! ** Save the Children! ** Save the Teachers ** Shifting Gears, and Curing Obesity ** Save the Marriage, Save the Family ** The Perfect Recreational Drug, *is not Alcohol!* ** Save the Country! ** A Better "Smart Bomb" ** Save the World! ** The Brotherhood of Solomon ** Ushering in the New Millennium ** Well, was that "Over the Top", or what? ** Charts and Graphs **

Book VII.... The Secret of Secrets...   **90**

** Herbs of Mysterious Virtue ** Ritual and Procedures ** The Spirit is Holy ** The Secret of the "Lost Word" ** The Bardo ** The Vagaries of the Mind ** Levels of Abstraction ** The Art and Science of Contemplation ** The Sacrament, the Gift of God ** Summation and Recommendations **

Book VIII.... The Training of the Mind...   **97**

** Consequences of an Untrained Mind ** Visions of Hell ** Escape to India ** The Technique ** the Life Breath ** Exercise in Concentration ** The Three Types of Thought ** Objectivity and Zen Absorption ** Subjectivity, Positive and Negative ** Training the Dog ** Seed Thoughts and Magic ** Discriminating Between Good and Bad Seeds ** Accent the Positive, Eliminate the Negative ** "The Great Work" ** The Way of the Western School ** The Voice of the Silence ** Your Purpose and Destiny ** For the Benefit of Mankind **

**** Treatise on the Sub-Conscious Mind ** A "New" Discovery ** A Separate and Distinct Entity ** A Faithful but Simple Animal Consciousness ** The Cognitive "Alpha" Alien ** The Ethnic Diversity of the Sub-Conscious ** Traumas to the Sub-Conscious, resulting in Phobias and Aberrations ** Desecration of the Temple; *Gay*, is a Lie! ** This Contagious Disease that Contaminates the Soul.., and Spreads.., *Exponentially* !! ** The Power of Suggestion ** Mans Best Friend, when Properly Trained **

**** These Original Findings, Supported by Scientific Contributions ** The "Split Brain" Experiments ** Two Separate Entities, One Body! ** The "Alien Hand" Phenomenon ** Single Mindedness, Wins! **

Book IX... The Great Debates...   **111**

** Debate at the Ashram ** The Swami Knows ** The question of God and the Soul ** Eastern school vs. Western school ** The Compendium of Knowledge ** Krishnamurti and the Epiphany ** Solution to the Zen Riddle ** The Shiva-Shakti "shift" and "one hand clapping" ** The Buddha Teaches ** The "Variegated Cloak" of Words **

**** Proofs of God ** Contradictions in Buddhism ** Buddha, Bodhisattvas, and Immortality ** The Test of Wisdom ** Our Hero Lives**

**** Buddhas, Bodhisattvas, Saints, and the Common Man** Out of body states ** Objectivity and Expansiveness ** Subjectivity and the Self-conscious Ego **

**** The "Pearl of Great Price" ** the Knowledge of the "Self" ** One in a Million **

**** Prayer to the "Root Guru" ** One God,.. a Multitude of Names **

**** The Philosophers Stone; the "Rock" of ages ** Spiritual Alchemy, and the "Living Word" ** Communion and Dialogue ** The "Ancient Way" **

**** Enlightenment ** All Knowledge and the Unified Field ** The "First Cause", and the spiders web matrix of correspondences ** The "Fifth Dimension", and the spectrum of "Universe-World-Chakras" ** Concepts Beyond Conception **

**** "The Last Days" ** The Four Horsemen ** Is this a Joke? ** "The Time is Near" (2000 Years Later, and still counting) ** "So What"??? ** Corroboration.., by the Buddha! ** The "True" Signs of the Last Days ** The Time is;.. *"Now"*!!... **

Book X....   Nepal.., and Meetings with Remarkable Minds…   136

** Bus ride to the roof of the World ** Looking down on Shangri-La ** Trade route and cross-roads to ancient Kingdoms and Mystical Realms ** A Meeting of Minds ** Stories, Smoke, and Laughter ** The Secret Revealed; The Most "High" God ** Journey to The 14th Century, B.C.E. ** The Luckiest of mortal men ** The Temple of "Swayambhu" ** An unlocked door to the ancient "Space Age" Science ** The Liberation of the Soul through Sound ** The Scientific appeal of Buddhism ** Christianity doesn't have that! ** The "Stargate" to inner realms ** Christians never go there! ** Herbs of Mysterious Virtue ** Conspicuousness by Absence ** The Barefoot Holy Man, and the Face on the Shroud ** Shakespearian eloquence, and the voice of authority ** The "Father" speaks: from the Nuclear, to the Astro-Galactic, to the Metaphysical ** Power beyond charisma ** Voices of dissent ** A Quandary of Contradictions ** Consultation with an Urban Legend ** Decision at the cross-road of life ** The Confrontation ** The Road not taken; the Quandary deepens ** Escape from Nepal**

**** Introspections in Retrospect ** What would you have done? ** The fork in the road ** Televangelism and the true believer ** An avalanche of words; diced, spliced, dissected, translated, etc. ** The "Living Word" has become the "Lost Word" ** "The Way" ** Jesus Christ finger suckers ** Standing with the Martyrs ** Who knows **

**** The Bible; (Paraphrased, Simplified, Condensed) ** Rene Descartes; logical and empirical conclusions ** Genesis Exonerated ** "Let *Us*" make Man" ** The fall of Satan ** The Trees of Good and Evil ** The fall of Mankind ** Sodom and Gomorra ** The Prophesy; to rescue Mankind ** The Epic Battle ** The Greatest Love Story ever told ** Prophesies fulfilled & Satan's vengeance ** Teach your children ** Discriminate! Choose Life!

**** The Intellectual's "Intellectual" ** Shakespeare and Jeremiah ** Literary styles compared ** "Tales told by an Idiot" Vs. "Historic Parables" ** "To Be, or Not to Be" **

**** The Proverbial "Philosophical Coin" ** Which side of this coin? ** "Ye must Believe" ** The "Written Word" Vs. the "Living Word" ** The Bible as a Testimonial; ("Old" & "New") ** Belief, a poor substitute for Knowledge ** The "Ego" is not welcome here ** "Communion" and Absorption ** What Life is all about! ** Methodology **

**** "From Out of the Mouths of Babes" ** The cult of the "Bwiti" ** The Cross and the Book; The Religion of the "Whites" ** To Hear with the ears, or to "See" with the eyes ** "Eboga" the Sacrament that enables us to see ** One picture is worth a thousand words, one "Vision"; Priceless ** Vision Equals Knowledge transcendent over belief ** The Religious Experience that cures addictions ** The Science of "Altered States" ** Search and Research; in the interest of Science and Humanity ** A Plethora of Religions and a plethora of Sacraments ** Only the Brave should Enter Here ** Back to the Future **

Book XI.... Thailand, the Sexual Oasis... _____162

    ** Meandering through the Sangsara ** Sin City #2 ** The Sexual Oasis ** Householders, Celibates, and Me ** The Drug of Sex ** The "Specialist" ** The Middle Way **

    ****Timeline; MDA, the "Love Drug" ** Her naked glory, and the "polar opposite"! ** The Secret of Profound Meditation ** The Sky Opens, a Fifth Dimensional Experience ** Religious experience vs. the Secular mind ** The Question remains; "What if "? ** Expanded Consciousness, personal ethics, and objectives **

    **** The Mystery of Women ** Damned liars and idiots ** The Grand Scheme ** Vive la Difference, vive la Mystery **

    ****Buddha Grass and the Unified Field ** Prison!., The Million Dollar Experience ** Advice to Travelers ** Yoga, Zen and the Martial Arts ** The Ultimate Wisdom ** Muscle Tone, Mental Tone, and the Bodi Tree ** The Exit Railroad ** Beautiful Bangkok.., My Heart Grieves **

Book XII.... Incident in Laos... _____172

    ** Idyllic Train Ride to idyllic times ** Aftermath and prelude to war ** Rickshaw to Opium land ** The "Pipe" and procedures ** The Sweetly Perfumed Essence of Seduction ** Speculations about the Buddha ** Mind-Body Separation and the "Isolation" of Soul from Mind ** The Profound Centeredness and Gengis Khan ** To rule the World,.. or Not ** Alternate realities and Worlds of Deception ** Questions of Reality ** The Pagoda of Converging Dimensions ** Humility ** Buddha's Law, and Dreams of Reality ** The "Root Guru", and the "Pranja Paramita" **

    **** The Politics of Opium/Heroin ** The War of "Good vs Evil" ** Opportunities Missed ** Alchemy and World Peace ** The Gospel of "Dame Cicily" ** Let Wisdom prevail **

Book XIII.... Incident in Singapore... _____187

    ** The Boom Town of the Orient ** The Jungles of Sumatra, and the Search for Oil ** The Best of Friends, and Tragic Misunderstandings ** Samadii; The "Father" Speaks.., the Vision unfolds ** The Contagious Disease that Contaminates the Soul ** Satan, and the Mark of the Beast! ** We are at War! ** Abominations on the march ** The Unthinkable.., has Happened **

Book XIV.... Seership and Obligations... _____200

    ** Interrogation at Boogie St. ** The Question of Seership ** Only the Hand Without a Wound.., can Safely handle Poison ** A Revelation within a Revelation, Within a Fraction of a Moment ** All Men are Seers, if Only they Knew ** The "First Cause", and the Key to Genius ** To Write!., or be Derelict in my Duty ** A 30 Minute Flight; from Jet Age to the Dawn of Civilization ** Hacking and Slashing in the Arm-Pit of the World ** The Devil; a Stumbling-Block, a Reality, *and a Faggot.!.* ** My Best Friend, Runs Away from me! ** A Curse; to See into the Hearts of Men ** What is the Point? ** Don't Go There **

    **** "Gratitude in Retrospect" ** Raised in the Era of "Happy Days" ** Good Teachers, and Queer Encounters ** Casualties of "the Dark Side" ** The Adventure Begins; Life on the Road ** Journey to Manhood ** I, "Iron Owl the Lucky" ** The Forewarning.., I Hope I'm not Too Late! ** Life in the Suburbs, and Faggot Lies **

    **** "Political Correctness" and the "Flat Earth" Mentality ** Instant Notoriety; in exchange for your Soul ** Marching under a banner (gay).., *that is a lie!* ** The "Supreme" Court, Vs. The Founding Fathers ** The "Rude and Crude" Truth of the matter ** The Desecration of the Temple ** This is War!, Choose Your Side ** Discriminate Wisely, Serve the Lord, and Vote! **

**** The Boy Scouts of America ** Under attack!, by Perverts, Atheists, and other "Liberals" ** Perverted Intentions: *Scouting for Boys!* ** The Blatant Disregard; for God, Reverence, and Moral Straightness ** Stand Your Ground, and "Be Prepared" **

Book XV.... Episode in Singapore... _____ **211**

** The World of "Work", and Life's Lessons ** Rough-necking for Oil in the South China Sea ** Massive Proportions, Massive Power ** The Choreographed Ballet of "Tripping the Pipe" ** Leave-time in Singapore.., and then I saw "Her"! ** The Archetypal Zen Beauty Anomaly ** A "Warrior Queen", and "Alpha" Female ** A Cosmic Conspiracy, Slap-stick Comedy, and "I", the Clown ** Humiliation, Rejection, Retribution, and Poetic Justice ** Wounded in Love, (or whatever) ** *Sha-zam!!*. The Utterance of the Magic Words of the Magic Formula ** Restoration and Celebration ** I had lamented too loudly, *and I had been heard!* ** The *Defiant* Solution to the Universal Problem ** To Present to the Lord.., Gifts.., of Men ** Ibogaine; "The Healing Drug" ** Ancient Yesterday; No bearing on Today ** Meanwhile, Back in Singapore ** the Roughneck Haven; the Night-club ** An Act of Bravado ** The Clown/Buffoon ** The Reality check ** You Win some, You Lose some ** The Lesson of Solomon ** Some Things Never Change ** Moving on **

Book XVI.... Scope and Limitations... _____ **222**

** (An Overview) ** The Indonesian Holy Man ** The Cult of "Subud". and the Initiation in Calcutta ** Going the "Extra Mile", etc., and etc. ** Pissing off everyone equally ** The Parting of the Red Sea, but not the Railroad Tracks that lead to Auschwitz ** Enormous Trivialities, and the mental "Mind-Fuck Trap" ** "My Kingdom is not of this World", *and neither is yours!* **

**** Is this a book about Religion?? ** The Comprehensive Whole, and the Complete Body of Knowledge ** *Aha!!* The Question of all questions ** The Key to the Vault, and just *What* does the Treasure Consist of? ** The Folly of "Casting Pearls before Swine" ** The Treasure map Revealed, but will *You* Possess the Treasure? ** Stay Tuned **

**** Is this book a Biography?? (*Heavens No!!*) ** The Quest, common to all of Mankind ** Many stories to tell ** The Quest Continues **

**** Is this a book of Adventure and Travelogue?? ** The Quest to Know, the Adventure of a Lifetime ** To the far Corners of the Earth, *and Beyond!* ** The plane of "High Adventure" **

****Is this Book of "High Adventure" about Drugs?? ** Research Professionals, Prejudice, and the non-experienced ** Lets get Real ** The Critical Factor ** Uppers, Downers, and Sideways ** Getting "High" vs. getting "Stoned" ** Assholes and extremes of Stupidity ** A Diametrically Opposed different Purpose in Mind ** For the Edification of the Few ** The Oldest Document in the World!! ** This is going to Piss-Off a lot of people!! ** The "Key" that Unlocks the Vault ** The Treasure Revealed!! ** This is the *"Truth"* about the Soul **

**** Is this book a Belief System?? ** I don't believe.., *In Belief !* ** The Endless *Blood-bath*, of Armies of Believers! ** Do you really believe, or do you only believe that you believe? ** Show me the "Signs" ** The Difference between simple "Faith", and complicated theology ** In the face of not knowing (*ignorance*), you're going to believe "something" ** You must be very careful what you believe ** "Talking the talk", vs. "Walking the walk" **

**** Is this a book of Science?? ** *Oh Yes* !! Examine and evaluate my findings ** The Multi-Dimensional aspects of an Infinite Universe ** The Reality of the "Fifth Dimension", and "Facts" that are non conceptual ** Secular Science; working feverishly to prove the non-existence of God!! ** Absurdity; the basis of all humor (Pardon me for laughing) ** Experiments of that "mad" scientist: "Iron Owl; the Facetious" ** The *Timeless*-Space Continuum ** The Eternal, ever present.., *Now!!* **

Worm-holes through space; the ultimate "Oxymoron" ** The First Law of Thermodynamics; Violated! ** The "Self Generating" energy source, the energy/matter conversion, and "space dust" ** Theoretical Astrophysics, and the Physical/Metaphysical convergence; (a foregone conclusion) ** The "Fifth Law" of Thermodynamics: "The Quintessential Law of the Primordial Quintessence" ("Life", in the Universe) ** But does it really matter?? (Oh Yes!) ** Books have been written, battle lines have been drawn ** The Supreme Court, and the *antithesis* of Thomas Jefferson's intentions ** Pissing-off everybody (again) ** The "Abomination that causes Desolation": Constitutionally Protected by the Supreme Court! ** ***"God"!*** ; a *Scientific fact* outside of and beyond Belief or Religion ** One more Scientific fact to present: (*the obligations of Duty*) ** In the course of my research.., *I encountered an "**Entity**"* ** The preeminent "Flaming Faggot" of all Time; the personification of Evil ** "Star Wars"; (The Epic Struggle): "The Supremely Good" vs. "The Diabolically Evil" ** Will you be the Hero of your life, or will you be the "Asshole"? ** Choose Now, to which side you belong, and whom will you serve ** A "Fair Witness" testimony ** But will the world of Secular Science acknowledge my findings? …What do you think?? **

**** So.., just what is the "Scope" of this book??.   ** To solve the Riddle of the Universe, to see the Scheme Entire ** All Knowledge, and the Unified Field ** The Matrix/Paradigm of Genius, (a.k.a.: "Enlightenment") ** Everything Relates!., (except errors and lies) ** Did you think that Heaven was merely a "*Place*" ?? ** This ***"Event"***, that is the death and rebirth of the "New Man" ** A "Champion", able to traverse the seven planes of existence ** ***This..,*** is the scope of this book! **

**** So.., just what are the "Limitations" of this book??   ** The Scope is too great, the ability of the author; too small ** No natural talent, no editor, no research dept., no feedback, no proof-reader, organization is "after the fact", and no publisher (yet) ** Condensing the Elaborations, limiting the tangents, and holding my tongue ** Too many, but not enough pages **

**** So.., is this a book of the Mind??   ** Preeminently a book of the Mind, Primarily a book of the Soul ** Mind as the "organ" of the Soul ** Mind; as contrasted with Matter ** "String Theorists", and the "11th dimension" ** Zeno's Paradox, or the Absolute Void ** Does the "String" utter the Sound, or does the "Sound" utter the String? ** A multi-ordinal term, with a multitude of meanings, lacking substance ** A Mystery contained in a riddle, contained in a paradox ** The word-trap quagmire ** The Zen state of mind: *"Named", and claimed!!* ** Identifying and *Naming* the various states of mind (gives you power and control over them!) ** Guilt, and the "Wounded Ego"; (the strongest "locked in" ego state) ** A precursor to disease in the body ** Zen "Enlightenment" and the "Born again" experience ** East meets West, the crowning achievement! ** No Yin without Yang.., no Siva without Sakti ** Doctrinal Errors resolved, the Soul (and the Primordial "Essence") discovered, and: ***"Aha!"*** ** Transformation!., at the gut-wrenching level of the emotions (the "Born Again" catharsis) ** West meets East: Zen objectivity and the doorway to the "Fifth Dimension" ** Welcome, to the Kingdom of God! **

**** Treatise on the Sub-conscious Mind ** Our Faithful animal companion and counterpart ** Those things and practices that are detrimental to our sub-conscious well being ** The perverted, the "secularly naïve", and degradation to the "sub-status" of "surrogate female" ** Limp-wristed, effeminate, and submissive ** The desecration of the Holy Temple; (the "Abomination") ** The "Sick" game of domination and subjugation that spreads this "Disease" ***exponentially!!*** ** The "Queering of America"; their unstated goal ** This "Unholy Movement", and sedition from within ** This Nation could fall!, like Greece and Rome fell, like Sodom and Gomorra fell ** Blind Belief vs. Blind Unbelief ** Condensing *This* Book, into just one paragraph ** The Interplay between the Conscious and Sub-Conscious ** A Marvel of Unity and the Crowning Achievement of Life on Earth ** The "Isolation" (abstraction) of Soul from Mind (a.k.a.: "the Unmodified state") ** The "Zen shift" takes on a whole new dimension (words fail to convey) ** Spiritual Alchemy and Tradition ** Both Teachers and Candidates of the "Way" are in short supply ** Applications are now being taken.., Apply Within… **

**** So, Why did I write this book?? ** Being "Thrice Blessed" in the "Crap Shoot" of life ** Confrontation with Mortality ** My Legacy; a tempest in a tea cup ** The "Bodhisattva Vow", and *abject failure!* ** Yes, Assholes *could* become Hero's!., and be "Born Again" ** Telling what I Know ** Not for your intellectual assimilation, but for you to verify for yourself, by your own experiences ** Keep the Commandments, and do good.., every chance you get ** Amen **

Book XVII.... Purgatory... _____**248**

** The Purging ** Alone with my Soul, drifting in and out of a fifth dimensional reality ** Symbols, Visions, and the Spoken Word, punctuated by bouts of nausea ** "I see dead people" ** Zombies in Limbo ** The "Bardo of the After-Death state" ** Fear and Trepidation (one just doesn't go to see the Lord as an afterthought) ** The Punishment: *"Here* (in Purgatory), *is where you will serve"!!.., and stop smoking pot!!.* (*Oh no, oh no, Oh God, no!!* ** The Bitter Pill: (severely reprimanded, dismal despair) ** Being put to the Test! ** Drifting in and out of that terrible place of the dead.., *and the dead were looking to me!!* ** Through the Veil, and setting foot on the Earth.., *but it wasn't Earth!!* ** Trying to make sense of it all ** Decision at the Alligator Swamp ** So clever that I outsmarted myself ** Déjà vu, Déjà vu.., Oh no, oh no, I will not make that same mistake again ** Like the Sun emerging from the clouds, the "New Heaven" and the "New Earth" ** Doing rescue missions into the Bardo.. Send me!., I will go.., *I WILL GO!!!* ** Obedience to the Lord; the height of Wisdom ** Something to think about **

**** To repeat the experience.., one year later ** A very strange fellow, a very spooky place ** A suicide note, just in case I should die ** The Search for Knowledge; not a simple walk in the park ** Interruption at the most crucial moment ** Missing the "Peak" ** Journey to Sodom and Gomorrah ** Ugh!.. Why should *"I"* be shown *"this"*?? ** Three Times!!. **Enough!!,** I said... Why me?? ** I have no intention of becoming an activist, or crusader, or anything like that! ** The truly frightening thing ** The loss of a friend, and access to Ibogaine ** Psychic Dreams, symbolism interpreted ** The *"Comforter",* thank God…

**** A Diplomatic Endeavor, a letter of apology ** The same road, different conclusions ** Astrology, and other subjects relevant to this book ** The "Riddle of the Sphinx" ** The Prophesy; the Epic Struggle depicted in the Stars ** Astrological profiling and "handicapping" the horses ** The **Big** question: "Who" screwed it up? ** The "Tower of Babble" is a metaphor ** The "Diaspora" ** "Somebody" has to say *"Something"*! ** The Long and Winding Road, vs. the "Straight" and Narrow ** Simple Logical Deductions ** "Shit Happens", what can I say? ** Apology rejected.., End of story.., temporarily **

**** Artwork and the Tarot ** the Game of Life ** the Tower of Babble ** the Alchemist ** the Fool's Return ** the New Earth **

Book XVIII.... The Preliminary Prerequisite... _____**271**

** The Journey begins with "That *Mandatory* Preliminary First Step".., (that is the Last Chapter of this Book) ** A Martyr to goodness, ensnared in a web of trivialities ** I *"hated"* that legless, sorrowful, little old man ** My New Philosophy: "Self Righteous Selfishness" ** Confrontation with that "Little Old Man" ** The Transformation: "His".., and mine! ** The Art (and virtue) of Selfishness ** The Martyr exposed; a sham and a tragedy ** The very best day.., of my entire life! ** Adam Smith, and "The Wealth of Nations" ** Economics and the Bottom Line ** "To Thine Own Self Be True" **

**** The Fork in the Road; the change of heart ** This *most significant* change of heart, and the *most significant* "External Event" **: "The Baptism of Fire" (for Serious Students only) **

**** The "Game of Life" ** The Ultimate Game, propounded by the "Ultimate Gamesman" ** The "crapshoot" (just the luck of the draw) ** Your Role in the game (and how well will you play) ** The Rewards (or Losses) in the Game ** The Obstacles in the Game ** The Objectives of the Game ** The Ultimate "Scavenger Hunt" ** This is a very serious game (for real) ** Discovering: "The Great Mystic Faith in it's Entirety" ** The only "Way" out of the Game.., lies Within ** Heaven lies Within you **

**** The End! ** "Death"; the Grand Illusion ** Surprise, surprise, the Joke is on you! ** Selfishness, Sincerity, and the "Will to Good" ** The Closing Statement of this Book! ** Hallelujah!.., Go With God!.. **

**** Well.., If that was the closing statement, why am I still writing?? ** "The Never Ending Book" (always another chapter left to write) ** One more story to tell ** Conversation with a "Mongoloid Idiot" ** The Pool Game from "Outer Mongolia"!! ** An impossibility, three times in a row! ** What the Hell just happened here?? ** Just when you think you "Know It All" ** Lesson from a Mongoloid: "You don't know "Jack Shit" ** Vanished without a trace ** The Lord has a sense of Humor!! ** The Universe Laughs **

Addendum…. Conversations with the Devils Advocates…   **282**

** Objections to this book, by the "D.A." (publisher, critics, etc.) ** "I can't publish this"! ** Inflammatory Words vs. the Inflammatory Truth ** To be a commercial success (or not) ** Making common place and acceptable *those things which are Expressly Forbidden* ** Instant Notoriety, by lowering the bar of the unacceptable ** A "face to face" encounter ** This expose falls to me ** Fanaticism and Truth ** I have to say **Something**, **Somebody** has to say **Something!** ** Gullibility to the point of Criminality ** Homophobia, and the "Mark of the Beast ** This is not mental health.., not what you want for your children. ** In defiance of the will of "**We the People**" ** There is a "Flaw in the System" ** "**Failure to Discriminate**"!.. A Crime of the First Magnitude ** Sodomite "marriage", *opens up a whole new can of worms* ** The Pandering and Procuring of Children (into the hands of sexual deviants) ** The "A.C.L.U."., and "Un-American Activities" ** **Take a Stand!** Refuse your Vote, and refuse your business ** Drug Laws, for the Edification of the *Many* ** Altered States and the "Underground Audience" ** The "Flat Earther" will explain away everything, and never "Know" (but will always condemn) **

*** The Debate goes on.., the Debate never ends ***

* * *

*** INTRODUCTION ***

This book is unique in this one respect… It is a book of first-hand experiences that qualify the author as being a "Seer"… One doesn't become a Seer over-night, but only as a consequence of having had a multitude of experiences and seeing first-hand those things that are largely hidden from the view of the common man who has no interest in seeing… To become a Seer, one must first become a Seeker… Seek and Ye shall find", is the universal dictum, but rare indeed is the Seeker after "Truth", and just where indeed, may that "Truth" be found??.

Some people say that the Truth can't be known, that Truth is whatever you believe… There is my truth, your truth, his truth, their truth, the Christian truth, the Hindu, Buddhist, Moslem, etc., and etc… So.., can the Truth be known??.

Yes, the Truth can be known.., because the Truth is an "outside" event, and it is not in the least influenced by what you believe or don't believe… The "Truth" stands alone…

For all of recorded time, and before, mankind believed that the Sun traveled every day, around the Earth… It was even a religious precept!.. But never once did the planet Earth refrain from its journey around the Sun… Never once did the Sun try to accommodate the beliefs of man!.. This is an "outside" event, and not effected by what you think or believe… Believing otherwise doesn't make it so… It is what it is, and that's the truth… Anything that isn't the truth is an error.., or a lie… History records the harsh treatment given to Galileo when he told them the truth…

And the Truth is unforgiving!.. If you are lost in the desert, and believe the Oasis to be in the North, and it is not, your bones will bleach in the Sun… Most of mankind is lost in the desert… Some think the Oasis lies in their own particular religious direction… Some think that the Oasis is a lie, that there is no Oasis… Some don't know about the Oasis… Some intellectualize about the Oasis… Most just don't care… Most don't realize they are lost in the desert!.. Only a handful ever set out on their own journey to the Oasis.., only a few ever get there…

But directions are lacking!.. Our Hero *(yourself)*, the intrepid explorer, must research all the pertinent information available, separating truth from fiction, and come to a reasoned conclusion as to the truth of the matter, and proceed with cautioned determination towards that goal.., praying that his reasoned conclusions somewhat approximate the Truth…

So what are we talking about here??. Are we talking about replacing one set of beliefs.., for another set of beliefs??. *No, No, **No..!*** Belief is the *antithesis* of Knowledge!!. To say that you believe.., is to say that you don't know… *We are talking about **Knowing..,*** and the only way to truly Know, is to have the direct first-hand ***experience*** for yourself!!!.. Anything less than this *first-hand direct experience* will not satisfy "Our Intrepid Hero".., the Seeker of the "Truth"…

The interesting thing about becoming a Seer, is that with every experience, you get to see a little more, and progressively, the more you see, the greater becomes your scope of Vision, and even more importantly, you develop the ability of ; "Inner Hearing"… ***This!.,*** is the secret of all Secrets.., because what you hear with your "Inner Hearing.., is the "Inner Voice"!!!… This "Inner Voice" is the same Voice heard by Abraham, Isaac, and Jacob… It is no less than the Voice of the Lord!… The entire Bible, from beginning to end, Old Testament and New, Bibles from other Religions.., all testify to this fact.., and interestingly enough, this is the most "overlooked fact" of the entire Bible, with good men searching diligently, reading the "printed Word", and missing the point of actually "Hearing" the "Living Word", spoken by the Living God, to living men.., and as ***That*** Voice speaks, there is Vision, and the Vision is revelation, the revelation is Knowledge.., and you will Know!… ***All*** men are Seers.., *if only they Knew…*

So this is a book of experiences!.. But more importantly than that, it is a book of **directions** that lead to the experiences.., and you are being invited to experience the *"Magnificent Experience"*.., that you may validate the Truth for yourself.., and you will **Know**!!. Belief is relative.., but Knowledge is absolute!!. Without Knowledge, there is no Wisdom… **Wisdom reigns Supreme!!…** The beginning of Wisdom, is; "get Wisdom"… As Knowledge is the prerequisite to Wisdom, so too, *Experience* is the prerequisite to Knowledge…

The Knowledge of the "Way", is priceless information that can prevent my people from getting lost in negative pursuits, and instead, direct their energies into the most important work on Earth.., the Enlightenment of their Souls, for their own benefit, and more importantly, for the benefit of all humanity… This *transformation*, is known as "The Great Work", and it is the reason and purpose for your existence on this Earth… Wisdom dictates.., that you follow the "Way"…

This information has been a closely guarded secret, traditionally handed down from teacher to student… There is a shortage of both teachers and students… It is a secret to the vast majority of humanity because they simply do not care!.. It remains a secret to the rest of humanity because they are locked into "belief systems" that precludes any chance of a real first-hand experience whereby the Truth may be known…

Thee "Inner Voice" asked; "Would you want to be a savior to your people"??. I contemplated the matter deeply (*for a fraction of a second*), and I answered; **"Sure"!!…** This book is a response to that question…

Who are "my people"?.. My people are their own people!.. Those people of independent thought, who hear my words and take them to heart… Those people who make a choice to follow the path of Wisdom, and depart from error… My people are those people who are driven beyond the limits of belief, and seek with all their hearts.., **to Know!..**

This book is dedicated to the Spirit of those people who want to "Know"…

* * * * * * *

BOOK I

"The Legacy of the Owl"

It was the 1960's.., and it was a unique time, like no other time in history!.. It was "Revolution American Style", and it took a myriad of forms, with a myriad of Hero's and Anti-Hero's.., and their weapons weren't guns and bullets.., their weapons were "Ideas".., and every faction was represented: Left, Right, and Center… Their leaders took the form, not of Generals and Politicians, but of Poets, Songwriters, Intellectuals, Book Authors, College Professors, Holy Men, and Radicals, marching in the streets, carrying placards and shouting slogans… It was called a "Cultural Revolution", and the spark that lit the fuse was the discovery of a new class of drugs that were called; "Psychedelics".., and they were available to everybody…

They had done it!.. They had actually done it!!. It was called (by some) the greatest achievement of the 20th Century… They had actually synthesized the legendary "Elixir of Immortality".., The "Soma".., "The Drink of the Gods"; that opened the portals of the Soul, cleansed the "Doors of Perception", and opened those doors onto a "New Reality".., an "Inner Reality".., and the World changed.., and it would never be the same again…

Whether that change was for the better or the worse has been hotly debated ever since…

* * * * * * *

"To Know Thyself " was the great dictum of the ancient philosophers… My first few LSD experiences were in the company of a good and trusted friend, but now it was time to go into my own mind on a solitary mission, just to see what there was to see… To embark on this solitary mission required a place of solitude. Solitude is not that easy to find!.. I could not find solitude in my own home, there were just too many distractions, too many interruptions. Solitude could not be found in the countryside. If the flies and mosquitoes didn't bother you, someone would come by and want to know; "What are you doing out here all alone?". I finally decided to rent a motel room, lock myself in, and lock the outside world out. It was early in the day, as I checked into the motel. I waited, as the motel manager had one of the cleaning ladies hastily make up the room for me. I went in, locked the door behind me and imbibed the magical elixir. I was sitting cross-legged on the bed with the pillows positioned to support me in a meditative posture, waiting for the drug to take effect. There was a knock on the door. It was the manager, bringing me some clean towels and a room service menu. I thanked him, and as I locked the door behind him, I hung out the "do not disturb" sign, and I gave it a half twist to make it stand out prominently. About 15 minutes into the session the drug was just beginning to take effect when I heard a key being inserted into the lock and the door opened. It was another cleaning lady, intent on making up the room. "Oh, I'm so sorry", she said, apologizing profusely, "I didn't know this room was occupied! The sign was twisted, and I thought that probably happened when the previous guest left this morning". I assured her that no harm was done, and I untwisted the sign as I locked the door behind her...   Solitude is a very precious commodity, difficult to obtain…

I repositioned myself in the meditative posture and proceeded to go into the domain of my own being. After some time, I felt myself rising up out of my body, through the top of my head, and it was as though I had oozed up out of the ground.., and I was in a different place!.. I was viewing the landscape from a small hill, overlooking a tribal encampment of American Indians spread out in the valley below. On a hill of the far horizon, silhouetted against the red sky of the setting sun, stood a great statue of the "Great Horned Owl".., dark gray in color... "Where am I"?, I said in wonderment, with the voice of my mind. The second question proceeded the first in rapid succession. *"Where am "I"?..* The second question was more important than the first, and I made a diligent search for myself.., and I couldn't be found! There was nothing!., ...no substance whatever! I was amazed and perplexed. I returned to the first question, and as I surveyed my surroundings, my attention was captured by that great gray statue of the Great Owl. What was it's purpose?.. What was it's meaning?.. It seemed the natural course of events that as I was pondering these questions about the Owl, I moved towards it, and with unimpeded motion I penetrated to the inside of the great statue, and perceived that it was made of thick metal, like armor plate, and the

"The Sacred Dream-Vision"

interior of the statue was total darkness, but I could see by my own light, and I saw that it was hollow and empty on the inside, and I perceived that I was also of the nature of emptiness, being totally vacuous and without substance, and I could not be found!

An instantaneous and profound realization hit me, and I exclaimed in stunned disappointment..; "Is that it"?.. "Is that what I am"?.. "Is that all that I am"?.. "A façade!., of nothingness!!, clothed in a facade of greatness"??? I was distressed and disappointed... As if in response to my question, a pillar of flames of fire rose up from the base of the statue to its top, and spread out through the statue filling it entirely with flames of fire, and as I watched from my *"nowhere"* vantage point, the fire did me no harm, and I heard a voice in the distance, and it said: "there's a long fly ball to center field, and Jones is under it in time for the out, and the side is retired"... "what?", I said, not comprehending... "This program is brought to you by the makers of "Such and Soforth" Beer, the beer that will refresh you and make you famous". etc. etc.. *"WHAT"???,* I shouted, in an instant rage. I left my lofty vantage point and descended back into my body, seething with rage.., that the most sacred and precious moment of my life should be interrupted.., by the trivial and the profane... I cursed the "Redneck" asshole son of a bitch and the "God damned" television set in the next room. I raised my hand to strike the wall and shout profanities, but I quickly assessed the situation and realized the futility of dealing with Redneck assholes in such a manner. Regaining my composure, I tried to ignore the television and get back to my previous lofty abode, but it was no use… I left the motel... ...I hate cheap motels...

I recognized the experience as typical to that of the American Indians. It is a rite of passage, and the most important event in the life of the young "Brave" approaching manhood. He goes out from the tribe to a place of solitude, fasting and praying, cleansing himself in the steam bath of the sweat lodge, partaking of the sacrament of Peyote given to his people, and imploring "That Great Spirit", his Maker, to give him a vision of the man and the warrior that he is to become. He will stay in his secluded retreat until he has had his vision, or until his death, whichever comes first. The vision comes in the form of his "Totem Animal", who's name will become his name, and who's qualities of bravery, cunning, strength, swiftness, etc., will become the qualities that he will be endowed with as a result of this vision. His vision will be a determining factor to his status in the tribe. He will come back to the tribe with a new name, and he will have made the transition from a boy to a man, and be recognized as such.

The young warrior returns to the tribe with a sense of fulfillment, having had his vision. I did not have that sense of fulfillment, I had a sense of.., …emptiness!.. I had been seeking answers, and I was left with questions... Although the vision seemed very natural and appropriate as it was unfolding, I had to wonder why it was in the format of the native American Indian. Was the experience, as it was unfolding, really interrupted by the trivial and the profane circumstances of life.., or.., did it unfold exactly as planned? If it did unfold exactly as planned, was it prophetic in nature, and was it my destiny to be plagued by the trivial and the profane as I wandered the face of the Earth in the pursuit of that which was true and sacred? I was almost despondent at the prospect that this would be the case. And what was my mission?.. What was my purpose in life? I was seeking direction, and purpose.., a mission to be accomplished.., and what I got was.., absolute freedom!.. I had no purpose other than what purpose I selected, no mission except that of my own choosing, no direction other than that in which I chose to go. I was not happy with absolute freedom.!. I would have preferred a task of heroic proportions, but alas, I found total freedom to be a far greater challenge... …And what was my name?..

In the wake of my interrupted vision, in my disappointed state of mind, I mocked myself with my names for myself. Who was I?.. Hoo?., Hoo..? Perhaps I should call myself "Screech Owl", for the manner in which I made my reentry from the vision world back to this world, or "Hoot Owl", or maybe "Fire Owl", each of those names evoked a sense of absurdity… Or maybe "Grey Owl", which seemed to be the real theme of the experience, but that name had already been taken, and had a commonality about it, like Smith, or Jones... Perhaps "Iron Owl" should be my name....

I didn't select a name for myself at this time. I didn't wear any Owl feathers in my hair, I didn't have an Owl engraved on my belt buckle, I didn't have my pick-up truck adorned with Owl icons, etc. I didn't even tell anyone about the experience. It was a private matter, of concern only to me. It seemed a bad omen, to have one's sacred dream-vision interrupted in such a manner. Mostly, I tried to forget the whole experience.

Many years have gone by since this experience, and for many years I have pondered the significance of it. I have decided that the vision had indeed unfolded exactly as planned, and the trivial and profane are indeed my adversaries in life. Other experiences (worlds within worlds within worlds) had unfolded with such precision, that it seemed to bear this out. But whatever, it happened the way it happened.., and that's the way it is...

And what of my mission in life?.. There was really no question about that. I had to know!.. Not by reading about someone else's experiences, (although I read voraciously on the subject), not by mere belief, (although I consumed volumes of all the beliefs of all the religions of the world).., but by experiencing for myself, first hand, that which was the "Truth" to be known. This was the "prime directive" of my Soul!.. This inner drive.., "To Know".., by first hand experience, is considered sacred by the "Western School", and is a manifestation of the "Thee Within Me".., more commonly known as: "The Calling"...

This.., was that "Sacred Fire".., that burned in the belly of the Owl... This was the "Spirit" of the "Soul that wants to Know"… And this was not something that just one day came upon me.., It always was...

My name?.. What name should I adopt, as a result of my vision? Grey Owl, seemed to be the most appropriate name here, but I didn't feel comfortable adopting a name that had already been in use by a great Chief... No, I couldn't trade on another man's name...

I am "Iron Owl".., Grey in color, Empty on the Inside, and Filled with Fire"... I see things from a height.., I can turn my head and see in all directions.., my vision penetrates the darkness... With tufted ears, my keen hearing detects the most subtle of sounds.., and the name of my God is: **"Wisdom"**…

**"Wisdom".., ** is the highest aspect of consciousness… Profound Wisdom presupposes "All Knowledge"... It is because of Wisdom.., that there is Love.., and Compassion... It is because of Wisdom.., that the chief characteristic of God is known as: "The Will to Good"... There is nothing that surpasses Wisdom, and if there were.., It is Wisdom that would seek it out and grasp it... This is the excellence of Wisdom...

Absolute emptiness.., is the nature of my Soul... Beyond time and place, beyond planet Earth, beyond substance.., …I am... "Existence".., pure and simple… "I think, therefore I am".., …and I am immortal...

This is the "Truth" about the Soul. This is the truth about my Soul, and about your Soul. You do not possess a Soul, you ARE the Soul... Three times, on two separate occasions, I have made diligent searches for my "Self", the Soul, and each and every time.., there was: "NOTHING"... …and yet.., I am... This is the fact!.. In the pristine purity of absolute nothingness.., "I am"... The implications of this fact.., are astounding….

My color is gray... In the ancient language of symbolism, the color gray represents the merging of opposites. Whenever two opposite colors (red & green, blue & yellow, black & white, etc.) are mixed together, the resultant color is.., gray... In this case, it is the mixture of religions.., ALL religions.., not by mere academic study, but by immersion into each religion, with the fire of passion, and in the countries of their origin... And the Opium dens, the Hashish bazaars, the Buddha grass, the Mushrooms, the dens of iniquity, the towers of babble, the trivial and the profane... Not all at the same time, of course, but each in it's turn...

Firm in the knowledge of "The One Supreme Consciousness", that is the "First Cause" of all cause and effect, I felt free to explore the "Truths" that are unique to each religion, and general to all religions. There is not one religion that has an exclusive monopoly on all aspects of the truth. The "Truth" is where you find it. Ultimately, the truth, the real "Truth", is not discovered in the ancient texts of scriptures or scrolls, to be debated about by men.., nor in the temples, mosque, synagogues, cathedrals, monasteries, etc., built by men... No, the "Truth" is to be found in the temple made without hands, in the temple of the Soul, and it is not simply discovered.., it is experienced...

That is not to say that the scriptures and the scrolls, the temples, monasteries, cathedrals, etc. are of no use or importance. They are of great importance, as rules of conduct, of example, of inspiration and of aspiration. All of this is needed in the approach to

"The Iron Owl"

that "Holy of Holies", the Inner Sanctum of the Temple within... Reverence.., is the criteria of the sincerity of your purpose, exercised in the temple without, and the temple within...

Not only did I explore the religions of the East, but also that great religion of the West:., Science, in all of it's aspects, and the writings of all the great philosophers, and in the tradition of the philosophers I traveled the face of the Earth in search of knowledge. For 12 years of my life and in 33 countries... And if all that I had to report to you was travelogue.., I wouldn't bother...

"Seek and You Shall Find".., another great dictum. What happens when a person really honestly and sincerely seeks for the "Truth"?.. I offer you the neutrality of the color "Grey".., the neutrality of a fair and impartial witness.., the testimony of the Owl.., who's vision has penetrated through the darkness, and has seen the light of a "fifth dimension"... Who has turned his head in all directions and examined all viewpoints, and from the vantage point of "On High" has seen the *"Wisdom"*, of the Ultimate Viewpoint.., and who, with his inner hearing has heard that subtle *"Inner Voice"*.., and as that *"Inner Voice"* speaks, there is Vision, and the Vision is Revelation, and the Revelation is Knowledge.., and it is experienced, assimilated and KNOWN.., to be the ""TRUTH"...

And let us not forget the purpose and "prime directive" of the Owl... It is to keep in check those elements of earth that seek to overrun it like a pestilence.., those "rats" and "vermin" that eat away at the harvest of the earth, and what they don't consume and destroy, they infect with their filth... But the Owl is watching, and waiting... So let the vermin of earth fear the Owl.., because he flies by night, on wings of stealth, soundlessly, and the first indication of his presence.., is the talons that rip open their flesh...

Now, that person who seeks for the truth, and finds the truth, and tells the truth.., is bound to piss off a lot of people!.. Especially if he is not motivated by profit!.. Especially if he is not running for public office. Especially if he seeks not fame, but prefers solitude. Especially if he speaks to the common man in the vernacular of the common man. Especially if he has no regard for "political correctness"...

Such a person could be regarded as "dangerous".., and "subversive"... His metal will be tested... Such a person must be prepared to suffer the outrage of the "Secular Humanists", who know better than God, and are more humanitarian than God... The Saints can bear witness... But I claim not Sainthood, and the harsh words of criticism will roll off me like water off of a statue of an Owl made of iron, empty on the inside.., and coming from that emptiness in the belly of the Owl, you will hear; *Laughter!..*

Any research scientist engaged in the process of discovery must leave behind him a record of his discoveries, so that those who follow in his footsteps do not have to "plow the same ground".., and can avoid the pitfalls, the wrong turns, the dead ends, and the mistakes on the road of life... What I have sought for, and what I have found, I give to you.., first, for you to verify, and then for you to proceed on to greater heights of "Self Realization".., and not simply for your own gratification, but that you might be a light unto your fellow men, bearing witness to the truth, and showing the "Way"... This is the "Legacy" that it is my great pleasure, my joy, my honor, and my duty.., to leave to you. I am Iron Owl,.. I am your servant.

* * *   * * *   * * *

Chronology of Events

The reader may have noticed that the events described herein are not in their consecutive order, but more in the order of importance. To make evident the progressive nature of the unfoldment process, I will regress to a point near the beginning, and show the progression in a more consecutive manner:..

It was one of my first LSD experiences. I was in the company of my good friend, "Geno", a fellow "seeker of the Truth". We were the best of friends, and although we were on the same spiritual exploration, we disagreed about almost everything. Our contrasting viewpoints on matters of religion and philosophy, and the heated debates that ensued, were the firm basis of our friendship. "Geno", was about 15 years older than myself, a war hero, college educated, a hypno-therapist by occupation, and assisted at a medical facility that was using LSD for therapeutic purposes.., and as far as LSD, the sub-conscious mind, and hypnosis was concerned, he was my Mentor...

By natural inclination, I was prone to abstract contemplation... Under the influence of the LSD, sitting on a cushion on the floor in a cross-legged position, I went into deep contemplation. Suddenly, I jumped up and announced in a loud and startled voice: "I saw it!., I saw it"!.. What did you see?, asked Geno. "I saw it", I repeated, "I saw the Void"!..

"You saw the Void", Geno repeated thoughtfully... "And what did it look like"?, he asked... I was stymied by the question... It was a paradoxical absurdity.., a Cosmic joke. I couldn't stop laughing. The laughter was contagious.!. Geno was laughing. Presently.., I regained my composure, and wiping the tears of laughter from my eyes, I said, "I saw it in my mind's eye".., "I saw and understood it in my mind's eye"…

Actually, I had seen it, the "Void", with the eye of the Soul, but I wouldn't learn of the distinction till later in the future, so, more than discovering the Void, I had discovered that fabled "Third Eye".., the eye of *"in-sight"*...

So, with the "Third Eye", the eye of insight, the eye that is the "I" of the Soul, I had penetrated into the "Void" itself.., but how to explain it?..

In our customary frame of reference, we stand on the Earth and look out into space, at the stars. The men of science tell us that as we are looking outward into space, we are also looking backward in time, that we are seeing the stars, not as they are at this moment, but as they were, light-years ago. They call it the "Space-Time Continuum", as though space and time were inextricably woven together.

But, in your minds eye.., reverse this perspective, and stand out in space, and look back at the planet Earth. You will observe that the Earth is a three dimensional object (having height, width, and depth), floating in this vast sea of nothingness (the fourth dimension) that we call space...

Space.., is the fourth dimension. Space, (nothingness) is very difficult to conceptualize. We can only think of space in relation to an object that occupies space. Even our language betrays us. Space is the subject in our sentence, and as such, it is a Noun. A Noun, by definition, is a person, place, or thing.., and Space, by definition, is the total absence of a person, place, or thing... So we refer to Space as though it were something to be reckoned with, when in reality it is *"Nothingness".., * and "Time".., does not touch it...

"Time".., belongs to "Matter"... Only "things" have time. Only "things" have a birth, life-span, and dissolution. Only Matter has a consistent molecular breakdown that can be carbon dated as to time. Even light (photons) is matter, and can be effected by magnetic fields, and "timed" as to distance traveled. It is the "Light-Distance-Time Continuum"... Light travels through space (nothingness) unhindered and unopposed, and the nothingness of space is untouched and unperturbed...

So, what time is it in space?.. It's the same time it has always been... It is the eternal, ever present, "NOW"... So, no matter what time it is, it is always "NOW"... It is: "The Timeless-Space Continuum".., and the concept of "time travel" (backwards and forward in time), will always remain science fiction because it is always NOW, and cannot be otherwise. The "Akashic Records" (cosmic memory) can be observed with the "minds eye", but cannot be entered into or altered... Similarly,.. "Worm Holes" in space (as a shortcut from point "A" to point "B", because the "fabric" of space has a "warp" in it), is also laughable science fiction. There is no fabric to the nothingness that is space, and therefore no warps exist... A "hole" through nothingness is an absurdity!...

But there IS one thing in the universe that is faster than light... There IS one thing in the universe that can penetrate the "Distance-Time" barrier!.. It takes approx. 8.33 seconds for light to get from the Sun to the Moon, but a thought can go from the Sun to the Moon immediately.., and the *"Soul".., * is even quicker than thought.!.

So, the "Void" is to be understood from the point of view of "Space", looking back at Earth, instead of from Earth looking out at Space. It is the "fourth dimension" looking back on three dimensional physical reality. And the reality (or non-reality) of "Space" is everywhere (or nowhere) present (or not present)... It is (or is not) present (or not) between Galaxies, molecules, and atoms, etc…

It was at this point in my contemplation that as "I" was viewing the three dimensional from the fourth dimensional aspect, that my viewpoint shifted.., from the Macro-Cosmic to the Micro-Cosmic.., and back again... And the objects of the three dimensional changed their relative size from miniscule to magnific, and back again.., and I could not ascertain the size of anything, because it was relative from my viewpoint of either magnitude or parvitude, with infinity in both directions... I had no yardstick of measurement in this dimension, and as I momentarily pondered this paradox of relativity, I registered both surprise and confoundment.., and it was in that moment that I jumped up from my meditation cushion and shouted: *"I saw it"!..*

Have I communicated the "Void" to you?.. Probably not... I explained my experience of the Void to a Physicist, schooled in both nuclear and astral physics, and his response was that the Void is not Void at all, because it contains Galaxies, stars, worlds, energy, etc. He could not conceive of the Void in it's pristine purity, but only in it's relationship to matter.., but matter is not void.., and the "Void" is not matter... A very subtle point.., but this gives rise to a question... From whence cometh matter?.. Science doesn't have a clue. Einstein considered the assumption that matter just was, (without a cause), to have been his greatest mistake as a theoretical mathematician... But mathematics can illustrate that it comes from the Void... $0 = (+1) + (-1)$. From out of nothing, came everything... But what was the "First Cause"..?

The ancient Greeks speculated about the smallest particle of matter; the atom.., but the ancient Buddhists speculated about the Void... The Buddha, when asked about the Void, replied that the Void could be described only in negative terms: "It is not this.., it is not that"...

But this "Void" that I saw.., was it the Void of outer space.., or was it the Void of "inner space" ?.. And if it be the Void of inner space.., from whence cometh thought?.. and from whence cometh the power to create.., in my imagination?.. And that which I see projected in my imagination.., where is the projector?.. Where is the observer?.. And Where am "I" ?.. The "I" that is the "Eye" of the Soul.., the Eye of insight?.. My nature and my substance.., is Voidness... "I think.., therefore I am".., ...in the image of my Creator...

You will observe that the Voidness of outer space (the fourth dimension) and the Voidness of inner space (the fifth dimension) have similarities in common. Both inner and outer have their source in the "Absolute" Void, (of which the terms "inner" and "outer" do not apply)... We have not yet penetrated to the Essence of the Void.., but those Seers and Saints who have, have this to report: (in essence): There IS one characteristic of the Void that can be known.., and that is it's "sound"... It is the "Sound of Silence"... In a condition of Absolute emptiness there is a sound that is spontaneously produced, and it can be heard with the "Inner Ear"..,of the Soul... This "Sound of the Silence" originates from no particular source, but is everywhere present and all pervasive. Because of this sound emanating throughout the Void.., *because* of the Void.., "HE".., heard that Sound, and "HE KNEW THAT HE WAS".., AND HE WAS THAT SOUND.., and by the articulation of that sound, HE spoke the Worlds into existence!.. And since the Void always was, and the Sound of the Voidness always was.., HE.., who was the Voidness and the Voice of the Voidness.., always was.., and IS.., and forever will be...

So this "Primordial Sound", the first emanation from the Void, is held to be Sacred by the Hindu Religion, as the "Mystical Name" of God.., which is: "Om", (or "AUM").., (consisting of three and a half prosodial moments)... The repetition of this Name, and the reflection on its source and meaning, are very conducive to abstract meditation.

You must notice the similarity here between the Hindu and the Biblical version of: "In the beginning was the "Word" (emanation), and the "Word" (sound) was with God, and the "Word" (sound) was God"... Amen...

The Hindu's point to this passage from "John 1", and the repetition of the word "Amen", as confirmation of their own religious convictions and the universality of "Truth", no matter in which religion it may be found.., and there is much Truth to be found in the Hindu religion... Amen...

* * *   * * *   * * *

As a matter of procedure, I would enter into my "Sacramentally induced" meditations by way of the music of the great symphonic Masters, as well as contemporary Masters, of instrumental music... The music of "sounds".., not words... Melodic sound.., has a power......

I reclined back in the big overstuffed chair and let myself be drawn into the sounds produced by the Masters of the Sitar, and the Tabla.., the complete library of sounds produced by the Hammond

Organ.., the rhythms of jungle drums.., the cadence of the Marches.., the Trumpets.., the Cymbals, etc...

I could feel each sound as it penetrated through my being, evoking a psychological and emotional response, from laughter to tears, from hope to inspiration, from reverence to exaltation... Across the screen of my inner vision there would play out a scenario in full regalia,.. "The Charge of the Light Brigade", the clash of battle, in full glory, with the appropriate music to accompany it... "The Saber Dance", performed live, in the domain of my imagination... Black natives, adorned with beads, plumage and furs, would be performing ritual tribal dances in response to jungle drums. I would struggle through the ups and downs of treacherous terrain in response to the ups and downs of the music, to emerge victorious as the music reached it's crescendo...

I observed that the manifestation of phenomena in my imagination was the direct result of the music that was being played... Sound, produced a visual response... What that visual response would be, I could not know, I could only observe.., and be amazed... And the visual response would be produced spontaneously with the sound. There was no time delay, the sound and the sight were simultaneous.

There was something very profound here... Something to do with creation.., where the sound.., spoken in the voidness of primeval consciousness, produced: form!!. A relationship between a vibratory tonality and the form it produced... Here was Divine Mystery... The linear-logical mind of the secular "flat earth" society couldn't come here... No, the evolutionists and the Atheists couldn't come here... It was evident that both form and consciousness in the realm of mind preceded form and consciousness in the realm of the physical... *Essence*".., precedes Existence!..

And I would dance... The music would touch my Soul, and energize my Spirit, and I would dance... Becoming absorbed in the music, becoming the music.., I would dance around my living room in perfect response to the rhythm of the music, at times leaping from chairs and sofa, doing pirouettes in mid air, landing in a perfect martial arts stance, in perfect time to the music. Its effect was cleansing...

And laughter..! With intuitive insight I could see.., that the basis of all laughter.., was absurdity... And the basis of all tragedy, was also absurdity, and I could laugh at the absurdities of life.., and laughter was good for the Soul...

Words do not adequately convey.., because there is nothing in your own experience to relate this to, but for brief moments, a particular sound would completely capture my attention, and I would instantly become "one" with that sound.., I would become, and identify with that particular sound, as it vibrated out from my stereo speakers... A momentary "transference of consciousness", away from my body and directly into the vibratory essence of the sound itself.!.

Because the nature of the Soul is "Voidness".., being totally without form or substance.., it has the unique ability to enter into any substance.., and assume that form.., and to become one with, identify with, and get lost in.., some particular sounds, that because of their uniqueness, have the ability to momentarily capture the undivided attention, and the presence of the Soul itself...

At the moment, the Soul has entered into your body and taken that form... But,.. if you can achieve a "level of abstraction", great enough to isolate the Soul from the body, and your attention be focused on something else, to the exclusion of everything else, you can experience a "transference of consciousness" into what has "captured" your attention.., and there are "certain sounds" that can capture your attention, and you can be absorbed into the sound and become "one" with that sound... A unique experience!..

Within the Buddhist community, there are "schools" that utilize this principle of "certain sounds" that have the ability to "capture" the "consciousness principle" and effect this "transference of consciousness".., and liberate the Soul from it's bondage to the body... A liberating experience!..

Years later.., I sat for meditation on the grounds of the large Buddhist temple that sits on the hill overlooking the valley of Katmandu, in Nepal... I explored around the temple grounds, and I found a door on which someone had neglected to replace the padlock... Seized by curiosity, I opened the door and looked in... It was a room that was used for storage, and stored in this room were those unique musical instruments that could produce those unique sounds... There was a hammered metal "gong", about five or six feet in diameter, suspended from a transportable framework.., and a drum, about four feet in diameter also suspended from a transportable framework, and the body of the drum narrowed down and fluted out into a trumpet shape, to amplify and direct the sound from the drum.., a veritable "sound cannon"... There were horns and trumpets, and hollow bones that would produce a hollow "clacking" sound... cymbals and bells of various sizes and shapes.., Bowls of various sizes, that produced an enchanting harmonic resonance, when the rim was rubbed with the finger tips.., and the human thigh bone trumpets that were used in ceremonies for the dead.., and to remind the living of the inevitability of death...

I did not enter the room, but just stood there in the doorway.., fascinated.., and as I looked.., I knew... These were those unique musical instruments, that could produce those unique sounds used in the ritual "consciousness transference" ceremony... I thought to myself, as I viewed these instruments, that I was viewing advanced "space age" technology from a time in the past, and a science that is to be resurrected in a future time, but, for the present time.., is here in storage... I closed the door, replaced the padlock, and went back to my meditation.

* * * * * * * *

It was early morning. I was alone in the house, seated on a cushion on the dining room floor. I had taken that magic potion about 30 minutes earlier, and I was awaiting the effects. The house was quiet... Suddenly, the refrigerator in the kitchen kicked on. The electric motor started it's mechanical compressor pushing a cooling agent through the condensing coils. It was a rhythmic mechanical vibration.., and I could see the sound it made, on the field of my inner vision... I could see the sound that the refrigerator was making... It had a shape, and a color, and movement…

A procession of bright yellow rectangles, like bricks, marched in cadence in both directions, right and left, away from a bright yellow center. It was like a flowing brick wall, flowing and undulating away from that bright yellow center in mechanical cadence, in response to the mechanical sound of the electric motor and compressor. The sound and the visual sight of the sound were simultaneous.., there was no time delay... I could see sound, and this is what the sound of the refrigerator looked like...

I went into the living room and turned on the stereo. I was bathed in the music of the great symphonic orchestras. I would be carried along by the music, experiencing the emotional impacts of the crescendos, etc. and for brief moments, the sound would completely capture my attention, and I would become "one" with the music, and I could *"see"* the sound that the music made.., on the oscilloscope of my mind.., and I recognized the sound that I saw,.. and it was: ***Arabic!!...***

This was a surprise to me... I had studied all the great Religions.., from Christianity, through Hinduism, through Buddhism, through Judaism, through Mysticism, etc., through all the "new age" and old age philosophies, and offshoot belief systems, from Spiritualism to Voodoo, etc... My knowledge of the Moslem religion was superficial at best.., but this really had nothing to do with religion... I saw the shape and form of sound.., and it was Arabic!

I had often wondered about the source of written languages. What was the basis for the construction and design of letters.., the consonants, and the vowels?.. Were their designs just arbitrary, or was there a methodology of reason involved?.. Did it just evolve and develop from simple x's and o's, or was there a hidden logic to it?.. and if there was a logic to it, what was it?.. What was the first written language?.. Was it Aramaic?., the language that the Bible was written in, and if so, was it given to man by God?.. Did it have a Divine origin?..

There were so many styles of written languages;., the Egyptian "knowledge-picture-symbols" (hieroglyphics).., the Greek letters.., was there a deeper meaning behind the symbols than mere phonic sounds?.. The Latin letters, and the Russian alphabet, with it's backward letters.., was there dyslexia involved?, a different way of seeing things?.. The Inca, the Aztec, and the Mayan?.. The complicated and stylized letters of Sanskrit?.. The picture-words of the Chinese?.. Etc. and etc...

It had been a mystery to me.., but now I had an answer, and it came in the form of sounds that created a visual impression on the inner screen of my consciousness, that I could see with the eye of my mind.., and it was beautiful.., and it was Arabic!..

This is what I saw, and because I saw.., I know... Beyond this, I can only speculate...

Before the Moslem religion descended into the dogmatic extremism of today, there were the "Wise

Men" from the East... The "Sufi" masters... It was they, who could see the shape and form of sound, with the eye of the mind.., the eye of insight... It was these "Holy Men" who transcribed these sounds that they saw into their unique alphabet, and wrote down the Holy words, to be read by generations of posterity... It was they, with their Divinely inspired insight, who wrote the songs, the poetry, and scriptures... It was they, who developed the science of mathematics, the numerical system, algebra and geometry.., while the rest of humanity was still counting on their fingers and toes...

This gift, this ability to see sound, is a rare faculty, but it is not extinct... Just as there are people with the rare gift of a photographic memory, there are also people with the gift of being able to see sound, on the oscilloscope of the mind... They are rare, but they are not extinct[1]...

I suspect.., I speculate.., that there are several alphabet systems that spring from this Divine "source"... I can look at the Sanskrit alphabet, and I see the same stylized beauty and fluidity that I saw in the Arabic... This may also be true of the Aramaic, the Hebrew, and Latin... But it is interesting to note, that the numerical system, mathematics, algebra, geometry, etc., were developed by the Arabic system.., which the world has adopted... While the Aramaic, the Hebrew, and the Greek systems used the letters of their alphabet as a substitute for numbers, which were cumbersome and inefficient, and degenerated into the pseudo sciences of Gematria and Numerology...

This was a "one time" experience for me... It came as a gift that I did not have the ability to control or repeat, and while it answered the major question of the "Source" of alphabets, it did not conclusively give me the answers to all the questions that I posed above.., nor did it give me the "source" language developed by Adam, who I am sure had this ability to see the form and shape of sound in his minds eye…

* * * * * * *

I list this next event as a separate experience, and it is a separate event, but it immediately followed the experience of the "the ability to see the shape and form of sound in the minds eye", as related above...

---

[1] This ability to see sound (in the mind's eye) is termed "Synesthesia", and it is estimated that about 1 in 2000 people have this ability…

And perhaps this "opening" of that "Third Eye", the eye of insight, the minds eye.., had something to do with it... But this event, I saw with my two eyes open, standing in front of me, not twelve feet away.., in my living room...

He appeared instantly, was there for only a second, and just as instantly.., vanished!.. I saw him clearly, in every detail, and there was no mistaking who he was... It was Satan himself.., standing in front of me.., in my living room...

He was tall and lean, impeccably dressed, in flamboyant style... His black and silver hair was parted on the right side, and combed back, rippling with kinky wavelets, and had a high sheen, as though well oiled.., his sideburns came down below his ears, spit-curling counter-clockwise, forward, inward and down... He had on a black cape, with a high collar, fastened below his neck with a silver linked clasp... The color scheme of his dress was black and silver... He was clean shaven, with a prominent chin that was cradled in his right hand, his left hand reaching across his waist, cradling his right elbow... His reddish effeminate lips curled up in a faint smile... *It was the "Joker"!.,* the "Evil Nemesis" himself.., but his face bore a close resemblance to the face.., of.., "Liberace" (the famous pianist)!.. His attitude seemed to be one of contemplation, ...of how best to bring me down... I did not see his feet...

I said; "Huh", in surprise... It did not surprise me that the Devil was obviously a "flaming faggot".., Somehow that figured... It did not surprise me that he appeared as that "Evil Nemesis"; the **"Joker"**, with the ability to "morph" his appearance into a resemblance of "Liberace", both in facial features and flamboyant attire... What surprised me, was that he seemed.., a gentleman.!.

If someone had asked me to describe Satan, the Devil, I would have said that he was a reddish brute with two horns and a pointed tail.., and not a gentleman...

As I write these words, I am presented with a dilemma... Most people don't even believe in the Devil... Anyone that would say that he has seen the Devil.., face to face.., immediately loses all credibility... To say further that the Devil is the "Joker", and looks like "Liberace".., is laughable... To further say that he was a "flaming faggot", flamboyantly attired.., and seemed a gentleman.., is to invite ridicule...

It would be much easier for me to eliminate these few paragraphs from this manuscript, and maintain a semblance of credibility... But, I must include this episode, because it is the absolute "Truth".., and you have to know.., and have no doubt about it... HE EXISTS!.. I saw him clearly.., and he IS a "flaming faggot".., and his resemblance to a gentleman.., is a lie...

As I look back on this episode, I must admit to having been very naive, to say the least... I brushed off this encounter as of no consequence, when in reality.., it was a warning... I should have been on my guard, because his purpose was.., to bring me down.!. I didn't realize it at the time, but I had approached the Divine, on the threshold of transcendence.., and he was there to bring me down.., to engineer my fall from grace.., and I fell... It was no contest.., and I fell.., through my own naive stupidity...

The Bible records.., the trials of Job.., at the hands of that evil one; the Devil... Job prevailed, and his victory is recorded, for all to see, for eternity... Jesus was tempted.., weakened, after fasting for 40 days... His victory is recorded, and the story will be told and retold, forever and ever...

I am not Job... I am not Jesus... Not even close... I am "Iron Owl the Stupid".., "Iron Owl the Naïve"... I had been that "Samaritan", on the Road to Damascus, (metaphorically speaking) and a fellow traveler, a woman, had held out her hand to me, and said; "Help"... A voice whispered in my ear, and said; "never mind", "don't get involved", "think about other things".., and, without another thought about it, I did just that... I turned my back and walked away...

How easily I had been tricked... How easily I had been deceived... I couldn't believe my own naive stupidity... A moment of non caring carelessness, and that sleazy voice whispered in my ear.., and I blocked out the significance of the situation... That poor woman, used and abused, injured by a non caring world, in despair.., held out her hand to me, looked me in the eye, and pleaded for help.., and I turned and walked away.!. To her grief and despair, I had added rejection and hopelessness... How could I have done that?..

I, who had been blessed by God.., how could I have done that?.. I walked on down the road, not looking back... Presently, I looked back, reviewing the situation in my minds eye, and I was horrified by my own callousness... With my minds eye, I looked again into that woman's eyes, and I felt her pain, her grief and despair.., it was overwhelming.., and now.., it was mine... I wept bitter tears.., too late.., too late... I could have been the Hero of this situation... With no effort, no expense, no trouble at all, I could have been the Hero of the moment, I had only to act... But, because that voice whispered to my inner ear, I turned my back and walked away... And now I knew.., that voice that I had so carelessly acquiesced to.., it was that evil one.., and he had tricked me... But he did it much too easily...

Do you want to know the secret of personal Power?.. *It is a clear conscience.* If you can see righteousness, and do that which is righteous, with a clear conscience.., you do it with conviction, and you do it with **Power...** But if you have guilt on your conscience, from having acted contrary to your convictions, how can you lead the charge of righteousness, when you know in your heart that you are less than righteous? Guilt, will bring you down.., from a leader to a follower...

Know this to be a fact:.. There is War in Heaven... The "Fifth Dimension" is divided... The Evil one.., Satan, rules over the "Hellish" realms of the "Fifth Dimension", and is alive and well on planet Earth.., and he vies for the Souls of Men... It is the classic struggle of Good against Evil, and it goes on in the hearts of men, in the streets of our cities, and on the battlefields of Earth...

So.., We have this situation... That evil one had seen his opportunity, and with a few choice words, had set the trap, and our bumbling hero, "Iron Owl the Dupe".., had been duped... Just like "Adam and Eve" had been duped with a few choice words and expelled from Paradise, so too our hero, "Iron Owl the Zen Warrior", had been expelled from the crisp clean clear rarified air of the Zen-Objective state of mind.., down.., down.., through the "positive-subjective" state of mind of the Common Man.., down.., down.., to the "negative-subjective" state of mind.., of the Guilty...

Guilt will bring you down... Guilt.., and the Zen-Objective state of mind, are not compatible... "Adam", because of guilt, fell from that high Zen state, down to the self-conscious/subjective state, and covered himself, because he was naked.., and self conscious... So too, our hero; "Iron Owl the Sorry", stood naked and condemned, covered in shame, guilt and sorrow... Could he ever be forgiven?.. Could that poor helpless woman ever forgive him?.. No, she would stand there, before God, on judgment day, and point a bony finger; "There he is.., That's him"... "That's the Asshole that turned his back on me, in my hour of need".., ...and he would be condemned... Could God forgive him?.. Oh, yes.., but then again.., why should He?.. Why indeed?.. Wasn't this the very parable?., spoken of by the Savior, whereby the good Samaritans and the Assholes come to a fork in the road, and each chooses his own direction?.. And the "Evil one" would be there, and say: "He did my bidding, he belongs to me".., and he would be condemned... Could "Iron Owl the Wretched" ever forgive himself?.. No.., even if God forgave him.., even if the woman forgave him.., he could not forgive himself... His state of mind was self-condemnation...

Oh, The tragedy of it all.!. A double tragedy, for the woman, and for our hero.., because the law of love had been ignored... So.., what now?.. Our valiant hero.., is he condemned to roam the face of the Earth in a perpetual state of "mind-fuck".., or.., is there a way out.?.

Our hero analyses the situation, and perceives that the only difference between himself and other mortal men, is the content of his mind.., which is guilt and remorse... He further perceives that the "mind-fuck" content of his mind has been brought about by the "Adversary", that Evil one, called "Satan"... He further perceives that this is no ordinary back yard brawl... No, this is a fight to the death.., Winner takes all... A Universe is at stake!., and it is the Universe called "Iron Owl"...

Can he do it ?.. Can our hero find his way out of the "mind-fuck maze" ?.. Can he possibly forgive himself, and erase this incident from his mind ?..

With a mighty and defiant war-cry, our hero "Iron Owl the Pissed-Off" declares: ***"NO"***... "No I will not"... I choose to never forget.., nor will I ever forgive myself... Never.., never, never, *ever*, will I forget this woman.., and though I live a thousand lifetimes I will cherish her memory, and I will be her Champion... Because of Her.., I do hereby take the "Bodhisattva Vow"... Even though I be offered entrance into that "Final Nirvana", the "Seventh Heaven".., I will refuse it... Not until every being on Earth has achieved it, will I partake of it... This is the Vow of the Bodhisattva Warrior... With Joy in my heart, I will offer help and assistance to my fellow man.., and woman... Where that Evil one had won a victory, I will win a thousand victories.., Nay, tens of thousands of victories, and I will break bread, and drink wine.., and offer a toast in memory of *That* "Bodhisattva of all Bodhisattvas".., HE, who is called "Worthy".., HE.., who laid down his life, that all men may live... "And I will live in a house by the side of the road, and be a friend to man".., always.!. ...Thus spake "Iron Owl.., the Redeemed "...

The point of this story is not the fall and redemption of "Iron Owl the Grateful",.. although there is much to be learned here... The point of this story is that the Evil one.., Exists!.. Make no mistake about this... He is the Adversary.., and if you are on a spiritual quest, and approaching the Divine.., he will attempt to bring you down... Take heed... A battle rages... Unseen and largely unknown to mortal man, a battle rages, and YOU are the Prize!.. His weapons are cunning lies and deceit.., and he will deceive you by your own weaknesses, be they greed, hatred, lust, or lack of integrity... Take heed, lest you fall...

The central theme of this book, is the same as the central theme of the "Old Testament", and that central theme continues unbroken through the "New Testament", and that central theme is this: God speaks to man!.. There is dialogue between God and Man!.. The Bible is a record kept of this dialogue between God and Man.., and the consequences of responding to, or of failing to respond to, that spoken word...

The Bible is referred to as "the word of God", but it is only the shadow of that word, the history recorded of that word, as it was spoken to Adam, Job, Abraham, Isaac, Jacob, Jesus, all the Prophets, etc... The real word, "The Living Word", is that which is spoken directly to you, in the inner sanctum of your own Soul... So the very first of the "Superhuman Faculties" developed by the spiritual aspirant absorbed in rapt contemplation, is the faculty of "inner hearing"... "Wisdom commeth by HEARING, and Hearing by the word of God"... This, and no other, is the "Living Word"...

But beware.., having developed the faculty of inner hearing can leave you vulnerable to deceptions from the "Dark Side" of the fifth dimension... You must discriminate!.. You must be aware.., lest you be deceived...

* * *   * * *   * * *

BOOK II

"The Experience"

This was probably my seventh or eighth experiment with profound (LSD induced) meditation, and it would not be my last. With my lady-friend in attendance, to prevent my experiment/meditation from being disturbed, or intruded upon, I embarked on my inner solitary journey. The experience customarily lasts for approximately eight hours with a profoundly enhanced appreciation for music, in my case it was a classical instrumental selection with a heavy base that had the effect of drawing the mind into the music, and for brief moments becoming absorbed in the music. This is an experience that cannot easily be described, of becoming one with the music, of becoming the music, where nothing but the music existed (especially not I). So how could you explain to someone that music could be heard, felt, seen, and experienced with the mind alone? Yet, this is a relatively common experience with this category of profound meditation.

It should become obvious to the reader that there are more capabilities to human consciousness (the Soul) than are normally recognized.

Having gone through the peak of the experience while listening to the music, having experienced the power and majesty, the exhilaration, the inspiration, the splendor, the profound awe.., the feeling that I was on the verge of a great revelation, a great discovery.., that never came...

I was coming down from my lofty experience. The music was returning to normal. My perceptions were returning to normal. Despite the grandeur of the experience, I had a feeling of.., something left undone.., a mission not accomplished...

I turned off the music. I was sitting in a big easy chair, and my mind turned to natural contemplation. The eternal questions that plague the Soul... The who, the how, the why of existence. I watched as my mind raced to answer these questions. There were answers, there were profound insights, there were ...Aha's. It seemed I was on the threshold of solving the riddle of the Universe... On the threshold, but never quite there… Again the feeling of a mission not accomplished.., almost grasping the infinite.., but not quite...

A mystery not solved, a threshold not crossed, a great and magnificent promise.., left unfulfilled. I had been there before, many times, in fact, every time... I pondered this fact. It seemed this experience was a repetition of the last experience, and the one before that, and the one before that… I wondered.., is this as far as I can go?..

Not to belittle the experience, by any means, because it was a confirmation of something far greater and more profound than anything else I had ever experienced in my life. There are Holy Men who have meditated for years, Monks in monasteries, Priests and Rabbis, dedicated and sincere people who have prayed for and not received the gift that I was taking for granted. But I was a seeker after truth, and the answers to the big questions still eluded me. Should I go on?.. I had no choice. Of course I would go on. There were questions that hadn't been answered. There was a threshold to be crossed. There was a promise not yet fulfilled.., but it was a promise, and I was driven by that promise.

The experience was nearing it's close. It was an eight hour experience, and time was almost up. I watched a little television. How utterly trivial. The commercials were so absurd I laughed out loud. I turned off the television. The clock on the wall confirmed that eight hours had gone by and I was back to my normal self. I sat there in the chair and closed my eyes. As I sat there I noticed a soft, white light on the screen of my inner vision. It wasn't a bright light at all, it was just soft and white.., and it was blinking on and off... Interesting, I thought...

To be sure, the experience itself is a profound type of meditation... First, absorption on an external source, the music.., and second, the practice of profound contemplation, in which secrets are revealed and knowledge is gained… But there are other types of meditation...

I decided to capitalize on this interesting internal strobe light, and utilize it as a focal point for a disciplined attempt at focusing my concentration, and lengthening my attention span.., and who knows, there may still be a residual effect from the drug.

I went into the bedroom and seated myself on a pillow in the middle of the bed, in the traditional meditation posture and proceeded to focus my attention on this internal phenomena. I wasn't having much success. It seemed that the more intently I focused my attention on this pulsating soft white light, the more it faded from view, and when I had almost forgotten about it, it would come on strong!.. I was also having difficulty holding my concentration, as my mind kept wandering off in all different directions. I soon tired of the effort, and my body reclined itself on the bed with the pillow under my head.

I wasn't sleepy at all. In fact, I was very much awake and alert.., and, with eyes closed, the pulsating white light still presented itself to my internal view. With renewed determination, I focused my attention on the pulsating white light, but thoughts kept invading and intruding themselves. I made the observation that I, and my mind.., were two separate and distinct things. I was the observer, and my mind was.., what?.. an obedient servant that presented to me in visual form my every whim.., but if I failed to pay attention.., it would wander off of its own accord in every conceivable direction, recalling past events, projecting future events, etc., and forever restless…

My task at the moment was to bring this restless mind.., ...to rest... I employed a meditation technique known as "chopping the roots". The thoughts seemed to be coming into my field of vision from somewhere outside of me, invading my inner space, and carrying me off on a train of thought. The technique involves maintaining constant vigilance, and as the thoughts spring up, to catch them at their source and chop them at their root before they develop into trains of thought. In response to this effort my mind produced for me an analog readout in symbolic form. Just to the left of my inner field of vision, in my peripheral vision, was a glass fish tank filled with water, and an air tube that lay across the bottom of the tank. There were five pin holes evenly spaced across the top surface of the tube from which tiny bubbles of air would escape, expanding in size until they burst forth on the surface of the water.., as a full blown thought!.. The emergence of a bubble at the bottom of the glass tank and the emergence of a thought were simultaneous. With the aid of this visual display, I could catch and stop the though before it got started, just by willing it. The bubbles and the thoughts came profusely at first, and I was actively engaged in chopping them at their root. A few thoughts got by me, at first. How clever my mind was to create and produce this fish tank display, I thought.., as the bubble burst forth on the surface of the fish tank! I renewed my efforts, and the production of thoughts slowed down and finally stopped, for a couple of seconds, then they started anew, only fewer and slower. I chopped some more, they stopped for five seconds, and a few thoughts bubbled up, but fewer and slower again. Again I chopped, until they stopped. I waited.., no thoughts!.. The glass tank lay quiet and still. I was thought free... I just was...

Freed from thought now, I turned my attention back to the pulsating soft white light, and I just observed it. The more intensely I focused my attention the more the light diminished in intensity. The less intently I observed it, the more intense the light became. I finally reached a point of equilibrium, where I was observing this internal phenomena from a disinterested, dispassionate, unconcerned, and effortless point of view. I was watching it, without paying attention to it. And then, it seemed, I forgot I was even watching it. I wasn't even there. Only the pulsating soft white light was there... And then it happened!..

There was a brilliant flash of light, as though a flash bulb went off in front of my eyes, a rush of air, and a soft thud, as though a large book had closed shut as the air rushed from between the pages, cushioning the close of the book to a soft gentle "thud".., **...and I was - - "There"!..** And I was astonished!..

A brilliant, momentary flash of light, a rush of air, followed by a gentle thud, and I was projected, bodiless, into a different universe.., and I was astonished at the sight that spread out in panoramic view before my perfectly clear vision. My vision was perfectly clear because it wasn't dependent on the intermediate agency of an eyeball, retina, optic nerve, etc. No, my vision was perfectly clear because "**I**", was the eye, and my eye was "**I**", and nothing obstructed my perfectly clear vision! My mind was also exceptionally clear, as it worked at high speed efficiency to assimilate the information presented and recover my equilibrium from the astonishment.

I had been projected into this new universe. I arrived bodiless, at birds-eye height from the ground, and with a birds-eye view. I was on the outskirts of a village, or city, where the lush forest met the spectacular green fields, and where the fields met the city. The first rays of sunlight were streaking over the horizon. The colors were rich with iridescences and opalescence's. The populace was still asleep. My initial astonishment turned to wonderment as I viewed the architecture of the city. *It was Pagoda!.,* and one of the principal building materials.., was gold!.. The pagoda style roofs of the houses were shingled with gold. The trim was gold. The decorations were gold. The craftsmanship was exotic perfection.., and it was a solid reality...

My mind was racing at super quick speed. I took in the entire scene at a glance. My first reaction was to speak to myself with the voice of my mind, and in my astonishment I said... "Wha- "...???!!!! Before I could even finish the word my mind was racing to comprehend the situation. "Where is this place?", I asked, in amazed wonderment, with the voice of my mind... Within a fraction of a second my mind searched through my entire memory store, gathered all the relevant information that I had ever seen, heard, or read about, assimilated and related the information and presented three possibilities.., and I could see this process working in my mind as it was happening.., and I was amazed!..

The three possibilities were that this was some secret hidden Shangri-la type Mystery School on planet Earth, possibly somewhere in Tibet, or Mongolia, judging from the architecture, ...or a civilization existing on another planet, outside our solar system.., or, that it existed in another dimension entirely.., *within the realm of mind!!.*

I left the first question unanswered to ask the second outstanding question.... Where am "**I**"?.. I made a diligent search for myself... I could not be found!.. Not a pinpoint center, not a cross-hair location, not a circumference, no trace of anything... Nothing!.. and yet,.. I was! There was only;.. "I think, therefore, I am"..

The third outstanding question presented itself; "What about my body"?.. Instantaneously I was back in my body. I didn't "Go" back to my body. I just instantaneously "happened" there. I was back in my body and also examining it at the same time from an abstract view-point... I was relaxed and at ease, lying on the bed. All systems were functioning normally with one notable exception.., my breathing.., It was perfectly relaxed and normal…

Breathing is part of the autonomic nervous system. It takes care of itself automatically, without you having to think about it, but if you become aware of it, you automatically assume control of your breathing. I was aware of my breathing, but I left it under its own autonomic control. The question presented itself; did I have control? I opened my eyes. I was in the bedroom. I closed my eyes, the other reality was still there. I opened and closed my eyes rapidly several times. I was blinking back and forth between the two realities. Satisfied that my body was in no danger, I made a conscious decision... I closed my eyes...

The entire scan-analysis of my body, including the conclusions, deductions, and a decision, was accomplished in less time than it took to blink my eyes... So quick and clear were the workings of my mind!

I came back to my lofty vantage point, not as a religionist, but as a scientist, awed by the splendor and filled with wonderment, but seeking to solve the mystery of; "Where is this place"?.. I was questioning myself as to what I should do first, and reached a conclusion before I finished asking the question.

I searched for myself again, for the second time, only I tried more diligently this time. Sensing that I had the power of expansion and contraction, I scrunched down within myself, condensing myself to the smallest possible dimension, to the smallest possible pin point.., and there was nothing!.. I accepted the conclusion that I was.., *without substance!..*

I abandoned the self-search in favor of solving the problem of "Where is this place?" I suspected that this was not a place on planet Earth, and I didn't think you could get here by rocket ship, so that left only "the realm of the mind", but how could I know?.. I was looking at an unmistakable solid reality! What clue should I be looking for?..

By the process of deduction, quicker than asking the question, I had the answer. A flaw... I would look for a flaw. If I could find a flaw, evidence of decay, a crumbled wall, any kind of material breakdown, then this would be evidence that it was of material construction, and if there were no flaws.., it would be in the realm of mind...

With unimpeded motion, I descended down to the edge of the village. Wherever I focused my attention, there I would be. I marveled at the beauty of the dwellings. I was drawn to the architecture of a particular dwelling, where the upturned corner of the pagoda style roof was supported by a decorative angle support that resembled a deer-antler, crafted from the purest gold.., a simple corner brace, but it was artistic perfection... I observed in awe... On the fascia board of the roof edging was a golden crest, about the size and shape of a human heart, like a coat of arms.., inscribed with an emblem I didn't recognize, and there were four peacock feathers that protruded from atop the crest... It was an exquisite work of art. It's beauty and craftsmanship were perfection, it was.., *flawless...* I was caught up in appreciating the beauty of the corner brace and the crest, wondering if it had symbolic purpose as well as decor---. (...I suddenly had that feeling you get when you realize some one is watching you).., I made a half turn to see.., *and I was astounded!..*

I was astounded!.. I was literally blown backwards by the effect of being astounded by what I saw. The super quick calculations that my mind was performing had a time factor, a fraction of a second, but what I saw was the missing piece of the puzzle that instantaneous slammed together all the theories, loose ends, clues, and unanswered questions in one astounding mega-conclusion, *instantly..,* and I was astounded!

I had never been astounded before. I was blown back by the effect, back into my body, and my body instantly catapulted itself off the bed over the foot rail, to the door of the bedroom, and I shouted to my lady-friend, "Come see"!... I realized the absurdity of the statement before I could stop the words from coming out, but it was obvious to my lady-friend that I was in a hyper excited state of mind. I had briefed her before hand that she was assisting me in my experimentation, with the possibility of uncertain results. She was there to prevent my being disturbed by trivialities, a knock on the door, food preparation, etc., and to be a down to earth stable support if I should need it.

I was rapidly trying to explain, in my hyper excited way, the reason for my hyper excited condition, and she was doing her best to try to calm me down, saying; It's o.k., you didn't see anything, it was just your imagination, only a hallucination, nothing happened... I backed away from her with my hands outstretched, palms forward, protecting myself from the heresy she was speaking, as though warding off Dracula with a crucifix.

I calmed myself down for her sake. I had a cup of coffee, briefly explained that I had taken a trip to somewhere else, but I was back now, and all was back to normal. Satisfied that I was alright, she excused herself to go to her evening job. I thanked her for her help, and see you later, etc... I was greatly relieved when she walked out the door.

I went back to the bedroom, to try to get back to where I had been, but it was no use. I could not calm myself down enough. I could not lay down, I could not sit down. I went back to the living room and paced the floor. Pacing the floor is a form of meditation known as "walking meditation", where the body is occupied with an activity so that the mind can be free to contemplate. I was contemplating the scene that had astounded me back to earth...

I had seen a youth, a boy, of about fourteen or fifteen years of age. He was not a God, or spirit, or prince, or anything like that. He was simply a citizen of this realm... He had jet-black hair piled up on his head in three concentric donuts, the largest on the bottom, smaller in the middle, and the smallest on the top. His facial features were Mongol/Oriental/Exotic, his limbs were of the correct proportions, he was naked from the waist up, his skin was the color of bronze with a soft textured sheen, and he was looking at me, from about thirty feet away, with dark almond shaped eyes and a puzzled look on his face, as though he was seeing something that he couldn't explain.....

It was totally unexpected. All I got was that first glance, and with an instantaneous flash of recognition I knew what he was and where I was. I aspirated an astounded "Haaa", as though I had seen a ghost, and as I was rebounding back from the shock, I was wondering what it was that he could see.., *of me??.*

I recognized his facial features and hair style from some art work that I had seen in a book. I had seen an inhabitant of the Deva world, face to face. I had been to the realm of the Devas...

But does the realm of the Devas really exist? Oh yes, it exists. I am an eye witness... All the temples and monasteries in Asia are built on the pagoda style of architecture that is copied from that realm. Pictures of Devas adorn the walls... The evidence is abundant. The documentation is abundant. It is obvious. I am not the only one that has been there...

"The Deva World"

But where does it exist?.. It does not exist in the fourth dimension of timeless space. It cannot be located with the Hubble telescope. It is located where the linear-logical-secular scientists have failed to look!.. It is located in a different dimension altogether!!. A "fifth dimension";.. *the realm of mind!!...* With the discovery of the fifth dimension, my infinite universe.., had just doubled in size...

I laughed out loud. *The irony of it all...* The scientists had looked deep into space, at what they called "their creationless universe". They looked at the "Big Bang" and said that they had "looked at the face of God"!.. Such mockery... There are so many missing links to their creationless theory of evolution. I laughed again. I had found the missing link to the Creation theory. I had found a fifth dimension, and unlike the sterile universe of the fourth dimension.., *It was teeming with life!..*

I thought again, about the boy Deva... His skin, the color of bronze, with its soft textured sheen... It looked exactly like, .., *women's nylon stockings.!!* I laughed again, I laughed long and hard!.. This was information that the behavioral psychologists do not have. They seek to explain the behavior of mankind in terms of evolutionary theory. We are merely reacting to subconscious programming learned over the history of our evolution as survival mechanisms.., like rats in a maze.., We evolved by "Ratamorphosis"... It is a joke.., and the joke is on the behavioral scientists.

Women-kind, at least, are not responding to subconscious programming. They are responding to the super-conscious... They are making themselves more attractive to men by emulating the exotic beauty of the Devas. The bronze colored soft textured sheen of their skin is achieved by wearing nylons, their facial features are made more exotic with lipstick, rouge, eye shadow, etc... They are, without being aware of it.., attempting to look like "Divas".., and men are attracted to them.., because Divas.., are very attractive...

I looked again at the question, "Where is this place"? Despite my eye witness testimony, despite the physical evidence of entire cultures that have emulated the Pagoda style of architecture for their most important buildings, their temples and monasteries, despite the enormous amount of art work and ceremonies depicting the grace and beauty of the Deva world.., despite the eye witness testimony of Prophets and Seers, despite the documentation in the Buddhist, Hindu, Old and New Testaments.., despite all that.., "They".., the scientists, astronomers, behaviorists, evolutionists.., Secular Humanists, etc.., are just not going to believe it!.. They aren't even going to consider it!.. If they can't get it under their microscope, if they can't focus it in their telescope, it simply doesn't exist!!. They will land their space ships on barren distant planets, before they will look into the realm of their own mind and Soul.!. To ignore the realm of the mind and Soul.., is ignorance indeed...

Even though I had just returned from there, there was still a puzzlement in my own mind. It is so difficult for the linear-logical-material mentality to grasp. *"How"?.,* could there be a physical, solid, three dimensional world, existing in the fifth dimension of the realm of mind, and it not exist in forth dimensional timeless space??...

As I was pondering this question, deep in thought, I was also rummaging through the kitchen to appease my hunger for a snack. I spotted a packet of saltine crackers, and still deep in thought I sat there eating them. I got up and was returning to the living room to continue my pacing.., and suddenly, without reason, I stopped, and was standing there, in a pose... I was so deep in thought that I didn't realize that I was standing there.., in a pose. Eventually I became aware, and I asked myself;.. "Why am I standing here, in this pose"?.. I was standing there, with my right hand raised in front of my face, three fingers and thumb curled into my palm, index finger straight up. I gazed at my index finger, *and there it was!!.,* right on the tip of my index finger!..

It was a cracker crumb, perched on the tip of my index finger. I looked into the cracker crumb, and saw that it was a world.., and on this world there was a being, standing there in a pose, with his finger in the air, and there was a cracker crumb on the tip of his finger, and the cracker crumb was a world.., and on this world, there was a being, with his finger in the air.., ...I reeled from the concept!!. The implications stagger the mind...

My first reaction was to reject it. *"No.., it just couldn't be"!.,* I said, with my linear-logical mind, based in the laws of physics as they apply to the material world... But I had just returned from a physically material world that existed in a non-material universe, a universe of mind, a universe in which the laws of physics do not apply... The realm of mind has it's own laws.., ...and nothing is impossible!..

Now, there was another thing for my linear-logical mind to try to cope with;.. the manner in which the concept came to me. How did it happen that my body stood there in a pose, not of my own making, without my even being aware of it?.. How did it happen that there was a cracker crumb placed exactly on the tip of my finger?.. It appeared that there was even another dimension, of even greater importance, to this experience... We are not alone.!. *There **IS..**,* an "Overseeing Intelligence"...

I cannot remember ever having been astonished or astounded before in my life. This experience, from astonishment, through amazement, to astoundment, took far less time to happen than it does to tell about it... Probably about ten seconds.., maybe less. The amazing part, was the quickness of my mind. By the process of deduction, questions were answered faster than they could be asked.., analyses made, decisions reached, in a fraction of a second... If only my mind worked that efficiently all the time. A lot happened in those few seconds.

I went over to see a friend of mine, and told him of the experience. "Oh Wow", he said. "That's really is an amazing story! You should maybe write a book about it, or something... Would I like to have a beer?.. Did I know what the baseball score was"?..

      *   *   *   *   *   *

BOOK III

"Analysis of the Experience"

I have lost faith in the spoken word. I have told and retold this experience to those people.., friends.., whom I thought would have a keen interest. They did have an interest, a fascination of the moment, with exclamations of "Wow", and "far out'", etc., but it never went any farther than that. The spoken word was launched out into open space, momentarily reverberating off an eardrum, with a momentary reaction. Sometimes the story survived a retelling, and there would be.., distortions. I have been misquoted.., and there has been derision...

The spoken word is spent and dead and forgotten. The momentary reaction to the spoken word is also soon spent and forgotten. Nobody asked any pertinent questions. Nobody brought up the subject again. The outcome was always the same; "Did I know what the baseball score was?, would I like to have a beer"?... The spoken word was launched into open space.., and it evaporated!..

So I have chosen as my medium of communication, the printed word. The printed word is solid and tangible. It can be quoted, but not misquoted. It cannot be distorted, and it will not evaporate. But, it carries with it an obligation. An obligation to be accurate, concise, and to the point. Of the utmost importance is Truth.., as the bottom line...

I have rendered the facts of this experience as faithfully as I can, but with time I have found that there is a multitude of corroborating evidence. "Swami Sri Yukteswar", writes of this experience[1]: "One who has this experience, is as though he were born again". I don't know about being born again, but for sure, *life would never be the same!!*. I have a point of reference that is shared by very few people, the reality of what I call; "the fifth dimension"...

Other people may have called it "Heaven", or a "parallel universe", or "the fine material plane", or whatever... There are references to it in all the religions of the world and spoken of by all the great Teachers and Masters who have crossed that threshold. This is the "Missing Link" of creation, and it is the death of Existentialism... *Essence..,* does indeed.., precede existence.

Look around you, if you will, and examine the evidence. Every man made product and invention that you see was first a creation in the mind... From a non-material realm, out of nothing, came something... An idea! The idea was transferred to the two dimensional plane.., plans on paper. Materials were gathered and assembled, and Viola! A three dimensional object now exists on planet Earth, in a four dimensional universe... With the exception of plans on paper, does this not sound remarkably like the process whereby "Adam" set foot on Earth?.... The concept of "Man", (Adam).., was already a reality in the fifth dimension. With a few "adaptive modifications", he was made a reality on Earth.

The ability of "adaptive modifications", the process whereby mankind can adapt to changes in his environment, is an inborn, pre-programmed in, genetic trait. The potential is always there in the genetic variables, the dominant and recessive genes. Given a new set of circumstances, a recessive gene will become dominant. Given the genetic mix of male and female, all of humankind is a variation , one from another, all uniquely different, yet all uniquely the same.., the family of "Man"... Science has mistaken *adaptation*.., ...for evolution!..

There is a fundamental difference between adaptation and evolution. There is also a fundamental difference between Genotypes. The lizard, for instance, is a different genotype than a rabbit, and the rabbit is a different genotype than a gazelle... The lizards can live in the forests, and they can live in the deserts. The forest lizard will undergo certain modifications, and recessive genes will come into play, and the lizard will adapt to his environment, and turn green... The desert lizard will likewise adapt to his environment, and turn brown, like sand.. Where the desert meets the forest,

---

[1] A priceless little book, called: "The Holy Science" written by the Hindu Saint; Swami Sri Yuketswar (published 1949, by the "Self Realization Fellowship of America")... I have also quoted from his book, the phrase: "the variegated cloak of words", which I have seen the truth of, and which I use in several places throughout this book... The Swami is best known for his role as being the Spiritual Master (Guru) of his illustrious disciple; "Paramhansa Yogananda"...

these two lizards meet and out of dozen little lizard eggs comes a dozen little lizards. Three are green, three are brown, three are speckled green and brown, and three can change their color from green to brown at will. The green lizard is camouflaged in the forest, the brown in the desert, the "chameleon" in both the forest and desert, and the green and brown in neither the forest or the desert. The genetic dice have been rolled, and there are now four species of lizard. The non-camouflaged specie becomes part of the food chain, so there are only three species... Actually, there are 3,500 different species of lizards, each one a modified *adaptation*.., but they are all from the Genus "Lizard", and are "Lizard Specific" to their genetic genotype... While there are many adaptive modifications that go on within the lizard genotype, there are no evolutionary jumps beyond it! The genetic code of each genotype is "genus specific" to that genotype, and cannot propagate with any other genetic code that is not of the same genotype... A lizard, no matter what the adaptive modifications, will always be a lizard, and will not evolve into a rabbit, and the rabbit will always be a rabbit and will not evolve into a gazelle. There is no "genetic chain of events" that would link a lizard with a rabbit. There is no "genetic chain of events" that would suggest an evolutionary jump from one genotype into another genotype. The "Missing links", are missing because they never existed...

Or would you rather believe that a primordial sea slug crawled out of the ocean and the sun shined on it, so it developed an eyeball to see, but it took millions of years of evolutionary effort. Do I detect a "missing link" here? But even so, that's still pretty good for a sea slug, I mean, to figure out that it needed an eyeball in the first place, and then to extract the nutrient properties from the slime of the earth that it sucked on, converted them to compounds, and proceeded to build an eyeball. And not just any eyeball, this eyeball must be made of a very strong material, and yet be flexible and resilient. It must be fitted with a perfectly curved, flawlessly transparent, insta/automatic adjustable focal point, to see things near or far away. This is made possible by a network of muscle fibers that may be tinted various shades of color, so as to be more attractive to a mate. The focal point must be perfectly positioned to focus the incoming light on a network of retina perfectly positioned to receive it. It's got to be able to make adjustments for bright or dim light, and in some cases it will inject a florescent into its inner aqueous solution to enhance night vision. Then Its got to have an eyelid that will open and close to protect it from harm and block out the light when it wants to sleep. The eyelid must be lubricated with special lubricants, so as not to scratch the lens, and come equipped with eyelashes, with touch sensors, to brush away debris.., in the blink of an eye.., *automatically*!!.

I see another "missing link" here. This is very "High Tech"!!. Too high tech for a sea slug.., or a human being…

There is a missing link here at every step of this process, and there is a mega missing link in the assembly and orchestration of the components into a functioning bio-technical organism that allows us to see.., *effortlessly*!!.

The key word here is "orchestration"!.. Just one missing link in this orchestrated chain of events.., and the final result.., sight.., (and "Man").., does not happen!!!

This is at the surface level. We can delve deeper into this mystery, we can examine the make-up of any component at the cellular level. The retina, for instance, composed of photo sensitive cells able to transform light into electro-sensitive nerve impulses and relay them with the speed of light to a central intelligence component that comprehends what it sees.., (more or less)?...

All of this vast network of cells is nourished by another vast network of blood vessels, arteries, veins, capillaries.., exchanging oxygen molecules for carbon dioxide, supplying nutrients, carrying away waste, repairing, replacing.., etc. We can go down to the molecular level, and view the mysteries and wonders that go on there.., and be amazed!!. Down to the atomic level, and to the sub-atomic level.., where the physicists numbers have very large exponents, and the finest of all particles are referred to as.., "mind stuff".., and the mysteries deepen.., *profoundly*!

Hearts, pumping blood.., lungs, pumping oxygen.., digestive systems, pumping nutrients.., elimination systems, pumping waste.., immune systems, warding off disease.., sensory systems, pumping information!.. All systems working independently, as if they had a mind of their own. All those specialized cells, just doing their jobs, and all working together with precision and harmony, each phase blending into the next, to one grand objective.., the miracle of sight!... Do I hear any applause? Is there any appreciation? Is there even any recognition?...

The missing link here is;., "Intelligence". It should be obvious to a blind person that there is intelligence involved here. It should be obvious that the intelligence is beyond the capacity and capability of the sea slug, or of a human being.., who cannot by the force of his will, alter one single hair on his head!!.

Did blind evolution bring about the miracle of sight? The evolutionists would have you believe so. With smug certainty they will point out that eyeballs are a very common occurrence, every creature on earth that has an asshole has two eyeballs, so there are twice as many eyeballs as there are assholes. No miracle about it!.. So how did evolution bring about the eyeball? Well, by evolution of course!.. Everybody knows that!.. The key words here, are;., "smug certainty"...

We could continue our analysis in the opposite direction, away from the microcosm.., into the macrocosm…

Add a second eye.., add stereoscopic vision and depth perception. Add a skull, to house and protect the eyes and the central intelligence component... (Mystery Divine)... Add a body, for mobility. Add a thousand support systems necessary to the eye. Add The additional sensory components; Nostrils;., that can detect and identify the faintest of odors, measured in parts per million!.. Touch;., so sensitive that it can detect the caress of a gentle breeze, or read in total darkness, with the finger tips, and with a reaction time measured in hundredths of a second!.. Hearing;., that can locate the source of sound, and give identity to things not seen!.. Taste;., the ability to detect the subtle differences in flavor, and identify it's nature and composition!.. Add the intuitive faculties, add fluidity and grace or movement, add poise, symmetry, beauty.., a face!., that will express it's innermost feelings in a thousand different faces, from laughter to sadness, from love to hate, from pleasure to pain, from anger to compassion... Add an identity, add a name, add the opposite sex, add articulate speech, add the twinkle in a lovers eye!.. Add laughter!.. Add the Earth on which to stand, add the Sun in the morning and the Moon at night, add starlit skies and sandy beaches, add a magnificent steed on which to ride, tall ships to sail the seas.., and worlds to conquer!

Add that all up, and what do you find? I find the unmistakable evidence of an intelligence so.., "*SUBLIME*"!!. Even the linear-logical mind must stand in reverential AWE at the ***magnificence of this "Grand Design"!..*** We are looking at the handiwork of a Master architect, artist, and builder. I see beyond intelligence here. I see;., *Poetry*!!. I see Beauty. I see Art. I see Ability. I see Genius. I see Brilliance. I see Splendor. I see Mystery and Majesty.., and More!., and so much more....

The ancient Bedouins, famed for their ability of tracking man and beast over desolate terrain, when asked how they knew there was a God, answered;., "I know there is a God because I see His tracks.., everywhere"!!. His tracks are everywhere...

***   ***   ***

If the men of science, in their laboratories, were to transform sunlight into matter, they would award themselves with Nobel Prizes and congratulate themselves, and call each other;., "Genius"!!. The World would applaud...

The simplest life forms of the vegetable kingdom, a blade of grass, has the ability of transforming sunlight into matter, without the by-product of heat, and with the by-product of; ...oxygen... and it spreads forth a thousand fold, the tiniest of seeds, which brings forth new plants of it's own kind, and it is alive, and it is;., "Food"!!. Life, consumes life, to maintain life, to propagate life!!. Do I detect a Cosmic conspiracy here?..

It turns out that the simplest life forms of the plant kingdom are not really that simple after all. The processes that go on within the plants are really quite ingenious. An army of scientists, with microscopes in hand, spend their entire lives researching and cataloguing the processes that are unique to each plant, filling up biology books that fill up libraries, and they will readily admit that they have barely scratched the surface.

The symbiotic relationships between the plant kingdom and the insect, animal, and human kingdoms, again show the unmistakable characteristics of the hand of intelligence…

There are the plants that produce flowers.., of beauty, color, symmetry, sweet smelling and tasty.., that attract the bees, that spread the pollen, that propagates the species!.. Very intelligent for a plant, very necessary for the bees... There are the plants that produce the berries.., that feed the birds that fly through the air and expel the seeds to earth, wrapped in a dollop of rich fertilizer!!. Very clever of the plant, and very nutritious for the birds. There are the plants that produce sweet and nutritious fruit, that are eaten by animals that also expel the seeds in fertilized packets. Other plants send their seeds aloft with little parachute like devices that catch the wind and ride the breeze!.. Still others snag onto a passing animal and hitch a ride until dropped in a new location... All of these examples are evidence of an intelligence that is beyond the capabilities of the plant itself.

Not to be overlooked is the mathematical probability factor of seed production. Some seeds will be consumed as food by animals and insects. Others will be attacked by bacteria and fungus. Some will fall on barren land and be dried out by the sun. Others will germinate, but will not survive long enough to reproduce itself. Only a small percentage will find favorable conditions for germination and reproduction. The plant knows the odds.., and plays the percentages...

And speaking of mathematics!!, again we see the hand of **"That"** Master Architect at work!!... Incorporated into the **design** of the "lowly plant" *(and indeed, in all of nature!)* can be found the "Sacred Geometry" of the most advanced and esoteric mathematical principles of:., *"Projective Geometry".., "Harmonic Proportion".., the "Golden Section".., the "Fibonacci Series".., the "Logarithmic Spiral"..,* etc. and etc.!!! **So you see..,** beauty is not simply in the eye of the beholder, but is intentionally designed into the "art and architecture" of all of Nature!!... *Think on these things!.[2].*

Also not to be overlooked is the astounding Intelligent foresight that has been built into our planet from the dawn of time itself! Oil!., that is indispensable to our modern way of life, that powers our factories, lights our cities, heats our homes, and propels us through the skies and across the face of the earth! Oil.., and coal.., are not minerals, as you might suppose, but are in fact the prehistoric remains of vast forests that have been buried under miles of sediment earth, beneath oceans, mountains and plains!!, evidence of cataclysmic Earth changes (and the Great Flood?)!.. "There is far more (Intelligent Foresight) than is dreamt about in your philosophy, (Horatio)"!..

Plants;., besides being the basic foundational food supply for all life forms, besides being the primary source of energy on this planet, besides providing for the very air that we breathe.., the fibers that we weave into clothing.., the timbers with which we build our homes.., for all of which humankind is the direct beneficiary.., besides all that, we have to take a closer look at the processes that go on within the plants themselves...

Processes that are as mysterious and profound as they are complicated and wonderful... I have heard it stated, that if scientists could duplicate the process of photosynthesis in the laboratory, they could put an end to world hunger! To my knowledge, they haven't been able to duplicate the process that nature does so effortlessly and efficiently. Just to take common dead earth, and mix it with sunlight to produce living matter, is a feat that should inspire us to reverence, if we could ever develop the capacity to appreciate it, but it is so common that we overlook its significance...

The sheer volume and variety of compounds that are produced in the laboratories of the plant kingdom stagger the mind. Complicated chains of molecules that combine the rare elements of minerals, gases, liquids, proteins, sugars, acids, alkaloids, carbons, etc., and fashion them into geometric patterns of cubes, triangles, pyramids, spheres, octagons, dodecahedrons, etc., at the atomic and sub atomic levels.., producing a pharmacopoeia of exotic compounds that we use to cure our illnesses, remove our pains, induce us to sleep, keep us awake, improve our health, etc.

Beyond all this.., "Nature", "In Her Infinite Wisdom", has provided us with a special class of:.; "Herbs of Mysterious Virtue"... Plants, with special properties.., that can transport us to higher levels of consciousness!.. To elevate our thinking, to be able to comprehend the mysteries of the universe, to be

---

[2] One paragraph (or one book) is not enough to fully appreciate the significance of this "Sacred Geometry" that is incorporated into all of Nature, and most significantly.., in the human body!… The temple of Karnak, in Egypt (for instance) was built (1400 B.C.) in accordance with this "Divine Geometry", and just being in this temple, surrounded by these "Divine Proportions" would effect, *and raise*, the consciousness of those who entered into it… This same principle has been used by the great architects of modern times (our Cathedrals, Capital buildings, etc.) as well as in ancient times (the Parthenon, etc.)… For a greater appreciation of these principles, read: "Projective Geometry", by Rudolph Steiner..., and etc…

able to discover the Nobility of Mankind, and the Nobility within ourselves... These plants were known as;., "The Plants of the Gods" [3] ...

This might be called the supreme achievement of the plant kingdom. The discovery and synthesis of these compounds has been called.., by some scientists and theologians.., the greatest and most significant discovery of the 20th Century!... That is a very bold statement, considering that we conquered flight, landed a man on the Moon, completed the periodic table of the elements, utilized Nuclear energy, mapped the human genome, etc., and etc...

Of course, not everyone agrees with this viewpoint. The American government, for one, has outlawed the use of this "mind expanding" class of "psychedelic" drugs, and puts it in the "schedule one" category, which includes such Narcotic drugs as heroine, crack-cocaine, etc. Never mind that these mind expanding substances are neither addictive nor habit forming. Never mind that they have therapeutic value, and can be used to cure many of societies psychological ills. Never mind that the cure for heroine addiction has been found, and the victim can be freed from his addiction.., AND the withdrawal symptoms.., by just one or two sessions with the psycho-active alkaloid called;., "Ibogaine".., which is manufactured in that "mysterious alchemical laboratory", located in the root of the "Iboga" plant.

The heroine addict, while under the full influence of heroine intoxication, takes the drug "Ibogaine", and for the next 36 hours drifts in and out of a deep reverie. There is a disassociation of mind from body, and the participant views his entire life from a "higher" objective viewpoint. A "Zen" perspective, if you will. The "viewer", while analyzing his past life, will frequently have conversations with "persons unseen" that are there to assist the participant in the "healing process". Immature attitudes are analyzed in the light of objective truth.., and discarded. Maturity.., is gained, and with this new maturity, a new outlook on life is gained. The Truth has been seen, and the Truth.., will set you free. The participant has no desire to repeat the sins of the past, and is in fact.., "Healed"... Not only is the person healed in his mind and his Soul, but his body, that would normally undergo excruciating and almost unbearable withdrawal symptoms from the heroine addiction, has also been healed!.. This is a spiritual healing, and there are no withdrawal symptoms... The healing has been complete!..

Ibogaine has been called; "The Healing Drug", and it has been shown to be almost 100 percent effective in curing heroine addiction. Rarely is a second session required.

Heroine addiction is only one of a host of addictions that mankind is plagued with. Ibogaine has been found to be equally successful with these other addictions as well. Let it be understood, that Ibogaine itself cures nothing. It permits access to a fifth dimensional realm, and the healing comes from there. The full potential of this healing process has yet to be explored.., and that would require the existence of a fifth dimensional reality to be recognized, as a fact...

The Iboga plant is just one of less than one-hundred plants with psycho-active properties. This plant is indigenous to West-central Africa, and although there are many different tribes that inhabit that area, they are united in brotherhood by their common use of the Iboga plant in their religion and culture. The Christian and Islamic missionaries have been unsuccessful in their attempts at converting these people.., who already have direct access to the spirit world!..

* * *   * * *   * * *

All life forms, from insects to alligators, from plants to animals, from serpents to elephants, from birds to buffalo, from fish to fishermen.., all display a uniqueness of design that can only be described as;., *creative!..*

Creativity.., from an inexhaustible effervescent life/energy source that manifests itself in 27,000 different species of insects, 3,500 different species of lizards, 2,500 different species of snakes.., etc. and etc. I could go on and on... Each and every one of these species, in their form and in their function, displays evidence of a creative, artistic intelligence...

The lowly skunk.., Natures little clown.., gaily bedecked in his black and white striped clown suit, prances through the forest with his tail held aloft, like a proud flag waving in the breeze.., cocked at the ready... The skunk has a secret;., an obnoxious

---

[3] The "Plants of the Gods", origins of hallucinogenic use.., by Richard Evans Schultes, and Albert Hofmann... 1979...

potion, "secreted" in that secret laboratory of internal glands, ready to be expelled, with accuracy, in the face of a hungry predator, who immediately loses his appetite for skunk... The formula for this secret obnoxious potion (patent pending), is a secret from even the skunk!.. The formula for this secret potion, is KNOWLEDGE!.. I ask the scientist and the evolutionist: "From whence commeth this Knowledge"?.. The knowledge of the formula, and the knowledge of it's manufacture... From whence commeth this Knowledge?..

The deadly poison of the serpent, efficiently delivered through hypodermic fangs?.. I see Genius in the design and manufacture.., and Knowledge in the deadly formula... And the formula for the simple secretion of stomach acids, that can etch metal, dissolve teeth, flesh and bones!., while encased within a fleshly organ that is impervious to it?..

And the formula for the production of "Endorphins", that opium-like compound secreted in the brain, that can alleviate pain, and stimulate higher mind functions, and the body has opiate receptors to receive the endorphin production.., or the production of the Poppy fields.., and this too is a secret formula, manufactured by a plant... *Now isn't that coincidental.!?.*

Evolutionist theory breaks down here;.. not only does it break down,.. it falls apart... When it comes to the production of endorphins, seratonin, dopamine, secretions of the pineal gland, etc. and etc.., those mysterious compounds involved in higher mind functions.., the explanation that "evolution did it", is an insult to the intelligence... What the evolutionists cannot explain, they ignore!.. This is called: *"Ignor-ence"*...

What is the source of this Knowledge?.. This question is never answered, because it is never asked... This is beyond the limits of the linear-logical "flat earth" mentality of the scientists and evolutionists... The source of this Knowledge is never recognized, never acknowledged, never even considered!!, Obviously brilliant, obviously intelligent, IT is never ever NAMED... To not ask, and not answer this question is *very* **unscientific!**.. For all of their intellectual sophistication.., *they are SHALLOW*...

They would have you believe that evolution designed and produced the brain, without a concept, without a plan, by random chance.., so that it could think (about evolution, no doubt?)!!. Always, and without apology, they put the "cart before the horse"!.. It would seem that evolutionary theory is dependent on always "lifting itself up by it's boot straps" *(an impossibility),* not only by contradicting the force of gravity, but by ignoring it altogether...

It is not conceivable, to the mechanical linear-logical mentality, that there could exist a "First Cause" that is consciousness based, rather than a "cosmic accident" that is materially based... What is the material-mechanical basis for the imagination?., and for the stuff of dreams?., and Who is the Mechanical Genius behind this magnificent orchestration that I see before me?.. The linear-logical-material-mechanical mentality cannot conceive of or acknowledge an intelligence greater than its own, so it doesn't ask these questions.., and it is not arrogance, as much as it is ignorance...

In a court of law, when two or more "eye witnesses" testify to the truth of a certain event, it is held to be the Truth and a fact... There have been countless "eye witness" testimonies to the similarities of the "near death" experience.. "spontaneous healings".., "visitations" of Saints and departed Souls, bona-fide "Miracles", and the reality of a Fifth Dimensional **"Essence"**.., that precedes Existence... In any other branch of science this abundance of testimony would be classified as "Empirical Evidence"... And if Science be truly scientific, I expect that by the force of logic, it will take that "Intuitive Leap" into the fifth dimension, and the headlines of the "Scientific Journals" will one day read: ...By the Preponderance of the Evidence;., "God".., **"Is"**...

There is *Genius* in the design and construction of a butterfly's wing! There is *Mystery* in the metamorphosis of the caterpillar.., into a butterfly!., and a child can see it and say;., *"It is Beautiful"!!.* With our shallow mentality, we have a poor concept of what constitutes "Glory", but the butterfly wears it's glory proudly, as though a masterpiece, signed by the Artist... This work of Art, of Mystery, and of Genius, is child's play, when compared to the Sublime Achievement of Cognitive Intelligence in the Magnificent Body of;., "Man"!!. What other purpose could there be for all of creation if there were not Mankind to comprehend it, and say;.., *"It is Beautiful"!!!*

***   ***   ***

"The Theory of De-evolution"

There are many different theories of evolution. Few things have evolved as much as the continuously evolving theory of evolution. Consider If you will.., an alternate theory. The theory of "De-evolution"...

De-evolution is very easy to bring about. Suppose we were to swap the new born children of a college educated community with the new born children of a primitive cave dwelling tribe. The children from the cave dwelling parents would become college graduates, but the children from the educated parents would be killing their food with rocks. How many millennium would go by before they discovered the wheel? How many more millennium would go by before they discovered the existence of.., a fifth dimension?... De-evolution from the space age back to the stone age would be brought about *immediately..*, by the loss of knowledge...

I see other evidence of de-evolution, in the physical sense. Again, the evidence is obvious and abundant. I see the weakening of the human race.., by inbreeding!!. When two identical gene sequences are paired up, one of two consequences result... Either the genetic trait is cancelled out completely, (you cannot shake hands with your mirror image) resulting in a defect, or.., in rare cases, the genetic trait is doubled, resulting in an abnormality or a deformity!.. (big noses, etc.)...

I see:., male pattern baldness. I see cleft palates. I see imperfections of the cornea, in the eye. I see genetically inherited diseases of the blood, the inability to metabolize certain foods, allergies, deformities, a weakening of the immune system.., cancers.., etc... Any deviation away from perfection is towards imperfection.., and no one.., lives to the age of Methuselah any more!!.

In the theory of De-evolution,[4] Adam.., with Eve, is seen as the perfect creation of God. Genetically perfect. Adam had it all... The perfect clarity of mind that we would call the "Zen" state of mind. A perfectly integrated personality, a true "Alpha"... He functioned from the center of his being, with purpose, and without a trace of self doubt. A Zen Master.., before there was a concept!..

His memory was photographic. His imagination was illumined inner vision. His immune system warded off any possibility of disease. Genetic diseases were unknown. Physical perfection, a wonder to behold, with strength of body and clarity of mind. The first man, was;., the "Omega Man"!!. Genetic Perfection!..

Enter.., an enemy!., from the dark side of the realm of the fifth dimension! That evil one, called "Satan", in the form of the serpent, seduced first Eve, and through Eve, then Adam, causing their fall. Their fall, was from the Zen state of mind.., to the "self conscious" state of mind. They became self conscious, and hid themselves.., because they discovered.., they were naked!...

The two trees of the garden, the "Tree of Life" and the "Tree of the Knowledge of Good and Evil" were not your simple ordinary fruit trees. The Tree of Life had consciousness expanding properties, where the "Doors of Perception"[5] were opened and the grandeur and majesty of all of creation could be seen, examined and appreciated, at the atomic level or at the galactic level, with the eye of insight, the eye of the mind, where the observer and that which was observed.., became One!.. The fruit of this tree

---

[4] It may seem that the author has taken "liberties", and "poetic license" with the classically understood story of Adam and Eve in the Garden of Eden, the "Tree of Life", and the "Tree of the Knowledge of Good and Evil".., but the author gives to the reader here, his insights and knowledge of the reality of "altered states" of consciousness as well as the understanding of the Zen-objective (Superior) state of mind, and the "Fall" from grace into the "negative- subjective" (inferior) state of mind, which may seem unfamiliar to the reader who has never identified these states, and therefore.., lacks the "intuitive insight" that is the product of the (herbally induced) altered state of expanded consciousness... Also, the "Tree of Life" is again referred to in the book of Revelations: 22-2.., where: "the leaves of the Tree (*an herbal remedy*) are for the healing of nations"!..

[5] "The Doors of Perception", by Aldous Huxley, 1952

was akin to the class of drugs we would today call; "mind expanding"…

The fruit of the "Tree of the Knowledge of Good and Evil" was probably akin to the "nicotine" class of drugs that we would today call "downers", where the consciousness of the partakers becomes "self conscious" (subjectivity), and that which is observed is "other" than ourselves. The world of hard and harsh reality. The world of "duality". The world of "us" and "them", good and bad, right and wrong, beauty and ugliness, pleasure and pain, health and sickness, innocence and guilt, life.., and ultimately.., death!.. *Otherwise known as:* **the "Ego-centered life"!!…**

The Zen state of mind, is the totally objective state of mind. To experience guilt, or doubt, or fear, or any emotion relating to self is to be in the self conscious, subjective state of mind, and true objectivity is clouded by personal motives of "self" survival. Self consciousness is very inhibiting, and the "natural" state is lost. That graceful state (the "state of grace"), the Zen state,... is lost!..

What need now for a photographic memory? To be able to recall in perfect detail the scene of the "fall"? To experience again and again the guilt and shame of the loss of innocence? A perfect memory is now a source of pain. Better to be able to forget.., if only they could...

A photographic memory is genetically inherited. I knew personally, a family that had this genetic trait. The mother had it, and the two daughters had it, but the son didn't have it, and the father didn't have it. The one daughter became a lawyer. I asked her what it was like to have a photographic memory. She said,.. "It doesn't make me any smarter than anybody else, but I can call up and see before me in my minds eye every word on every page of every book I ever read!"... She continued; "I may not have even understood what I read when I read it the first time, but I can recall it up and reread it until I understand it. I felt guilty about it when I was going to school, because it was like reading from the book when I took my tests"... Most people have no concept at all of what it's like to have a photographic memory... The other daughter lived at home with her parents, and was very reclusive. I presumed that she had had some bad experiences with life, that left her with some indelible "bad memories", but I really don't know the real story.

A photographic memory is a genetically inherited trait... It is not a trait that is evolving up... It is a trait that is handed down... It has all but died out, due to
inbreeding and the loss of the "Zen" state of mind, but in many cases, it is still there in the recessive genes. It may well be the geneticist that will, in some future time, lead us back to that "Brave New World" of the genetically perfect "Omega Man", and the elimination of all genetically inherited diseases and defects.

What does the Zen state of mind have to do with memory? The secret of a good memory is;., focused concentration. You can't really remember something if you aren't really paying attention to it. It doesn't imprint properly.

In the "self conscious" state of mind, The faculty of concentration is divided into two parts; the observer, and the thing which he observes, (be it an external object or an internal subject of contemplation)... In the Zen state of mind, the only thing that exists; is that thing which is observed... This is the key to the understanding of Zen, and it is the key to perfect, effortless concentration...

So the fall of Man from the Zen-objective state of "object oriented" observation, to the guilt ridden state of "self-oriented" observation, is the fall from grace, the expulsion from the guilt-free Zen-objective garden of paradise, and the loss of the fruit of the "Tree of Life" that afforded the "Third Eye" insightful view of the Microcosmic mysteries and the Macrocosmic splendors...

There were two methods by which procreation was possible. By a spiritual process, or by an animal process. The first process was lost in the fall, and the animal process was the only means left... The rest is genetic history, a history of inbreeding away from perfection, a history of De-evolution...

* * *   * * *   * * *

This was not my first experience with a mind altering substance, nor was it to be my last. One may ask the question, "What is a Western educated, Caucasian-American, essentially Christian man doing.., having what is essentially an Eastern (Hindu-Buddhist) religious experience"?..

Suffice it to say, I am a student of the mind and the Soul of all religions, not by choice, or as an academic pursuit, but as a natural bent of my personality. I have no choice, and if I had a choice, this is what I would choose. This is who I am!.. I am looking for the Truth, wherever it may be found, and as the natural bent of my personality dictates.., I have to look everywhere!..

No one religion has an exclusive on the truth, and there is no religion that is free from error. If the truth is to be found, it will show up as the same truth in all religions as "universals". The universal truths that stand by themselves, beyond the labels of any particular religion. Where there is conflict between the truths of different religions, this is where error lies, or a misunderstanding, or a misinterpretation. There may be conflicts between different religions, but there is no conflict in the Truth. The Truth stands alone. The Truth is absolute...

The truth cannot be known at the intellectual level. Indeed, intellectuals are suspect!.. There are passionate intellectuals that are Communists, Socialists, Atheists, Evolutionists, Secular-Humanists, and even Religionists.

Nor can the truth be known at the religious level. Regardless of your fervent faith, or how deeply you believe, You cannot say; "I know". You can only say; "I believe". Men will die for what they believe. Men will kill each other for what they believe. Belief is no substitute for knowledge. In the absence of knowledge, you are going to believe "something"... You must be very careful what you believe...

The truth can be known only at the experiential level... Only when you have experienced it yourself, can you say for a fact, "I know". Up until that time, the best you can hope for is a reasoned conclusion, and pray that your conclusions somewhat resemble the truth. The problem is, we don't even have enough facts to arrive at a reasoned conclusion!.. Information is lacking. We're not playing with a full deck!..

The purpose of this book, is to supply the reader with the information that is lacking.., by way of direct knowledge gained at the experiential level. I am not telling you what I think, or what I believe, I am telling you what I know through direct first-hand experience. Without this knowledge.., Science, Religion, and Philosophy have arrived at misleading and incorrect conclusions.

With the inclusion of this knowledge into our otherwise incomplete equation, we can arrive at more complete and correct conclusions. We can cross reference these conclusions with what is known in the various disciplines of Science, the doctrines of various religions and philosophies. We can corroborate our findings... We can gain perspective.

* * *   * * *   * * *

(Quoting Myself)

How could you explain to someone that music could be heard, felt, "Seen", and ***"experienced"..,*** with the mind alone.?. "I ***"was"*** the music"! * * *

"My vision was perfectly clear because **"I"** was the eye, and my eye was **"I"**. * * *

"I made a diligent search for myself… I could not be found!.. Not a pin-point center, not a cross-hair location, not a circumference, no trace of anything…. *Nothing*!.. and yet.., ***I was!*** There was only;., *"I think, therefore, I am"*!.. * * *

(End Quote)

These are first-hand, direct, "out of body" ***experiences..,*** of the ***reality*** of the Soul…

* * *   * * *   * * *

…..Let us bring ourselves up to date on the latest Scientific facts: ... After extensive genetic testing of all the races of mankind throughout the world, it was determined that there were five distinct genetic families of man. Using computers, the scientists played with the mathematics of the genetic codes and soon the five distinct strains dissolved into only three genetic strains. More research into the mathematics and.., "Viola"!!, the three genetic strains merged into only ***one!.,*** proving conclusively, scientifically, and empirically, that we are all truly.., one family of man!..

This lead to the unmistakable, scientific, and empirical conclusion.., that the entire human race.., descended "exclusively" from just "one" ancestral Mother.., that they embarrassingly called;., "Eve"!..

Furthermore, with their new genetic science, they were able to determine that the bones they had dug up of prehistoric man, Neanderthal man, Peking man, etc., were in fact.., not man at all!!. No relation to the offspring of Eve!., and in fact.., not related to the human family!!. Their new guesstimate conclusion is that mankind goes back in time no further than two hundred thousand years (that is 200,000... *and Not 200 million*).., at the most!!...

Oops!.. Update; (2002), The most recent guess/estimate puts Man (Homo-Sapiens) on Earth about One hundred thousand years ago (Evolution evolves again)[6].., while the shark has not changed in two hundred million years!!.

The cornerstone of evolutionary theory, "Piltdown Man", with the skull of a man and the jawbone of an ape, touted as the "missing link", was found to be;., a hoax and a fraud! For forty two years (1911 to 1953) science pointed at this counterfeit and accepted it without question as scientific proof!.. For forty two years all the text books in all the schools of all the world published this fraud as the fact, and to believe otherwise was just unscientific... Their cornerstones have crumbled into dust, and their house was built on sand, but their text books.., remain the same...

* * *   * * *   * * *

It is a postulate of evolutionary theory, that all development results in response to a need, but there are several examples in nature that seem to contradict this postulate.

Take for example the Salmon of North America. They are spawned in the inland streams and rivers of North America, and begin their long journey down stream and down rivers, to the sea... Approximately four years and 10,000 miles later, this fish, finds it's way back to that very river, and swimming up river against the current, (a Herculean feat) sometimes hundreds of miles inland, will find the very stream from which they descended, and proceeds upstream to that very place from which they were spawned, and they spawn!!, replenishing the stream and their population with a new generation... This is a brilliant feat of navigation.., for a fish!!.

I'm sure, that the fish doesn't know how he does it, or even why. There seems to be *another* force at work!..

This remarkable fish, with a genius for navigation and Herculean strength, could just swim inland to the first fresh water lake and spawn there, or simply adapt to spawning in the ocean.., but no, this fish swims his heart out!., up every river, tributary, stream and creek.., against the current!.. The result of this epic event is quite remarkable to behold...

The fast running streams and rivers would soon wash this fish out to sea, and the streams and rivers would be barren of fish and sparse of life.., but because this fish is obeying a dictate of nature that is beyond his capacity to comprehend, and beyond any evolutionary needs, the streams and rivers are teeming with life and abundance!.. All the creatures of the forests and the villages come to the river to replenish themselves. Because of this fish, food is abundant and life is prosperous...

This fish is responding to a higher law than would be dictated simply by mindless evolution. It plays a crucial role in the ecology of the environmental food chain. Not a morsel of food is wasted, all creatures are benefited, abundance is the result, and the river.., teems with life!!.

* * *   * * *   * * *   * * *

A second example in which the postulate of evolutionary advancement as dictated by need, is violated.., is the human brain itself!.. Science tells us that we utilize less than ten percent of the brains potential, probably about seven percent. So ninety three percent of our brain.., goes unused! Ninety three percent of our brain.., has "evolved" (in defiance of the postulate) far in excess of any previous or current needs!...

This fact was dramatically demonstrated by the invention of the "drainage shunt" that has saved the lives of many new born babies who were afflicted with "Hydrocephalus" (water on the brain)... The build-up of water pressure in the cranial cavity causes the head of the baby to double in size, and the pressure kills the brain and the baby!.. The drainage shunt relieves the pressure and allows the baby to live... With the recent invention of the "CAT scan" X-ray, they took a look at many of the

---

[6] From the series: "Evolution"; "Theories & scientific developments since Darwin's initial philosophies"... TV Documentary ; The Science Channel, year 2002…

children that were saved as a result of the "drainage shunt", and they found, to their amazement, that in many cases the entire central core of the brain had been killed by the pressure, and only the outer areas of the brain (the cerebral cortex) were functioning!.. The children weren't aware of this, and went on to colleges of higher learning, excelling in languages, mathematics, etc...

And more recently, a three year old girl child, named "Jodi" was afflicted with "Rasmussens" disease, and to save her life, the right hemisphere of her brain was removed (a split-brain-ectomy). The left side of her brain being more than adequate, Jodi is a very intelligent young girl, normal in every way, with only a slight impairment to her left arm. It is also interesting to note, that there has been no personality change in this child as a result of the loss of half of her brain... [7]

* * *   * * *   * * *

*** The "Intellectual" Religion ***

The school of "Behaviorism", like the school of "Evolutionism", stems from the same basic premise, which simply stated is;.. There is no God... There is no Creator. There is no creation. The supreme intelligence in the universe is, after all;.., Man!.. Everything in the universe has a logical and evolutionary cause and effect, from the sub-atomic to the atomic, to the molecular, to the cellular, to the glandular, to the vascular, to the muscular, to the structural, to the optical, to the etc., and the etc., and more etc.'s..., *to the intellectual!!.* (Pardon me for laughing)... This is the end result of their intellectualism; the modern day version of.., "The Flat Earth Society"...

It seems that there is a vast difference between intellectualism and intelligence.... Intellect be damned! It is intelligence that sees the greater picture.

It has always amazed me.., take any two people, expose them both to the same identical information,

---

[7] The story of "Jodi" was told in a television documentary (1999)... A similar story is told in a Readers Digest article (Nov., 1995)... The theme of the extraordinary development of the human brain (far in excess of any evolutionary need) was developed and explored by "Arthur Koestler", in his book entitled: "The Ghost in the Machine"... He also coined the term; "ratamorphosis", which I have used in this book...

and you will have two opposing view-points! Two diametrically opposing view-points, with almost no hope of reconciliation. The one will be a Conservative, the other will be a Liberal. The one will be a Creationist, the other will be an Evolutionist. The one will be a Deist, the other will be an Atheist. The one will be on the "Right", and the other will be on the "Left"…

It seems that in this world of dualism, the very mind of mankind is split into two factions. Each side is blind.., literally incapable of seeing.., the viewpoint from the other side. We argue our viewpoints with such tenacity that we become crystallized in them, and will defend them even to the death, with smug certainty.., without ever really knowing!!.

What is the determining factor? What is it that makes one person see things from a Religio/Mystical view point, and another person will see everything as having evolved from a strictly materialistic, cause and effect, random chance event, with no inner significance whatsoever? Was the die cast at the moment of birth? A simple toss of the coin? Just random chance? Or, did we at some point in our life experience make a conscious decision? Can we even be held accountable for what we believe? We may decide to believe either This or That, but in our heart of hearts, we will believe what we believe, and we will doubt what we doubt...

Certainly, a religious upbringing, or the lack of one, can be an influencing factor, but then.., what religion?..

A religious upbringing can produce an Atheist. A secular upbringing can produce a seeker of the truth. We would say of the one, "he has lost his faith", and of the other one we would say he has been "born again"...

The secularist is in a similar predicament. If there is no God, then every man can decide for himself how he should live his life, because nobody is keeping score. Philosophies abound; Existentialism can turn into Pacifism or Nazism… Abortion clinics and extermination camps can be looked upon as for "the greater good"… Perversion can be looked upon as an "alternate lifestyle". Libertarians can be looked upon as patriots or subversives. There is no "Pillar of Truth" on which to set anchor. Everything can be rationalized.

But wait.., we are no longer talking about view-points. No, we have gone beyond view-points, we are now talking about what is the Truth.., and what is the Lie. We are down to the nitty-gritty, here. We are down to the "foundational basic premise" of our computer based logic/memory system. All deductions made henceforth must agree with that foundational basic premise, or they must be discarded. All future thought and concepts must fall in line with which-ever foundational basic premise that you decide to adopt as the truth. Both are belief systems, and therefore.., both are religions...

It is very important that this religion of the "Left".., **be *Named!*..** This "World Wide Religion".., of the "last days".., spoken of in the "Book of Revelation" as the religion of the Anti-Christ.., it must be named!..

To name something is to identify it, and that which is abstract and illusive becomes real and tangible.

On (such and such a day), in (such and such year), The Supreme Court of the United States (should) declare **"Secular Humanism"** (Atheism) to be classified and recognized.., *as a Religion!!*. A belief system that recognizes only human-kind as the supreme intelligence in the universe, (an accident of nature) and we should be good and humanitarian to one another, because that's the human thing to do!!. What is good and humanitarian is subject to your own interpretation.., and rationalization... The only requirement to belong to this religion is that you don't belong to any other. Since non-attendance is the requirement of this religion, a vast number belong to it simply by default, and the belief in their heart of hearts.., that there is no God... Others belong to this religion just by ignoring the whole question!..

To which religion do *You* belong.., really?..

***   ***   ***

BOOK IV

"The Reality of the Fifth Dimension"

I went into the Deva Realm, not as a Religionist, but as a Scientist... I gave it a scientific name.., I called it the "Fifth Dimension"...

My first thought and question when I entered this Realm was;.. "Where is this place"?.. This was a scientific question requiring a scientific answer... Was it a "secret city/mystery school" located on planet Earth?.. Or was it a city existing on a material planet, floating within that vast ocean of fourth dimensional nothingness that we call "space", within or beyond our solar system.., or did it exist in another dimension all together.., in the Realm of Mind"?..

It was this question that I pondered, as I was caught in mid stride, between my kitchen and living room, and stood transfixed in a pose, like a statue.., three fingers and thumb clenched in to the palm of my hand, index finger raised, with a cracker crumb perched precisely on the tip.., in front of my gaze...

I marvel till yet.., the profound orchestration of this event, that was produced spontaneously by a force and intelligence that was other than myself.., beyond my understanding... I was not alone, as I stood there, gazing at the cracker crumb, on the tip of my finger.., Transfixed...

(Quoting myself).., "It was a cracker crumb, perched on the tip of my index finger. I looked into the cracker crumb, and saw that it was a world.., and on this world there was a being, standing there in a pose, with his finger in the air, and there was a cracker crumb on the tip of his finger, and the cracker crumb was a world.., and on this world, there was a being, with his finger in the air.., (etc. and etc.)... I reeled from the concept... The implications stagger the mind...

My first reaction was to reject it. "No.., it just couldn't be"!., I said, with my linear-logical mind, based in the laws of physics as they apply to the material world.., but I had just returned from a physically material world that existed in a non material universe, a universe of mind, a universe in which the laws of physics do not apply... The realm of mind has it's own laws.., and nothing is impossible"... (end quote)...

In the realm of public opinion, the majority of Mankind believes in a fifth dimension;.. Heaven, Hell, the Afterlife, etc... Great thinkers, shallow thinkers, and scientists alike, have gone to bed at night and entered the "dream world" (a world of the mind, having no physical reality) reporting amazing adventures and terrifying nightmares, and for the time that they were dreaming, the dream world was a solid reality... Now let us suppose.., (for the sake of supposition) that as the dreamer was "involved" in his dream (a seemingly solid reality), that the dreamer died in his sleep.., but the dream continued... Now locked within the seeming reality of his dream world, (which he cannot by any means disprove) he recalls his former brief lifespan (which is now over) and he continues on in the reality of the dream world which is now truly real.., and his former life (which is now over) was the dream!.. You would have to conclude that the life that continued on, was the real reality, and the life that died was only a dream... Or.., that they were both realities.., Or both dreams.., Or a dream within a dream.., Or just a dream of reality.., Or..,??? etc…

And lest we forget.., our hypothetical supposition will one day be a reality... So let us live our lives in such a manner that the dream/reality of the after-death state (the "Bardo").., won't be a nightmare...

The Buddha was asked the question;.. (in essence).., "This world that we see before us, is it reality, or is it illusion"?.. The Buddha replied;.. (in essence).., "It is *All illusion*, but the illusion being all there is, it is therefore reality"... We will herein-after refer to this principle as:.. "Buddha's Law of Reality"...

Similarly;.. you can close your eyes and imagine (for instance) a ship.., on a sea just as deep or deeper, on a world just as big or bigger, with a sky just as high or higher, in a universe even more vast.., and you can get lost in your imagination, and for the brief time that you are there, it is real, and truly.., it is a universe even more vast... But where is it..? A Universe within a Universe..?

If I had to explain it to the linear-logical mentality, I would use the facsimile of octaves.., vibratory frequencies operating on different wave lengths, like different channels on a television set, all existing simultaneously, but only one channel being evident according to the particular frequency calibration of the receiving set. The "sleep/dream" reality would be a particular frequency setting.., the "Alive on Planet Earth" reality would be operating at a different frequency setting, as would be the journeys into "flights of imagination" at yet another frequency setting... Beyond this, (if the consciousness be directed inward) at yet a "higher" frequency setting, there is a higher frequency Universe.., and higher frequency realities.., etc...

These higher frequency realities do indeed exist... If I sleep and dream, that could be considered a personal reality, of myself alone, and the same can be said for "flights of imagination".., but if I go to a higher frequency reality that is common to all of mankind, then this is not a personal reality.., This is an objectively real reality... I went to the Deva World... It exists!.. This book is a result of that event... I am an eye witness... There have been other eye witnesses, their works of art and paintings depicting the Deva Realm are common throughout the temples and monasteries of Asia. The Pagoda style of architecture is a direct emulation of that realm.

There are other dimensions beyond the fifth, but I use the term; "fifth dimension" inclusively, to include all the various frequency/dimensions that exist outside of the commonly perceived fourth dimensional Universe, be they Heavens, Hells.., or Purgatories...

To the Western mind, this is unknown and uncharted territory, with only vague references found in the Bible. But with the same tenacity that the "Western School" has pursued the exoteric sciences and outer space, the "Eastern School" (Hinduism-Buddhism) has pursued the esoteric science of the "Inner Realms".., with the Soul as "Voyager"...

That "Ancient Science" of adjusting frequency settings to "Higher" calibrations, is the art and science of "Yoga"... A finely tuned mind.., in the finely tuned body.., of a Worthy Soul...

Of particular interest is the art and science of "Kundalini Yoga", which seeks to awaken the occult and mysterious "Serpent Power" (so called because of it's serpentine movement), that lies dormant within the being of the Yogin. Awakening this energy source to raise the frequency level to higher octaves (Chakras) gives the Yogin the experience of "Life" in a higher frequency Universe.., a Universe of Mind.., the "Fifth Dimension"...

Likewise, in the art and science of "Nada Yoga" (the Yoga of the "Sound Current"), the practitioner focuses his unbroken attention, listening intently to the sounds that exist interiorly, within the field of mind, following the "Sound Current" to higher and higher frequencies, corresponding to higher and higher levels of consciousness.., and higher and higher realities.

Likewise again, in the "Bardo" of the after-death state (Buddhism), the Yoga practitioner is trained in the art and science of recognizing the corresponding "colors of the light" emanating from the octave-spectrum of the various "wave-length frequency dimensions" that are the "Chakras" corresponding to the various "World-Dimension-Universes" that occupy the "vastness beyond comprehension".., which make up the "Kingdoms of God"... ("Beware the "smoky red" light emanating from the Hellish worlds, and seek Ye the "Clear light" of the Ultimate reality".., etc.)...

And likewise again, in the art and science of "Mantra Yoga", the practitioner repeats the melodic and harmonic vibratory sequence of words (sounds) that raises the "Kundalini" energy level corresponding to the (wave-length frequency) level of the specific "Chakra" as well as the refinement of the "consciousness principle" (Soul) that progresses upward on this interior journey...

Now, there are two schools of thought regarding this process of raising the level of consciousness to each individual Chakra in it's turn, as well of the corresponding refinement of the Consciousness Principle, that grows in Understanding, Knowledge, Wisdom and Abilities... The first "school" aims at the direct stimulation of this "mysteriously secret energy" inducing it upwards (and inwards), carrying with it the "consciousness principle" that is progressively refined into the abilities and powers of abstract thought and the comprehension of the laws and mysteries of the interior dimensions.., of which the individual Soul in question may have had little previous aptitude or inclination thereof...

The "second" school of thought holds that the movement upwards of the refining energy of the Kundalini should be a "natural response" to the contemplative nature of the "Soul that wants to

Know".., as a "natural response" to the Soul that loses itself in devotion to the Lord...

Interestingly enough, "Pantanjali" (the father of the Yoga systems) regards this "Bhakti Yoga".., (the path of devotion) as the "Easy Way".., and it is the Easy Way, inasmuch as the Soul easily achieves the "one pointed concentration" of the "Zen" state of mind, completely bypassing the "Ego" barrier, and is absorbed in "Communion" with the Lord (*Thee Ultimate Guru*), and there is dialogue and conversation with the Lord, and all of your questions will be answered, and nothing will be hidden from you... This path is open to all devotees of every religion who honestly and sincerely seek to know the Lord...

And there is a further sub-division within these two schools of thought;.. the one school holding that the Kundalini (energy factor), along with the accompanying "consciousness principle" (the Soul) should penetrate and explore each Chakra on it's way up to the "Ultimate Reality" (ecstatic Union with the Lord)...

The other school of thought holding that the consciousness principle become only superficially acquainted with each Chakra, developing only the intuitive capacity and the "super-human" faculties of the Soul, and instead concentrate directly on the ecstatic Union (Communion) with the Lord, which is the true Goal of the Yoga (Union), and instead explore each Chakra on it's return voyage... it is further held (by the latter school) that this is the much safer and direct approach, as the Soul could easily become distracted by the multi-faceted wonders of these interior reality-dimensions, possibly even mistaking one of the "Pleasure Realms" as Heaven, becoming trapped in this dimension, to the detriment of his physical body and his failure to reach the "Ultimate" goal...

And then there is the "Raja Yoga".., considered the King of Yogas (another school of thought), because it is the "combined multiple approach" of the other Yogas, incorporating first of all a Worthy Soul of high intelligence, capable of abstract contemplation.., coupled with an intense desire for Union with, and devotion to the Lord.., and incorporating the actual physical practices of awakening the "Kundalini" energy factor that carries the Soul upwards and inwards on it's interior journey...

Each one of these several Yogas is an approach to the Divine, with it's own philosophical "school of thought", and with each Yoga being appropriate to a different personality type... You should pick the one most appropriate to you...

A word of caution here[1];.. Tampering with this Mysterious Kundalini energy factor is not for amateurs!.. Only the most dedicated of aspirants, having taken the vows of a religious order, and under the tutelage of an enlightened teacher (which is extremely rare) should undergo this training... It is much more preferable that the activity of this energy source be a "natural response" to that Soul who is "naturally inclined" to deep and profound contemplation, and dedicated to the Lord... This is the "Way" of the "Western School", and there is nothing wrong with it, although very few actually achieve it.., *(mostly because introspection becomes intellectual, rather than the "pure" (Zen) immersion into the contemplative devotional state that is required for "Communion")*...

This is the Noble path... This is the path of Hero's... This is the destiny for which we were created... It is the "Soul" (as "Voyager")., as it makes it's way up that ancient interior pathway.., as it is progressively refined and purified.., by correspondingly higher and higher frequency modulations.., gaining in Knowledge, Insight, and the development of the "Super Human" faculties and abilities.., ultimately merging into the Clear Light of the Ultimate Reality, which is the ecstatic Union with the Divine... Halleluiah!.. Halleluiah!..

The Soul that has mastered this science, and is able to enter into whichever Chakra, (frequency-World-Universe) that he chooses (by intention), and experiences life there, and can go up and down this "ladder" of Universe-Worlds at will, is called an "Adept"... *(And what would be YOUR definition of Heaven?)*...

It should be evident that the body is far more profoundly the "Temple of God" than we had supposed.., and our Crime:.. We have viewed GOD.., and HIS Kingdoms.., *"too small"*... If only we knew...

** * * * **

---

[1] Before the student attempts to "awaken" his Kundalini power, it is recommended that you read (case in point) the book: "Kundalini", by Gopi Krishna... (Shambala Publications Inc., 1971)...

35

The Chakras

This subject;., of the "Fifth Dimension", would not be complete without a more in depth discussion of the Chakras...

I had lived in India for one year, during which time I studied meditation techniques under three different teachers, and I learned eight different techniques, in addition to techniques for activating and raising the Kundalini... The techniques for raising the Kundalini have to do with visualization exercises in the imagination, focusing the consciousness and working it repeatedly through the body from the base of the spine up through the Chakra centers and out through the top of the head, accompanied with mantras, breathing exercises, bodily postures, etc... These visualization exercises are referred to as "cleansing techniques" (Kria Yoga), cleansing the pathway for the Kundalini, should it become awakened... And although I have had extensive experiences with the Kundalini.., *I have never seen a Chakra!!.* So whether the Chakras exist as an interior reality, or whether they are symbolic representations for use in the visualization exercises, I cannot say for sure.., but I suspect that they are the latter...

The very serious (committed) student will undertake the study of the Chakras in order to be able to identify into which interior (fifth dimensional) realm he has entered... The symbolism of the Chakras contain "identity markers" (specific colors, sounds, animals indigenous to this realm, the form of the Deity personages, certain "Superhuman faculties" (eloquent speech, intuitive insight, wisdom, etc.) and may even make reference to which "Herb of Mysterious Virtue" that will grant you entry into this realm... But there is a kind of "Catch 22" to all of this, because it is a mistake to try to comprehend this literally when the symbols point to a more esoteric meaning which requires the intuitive faculty.., which further requires the raising of the Kundalini to acquire the ability of intuitive comprehension!.. To try to explain "levels of consciousness" to a person who has never had the experience of an "altered state", is like trying to explain color to a man "blind from birth"!.. There is a sense of futility here that requires an "intuitive leap" on the part of the reader [2]…

If we were to view our Solar system from above (or below), we would see that the planets revolve around the sun, all moving in the same direction, and all in the same plane... This is a "Chakra" (described as "wheels")... In both the Hindu and the Buddhist Cosmology, these "Chakras" (Universe-World-systems) are (*representationally*) seen as being strung along the spinal column in which the mysterious "Serpent Power" [3] (vital psychic energy) is raised to the "wave-length frequency setting" (*figuratively speaking*) corresponding to each "Chakra-Universe-World system"...

At the moment, the "Kundalini" resides in the "Muladhara" Chakra (at the base of the spine), which is the corresponding wave length frequency setting of "Planet Earth" and our particular solar system...

These chakras, or wheels, (or planetary Solar systems) are to be ***visualized*** as if strung along the thirty-four vertebrae of the spinal column, equidistant from one another, extending through 21 of these charkas, to the exit at the "Aperture of Brahma" at the top of the head [4]... Of these 21 Chakras, six (6) are considered to be of major importance, and the seventh (the Aperture of Brahma) (*symbolically represented as; the "Thousand Petaled Lotus"*) in which the "Soul" (the "Consciousness Principal") exits from the worlds of manifestation (the Sangsara) to merge with the "Clear Light of the Ultimate Reality" (Brahma).., which is the culmination of the "Yoga" (Union)... The "Enlightened Soul" then returns to the "Worlds of manifestation" (*whichever one He chooses*) as a **"God-Man"**, (a Saint, or a Christ, or a Buddha) endowed with Wisdom, Understanding, Powers, and abilities.., for the purpose of the

---

[2] At this point, the reader may ask: "Why do I need to know this if I do not have the intuitive ability to comprehend it"?.. Answer: "Because it is the indispensable **road-map** of the Fifth Dimension, and if you intend to take this journey, the knowledge of the symbols & etc. will become evident as you progress on this interior journey, and without which, you could be "lost and confused" as to where you are in this vast interior universe"…

[3] The classic work on this subject is the book: "The Serpent Power".., written by; Sir John Woodroffe (writing under the pen name of; Arthur Avalon), and first published in 1918... This is a direct translation from the Sanskrit *"Tantra Sastra"*...

[4] See; "Tibetan Yoga and Secret Doctrines", (page 247, fn. 2)…

"The Three Worlds"

salvation of the Souls of humanity *(Compassion)* by which Saints are recognized...

Within these 21 Chakras, there exists 33 worlds (Buddhist cosmology), *or "planes of being"..,* of which some are considered "Pleasure Realms".., and some are "not desirable" (because religion does not prevail there).., some are "Spiritual beyond human conception" (the indescribable regions of formlessness).., there are "Purgatories".., and there are "Hells".., one is described as "the region of unhappy ghosts", and etc... These inner worlds (of reality) are populated with peoples and cities, located on continents, separated by mountains and oceans.., and wars!., etc...

Even though the religion and people of India are basically monotheistic (the one God; *"Brahma"),* each one of these inner worlds has a "Ruler" (or King) which is revered by the "simple folk" of India as; "lesser Gods", and homage is paid to them, because; *"you never know where (after death) you're gonna go"!!!...* The "West" looks at this as a polytheistic religion of "many Gods", because they have no knowledge or concept of inner worlds or dimensions, because their vision is external... Even though "Heaven lies within you".., they never look there!..

I could get into a lengthy discussion of each of the six (and seventh) charkas, but this would require a "book within a book", and these books have already been written[5], and I refer you to them for your further in-depth study...

This is the "Holy Science"... It is the most esoteric and secret of sciences, and it is the rare individual that encounters it... It has always been clothed in secrecy and symbolism, and any serious student that attempts to understand it (let alone accomplish it) is confronted with both the language of Sanskrit, and the even more esoteric language of symbolism...

* * *   * * *   * * *

So.., the question arises??.., **Why??.,** is this not part of the Christian tradition.., or the Hebrew.., or the Muslim, or etc??... The answer to this question may be offensive to Christians, Jews, Muslims, and etc.., each of whom consider their particular religion to be the "Only" true religion.., *and who's wrath I will undoubtedly incur...* (So, what else is new?)...

The answer to this perplexing question is;.., that *"all"* the "Religions" (Scripturally based belief systems), are (generally speaking) *for the "Masses"...* If you are still trying to find God between the pages of your "Bible", and arguing the superiority of your "Religion" over all others, and have rarely (if ever) sat in "rapt contemplation" for an extended period of time.., consider yourself just one of the *"mass"* within the *"masses"* of humanity... It has been said; *"That the masses just live and die, so that one "Beethoven" (or one Christ, or one Buddha. Or etc.) may be born"...* ***Think about it!!.*** YOU.., are so spiritually *"dense"* that *a* "Savior" has to incarnate and die on a cross, just to get you to turn your life around and act righteously (the fundamental *"Born Again"* experience), *(the "first step" of a multi-step process),* just to save your sorry ass from Hell and damnation!!...

Where Religion in general, and Western science and civilization in particular.., has explored and catalogued the history and phenomenon of the *"EXTERNAL World"..,* with that same tenacity, the East (and only a small fraction thereof), has developed the *Science* of abstract contemplation and meditation, exploring the multi-dimensional Realms of "INNER" Space, and the nature of the Soul, with the potential of "Ecstatic Union" with the ***Divine Mystery of it All..,*** and returning to the external world a ***"Saint",*** where a sinner once stood!!...

Consider (for example) the Eskimo.., he has a vocabulary of approximately 27 words (and probably more) just to describe "snow"!., because he is very experienced with snow... The ability to conceive of and communicate esoteric and abstract thought is much more enhanced (even though rare) in Sanskrit than in the "English" language, because (due to their explorations into "inner Space"), they are very experienced with abstract concepts... Similarly, consider (for example) the simplicity of the Hebrew Alphabet (containing 22 letters and no vowels), or the "English" (Western) alphabet (containing 26 letters, including vowels), as compared to the "Sanskrit" alphabet (containing 51 letters of which 16 are vowels)!!... While words in the English language have a dictionary definition, words in Sanskrit may require a book to fathom, and then only with recourse to more Sanskrit

---

[5] "The Serpent Power", by Sir John Woodroffe..., "Tibetan Yoga and Secret Doctrines"..., "The Tibetan Book of the Great Liberation"..., "The Tibetan Book of the Dead" (by Evans-Wentz).., and others…

words... Few people have the dedication required for just an "intellectual" understanding of this Science!.. Intuition is required!!... Furthermore; each individual letter of the Sanskrit alphabet has a meaning of it's own (as does the Hebrew), and the words (many, not all) are formed as a consequence of these combined meanings!.. To reiterate; the meanings of the words are revealed by dissecting the individual meanings of the letters!!. Again, intuition is required... And furthermore (again), each individual letter has it's own distinct sound, which as a combination of sounds, as "uttered speech", conjures up in the mind the visual manifestation (image) of thought, which combined with the rhythmic and melodic "vibratory-wave length-frequency"; is a "Mantra"!!... The repetition of Mantra (Japa) is compared to the action of a man shaking a sleeper to wake him up!... Each Chakra has it's own Mantra...

The intellectual comprehension of these highly abstract concepts is almost impossible *without the awakening and subsequent raising of the Kundalini to a correspondingly "higher" level of consciousness!!!*... Without this "awakening".., the (so called) "intellectual understanding" is an exercise in futility... Furthermore, there are "words" for concepts, for which the "West" has not even developed the concept!!., and furthermore again.., these concepts have been reduced to symbolic form, which is (again) only comprehensible if you know the meaning of the symbols!!!... This is basically "insider information", reserved for the dedicated and committed practitioner, and hidden from the intellectually curious.., and definitely *Not* for the masses!..

A "Western" man (one of the masses) looking at the "symbolism" and the arcane language would be totally bewildered!!. Confined to his own sphere of "Religiosity", he would probably reject the whole idea as outside of his religious framework, and therefore foreign and heretical...

Although an overview understanding is required to enter into this science, all of the intellectual understanding in the world is futility, without the experience...

So the question arises;., am I qualified to speak on this subject.?. The answer is "No"[6], not adequately,

but this is a book of "EXPERIENCES".., and I have had *extensive* experiences with the Kundilini.., and I can testify to the reality of this subject.., but these experiences were not entered into in a conscious and systematic way, but more in random chance episodes, as a natural response to "in depth" abstract contemplations, under the influence of "conscious expanding" (psychedelic) drugs (LSD), (and subsequently Hashish) while seated in the "Lotus Posture" for extended periods of time... So I have had more experiences of this "most profound" event, than I have knowledge about it!!. Furthermore, these "random chance" interior journeys are beyond the ability of verbal communication (words fail to convey), and to attempt to convey the experience is to cheapen it... But the transition from external consciousness to the "Inner Dimensions" is not accomplished without the body entering into a state of "trance"... On most occasions the spinal activity was barely perceptible (subtle), but on a few occasions it was electric, dramatic, and **terrifying,** with my "self" clinging to external Consciousness, and the Inner pathway opening up and threatening to propel me into "Inner Realms" in a "Quantum Leap" manner, into the unknown, which was **terrifying,** and I

---

[6] I have answered "No" to this question, even though I have had more personal experiences with it than anyone I know about!!. To complete this yoga, is to become "One" with the Divine.., in other words, a "Realized Saint" (a Buddha).., and I don't believe I have ever met one, and for sure I am not one.., because I have not taken this yoga to it's "Ultimate" conclusion… To explain further.., (and I have never explained this to anyone before, because it is a "failing" on my part).., the Spiritual journey "inwards" can be perilous if you don't know what you are doing, and this particular "Yoga" is generally not even attempted without a "Master" to guide you (but where to find such a "Realized Master?")… Prior to this "awakening of the Kundalini", I had had "Communion" with the Lord.., as my "Inner Guide".., and (to make a long story short).., *I blew it!!. Through my own stupidity.., I blew it!!*... As a consequence of this transgression, I was shown "Hell" (by the Lord) as an object lesson.., and to see Hell.., is to experience **"Unspeakable Terror"…** As a consequence of this (most traumatic) experience I was "wounded"… I had been courageous to the point of recklessness.., and now I knew "Unspeakable Terror"… This created a conflict in my soul that I refer to as; "The Dark Night of the Soul"… It was a quandary!!. I could not acquiesce to this "barrier of fear" that impeded my Spiritual progress, and yet I could not go beyond this barrier!!. I was driven to face this fear on a regular basis, (by getting "High" with Hashish) and each time I was stymied by terrifying fear!.. This went on for approximately 18 months, before the Kundilini went back into dormancy...

wasn't psychologically prepared [7] for it! A gradual and systematic progression would have been preferable, but to just "let go" and leave this dimension *completely*, without any knowledge of "where", of how to get back, or even if I could get back.., was terrifying!!... It got to be that every time I got "High", the Kundilini became active, taking me higher than I was prepared to go, but I learned to control it... I found that if I sat in the upright (cross legged) *semi*-Lotus posture, the Kundilini energy would race upwards, but if I lay in a reclining position, the upward movement would be arrested, and I could control just how High (in terms of my level of abstraction) I wanted to go... It was during this period that I got "glimpses" of inner realms, without actually making the full transition to go there... Eventually (after about 18 months), the Kundilini returned to dormancy...

So.., I am not here to advocate any one religion over another, as basically, they are all belief systems *(for the masses)* devoid of any **actual** "experiential" knowledge... The point that I am trying to make here, **and that I am advocating,** is the inclusion and practice of "Meditation".., which is compatible with all religions!.. If you are going to search for buried treasure, you have to look *within* the "field" in which it is buried *(Mt 13:44)*!.. That field of research is within the realm of your own being... Heaven lies within you...

Meditation.., is not about thinking *(as the mind will wander into endless trivialities)..,* nor is it about praying *(although a prayer going into meditation is appropriate and advisable)...* It is about **"receiving"...** **"Be still.., and know that I am God";** is the admonition... So meditation has to be approached Religiously *and* Scientifically... It is the Science of "going within"...

* * *

Throughout this book there are instructions in the art and science of meditation, but I like to include some practical tips that I have observed and developed (from experience) along the way... The "trick" of a successful meditation is that you get completely immersed into contemplation.., and you can only do that if you lose awareness of your "Self", your body, and your immediate surroundings *(a.k.a..: the "Zen" state)...* So the first barrier is; "body consciousness"...

The most generally accepted body posture conducive to meditation is the cross-legged semi-lotus seated position, *if you are an Indian from India!!.* What is not generally known, is that until the British occupation of India, there were no "table and chairs" in India!.. Everyone sat cross-legged on the floor! The women prepared meals from a flat-footed, full squat posture at floor level, and all meals were eaten while seated cross-legged on the floor... A straw mat on the floor served as their table, with tea pots, water pitchers, cups, glasses, dishes, condiments and etc., placed appropriately.., but no silverware!.. The food was (and still is) eaten with the fingers, and then only with the right hand.., as the left hand is considered "unclean" (there was no toilet paper in India)!.. This daily act of elimination is also done in the flat-footed, full squat position, cleansing the rectum by washing with cold water, with the left hand (very refreshing on a hot day), and then washing the hands… The bed also consists of a mattress on the floor, as a raised bed is considered "decadent"... The food, by the way, could be described as "superbly excellent cuisine", and the furnishings could be lavish, with wall hangings, religious and family portraits, Persian type carpets, fine furniture dressers (with drawers), televisions, etc. !!.. This "floor-level" culture of India is the same for rich and poor alike, and whether it be based on practical or religious principals, I don't know!.. But the point here is that the cross-legged seated posture is very comfortable and natural for Indians.., but not for Western man...

Unfortunately, it took me about a dozen years to figure this out!.. Meditations were rarely successful because of the "pain" factor!.. After a short period of time, the back muscles begin to ache, there is torque at the hip joints, the circulation is cut off below the knees, pressure points where the legs cross, the feet fall asleep, etc., and etc... Making the transition to the Zen contemplative state eliminates all pain and bodily consciousness, but the preliminary bodily discomfort is an impediment to ever reaching that Zen state... For the meditation to be successful, you must maintain a bodily posture, ***fixed and unmoving****, for an extended period of time!!.* So achieving a suitable, comfortable, and stable posture conducive to a successful meditation is the first prerequisite!..

---

[7] The reader should be aware, that it is impossible to write this book in a totally sequential order.., and there were "experiences" here that "cannot be told", that had a bearing on the ***terror*** that I was experiencing.., experiences having to do with; "the Dark Night of the Soul"...

Necessity being the mother of invention, I have developed this method which will save you a lot of discomfort and facilitate your success in meditation... It requires three large and firm cushions (or facsimile thereof:; *folded blankets*, or whatever) that will elevate your body at least 8 inches off the floor... One cushion you sit on, and the other two go under your knees, supporting their weight and relieving the torque at the hip joints... The lower legs are crossed inwards, and they don't even have to touch, relieving this pressure point, and the circulation is not impaired... Now, most people have a tendency to lean forward with this semi-lotus posture, which results in muscle fatigue, and the head droops downwards, causing drowsiness, etc., but there is a "spot" of equilibrium that is perfectly balanced (like a tall stack of books) in the military *("at attention")* upright posture that is the most conducive to the meditation, and the least taxing on the muscles for support... Find this spot!!... Finding this perfectly balanced upright posture is the most critical factor in the meditation...

For the Western student who may not find this cross-legged posture appealing, there is an alternative meditative posture... Seated upright in a straight backed chair, in the "at attention" posture, leaning slightly forward with your elbows on the table, supporting your upper body.., or seated without the table.., or however!.. The whole point of these meditative postures, is that you *forget about your body*, **completely!..** Your whole and complete attention is *"absorbed"* in the meditation.., to the exclusion or your "Self", your body, and your immediate surroundings...

A second factor in the Science of meditation, is the Sciences of "Mudras", which has to do with (by an etymological coincidence) your "mood", while in the meditative state... For instance; lying down is the "Mudra" (bodily posture) for sleep, and is therefore not conducive to meditation... Seated with your hands folded in your lap, is the Mudra for peace, and will put you in a peaceful and tranquil state... Seated with the hands "palms up" (on your thighs), is the Mudra of beseeching and receiving, and will put you in a very humble receptive mood... Seated with the palms down on your thighs (or knees), is the Mudra of "authority", and will put you in a very composed and "centered" frame of mind... Seated with your head bowed, is the Mudra of drowsiness, and will cause your mind to wander.., etc... These particular Mudras are, in effect, the reverse application of "body language",

and the student will find it a very interesting experiment!..

The various scriptures (Hindu/ Buddhist) have differing recommendations concerning the *"at ease"* focal point of your *closed* eyes... some recommend the focal point to be at the tip of your nose, others recommend a point about a foot or so beyond the tip of the nose, and others recommend that the *attention* be focused outward, at a point above and between your *closed* eyes... I personally prefer the latter recommendation, but there should be no eye strain involved here... [8]

Minor aches and pains can be alleviated by taking an aspirin, and a sluggish, drowsy mentality can be alleviated by taking a **mild** stimulant, (try: Ginkgo Biloba and Ginseng, washed down with Green Tea, as a daily regimen, well prior to the meditation), or something stronger *(you want to be alert, but you don't want to be "wired"),* and if, after several attempts, you fail to reach a detached level of abstraction, you can take a **mild** *"enhancement"* (one or two "tokes" *only,* will do)... If the mind starts to race, this is counter productive!.. You are looking for that "steady state", where you can rise above the thought process and view it from a detached and dispassionate point of observation.., and you will realize that *YOU are NOT your mind!!...* YOU are in fact the *"Observer"* of your mind!.. Halleluiah!!... **This is an achievement!..** To reach this level of abstraction is known as; "Isolation".., and is called; "The First Resting Place".., and it has a very "Zen" (integrating) effect on your life and your relationship with the Divine... This is a very good beginning!.

It takes about 20 minutes or so just to get to the "settled" contemplative state, so for the meditation to be of any value, it should last *a minimum* of twice this long, and preferably *much* longer... To focus your attention, begin with the breathing exercises, watching your breath, as it comes in and

---

[8] There are Mudras.., and then there are "Maha Mudras" ("Great" Mudras)... Maha Mudras are generally given only at the time of initation, and are considered advanced techniques for dedicated students of the "Inner" Science... The focal point above and between the eyes is considered a Maha Mudra in that it is the convergence point of the Left and Right psychic nerve currents, called: the "Ida" and the "Pingala" (a.k.a. the Sun and Moon.., or: positive and negative)... This point of convergence is at the "Agni Chakra", which is considered a "Doorway" Chakra... There *are* other Maha Mudras not discussed here...

as it goes out, **screening out** *(with vigilance)* any random extraneous "self generating" thoughts, and progress to abdominal breathing until you reach a calm and centered state of mind... additional focusing exercises could include a mantra, which is the continuous repetition of (for instance) the Name of God.., or the continuous repetition of a phrase, such as; "I am here, I am aware, I am alert, I am vigilant", (etc., and etc.)... The purpose is to bring the self-generating thought process;., *to a stop!!,* until "Self" rests in "Self" alone... It is at this point that the "Self" is itself transcended!., by the shift from self consciousness into the Zen-objective state of *Absorption* into the subject of your contemplation, which will spontaneously present itself as a natural response to: "The Soul that wants to know"....

So prepare yourself!.. When you come to this place of meditation, come with a prayer in your heart, with reverence and sincerity of purpose, walking in the ways of virtue and charity, with a will to good.., *and do good!,* every chance you get!..

And remember.., this is a science!!. It is the Science of transformation.., and You are the Alchemist!!. You are in the process of transforming the "base metal" (lead) of your "Self" into the pure Gold of the "Selfless" being that describes himself as a "servant of the Lord", but in reality, he is a King among men, and he does his own will, which is in perfect harmony with the Divine will, of which he is part and parcel, and in whom there is no guile or duplicity...

The student should be aware that we are taking a very broad (and not necessarily comprehensive) overview of the most esoteric subjects on Earth.., namely; the reality of "The Fifth Dimension" in general, the science of Kundalini Yoga, the Chakras, Meditation, Mudras, and etc... Each one of these subjects is a science unto itself, and would require a multitude of books to acquire even a superficial understanding.., but, **"The proof of the pudding, lies in the tasting"!!.** You now know what the "Mass" of humanity doesn't know.., namely; that Heaven lies within you, and this is the "field" of your search and research... Seek ye first the Kingdom of God and HIS righteousness!!... Everything else.., *is a triviality!..* **Taste and see!!...**

Meditation is like fishing!.. You never know what you are going to get... Good luck and Godspeed... Amen...

*   * * *   *

BOOK V

"The Bardo"

Other books may give you theories, beliefs, conjecture, suppositions, etc.., backed up by the scriptures of this or that religion, and speculated upon by this or that learned doctor, philosopher, scientist.., graduated from this or that prestigious University, and having read all the written material available from previous doctors, philosophers, scientists, who wrote their books based upon the theories, conjecture and experiences of others, etc. and etc.., all of which you may believe or disbelieve, or speculate about.., or write your own theories and speculations to be read by other doctors, philosophers, scientists, etc.., but first hand experience is lacking... Actual Knowledge.., is lacking...

So.., this is a book of experiences.., based upon the approximate 35 or more times that I have ventured into the inner realms of my own mind, aided by a powerful psychedelic (usually LSD) and other "Herbs of Mysterious Virtue"...

While I am certainly not alone or unique in my experimentations with these powerful drugs.., there is one thing different about my experiences, and that is the difference that "intention" makes... Whereas most of the participants bombard their senses with the experiences of a party atmosphere, at "Rock" concerts, or the visual displays of Nature, or sexual encounters, good music, good times, etc.., all externalized activities.., while I (on the other hand), chose.., "the road less traveled"...

The road less traveled, is the road that leads within... In the privacy of solitude.., in the darkness of night, when silence was at it's height.., seated in a meditation posture, practicing meditation techniques aimed at suppressing the thought process.., eyes closed in darkness.., ears closed in silence.., immobile.., complete sensory deprivation... Encountering.., The "Bardo"...

The "Bardo" is a transition phase between two levels of consciousness...

It is not an easy thing.., to go from the externalized, mundane level of consciousness, stabilized by the physical body in its familiar external reality.., to an internalized level of consciousness, characterized by instability, of having no familiar environment to relate to, no solidity, in a disembodied state, as a "consciousness principle" only.., floating in a maelstrom of thoughts and images, with nothing to hang on to, and only your disembodied self, which cannot be found or located... It can be terrifying... The faint of heart cannot enter here...

To be terrified by the disorientation and instability of the Bardo, is to invite terrifying images, of nightmarish qualities... Many there are, who experience the Bardo, are terrified, and retreat in panic, fleeing back to the safety of their external reality.., never to approach the Bardo again...

To navigate through the Bardo requires a sincere and courageous heart, of acceptable character, good karma.., and knowledge... I can give you the knowledge...

Or rather, I can give you the information... True knowledge is gained only by the experience... I can give you the information, that leads to the experience, that is the substance of knowledge...

Upon entering the Bardo.., tumbling through the maelstrom of thoughts and images, sights and sounds, bombarding your disoriented and disembodied consciousness, you must remember this: (the first rule of the Bardo) you must remember that you are in the transition state of the Bardo, and that it is a temporary state, and come what may, it will eventually be over... You must not forget, that the terrifying images (or whatever) that you are seeing (experiencing) are illusory in nature, and a testing of your courage, determination and worthiness to proceed in this transition through the temporary state of the Bardo... You must always be able to say;., "Oh.., this is the Bardo"...

Of course you can always "option out" of the Bardo by opening your eyes, breaking off the meditation and returning to the comfortable (mundane) world of reality (?) that you left behind, but this is to "miss the point" of your endeavors...

The better course of action is instead to "hold fast" to yourself in the disembodied state of the Bardo (rule number two).., and do not let your concentration be scattered by fear and terror (not good)... You must maintain your self awareness while in the state of the Bardo, and do not let yourself be carried off by the mundane thought process... This would be to lose direction while in the Bardo, and come out through the same door that you went in.., and be robbed of your goal of a higher consciousness...

Now this (rule number two) is where most people fail on their journey through the Bardo... They lose sight of their "intention" (or they don't have one), and allow their "consciousness principle" to get caught up in the mundane thought process, and ride a thought train back out of the Bardo.!. This is called;.., the "Thought Barrier"...

"Serious students".., sit for meditation daily in committed practice, the objective of which is "Isolation"... To isolate the "consciousness principle" (soul) from the mundane thought process, and to see the thought process as other than your "Self", is the objective of your meditations... If it was easy, everyone would do it... The LSD is a great assist to this objective, (provided that you know and understand what the objective is)... The LSD is a "Sacrament", and should be viewed as such, because it will allow you to rise above the thought process (if you understand the objective).., because your real objective is the "Reality Beyond Thought"...

The best course of action (rule number three) is.., "to pray fervently to the Lord"... This is the test of your faith... In this trial of uncertainty and disembodied instability, being tested by the "Wrathful Deities" (*).., you must call upon the Name of the Lord, repeating it endlessly if need be, maintaining your integrity and concentration on your journey through the Bardo, and if you are very lucky, and worthy, you will reach a place of stability and tranquility.., and the "Lord" will answer your prayer and your questions.., and speak to you in vision...

If you should reach this place of stability and tranquility, and hear the "Voice of the Lord".., all is well, and you will be guided and protected... You should be mindful of this "Supreme Goal".., and pray for it's occurrence...

But there is a "fourth" (rule of the Bardo) that you must be aware of.., and that is the possibility that you might emerge from the Bardo.., into a different Realm.!. To emerge into a different Realm, in a different dimension, is not bad in itself, but there is "danger" here... The danger is that you may become so enamored with this "alternate reality", that you will become trapped in the "truly real" reality of it, to the detriment of your physical body.., which may have to be carried off to the local "looney bin" and be maintained (by others) in a vegetative state, a body devoid of it's consciousness principal (Soul)... Or worse yet.., your corpse will have to be disposed of.!.

While this is a very rare occurrence, it has happened.., even to enlightened "Adepts"... Observe the Biblical narrative of "1 Kings:13" (never before interpreted)...

(Paraphrased): "And behold, there came a man of God (an unnamed Adept who arrived via the Bardo) on a mission to convert (and save) an idolatrous king and his people, and restore them to the true faith in the true God... The Adept was instructed (by God) in the "fourth rule of the Bardo", which is: You cannot go back the way you came (You cannot leave the Earth Realm by re-entering the Bardo at the point from which you exited it).., and you must not eat the food or drink the beverages... (for the Adept to eat or drink the food or beverage of the Earth Realm causes the Earth Realm to assume the appearance of reality, and the Adept would become trapped in this "Alternate Reality")... As the story goes, this is exactly what happened... The Adept was tricked into accepting the hospitality of a well meaning but devious pseudo "holy man", who sought to gain merit and prestige through his hospitality to a true "Holy Man"... The Adept became trapped in the Earth Realm and had to be rescued by the Lord, who assumed the form of a Lion which killed the Adept, releasing him from his entrapment in the Earth Realm.., but his body remained to be buried in this "foreign soil"... The scriptures record that the Lion did not devour the Adepts body, but stayed with it to prevent it from being eaten by other scavengers... Nor did the Adepts mount (an ass) flee from the Lion (most unusual).., and the idolatrous king and his people (observing the Adepts death) returned to their idolatrous ways... The fourth rule of the Bardo had been broken.., and the mission was a failure...

Also, in Greek mythology (an allegory), Persephone, the granddaughter of Zeus, was kidnapped by Hades, the lord of the Underworld... Zeus sent Hermes to rescue her from Hades, but before Hades would let her go, he required her to eat a single pomegranate seed... Because of this, she had to spend four months of every year in the Underworld, emerging into the Outer-world in the Spring, for the remaining two-thirds of the year, perpetually alternating between these two "realities"... While this may be allegory, it bears an unhealthy resemblance to the "Manic-Depressive" state of mind... A harsh penalty to pay for violating this fourth rule of the Bardo... Take heed...

While there are many "Alternate Reality" Realms on the far side of the Bardo, some of which may be described as "Pleasure Realms", with Celestial Nymphs of exceedingly voluptuous beauty, offering golden goblets of exotic elixirs, delicious fruits and spices, etc.., you must decline their offer (as did the Buddha), because your goal is "Enlightenment".., and the mere attainment of life in the Pleasure Realm is death on Earth, and eventually death in the Pleasure Realm.., and rebirth (eventually) back on Earth (or wherever), and in who knows what circumstance.!.

So remember your purpose.., which is "Enlightenment".!. This is your first and foremost priority... It is generally conceded that these other Realms are a distraction and a diversion on the path of Enlightenment, and if you should happen to enter into one (of many) of these alternate realities, it is as a tourist only.., and you must not forget this fourth rule of the Bardo, which is:., You cannot retrace your steps and go back via the same route by which you entered this Realm (because the Bardo "door" closes behind you), You must not eat the food or drink the beverages of this Realm, and you must not allow yourself to become involved with the voluptuous beauties of this realm who may try to seduce you... To break this fourth rule of the Bardo would be to make your stay in this Alternate Reality permanent, your goal of Enlightenment will be thwarted.., and your life on Earth may be over.!.

Your exit from this alternate reality is usually accomplished by a call from your physical body, which will eventually emerge from it's "trance" state by rolling over in bed, due to discomfort or a "call of nature", or whatever...

This is the Bardo of the "Living".., which is somewhat different from the Bardo of the "After-Death" state [1]... Obviously, in the Bardo of the "after-death" state, there is no returning to your physical body, and your course through the Bardo (and your destination) is determined by the preponderance of the good or evil deeds that you performed while yet alive.!.

By special training in the "Yogic" science of the Bardo of the after-death state, it is (theoretically) possible to navigate through the Bardo, and refuse to enter into any of these alternate reality dimensions, and instead to merge into the "Clear Light" of the "Ultimate Reality", thereby achieving the Enlightenment after death, that you were unable to attain during life...

Even so.., whether it be the Bardo of the Living, or the Bardo of the after-death state.., these four rules [2] of the Bardo must be adhered to.., with special emphasis on "Rule number three"... It is by rule number three that the Enlightenment is attained, which is:.. By earnest and sincere supplication to the Lord, maintaining the focus of your concentration, praying fervently to hear His "Holy Voice", and losing yourself.., in Communion with HIM...

Be advised;.. You WILL go through the Bardo.!. Be Ye alive or be Ye dead.., you will go through the Bardo... How much better it is, to achieve this Communion with the Lord while yet alive (the Bardo of the Living).., and to become a servant of the Lord, bearing witness, yielding tangible fruit

---

[1] This subject is extensively dealt with in the book called: "The Tibetan Book of the Dead", by W.Y. Evans Wents, and it is the English translation (by the late; Lama Kazi Dawa-Samdup) of the ancient Buddhist scriptural texts... It is required reading for the serious student of the inner path (called: "The Way")...

[2] And there is a "fifth rule", that you must take into consideration when dealing with the psychedelic experience... This is not necessarily a rule of the Bardo, but it is a rule regarding the psychedelic experience.., and that is; you must never go to sleep while under the influence of a psychedelic... The normal experience is awake and alert.., and sleepiness is an indication of a serious problem, usually (in most cases) the drug that you took is a counterfeit, and not pure, or an overdose, or the result of a physical condition... To go to sleep in this state raises the possibility that you could simply "Die", and you journey on the "Way" would be over!.. You may encounter "Death" as an intriguing and attractive possibility, but it is the most ancient of deceptions, and if you are enticed into it, you die!.., and death is easy!., (not terrifying or ugly), all you have to do, is go to sleep!.. You must realize(at this point), that you are in great danger, and seek help, but whatever you do, do not go to sleep... This is "Survival Information" - *from a survivor* - (you get no feedback from the dead)!.. Take heed...

(the parable of the fig tree)... This is Wisdom... Hear Ye... Hear Ye...

* * * * *

But it is not at all certain or necessary that you will be confronted by the terrors of the Bardo... It is a possibility that you must be aware of, and prepared for, but it is by no means a necessity... On the contrary, if you be a good person, with good karma, the Bardo can be a very interesting and intriguing experience...

In my own case.., with the courage and fearlessness born of ignorance.., I entered the state of the Bardo.., and found it to be a very interesting and intriguing experience... If I had had enough intelligence to be apprehensive and fearful, I might have had to face my fears in the form of terrifying images (the "Wrathful Deities"), but I was blissfully ignorant and of good karma, and the benevolence of the Lord guided my steps...

The Bardo is different for everyone... In my own case.., as I tumbled through the maelstrom of thoughts and images, sights and sounds, disembodied and disoriented.., it seemed that I moved, stage by stage, through different scenarios.., birth memories, childhood memories, random memories.., a "Jurassic" period, with dinosaurs and lizards.., a "cartoon" phase, with cartoon characters in model trains, cars and biplanes.., a "patriotic" phase, with stars, stripes and fireworks.., observing the mysteries of bodily processes and electronic wizardry.., intricate patterns.., flashes of brilliance.., momentary revelations, insights, etc., and etc.., finally arriving at a place of stability and tranquility.., contemplating the Infinite...

Memories of the maelstrom of the Bardo are vague, but there are three memories that I will not forget...

Tumbling through the maelstrom, I became aware that I was observing the womb of creation, and I saw the male sperm swimming on their journey to union with the female egg, and I thought about those hundreds of millions of sperm, each one containing that mysterious spark of life, of a new being, and only one of those sperm will make contact with the egg.., and I wondered about the mysterious mechanism that produced the profuse abundance of "spark of life" sperm cells, as though the phenomena of life was as abundant as grains of sand in the desert... What was the mechanism of this gland, this "cornucopia".., that spewed forth sperm cells imbued with life.., how was the sperm cell created with it's form and function.?, and how did it get imbued with life.?. From whence cometh this life.?, and I sought to understand the mystery of the Union of Life with flesh, and Soul with body.., and as I penetrated into the cornucopia;., I saw a beautiful young child, a boy, with blond tousled hair, in a navy blue suit, with white collar and cuffs trimmed in lace, and he dipped a circular wand into a glass bottle.., he withdrew the wand, and with his breath, he blew forth a stream of bubbles.., and each bubble was an individual entity.., and I realized that I had reached the limit of my comprehension.., which was "child's play".., to the Lord...

On another occasion, tumbling through the maelstrom, I encountered what seemed to be a "manhole cover".?. I pushed against it from underneath, and the heavy lid suddenly released, opened about six inches and fell back closed... All that I got, was that one momentary glimpse through that six inch opening.., that was a hatch cover.!. In that momentary glimpse I saw that the hatch cover opened into the control room of a spacecraft of high technology, with a uniformed crew standing at their control panels, but standing at attention, facing the hatch cover, awaiting my arrival...

I was so amazed at this completely unexpected occurrence that I lost my concentration and the thought process ran rampant, and I never did make the transition from the Bardo into the spacecraft... All I got was that one glimpse...

I don't like to speculate about things that I don't know anything about... I know nothing about spacecraft or flying saucers... I have never seen, nor looked for, nor believed in flying saucers, etc... Because of the light speed barrier (hundreds and thousands of light years to the nearest star, etc.).., I dismissed any possibility of inter-stellar travel... However, (if I may speculate just a little).., I am an "eye witness" to inter-dimensional travel...

Who is to say.., that in the same way that I climbed the wavelength-mind-frequency spectrum into different dimensions in the realm of mind, and beyond mind.., that beings in those different dimensions likewise sought to come here.?. Who is to say.., what technologically advanced marvels may exist in a higher frequency dimension within the realm of Mind.?. This may explain why those people who claim to have had encounters (abductions, etc.) with Alien beings and spacecraft are always returned to their point of departure, usually in their car, or still tucked in bed, etc...

And who am I to say.?. I cannot say anything for certain, only this speculation, based on a glimpse, while tumbling through the Bardo...

And a third memorable incident.., that icon of Chinese culture and mythology.., the "Dragon"... While cascading through the Bardo, I literally "bumped" into this huge, undulating, magnificent Celestial creature... I bumped into him broadside, in his midsection, and being non-substantive (bodiless), I slipped myself up beneath the creatures bright green scales, penetrating through the creature and out the other side, continuing on my journey, tumbling through the Bardo... The Celestial Dragon also continuing on his way, unperturbed by the encounter...

Now.., this was Not the "Red" dragon.., with seven heads and ten horns.., spoken of in the book of Revelations (Rev. 12-3)... This was the "Green" dragon of Chinese mythology.., which is associated with good fortune and prosperity, and it is paraded through the streets in the famous "dragon dance" celebrations, amid the sounds of booming drums, clashing cymbals and fireworks, in "New Years day" celebrations and on other auspicious occasions...

I know Not the meaning and significance of this incredibly beautiful and magnificent creature, only that the mythology has a basis in the fact that it exists.., and it's resident domain.., is in the Bardo of the Mind...

So, the Bardo was friendly to me.., as was the Lord...

Attribute it to the rarity of the adventurer, who takes the road less traveled... Attribute it to my intense desire to know... Attribute it to the fulfillment of the promise of; "Seek and you will find"... Attribute it to the "Truth" that is the underlying basis of all the scriptures and the fulfillment of them... Attribute it to the delight of a loving Father.., who takes pleasure in the dispensing of Knowledge to a son who sincerely asks to be shown... Attribute it to "unmerited favor".., but the fact of the matter was;., I asked.., and the Lord answered...

I had gone through the initiatory experiences, the Iron Owl experience, the Diva realm experience, etc... I had become an experienced traveler, through the Bardo, and to that place of tranquility and centeredness.., that place of contemplation and of "Communion"...

I was; "the Soul that wanted to know"... I had asked the profound questions that came spontaneously from my Soul.., and absorbed in my contemplations, I became absorbed in "Communion".., and within the "Inner Sanctum" of my Soul, I heard that subtle "Inner Voice", and I asked, and HE answered, and there was dialogue.., and my profound questions were profoundly answered.., in a manner that was even more profound...

Lost in contemplation.., I heard that subtle "Inner Voice" that spoke the words that manifested in vision, and with the third eye of insight, I could see, and the vision was revelation.., of those things that had been hidden from the dawn of creation.., not because they were secret, but because they were beyond the comprehension and understanding of the linear-logical mundane mind... To speak of such things with mere words, would be a befuddlement and a sacrilege... Mere words.., fail to convey...

But not all of my questions were of this highly abstract nature... On one occasion I asked the question: "What is it with Christ".?. This wasn't even good grammar, and the response from the Inner Voice was: "Is this a serious question".?. (with good humor, HE toyed with me.!.)...

Never once did it occur to me to ask the question:.. "To Whom am I speaking?"... To have asked that question would have been to be aware of the distinction of "I", and "Thou".., and only the consciousness of "Ego" could have made that distinction.., and (almost) never does HE speak to the Ego consciousness... No.., the Zen-objective state (of absorption) is devoid of Ego.., and it was the nature of the "Communion" to convey emotionally, empathetically, telepathically, visually, intuitively and "experientially" that which was revealed.., and it was "Known"...

But I had asked the question.., "What is it with Christ".?. The response of; "Is this a serious question".?, should have revealed to me the absurdity of the question, but it did not, and I responded with; "Yes, it's a serious question.., I don't get it"...

"Journeys Through the Bardo"

….."I don't get it".., I grew up in a Catholic home, I went four years to a Catholic school, I memorized the entire Baltimore catechism by rote, attended all the masses, the rituals, the sacraments, etc., I prayed, I fasted, and NOTHING.!. "I don't get it"... I had seen the Void of Buddhism, I had traversed the Bardo, I had seen the Diva realm of the Hindus, I had the "dream vision" of the American Indians, I had solved the Zen riddle, I had even seen the Chinese Dragon.., I have had visions and revelations, but about Jesus Christ.., Nothing.!. As a matter of fact.., If it had not been for the intensity of my quest and the introduction of these powerful psychedelic "drugs", I would have seen NONE of the above.!. Without the consciousness expanding properties of the "drugs", the religions were meaningless... I owed more to the drugs than to the religions... I had verified the truths behind the religions, but about Jesus Christ.., nothing...

I didn't say all of the above, but it was implied... All that I said was.., "I don't get it"...

The Inner Voice spoke:.. "HE came to remove guilt" ... That's all that was said, but the vision commenced.., and I could "*see*"; "guilt".!, and it looked like "gilt"... This "gilt" looked like the superficial decorative "edge trimming" that you see on cheap ornaments, but this gilt.., was on people... This gilt, this superficial and superfluous edge trimming took away from the natural grace and beauty of the people, like a prostitute with too much make-up.., like an embarrassment.!. It gave a superficiality to the person, which was the substance of the Ego, and presented a barrier to the state of absorption necessary to Communion...

I saw it clearly.., "guilt", was the fall from "grace"... "Adam", was naked in the garden, but he was not in the least "self conscious"... He was super-conscious of everything in the garden, but he was not self conscious... It was only after he had experienced guilt that he became self conscious, and realized that he was naked...

Words fail to convey... It seems almost a travesty to repeat this conversation with the "Most High"... To just repeat the words, is to trivialize it... But the reader must make that "intuitive leap" here, and be aware that the words of this conversation were almost secondary to the nature of the "Communion".., that transmitted a complete "body of knowledge" (visually, emotionally, empathetically, intuitively, and experientially).., in just a few words... Just a few words.., that were assimilated into my being.., and became a "well-spring" of knowledge.., that continues to flow...

"HE".., could have said;.., that "HE" (Jesus) came as a sacrifice to buy back that which was lost".., or.., "He came as a recompense for sin".., or.., (whatever) is the commonly parroted "phrase of the day".., but "HE" didn't say that... "HE" said:.. "HE came to remove guilt".., which is far more precisely to the point... What I didn't realize at the time, was that this was more than just "general" objective knowledge (to demonstrate the subtlety).., this was "personal".., for myself.., for a guilt yet to come...

And so it went... Episode by episode.., and each episode building on the knowledge of previous episodes... This was the "Yoga of Knowledge".., and I was climbing the ladder of knowledge (figuratively speaking) to higher and higher plateaus... Through experimentation I found that it was best to space out these episodes at two week intervals, which gave the highest "High", and allowed time for the knowledge gained to be properly assimilated... Sometimes, I would have a vision of the next "plateau" (figuratively speaking), and in the following episode, I would be on that higher plateau, comprehending a higher Knowledge...

Over a period of several months, I progressed up this ladder of the Yoga of Knowledge, guided by the Inner Voice, that spoke to me in vision, revealing to me revelations upon revelations, which I accepted without question.., as though it was my divine right.., as though I really deserved this special attention.., of a loving "Father" who delighted in the dispensing of revelations to a wayward son that had crossed the Bardo in search of Knowledge...

I had reached the "Threshold"... I had reached the plateau of the Threshold, and I could see (intuitively) the next plateau, which was on the other side of the Threshold, but it required a "leap of faith" to cross that Threshold, to that other dimension, and not simply to "be" in that other dimension, but to achieve that exalted state of absorption while in **"THAT"** Primordial Dimension, known as "The Clear Light" of the Ultimate Reality, which is the "Realm of Brahma".., The Domain of God...

To "be" in that Exalted Dimension, is to attain Sainthood... To become One (absorption) with that Exalted Dimension.., is to become a Buddha...

I stood on the Threshold of Sainthood... I could look across that Threshold and see into "forever" through the Clear Light of the Ultimate Reality, but I could not make that "Leap of Faith" into it... Three times!., three times I reached that "jumping off" place.., and three times I hesitated... Why.?. Why did I hesitate.?. Fear that "I" might lose something in the transition.?. My "identity" maybe?!. My fears were groundless, but I doubted.., and I hesitated... Why.?. I don't know... I don't know...

This "grade" among the initiates is referred to as the grade of; "Dweller on the Threshold"...

Then came that fateful day... I imbibed the newly purchased capsule of that magical elixir, and waited for the transition stage of the Bardo.., but nothing happened... Nothing happened, but I could feel a presence there in the room with me, but not a "word" was spoken... There was only silence, but I could feel.., that I was "in the presence"... I could feel that I was being silently observed... The silence continued, and I guess I became frustrated... "Do Something"!., I shouted.., in a rather disrespectful manner...

"Do Something", I had shouted to this unseen Presence... It was an "expression of the day".., commonly used (among equals) when things have reached an impasse.., but most inappropriate in the presence of exalted company...

There were about three seconds of unbearable silence followed by a single word reply..., which was audible to my external ears.., which was just a sound.., which was a word.., a word/sound.., which reverberated through my soul, and which I will never ever forget... That word/sound was: "Humph"...

"Humph"... This is a word, a sound really, spoken with the mouth closed... It expresses an attitude of disdain.., a response to insolence.!. A reply to arrogance... A response to ill mannered presumptiveness...

"Humph"... That's all that was said.., and then this unseen Presence departed.., leaving behind a profound "emptiness"... Hell has been described as the "absence of God".., and I can verify this... There was a sense of loss, so profound.., an emptiness so complete... I hadn't experienced anything like this since--, since I was a child, lost.., at the county fair!.. And this profound sense of loss and emptiness didn't go away.!, and it was almost unbearable...

Oh yes.!. Leave to me.!. If anybody could piss-off God, it would be me.!. Oh yes.., Iron Owl the Intrepid Buffoon.., Iron Owl the Clumsy.!. There are some people who just don't know how to act in the presence of Royalty, and that's me.!. Oh yes.!. Just leave it to me, to be the Fool of all fools.., to commit the sin of "Presumption", while in the court of the "Most High".., while in the presence of God... Only "I", Iron Owl the Buffoon.., could do this...

I could not get over my incredible stupidity... I berated myself night and day... The sense of loss and emptiness pervaded my soul... How could I do such a thing?..

A week passed, and still that unbearable emptiness persisted... I had to do something.!. I ingested a capsule of LSD, and waited for the Bardo, but again, nothing happened, except that I felt inebriated.., drunk... My speech was slurred and my equilibrium was unstable... You can't trust what you buy off the street anymore, I lamented... Because of the government restrictions, you were forced to buy "bootleg" stuff that may not be pure, or even the real stuff! Or maybe it's just me... I decided to push the envelope, and I took a second capsule of what I hoped was LSD, and I just got more drunk and more unstable... My reasoning faculties seemed to be clear, but my speech was still slurred and my equilibrium was off... Well, I didn't plan on talking to anyone, and I wasn't going to walk anywhere, so undaunted, I reached for my hash pipe... I had acquired this "dynamite" kick-ass hashish that was almost as powerful as the LSD!.. This should get things started, I said to myself...

I lay back on my pillow, and observed the screen of my inner vision.., and it was chaos!.. There was a conflict between my mind and my soul... My mind was pouring out a profusion of thoughts in random disorder... So quickly they came, and before I could complete a thought, a new one started, and before completion, another new one, and on and on... I said to myself with the voice of my soul; "If I can't complete a thought, *I can't think!*.. I'm in trouble"!.. But the thoughts continued coming, only faster than before, and with the voice of my soul I said; "This is craziness, I can't complete a thought! *I'm in trouble"!..* The thoughts continued in rapid profusion, at the rate of dozens a second, and I realized again, that "I'm in serious trouble"!.. I was becoming fatigued maintaining my separation from the flow of these chaotic thoughts, and in my soul I recalled that "there is no rest for the wicked"... I knew that if I allowed "myself" to get caught up in these chaotic thoughts, I would go insane, and I was getting fatigued maintaining my concentration, and if I "let go", I would fall into this chaos, and I would go insane!., *and I thought about "letting go"*...

"Don't Let Go".., that familiar "Inner Voice" spoke to me... But I argued with HIM.!. "But I read in a book that you had to go through insanity to reach enlightenment" I said... "Don't Let Go".., the "Inner Voice" repeated, with stern authority, accompanied by the vision of the Earth spinning, and I was holding on to a rope at the Equator, and if I "let go", I would be flung from the Earth into outer space, and lost.!. "But the book - -".., I protested.., "DON'T LET GO".., The "Inner Voice" repeated, with an attitude of reproach at this "not very bright" recalcitrant student, as the second vision started:.. I had fallen off a ship, crossing the ocean, but I was holding on to a rope trailing behind the ship, and the sharks were attacking, but I couldn't die, and I would be saved as long as I didn't "let go" of the rope... "O.K.", I said... "I won't let go"...

I got up from my resting place and went to the kitchen... I focused my thoughts on making a cup of instant coffee... The chaotic thoughts swirled through my head as I ran the water into the tea kettle... What was I doing?, oh yes, making a cup of coffee... I put the tea-kettle on the stove... The thoughts swirled... I brought my self back to the cup, and lost my concentration as the thoughts swirled... I procured a spoon, and lost my concentration as the thoughts swirled... I brought myself back to the coffee jar, and lost my concentration as the profusion of thoughts swirled through my head... Step by step, with great effort, I brought myself back again and again until I completed the simple task of making a cup of instant coffee...

If I closed my eyes, I could see the chaotic thoughts swirling through my mind in uncontrolled torrents of nonsensical activity, so I purposely occupied myself with external activities, focusing my attention on the step by step process of accomplishing simple household tasks, while fighting off this drunken stupor... Several hours passed, and eventually I returned to normal.., but was I really back to normal.?. I went out to a restaurant that evening and I noticed that my mind would wander from subject to subject much too frequently... My normally very focused concentration was now "scattered"...

.....My involvement with LSD was not just a haphazard thing... No, on the contrary, it was just part of a very disciplined program which I took very seriously, and to which I was totally committed... One doesn't just cross the great expanse of the Bardo to that inner shore, climb the ladder of the "Yoga of Knowledge", and attain the level of "Dweller on the Threshold" by haphazard happenstance...

I was a serious student... I was the most serious of serious students.!. My discipline was the "martial arts", and my teacher was a Japanese Sensei who was "the best by contest", and I was proud to be his student... I wasn't a "black belt" (which requires years of training), but I was very good and exceptionally quick... I rose in rank through long hours, many days and many many months of consistent disciplined practice... An integral part of the discipline was the Zen meditation, which I practiced daily, beyond the scope of what was required... I was at the pinnacle of my physical strength and mental conditioning... I was the quintessential "Zen Warrior"...

Above and beyond the physical and mental training, I was well schooled in (almost) all the religions of the world, as well as the esoteric sciences, the mystery religions, the history and philosophies of various cultures, etc. and etc... I devoured books, and not as an academic pursuit, but as the craving of my soul... It was not a thought out course of action that I followed.., it was my very nature...

The LSD was not a recreational pastime.., no.., it was the missing ingredient of the "alchemical formula" whereby the "Magician" turns the "lead" of the base personality into the "gold" of the Enlightened being... This was "Spiritual Alchemy"., and I was totally committed...

But there was one aspect of my quest that was purposely concealed from me.., and that was the "Identity" of the "Inner Voice"... It was such a natural thing, that I just accepted it without question, and even debated with "HIM" in natural conversation, because the nature of the conversation was "Communion", and there was no awareness of the distinction between "I" and "THOU"...

The reader should always be skeptical.., but I swear to you that I didn't know.., that my Spiritual Teacher.., The "Voice Within".., that spoke to me in natural conversation and revealed to me in vision.., was none other than the "Lord God" Himself... It is only in retrospect that I know this...

This is the "Great Teaching" of the "Western School"... This is the "substance" of the Bible, from beginning to end.., Old Testament and New.., the testimony of all the Prophets.., of Abraham, Isaac and Jacob.., of Adam, of Job, of Enoch.., of Moses, of David.., of Hagar, etc. and etc.., and of Jesus, the Christ... If you learn nothing else from this book, learn this:.. That the Lord God speaks to men.., and HIS "Inner Voice" is the true "Living Word"... The Bible is only the "written word", bearing the testimony of the prophets to the fact of a Living God, that speaks to living men, and there is dialogue... And I;., "Iron Owl the Intrepid Fool".., I also have heard that "Inner Voice".., the Living Word of the Living God.., and I also testify...

But I had shown myself to be unworthy of the great privilege bestowed on me... I had committed the great sin of "presumption" and insolence, while in the court of the "Most High".., and the Lord had departed from me, leaving behind a terrible emptiness.., but HE had not abandoned me...

Truly unworthy though I was.., and only one week had passed by since HE had departed from me.., and already I stood on the brink of certain disaster.., on the brink of a great precipice.., and I had contemplated stepping off into that precipice.., of insanity.., and HE rescued me.!. I stood on the edge of the Pit.!, the great Abyss.!, and "argued" with the Lord!., and yet HE saved me!?... Truly unworthy though I was.., and yet.., HE saved me...

I had been saved from certain disaster, but there was still a price to pay... I had been weakened by the experience... My focused concentration had been scattered, and my "psychic energy" was at low ebb... That night, still distraught over the drama of the days activities, I lay down to sleep... There is a stage of "twilight sleep" that you go through just before you enter deep sleep... This stage of twilight sleep is a very "suggestible" and hypnotic level of consciousness where the activity of the rational conscious mind is temporarily suspended... I was in this stage of sleep when I heard this "voice" whispering in my ear...

It was a very deep, guttural and raspy voice that came up from a cess-pool, through a gravel pit, and "reeked" of evil!.. That gravelly, evil voice whispered into my ear, "that I should take another "trip" with this LSD, and that it would be a "bad" trip, but everything would work out just fine".., and with the third eye of "insight", I could see this creature, with his upper body protruding through a rip in this "membrane", and he had the head of a jackal, and the body of a hairy monkey about four feet tall, and I could see the grotesque shapes of other bodies pressed against the membrane, waiting for the membrane to rupture, so that they could spill forth from their evil dimension.., into mine!!.

But I became aware.., and like the proverbial "junkyard dog", that rouses from a deep sleep into attack mode.., I too.., instantly!, roused from deep sleep, up into combat stance, and in a voice even lower and more raspy, that came up from the gravel pit of my bowels, emerged from the grave, "reeked" of Death, and exploded in a crescendo of wrath, as I described to this impish demon the manner in which I would distribute his body parts...

My reaction was beyond quick!.,. it was instantaneous!.. It was the "Zen moment".., the moment that I had trained for.., and it was no idle threat that I gave to this demon, because if I could have laid hands on him, I would have ripped his throat out.!. The demon recoiled in terror, back through the rip in the membrane, and the rip sealed up.!.

I had terrorized a demon!.. I laughed at the ironic absurdity of it... But this demon, more clever than the rest.., had attempted to give me a "Post-Hypnotic Suggestion".., to the effect that my next "trip" with this "bogus" LSD, would be a bad trip, which would have surely ruptured the membrane that separated that evil dimension (in the realm of mind), from the personal dimension of my own mind.., and I would have been invaded by a "Legion" of demons!!. I had just narrowly missed the fate of that poor wretched soul spoken of in "Mark. 5:9"...

The demon might have been successful, with his "post-hypnotic suggestion", except for one fact;., I couldn't be hypnotized!.. It was probably the greatest disappointment of my young life, that I couldn't be hypnotized... Being a student of the

"The Demon Encounter"

mind, hypnosis was my first love... I tried a thousand times at self hypnosis, I hired professionals to hypnotize me, I even underwent sodium-pentathol with a professional hypnotist to achieve the hypnotic state, thinking that the hypnotic state was the "doorway" to higher states of consciousness.., and nothing... This inability to become hypnotized had a higher purpose, and probably saved me from a fate far worse than death...

Twice in the same day, I had just narrowly averted a fate worse than death... I had been sabotaged!!. I don't know what that "bogus" shit was, but it wasn't LSD... I took the remaining capsules of that "bootleg" bathtub, home made concoction, and flushed them down the toilet... Again, I was the victim of government interference.!. They had outlawed the legitimate sources of LSD, and opened up the door to bootleg amateurs, that produced an inferior (and mind- bending) product... I am sure that most (if not all) of these so-called "bad trips" are directly attributable to these counterfeit bootleg recipes...

So.., by the "Grace of God".., I had averted the most profound of tragedies... It was the following day before I got any sleep, and I slept.., and I dreamed...

If I were to include in this book a chronology of dream activity, it would fill many volumes, but I kept no such chronology... Suffice it to say, that any student of the "Inner Path" will have a wealth of dream experience... There are many types of dreams.., the nonsensical "random access" type of dreams, dreams stimulated by those things that we fear.., dreams stimulated by events of the day, emotions, indigestion, etc., and then there are the "Psychic Dreams"... It is these Psychic dreams that are of interest to the student of the inner path... These dreams are characterized by their "symbolic" content, and the fact that you usually awaken immediately from the dream with clear recollection[3]... The symbolic nature of the dream content requires interpretation, and the best person to interpret the dream is you yourself.., because they are *Your* symbols...

---

[3] Required reading for the student "of the inner path", is the book: "The Symbolic and the Real", by Ira Progoff (1973), which is an in-depth study of the nature and meaning of "Psychic Dreams"..., as a method of communication between the Super-conscious and the Conscious mind, by way of symbolic dreams…

But I slept, and I dreamed... In my dream, I was visited by a beautiful black "Nubian" dressed in colorful attire, and she was explaining that the film-strip had unwound from it's intricate course through my movie projector and become unspooled, and she had rethreaded the film strip through the projector and now it was working fine... I was more than appreciative.., and she was very desirable... She looked heavenward, and with her arms in the air, amid surprise and gleeful laughter, she exclaimed;., "He wants to make love to me"?!! Apparently, consent was given, and we made love... When I awoke, there was a wet spot on the bed... I have vivid dreams...

The symbolism of the "movie projector", that had become "unspooled", is readily apparent... Why she was a "black Nubian" is just the exotic creativity of the mystery of dreams themselves, a tribute to the Dream-maker... Why did I make love to her?., because she was a work of perfection, and exquisitely desirable...

So.., with the help of the Lord.., I was restored!.. But the sin of "presumption".., is a great sin.., and a great sin has profound consequences... I had proved myself unworthy, and I was to be tested further... My greatest test was yet to come...

I allowed myself about a two week respite from my "Alchemically enhanced" profound meditations... I had been restored to normal, with apparently no ill effects, but that profound sense of loss and emptiness still prevailed... I reached for my hashish pipe... My faithful hashish pipe, that never failed to open up to me the "Doors of Perception'... It had been my practice.., that after I had traversed the Bardo with the aid of LSD, and sat in "Communion" with the Lord.., Who revealed to me in vision, the profoundest of mysteries.., that I would sit in contemplation for the next two weeks, processing and assimilating the Knowledge and information that had been shown to me...

This had been the most joyous of times... The Communion of the Lord, the revelations, the climbing of the ladder of the Yoga of knowledge, ever higher and higher plateaus, and sitting on the "Threshold".., looking out into forever and forever, with the greatest promise yet to come;., Oneness.., with the Lord... The Supreme goal of all the Adepts...

But now.., I was back on Earth... I had allowed myself a two week respite from my wayward journey, just to allow myself a "balancing out" period... Firmly back on "Terra Firma", I reached for my faithful hashish pipe... Two tokes only.., and the veil dropped from my eyes.., and with the "third eye of insight".., I could see!!. Oh God, did I see!., and what I saw.., no man should ever see!!...

* * * * * *

"The Dark Night of the Soul"

Locked into the Samadii of deep contemplation, I looked again into the "Pit", on the brink of which I had stood, and I had argued with the Lord, as I contemplated stepping off into it, because of a book that I had read... But now, with the third eye of insight fully opened, I looked down into the Pit.., and I recoiled in terror!.. This was not just your everyday sort of terror.., this was TERROR.., the simpering, whimpering, trembling, fall on your face and beg for mercy.., kind of TERROR, that you never forget, and it harms your Spirit, and is a "Trauma" to your Soul!..

Let me explain about the "Third Eye", the eye of "insight"... It is much more than the simple ability to see... It is "absorption" into that which is seen.., and the knowledge gained is experienced directly, and absorbed into your Soul, and the understanding is intuitive and complete.., and I had looked into the Pit.., the great Abyss.., with intuitive insight.., and I saw.., what no man should ever see!.. This is forbidden knowledge.., forbidden.., because it is harmful to the Soul...

There is a negative aspect to "Truth"... I.., Iron Owl the Intrepid Explorer, had asked to see "Truth"... I had navigated the great Bardo, in search of "Truth"... I had climbed the ladder of the Yoga of Knowledge, and stood on the threshold of the "Ultimate Truth"·.., and now.., now I had fallen from that great height.., to the equivalent greatest depth.., and now I stood.., on the threshold of "Hell"...

With the "Eye of Insight" fully opened, I had looked down into the great Abyss... Just one glance.., and my life would be changed forever!.. I recoiled in absolute Terror!..

The eye hath not seen.., the ear hath not heard.., and mere "words", fail to convey... Be thankful for this... I can describe to you what I have seen.., but the description will not adequately describe, nor will the understanding fully comprehend... Be thankful for this... The emotional impact will not be there... Be "Oh so grateful" for this...

I would very much like to report to you that there is no such place as "Hell".., that it is a fiction.., but I cannot do that!.. To my great misfortune, I have seen it with my own "inner eye"... What follows, is my "eye witness" testimony...

Locked into the trance state of deep samadii, I peered again into the great abyss... For just a single moment I looked down into the face of lost souls... Souls in torment.., suffering a mental anguish that was far worse than any physical pain..; *Insanity*!.. Without the ability to string together the consecutive moments of a coherent thought.., totally insane!.. Wailing and moaning in their mental agony, with an overwhelming sense of despair so complete.., a hopelessness so complete.., a profound vacant emptiness so complete.., because of the absence of God!!. It was the abomination of desolation, and in spite of their insanity, they knew and had the sense of absolute hopelessness.., and they could never die...

Death would have been a reprieve.!. Fire and brimstone would have been a reprieve.!. But I saw no death.., I saw no fire and brimstone.., what I saw was insanity, and the absence of God... How do you communicate the absence of God?., except to compare it to the experience of being "LOST".., like a child.., at the county fair... It was this profound sense of "Loss", and the utter despair and hopelessness that touched my soul, and sent me retreating back from the edge of that abysmal Pit, horrified and terrified, quivering and trembling, and crying; "Oh no, oh no, no, Oh God, No"... But my sojourn through Hell had only just begun...

Like a disobedient child, that had been grasped by the ear with the thumb and forefinger of his Fathers strong right hand.., I was marched down through the corridors of that insane asylum called;., "Hell"... Horrified and terrified, I was made to look in upon those wretched souls in the various stages of Hell.., the various stages of insanity.., from the schizoids to the paranoids, to the psychotics, to the criminally insane, from dementia to madness, and etc.., and all the while that I am viewing this terrifying menagerie, there is a voice in the background reciting a nursery rhyme:..

"Humpty Dumpty sat on a wall.., Humpty Dumpty had a great fall.., All the Kings horses, and all the Kings men.., couldn't put Humpty Dumpty together again"...

I had recited this nursery rhyme as a child, but never before had it had such tragic implications, and to my horror, I realized (but for the intervention and the grace of God), that "I".., was Humpty Dumpty.!.

And still, my sojourn through Hell was not over, as I viewed ghostly apparitions;., the "Haunts".., and the "Haints"... With my soul, I reached out and touched the "Haint".., and I withdrew in terror.!. How could I ever explain it?., except to say that the Haint.., "ain't".., but with a capitol "H".!. It was like "antimatter" to the soul; the essence of vacant emptiness, hopelessness and despair... I was horrified... Only the insane see these things... Only those poor souls that have ruptured the membranes that separate the domains of Hell from the domain of their own minds.., and here.., but for the grace of God.., was I...

I came out of my samadii, and I ran out of the house.!. I ran down the street to the highway, and I ran down the highway.!. I ran at high speed until I could run no more, and then I walked, as fast as I could, and then I ran some more, and then I walked, and then I ran, and I walked and I ran, and I walked and I ran, for many miles and several hours, I walked and I ran.., trying to distance myself from the terrible horror of the vision of Hell that I had just witnessed, and the realization of how close I had come.., to permanent residency...

Understand this:... It was not the experience of the "mind bending" bootleg bad acid.., nor was it the mind benumbing torrent of incomplete thoughts that swept through my mind like a chaotic whirlwind, robbing me of the ability to think.., nor was it the standing on the brink of the Abyss and arguing with God.., nor was it the depletion of psychic energy and the confrontation with the demon... No.., I had survived these perils and emerged unscathed... It was the subsequent vision of Hell, and the realization of just how close I had come to going there, that scarred my soul.!.

I had been Invincible!!. I was the "Zen Warrior".., with a mind like a steel trap and razor sharp mental focus, fearless, unshakable.., and arrogant... But now, I had been shaken to the core of my being... I had never before seen such horror or known such terror... Now I realized my vulnerability... Now I trembled with unspeakable fear...

I was haunted by that terrible vision... I could not erase it from my minds eye... It was unforgettable horror... I could not enter the Bardo without these terrible visions presenting themselves to my minds eye, reducing me to quivering terror... My way had been blocked be fear... My reason for being had been thwarted... I had been rejected by the Lord... Woe is me.., woe is me... No one had ever lost what I had lost... Rich men had lost fortunes, Emperors had lost empires, but I had lost the Communion of the Lord... I had gone from the "Dweller on the Threshold" to the gates of Hell, and it was my own doing... Woe is me...

I plunged into deep, dark despair... I had no reason to live... Emptiness and abandonment pervaded my soul.., and that profound sense of loss.., like a child, at the county fair... I went into a deep, dark, morbid depression... Thoughts of suicide crossed my mind, but were quickly abandoned, knowing that there was no death, and that such an action would surely put me into that unspeakable Hell... My only consolation was that every day that passed was one day closer to my death... I was 28 years old... I prayed to die...

But nobody knew, except me... I confided in no one.!. Work was my salvation... If I had allowed myself to dwell on my situation, I would have spiraled ever downward, and I would not allow myself to do that... The only thing I could do was to occupy my every waking hour with work... I worked as though possessed... from dawn to darkness, I worked at the floor covering trade, installing wall-to-wall carpeting in row after row of newly constructed apartment buildings, playing the radio loudly, to drown out the emptiness that pervaded my soul... I had no appetite, but forced myself to eat, only to be able to work, to distract my mind from that terrible vision, and at the end of the day, I fell into bed, to a restless sleep, and up at dawn, to escape into work...

And then.., miraculously.., the pendulum swung.!. After about two months of enduring this living hell, the pendulum had swung, and I was again in the land of the living, in the presence of God... Reprieve.!. Oh Yes!!. God, thank you, thank you... Still, I could not enter the Bardo, the wound was too deep, too fresh.., but just the mere remembrance of the heights that I had visited, and the presence of the Lord, would transport me to intoxicating heights

"Sojourn Through Hell"

of inspiration... For about two months, the sun shown, with bright days.., and then the pendulum swung back.., plunging me again into that deep dark pit of morbid despair...

And again I worked, as though possessed, to escape the emptiness that pervaded my soul, for about six weeks.., and then the pendulum swung again to sunny days and ecstatic remembrances.., before swinging back again, to that deep, dark pit of emptiness and despair...

It wasn't until after the third set of reciprocal swings of the pendulum that I noticed the pattern... Just like a pendulum.., on a clock winding down.., the pendulum would swing from side to side, from the depths of morbid despair to the other side, of bright sunny days and ecstatic remembrances, but with each swing, the ark of the swing became less, just like a clock winding down... and I could see that eventually there would come and end to my punishment, and that eventually, the pendulum would come to rest...

It took the better part of a year.., before the pendulum finally came to rest... After observing the pattern, and knowing that it would eventually come to an end, it was more bearable.., at least as bearable as an almost unbearable situation could be... Again, words fail to convey the agony and emptiness of morbid despair, which I fought against with unceasing involvement in work, and the ever present radio blaring loudly in my ears... Work was my salvation.., what would I have done without work.?.

At the end, I watched the pendulum like a scientist, as it swung to and fro, from despair to gladness.., the last week, then days, then a day, then hours, and then minutes, then a minute, and as it oscillated in seconds, and then, like a dagger thrown and stuck into heavy timber, it vibrated to a close, at rest... The sentence had been carried out.., "to the last jot and tittle"!., and it was over...

I emerged a much wiser, but sadder man... Definitely a more humble man.., but only a man... No longer was I a "Dweller on the Threshold"..., and no longer did I have at my pleasure the Communion of the Lord.., and I had the knowledge and vision of Hell.., which was a burden to my soul.., and for sure, I knew the difference between the Lords presence.., and HIS absence... Also, I had a profound appreciation.., of just how magnificent a gift it is.., to be able to string together the consecutive moments of a thought, into a complete thought.., and to be able to relate that thought to previous thoughts... Cognitive intelligence.!. How few there are, who appreciate the magnificence of this phenomenon...

My only consolation: "Hebrews 12:5-7"... "My son, do not disdain the discipline of the Lord, or lose heart when reproved by HIM. For whom the Lord loves, HE disciplines. HE scourges every son HE acknowledges"...

"Endure your trials as discipline, for God treats you as sons, for what son is there whom his father does not discipline? At the time, all discipline seems a cause not for joy, but for pain, yet it brings the peaceful fruit of righteousness to those who are trained by it"...

Well,.. I had no feelings of righteousness... I had been, after all, the "Fool" of all fools... The absurdity of it.., to stand on the brink of the Abyss, and argue with the Lord.!, about whether I should step off into it.!. I had forced the Lords hand.!. HE saved me.., and it was "absolute" justice.., that HE show me from what... My "discipline" from the Lord had lasted almost a year, and I suffered it in silence, telling no one about it, except for now, and I tell You.., so that you might learn from my experience.., and NOT commit the great sin of presumption...

Although the period of discipline was over, the "horror" of what I had seen was still fresh in my mind, and it was a trauma to my soul.., I had been traumatized by fear.., and fear is a barrier... The Bardo "door" was still open to me, but I was unable to traverse it.., because of fear...

Strangely enough, that spinal energy factor (Kundalini), was stronger than ever, threatening to take me to higher and ever higher levels of consciousness, but it was like walking a tightrope, and one slip would send me careening into that dreaded Abyss, and I would retreat from it, trembling and shaking, petrified with fear...

I have had much more experience with the mysterious Kundalini than I have knowledge about it.., but I found that I could control it by my body positions... It functions similarly to a chimney.., If I sit up straight in a meditation posture, it's flow is unobstructed, and it carries you (the consciousness principle) upward and inward to higher levels of consciousness as well as to interior (fifth dimensional) Realms of being... But by reclining, I could inhibit it's flow, and regulate the level at which I felt safe... By lying down, I could arrest the flow completely...

It was a dilemma... I was compelled.., by my inborn "prime directive".., to solve the "Riddle of the Universe", to "Know my Creator".!. It was the reason I was born.., It was my reason for being, and I couldn't stop trying, at least twice weekly, with the aid of my trusted hashish pipe, that never failed to lift the veil from my eyes, and give me insights into the nature of my soul, and to progress upward.., only to hit that wall of fear.., and retreat in panic... Again and again, I stormed the gates of the Bardo, and again and again I retreated, drenched with sweat, trembling with fear...

I was in a quandary... Compelled to go on.., and stymied by that terrifying "abysmal" fear... It is humiliating to be blocked by the barrier of fear, but the wound was still too fresh in my mind, and too deep... I could not close my eyes without conjuring up that terrible vision... I was haunted by it... It was a plague to my soul...

I could see no way out of my dilemma... I needed help!.. Not medical help.., not psychological help.., No, I needed spiritual help, but who was qualified?.. Who was there, that knew more about my specific spiritual dilemma than me?.. Who else was there, that had crossed the Bardo, encountered and defeated a demon, viewed Hell, and had discourse with the Lord?.. Who could I turn to that knew more than I.?, and would be willing to teach me?.. There was no one.., I was alone... But I couldn't continue to live in this defeated situation... I couldn't live and be defeated by fear... I would not give up, I would not surrender to this dilemma...

There had to be someone I could turn to.., and if not in this country, then in India.!. Yes.., About a year before, I had met the Swami.!, He was lecturing in the U.S., and he had invited me to attend his "School of Yoga" in India... It was a fortuitous meeting... Yes.., I would go to India...

* * *

* * *   * * *

....I have been very brief with my description of Hell. It is not good for me to recall this event... I have spent these many years trying to forget the horror of what I had seen.., so believe me.., you do NOT want to go there... Take every precaution...

BOOK VI

"Wanderings Through the Sangsara"

It was the latter part of the 1960's when I left the United States... I had sold all of my worldly possessions, my lifetime of accumulations, for the princely sum of approximately three thousand dollars in travelers checks... My destination was India, but my reasons for going were vague and undefined. I was wandering around like a lost Soul, with a sense of emptiness and purposelessness. I picked up a used back-pack at the Army surplus store and packed it with the barest of essentials; a few changes of clothes, a few good books, and a sleeping bag. I bought a one way ticket to Europe on the cheapest flight I could find, which was by way of Reykjavik, Iceland, landing in Luxembourg.

There was a new phenomenon happening.., an explosion of international travel by a new class of tourist; the American "Hippie", with whom I was identified and whose lifestyle I adopted, because it was the most economical. I didn't have the financial resources to afford hotel accommodations, so wherever I found an empty space, that's where I would unroll my sleeping bag, usually in the company of several other sleeping bags, in the park, or wherever. This carnival atmosphere was attractive to the Europeans as well, and soon the "Hippie" phenomenon was also an European phenomenon that incorporated young travelers from all countries that were identified under the "Hippie" banner, motivated by "free love" and the adventures of the "open road"...

This was my first time in Europe, so I thought I might as well explore. By bus, by train, and sometimes by hitch-hiking, I meandered through Germany, Denmark, Switzerland, France, Italy, the Vatican, etc. By boat, over to Greece, and by train to the Bosporus, a short ferry boat ride across the channel, and I stepped off into Asia... A transition.., from Europe to Asia, and from the age of 29, to the age of 30. I celebrated my 30th birthday in Istanbul... I took a train from Istanbul to the South of Turkey, where I caught a Russian passenger boat to the island nation of Cypress, intending to go to Israel, but the border was closed because of war... I took the same passenger boat over to Lebanon, intending to go to Israel from there, but that border was also closed, so I took a short flight over to Jordan, but the border had been closed only the day before, and the Jordanian military was openly hostile to Americans, and I escaped with my life by taking a flight to Tehran, Iran. Iran was, at that time, still under the rulership of the Shah, and the Iranians and the Americans were the best of friends and allies. Another long bus ride to the Iran-Afghanistan border, which was a wide shallow river with no bridge, and temporarily closed, because the buses had to ford the river through two feet of water, and there was room enough for only a single lane of traffic in only one direction at a time, and there was a bus load of passengers from Afghanistan and the busload that I was on from Iran, head to head, in the middle of the river, and each refusing to back-up and let the other through... It was a matter of national pride, and they were screaming obscenities at each other, and then they were picking up rocks from the river bed and throwing them at each other. This had been going on the whole day.. I don't know how the situation was resolved, because I walked across the river to the Afghan side, and hitched a ride with a Pakistani trader to the city of Herat, then on into Qandahar, and then all the way on into the capitol city of Kabol... I spent a few days in each city and about a week in Kabol, and then another bus ride through the Khyber Pass, into Pakistan, and finally a train ride on into India...

The trip overland, through Europe, the Middle East, and into India took approximately three months...

The trip to India was not for the purpose of tourism, but was more an act of desperation... I had been wrestling with "internal demons" in the depths of my soul... I had to find "someone" who knew more about the realms of "inner space" than I did. I had no other concern than this. I cared for nothing beyond this. This was my purpose and my destination, with no provision for failure, and no provision for return…

I had previously met the "Swami" in the U.S., where he had been invited to speak to a small society of "spiritually minded" individuals that had come together by virtue of their common interest in Yoga and "spiritual integration". The Swami was on a mission to bring the science of Yoga to the Western world, which was badly in need of this spiritual integration. The Swami had founded the "School of Yoga" in India with the purpose of recruiting dedicated aspirants from the Western cultures, training them in the science of "Kriya Yoga" and having them return to their Western cultures and hopefully, convey the knowledge of this technique to bring this "inner light" to a world in darkness. A very noble mission, indeed...

I studied the Swami. He came without pretense or fanfare. He spoke with a quiet and sincere nobility, a humble nobility, without a trace of self doubt in his make-up. His speech was both eloquent and simple at the same time. He was an "integrated personality"...

I felt called, but there was no way. India was just too far away. Circumstances just wouldn't permit... More than a year later I arrived on his doorstep, unannounced.., and joined the class in progress.

The experience at the ashram proved very beneficial. The Swami was a man of deep experiences and dedication and we (myself and other students) had many intriguing discussions that lasted well into the evening, sitting by the fireside, under the canopy of an octagon shaped pavilion.

The Swami took no full time students, but merely communicated the techniques of Kriya Yoga as he himself had been taught, by the process of total immersion into the techniques for 10 to 12 hours a day for a period of approximately 3 months. After that, the individuals progress was dependent on the individuals initiative.

I characterized the technique as "the combined multiple approach"... By combining daily aerobic exercise, proper diet, breathing techniques, visualization exercises, Yoga postures, contemplation, etc., into a concentrated effort of undisturbed and immobile meditation for an extended period of time, results could be achieved, but patience is required.

I must admit to a flaw in my character. I am by nature not a very patient person. When I sit immobile for a 3 hour stretch twice daily, over a 2 month period of time, I want something to happen! Things were happening, but not fast enough or dramatically enough to suit me. I was not a beginner at meditation, having previously been initiated into the "Yoga of the Sound Current" (Nada Yoga), under the direction of "Shri Kirpal Singh Gi Maharaj", the leader of the Seik religion (I never met the man, the initiation was by proxy, in the U.S.). I was also an avid student and practitioner of the Martial arts, Karate in particular, of which Zen meditations played an integral part. I was also deeply involved in Buddhist meditations, extracted from the Mahayana texts, as translated by Evans-Wentz. I read voraciously on all the exoteric sciences, physics, psychology, philosophy, the "Religions of the World", etc.. I was also taking correspondence courses in the Jewish Kabala, and the "Tree of Life". I had been a student of Hypnosis and self-hypnosis for years (perhaps my greatest disappointment in life was that I, personally.., could not be hypnotized). I dabbled in the so-called "Mystical" sciences, of alchemy, astrology, and etc... I sought to solve the riddle of the universe, to "see the scheme entire", and to see it organized into a movable matrix system that could be brought down to earth and comprehended by dividing all the sciences into 22 different categories, reducing the knowledge of these sciences into symbolic form, and presenting them as a comprehensive whole, known as the Tarot, (not profanely used to tell the future), but to be able to see the "Scheme of Life Entire"... This.., was the fire.., that burned in the belly of the Owl... No less than this, was my goal...

I could appreciate the concept of the combined multiple approach. I considered it to be "my way", and I added to it by incorporating in another factor; I smoked some Hashish. I broke the rules, very discretely, on my own time, when I should have been sleeping. But when I could not, I sat in my hashish induced meditation. The effects were dramatic. The two months of disciplined preparation proved to be very rewarding. I went into deep contemplation, and I saw my life in a previous time. I was a native American Indian, somewhere in the South Eastern part of colonial America... There was an uneasy truce between the white settlers and the warrior savages that inhabited the deep forests. Each viewed the other with suspicion, and there was just cause on both sides for these suspicions, as each had suffered at the hands of the other. I was a warrior and a hunter, and I had no fear of the white man with whom I had had dealings on previous occasions. I did not consider us to be friends, but neither did I consider us to be enemies at this time. I walked into their compound in the light of day, clad in buckskin from the waist down, naked from the waist up. I was there to trade. The white man had many interesting tools, knives of steel, steel hatchets that could cut trees, long rifles, blankets, etc. As I walked into the compound

I saw the faces of suspicion and hatred. I could feel their animosity. Something had been stolen. They looked upon me as a thief, scouting out in the daytime so that I could come back and steal in the night, as only an Indian could. I sensed their hostility. I turned to leave their compound. I heard men shouting, I saw men with long rifles. I ran as fast as I could, into the swamp where I thought to elude them. This only confirmed their suspicions that I was the thief that had stolen from them in the middle of the night. They pursued me into the swamp. I was on foot, and they had a flat-bottomed boat with oars. There was three of them. I could not outrun them, the swamp was chest deep with dense vegetation. I thought to conceal myself in the dense growth, but they found my hiding place, and I was captured. I was tied hands and feet, and my arms were bound tightly against my upper body. I could not move. A discussion followed; "We captured him, now, what should we do with him"? "Let's see if he can swim", came the jeering reply. I was pushed and kicked from the boat, into the murky water. I heard laughter. I fought and kicked against the ropes that held me, to no avail. I was coughing and spitting. The murky water was in my nose and down my throat, into my lungs. I was drowning... This was not a good death!.. Especially for a warrior, this was not a good death. I watched.., as I fought against the murky waters that engulfed me. I watched.., as my body kicked and jerked, as the life was suffocated out of me... In distressed agony, repulsed by the witnessing of my own death, I spoke the words aloud; "Oh God, I don't want to see this"... An inner voice answered; "That's why you can't see it"...

I accepted that statement as a fact. I had seen enough... I had been murdered!.. This was just another episode of frontier life in Colonial America. I'm sure the early settlers felt entirely justified in their actions. Life was hard, and life was cheap, especially among the heathen savages. Just another episode of frontier justice, it happened every day, not worth mentioning.

I sat there in the dark, contemplating the meaning of this past life experience I had just witnessed. It explained the "Iron Owl" episode. The reason it was in the traditional American Indian format, where the young braves retreat to a place of solitude, fasting and praying until he receives his "dream-vision" of the animal that will be his "Totem", the animal that will determine what name he will henceforth be known by, the animal that he will henceforth embody the qualities of, the qualities of cunning, stealth, swiftness, bravery, strength, etc. His vision determines his status in the tribe, and his vision is true to his nature and personality...

This past life vision had brought understanding to the Iron Owl experience, but it also brought something else.., something I wasn't prepared for... The nights were very cool at the ashram, and I slipped back into my sleeping bag and zipped it up. Panic gripped me.., I couldn't breathe. I unzipped the sleeping bag and lay there, not understanding. Soon I was chilled by the cold night air. Again I zipped up the sleeping bag, and again I was gripped by panic. I was claustrophobic! For the very first time in my life I was experiencing claustrophobia. Alternating between freezing and suffocating, I zipped and unzipped my sleeping bag many times during that restless night. I would never again be able to sleep zipped up in a sleeping bag... The following day I went down to the village and bought some blankets. I slept on top of the sleeping bag and covered myself with the blankets...

There is good reason why we cannot remember our past lives. We have enough burdens in this life, without dragging into it the burdens of past lives. There are many people who cannot bear the burden of sins committed in this life, and seek solace in a drunken stupor... It is a blessing not to remember. The slate is wiped clean. We start life fresh and unencumbered by the sins and heartaches of the past. A clean slate, a fresh start, it is a blessing...

I had ample time to contemplate the meanings of this past life experience. I had never been really sure about the theory of reincarnation, and as such, I never really arrived at any definitive conclusions about it. There is a blurry line between what is memory and what is imagination, and that which is imagined can be entered into memory, and that which is retrieved from memory can be elaborated on by imagination. The theorists from both camps (pro and con reincarnation) have no real understanding of the mechanics of either memory or imagination, or even dreams, for that matter. They can observe the phenomena, but their explanations are only theoretical. Their theories do not even approach the "Akashic records", (the cosmic memory), or higher mind functions.

The "hypnotic age regression" experiments have only served to exacerbate the argument; the pro reincarnationists saying: Aha, under hypnosis the subject can remember past lives, therefore proving my point! The con reincarnationists saying: Aha, Under hypnosis the subject will imagine and invent a past life scenario in response to suggestion, therefore proving my point!

The "Eastern world" of Hinduism, Buddhism, etc., accepts the concept of reincarnation without question. The Buddha (Sidhartha Gotoma) is said to have had perfect recollection of over 500 past lives! Which raises the question:., If the Soul really is immortal, (and I say that it is), what does it do with an infinite life span? How does the soul occupy itself with an infinite life span?..

It has been stated that the purpose of life on earth, and the purpose of the vehicle of the body.., is for the experience of the Soul!.. That the Soul passes through the "Veil of Forgetfulness" and enters into life again and again, for the purpose of testing. The purpose of the test.., is to separate the "Good Samaritans", from the "Assholes", because Heaven wouldn't really be heaven, if it were populated by Assholes!.. There is a special place reserved for the assholes.., who also have an infinite life span...

The above paragraph is the conclusion and summation of volumes of books and religious/philosophical treatises. You could elaborate on the above paragraph and write volumes of books and religious/philosophical treatises, so, this is the definitive bottom line. No need to waste words... Which gives rise to the next question; Are you a Good Samaritan, that is concerned with the welfare of his fellow man, that will go out of his way to extend a helping hand, that will extend charity to the poor, that will forgive those that have transgressed against you, that will love thy neighbor as thyself, etc.? Or.., are you an asshole, who will cheat on his wife, who will fuck his neighbor's wife and screw his neighbor, if he can.., who scoffs.., at the 10 commandments.., whose nature is greed and selfishness, etc... No need to waste words...

Know this: If you are involved in meditation, you are on a religious quest. If you enter into the realms of inner space, you are entering the realm of your own Soul. You are on Holy Ground. The profane dare not enter! Act accordingly, and take this advice from Iron Owl;.. Do Good!.. Every chance you get, do good. Go out of your way to do good. You may not get that many chances to do good, and a chance missed is an opportunity lost. And the second directive is like unto the first;.. Refrain from doing that which is evil… Shun the company of those that do harmful and hurtful acts. Avoid defilements.., and this is Wisdom;., FLEE from temptations... Fools rush in... Discretion is the better part of valor... A word to the wise here, should be sufficient. Etc…

Before we leave the subject of reincarnation, I must tell you of another incident that happened years before;.. An "Itinerant Preacher" came through the town where I was living, and he had no place to stay, so, as chance would have it, I had a spare bedroom, so he spent a few days in my home. The subject of reincarnation came up, and he made one of the most startling statements that I had ever heard! He maintained that the entire Bible, Old Testament and New, was about Jesus Christ in his various incarnations! He had been Able, slain by his brother; Cain... He had been Job, tested and tried by Satan... He had been Isaac, who had obediently consented to be put on the alter and offered up as a sacrifice to the Lord at the hand of his own Father, Abraham (a forerunner to the crucifixion, (??)... He was Enoch, who walked and talked with the lord... He had been (???), who fell in love, was married, and nothing else was written of him. (?)... He was not Moses... He had been Aaron, who participated in the slaying of 40,000 of his own people who committed the sin of idolatry by worshiping the golden calf... He had been Joshua, who had gone into battle at the direction of the Lord and slew Jericho; men, woman, children, *babies,* cattle, sheep, dogs, cats, chickens, pigs, asses,.. *and all things that drew breath!!. (Who will judge the Lord?.. Don't piss off the Lord)...* Etc. and etc... I don't remember the entire list of incarnations... Is this the truth?? I don't know, but it is an interesting concept! About the only thing that I will really commit to that I know for sure, is;., I can no longer sleep zipped up in my sleeping bag!..

* * *

Post Script: (This is an insertion.., added long after the above was written)... You may remember.., that in a previous chapter I told the story of the "Dream Vision".., which is the "rite of passage" of the American Indian, when he is given his "Warrior Name" in accordance with the vision of the animal that he has the vision of, and he embodies the characteristics of his "Totem" animal counterpart (speed, cunning, bravery, stealth, etc.).., and I had the vision of the Owl.., dark gray in color... I would have selected the name "Grey Owl".., except for the fact that that name had already been taken, and I didn't want to plagiarize the name already made famous by another... So.., when the motion picture; "Grey Owl" came out, I had to go see it!.. It was the story of Archie Belaney, a very idealistic young Englishman, enraptured and captured by the noble spirit of the American Indian... Pursuing his dream, he left England for Canada and became adopted into the "Ojibway" Indian tribe, where he lived his life as an Indian, learning the ways of the wilderness, and communing with the wild nature that he loved... He was given the name "Grey Owl", and he married into the tribe... Fortunately (for the rest of us), he had the gift of authorship, and he was able to eloquently put down on paper his insights and experiences into the life of the truly "Noble Savage" that inhabited the deep forests of the Canadian wilderness... He showed that the Native American Indians were far more Noble than they were savage, with an inborn "Warriors" code of ethics, a reverence for God, and a respect for nature that "we" had lost sight of... He touched our hearts with his words, and he became one of the first "conservationists"...

I identified with the person of Archie Belaney!.. I too, had been an idealistic youth, captured and enraptured by the nobility, courage and resourcefulness of the American Indian, that lived in communion and harmony with God and nature... When other boys were into baseball, quoting statistics, batting averages, the baseball "Greats", etc., and etc.., I could name all the Tribes of North America, the great warriors and chieftains, the lore of the wilderness, and I hunted, fished, and ran my trap-lines... The American Indian was my hero and my role model, and I aspired to run away from home, join an Indian tribe, and live as an Indian.., but Archie Belaney had actually done it!.. He had lived my boyhood dream!..

So.., although it is unusual for a "white man" to go through the "rite of passage" of the American Indian, and have the "dream/vision".., and be given the Warrior name of his "Totum" animal counterpart.., in my case, it really wasn't that unusual, because the Lord knew the essence of my heart!..

So I identified with the person of Archie Belaney, and I knew the essence of his heart, because it so closely paralleled my own!.. But the "kicker" came at the end of the movie, when "Grey Owl" died.., *and "Iron Owl" was born!!..*

Within two days, after Grey Owls death.., Iron Owl was born!!. Is it coincidence?., *or is it Reincarnation??*. ***I don't know?..*** I don't know, but I am coming down on the side of coincidence... It is an amazing coincidence (perhaps), but just like I wouldn't usurp his name, neither will I usurp his identity!!. Grey Owl died!., may he rest in peace... Iron Owl is a different person...

Now.., I haven't reached a definitive conclusion about the truth or fallacy of the doctrine of reincarnation... There is much evidence to support it, including my own experience, witnessing my death as an American Indian, a vision so powerful that it caused me claustrophobia!.. But I have *intentionally* not reached a conclusion on this subject because I am prejudiced!!. *I **Hate** the doctrine of Reincarnation and Karma!!.*

Even though the doctrine may be true.., the ***belief*** in this doctrine is counter productive!.. It is an immediate rationalization and justification for any and all circumstances!.. Case in point: "India"!.. I blame this doctrine for the stagnation and poverty that is India!!. Ask anyone; "Why are you in such poor circumstances"?.. Oh, it is my karma, I must have abused my riches in a past life, therefore I must endure the poverty of this life!!! "Why do you beat your wife"?.. It is her karma, she was probably unfaithful in her past life!!! "Why did you kill this man"?.. because he killed me in a past life.., it was his karma!!! Why are you an "*Untouchable*"?, living your life as an outcast??? "It is my *Karma*"!.. Etc., etc., and etc... This doctrine promotes an acceptance of your circumstances and rationalizes them, and to try to get beyond them is to interfere with karma!!. It is "fuzzy logic", and it doesn't compute!!.

Forget about your past life!.. It's over, and the slate is wiped clean!.. Be grateful for that, and do the best you can, now.., and be the best you can be, and do good every chance you get.., because.., "What goes around.., comes around"...

*   *   *

A week or so passed, and again I experimented with a hashish induced meditation, on my own time, in the middle of the night. I wouldn't exactly call it a successful meditation, but it was memorable... It seemed, that I was penetrating into.., the nucleus of the atom, (or a fifth dimensional facsimile ?). I was sitting cross legged in the meditative posture with my hands palm down on my thighs. "I" was into the inner realm of mind, and as such "I" existed as sight only, without substance and without a center of location. It was similar to the "moth and the flame". There was this brilliant center that I was hovering around, and it seemed that I should merge myself into this brilliant center of the atom, just to experience the indestructibility of the Soul, because that's what I really and truly was.., but it was terrifying. Not only was it terrifying to myself, the Soul, but my body was also terrified! My hands would not stay positioned on my thighs, but came up to my chest and were twining around themselves in constant revolutions, like twiddling thumbs, but it was my hands that were writhing around themselves in terrified agitation. My breath was coming in short rapid staccato pulsations. I kept coming back to my body trying to calm it down, trying to control my breathing, forcing my hands back to my thighs, and trying again to go inside and penetrate the heart of the atom, but my body would not cooperate... Again and again I tried to get my body to calm itself down, but it would not.., my body was terrified, and "I" wasn't all that confident about it either, so the attempt was not successful... There was, I am sure, something far more profound about this experience than what I have the knowledge of, or the ability to communicate here.

....But notice here the distinct separation of Soul consciousness from body consciousness (a.k.a. sub-consciousness)...

I wanted to confide my experiences to the Swami, but I felt really guilty for having broken the rules, and a private audience with him wasn't that easy to arrange. So, during one of the fireside chats, I asked him if he had ever meditated while using hashish... "Oh yes", he said, "One winter I went up to the mountains and spent the whole winter snowed in, in this mountain cabin. I had enough provisions for the whole winter and enough hashish to last me for the whole winter. It was so cold that I couldn't go outside for the whole winter. I had to relieve myself on a shovel and pitch it out the window"! The audience of about 35 students roared with laughter. So, he continued; "I spent the whole winter there, doing my sadana (meditations, etc.) and smoking hashish. When the winter was over, I hadn't made much progress, and I didn't remember that much about it! So, I don't recommend it."...

There was a quality of unassuming honesty about the Swami, as well as a down to earth practical humanity that inspires me to say; "He was a man after my own heart".

My own experiences with hashish were in contrast to the Swami's. But you must remember, I had had extensive and profound previous experiences with the drug LSD, and the parameters of my inner consciousness had been greatly expanded. The hashish acted as a catalyst that could put me back into that realm almost as effectively as the LSD itself, and I could remember everything. Without this catalyst, my meditations were practically a waste of time. So, my experiences with hashish were outside the normal range of experience, but, every persons experience is different, and most people experience an expanded state of consciousness that borders on the profound. So, in the final analysis I would recommend it. Everything has it's use, and everything can be abused. Dosage is a critical factor, frequency of use is a critical factor. But, intent.., is the most critical factor of all. It is the determining factor... Are you serious about what you are doing, or are you just blowing smoke?...

I have watched good men, sincere and dedicated men, with much more patience and tenacity than myself, sit on their meditation cushions for hours a day, over a period of months that stretched into years, only to one day realize that they had spent the most productive years of their life sitting on their ass, on a cushion on the ground, and they never could get off the ground!.. Such cases are not rare, in fact I would say that most of the time this is the rule! Entire monasteries, filled with serious and dedicated aspirants, sitting for hours, and days, for years!.. Benefits are reported, but I, Iron Owl, have to ask this question: "Where are all the Buddhas"?...

If you are really serious about meditation, you must at some point experiment with a catalyst... I would question the sincerity and dedication of any "man of the cloth" who would not experiment with an altered state of consciousness, be it by use of a psychedelic, or by fasting for 40 days, as did Jesus Christ... There is no successful meditation without an altered state of consciousness. It is not an easy transition to go from the externalized state of consciousness to the inner state, and it won't happen the first time you try it. It is a gradual process of progressive advancement, (remember the parable of the new wine in old wine skins). The *occasional* use of a catalyst can be the determining factor, if your motives are pure. If you have the right intentions and if you have the proper dosage. *This is the real science of Alchemy!..* Do not make the mistake of believing that the catalyst alone will do the trick. It still requires you the practitioner to excel in disciplined meditation. The catalyst by itself is not the way, it is just a tool, and you are the craftsman... The tool should never become a crutch. ***This..,* is the real science of Alchemy... *I have told you a great secret, do not abuse it..*[1].**

You have my opinion about the use of hashish (and other THC class drugs, marijuana, etc.).., and you have the Swami's opinion. Both opinions are correct, as far as they go, and as far as this particular drug is concerned. It has limited use. It can take you just so far, but it won't take you all the way. It can give you insights that you may otherwise never have, and that is its' value, if it is used in this way and for that purpose. The insights can be profound, intuitive faculties can be enhanced, different viewpoints can be objectively seen and explored, communication can border on the telepathic. This is it's value... This is it's potential...

But, generally speaking, this is not the way it is used. The noble intentions are lacking, There is no disciplined meditation. No, it is party time, and it's use is "recreational"… Even so, I, personally do not find this objectionable. Remember this poetry from the "Rubaiyat" of "Omar Khayyam":..

"And this I know: Whether the one true light
Kindle to love, or Wrath consume me quite,
One glimpse of ***"IT "***.., *within the tavern..,*
caught!
Better than in the temple.., lost outright."

Truth is where you find it, and, if you give it an opportunity, it may find you... In this modern society, where stress is a recognized killer, recreation can be the antidote.

I will always remember the first time I smoked a "joint" of marijuana. It was a sort of "initiation", one of those milestones of life that you never forget... We, my friends and I, had just finished a hard days work of installing wall-to-wall carpeting in an apartment housing complex. After work we went to the local bar to quench our thirst and flirt with the barmaids. Before we went in, one of my friends lit up a joint of marijuana and passed it around. I was almost totally ignorant of what it was, and I said; "No thank you, I don't smoke". "Well", he said, "Neither do I, but this is different. You have to try this"! So, I tried it. No big deal, I thought to myself. We went into the bar and sat down at the table. The waitress brought us a pitcher of beer, we joked with the waitress, she joked back. The music on the juke box had a quality that I had not recognized or appreciated before. It seemed as though I was hearing it, ...really hearing it.., for the first time! I tasted the beer. I didn't really like the taste of beer and rarely ever drank it, but now I was tasting it, and objectively analyzing the taste!.. Interesting, I thought... My friends were laughing and telling jokes. I laughed. It was one of the funniest jokes I had ever heard! I laughed and laughed as the jokes continued one after the other. I laughed so hard that the muscles in my cheeks ached, and I realized that I had never laughed so hard in my life!.. And then I heard it!.. That Inner Voice.., and it said, very matter-of-factly: *"Laughter.., is good for the Soul"*... With a sudden flash of insight, I abruptly stood up!.. I didn't slide my chair back from the table, I just stood up!.. The table almost tipped over, glasses fell to the floor, somebody grabbed the pitcher of beer. The truth spoken by that Inner Voice was immediately apparent, and as I stood up, I announced in a loud angry voice:.. ***"They lied to me"!!.*** My friends scrambled for cover, fearing that I was, for some unknown reason, becoming violent. "Who lied to you?", my friend asked. "Everybody, They all lied to me, the media, the television, newspapers, radio.., the government"!!. "They all lied to me"!...

I had sampled the dreaded evil weed, the weed that was supposed to numb my senses, rob me of my faculties, and make me stupid. Instead, the exact opposite happened! I heard sounds, music, like I had never heard it before! I tasted things, with the objective analysis of the connoisseur! All my faculties were enhanced. Inner thought processes were almost tangible. I processed new information and related it with other information and came up with new conclusions that I had never even thought of before!., I heard *Thee* "Inner Voice".., that spoke the simple blatant Truth.., And there was laughter.., genuine laughter.., laughter that came from the depths of my Soul.., and I judged it, and it was:., ***Good!!.***

---

[1] Again.., let me emphasize: "Dosage is the critical factor"… It is a mistake to think that you can take a double or triple dosage of a psychedelic catalyst.., and "Storm the Gates of Heaven".., and gain entrance!.. This is dangerous folly… You cannot command or demand an audience with the Most High!.. The Science of "going within" is one of disciplined meditation with a sincere and reverential attitude… It is termed a "Receiving".., not a grasping…

So, I had been lied to... The next obvious question that occupied my mind, was:., "What else have they lied to me about"?.. Herein lies the danger!..

* * * * * * *

"Drugs of Virtue.., Drugs of Vice"

I do not believe that the Government has sinister intent. On the contrary, I am sure that their intentions are mostly honorable and well meaning. They have a very expensive propaganda program aimed at the youth of America to "Just say No", to drugs. If this works, all well and good.., maybe.., but at some point, just as surely as Eve ate the apple, they are going to take that first taste of the forbidden fruit, and they are going to say;., "They lied to me"!.. All that expensive and well meaning propaganda program will come crashing to the ground like a house of cards, as they experience an alternate state of consciousness!!. Something that no one even has a concept of until it happens.., and when it happens, it is a major discovery.., a revelation.., and they will announce it to their peers, with the invitation of: "Come see"!., "You have to try this"!., and then they are going to experience the "experience", and then they will say;., "They lied to me"!!., "What else have they lied to me about"?.. Herein lies the danger...

There is a very "bizarre" and strange sequence of events that comes into play here:.. The government has decided that any "use" of the benevolent herb "Marijuana", should be considered "abuse" (the lie), and therefore be illegal!.. Even though it is neither addictive or habit forming... Even though there is no possibility of death from overdose... Even though there are no "hangover" after effects... Even though it can enhance your faculties and give you insights that you may otherwise never have... Even though it will enhance your appreciation for art and music... Even though it can cause you to look inside yourself and be honest with yourself... Even though it can enhance communication between husband and wife, and save your marriage... Even though it can restore the sex act to a union of hearts and minds, instead of just bodies... Even though it can focus your concentration and allow you to "reap rewards" from your academic studies, with insights.., and the Holy Scriptures, with insights... Even though the participants are prone to peace and harmony, and abhor violence... Even though it can allow you to "rise above" your pain and suffering... Even though it has a salutary effect on the human body, and promotes restful sleep... Even though it has been used as an healing herb for millennia... Even though the participants are otherwise good, hard working, tax paying AMERICANS exercising their *inalienable* God given rights of Life, LIBERTY, and the pursuit of happiness... Even though it can bring you "Nearer my God to Thee".., if the participant be so inclined...

So WHY has the government put itself in the position of being an "Enemy of the Constitution"?.. Why would the otherwise good government of a free people make criminals of otherwise law abiding citizens?.. Why would they go to the extremes of denying you your freedom, your liberty, and even your LIFE, to prevent you from "experiencing" this benevolent herb?.. Why would they perpetrate atrocities, like sentencing a productive father of four children to 93 years in prison, for growing Marijuana (a cottage industry) in his own home (Texas), making his children fatherless and reducing the family to poverty.., while murderers, thieves, rapists and child molesters are released in 7 to 10 years?.. Why are they building more prisons, and imprisoning more people.., while rampant perversion is marching in the streets, under the guise of liberty?.. What is wrong with this picture?..

It has always amazed me, that the shrill sanctimonious voice of condemnation comes from those who have the least knowledge of, and no "experience" of this particular herb. If they had had the "experience", they would know better, but they haven't, and they don't.., and they won't!.. They erroneously suppose that the level of consciousness that they themselves portray is the highest, and any "altered state" from their state has got to be in the direction of dementia. It just doesn't occur to them that an "altered state" could be an "enhanced state", superior to their "normal" state... They just do not know!.. But they could ask the "Whiz Kids" of Silicon Valley, who attribute much of their technological wizardry to insights gained through the use of both LSD and Marijuana [2]...

---

[2]   (Copyright; August 8, 2004, Associated Newspapers Ltd. Mail on Sunday, London)...
HEADLINE: "Nobel Prize genius Crick was high on LSD when he discovered the secret of life"... (BYLINE: Alun Rees): Francis Crick, the Nobel Prize winning father of modern genetics, was under the influence of LSD when he first deduced the double helix structure of DNA nearly 50 years ago... Crick, who died 10 days

So why?.. The governments position is that Marijuana is a "gateway drug".., and if you go through that gateway and discover the "experience" of an "altered state"..., and it is a good experience *(and that you were lied to!)*.., then you are prone to experiment with other, more sinister substances, such as heroin, cocaine, crack cocaine, etc... Herein lies the danger... The government's point of view is not without merit.., but at what cost?.. To what extremes will they go to, to save you from yourself?.. And is it working?...

The sequence of events gets even more bizarre and strange... The cost is beyond enormous, It's beyond comprehension.., and not only is it not working.., it is enormously counter-productive...

The moment these substances were made illegal, they became a "black market" item, and the price went up!.. The profit potential became a driving force. The illegality of these substances, and the publicity surrounding them, made them mysteriously attractive to a curious, and consequently growing, clientele.., who had no qualms about violating laws that violated their freedoms... At taxpayer expense, the government doubled it's law enforcements efforts, driving the prices up, and making the drug trade enormously profitable!.. The traffic in illegal drugs went from a trickle.., to a Torrent!.. By airplane, by boat, by truck, and by car.., hundreds of tons of illegal drugs flooded into the U.S.A., and a river of dollars.., hard currency.., left the Country!.. THIS.., IS THE REAL CRIME!.. Besides weakening the U.S. financially and economically, this river of hard currency has financed left wing dictatorships, subverted and corrupted governments, funded communist gorilla organizations, and wars... Entire governments based their economy, their cash crop production of marijuana, cocaine, and heroin.., on exports to the U.S... And all of this was done at taxpayer expense, and with the good intentions of the U.S. government.., who has declared war on drugs, and made it all possible!!., in truth;., "Aiding and Abetting"!.. And it continues.., year after year after year...

Meanwhile, back in the U.S.A., the availability of drugs has not lessened, the demand has increased, and a crime wave of unprecedented proportions is sweeping the country... Heroine addicts, will lie, cheat, steal, prostitute themselves, and kill.., to support their addiction that has now been priced beyond their ability to pay. Cocaine use is rampant in middle America and Corporate America, funneling off huge amounts of money. Crack-cocaine is an insidious addiction that allies itself with "sexual addiction", causing all sorts of aberrations that make it worse than heroin and cocaine combined, and it is available at ghetto prices.., and is being sold, even by children... Large sums of money change hands... Guns and death are just part of the business... Gangs, turf wars, drive by shootings, death of innocent bystanders!.. What to do?.. What to do?.. More and bigger law enforcement? More sophisticated technology? More drug rehab programs? More laws? More telephone taps? More court cases? More lawyers? More prisons? More prisoners, (approaching a *half-million* at this writing).., that have to be guarded, housed, fed, clothed, and doctored.., at taxpayer expense.., and another *half-million* that transit the "Halls of Justice" *yearly!!?*... The cost is in the *Billions*... And the result.., is a "POLICE STATE".., where the police can stop you and search you, your car, your home.., with *dogs!*., listen in on your telephone conversations, examine your bank records, examine your bodily fluids!,. etc.., just for looking suspicious! (Shades of Nazi Germany!)... Where the people are becoming more and more distrustful of the government.., where armed militia are threatening open revolt.., and terrorism...

You can plot this bizarre and strange sequence of events on a graph.., and project its course into the future.., and the future is chaos.., anarchy!!, If the trend continues...

---

ago, aged 88.., (Etc.., lengthy article)… ***And also;*** (from "Wired's" recap of; "LSD: Problem Child and Wonder Drug"), (at the International Symposium on the occasion of the 100th birthday of Albert Hofmann): Steve Jobs told a NY Times reporter that taking LSD was "one of the two or three most important things he has done in his life"… Nobel Prize winning chemist Kary Mullis told Hofmann that LSD helped him develop the polymerase chain reaction that helps amplify specific DNA sequences… Kevin Herbert, an early Cisco employee, fought to ban drug testing of technologists at the company because, as he put it, "When I am on LSD and hearing something that is pure rhythm, it takes me to another world and into another brain state where I've stopped thinking and started Knowing"… Hofmann, who's still alive, says, "There's a global healing in these compounds which have been used for millennia by indigenous peoples that have much to teach modern man and woman"…

What to do?.. What to do?.. Well.., It's one thing to take a few paragraphs and present the problem... But.., can I take a few paragraphs and present a solution?.. I can give you "The Iron Owl Perspective".., but will it be implemented?.. Probably not... Will reason prevail?.. Probably not...

Legalize Marijuana.., and tax it... This will have the effect of slowing the imports from outside countries to a trickle, slowing the river of hard currency out of the country, and providing a bounty of tax revenue to the government that may cancel the National Debt!.. With the availability and legality of a non-addictive substance that is conducive to harmony, conversation, sex, appetite, insight and laughter.., with restful sleep and no hangover!!, it will dramatically cut into the use of those really bad and objectionable drugs;.., **the Legal ones**... Such as Alcohol; ...that causes you to lose your common sense, your manners, your morals, and your equilibrium, reducing you to a babbling idiot that will wreck his car, kill innocent people, beat his wife, wreck his marriage, lose his job, fall asleep in bed with a cigarette in his hand and burn down his house!., or his apartment building, or hotel, etc... This is no exaggeration, it is an understatement! The cost to the individual, the American tax paying public[3], and the government, probably exceeds the annual military budget!.. And that's just the dollar amount, it doesn't take into account the lives lost, the lives ruined, the sorrow, and the grief... ....And cigarettes, an insidious addiction that gives you nothing in return, but cancer, emphysema, heart attacks, an impaired and shortened life, etc.., and a miserable death... (You can already guess where the opposition to *this* plan will come from)...

So release the non-violent drug offenders from the prisons (nearly a *half-million*) and let them be reunited with their families and children, and again become productive, tax paying members of society.., and relieve the burden and the expense of the court systems, the prison systems, and the law enforcement systems.., freeing them up to pursue real crimes.., and real criminals... And instead of building more and more prisons, build more schools and universities...

---

[3] It is estimated that it costs the U.S. "One Hundred Eighty **Billion** Dollars" yearly.., and that 50% drink alcohol excessively, and a sizable percentage of these drinkers are *underage!!*. (Source: Channel 8, mid-day news.., WFLA, Tampa Fl... 2/26/03)

Next, the government should buy up all the raw cocaine and opium/heroin base, at the source of production.., for pennies on the thousands of dollars.., legalize it, and distribute it through licensed clinics that can monitor usage and evaluate health concerns.., eliminating death from overdose.., eliminating the acts of desperation, degradation, crime and violence, that drives those enslaved by this addiction.., eliminating death in the streets from organized crime syndicates, and the mayhem of disorganized crime.., eliminating the spread of this addiction by those "whores" who are forced to sell this addiction, in order to be able to use it.., eliminating this avenue of misery and death from the "Aids" virus, that is spread by the needles, perversion, prostitution, and degradation surrounding it.., eliminating the cash flow river of hard currency that supports this "evil empire", both here and abroad...

Make no mistake, the heroin addict is a victim, a willing victim in most cases, but still a victim... I have seen strong willed people get into heroin, and they get into it with a strong will!.. I have known businessmen, craftsmen, and family men.., good people, who were heroin addicts, who could maintain, and be productive citizens, until the government produced "black market" forced them into acts of desperation.., and "trafficking"... ("It is criminal", they complain of the government, "the actual cost of this addiction is pennies, but the government produced black market drives the cost up to exorbitant levels")... And it (the government) is the cause of the crime, the violence, the spread of this addiction, and the "War" that it is fighting.., and losing!..

There is another aspect of this ironic tragedy that has to be addressed... The subject of "chronic pain"... There are millions of good common citizens, the elderly, accident victims, people facing death, dying of cancer, aids, etc., incapacitated by chronic, unbearable pain... They are medicated with everything imaginable, and still the pain persists, and the mental pain is more excruciating than the physical pain... Because of the government restrictions, prohibitions, red-tape, addictive potential and prejudice.., they are largely denied the one true pain reliever that could restore them to a degree of physical functionality and mental peace:.. Morphine!.. As if the patient were not already addicted, because of his pain, to a host of "pain killers" with side effects, that reduce him to the status of "vegetable", draining the family bank account.., and they aren't working...

Everything has it's use, and everything can be abused... I have heard it said, that the government of Canada, at one time, contemplated the stockpiling of morphine/heroin etc., as the only effective remedy, to be used in the aftermath of a nuclear attack... To deny use, to victims in terrible pain, is to be without mercy... It is merciless... it is unconscionable...

I don't like heroin... Not at all... It is a perversion... But the fact remains, that those people so inclined are going to use it, without regard to consequences, cost, or what they have to do to get it.., and as long as there is this "demand".., there will be a supplier; the black market, with all it's evil consequences.., or.., government controlled clinics that will reduce the spread of this plague.., and choke off the river of hard currency that feeds it... And, at the same time, at the same clinic.., PROVIDE A CURE FOR HEROIN ADDICTION!..

Yes, there is a cure for heroin addiction!.. But the government, in their infinite "criminal stupidity", has not only withheld this cure from the victims of heroin, and the many good people involved in the humanitarian work of trying to redeem these victims, but has made the cure.., illegal!.. ...The government has made the "cure" for heroin addiction illegal, and unavailable, because it involves the "one time" use of a psychedelic called "Ibogaine", that is neither addictive or habit forming, and has no side effects, other than the possibility that the recipient might "find God", talk to Angels and departed ancestors, gain maturity, and a whole new perspective and attitude about life!., and as an added benefit, be cured of his heroin addiction.., and the horrendous withdrawal symptoms that usually accompany it!.. It seems a miracle, an answer to a prayer.., and not only heroin addiction, but other addictions as well, including alcohol and nicotine!.. And it is illegal!..

What in "Hell" could the government be thinking?.. What could possibly be their rationale?.. Could they really be so.. *Blind*??. Have they no intelligence?., no ability to discriminate between Smart and Stupid??, between what is humanitarian and what is criminal??... I guess not...

The Supreme Court has declared the use of the herbal "Sacrament" of the Native American Indian peoples religious ceremony.., to be illegal!.. The Sacramental herb "Peyote", a psychedelic.., central to the religion of the American Indians, given to them by God.., and taken away by the Supreme Court of the United States... A clear, blatant, and criminal violation of the Constitution!.. An open and shameless attack on the "Freedom of Religion"., the ultimate and final insult.., on the last bastion of retreat;., the reservation... **But alcohol.., which ravages and decimates my people..,** *is everywhere available!!...*

Hear me!!, You El Supremo Assholes!!... I am Iron Owl.., and I am an American!., with all that that name and that designation implies... DO NOT expect compliance... In this land of the free, and the home of the brave.., if you want to be free, apparently, you still have to be brave...

And what about cocaine?.. Should we legalize cocaine as well?.. The drug of the movie stars and the jet set. The "feel good" drug of the 80's and 90's... Praised by a Pope,[4] and used by Egyptian Pharaohs... The drug of seduction, that ultimately seduces the seducer.., turning men into whoremongers, and women into sluts? To what extents will we go in the pursuit of pleasure?., in the pursuit of lust? The carnal minded will always go too far. Cocaine addiction amplifies sexual addiction, and the combination is seductive and destructive, leading to physical, moral, financial, and spiritual disaster... *This is not the path of Wisdom...*

The native peoples of Peru, chew the leaves of the coca plant, a stimulant, that enables them to withstand the rigors of the chilled mountain climate in which they live, fortifying them against the cold and giving them remarkable stamina, enabling them to carry large bundles of produce, etc., up the steep slopes of the mountainous terrain in which they live. This constitutes proper "use"... To multiply the dosage many times by concentrating it into a powder and ingesting it all at once, can stimulate both mind and body to greater mental and physical accomplishments, and it is euphoric!.. This euphoric feeling of both physical and mental superiority *(Hello, Sherlock Holmes),* is very psychologically addicting. This is the seductively subtle nature of this addiction... Soon, this

---

[4] His Holiness, Pope Leo XIII carried a personal hipflask of coca wine to fortify himself in time of need. The grateful Pope awarded a Vatican gold medal to its distinguished originator, the Corsican-born pharmacist and businessman, Angelo Mariani…

Harlem Protest Demonstration, sponsored by "Cures-Not-Wars" coalition. (May, 1993)

"superior" person is ingesting more and more of this drug daily, all day, every day, to maintain this euphoric feeling of superiority.., (lesser amounts are given to horses to win horse races), depleting both his bank account and his health, ultimately resulting in paranoid inferiority and financial ruin. This is the result of abuse.

I had a good and intelligent friend. He started smoking Cocaine (freebasing)... This is to take already highly concentrated cocaine of high purity, put it into a pipe and smoke it!.., This is extremely expensive and wasteful... At this massive concentration, you are no longer doing this drug, the drug is doing you!.. Within a period of 6 months, he spent a quarter of a million dollars, lost his wife and his children, his home, and his freedom... Eight years in prison... And the irony is, that he was "rescued" from his path of destruction.., by prison!.. This story is not unusual, it is typical... I can tell you from personal experience, if you ride the crest of this wave, you will crash on the rocks... ...*This is not the path of wisdom...*

From personal experience.., I have done this drug to excess!!. Having been "in the flow", I consumed large quantities of this drug over an extended period of time, and I never considered it to be addictive, and when I didn't have it, I didn't miss it!.. But there are some people that are classified as "addictive personalities".., and (I guess) if you have no purpose in life, then this (or any) drug could be your only purpose in life, hence; addiction!!. It was while at a freebasing party.., while freebasing.., that I observed; that the only thing that I got from this drug, was the desire to take another hit on the pipe (ad infinitum).., and it became evident that at this point "I" wasn't doing this drug.., this drug was doing me!!. It was at this point.., in the middle of this freebasing session.., that I decided that it was just plain stupid.., and I stopped!!.., to the bewilderment of my fellow party-goers!!... I had taken this drug to it's maximum limit, and found it to be; *way* over-rated, *way* over-hyped, and *way* over-priced!!... "Cocaine is God's way of telling you that you have too much money" (*end- quote*).., (and we all know about "fools" and their money)...

So.., the question arises: What is it?., that makes one person be a casual user.., able to pick it up, and put it down.., and walk away..., while another person will become hopelessly addicted?.?.. This is not a simple question, with a one line simple answer!., but we can look at some "bottom line" generalities... It would seem that "intelligence" alone would be a determining factor, because to become addicted to a drug (or anything), knowing in advance of the addictive potential, and observing the end results of addicted peoples.., is an exercise in stupidity!., and a downward spiral into a slow and excruciating early demise... *Clearly.., this is not the path of Wisdom...* But we have all, at one time or another, engaged in an activity of short term enjoyment with the potential of long term negative consequences *(just ask any unwed mother),* and some of us have been "lucky", and some of us have to live with the consequences... But the drug user/experimenter, with just a little foresight, can avoid the precipice of addiction.., and even if addicted.., it is a reversible condition!., for the intelligent person...

But let's face it.., some people are just stupid.., truly stupid.., and fools rush in... These are casualties in the making, and by their own hand.., *expendable...* A lesson to the rest of us... But let's say that we are dealing with the average "common man", that can be classified as neither "wise" or "foolish", but just lacking in knowledge, without direction, and without a higher purpose... This person is susceptible, because without purpose, by default, the drug becomes his only purpose, hence.., addiction...

It is the purpose of the Author, and the purpose of this book to supply the reader with the Knowledge of the Higher Purpose for his life.., which is the Truly Higher states of Mind, and the "Knowledge and Conversation" of the Divinity within all of us... "This is the Fork in the Road" that leads to degradation and addiction on the one hand.., and emancipation and enlightenment on the other... ***Choose Ye Now.., which path you will follow...***

But Yes, I would legalize it (cocaine), dilute it to acceptably safe and sane levels, control it and tax it, simply because this "Pursuit of Happiness" is guaranteed in the Constitution, as is "Liberty".., even if it is the freedom to "self destruct"... Laws, no matter how well intentioned they are, will not deter fools from their folly... All that we can hope to do here is to stop the spread of this dis-ease by eliminating the profit motive.., and divert this "River of Hard Currency" that is flowing out of this country, supporting evil empires and evil deeds, and channel this vast resource of wealth into benevolent good within this country...   ...We could probably abolish the income tax!..

The prohibition against cocaine has spawned the crack-cocaine "industry"... Just another example of the well meaning but counter-productive laws that were meant to save us from ourselves... This is a major setback, a defeat, and it hits us in the most vulnerable of places, among our young people... The great promise of our society, our youth, are being subverted by this most insidious addiction of all... There are no "redeeming qualities" to this drug, no "safe" levels of intoxication... It causes an immediate change of personality, appealing to our baser instincts, of lust, without love.., and it is immediately addicting, to fools... The horror stories abound:, of children being totally neglected and deprived of food, while the parent indulges themselves with this drug.., of women, disregarding their unborn fetus, and giving birth to physically and mentally impaired babies that are destined to be "wards of the state". Even abortions are not sought, because the money is spent on this debasing drug... These are crimes of violence, and should be dealt with in a violent manner.., The horror stories abound... Any possible good resulting from the prohibition, has been nullified by this latest scourge...

The exact same scenario is seen with the prescription medications of the amphetamine class... Dexedrine, a relatively innocuous stimulant that was prescribed mainly for weight loss.., and it worked!.. This medication, (or drug) would suppress hunger and appetite, and at the same time would provide an energy boost that was not only beneficial in terms of burning calories, but would increase the efficiency and productivity of the users daily lives and income potential.. Women, would "clean house" with a vengeance, run errands, take care of the kids, do the shopping, wash the car, etc., and do exercises with the time left over.., and lose weight!.. Men, doing "piece work" on the assembly lines, working tirelessly, without fatigue, watching their incomes dramatically increase, would come home from work.., and mow the lawn!.. Truck drivers, almost impervious to sleep, would do "coast to coast" runs, in record times.., and with record paychecks!.. Athletes were breaking records!.. Parties, would rage into the night, fortified against both alcohol consumption and sleep!.. The "nickname" for this remarkable substance was "Speed", and you can see why... Too much of a good thing? Yes, the government thought so...

Speed is good, but too much speed can kill you!.. There is the potential for abuse. While not physically addictive, it is psychologically habit forming. Life without speed can seem dull, slow, lethargic, and fattening!., hence the psychological impetus to continue its use to the point of excess, where sleeping pills are required to go to sleep, and speed is required to wake up... This is excessive use, and excessive use.., is abuse... But, while not everyone is guilty of abuse.., all are denied use!..

Sleep deprivation can go on for only so long, before the body rebels... Truck drivers can push themselves to such an extent that the drug will wear off too suddenly, and sleep will approach too swiftly, with fatal results... This is clearly abuse.., but intelligent use is not abuse... The nemesis of all truck drivers is drowsiness and boredom behind the wheel,.. *much more debilitating and deadly than alcohol!!*. The truck driver has a job to do, deadlines to meet, and sleep is the enemy... The one tool that effectively combats sleepiness behind the wheel, is speed, restoring the truck driver to peak alertness and efficiency... The time and the miles just fly by, at maximum safety... Abuse is not inherent in this particular drug, especially if prescribed by a doctor in non abusable dosages, but the potential for abuse is inherent in human nature...

The alternative strategy, as employed by the government, is to make this drug illegal and unavailable to everyone for any reason... In it's place, the government has instituted a very costly and cumbersome program of tracking the movements of every truck driver, of where and when he wakes up in the morning, to where and when he has lunch, and for how long, to the where and when of his final destination in the evening, how many miles he has traveled, and how much sleep he gets during the night, the day, etc., by the use of a "log book", that in effect has made documented liars of every truck driver... A literal army of inspectors are employed to randomly inspect this acknowledged "book of lies", and if it is not up to date, heavy fines are imposed... The question is:.. Has it prevented the truck driver from having to fight the debilitating boredom and sleepiness that he experiences every day behind the wheel?.. I can tell you from personal experience that it has not! Has it eliminated the horrendous accidents caused by falling asleep at the wheel?.. No, it has not eliminated either of these serious problems.., has this "alternative method" been more effective at combating this serious problem than would be the intelligent "use" of medically prescribed dosages of speed, to be used as needed?.. No, it has not!.. In fact, every accident caused by falling asleep at the wheel, and inattentiveness caused by drowsiness could have been prevented by the intelligent use of the "tool" of speed.

All of this carnage on our highways, caused by "sleep addiction" and drowsiness.., is preventable!.. The solution to the problem is blatantly obvious:.. Legalize the prescription use of mild forms of speed, and keep in place the "log book" monitoring system to prevent abuse!

If only the "intelligent use" of government could be implemented as easily.., but "abuse" is inherent in the system... This axiom still holds true: "The best government of the people.., is the least government of the people"...

The prohibition against amphetamines has spawned the "Meth-Amphetamine "INDUSTRY"... Just another example of the well-meaning but counter productive laws meant to save us from ourselves... (Does this sound repetitious?)... The relatively safe, medically prescribed diet pill "Dexadrine" is off the market, and "Crystal Meth".., is everywhere!.. Unregulated as to who and why, uncontrolled as to dosage and method of ingestion (orally, snorted, smoked, and injected), etc., and etc... Is this progress?.. The government must answer the question: "Is this progress?" ...No "slick answers" will suffice to negate the obvious...

An observation;.. It is a natural predilection of human nature to alter the normal state of consciousness, to get away from the ordinary, be it by alcohol, smoke, or whatever... The reasons for this can be speculated on endlessly, but the predilection is there.., and when a vacuum is created, by making a substance illegal, unavailable, or unaffordable.., human nature dictates that the laws against prohibition will be ignored.., or.., that person will move on to the next available drug... Observe this maxim:.. When code law, conflicts with natural law, natural law prevails... Always!.. And this is basically good.., this is why communism failed, and free enterprise prevailed... So the solution is to work in harmony with natural law!..

The principles of both "Natural Law" and "Constitutional Law" (one and the same), have been violated in this "War on Drugs", and since Natural Law always prevails.., this war will eventually be lost, or.., it will go on forever!.. Every time a drug is taken illegally, it is a "vote" cast in favor of ending the prohibition...

If you are going to fight a war, at the end of every day you have to tally up the score, to determine whether you are winning or losing!.. Every day, there are more and more civilian casualties... Every day, there are more and more "defectors"... Every day, more and more Americans are incarcerated, and become liabilities... Every day, more and more of the "enemy" are incarcerated, and become liabilities, but their ranks never diminish... Every day, the American tax-payer is "raped"... Every day, the "River of Hard Currency" leaves our shores... Every day the coffers of the "Army of Darkness" are filled to overflowing... Every day that we fight this war, we show a loss in terms of human casualties, financial resources, and victims of crime... And every day.., "The Army of Darkness".., shows a profit!!.

Wars are not won simply because of a determination to fight on endlessly. The determining factor in any war.., is strategy... We are fighting our own people! Even if we win, we still lose... This is a losing strategy!..

A new strategy has to be implemented:.. The "Army of Darkness" has to be strangled to death by choking off the "River of Hard Currency" that is it's life blood!.. This can only be done by replacing the "black market" with a "white market". The government can out bid, out muscle, and politically out maneuver the black market at the source of supply.., then legalize, medically prescribe, educate, tax, and sell.., marijuana, cocaine, dexedrine, heroine, and the psychedelics.., at consistently lower prices than the black market competition... And at the same time, concentrating law enforcement efforts on obliterating the crack-cocaine and meth-amphetamine substitute markets...

With the consumer being given the choice between a legalized, medically prescribed and relatively safe drug, and the illegally made "bath-tub" substitute that carries harsh penalties, the choice will be self evident... This scourge will be no more! It then becomes the duty of the government to EDUCATE the consumer (instead of propagandizing) as to the difference between what is "use", and what is "abuse" of these substances, and to up-grade the "re-hab" clinics to the "Ibogaine Cure" facilities... There will be a legal age of consumption as well as a "High School graduation" requirement for most of these substances, (excluding marijuana, which will largely replace alcohol and cigarettes, to the benefit of humanity)... The requirements for the use of psychedelics would include college courses in psychology and comparative religion, as well as affiliation with an educational and/or religious organization licensed to distribute these substances.

Harsh penalties, including caneing (at the discretion of the judge), as well as jail time, will be imposed on anyone selling to under age or unqualified persons, etc...

These few paragraphs, outlining the "Iron Owl perspective", constitutes an overview, and as such it does not address all the details that would have to be worked out with such an approach to this problem. It is outside the scope of this book to do so, but I offer it as a contribution to both the government for their consideration, and the consumer, for their information. I am NOT advocating the indiscriminate use of any and all drugs. On the contrary, ...for the trivial minded, the carnal minded, the immature, and the recklessly stupid.., this can be a disastrous (if not fatal) mistake, (let the buyer beware)... These are the circumstances as they exist at the moment.., and that I am attempting to rectify...

Do not mistake these few paragraphs as being the substance of this book... It is not... This is my own personal viewpoint, arrived at by having walked many miles in these shoes.

Everything can be abused.., Even Liberty... The misuse of Liberty is "Abuse of Liberty"... To use a drug is the exercise of Liberty. But, Liberty is not license. Liberty carries with it a responsibility. To misuse a drug is drug abuse, which is not only punishable by civil law, but it is also punishable by Natural Law.

"Discipline without Freedom is tyranny;.. Freedom without discipline is chaos"... Are you really worthy of Liberty and Freedom?., Or, is the government doing you a service by saving you from yourself, or by saving other innocent people.., from you?.. Who is going to save you from your own stupidity and recklessness?.. Will it be the police officer that takes you to jail, or the emergency room at the hospital that resuscitates you back to life from the brink of death?.. Or, will you just die from an overdose of stupidity?..

So Where do you draw the line.?. Where do I "Iron Owl", draw the line.?.

I draw the line at addiction... Addiction is tantamount to slavery... I have experienced most of the drugs, just for the experience, extensively, just to see what there was to see, and I have found nothing worthy of addiction... I am too much of a Free Soul to permit myself enslavement by addiction...

I draw the line at stupidity... Enslavement by addiction is stupidity.., death by overdose is stupidity... Dosage is the critical factor... Frequency of use is a critical factor... but the most critical factor of all is "*intention*". Why are you doing this.?. Are you exploring the parameters of your mind, the potentialities of your abilities, the enhancement of your faculties, or are you just "blowing it"?..

I draw the line by discrimination... You MUST DISCRIMINATE.!. There are things that get you high, and there are things that bring you down, and you must wisely discriminate between the two... There are things that get you high for awhile, but ultimately, they bring you down... And there are other drugs that get you neither up or down, just "sideways" (not good)... Is your purpose to enhance your faculties and capabilities.., or to wallow in degradation.?. Some people choose the latter, consciously.!. At this moment, as I write these words, there are millions of people in a drunken alcoholic stupor, by choice.!. What will you choose.?.

I draw the line at the needle... There are two ways to learn about things, and experience is not always the best teacher... If you can learn from other peoples experiences (the hand on the hot stove), you can eliminate a lot of pain for yourself. The essence of Wisdom; is the elimination of pain which is not yet come...

I had a friend, in India, who confided in me about his use of morphine.., and the needle... "Even when I don't have the morphine", he said, "I will boot up water with the needle, jacking the water and blood in and out of the syringe, while hiding, where nobody can see me"... His confiding in me was a cry for help... He was hopelessly addicted to morphine.., and the needle had become the sexual replacement for women... He was masturbating with the needle.!. I was stunned and appalled by his admission. This was a perversion... I would have helped him if I could, but I was at a loss... He was on the road to oblivion, and I couldn't help him... I lost a friend.., to the needle... I hate that!.. I really hate that... When you are fooling around with something that is more seductive than sex, that is a sexual replacement, you are in the gravest of dangers... This is the legendary "Siren", that leads men down the slippery slope of sensual gratification, promising ecstasy, but giving death!.. This is Cosmic quicksand...

I draw the line at excess... Dosage is a critical factor... The needle is excess... To "slam" a drug, that is a hundred times more powerful than it's natural state, directly into a vein, is excess...

I draw the line at the loss of the critical faculty... The loss of the ability to discriminate... The loss of the ability to choose... The loss of the ability to think!.. Only once did I lose this ability (with alcohol), and once was one time too many... I absolutely detest the state of mind of insensibility.., drunkenness.., the loss of motor control... I never understood this... Why?.. Why would anyone consciously choose to obliterate his critical faculties?.. Is life so empty?.. So meaningless?.. The hangover is definitely empty and meaningless...

You must discriminate wisely... This is the test of your life.!. You must choose.., you must choose between the good and the bad.., between the right and the wrong.., between the smart and the stupid.., between that which is Holy, and that which is unholy and unwholesome... If you fail at this test, you fail at the game of life... As you walk down this road of life, you will step over the bodies of those who have gone before you and failed the test... The landscape is littered with the bodies of failure, of those who have failed to discriminate... There are some things that are absolutely forbidden (perversions, defilements, etc.).., and of those things that are not expressly forbidden, **"Moderation".., is the rule!!!**

There are those things which are for; *"the Edification of the few, and the Destruction of many"*... The determining factor is your ability to discriminate... Choose the right, the good, and the true.., choose Edification!.. If you fail to discriminate wisely, you will be discriminated against.., and your name will be stricken from the "Book of Life"... Yours is the choice between Life and Death!.. Choose Life...

The Ultimate High.., is the Spiritual High... Go with God... Amen...

*   *   *   *   *   *

But will my recommendations be implemented?.. Probably not... Will reason prevail??. Probably not...

I might just as well turn my attention to something more practical.., something more worthwhile.., to.., say..; saving an endangered species from extinction!..

The "Black Rhino".., inhabiting the jungles of Sumatra, has been hunted to the brink of extinction!. This magnificent animal is relentlessly hunted down and killed.., for the horn on the end of it's nose!!. Why??, because the horn on the end of it's nose is a replica.., of the "Shiva Lingam"; the "erect penis" of the Hindu God; "Shiva"!!, and as such, it is reported to contain the essence of the sexual prowess.., of a God!!! On the Asian black market, this horn will fetch upwards of 10,000 dollars!.., with "minute scrapings" of this horn generating retail sales of probably ten times that amount!.. And by implication, the African Rhino is also hunted for his horn, even though the resemblance to "Shiva's Penis" is less obvious.., and following the same line of absurd "illogical logic", the testicles and penis of the great Bengal and African Tigers (also on the brink of extinction) are also worth a small fortune!..

Such is the lust.., for ever greater lust!!. We will hunt and kill these magnificent animals to extinction, for a bigger, better, and longer lasting erection!!. This would be hilariously funny, if it wasn't so tragic...

And does it work??. I seriously doubt it.., but if your belief is strong enough to pay big bucks for powdered tiger penis and horn scrapings, then perhaps belief is the key!!. Who knows?.. I don't...

Enter into this picture, the drug; "Viagra"!..

That technological breakthrough "marvel" of modern science that actually delivers what powdered penis and horn scrapings only promise.., and at a fraction of the cost.., and it's legal!.., and it undermines the black market, and the profit incentive of the poachers.., and the Rhino is saved from extinction!!!

"What"??.., (you ask)... Do you mean to tell me that the Rhino is being saved from extinction;., *by a*

drug??!!... Yes.., as incredible as it sounds.., that's the fact!!.

But this fact points the way.., to an even greater breakthrough "Principle"!.. A breakthrough principle that may be the answer and the solution to a host of problems that plague humanity.., an end and a "Victory".., to the war on drugs.., and possibly an **End to War**.., and the ushering in of a "New Era" of advancements in education and creative thinking.., with wonders to behold!!, and advancements in Religion.., with greater insights, where beliefs would be replaced by Knowledge gained experientially.., in a World that was "Nearer my God to Thee"!!!... The potential of mankind is far greater than what we can conjecture...

Before I get carried away, here.., and accused of having "Illusions of Grandeur" etc., and etc.., The above paragraph has to be taken apart, one assertion at a time.., and just what is the "Principle" that we are talking about??. It's the principle of *"the better mousetrap"*!!. "Build a better mousetrap, and the World will beat a path to your door"!.. How does this apply to the war on drugs??. Well, instead of trying to stop the influx of drugs from foreign countries, losing exorbitant amounts of hard currency daily, killing and incarcerating drug traffickers and offenders, enormous expenses, legal fees, courts, prisons, etc., and etc.., BUILD A BETTER DRUG!!... Think about it!!. It cant be that difficult!.. A drug that will get you "high", without getting you drunk!., a drug that will expand your consciousness and open the doors of perception, a drug without side effects or addictive properties, containing vitamins, that will enhance your mood, your endurance, and your awareness!.. etc... A drug that is "legal" and better!!. The savings and benefits would be enormous, and we could even export it!!! Perhaps.., that river of hard currency could beat a path back to our shores!..

* * *

Save the Rhino.., and save our children!..

There are some three million children suffering with the modern day malady known as "Attention Deficit Hyperactivity Disorder" (ADHD)... The causes of this disorder are not known, but the effects are disastrous to the child (doomed to failure), his parents and siblings (stressed out to wit's end), and to his teachers (who's classroom he disrupts to the detriment of all students)!..

Enter into this picture the drug; "Ritalin"...

"Ritalin" is a mild form of "speed"[5] that speeds up the child's mind to where it is "in sync" with his youthful exuberance, with the result that the child's previously scattered attention becomes focused, where he was a scholastic failure, he is now an achiever, where he had low self esteem and no friends, he is now optimistic and popular, excelling in sports, weight under control, etc., and where he would have been a social drop-out and misfit (possibly criminal), he is now on his way to college and a career!!. The child has been literally "*Saved*" by a ("meth" class) mind-altering drug!!! I love success stories!.. I love happy ending!!. And the latest studies show that he will eventually outgrow his disorder, and without a predisposition to drug use!..

But of course, Ritalin is not right for every child, and there are parents groups (usually religious based) that are opposed to the "drugging" of their children, and prefer to "tough it out" at the child's expense, but if you want an objective overview.., *ask the Teachers...*

* * *

Save the Teachers!!... I have to defend the Teachers...

It is a rewarding vocation to be a teacher; to be instrumental in the lives of children, to see them progress to the next level, to see them graduate... But the modern day classroom has become, in many cases, a "battlefield"!.. And it is a battlefield in which the Teacher is rendered "powerless".., *by Law*!!. The Teacher is victimized, denigrated, and disrespected by her students, and she is forbidden by law to exercise discipline... She cannot excessively berate the student, she cannot make him "stand in the corner", and God forbid that she "touch" the student in any kind of a disciplinary fashion!.. To do so would result in her immediate

---

[5] "Ritalin"; (methylphenidate), a stimulant (note the "meth" designation).., (and more recently, a "timed release" version) has been safely used for decades, and is being improved upon as we speak!.. At this writing (2006), it is conceded that Ritalin is not a perfect solution, and other similar drugs (Adderall & Concerta) are also popular...The point that I am trying to make (in this emotionally charged controversy), is that whether a substance is classified as a "drug", or a "medication", depends upon the use to which it is put...

dismissal, loss of her profession, and a law suit from the parents.., who are also (incidentally) forbidden *by Law* to impose any type of "corporal punishment" on their child!..

This is insane!., and it is Government mandated insanity!!. The end result of this insanity is that the "children" are undisciplined disrespectful "vandals" that are failing and dropping out of school, and the parents are suing the teachers and schools because their children are failing, with the result that the children are promoted and graduate, and cannot read their diploma!!! If there was ever a "diabolical plot" to destroy this Nation from within!., this is it!!!

How fortunate I am.., to have been raised in an era when "Big Brother" did not impose itself into the family!!. I can remember the first time that I came home from school, in the first grade, and told my father that I had been "spanked" by the teacher... *He spanked me again!!...* "How dare I disrupt the class with my shenanigans"!!. (How different is this attitude from the present day.., when the Teacher will be sued by the irate parent, for touching their child)...

On rare occasions, I got "the belt" from my father, and I deserved it... Discipline was strict at the Parochial school that I attended, and I got the (palm side) of my fingers whacked with the edge of a heavy ruler for not doing my home work, and for even missing spelling words (because "I was better than that"), *and I won spelling-bee's*!!. And I got whacked with the yardstick all through grade school (I didn't tell my father), and even as a Freshman in (Public) High School, I received the "Board of Education" (for insubordination) which was a finely crafted (from shop class) two foot long, one inch thick, polished maple "paddle" with holes drilled through it to cut down on wind resistance!!.

Can you imagine??, I got "spanked" in High School, by the football coach.., for insubordination!!. Unheard of today!.. And I am grateful!!. And I was (by today's standards) a good kid!!. I *never* sassed my father (under pain of *death*), and to this day, my parents have *never* heard me utter a four-letter word!!. It just wasn't done!!. And I am so grateful to my parents, and *I REVERE my teachers*... How different from today... This was an era nostalgically referred to as; "Happy Days"!..

My sister is a teacher of the primary grades... She suffers from migraines!.. The teacher has a class of about 20 or more children whom she is teaching the fine arts of reading, writing, etc., and she is supposed to be the center of attention for the children, but too often she is not!.. Too often, there are one or two children that usurp the attention of the whole class and the teacher, because they will not listen, they will not learn, they will not sit down, they will not shut up, and are defiant to the teacher!!. To try to assert any type of discipline to these children (who are a detriment to the other students) brings a confrontation and threat of law-suits from the irate parent!..

It is to these "irate parents" that I speak... If your child is *not* suffering from ADD or ADHD [6].., then *why* is he so unruly and disrespectful... If he is not suffering from ADD, then you have failed to teach your child discipline, manners, respect, etc., and you have doomed him to failure in his education, his place in society, and with no respect for authority, they will eventually "put him away"!... So which is it?., a disorder for which there is a treatment, or your failure as a parent??. To blame and threaten the teachers is to add to your list of incompetence, and is unfair and unjust...

If you do not love your child, you should not beat him... It is only the loving parent that has the right *and duty **(a sacred obligation)*** to discipline his child, and if he is a disrespectful child.., *beat his ass,* until he learns respect!!. His future, *and yours*, depends upon it.., and work with his teachers, and assist them... The world will be a much better place...

*   *   *

Save our Teachers, save the Parents, save the Children, save the Military, and save the *Health and Dignity* of the People!..

But of course.., amphetamine class drugs (speed) are given to our combat soldiers, who must function

---

[6] It must be pointed out that not all learning disorders are ADD or ADHD related, and should therefore *Not* be treated with Ritalin… The learning disorders (LD) include everything from hearing and sight problems, to dyslexia, dysgraphia, comprehension, etc., which afflict approx. 7% of children… (Source: www.focusonlearning.org)… The topic of our conversation here is Behavioral, Discipline, and Learning problems resulting from ADD…

at peak performance because their lives depend on it, and they are in charge of million dollar equipment.., and our fighter pilots, who must also function at peak performance, and they are in charge of *Billion* dollar equipment, etc., but "use" by the common man is termed "abuse"!!.

The number one health problem in America, is **Obesity!!.** The number one cause of *Death* in America, is Obesity!!. The number one *Image* problem of America (as viewed by the rest of the world).., is Obesity!!. The number one addiction in America, is *sugar and refined carbohydrates!!!* Our modern world is functioning at light-speed, and we are waddling around like ducks, encased in fat!.., *burning sugar for energy.., and storing fat!!.* Obesity is embarrassing!!. As an American, I am embarrassed by this National tragedy!!. And it is a personal tragedy of disfiguring, embarrassing, vexing, and costly consequences... The cost to the Nation *exceeds the National debt!!!* And we have outlawed the one drug (amphetamines) that effectively combats obesity!!! Just how smart are we??.

What kills more people?., Obesity or Speed??. The death rate for speed is practically negligible... The death rate for Obesity related illnesses is *two-thirds of the population!!.* In a world that is speeding up.., we are falling behind!!. *It is time!., for the People of this Nation to slim down, shape up, and shift gears into a higher energy,*[7] *higher efficiency, less hungry, and more productive mode..,* to the benefit of the Nation!!.

How about a (better mousetrap) *"timed-release, buffered amphetamine", combined with a nutritional support supplement!!,* ...that would restore you to alertness (probably saving your life)[8], increasing efficiency, productivity, etc., raising your energy level, burning more calories, controlling your appetite.., and wear off by bed-time to a deeper more restful sleep??. This is very do-able!!. Why not??.

I shouldn't have to say this (again).., but I will... I am not advocating this as a way of life, on a daily basis, but only as a supplement in *critically measured dosages..,* to be used as needed.., discriminating wisely.., as an adjunct to a disciplined regimen of diet (*no sugar-low carb*) and exercise, etc.[9]...

A little bit of speed can enhance your life.., but this rule; *"Moderation in all things" must* be followed!!. This is the rule... Words to "*Live*" by [10]...

* * *

Save the Parents.., save the Marriage.., and save the Family!!.

---

[7] Case history: "Because of a tendency towards obesity, I was put on a Dr. prescribed (mild amphetamine) medication for weight control. I was in college at the time, working toward my R.N. degree... I looked the best I ever looked, I felt the best I ever felt, I excelled at my studies, I was organized, efficient, and "addiction" was never a problem or even considered... Now, several years later, this medication has been banned, and I am obese!.. I look bad, I feel bad, I am unorganized, exhausted, my life is chaos and my house is a mess.., *and I am addicted for life,* to blood pressure, cholesterol, and pain medications, with diabetes and insulin injections looming on the horizon!., and with all the side effects that these medications and obesity causes... As an R.N., I can tell you that the principle cause of weight gain is a sluggish metabolism, and the outstanding cure is amphetamine class medications... My life has been sabotaged (and shortened) by banning this life saving medication"... Ms.T., R.N., Ohio

[8] I don't know what the statistics are, concerning death on the highways, but I would bet that 50% of them can be attributed to falling asleep, or inattentiveness at the wheel due to drowsiness, as well as industrial accidents.., *all of which are preventable..,* saving ***thousands*** of lives each year!.... To not implement this strategy.., is criminal (homicidal) negligence!!.

[9] Now.., of course, **"The Powers That Be"**, are going to say that there are better ways and methods to achieve weight loss and etc.., but which "Medical Association", or "Dr's Guild", or "Pharmaceutical Company'" or "Legislative Body", is going to stand up and take credit for the ban on amphetamines.., and **the TENS of MILLIONS of** (largely preventable) **DEATHS** from Obesity related diseases and traffic fatalities that have occurred since the ban has been implemented???... (Hello??? Is anybody out there???)... The very fact that there is an "Obesity Epidemic" in this country dramatically demonstrates the **failure** of the "Medical/Pharmaceutical/Legislative" community in which we have (mistakenly) placed our trust...

[10] And, of course.., the caveat "disclaimer" has to be entered here:.. This (or any) drug should not be taken by anyone that has "contra-indications" that conflict with the health or well being of that person... Namely; a health, medical, or psychological situation *that is more life threatening* (deadly) *than your Obesity!!...* Always consult your health-care professional before taking any drugs or undergoing a weight-loss program, etc...

"Communication", is the Key to a better marriage and the solidity of the family... *But let's **"Get Real"*** here!!, and face the facts!.. *We are not communicating!!*... Over fifty percent of the marriages end in divorce, and the children of broken homes are roaming the streets and getting into trouble, and not just ordinary trouble, but troubles that compound themselves into the next generation of unwed mothers and fatherless children.., undisciplined children, abandoned children, children being raised by children that are having more children.., etc and etc... This is an egregious **"failure"** at the fundamental level of our society, and it is a *"Shame"*...

Can anyone doubt?., that this is an "altered state" of consciousness that is *not in harmony* with the "Grand Design"... *Obviously*.., the six-pack of beer, the mixed drinks, the pills, tranquilizers, binging on food, cigarettes, etc., in front of the television.., *is not working!!*. The state of consciousness that you call "normal", is actually a very low "altered state" level of consciousness.., and you are not communicating!.. You are alone and isolated.., and your marriage.., *is not working!!*. The "bumping" together of bodies in the marriage bed, *without the "communion" of hearts and minds*, **is not working!..** Your ego centered mentality, *alone in the midst of people..,* is not communicating on a "heart to heart" basis!., and your marriage is failing!!.

Now.., at this point in our conversation, I have to make the point that I am "eminently unqualified" (God knows) as a marriage councilor, and I cannot hope to solve the problems of marriage in a few paragraphs when volumes of books have been written on the subject, and still the problem persists!.. (But actually, *I do hope!*)... A "new approach" is needed... The reader should know by now, that the purpose of this book is to "elevate" the level of consciousness and "open" the Doors of Perception", and to reintegrate the harmony of the Grand Design, of which the "Family" is an integral part...

Simply stated; we have the situation where two individual (ego centered and isolated) "Souls" are standing together, "face to face" (a confrontation), shouting at each other, and not communicating!.. This is bad psychology and worse philosophy!.. Even the "better mousetrap" is no match for a fundamentally flawed philosophy that lacks "integrity" ("Cheaters never prosper")... The "new approach" is that your marriage is of *secondary* importance, and your relationship with God is of *primary* importance!!. You stand "face to face" with God.., and shoulder to shoulder in your marriage.., *facing in the same direction!!*. If even one of you adopts this "new approach", your chances for a successful marriage have improved *more* than fifty percent!., and a *thousand* percent improvement as a success in life!!...

Getting your priorities in order is the first step, and elevating your level of consciousness (and communication) is the second step... Now, **as a true and passionate scientist,** let it be known.., that I have endeavored, by every method known to man, to climb that "ladder of consciousness"!!. I had prayed devoutly, I had studied the scriptures intently, I had secluded myself in monasteries, I had fasted (my longest fast was for 21 days, liquids only) (I *do NOT* recommend this), I had stood on my head and twisted my body like a pretzel, I did breathing exercises, and I sat cross-legged in meditation for *hundreds* of hours.., **and my prayers were answered!!!** Oh Yes!!, my efforts had not gone unnoticed by the Lord!!. The situation arouse where I took two "tokes" from a joint of marijuana, went into the local tavern to have a beer with friends.., my consciousness was raised, *and the Lord GOD **spoke** to me!!!*... Truly, the Lord works in mysterious ways!!. The "better mousetrap" had been found...

It is difficult to realize *(if you have no basis for comparison)..,* that the level of consciousness that you perceive as "normal" is actually (relatively speaking) a very "shallow" level of consciousness in which you stand "isolated" in your subjectively self centered "self consciousness".., with all of the negative connotations that "self consciousness" implies!.. You are, *at this moment*, in an "altered state" of consciousness!., and there is a "vast conspiracy" to keep you there *(with no basis for comparison)!!.*

This is called the "modified state", and you can further modify this state with alcohol, tobacco, pills, selfishness, and "guilt" (from transgressions), etc.., all of which further condenses your consciousness into self oriented isolation.., ***or..,*** you can exercise a little insight and see through the restrictions of this "modified" "altered state", and take the necessary steps in the direction of a more "expansive" consciousness, which in it's ultimate "liberated" state is called; "The Unmodified State", and it is the "Self Assured" but *objectively oriented* (selfless)(Zen) state that is the characteristic of Hero's and Saints.., and as a child of God.., it is your destiny!!.

So forget the booze, cigarettes, tranquilizers, pills, and etc., *(all of which are "downers", but "legal")*, and take a deliberate step in the direction of a more "expansive" consciousness *(a.k.a. "getting high", which is "illegal"??!)* **(Go figure!!)**... and does anyone deny that alcohol produces an "altered state"??? There is something very "Oxy-Moronic" *(and sinister)* about this double standard of (illogical) logic.., **and it does not compute!!**.

Actually, it's not that difficult to figure out!.. The Liquor Dynasties, the Tobacco Barons, and the Pharmaceutical Drug "Cartels", that lobby Congress and make "huge donations" to their reelection campaigns (and etc.?), have a vested interest in promoting the "legality" of their "downward trending" *(and addictive)* level of consciousness, and promoting the "illegality" of a consciousness "expanding" substance of the "cottage industry" class (with no lobbies in Congress) **that would Negate them..**, and interfere with their profit margins!!.

So the "better mousetrap" *(by far and away!)* is your common garden variety (cottage industry) "Marijuana"... Just two or three "tokes" (at the most) of this wonderfully medicinal and therapeutic plant will elevate your consciousness, your level of **communication..**, *and save your marriage!!*.

This is *almost* [11] the perfect recreational drug for society in general, and the common man in particular... It's effects are dramatic, immediate, and *Welcomed!.*, as it relieves stress (a killer), increases awareness, focuses your attention, lifts your Spirit, gives you "intuitive" insights into things you never thought of before, enhances your appreciation for "Life" and your ability to communicate on a "heart to heart" basis.., which will restore the marriage bed to a union of hearts and minds, as well as bodies *(Ohh Yesss!!!)..*, **and save your marriage..**, *and with no drunkenness, no debilitating side effects, no addiction, no increase due to tolerance, no possibility of overdose.., and no hangover!!...* **And if the truth be told;** there are already a substantial number of educated and professional people (Doctors, Lawyers, Judges, Professors, Teachers, Law enforcement, *Surgeons*, Scientists, Researchers, Musicians, Computer Specialists, Military, *etc., and etc.!*) that regularly and clandestinely partake of this herb with enhancements to their life and careers!!...

Is there a down side to all of this??. Not really.., as *"abuse"* of this substance is almost impossible... But some people (idiots) manage!.. Excessive and constant use will deplete your "Psychic energy" (and the "B" vitamins), and cause you to become lethargic, and since sensory awareness becomes heightened (especially taste) this could cause you to "pig out" *(if you fail to exercise restraint)*, especially on spicy and salty foods.., and even the best consciousness expanding substances are no deterrent to "bad people", with bad philosophies, bad "intentions", and no integrity!...

So.., The next time you "toke up", thank God for the privilege, and for the beauty and "Mystery" of His Creation, and live your life in harmony with the ancient traditions of the Golden Rule, practice moderation in all things, stand face to face with God on a daily basis and shoulder to shoulder with your spouse, working together toward common goals... Take your family to church on Sundays, take your vitamins, keep your priorities in order, and do the right thing.., always... Priorities in order.., Communication restored.., marriage saved!...

As an adjunct to this.., the occasional use (on rare or special occasions) of a psychedelic (Ecstasy) can transport the marriage union to spiritual levels [12].., where communication becomes telepathic, where the hearts and minds of the individuals becomes truly entwined.., *"into one flesh"!..* (Words fail to convey)...

---

[11] The Marijuana plant has been used in scientific studies because of its mathematically precise relationship between exposure to sunlight and plant development… The common American (North and South) variety has a growing season of four months.., while the Asian variety (from Thailand) (a.k.a. Thai Sticks and Buddha Grass) has a growing season of six months, under intense sunlight… Therefore the Asian variety has a "higher ring" of Delta 9 THC and a lower ratio of the (sedative effect) CBD, which gives a very clean, clear, energetic, and "Spiritual" high.., and is therefore the even better "mousetrap", ("par- excellence")…

[12] In the "ABC" Documentary; "The War on Drugs", by John Stossel.., a segment of this documentary dealt with an estranged married couple that had been in "marriage counseling therapy" for many months, without results.., but only one session with "Ecstasy" restored their marriage "bond" to a spiritual union...

But a word of caution here... This drug (Ecstasy).., is in reality; a "Sacrament"!!, so remember your priorities, and have a "heart to heart" with God on an individual basis, and be "well established" in this **"Communion"..,** *before* you enter into this "transcendently" spiritual union with your spouse... Enough said...

And as a second adjunct to your life; there is a phenomenon that I have observed *(and you will find this observation and information nowhere else)..*, which has to do with the subject of meditation, which is communication *(Communion)* between you.., and God!.. I have observed;., that the act of sexual intercourse.., and Communion with God.., are at the complete opposite ends of the spectrum!!. But this observation can work to your advantage, because.., immediately following the *legitimate* act of sexual intercourse, there is a "bounce-back" effect to the opposite end of the spectrum, which is characterized by a serene and peaceful state of mind, a state of steadiness, tranquility, and quiet.., so profound.., that the Voice of the Lord.., may be heard!.. Are you listening??...

The Ultimate High.., the "True High"., is the Spiritual High!!... Go with God... Amen...

* * *

And save our high school teen-agers and young adults...

Never.., in the History of the World.., have our young people been confronted *(bombarded)* with such a "plethora" *(a veritable "mine field")* of life threatening choices.., that are attractively disguised **lethal Traps!..** It is a testimony to the human spirit that they even survive this period of life, and of those that survive.., many are scarred!!.

Beamed down by satellite television and blared out by stereo loud speakers, they are "sold" the lethal poisons of the day!!. What will it be today, children??. Do you want to be "cool"?, Well then, emulate the lifestyle of this glamorous *Slut*, because sin is "in", and never you mind about the unwanted pregnancies, abortions, sexually transmitted *(and incurable)* diseases, failed marriages, abandoned children, etc., and etc.., and emulate this "rap star", and slap that Bitch, because Bitches are a dime a dozen, and he's cool, and sells millions of records.., and here's another rock star "Idol" that you can idolize and emulate.., or change the channel, and watch this "delicious" pornography, and if your Bitch doesn't do this.., get rid of her.., and "Hey Bitch", if you want to keep your man, "do this"!!, etc., and etc., and don't forget, this program is brought to you by "Slick Velvet" alcoholic beverage that will rid you of all your inhibitions and common sense... "Happy driving"!.. Yeah, and smoke these "cool" cigarettes, and welcome to "Cowboy Country" (a.k.a. the Cancer Ward).., and click on into the "Cyber World", and become introduced to sexual predators on line, and view these terrific porno sites, and have sex in cyberspace with a pervert masquerading as a "chick", and this porno site over here, and be sucked off in your imagination.., and how about these pedophiles with their own organizations and websites, and if you're not sucked in to "becoming" one of these, then maybe you can be a victim of one of them, and on into the "party-drug scene", and be drugged into incoherency and "date-raped" (whether male or female), and then you can spiral downward, into Heroine, Crack, Cocaine, perversion, drunkenness, misery.., and death...

Enter into this picture the "Designer Drug"; "Ecstasy"!.

(Unfortunately, not of U.S. manufacture)... Granted, it is not perfect, and it is viewed (by the "unknowing") as part of the problem.., but in an ever expanding Universe, with ever expanding information, knowledge, technology, *and perversions..,* a step forward into the field of expanded consciousness *may be* a step closer to a solution!!. Or is it just a coincidence that the Atomic Bomb and LSD (polar opposites) arrived on the scene simultaneously??.

Now.., I have reservations about this drug.., so don't misconstrue this to be a "blanket endorsement", because as with everything, there is "Use", and there is "Abuse"... This is a sophisticated drug, and I would prefer that it be taken by an adult and mature mind.., with mature and religious intent.., but my preferences do not hold sway in the public arena... All that I can do here is to interject a little "mature attitude" and religious intent!..

This is a psychedelic that is "consciousness expanding" *(and therefore a **"Sacrament")*** that gets you "high" in the Spiritual sense of the word.., *but it comes without a "Book of Directions" and it is too often used in an inappropriate manner* (the sins of youth)..., **but not always!..** There are some teen-agers that have had insights and revelations that television evangelists can only dream about!!. But of course.., the sanctimonious religious, and the "save you from yourself" unconstitutionally self-righteous law makers have decided that it is illegal to have "too much fun", and to get "high" and actually "feel" the presence of God in a public setting... *"Oh no!, we can't have that"*!!. So the Kevlar clad, door busting, battery ramming, "SWAT teams" are called in (no exaggeration) and a halt is called to the "evils of Ecstasy"... ***Again..,*** we have that *bizarre* scenario!!... Ecstasy is virtually removed from the market and a vacuum is created! What then??. Back to Cocaine, back to Heroin, Crack, Crystal Meth, alcohol, etc., and worse yet!!; a plethora of bootleg-bathtub counterfeit "concoctions" that really are detrimental to body, mind and Soul (these are the REAL criminals)[13].., and people are dying!!, *and Ecstasy gets the blame!!!* The law makers and police force have aided and abetted the (truly criminal) counterfeiters and participated in the resulting deaths of their victims!!! ***Hey!!,*** (shout the police)., "We're only doing our job"!!... Yeah, that's what the Nazi's said.., at Auschwitz!.. "But it is the LAW"!!. Yeah.., that's the defense that Eichmann used.., at the War Crimes trials... Truly bizarre!!.[14]

So.., even despite the "sins of youth".., the casualties from this drug are surprisingly light.., and the casualties are not from the drug, but from the irresponsibility (abuse) of the user... But casualties, are to be avoided!!. These are dangerous times.., especially for the immature, the careless, the immoral, and the stupid!.. So I caution the user.., first of all, make sure (by testing)[15] that you have the real drug, and not a boot-leg counterfeit!., don't double or triple dose, don't mix this with other drugs, alcohol, etc.. Don't disregard the simple laws of decency laid down from the beginnings of the Earth.., because;., ***Casualties are not acceptable!!!..,*** and to misuse a ***Sacrament,*** is a ***Sacrilege..,*** and to fuck-up at a high level of consciousness will leave a scar on your Soul that you will carry for a very long time!.. So show *Respect..,* because you are the hope of the future, and your expanded consciousness is necessary for the future, otherwise it wouldn't be happening!!... *So grow up!.. Follow the laws of decency laid down from the beginning of Time!!, be respectful of God and your fellow man.., and Grow up!!...*

It is not my purpose to promote the use of this drug or any drug.., it is out of my hands!.. The drugs are out there, and they are being used, and people are getting "High"... What I am promoting is the understanding and the proper use of that "High" which can put you on the wavelength to Communion with the "Most High", which can be the most significant and "Life Changing" experience of your life!.. So, when you are High and "feeling the beat", and "doing the dance", *And if you want to get really, REALLY HIGH..,* remember your Creator, and direct the energy of the dance to HIM, and the energy and rhythm of the dance will flow through you into a spiritual Union that can be ***transcendent!!!*** *(Words fail to convey)...* ***"This",*** is the true meaning of ***WORSHIP!!!*** *(Let me recommend to you* (for instance) *the enthusiastic beat* (pre-selected works)

---

[13]   I have seen this happen time after time, and again and again!.. ***There is a pattern here!..*** A truly uplifting and consciousness expanding Sacrament is produced.., capable of giving it's participants the experience of Transcendence, into the Holy Realm of the Spirit.., a truly Religious Experience!., and then.., look-alike counterfeit substances are produced, containing some very sinister and sophisticated substances, like: m-CPP, PMA, PMMA, MDHOET, Scopolamine, etc. and etc.!.. These are truly mind-bending substances, completely sabotaging the religious intent of the true sacrament, and instead, giving the hapless victim a hellish-drunken experience, often with lasting negative effects (including "death"), and then.., the propaganda media machine goes into effect, denouncing the true sacrament, never disclosing the fact that it was a malicious counterfeit that was intentionally released onto the unsuspecting public, and Law enforcement goes into action to stomp out this menace.., and it is all a diabolical lie, and with diabolical intent!.. ***Who is doing this???*** Is it the Government?., or the DEA?., *or a more Sinister Organization*, bent on suppressing a truly God oriented and uplifting experience that might result in Communion with a Higher Power, and a step forward toward a break-thru solution and cure for the Evils of Mankind, that they have an interest in thwarting, and is contrary to their diabolical intent??? This is an intentional, deliberate, and sophisticated conspiracy.., and I therefore implore the "good people" of Law Enforcement to focus their investigation on the counterfeiters who are the true menace.., ***and expose their motives…***

[14]   See the ABC documentary; "The War on Drugs", by John Stossel.., and if you really want to know the facts and the potential of this amazing psychedelic, read: "Ecstasy: the complete guide" by Julie Holland M.D. (24 chapters, 450+ pages) www.maps.org/xguide/

[15]   Check out the web-site: www.erowid.org .., for just about all the information you need on all classes of psychedelics, and etc.., and their related pill testing program… (see: www.dancesafe.org/erowid and www.Ecstacydata.org , for pill testing results)…

of "Black Gospel Music")!!... ***Feel the Spirit..,*** and Worship the Lord!.. Amen...

Whether a law be good or bad, depends on the results it produces... Obviously.., the law makers that opposed "Ecstasy" have never experienced "ecstasy", nor any "expansion of consciousness", and are totally *ignorant* of what that means!., with no insight into the possibilities presented, and no visions of the future potentialities!!. So what's the solution??. The solution is education!., and it has to begin with the Law-makers!.. The Law-Makers have to *experience* the expanded consciousness of "Ecstasy"., otherwise.., they *simply* don't know what they are talking about!!.

* * *

And save our Country!!...

Poor "Usama Bin Laden"!!?... Poor, tragic "Usama"... No Ecstasy!!. No mushrooms!!. Just think!, we are all the sum total of our experiences, and poor Usama has not experienced any Ecstasy in his life.., no expansion of consciousness.., only bitter *"Belief"*... *Just think about it..,* if Usama had taken only one "trip" with Ecstasy, his whole life would have changed!, the sum total of his life experiences would have been different, and he would have been a different person.., and all of this "unpleasantness" could have been avoided!.. "Really"... Just think about it...

Our current strategy (to save our country), is to rain down "smart bombs" on our enemies!.. But how about (a better mousetrap) ***"Really Smart Bombs"!!!*** Suppose we were to rain down on our enemies "Ecstasy Bombs".., that would burst overhead and rain down Ecstasy.., like M&M's, all over the ground!!. There would be dancing in the streets!!. There would be a mass expansion of consciousness, revelations, and a better understanding and communication about those things that are really important in life.., like; "Life".., and "Liberty".., and the "Pursuit of Happiness".., and they would understand that *Fundamentally* we are all the same.., and we all want the same things.., and tyranny would be overthrown!!.

What we really want to do.., is change people's minds, and all of the propaganda, and all of the bombs aren't going to do that, but one eye opening revelation will change people's hearts.., and as soon as this phenomenon takes root, it will sweep through the nation like wildfire.., ***and tyranny will be overthrown!!.*** The only "True Victory" is to make friends of our enemies!..

But of course, there is always option #2.., We can bomb the shit out of them, and blast them to smithereens... Which will it be???...

* * *

And save the World!!...

A Drug!!??., that would save the World??!!.. You can't be serious!!! "Oh No" (you say), it would take the "Second Coming" of Christ to do that!!.

At the risk of "Pissing Off" everybody, let's start with conjecture.., to save the World... Now.., the theologians conjecture that the world will be saved by the Second Coming of Christ!., when Christ will again walk the Earth!!. There is just something "unsettling" and "incongruous" about this concept, which I see as "beneath the dignity" of Jesus Christ!!. Maybe it's just me, but I cannot imagine Jesus Christ as "Superstar", being mobbed by adoring fans, shouting; "yeah Jesus", "go Jesus".., etc... A "Rock Star", yes.., Jesus Christ?., *No*!!. ....Breaking News!!; Jesus speaks to the children, wheelchairs block traffic... News flash!!; Jesus walks on water!!. News update!!; Jesus spotted in the clouds, flies through the air!!, *NO No No!!.* It's just too ludicrous!!, too obscene!.., I can't imagining it happening... Even when Jesus walked the Earth 2000 years ago, He healed the leper (Mk 1:40-45) and commanded him; "Don't tell anyone", but the leper told.., and Jesus was mobbed from then on... *"He could no longer enter a town openly, but stayed outside in lonely places"...* If Jesus came back to Earth today.., He would be forced into seclusion!!... And if He did come.., would *YOU* be granted an interview??, or personal contact??... Not very likely...

But then again, perhaps Jesus is already here, and in seclusion!.. I say that He is, and He grants interviews.., to selected people!.. So the second coming of Christ is an "Individual happening"., A personal experience!.. But *YOU* have to initiate the interview... This is not conjecture...

Now I am not disputing the second coming.., but what I am saying is that to "God" (The Pre-eminent Expanded Consciousness in the Universe), confinement in a mortal body has got to be a comedown.., and the only reason HE would do that!!:.., **is to** *save your sorry ass!!,* because you are *spiritually blind and deaf, with no insight, and you are of the "less blessed" that have to "see" in order to believe!!.,* and the first thing that HE is going to do, is **"KICK ASS".,** and rain down fire in the form of "ARMED-MEGATONS"., and wipe out all the assholes., so traumatizing the world;., that there will be peace for a 1000 Years!!... *DON'T PISS-OFF THE LORD!!...* But of course, this is all conjecture!!... *(Sarcasm intended)...*

But sarcasm aside., the most ancient of prophesies [16] foretells of the coming of the God-man., and HE doesn't come as a Lamb., **HE comes as a Lion!!!...**

So what would it take to save the World??. That is not as complicated a question as you might suppose!.. It would take every "Leader" of every Nation., **to agree!!!** But is that possible??... I say that it is possible, because everyone agrees., that there is only "One God", and consequently only one "Body of Truth", and it becomes incumbent upon every Leader of every Nation to have the **"Experience" of "Union" and "Communion" with GOD!.,** and every "Leader" of every Nation will be a "High Priest" and he will rule a Nation under God, and the "Body of Truth" will be known!!. When our Leaders know the Truth., there are no disagreements... Only then can it be said that Christ walks the Earth...

But is this just an Utopian dream., or is it really possible??!!.. I say that it is possible, and we must come to this realization, and it must happen **Soon!.. When you say your prayers; "Thy Kingdom come"., think about what you say!!.**

Here we come to a *barrier*!.. Here we have hit **"The Wall"!!.** This "Wall"., this "barrier"., is the limits to our understanding, the limit of our comprehension... The only thing that we can realize here., is the fact that this realization is beyond our comprehension!!. Here is where the theologians fail., here is where the law-makers fail, and here is where I fail, as an author., a failure to communicate, because words fail to convey., and the imagination cannot conceive., and even the memory of the event cannot adequately be retained., because it is just beyond the capacity of the mundane (linear-logical) mind...

That having been said, I must therefore call upon the reader to take that "intuitive leap", to grasp the import of what I am trying to convey, with the full knowledge that it cannot actually be conveyed!..

How can I say this?!. Where do I start??!!.. How does one go about initiating an interview with Almighty GOD ??. *For sure,* the "Ego" consciousness cannot do it!!. *For sure,* the "intellectual" cannot do it!! The "theologian" cannot do it!!. The seekers of Power and Fame cannot do it!!... The linear-logical mundane mind is just not capable of it... So how???... *OBVIOUSLY,* if the Ego centered linear-logical mundane mind is not capable of it, *IT MUST BE TRANSCENDED!!...* But who can do this??. Who can stop the mind??. It is a Herculean task to stop the incessant babble that continuously goes on in the mind, and bring the mind to a standstill., and we *Identify* with our mind., how can we rise above it??.

Enter into this picture; "Herbs of Mysterious Virtue"...

The modern day synthesis of these "Mysterious Herbs" are now called; "Psychedelics"., a class of "drug" referred to as; "Consciousness Expanding"... To classify these "substances" as "Drugs", is to fall victim to the trap of "words" (a.k.a. "The Variegated Cloak of Words")... The more correct designation would be to call them; **"Un-Drugs"**...

Those who have taken the "Un-Drugs" report that the "Doors of Perception"[17] have been "Opened"!., and "Cleansed"!., and there was a sense of "Mystery and Awe", with "Insights", and an "Appreciation" for the "Grand Design" that was now so abundantly self-evident!!... **By contrast**., when you "come down" from this "High State"., back down into the "puny" and "trivial" self-centered and Egotistical mundane mind, it is as though you have been "drugged" into a mundane and "modified" perception of a reality that is somehow "less" than the Grand Design!.. **But of course**., The "Supreme" Court, the law-makers,

---

[16] That most ancient of prophesies., written in the stars (pre Egyptian > *early Mesopotamian*)., and sometimes called: "The Gospel in the Stars" is depicted in the Zodiac., beginning with Virgo (the virgin birth) and ending with Leo (the Lion-King)... This prophesy has absolutely *nothing* to do with astrology., which is a total corruption of the prophesy…

[17] "The Doors of Perception", by Aldous Huxley… The famous and prolific author gives his first-hand account of his experience with the psychoactive drug, "Mescaline", derived from the "Peyote" cactus…

police force, news media, the public in general, and etc.., *have no knowledge or experience of this*, and are indeed **"Ignorant"** of this fact!!...

The very fact *of the existence* of these "Herbs of Mysterious Virtue".., is the proof positive (the "smoking gun" evidence) of the *existence* of GOD!!. *Contemplate the significance of this fact!!...* Since even before the *"fall"* of man.., the "doorway" back had been provided for!!.

But that is not to say that every "dumb-ass, ding-a-ling, yahoo" that can pick a plant or pop a pill can enter through that "Sacred Doorway"!!. No No ***No!!...*** "No one goes to the ***Father***".., no one can enter into the ***"Inner Sanctum", no one,*** except he who is qualified by the purity of his *"intention"*, as made evident by the *"Desire"* of his heart!!. The **"Gatekeeper"** will *NOT* refuse entrance to such a one as this, ***regardless of his Religious persuasion!!..***

So that "Ancient Doorway".., held Sacred and Secret by the Alchemists of Old.., is now (relatively speaking), common Knowledge!!... The alchemical ingredients of the Magical Herbs are known.., *but the Traditions of the Alchemists, the Rituals and Procedures of the Ancient Mystery Schools, the Rites of Initiation, and etc.., are not remembered!!...* So while entrance is granted into the outer "Courtyard" of the Holy Temple.., and the Doors of Perception are thrown open, and the World is seen in all it's magnificent splendor, and the participants dance in glee, some even being touched by the Holy Spirit, with revelations and insights.., it is still only the "Dedicated Aspirant" that proceeds on.., into the "Holy of Holies".., into the "Inner Realm" of the Fifth Dimension.., and the "Gatekeeper" is found to be.., none other than the Lord GOD "HIMSELF"... *(Words fail to convey!)*...

So.., only one who has had this "Experience" is worthy to be called (truly) the "Servant of God".., and only a true Servant of God is worthy to be the "Leader" of a Nation... *It is imperative..*, that every "Leader" of every Nation realize the folly and futility of his "Ego-Centric" exercise of power, be initiated into the *"Mysteries"*, step through that Portal, and Experience the "Oneness" of GOD, and of HIS Servants... **"This"..**, is the **"Wisdom of Solomon"..**, and it is a "Brotherhood" to which all "Leaders" must inevitably belong!..

Only when this "Brotherhood" of Nations[18] is established on Earth, will there be "Peace on Earth".., and only then can it be truly stated that the "Second Coming" of Christ is a functional Reality, ushering in the "New Millennium"...

"Peace be with you".., Amen...

* *   * * *   * *

Well.., was that "Over the Top", or what!??

Many people will say that I have gone too far, here.., that I am advocating the use of drugs... These drugs are present and available to any and all who would use them... What is lacking is the proper direction and intention... It is my attempt here, to supply the proper direction and intention.., and I am the *only one* advocating the "Ibogaine cure" for drug addiction... You have to ask yourself; *"Why is it"..*, that no one else is advocating this "cure" for drug addiction??. Could it be because the "cure" bypasses the conventional secular mentality, and may introduce the recipient to a "Higher" level of consciousness, *beyond secular capabilities??,* and may even put the recipient in the confrontational position of having an audience with *God!!.* (*Well now..,* we can't have *that!!,* now.., can we?)…

It may well be that this book will be an "Underground Classic" long before (and if ever) it becomes popular among the general population.., and that is as it should be.., because the Underground sub-culture has one distinct advantage that their Bible pounding counterparts do not have.., and that is their familiarity with altered states of consciousness… Of course, not all altered states are "Higher" states, and we have to make that clear, and discernment is required here.., and that is the reason and purpose of my writings… The drugs used (and approved) by the "general population" (alcohol, tobacco, prescriptions) definitely do not get you "High" in the Spiritual sense of the word, and could more correctly be described as "Downers"…

---

[18]   Is there a Biblical reference for this "Herbal Sacrament" that will bring about this "Brotherhood of Nations"??. YES!.. Revelations 22:1-5 describes the "Tree of Life", bearing fruit, *"and the leaves of the tree are for the healing of Nations"*... You cannot interpret the "Tree of Life" literally in "Genesis", and then metaphorically in Revelations!.. The verse means "literally" what it says…

The Bible pounding Evangelicals (or whatever) would be perfect candidates for the "Higher" states of mind, if they could ever get beyond their prejudices… They quote (Isa 55:8-9): "As the Heavens are higher than the Earth, so are my ways Higher than your ways, and my thoughts than your thoughts"…(declares the Lord)… They quote this, but they do not have a clue.., nor can they conceive of the Lord having a different view-point from their own!… (The *key word* here is: *"Higher"*)!!.

How truly ***ironic*** it is, that the young person, experimenting with psychedelics and "altered states", has a better chance of having a truly religious "spiritual experience" (and many have), than does his Bible pounding, self righteous counterpart… The Lord works in mysterious ways.., and he is not deceived by pretentiousness…

Now.., concerning the subject of "Altered States"… First of all, let me make the point that "States of Mind" cannot be communicated!.. To try to communicate a state of mind is like trying to communicate the concept of "color" to a man, blind from birth!., it cannot be done!.. This is true even for the person locked in to the drug induced state, and becoming familiar to that altered state, cannot conceive of the "normal" state… The drug induced state *becomes* his normal state of familiarity and comfort, and he will resist change from that state, back to his previously "normal" state.., *of which he can no longer conceive*!!. It's kind of like "Pain".., when you hit your finger with a hammer, your state of mind is "pain", and you are locked into it, but a week later, you can remember the incident, but you cannot recall (or put yourself back into) the state of mind of "pain"… You are in a different (pain free) state of mind, and can no longer conceive of the "state of pain"… Neither the memory or the imagination can conceive of , *or even recall,* the altered state of consciousness.., because if it could, you would no longer need the drug!..

So this is valuable information, to those who are in the business of drug rehabilitation, and to those who are addicted to drugs… The solution to the Drug addiction problem, is to distance yourself from the drugged state for a sufficient amount of time, until the non drugged state becomes your "norm", and you will remember, but not able to recall, *nor conceive of,* the drugged state… You can look back on it, and observe the "side effects cost" (debilitating health, purposelessness, ego eccentricities, etc.) of the drug induced state, and decide if that is where you want to be in your life… But just one "shift" back to that previous state, and you may be lost forever, or you will have to start the "kick" process all over again…

So, at the risk of being redundant, here.., I must emphasize to the reader, that if you have never experienced the (psychedelically induced) "altered state" of consciousness, there is just *NO WAY* that you can conceive of this state!!! All attempts at imagining or conceiving of this state *do not even approach* that state!.. Therefore, all of your arguments for or against or about these "altered states" originates in a condition (like the man born blind) of "not knowing", and all of your opinions (and laws) laid down by the law makers, and etc., have originated from the unaltered state of "ignorance"… Simply stated, if you have not *experienced..,* you do not **Know!.,** and are unqualified to pass judgments or make laws…

"Question": So what is it that I am really trying to do, here?.. This is a straight forward question.., and it requires and deserves a straight-forward answer…
"Answer": I am trying to give the "Underground drug sub-culture" the direction and the zeal of the "Evangelicals" (or whatever).., and I am trying to introduce to the "Evangelicals" (the "Men of the cloth" of whatever *God oriented* religion) to the "Chemical Key" (or; *the Alchemical Key*) of the Underground sub-culture!!! It is a paradox!!. The one has the Key, but not the direction.., and the other has the direction, but not the Key!!! I am trying to bring about a ***"Convergence"*** of these two cultures!.. Can you imagine the results of such a convergence!?. Can you??? *The World would be Transformed!!!..,* and that is **Really** what I am trying to do, here… I am trying to transform the World.., one person at a time.., beginning with YOU.., and not just for You yourself alone.., but exponentially, to others through you…

This is your time.., and your opportunity.., to pick up the torch of the Hero, and make a difference in the World.., to Champion the cause of the Good, the Right, and the True.., an "Agent of Universe" against the Forces of Evil.., against the Army of Darkness.., that you may prove to be a "Profitable Servant", and your name be entered into the Book of Life… *Is that "Over the Top"??…* Read on, dear Friend, Read on, and take the Journey with Iron Owl, here.., because it is just an incremental step in your own journey through life.., *and you are Called,* as we are all called, to be the Hero of our

DRUG WAR COSTS

The Financial Costs of the War on Drugs Dwarfs the Federal Annual Deficit

SUBSTANCE ABUSE RELATED DEATHS

Mortality from Major Forms of Abuse (per year)

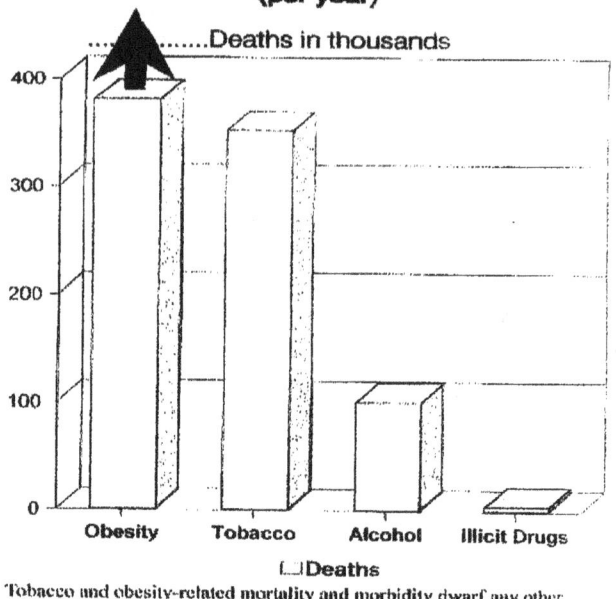

Tobacco and obesity-related mortality and morbidity dwarf any other factors in early death, disability, and medical care costs.

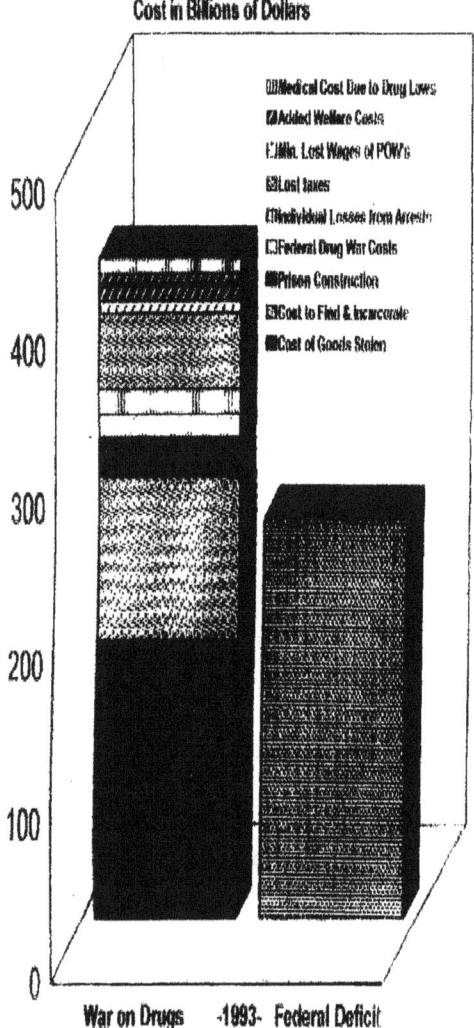

Source: Save Our Liberties, 187 Aculanes Dr., #14, Sunnyvale, CA. 94086-5520.
Note: Federal Deficit for 1993.

Graphs supplied courtesy of:
Schaffer Library of Drug Policy
For more information, go to:
http://www.druglibrary.org/schaffer/library/graphs/20.htm

So the Question is:

How Does This...

When Compared to This...

Justify This...

At the Expense of This...?

own lives, to our families, to our loved ones, to our friends and neighbors, and to all of those with whom we come in contact, as far as you can reach, and as far as you can imagine…

So.., I have gotten off the subject, here.., because the subject of drugs is not the main preoccupation or purpose of this book, and if it was, I have not said enough… But it isn't.., so perhaps I have said too much… Sometimes (it is said) it is necessary to exaggerate a point in order to make the point!… I don't think I have made any exaggerations at all.., but the "anti-drug coalition" (Government) has!!. The following charts and graphs are pretty much self explanatory, so I will make no further comments, other than to say; study the charts, and decide for yourself if the Multi-Mega-Billion dollar expenditures for this War on drugs (and the incursions on the rights and freedoms of the people) are justified.., and if you require any further information, visit the web-site… Keep the Faith.., I.O.

      ***   *   *   *   ***

BOOK VII

"THE SECRET OF SECRETS"

My concern here is with only one class of drugs (which in other circles are referred to as "Sacraments"). I am speaking mainly of that class of "Herbs of Mysterious Virtue", as referred to by that great teacher and sage, "Patanjali". That class of mind expanding drugs that we refer to as "psychedelics"... The mysterious "Soma", the elixir of immortality, as referred to in the Hindu scriptures. The alchemical compound "Mescaline", derived from the "Peyote" cactus, that opens and cleanses the "Doors of Perception"... The "Magic" mushroom.., the "Ayahusca".., the "Iboga.., etc.., and, of course, the much acclaimed and much abused synthesis of modern day alchemy; "LSD".

These "Herbs of Mysterious Virtue".., are Sacraments!.. ...and to misuse a sacrament.., is Sacrilege!.. This is the worst kind of drug abuse, and could lead to the worst kinds of punishment... The "law of man" being the least of the punishments, and the "Wrath of God" being by far the "most terrible"... He who has ears to hear, let him hear...

I have witnessed some very bizarre behavior;.. I was at a party where LSD was available to whomever cared to partake. I declined... This was not the proper atmosphere to partake of a sacrament. One of the participants took the LSD, followed by large amounts of alcohol, followed by marijuana, cigarettes, more alcohol, etc.., and was staggering around looking for a fight! I will never understand the mentality of this type of personality.., probably motivated by deep insecurities... Mercifully, the alcohol cancelled out the effects of the LSD, and no great harm was done (beyond liver damage and a few million brain cells murdered), but it could have been worse. It could have been much worse... There was not enough intelligence here to qualify as Sacrilege... It's even beyond stupidity... It's "criminal stupidity"...

On another occasion, a teenager of approx. 18 years of age, put a handful of capsules of LSD into a bottle of Coca-cola.., and drank it down!.. Just to see how much it would take to put him over the edge, beyond his ability to withstand the power of the drug.., as though it were a contest between himself and the drug!.. Apparently he did not reach that place where he literally "blew his mind", but he was acting strangely enough for someone to call the police and they took him away to medical treatment. I saw him a couple of days later, and he seemed none the worse for the experience... A tragedy had been averted... The amazing resilience of youth!.. But other people have not been so lucky... There have been a lot of tragedies out there, and not because of the drug, but because of stupidity... And strangely enough, this wasn't the first time that I heard someone mention the "contest" between themselves and their capacity to maintain control, as though it were a "Macho" thing to do... HEAR ME WELL.., there is a vast difference between courage and foolhardiness. When you partake of a Sacrament, you are on the threshold of the fifth dimension, and on the other side of that threshold there lies Heaven.., and there lies Hell…

For the foolhardy to cross that sacred threshold is to risk Hell!.. There are demons in Hell!.. There is insanity in Hell! There is terror beyond anything you can imagine! You do not want to go there!.. If you do not have the maturity to discriminate between that which is courage and that which is foolhardiness.., *DON'T GO THERE.!!*

I have seen it written down, in a popular book, that you have to go through insanity to reach enlightenment!.. ... THIS IS HERESY!.. The author of this heresy should be burned at the stake! There is an epidemic of stupidity out there. Ignorance is widespread... It's like a plague.., a deadly plague...

The primary purpose of putting yourself under the tutelage of a teacher, or Guru, is to prepare you to safely cross that threshold, and to prevent you from losing your balance.., lest you fall... If you were to fall, this would be a tragedy of Cosmic proportions.., as though an inhabited planet were blotted out of the universe...

You cannot "storm the gates" of heaven and expect admittance. You cannot put "new wine into old wineskins" without serious damage happening. Courage is a requirement, as is honesty, integrity, sincerity.., and a reverence for, and an understanding of what it is that you are doing here... There are procedures to follow... There is ritual to be observed...

Actually, considering the vast number of people who have experimented with the drug LSD, and the excessive number of times each participant has used and abused it, the number of mishaps has been mercifully slight.., and what mishaps there were have been blown out of proportion by the media... But that doesn't make the mishaps any less tragic... Mishaps, involving a sacrament, can have a lasting and detrimental effect on your personality and your spirit... A mishap, is a crime against the Spirit!.. The Spirit is Holy, and should be uplifted and sanctified...

The term "Spirit", as used here requires an explanation for clarification:.. A good horse is said to have spirit, a winning team is said to have spirit.., it is an adjective, not a noun... The error is so pervasive that even in Biblical translations, the Spirit of God has been mislabeled "The Holy Ghost", [a noun] instead of the more correct "The Holy Spirit", [which is BOTH adjective and noun at the same time]... Spirit is a quality of consciousness... So the essence of your "Self", the intangible Soul, is your Spirit... The Spirit can be harmed... There is nothing to be gained by a negative experience involving the Spirit... The Spirit can be harmed.., and crushed.., and broken.., ...and restored.., but it can never be killed.

The Spirit is Holy... It is the Essence of your being...

I have known people who have taken this sacrament on a regular basis.., three times a week! They would probably say that I am making too much of this.., that it is not as serious a thing as I portray... Their attention is focused on the external only, and as such they can see the beauty of the external world, and have insights, and listen to music, and they say; "Wow" a lot, and they "make love" while in this elevated state, and say; "Wow" some more.., and they could be in touch with the Divine.., And,.. the Divine could smile upon them, and grant blessings.., if they be good people, with good Karma... But what if you're an asshole?..

There is indeed, a negative aspect to "Truth"... The unworthy candidate could be confronted with the visions of his future;.. old age, sickness, misery, death.., and Hell... This is also the Truth... The undeniable Truth.., and it is meant as a warning, but the shock can be so severe that it will require extensive counseling and therapy.., but really, where could you find someone "qualified" to give you counsel regarding the condition of your Soul?.. "Saints" are very few, and very far between... This is not the proper drug for the trivial minded, the carnal minded, the immature, the recklessly stupid.., and assholes...

It is to prevent the possibility of a "Psychic injury" that I present to you here this information, for your consideration and implementation... The pharmacological aspects have to be considered... To take this sacrament too often and too casually is to flirt with disaster... Three times a week is dangerously abusive. There is a tolerance factor that lessens the effectiveness of this substance and defeats the purpose.., there are bodily processes that have to recoup, and be replenished, serotonin production, etc., there is a "Psychic energy" factor that must not be depleted.., there are "drug interactions" that should not be combined, etc.., your state of mind at the time of taking this drug.., even your external environment is of great importance.., and what is your purpose and intent?.. To take this sacrament under less than optimum conditions is to not have the proper respect!., and you could come to harm, even though you are basically a good person...

And.., I would never.., never, never ever.., use a Sacrament to indulge in sexual activities.., married or not… "Carnal pleasures", and the "Mysteries of the Soul" are at opposite ends of the spectrum... To bring the Sacred, down to the level of the carnal, is to invite both psychic injury and emotional damage resulting in suicidal depressions. If you want to enhance sexual pleasures, there are other drugs. Don't use a Sacrament...

If your intentions are frivolous.., so is your life. If you would view the inner realms of your own Soul, and uncover the great mysteries of life, you must present yourself to your Creator.., as a worthy candidate.., disciplined in mind and body.., with prayer and fasting.., and Reverence... This is the tradition... You must come to this alter alone and in solitude... Sensory deprivation is the key... Seated in a comfortable position, the senses are withdrawn from all outside stimuli, and focused within... You must neither succumb to or fight the vagaries of the mind, but observe them dispassionately and isolate your Self from them, and rise above them, to a place of solitude.., beyond the mind.., and if you are very lucky.., if you are very, very lucky.., you will hear.., "THAT Inner Voice"... That Inner Voice, is very subtle, and as That Voice speaks, ...simultaneously.., there is Vision, and the Vision is Revelation, and the Revelation.., is Knowledge... Mysteries will unfold.., step by step.., episode by episode.., you will be guided... Are you Worthy of this?...

Are you lucky?.. Oh yes, "Oh Thou of Noble Birth"... Fortunate indeed art Thou, to have been born "Man" (instead of animal) and to have before you the opportunity of "Enlightenment"... Do not waste this opportunity.., for That subtle "Inner Voice" that you hear, That "Revealer of Mysteries".., is the same Voice that was heard by Adam in the garden... It is the same Voice heard by Abraham, Isaac, and Jacob... It is the same Voice heard by Moses on Mount Sinai.., and it is the same Voice heard by Jesus, when he said; "As I hear, I judge, and my judgment is just"... This "Inner Voice" Is no less than the Voice of God, in the "formless form" of the "Holy Spirit", and it is the "sum and the substance" of the testimony of the Old Testament, and the testimony continued, unbroken and unchanged throughout the New Testament, and this is the testimony of Iron Owl.., unbroken and unchanged.., forever and ever.., Amen...

Are you lucky?.. Very fortunate indeed, are you to hear these words... Revealed to you here, is the "Summum Bonum" of the "Western School"... It is the "Secret of Secrets".., "The Pearl of Great Price".!. Many good men have sought to discover the mystery of "The Lost Word".., and did not find it... Many good men have searched the pages of the Bible, thinking this to be the "Word" of God, but it is only the History of the "Word", as spoken to the Prophets, and as such, it is of great value... But, hidden in plain sight, and overlooked by even the most diligent of students, is the True Word.., "THE LIVING WORD", spoken to you directly, revealing to you the mysteries.., of those things hidden since before the beginning of time... And more.., And even more than this, there is DIALOGUE... Of this it is written:.. "I stand at the door and knock. Any man hear my Voice and open the door, I will come in to him, and sup with him, and he with Me"... Are you worthy of this?.. Are you listening?..

"THAT" Inner Voice, of the "Holy Spirit".., is the Teacher of teachers... If you have a teacher, or Guru, and he doesn't introduce you to the Teacher within... "That Inner Voice".., get a new teacher...

Or better yet, prepare yourself as a worthy candidate, go within, still the mind.., and with rapt attention.., asking that most important question that springs from "the Soul that wants to know".., ..."listen"... You may find your-Self "absorbed" in conversation.., dialogue.., And the "Teacher Within" will answer your innermost question, and as That Voice speaks, there is Vision, and the Vision is Revelation, and the Revelation is Knowledge.., and you will Know... You will know...

A word of caution here... There are very few of us here that are truly worthy... Perhaps none of us.., and some of us will be tested... As you leave the "known" of the external world, and venture into the "unknown" of the inner realms, you may have to go through the "Bardo".., and be confronted by "The Wrathful Deities".., giving terrible visions.., and not all voices coming from that side of the "threshold" are benevolent... Beware of any voices that flatter you, or beguile you with promises of greatness, power, wealth, etc... Remember, there IS a "Dark Side" of the force that may try to bring you down, if you prove to be weak... Courage is required here, as is Wisdom, Humility, Sincerity, and Integrity... Stand firm.., and with the voice of your Soul, call out the Name of the Lord, and with firm faith and earnest prayer, request His presence... ...Do this regardless...

The "Bardo" is a transition phase between two levels of consciousness, and this period of adjustment can be fraught with all sorts of mental activity, either pleasant or terrifying, depending on your Karma.., but you must go through this experience, and be able to name and recognize it…

This is important: If you can name a state of mind, it gives you a certain power over it. You must be able to recognize this state as the "Bardo", and say: "This is the Bardo"...

There is another danger here.., that you might get caught up in the vagaries of the mind.., and start talking to yourself, and believe yourself.., and be mislead... What is the subject matter?.. If it be about your personal welfare, or your insecurities, or your wants, or your needs, etc., no matter how seemingly important.., they are trivialities... These are the vagaries of the mind... You do not bring "subjective" trivialities to the table of the Lord, and expect an audience... This is the "Mind Barrier"... If your "Way" be through contemplation (and this is a most excellent and natural way) your subject matter must be "objectively" outside of yourself, to those great and noble questions that arise spontaneously in the Soul, longing to be answered...

Overcoming the "Mind Barrier" is the name of the game... The mind barrier, is like a "flaming sword" turning every which way, blocking the way to the "Tree of Life"... It is like trying to find your way out of a labyrinth, with no exit.., except death.!. It is the propounder of riddles, the author of guile and trickery.., it confines you to the linear-logical-material.., and you cannot get behind the mind with mind... You can only "abstract" yourself from the mind...

It will become readily apparent that..; you are not your mind.!. It is extremely important to know the difference between your Self, and your mind... The modern day model for the mind, is the computer, a problem solving device. This is a good model in terms of function, but it leaves out the "dual nature" and also the "emotional nature" of the mind...

The ancient model for the mind, as symbolically depicted by the "mystery schools" of a by-gone era, has been.., the "dog"... The "dog", is shown as an unruly cur, antagonizing it's master, and biting at it's master's ankles... The purpose of this depiction is to show the unruly nature of the untrained mind and the consequences thereof... An untrained mind, like an untrained dog.., is an antagonist. With a little training, the dog can become a useful, productive, and joyful servant to his master, and indeed, man's best friend... The same is true of the mind. The mind can, and should be trained (more about this, later) to be the servant of man, ...and not the master...

The Soul, on the other hand... What could be the model for the Soul?.. There is not an adequate model for the depiction of the Soul... The nature of the Soul, your Soul, is Sublime, Magnificent and Mysterious... To "Know Thy Self", is to know the Soul, and at this point, you don't know who you are... You don't know the wondrous being that you are...

An inadequate model for the Soul, is the lens... A lens can be focused to view the ordinary, the mundane, the superficial.., if the lens be distorted, so is the view, but with an adjustment it can see beyond the ordinary, to the microscopic, the atomic, the sub-atomic, etc... With another adjustment it can view the Solar system, the Galaxy, the Cosmos, etc... That is the limit of the capability of the lens...

But the Soul, with another adjustment, can see and explore the inner realms of the fifth dimension.., and whatever it sees, that is where it is, instantly, effortlessly, with absolute freedom, and immortality... And yet, the Soul consists of nothing tangible, it cannot be found... It is "Spirit", (the adjective/noun) pure and simple... "I think, therefore I am"... That's all that can be said... And because of the vacuous nature of the Soul, it has another ability.., the ability of absorption...

The ability of the observer to become "one" with that which he observes... That is the ability of absorption. Because of the vacuous nature of the Soul, you are absorbed into this body that you identify with and call "yourself". You have literally "fore-gotten" your "Self" into the body of yourself for the experience of the Soul on Earth.., and this is in accordance with Divine plan... Because of the vacuous nature of the Soul, we can become absorbed in a good book, and for that moment, it is real... We know that a certain "movie" is good when it has the power to absorb us into it, and we can shed tears, and feel pain... We can become absorbed into our dreams, and experience an alternate reality, and for that moment, it is real... And because of the vacuous nature of the Soul, we can become lost in our thoughts, and if they be good thoughts, we will smile.., and if they be bad thoughts, we will clench our fists and grind our teeth, and relive that episode again and again, and pump adrenaline, and generate hate.., etc...

These are the vagaries of the mind... This is the aspect of the "untrained dog"... This is the "subjective" side of the "dual nature" of the mind... Any thoughts pertaining to our self, be they "good" and make us smile, or "bad" and make us hate.., are of the self-conscious, untrained, "subjective" mode of the mind, and as such..; are unfit for contemplation.

So, how do we "abstract" our Self from the vagaries of the "subjective" mind?.. The first step is to "step back" from the mind, (in meditation) and observe it's functioning's, and repetitive patterns.., dispassionately.., from an "abstract" vantage point, and as you observe the mind from your "abstract" vantage point, you will come to the realization that..; You.., are not this mind that you are observing... You are the observer.., and your mind is that "thing" which is being observed... That is, until you "fore get", and get reabsorbed into the mind, and are carried off on a "train of thought" on a roller coaster ride of emotional ups and downs, etc... Aha!.. AHA!..

It is a great day, a very auspicious occasion, when you first come to the realization that you, and your mind, are two separate things... It is not an easy thing to accomplish this "abstraction" directly, but with practice, and the proper "technique", it can be done. When the abstraction is complete, it is referred to in various metaphysical writings as "Isolation"... This "Isolation" of the Soul from the mind, and bringing the mind to a complete rest.., of absolute stillness.., is the aim and objective of meditation... This is the moment when illumination occurs... This is the moment of "absolute" stillness, when you "blink out" from here.., And "blink on".., in the Fifth Dimension... It is said that "Enoch" was master of this technique.., and he walked and talked with God... It is referred to in the Hindu scriptures as..: "When the Self rests in Self alone"...

I use the term "abstraction" here, because it has two meanings.., both of which apply... The first meaning is to separate out one thing from another, and the other meaning refers to "abstract thought"... This is a very important concept.!. The greater the "level of abstraction" of the "consciousness principal" (Soul) from the mind, the greater is the potential for abstract thought.., and conversely.., if abstract thought be pursued, abstraction of Self from the mind is accomplished...

This is the "Way of Contemplation", and it is a very excellent "Way"... The vagaries of the mind can be bypassed if the candidate has a natural "bent" for abstract thought... If the subject matter being contemplated be not of the "Subjective" variety, (pertaining to; I, Me, Mine, and why Me?, etc.).., and instead, be of the "Objective" variety of philosophical questions pertaining to the great mysteries of life... These types of "objective" philosophical questions have an affinity with the Soul, and indeed, spring from "the Soul that wants to know"... This is not an academic exercise where you "pick" a subject and decide to contemplate it... No, this is "the cry of the Soul that wants to know"... There is a "purity of intent" here , that is uncontaminated by motive... (It's a Zen thing)... But, be not dismayed.., the greater the "level of abstraction", The greater is the "natural" tendency of abstract thought, (and vice-versa).., because..; every Soul.., wants to know...

This is the "Art and Science" of Meditation, Contemplation, and Transcendence. We, of both the "Eastern School" and the "Western School", pride ourselves on our knowledge of "Art" and "Science", and often we approach our goal with an "Intellectual Sophistication" that is more of the "mind", than of the "Soul".., while the simplest and most primitive "Savage", will.., with the aid of his herbal "sacrament".., and with the innermost cry of "the Soul that wants to know".., transcend.., and have his "fifth dimensional" experience, etc... This is the birth of legend... This is the power of simple purity and sincerity of the Soul absorbed in rapt contemplation.., that yearns for, and longs to know and be known, by his Maker...

I find it interesting to note, that these "Herbs of Mysterious Virtue", have historically been given to the most remote and simple peoples.., those that are "the Pure of Heart"..,   the "unsophisticated"... While the "intellectual" is engaged in a wrestling match in the labyrinth of the mind... There is a "Cosmic Irony" to this.., the quintessential "Cosmic Joke", and it's on YOU!.. Ha Ha Ha... Nothing to do, but laugh.., and observe those qualities of the Soul that are found precious in the sight of God...

The "Sacrament", is truly the "Gift of God", and should be respected as such... What it gives to you is a "level of abstraction" that is greater and more profound than is normally possible, and with this profoundly enhanced ability of "absorption" into the abstract contemplations of "the Soul that wants to Know", you will hear "That Inner Voice", and you will become "absorbed" in conversation.., dialogue.., and all your questions will be answered, and you will Know, and you will be guided, step by step, episode by episode, to ever greater Revelations of ever greater Mysteries......

I have spoken all that I dare to speak... There is a point at which common language is inadequate to communicate. A point at which a greater level of abstraction is required for understanding... To go beyond this point with common language is to transgress...

I have lain before you the priceless "Secret of Secrets", which is: "The Knowledge and Conversation" of the "Holy Spirit", who is the "Teacher of teachers, Within"... I have explained to you the principle of the "Isolation" of the Soul from the mind, and the "abstract" contemplation of the "Soul that wants to know"... I have explained to you the "Vacuous nature of the Soul", and its ability of "absorption" into the object of it's contemplation, and into the "Conversation" (Communion) with

"The Alchemist-High Priest"

"The Holy Spirit".., and I have instructed you in the ritual use and purpose of the "Sacraments"... I cannot go beyond this... It is the province of the "Teacher Within" to go beyond this... "Heaven lies within you"... I wish you good luck, and Godspeed...

I would recommend a regimen of disciplined daily meditation, with a sacramentally induced meditation occurring not sooner than every seventh day, or ideally, every fourteenth day.., on the Sabbath...

These "herbs of mysterious virtue", are not an accident of nature... They are part of the Divine plan... Do not misuse them...

This is the testimony of Iron Owl... It is the most important information you will ever receive in this life or in any life... It is my pleasure, my honor, and the purpose of this book to impart to you this knowledge.., *which is the most Ancient and Sacred Knowledge...* It is the Knowledge of: **"The Way"...**

      Everything else is superfluous.

      * * *

BOOK VIII

"The Training of the Mind"

I have made mention of "the training of the mind", and to the fact that the mind can, and should be trained.., and that an untrained mind, like an untrained dog, is a vexation and an antagonist to it's owner... This is a gross understatement... Mental institutions.., and prisons.., are filled with people who are there as a result of untrained minds... Human "derelicts", forsaken and abandoned, are walking the streets in a drunken stupor, trying to blot out the pain of mental agony.., and guilt... Many people suffer silently, and just go on with their lives... Lives are shortened by the "stress" of this inner turmoil, and disease preys upon those who are at "dis-ease" in their mind... The silent agonies, and the vocal agonies, cry out in pain.., and violence... Victims, and victimizers.., of untrained minds... The toll is staggering.!. The weight of the pain of humanity is unbearable... And I too, was a victim of my own untrained mind...

I had suffered a "trauma", to my Soul... Through sheer stupidity, I had committed a great sin... The guilt was overwhelming, and the punishment was "absolutely" appropriate.., and devastating... I had seen Hell... Literally... I would like to be able to report to you that there is no such place as Hell, that it is fiction, but that is not the "Truth"... Unfortunately, Hell.., is a reality... It is not meant for mankind to see this... It is forbidden knowledge... Words fail to convey... It is more horrible and terrible than any nightmare you could possibly imagine.., and I saw it... The vision of Hell left me horrified and terrified, petrified by fear.., and paranoia.., that lasted for over three years... Please.., take every precaution… …Don't go there...

A "psychic injury", at a high level of abstraction, with only myself to blame, and only myself involved... Even though God could forgive me, I could not forgive myself... There was an unbearable emptiness.., cut off from the presence of God... My very purpose in life had been thwarted by my own stupidity... My only solace was that with each passing day, it was a day closer to my death, which I longed for... I was 28 years old... It was "the dark night of the Soul"... I have never spoken of this to any one in my entire life, until now, in this book, and I tell you, so that you don't accidentally commit the same stupidity, and suffer the same consequences…

My outward expression did not betray my inner hopelessness... No one knew... Work was my salvation. I worked as though possessed, from dawn to dusk, installing miles of wall to wall carpeting in row after row of new apartment buildings, playing the radio loudly, to drown out the emptiness in my Soul, falling into bed at night to a restless sleep... My mind never stopped replaying the scene, over and over and over again, of my "fall from grace", never stopped from berating myself for my stupidity... It just never stopped...

This was the burden that I carried, that sapped my strength, my energy, and my will to live... I could not go on like this... There had to be a solution to this problem... Perhaps in India, Perhaps the Swami, perhaps Yoga.., I had to try... I sold everything I had, and fled to India, with no provision for return, or failure... I arrived unannounced at the Swami's door, at his "School of Yoga", and I joined the class already in session. I did not confide my inner turmoil to the Swami, but I diligently applied myself to the curriculum at hand, which included a meditation exercise technique......., that had the dramatic effect of lifting this unbearable pall from my mind, and restoring my Soul.., and the process was so subtle, that I didn't realize it was happening!.. And it happened in approximately three weeks time...

So this is the technique that was given to me by the Swami, and this is the technique that I give to you... This is the technique for the training of the mind, and it is a preliminary technique to the "Isolation" of the Soul from the mind...

The first step in the practice of any technique of meditation, is "concentration"... This word has two meanings:., to reduce to a very small space, and to focus all attention on "something"... Both of these meanings apply here... The "something" that we will be using as the object of our focused concentration is.., "the Breath"...

The "Breath" is considered more than just a worthy object of our concentration... It has religious connotations as well... It is the "Holy Life Breath", that was breathed into Adam, by God.!. It is the point of contact between life and death, between the Super-conscious and the conscious awareness, and also between the conscious and subconscious minds (breathing is a sub-conscious process.., until consciously thought about).., and if your concentration be focused to the point of "absorption" into the "Life Breath".., it is a "breakthrough" experience... And it has the added facility of being always with you, and it is moving.., in and out... It is much easier to maintain concentration on something that is moving, than something that is stationary...

Seated in a comfortable position, in a darkened room, with no external distractions, the concentration is focused on the Breath... Observing the Breath, as it comes in, as it goes out, without interference, just observing.., a "detached" observation, without interfering, etc... It usually takes about 15 to 20 minutes to bring yourself to a "settled" relaxed and effective state of concentration.., and you will notice the correlation between the depth of concentration, and the "peacefulness" of the Breath...

To facilitate your practice of concentration on the Life Breath, focus your attention on "abdominal breathing"... This requires an added measure of awareness that will yield an added measure of results and "depth" to the process... How long can you maintain your concentration before your mind wanders.?. You can count the number of breaths in your preliminary practice, but you must refrain from counting after your preliminary introduction, and maintain mental silence... You are a silent and dispassionate observer to the process, observing your breath, as it goes in and out, observing your abdomen, as it rises and falls, warding off random thoughts, focusing, focusing, maintaining your concentration, observing, detached, dispassionate.., etc...

Your principle distraction will be.., "the mind"... It will seem as though the mind.., has a mind of its own... Without your permission, it will wander, at random, first to this subject, then to that one, then another, and another, constantly, like an "untrained dog"... And if you are not paying attention, you will be distracted away from the "Life Breath", and you will be following around your "untrained dog of a mind".., and it will be your master... As soon as you become aware that your concentration has wandered, bring it back to the Breath, and begin again, maintaining your concentration as long as possible... Again you will be distracted, again bring it back... Again and again it will wander, and again and again you must bring your "Self" back to the Breath, maintaining your concentration as long as possible each time... This is your "job"... This requires patience, diligence, and effort... A lazy consciousness will become absorbed in the mind, and be battered to and fro, like a helpless puppet, dragged around by an untrained dog... But remember.., this is a valuable dog, it can be trained to be a willing and loyal servant.., you must not fight the mind, or get angry at the mind, but gently abstract your Self from the mind and train the mind to go in the directions that you choose, and be it's Master...

This process will go on for several days, and as it does, you will become better at it... You will spend less and less time being "captured" by your mind, and more time
focused on the "Life Breath", and your "attention span" will increase... This has very positive rewards in all aspects of life, and especially in contemplation... As you continue this process (2 to 3 hours at a time, twice daily) you will come to view the mind as "other" than yourself... This is great progress... This is a "Level of abstraction", with the consequent refinement of the thought process... It is at this level of abstraction that we can train the mind...

As the candidates for higher knowledge sit in their meditative postures, having observed the workings of the mind "objectively", from an abstract viewpoint over a period of many hours and many days, they gain an intimate and detailed understanding of their thought processes, and several things become apparent.!.

You will observe that the thought process is almost continuous, unless interfered with by our technique of meditation...

You will observe that every time that you bring your "Self" back to the "Breath", for longer and longer periods of time, lengthening the attention span, eventually, you will lose your concentration and slip back into the thought process.., and because of your lengthened attention span, you may get involved more deeply in the thought process, before coming back again to the Breath...

You will observe that there are basically three categories of thought processes: those that are "good", pleasant, or inconsequential.., those that are "bad", unpleasant, and emotionally deleterious to our well being.., and those thoughts that are not about "us" at all, but instead are engaged in "scientific enquiry"… The "Tool" of the mind employed in it's most meaningful mode of conduct, as a "problem solving device"… The first two types of the thought process, the good thoughts, and the bad thoughts, are of the "self-conscious", "subjective" mode.., but the third type of thought process, the "scientific enquiry" types of thought, are of the "objective" class of thought, and it is the natural function and most productive use of the mind... This is what the "dog" should be trained to do…

You will observe, that every time your consciousness drifts off into one of the three modes, the selection is random and different each time… If you get into the "negative subjective", bad, "train of thought" process, and as this thought process goes on, we replay those negative events over and over again, feeling the hurt, plotting revenge, generating hate, pumping adrenaline, gritting our teeth and clenching our fists...

These negative thought processes are full of emotional impact, and we experience all the hurt, shame, guilt, anger, humiliation, frustration, anxiety, etc.., as though it were the first time... We continually replay these events of the past, as though it were a bad "soap opera", that we are forced to watch over and over and over again, but we embellish the events of the past, and make them even worse, and more hurtful than they originally were, and we project these events into the future, and imagine all sorts of scenarios in which we extract revenge on the party that injured us, etc., continually, and we are doing this while we are engaged in our daily work, and our work suffers from lack of full attention, and we walk around with a sour expression on our faces, and a bad attitude.., and none of it is real... It's all the result of negative thought processes that roam through our minds.., like an untrained dog.., driving us to drink, and greater involvement in the negative thought process, down the road to melancholia, depression, and failure.., to mental institutions.., and if we act on those negative thought impulses.., to prison...

That's a pretty dismal picture... So what happens when a person sits for hours at a time in meditation, daily, for many days, for hundreds of hours?.. What happens?.. What's going on?..

As you are sitting there, observing your thoughts from an abstract view point, you will notice the three types of thought: the "good" thoughts, that make us smile, or are of a practical nature, our wants, our needs, our duties, our work, or random thoughts that are of no consequence... ...The "scientific enquiry" type of thoughts, in which we are objectively looking at information, seeking for solutions to problems, making deductions, analyzing, arriving at conclusions, etc... You will notice that, with your lengthened attention span, you can take your "scientific enquiry" to greater heights of abstraction.., greater depths of absorption, and with greater results of your analysis... You may also notice that while you are engaged in this scientific enquiry type of thought, there is no emotional impact involved in it... You don't feel good, you don't feel bad, you don't feel anything at all... As your attention is focused entirely on the subject at hand, there is no consciousness of self at all... This is a very "Zen" type of thought process, and with a shift of focus to the spiritual, you can enter into the realm of abstract "contemplation", and become absorbed in your contemplations to the point of "Communion"... Good dog!..

And there is the "negative subjective" type of thought, and as you sit and watch from your abstract viewpoint, you will observe..; "There's that thought again, that's the same negative thought process that I had yesterday, and the day before, and every time I have these thoughts, I feel bad, and sorrow, and anger.., and there I go again, projecting a future scenario of revenge, gritting my teeth, clenching my fist", etc...   …Bad dog!...

There comes a time, eventually, when you have to ask yourself; "Why am I doing this? Why am I replaying this same old "soap opera" over and over again, feeling the pain, over and over again"?.. "This is futility.., this is masochistic.., this is "Bullshit"!.. Aha... AHA!..

From your "scientific enquiry" frame of reference you will analyze the situation, and with the newly honed scalpel of your lengthened attention span, you will penetrate into the "absurdity" of this "syndrome"...

It will become evident that an event that took place in the past cannot be changed, and all of our guilt, "nor piety, nor wit, nor tears, can wash out a line of it"... The only thing that we can really do, is learn from the experience, and determine to not ever do that again.., and determine to do better in the future... The past is dead, forget about what is past.!. There is no profit in replaying the past... Start anew today... This is the logic of the situation...

Beyond the logic, there is another aspect that has to be addressed... Forgiveness... Even though God will forgive us, we have great difficulty in forgiving ourselves... We can forgive our enemies, but not ourselves... Guilt, is the great barrier... Guilt, will hold you prisoner, and keep you in the "negative subjective" train of sorrowful thought... Forgiveness is the Gift of the Lord.., accept it.., and "Go, and sin no more"... Release yourself from your bondage, and accept the gift of the Lord... Pray the Lords prayer: "Forgive us our trespasses, as we forgive those who trespass against us"... Forgiveness is your salvation... Hold no grudges... Those that have trespassed against you.., wipe the slate clean... Live by this principle...

So, You have accepted the gift of the Lord..; which is forgiveness.., and you have extended this gift to all of humanity.., and you have realized the absurdity of continuing in your "negative subjective" sorrowful thought process habit pattern... This represents two-thirds of the cure... The other third of the cure, is the "technique", for the "training of the mind"...

As you are sitting in your meditation, practicing the technique, bringing your wandering mind back to the Breath, maintaining your attention on the breath for longer and longer periods of time, lengthening your attention span.., eventually.., you will drift off into one of the three modes of thought... If it goes into the "scientific enquiry" mode of thought.., let it go... If the "scientific enquiry" mode of thought be turned into religious/philosophical contemplations.., this is the greatest good.., let it go... Eventually you will become aware, and bring your "Self" back to the Breath, and start again...

If it wanders off into the "positive subjective" train of thought, this is not so bad... You will notice that the thought process goes from subject to subject to subject by a process of association, and as a mental exercise you can follow the associative process back to the point where you wandered off... If you can follow the associative process backward through seven successive subject changes, you have achieved good clarity of thought, as a result of your lengthened attention span... But bring your attention back to the Breath.., and start again...

If it wanders off into the "negative subjective" train of thought.., *catch it in the act,* and return immediately to the Breath... The "Life Breath", is your "life raft" in a stormy sea... You have seen the futility of allowing the mind to go down the negativity road... Don't go there... Come back to the Breath immediately, and start again... Every time you come back to the Breath, it is a fresh start, and the mind will wander off in a new direction each time... Each and every time that it wanders off into negativity, catch it immediately, and bring it back, and start again, effectively preventing the negative thought process from taking place... The repetition of this process is "the training of the dog"... It will soon become second nature to you, and a negative thought will trigger the immediate response of bringing your attention back to the Breath... Do this for all of your waking hours, while you are meditating and while you are going about your business...

Within a period of twenty one days, the dog can be trained... You will notice, as you are progressing in this meditation, you will be spending "progressively" less and less "time" in the negative thought processes, and consequently, more and more time in the positive mode, and in the "Zen-objective" mode of scientific enquiry... The consequent result of this is; you will be spending less and less "time" feeling bad about yourself, and consequently, more and more time feeling good, and interested in the subjects of your "scientific enquiry"... Both you, and your "dog", are progressively becoming happier and more interested in life... ...And you can observe your own progress...

Soon, because of your constant practice of preventing the mind from going in negative directions, and the rewards of going in positive directions, the mind will cease to go in those negative directions... Even after you have discontinued the practice of the meditation, the mind will have been trained to go in positive and productive directions, and if it should happen to slip back, you have developed the automatic habit of "catching it in the act", and bringing yourself back to the Breath... Lo and behold!.. ...The dog has been trained...

So, you had previously wasted much of your "time", every day, wallowing in self pity, anger, frustration, negativity, etc.., and now.., you have much more productive "time" on your hands...

What will you do with this "recaptured" new-found time?.. The dog has been trained to NOT go in negative directions, and now.., we must train the dog to go in more positive directions...

This is relatively easy, because this is the desire of your Soul... If the desire of your Soul be an academic pursuit.., study it... If the desire of your Soul be of a metaphysical or religious pursuit.., study that... This has a two-fold result on the training of the mind... The first is as a "diversion" from negative subject matter to positive subject matter, and in effect, replacing the negative with the positive... This "study time" should be integrated into the technique shortly after the "level of abstraction" has been achieved, between the meditation periods, and at our leisure... This is referred to as: "the meditation with "seed"...

The concept of the "seed" thought is pictured prominently in the tapestry of the ancient "mystery schools" [1] by the "pomegranate", which is a fruit of a seed, and the pomegranate is itself a seed pod with thousands of seeds, each capable of generating a tree with branches and seed pods, with countless other seeds, etc... The symbolism of the seed pod is quite clear, with respect to the mind... The Knowledge represented by the symbol of the pomegranate is this:.. You are responsible for what you see... If you would be master of your mind, and the master of your life, you must discriminate wisely about what are the "seed" thoughts and ideas that we let into our minds...

This is the message of the parable..; (Mt.13-52): "Like the Teacher (and student) of the "Law" (of the mind), who brings forth from his storeroom (memory), not only those things that are old, but also *treasures that are new!*" (the association of ideas, "new" invention!)...

If we let in filth and smut, these are the seeds that will grow, and produce a train of self reproductive thought, leading to consequences... If we let in trivia and gossip, these seeds will develop into trivial mindedness... If we open our minds to knowledge and truth.., these are the seed thoughts that will develop into a "Tree of Life", and yield "tangible fruit".., ("and the birds of the air will come and dwell in it's branches")... There is a type of Magic here, where a mere thought has sprouted into an idea, and that idea has become manifest as a physical reality[2]... You are expected to "work" this magic...

The second purpose of our "study time", is to stimulate the process of "scientific enquiry".., which is the most productive use of our minds... This is the "Zen-objective" state of mind.., and it has side effects... Because there is no sense of "self identity" involved in this thought process, it gives rest to an overwrought ego.., because there is no "self consciousness" to inhibit us, we have achieved the "natural" state.., and because we are in the "natural" stress free state, there is a harmonizing and healthful effect on our body.., and our personality...

With the virtual elimination of the negative states of mind, we will, as a result, be functioning in the "positive-subjective", and the "Zen-objective" states of mind... This will be the case, whether we are in deep meditation, or while we are going about our business... The "shift" from "positive subjective" to "Zen-objective", and back again, is a natural occurrence, and this will take place many times throughout the day, but the "shift" is so subtle that it will not be noticed... You will only become aware of this in *retrospect*, because there is no self awareness in the Zen-objective state...   ...The dog has been trained, and is our loyal companion...

---

[1] The "language" of symbolism figured prominently in the adornments of King Solomon's temple, especially the inner courtyard of the "Temple of the Lord" (1 Ki 7:12-22)… "He cast two bronze pillars (each 27 ft. high, and 18 ft. around), with two bowl-shaped capitals of cast bronze (7 ½ ft. high) (the capitals symbolizing the head, *possibly the Conscious and sub-conscious*), with seven sets of chain "networks" (symbolically representing the interlinking relationships of the thought process *matrix*), with two rows of pomegranates encircling each network, and above the capitals, above the bowl-shaped part, next to the networks, were 200 pomegranates in rows all around… The pillar to the South he named "Jakin" (HE establishes), and the pillar to the North he named "Boaz" (in HIM is strength)"… The design and construction of these pillars was commissioned to the master architect, craftsman, and *Mystic*; "Hiram Abiff", who is the symbolic founder of the master builders of "Freemasonry"…

[2] There is a principle of metaphysics here, as well as the result of prayerful request, that whatever you pray for, hope for, and wish for.., if you can be consistent and persistent in "imagining" the outcome of your desire (over time).., and take the steps necessary (work) toward the achievement of your desired outcome.., circumstances will order themselves in such a way (as if by magic) to bring about the fulfillment of your desire… Be careful what you wish for.., because if you apply this Law.., you will get it!..

How effective is this technique?.. Everyone that has the desire, and the ability to practice this technique.., will profit from it... The potential for a mass "Exodus" from mental institutions to mental health is there... To those that are afflicted, it is the Exodus from mental slavery.., to liberation... It is a life changing event...

This technique is best practiced in a class room atmosphere, with an instructor, to maintain the discipline and order necessary to the adherence to the program schedule... The instructor will lead his class in prayer, and there will be an attitude of "reverential respect" to the God that will deliver us from evil, forgive us our trespasses, and speak to us, in the inner sanctum of our Souls... There will be an evening discourse, a short inspirational sermon on the forgiveness of sin, the futility of the "soap opera" mentality, etc., and a question and answer period... The instructor will instruct his students in the art of silent prayer, to precede every meditation exercise... Silence, is maintained throughout the entire program... Not even eye contact will be made... Each student is there alone, to practice in solitude, the science of.; "The Mastery of the Mind"... This is no small accomplishment... It is a life changing event...

But there are those people.., (and I really shouldn't have to say this).., that may see this as a method to "block out" those pressing problems of the moment, and somehow, they will magically go away if you don't think about them.., that you can manipulate things away by manipulating your thought process to not think about these things... No, that cannot be done.., but you can pray for Wisdom... Wisdom is always paramount, and common sense is not dispensed with... A fresh wound will preoccupy the mind for awhile, and a severe trauma can bother us for years, but after a period of mourning.., and healing.., the negative impact of these experiences must be laid to rest...

But there are those people.., Those "Seekers after Wisdom", that will persist on with the meditation program, to greater and greater levels of abstract contemplation, and become absorbed in the contemplation to the exclusion of every other thing, including self... This is the "Noble Pursuit", and it will be your life's preoccupation, no matter what else you do... It is because of this preoccupation that you are sitting here, reading these words... This preoccupation is the call of the Soul, and it is considered a manifestation of the; "Thee Within Me".., that seeks to know itself... It is to those people, that I write these words...

The dedicated student will continue on with the meditation, becoming "established" in it... As the process continues, observing the Breath, the mind will wander off in one of the three modes... long buried negativities will occasionally rise to the surface.., and be discarded... This process is referred to as "cleaning the house" of the mind... But the main thrust of our meditations will be in the Zen-"objective" mode of "scientific enquiry"... If only academic pursuits are contemplated, you will excel... This is the "arena" of creativity, and you will excel...

But if the "longing" of the Soul be turned to contemplation.., in the form of "scientific enquiry".., of those questions that perturb "the Soul that wants to know".., "absorbed" in rapt contemplation.., this is the "arena" of "Communion"... This is the greatest good...

This is the **"Way"** of the "Western School"... It is called..; **"The Great Work"..,** and indeed, there is no greater work on earth that a man can aspire to... There is no greater accomplishment in life than this, and not for just "Self" alone, but for the benefit of all humanity, through you... The "Great Work", is not completed without this last step, of turning this benevolence back to Earth, and to humanity... Entrance is not granted to the ambitious, with motives of self aggrandizement and grandeur... This is vanity, and will prevent the "purity of intention" necessary to achieve the absorption of the "Zen-objective" states... It is the "Good Samaritan" with the giving heart, and the charitable nature, that is welcomed into the "Communion" of the "Knowledge and Conversation" of the "Holy Guardian Angel", Who is "The Holy Spirit".., the "Teacher of teachers" within... The "Voice of the Silence".., that speaks to man.., and there is Vision, and the Vision is Revelation, and the Revelation is Knowledge.., and you will Know..,. and you will be led, step by step, episode by episode, progressively.., and nothing will be hidden from you... This is your destiny, This is the purpose for which you were born, this is the purpose for life on Earth. This is the purpose of the Earth itself... "I HAVE SPOKEN; *YE ARE GODS* "!!. Thus sayeth the Lord... This is your destiny... Realize it.., and minister to mankind...

This is the testimony of all the scriptures, Old Testament, New Testament, Other Testaments of other religions, and of all the Prophets and all the Saints, and it is my "first hand" experience that I can personally testify to, that is the inspiration for this book, that be "turned back to Earth" for the benefit of mankind... Enough said...

* * *   * * *   * * *

Treatise on the Sub-Conscious Mind

This is a book of the mind.., and as such, no book of the mind is complete without a discussion of the Sub-Conscious mind...

The "Great Sub-Conscious" (as it has been called) is a relatively new discovery!!. Even though it has existed from the very beginning, it has remained (relatively speaking) unknown and undiscovered until about the eighteenth century, when Franz Anton Mesmer, an Austrian physician, "discovered" the hypnotic trance, for which he has come to be known as; "the Father of Hypnosis"...

.... Now.., in the Buddhist school of thought, there is a very important concept that we must utilize here, as well as elsewhere throughout this book, and it is this:.. If you can *"Name"* a certain thing.., then you have "power" over it!!... *This is especially true for states of mind...* So, until something is named, it is *(for all intents and purposes)* either non-existent, or so nebulas as to be out of reach and beyond our control...

So.., it is very recent in our history (the 18th century) that the "hypnotic state" had been discovered and named, and is now a tool of modern psychotherapy and etc.., and the same is also true for the "sub-conscious" mind... Until it had been named (in the 18th century).., it didn't exist!!.

Although it may have been somewhat understood by the ancient "mystery schools", it has remained one of the best kept secrets of all time... In the arcane language of symbolism, it is represented by the symbol of "the dog", and is referred to as "the dog consciousness", and as we will see.., this is a most appropriate designation.., because the dog is an *"animal"* that is (relatively speaking) very intelligent, but nowhere near the level of consciousness (i.e. *sub*-conscious) of "Man"... When properly trained, the dog is seen to be a faithful and devoted friend, companion, and servant of Man...

Being a student of the mind.., my first preoccupation was with the sub-conscious, and I read every book, article, publication, etc., on the subject, and I attended every performance by every stage hypnotist available, marveling at the skill of the hypnotist, the phenomenon of the hypnotic state, and the response to the suggestions of the hypnotist.., where the hypnotized subject sometimes displayed talents and behaviors that were beyond their "normal" functionings...

Perhaps my greatest disappointment in life, was that I myself, could not be hypnotized... The very subject of my intense investigations was not available to me!!. I could not achieve the hypnotic state, neither by self hypnosis, nor by being hypnotized by a professional hypnotist, and not even with the aid of the hypnotic drug; "Sodium Pentathol"...

So.., (the reader may ask?).., what can I add to the sum of knowledge regarding the sub-conscious mind?., or is this to be a distillation of hundreds of books already on the market, and what can I add in a few paragraphs that has not already been covered in these volumes of books??. Do I have anything "new" to add to the sum total of knowledge??. *Yes..,* I have a "new" contribution to make to the sum-total of knowledge regarding the sub-conscious mind...

This "discovery" occurred in the mid 1960's, when I first made the personal discovery that higher levels of consciousness could be achieved by the use of drugs... I was experimenting with the herbal sacrament (drug); "Hashish", and I *"knew not the strength of it"!!.* And, as chance would have it, I had to leave the scene of the "induction", and travel about 25 miles across the city of Los Angeles, during heavy rush hour traffic, via the freeway system.., which I felt capable of doing... Shortly after getting onto the freeway, the effects of the drug came on with full force, and I achieved a very high level of abstraction, lost in deep meditation, *contemplating the universe!!...* About 20 minutes later, I came back down to planet Earth and found myself in the midst of heavy traffic in downtown Los Angeles, which I knew very well, but I didn't know exactly "where" I was.., *because "I" hadn't been driving the car!!!...* I had to figure out where I was because I hadn't been driving the car, and I had no recollection of the last 20 miles of traffic or how I arrived at where I was now, but regaining command of the vehicle I continued on down the freeway, and after about five minutes, I again went into that high level of abstraction contemplating the universe, and I again relinquished control of the vehicle to that "unknown" driver!!. After about 20 more minutes I again came down from my lofty contemplation to planet Earth, and I again found myself behind the wheel not knowing exactly where I was or how I had unerringly negotiated the Los Angeles freeway system to arrive at this point.., which I discovered was about 10 miles beyond where I was supposed to get off!!, so I got off the freeway and back on again, going in the opposite direction to retrace the 10 miles to where my turnoff was.., and I again went into abstract contemplation and that "unknown" driver drove unerringly down the freeway.., 5 miles beyond where my turnoff was, and I had to again turn around and retrace the five miles to my turnoff, and I got off the freeway into the suburban city traffic.., but now my contemplations centered of the mystery of "Who" was driving the car, and "How"???... I went into deep contemplation (again) contemplating this mystery as I approached an intersection, with a car approaching from the right, and another approaching from the left, and the car stopped!., and the cars behind me started blowing their horns, and I came back down to Earth (again), and I realized that I had stopped for a green light!!!... Aha!!. *Aha!!!* Mystery solved!...

Oh Yes!!, I had just solved the mystery of what has got to be *the* best kept secret in the whole world!!! I had just discovered the Sub-Conscious mind!!... *I had just discovered "My" Sub-Conscious mind!!,* and the fact that: **the Conscious and the Sub-Conscious minds are two separate and distinct entities occupying the same body, and each is ignorant of the existence of the other!!!** I had **"Named"** *(described)* **it!!!...** This was my revelation...

The sub-conscious mind.., is the *animal* mind... This "Man-Animal" is really a very intelligent animal.., actually the most intelligent of all the animal species.., but it is, nevertheless, an animal!., and as such, it lacks that "cognitive faculty" that distinguishes "Alpha Man" the superior being, from the rest of the animal kingdom... So, when I approached that intersection.., "I" wasn't driving the car!.. "I" was gone into a high level of abstraction (result of the Hashish) and my sub-conscious mind, *my well trained animal,* was driving the car.., and where the Conscious mind would have been watching the street lights, the "animal" was watching the traffic, and stopped at the intersection for the cars approaching from the right and the left!!!

The same was true for the freeway.., the well trained animal, my sub-conscious mind, was very capable of driving the crowded freeway, as long as there were no deviations from the main thoroughfare, but the moment there was a decision to be made, the conscious mind was *instantly* called back from it's abstraction, to the scene.., and problem solved; the conscious mind returned to it's abstractions, and the sub-conscious resumed it's role of driving down the freeway, but lacking the conscious cognitive faculty, it was not cognizant of the turnoff...

The sub-conscious animal mind is a relatively "simple" mind, and as long as the road ahead is straight and uncomplicated, it will continue on, aware of the traffic, but not really cognizant of street signs and etc., but it responds to "stop" signs, pedestrians and etc., that have had a repetitive trained response, and it may even be aware of traffic lights, etc., but the physical environment takes precedence (hence; stopping for a green light)... I have observed that my own particular sub-conscious animal is very courteous, law abiding, and safety conscious.., *more so than my conscious mind!!..*

Now, although my experience here was an amplified and exaggerated experience (because of the Hashish) which extended the "time factor parameters" (20 minutes "gone" away from the scene), it allowed me to view the phenomena and arrive at these conclusions!!, which otherwise are *an entirely normal and commonplace occurrence!!.* We do this all the time!.. We are constantly shifting our attention back and forth from "the road" to thoughts that occupy the mind.., but we do this so rapidly, repetitively, and habitually, that the process goes on, undetected and unnoticed!..

But becoming aware of this process, you have to *marvel* at the beauty and mystery of it all!!. Just think.., if you had to be totally aware and cognizant of every thing and every detail of "the road", it would be an exhausting task just to navigate through life!.. But because we have this well trained and obedient animal ever by our side, we can delegate the mundane and repetitive tasks to this very capable, "simple" but intelligent animal that is our ever present companion and helper, freeing up the cognizant Human intelligence, to contemplate

"Higher things" (or whatever).., and life becomes leisurely...

Just like the "dog", that is "mans best friend", that delights in doing his masters will, and lives for the approval and affection of his masters hand that will give him an approving pat on the head.., so too the sub-conscious animal is willingly subservient to it's master; the "Alpha" master intelligence that is the Conscious mind.., but what the Alpha conscious mind is unaware of, is the **separate and distinct "Entity"** that *is* the sub-conscious "animal"!.. So you see.., the body of the "animal" that we call "our own", is occupied by an Alien intelligence.., and "We" (the Conscious mind) are the Alien!!! So too, the sub-conscious animal is also not cognizant of the **separate and distinct** nature of the Alpha intelligence occupying it's body, because it lacks the cognizing faculty and is habituated to this Alien presence, which it accepts without question...

To put it in more esoteric terms; the Soul Consciousness (a spiritual being), occupies this body of Man, (which is fearfully and wonderfully made).., for the purpose of experiencing Life on Earth!!.

But this animal sub-consciousness definitely does have a *mind of it's own!..* For instance; when you are busy explaining your concepts to a friend, the Conscious mind is occupied, and the sub-conscious mind is (literally) "scratching it's ass", because it is conscious of the itch at the body level, and the Conscious mind is totally unaware of this activity!.. Although the Conscious mind is on a diet (for instance), and while preoccupied with other things, the sub-conscious animal will be reaching for the cookies!.. Although you have given up the addiction to smoking cigarettes, the Animal sub-conscious is the one addicted, and may not share your intentions, and while you are not looking (preoccupied), it will be reaching for a cigarette!!. Etc., and etc...

Because of the close proximity of the Conscious and sub-conscious minds (occupying the same body), there is an *intuitive* "empathy" between them, or what you might call a "feed-back" effect, in which the influence of a sub-conscious "desire" is felt at the Conscious level (the cigarette addiction), and it is incumbent upon the Conscious mind to exercise "Authority and Alpha Mastery" of the animal consciousness, and it will be your faithful and willing servant.., **But,** *if the Alpha master should prove to be weak, and gives in to the desires of the animal mind, then it becomes an* **unruly cur,** *and exercises it's will over the conscious mind.., which could be disastrous!!!...*

Now.., having identified ("Named") the sub-conscious entity as "separate and distinct", we now can exercise *conscious control* (power) over it!.. We can train this "dog", (this valued and intelligent animal) by "conditioned response" (see: "Pavlov"), because there are certain things that this animal consciousness *is better at* than it's Alpha Conscious counterpart!.. For instance; *the survival instinct*, which will react in the animal consciousness even before the Conscious mind is aware of it!., and if the animal be trained (in the Martial Art *"Karate"*, for instance), then our faithful companion and protector (with *instant* response time) will be transformed into the proverbial "junk-yard dog" at a moments notice, saving you from harm or even death!!! The same is true with sports.., we practice and practice, training this sub-conscious animal to react in a certain way, and it will, if we don't interfere with it at the crucial moment *(read: Zen, and the Art of Archery)...* We can inhibit our performance by trying "too hard" at the Conscious level, when the sub-conscious has an *instinctual and effortless accuracy,* like the trained seal at the circus; catching, balancing, and tossing balls through hoops, with effortless precision and accuracy!.. It is the Conscious mind that learns the dance steps, but it is the sub-conscious that feels the rhythm, and does the dance in harmony with the beat... To do the dance consciously, is to have "two left feet"!., and incidentally.., the same is true of the sex act, which if done instinctually and naturally is harmonious and satisfying, but done "intellectually", is to have problems...

There are about 400 species in the dog family, with about 100 of these species having been produced (bred) within the last 100 years... Each and every one of these dogs; from the petite "Mexican Chihuahua" to the massive "St. Bernard".., and the short legged "Dachshund" to the swift "Greyhound".., are all the direct (or indirect) descendents of *"Canis Lupus"*; the "Wolf".., and each one of these breeds are a marvel of adaptation and specialization, having differing characteristics and personalities that guarantee their survival value as "man's best friend"... So flexible are these adaptive modifications, that variations will show up even in "purebred" species...

I am somewhat amused by Charles Darwin, who traveled around the world to the Galapagos Islands to observe the adaptive modifications of birds and lizards, which he attributed to his "theory" of Evolution *(a "cult" of the 20th Century)*, but he failed to notice the plethora of dog species in his own back yard!..

In the same way that dogs have the ability of adaptive modifications, so too the human animal also has this ability, although the modifications are within much narrower parameters... But nevertheless, we have the varieties of "color", and the characteristics of "ethnic diversification" which makes each and every one of us *a different animal with a different heritage*, which makes us all uniquely different *at the sub-conscious level!..* So all sub-consciousnesses are not alike!.. Each one of us has this "heritage" that *if we know about;* we can take into consideration and deal with, and sometimes even compensate for, which gives us a better understanding of just "Who" we are...

It must also be noted, that this sub-conscious animal (our "Temple" counterpart) can be harmed, and it's spirit broken!.. This can be completely independent of (and a vexation to) the Conscious mind... Dog trainers that train German Shepherds to be guard dogs know (for instance) that if a young dog is defeated in a dog fight with a larger dog.., or beaten severely by it's owner (made to "cower").., his pride and dignity have been compromised, and he will lose his "leader of the pack" Alpha male status.., and his ears will flop over!!. A floppy eared German Shepherd is not only a sad sight to behold, but his value as a guard dog is greatly diminished, as well as his aggressiveness, and he is less favored by the female dogs, who's instinct is to breed with the top Alpha male "leader of the pack"... So dog trainers are very careful to not let this type of incident happen, especially in the "formative year" of the young dog's life...

So too in the human animal (our sub-conscious "Temple" counterpart)... Any severe trauma, at any stage of life (but especially in the formative years) can leave a lasting "scar" on the psyche of the sub-conscious mind, resulting in a phobia (a deep set fear) of that which caused the trauma (such as a severe injury to the body, *or to the dignity,* of the human animal mind)!.. Generally speaking, the Conscious mind takes precedence and overrides the inclinations of the animal mind, but the deep-set fear (phobic result of injury) will cause the animal to react in ways inconsistent with and contrary to the intent of the Conscious mind!!. The Conscious mind may not even recall the traumatic incident and even be baffled by the illogic of these "irrational fears", but the sub-conscious knows only too well!.. Attempts made to psychoanalyze and rationalize these fears away at the Conscious level will be largely ineffective... The phobia must be dealt with at the sub-conscious level, either by hypnosis or by some type of gradual step-by-step confrontational therapy...

Now there is, at this present time in our history, a severe trauma to the sub-conscious mind, that *(due to ignorance)* is coming to be "accepted"*!!*. That severe trauma to the sub-conscious mind is **"Sodomy"!!**. The *"Supreme" Court* [3] has decided (in their infinite wisdom) that sodomy is o.k.!!! *Sodomy is NOT o.k.!!.*

This book is dedicated to the fact that the human body (our sub-conscious "animal" counterpart) is the ***Temple of God,*** housing the Spirit and Soul of Man, and sodomy, is the "desecration and defilement" of the Temple .., **a *Heinous* crime!.,** against both God and Man...

For the male animal to be sodomized *(profanely dominated, **(subjugated)** and violated by anal penetration)* [4], is to become **"used"** and "degraded" to the status of surrogate female!!. Having been "dominated" by another male, his pride and dignity have been crushed, his *spirit* has been broken, he loses his male status, his right to copulate with the females, and even the ability and desire!!. He has

---

[3] I don't think that there is any question that our "High Minded" forefathers.., who framed and signed the Constitution.., would be appalled at the recent Supreme Court decisions that ban "God", the "Ten Commandments", Religion and Morality in general from any influence (or even mention) from government.., or their secular decisions.., which opens the door to sodomy, pornography, perversion, abortion, profanity, etc. and etc... Our forefathers would have considered their Constitution to have been "hijacked", and the "hijackers" to be executed for moral "High Treason"... The "Spirit" of the law has been superceded by the "letter" of the law which can be interpreted to mean whatever the Supreme Court deems to be expedient!.. This "moral decay" has given our enemies (the terrorists) *"just cause"* against what they perceive as; "the Godless and immoral Infidel": ; America!!!

[4] I will be criticized for my "graphic language" here as being "politically incorrect" and offensive, by those who advocate the acceptance of this perversion as an alternate (and acceptable) "life style", with their duplicitous rationalization being:-- to describe this in plain language is (obviously) offensive and disgusting.., but it's o.k. to do it!..

been *"emasculated".!.* Despite the rationalizations of the Conscious mind, the sub-conscious animal mind knows and "feels" instinctively (at the gut level) that he has been degraded to surrogate female status, his psyche becomes confused, he begins to emulate female behavior, his movements become limp-wristed and swishy, his voice becomes sultry and effeminate, and his personality becomes; *"submissive"..,* etc., and etc... It is as though an "Alien" presence has taken over his personality.., and this is not a "gay" happening.., this is a *"Perversion"* and a tragedy!!. "Gay".., **is a lie!!...**

This *"lie"* can be accepted at the Conscious (intellectual) level under the guise of experimentation or sexual exploration, etc., without realizing the traumatic effect to the sub-conscious animal mind, and the realization comes only too late that he has been exploited and seduced by the clever words of a *liar.!.* He will watch in horror at the changes that become manifest in his personality, *(this is the true meaning of "homophobia")* and he will be forced into one of three options: he can acquiesce to the situation and become perverted into homosexuality.., he can become so despondent with self loathing that he commits suicide *(statistics are high)..,* or he can fight this "takeover" of his personality, and eventually come out of it (but the "scar" remains) and this "internal conflict" could go on for years, until the impact of the event is nullified by time...

There are several "aberrations" that can result from this trauma to the sub-conscious animal mind, *(which is part and counterpart of our being)...* The "victim" can join a religious order (Ministry, Monastery, Priesthood, etc.) to escape this perverted evil that threatens to consume his soul, only to eventually succumb to the perverted thoughts that invades his mind, and the Ministry, Monastery, Priesthood, etc. becomes contaminated... The victim can become married with children, and eventually succumb to the perversion, and the family is destroyed by this betrayal... Or the "Victim" can become so "twisted" by this perversion that he seeks to "dominate" other males, thereby soothing his wounded ego with this "ego boost", at the expense of weaker males, that are, in many cases, **Children!!!** It turns into a sick game of domination and subjugation, and those that have been subjugated seek to dominate, to soothe and bolster their wounded "Ego".., *with a series of serial seductions over their lifetime that can number into dozens, or hundreds!.,* and so.., this "sickness".., *this "contagious" disease..,* that contaminates even the Soul.., **spreads.., exponentially!!.**

So do not *ever* think that you can flirt with this perversion and remain unaffected!.. The archives of memory will not let you forget, and guilt and shame will pervade your soul, as you forever hide this shameful secret...

To be forewarned is to be forearmed... You have been warned!.. Knowledge is power, and there is power in the integrity of a clear conscience... Respect the dignity of your body, which is the "Temple" of the Lord... Enough said...

It is a mistake to think that the sub-conscious mind has anywhere near the discriminating or rationalizing capacity of the Conscious mind... It is similar in nature to the mind of a "dog", but with the ability of speech and with a greater capacity to learn simple tasks and repetitive procedures..; (for instance), it can learn to drive the car, and it knows the way home, and it will follow the flow of traffic very effectively, but if you want to stop at the grocery store on the way home, you better be paying attention, or you will pass it up and arrive home without your groceries!.. And (for instance:) the sub-conscious mind has learned to read, but with very little or no comprehension, and your Conscious mind can wander off, and the sub-conscious will continue reading (mentally sub-vocalizing), but with no absorption of content!., and you will have to re-read the material!.. And again (for instance), during hypnosis, the sub-conscious will obey commands to perform entertaining and even bizarre behaviors *without the questioning or discrimination that would be normal and obvious to the Conscious mind!!.* Without the Conscious mind to lead it, the sub-conscious is a very "simple-minded" animal...

To further illustrate the point (from my own experiences), although unable to experience the hypnotic state myself, I became adept at hypnotizing others, and this became known in my neighborhood and people would come to me for various self-improvement reasons (weight control, to stop smoking, etc.) and this mother came to me with her 12 year old daughter who was becoming "wild", and doing poorly in school, so I hypnotized her, giving her the post-hypnotic suggestions that she was a good girl and an excellent student in school, etc., and etc., and when she woke up she would be feeling good!.. She woke up totally drunk!!. She staggered around and giggled incoherently!!. I was in a panic.!. What had I done wrong!?? The mother explained that her father came home quite often "feeling good", and "feeling good" was a euphemism for being totally drunk!!. So I re-hypnotized her with the instruction that she would be feeling wonderful and refreshed!.. All was well... But the point being made here is that the sub-conscious is a simple and uncomplicated animal that will take things literally (this is called: a response to "organ language") instead of in the context intended.., so you must be careful how you frame your hypnotic suggestions, even for self hypnosis...

The sub-conscious mind, being a separate and distinct entity, is ever with us, and the relationship is one of "unified teamwork" under the direction of the Conscious mind, if the attention be focused.., but the perceptions and observations of the sub-conscious animal can be independent from the Conscious mind, especially if the Conscious mind be preoccupied... The sub-conscious is "body conscious", and self preservation conscious, aware of it's immediate environment, and may notice things that the Conscious mind is unaware of, (and vise-versa)... This sub-conscious memory record can sometimes be tapped as a resource (by hypnosis) as an adjunct to the Conscious memory record...

But caution must be exercised here, because the sub-conscious is very amenable to suggestion, and lacking the cognitive and discriminative faculties, it can be easily led down the road of imaginative "fantasy" in response to suggestion, and it can be very inventive!!. Lacking the cognitive and discriminative faculties, there isn't much difference between reality and fantasy, and being led by the suggestion of the hypnotist, the hypnotized subject will react to the fantasy scenario as though it were real!!. It is for this reason, that information extracted under hypnosis is not always reliable... So again, the trained hypnotist must be very careful about how the questions are framed, in order to prevent the "fantasy scenario" syndrome...

Whoever coined the term; "the power of suggestion".., knew what he was talking about!., because the suggestion is far more powerful and potent than a command!!. A command can be evaluated, disagreed with, and disobeyed.., but a suggestion is far more subtle, in that it *implies* a truth that is not consciously evaluated, but is *assumed* to be the truth, and you will act on that *assumption* as though it were the fact.., *and it may not be!!.* The advertising industry knows this only too well, and it is effectively aimed at both the Conscious and sub-conscious minds, and it is a form of mind control that is reminiscent of "black magic", and the casting of spells!!.., and the sub-conscious mind is even less discriminating than the Conscious mind, and is prone to act on the assumption!!... **But now you know!!..,** and now that you know, look at those advertisements again, and find the "hidden assumptions", beyond the words, that "imply" that if you smoke this kind of cigarette you will become this "rugged cowboy" type of individual, or if you drink this particular drink you will become this "svelte socialite".., etc., and etc., and just realize to what extent you have been influenced by suggestions.., *at the sub-conscious level!..* This *subliminal* influence of suggestion, the simple un-discriminated against acceptance of an *"assumption"*, is so powerful, and so pervasive, that double-blind testing of all drugs are required because "the placebo effect" can be more powerful than the drug itself!!. In other words, the medical remedy of the "Lipragus" pill can cure you of your disease!!... *("Lipragus" is "sugar pill" spelled backwards)!!...* "As a man believes in his heart, so he is"... It would amaze you, just how many of your Beliefs *(your most "potent" beliefs)* are really just simple assumptions... So.., do you believe (for instance) in astrology??.., that your destiny and your personality are dictated by the stars??., or are you just succumbing to the suggestion, and letting the stars dictate the content of your personality and the direction of your life, like a hypnotized subject, driven by the suggestions of the hypnotist??... You must be very careful what you believe....

And dreams.., We know that dogs, and animals dream, and so too the human animal sub-conscious mind dreams, and the dreams are often chaotic, random access memory fragments, directionless, and quite often the dreams are about "fears"... The conscious mind (while asleep) can observe these dreams, and try to make sense of them, but mostly it disregards them as the "fantasy dream world" of the sub-conscious, and forgets them... But the sub-conscious is the seat of the emotions, and it "feels" the emotional impact of anger and hatred (and pumps adrenaline), it feels embarrassment (and will blush), it feels sexual attraction (with physical responses), it feels even love and affection, it feels possessiveness, it feels jealousy, it feels rejection, it feels intimidation, it feels loss of dignity, etc., and etc., and it "fears" emotional pain... The analysis of dreams can reveal the content of these sub-conscious fears that may not be acknowledged at the Conscious level...

But the subject of dreams is far more complicated and differentiated than can be adequately covered in this brief treatise of the sub-conscious mind, with the "different types" of dreams, that link up to the imagination, and are quite creative, having involved plots and sub-plots, and there are those very special "Psychic Dreams".., *(where the Super-Conscious communicates with the Conscious mind via the sub-conscious dream state in symbolic form)*[5] that would require a "book within this book" to discuss.., and I am probably not adequately qualified to present myself as an authority on this subject.., even though I am keenly aware of my personal dream content, which is abundant!.. (I have *vivid* dreams)...

The Conscious mind (the Spiritual being) experiences "life" through the physical body, and gives it direction and purpose in accordance with the intelligence it possesses (or not?) and will hopefully guide it through the experience and adventure of life with a minimum of physical and emotional pain... So integrated are we into the body consciousness, that the distinction between Conscious and sub-conscious is not perceived, and "We" feel these emotions, and those things that we fear are revealed to us in our dreams, because we dream about what we fear!.. We dream about what the Conscious mind fears, and we dream about what the sub-conscious mind fears... So there is this feed-back effect, with the sub-conscious influencing the Conscious mind, and the Conscious mind influencing the sub-conscious.., and it seems to be an integrated whole, and for all intents and purposes, it is...

There are times when it may seem that the sub-conscious is working at cross-purposes to the Conscious mind, for instance; someone made the observation that it is very difficult for men and women to be "just friends" (not always true), but why is this?.. Because, although the relationship is intended (by the Conscious mind) to be "platonic".., the sub-conscious animal may feel sexual inclinations!., and this may be true for both the male and female "friends".., even though such a relationship would be inappropriate!.. There may be a direct communication between the two sub-conscious minds, with subliminal communications signaling willingness or non availability, attraction, or rejection, or non interest, etc., and this complete scenario can go on (and usually does) with the Conscious mind being totally unaware!!. The integrity of the Conscious mind must ever exercise authority over these sub-conscious instinctual inclinations... The sub-conscious is sometimes referred to as the "lower mind", and it is important to understand the mechanisms involved...

Similarly (for instance again), the Conscious mind may fancy itself as "the hero"!., only to find the sub-conscious instinct for self preservation so strong, that our "hero" turns tail and runs!!, and sometimes the opposite is true, and our timid hero (in the moment of self preservation) turns into the "junkyard dog" and vanquishes the foe, much to the surprise of the Conscious mind!.. Not all sub-conscious minds are created equal, but each one can be trained, and each one **should be trained** (by learning the "Martial Arts", good habits, good "instincts", etc.)... You will find the sub-conscious mind to be the most valuable, willing, and obedient servant, if you exercise the self discipline required to train it... Knowledge is power.., and *You are* the "Hero"!..

* * *   * * *

As far as I know.., my observations and conclusions about the "separate and distinct" roles of the Conscious and sub-conscious mind are an original finding, and having made these observations a long time ago (in the mid 1960's) has given me the opportunity to observe these interactions in many different circumstances, which support and explain my conclusions.., but there are many other contributions of science that support this evidence…

The first clue came with the "split brain" experiments at McGill University, in 1961 (?)... In order to cure the multiple daily occurrences of "grand mall" seizures that would no doubt have resulted in the death of the patient, a drastic operation was performed to save his life... The connecting "link" between the left and right hemispheres of the brain (the corpus callosum) was severed!.. The seizures stopped, and the patients life was saved, but with one very interesting side effect!; the patient now had two separate brains in one body!!. The only link now, between the left

---

[5] On this subject of "psychic dreams".., which has to do with the spiritual advancement of the Soul, on this journey through Life.., the reader is referred to the book: "The Symbolic and the Real", by "Ira Progoff"..., (McGraw-Hill, 1973)…

brain and the right brain, was through the eyes and ears, (which both saw and heard the same thing) and both brains having the same information, they cooperated as though normal.., but in subsequent tests, where the sight and sound was prevented.., the right hand and the left hand functioned independently of each other!.. The left hand did not know (literally) what the right hand was doing!.. Other anomalies occurred, as when the patient embraced his "lady friend" with his right arm, and his left arm rudely pushed her away!!. And in another patient there was the phenomenon called: "Alien Hand".., in which the left hand "entity" was antagonistic to the right hand "entity", as (for instance), when the right hand would attempt to write a letter, the left hand would do everything possible to prevent it!.. The patient described his life as: "living in Hell"!...

Generally speaking, the nature of the sub-conscious mind is subservience and cooperation to the Conscious mind, and mirrors the interests and intentions of the Conscious mind, because of it's training by association, and there is a constant "feedback" monitoring system in place (via the corpus callosum), but we can see from the above example the independent identity *and nature* of the sub-conscious, which may be influenced by an "Ethnic heritage", or harbors hidden motives (anger, jealousies, revenge, etc.) that the Conscious mind may be unaware of… In the final analysis (to reiterate).., "The Conscious mind must ever exercise authority over the subconscious instinctual inclinations"… Being aware of these independent sub-conscious inclinations gives the Conscious mind the opportunity and responsibility to utilize this feedback mechanism to program a healthy attitude and positive direction *training by association* into our sub-conscious minds.., and the resulting feedback from the healthy and positive sub-conscious to the Conscious is an added boost to our endeavors!!.. **Single minded teamwork.., Wins!!!..**

* * *

BOOK IX

"The Great Debates"

Meanwhile.., back at the ashram (pardon me for digressing), the course in Yoga at the School of Yoga[1], under the tutelage of the good Swami, was nearing its end. It was one of the last fireside chats, concerning states of awareness, and the Swami was coming to the end of his summation with the statement of:.. "You have to know that you know"... Without being recognized, I answered back;.. Yes, but after you "know that you know", then all that is necessary, is that you simply.., "just know"!.. Another of the students shot back at me; "Well it's for sure YOU don't know"!., expressing his indignation that I would presume to correct my teacher... No no no, the Swami interjected, it's alright... He welcomed the debate, and he was more than adequate to the challenge... It was my position that to "know that you know", represented a duality, and as such was an impediment to the state of absorption in which the knower and that which is known, becomes one... Yes, he answered back, but the knowledge resides in that thing which is to be known, and if you become absorbed without knowing that you know, where are you?.. We went back and forth a couple of times, but the Swami's logic was irrefutable, and I had to concede the point.., to the great glee of my classmates...

Considering the short period of time that I had spent under the Swami's tutelage, his effect on my life and thinking has been very profound and long lasting. I will always remember him with gratitude... The "little debate" that I had lost to him, had major consequences... I had become immersed in the teachings and philosophies of Buddhism, and this was the point of view that I was expressing in the debate… Without being aware of it, I had hit on the basic and fundamental conflict between Buddhism and Hinduism.., and also between Buddhism and Christianity, Judaism, Islam, etc.., which is;., the question of the Soul.., and of God...

This little debate continued to plague me for years afterward and interjected itself "in my face" every time I came upon an ambiguous viewpoint regarding "The Eastern School" of thought versus the "Western School" of thought.

Without ever directly confronting this conflict, I had adopted and embraced the teachings of Buddhism... I had spent time in Buddhist monasteries... I had been "initiated" into the "Sanga".., the community of meditators, and I had been given "secret" techniques of meditation that had been handed down for centuries, that were specific to Buddhism...

My "Bibles" of the moment were the Evans-Wentz translations of the texts of the "Mahayana" (Called the "Northern School" of Tibetan Buddhism).., the "Pali canon", and the "Vissudahmagga", which were the texts of the "Theravada" branch of Buddhism (referred to as the "Southern School" of Buddhism)... The "Theravada" or "Southern School" comprising most of Southern India, Sri Lanka, Burma, and Thailand... The "Northern School" of the "Mahayana" (Great Vehicle) traveled to Tibet, and on into China, Korea, and Japan, being modified into different schools by the influence of Hinduism, Taoism, Confucianism, Zen, etc., but they all have their roots in the historical Buddha.

It is interesting to note, that there are about as many different "sects" of Buddhism, as there are denominations of Christianity.., and each sect has it's own variation of the understanding of the Buddhist scriptures (called the "Pali" canon).., and each school has developed it's own technique of meditation... But they all have one thing in common.., they deny the existence of the Soul.., and of God...

How can this be?.. How can this possibly be?.. This is not just some variation of the understanding of scripture.., this is the basic fundamental "cornerstone", from which all other deductions and suppositions follow suit... There is no middle ground here.., there are only two possible

---

[1] It was the "Bihar School of Yoga", founded (in 1963) by my teacher (Guru) "Swami Satyananda Saraswati", that I attended and received a certificate of graduation, which qualified me to be a teacher of the fundamental principles of the Yoga and the techniques of meditation, some of which are presented here in this book…

conclusions... Absolutely true.., or Absolutely false...

I would like to think that if Jesus and Buddha were to ever meet, they would be the best of friends, and I am sure they would be, because the Truth is the Truth, and there would be no disagreements between them... So I can only attribute this discrepancy to a misunderstanding... But how did this misunderstanding come about?.. This is the question.

Prince Siddhartha Gotama.., gave up a throne to go in search of enlightenment, and having achieved it, became "Buddha".., (The Enlightened One)... He did not glory in it for himself alone, but spread the knowledge of this event to as much of mankind as he was able, so that all men.., and women.., could also achieve Enlightenment, and be emancipated...

The Buddha came approximately 500 years before the Birth of Christ, and He wrote nothing down himself, nor was there anything written concerning him for approximately 600 years after his death. His teachings were handed down through an oral tradition, until they were finally written down in the "Pali" language, which (like Latin) is no longer in use. Since then, there has been so much written about him that it is difficult to find the real Siddhartha Gotama from the idealized and romanticized legend [2]... Since the exact wording of the teachings of the Buddha are not recorded, all the teachings attributed to him begin with the statement: "Thus have I heard"..., etc.

Thus have I heard: The Conqueror, (Buddha)..,
….. Etc. & Etc…

---

[2] In the introduction to his very scholarly book; "Buddhist Scriptures" , (Penguin Books 1959) the eminent Professor " Edward Conze" (PhD., and Vice-President of the Buddhist Society) writes: "The bulk of authoritative Buddhist writings is truly enormous, and covers tens and hundreds of thousands of pages. The Pali Canon (Siamese Edition) fills 45 huge volumes, exclusive of commentaries. Both the Chinese and Japanese scriptures consist of 100 volumes of 1000 closely printed pages each, while the Tibetan extends to 325 volumes... The available material would, of course, be very much reduced if we could restrict ourselves to the words of the Buddha Himself, but alas, this cannot be done… For the first 500 years the Scriptures were orally transmitted, and only written down at the beginning of the Christian era (A.D. 100 and 400), in other words about 600 to 900 years after the Buddha's demise"…

.... As I wandered on (through the Sangsara) my collection of books grew... My personal library, in which I perused the writings of the great Buddhist, Hindu, and Zen thinkers and philosophers, as well as the Translations of the Mahayana and Pali texts, books on Buddhism, Buddha, the Upanashads, the Bhagdva-Gita, The Vedas, Patanjali's Yoga, etc... Books old, and books new... Soon I was traveling with a back pack on my back with books in it, and also a doctors valise that opened wide at the top, and had a wide flat bottom, filled with books... I have had many great teachers, most of them from books...

One of my teachers stated that; "It is better to read a good book twice, than a multitude of books just once"... There is a feed-back effect that happens when you read a book twice. All of the knowledge that you comprehended at the end of the book is re-introduced and reapplied into the book by a second reading, and comprehension and understanding are greatly increased, leading to contemplation and even greater understanding, leading to an intuitive leap!;.. Aha!... And when you read several books, in random rotational order, and then read them again, in random rotational order, the feed-back effect is overlapping, from one book to another, compounding itself into a "Compendium of Knowledge"... The Great;... "Aha"!.. Also known as;.. an "Epiphany"...

..... A couple of years had passed, since my "little debate" with the Swami, and I was living in Afghanistan at the time... I was smoking a lot of Hashish and re-reading the philosophical works of J. Krishnamurti... He was a philosopher-writer of many books, extolling the virtues of the selfless state of mind, over the selfish motivations of the Ego, and showing how these conflicting motivations work themselves out on the stage of life... His writings had that distinct "ring of truth" to them, and there was "no contest" with any of his conclusions, and you would say "Yeah", as you were reading the book.., but when you were done reading the book, you went back to your Ego centered life...

Krishnamurti was criticized for so brilliantly elucidating the problem, without providing a method for the solution to the problem, namely;.. How do you achieve this transition from the Ego centered consciousness to the much more desirable "Natural" state?.. Krishnamurti, frustrated by the question, was heard to reply; "You just do it, damn it"!!...

Krishnamurti was not known as a teacher of Zen, but I learned about Zen while reading his book!.. As I was reading, it suddenly occurred to me!., (I caught the thread that runs through his writings), and I said;., (out loud).., "He's saying the same thing"!.. Every chapter, paragraph, and sentence, he is saying the same thing!.. Every book he writes, every example he makes, he's saying the same thing!.. And I saw it clearly.., the solution to the Zen paradox...

And not only the understanding of Zen, but also the understanding of the Nature of consciousness, and with the understanding of that.., the solution to the paradox of Buddhism.., and the Soul... It was so simple.., and yet, so subtle.., so easily missed and so easily misunderstood...

I searched again the Mahayana scriptures, with new understanding.., and it was there!!. I searched through the Hindu scriptures, the interplay of Shiva-Shakti.., and it was there!!. I searched through the writings of the Zen masters, of the Yin and the Yang.., and it was there!!. I searched through the Old Testament, to the fall of Adam and Eve.., and it was there!!. I searched through the New Testament, to the "State of Grace", and the "Pure State", ...and it was there!!... I searched the Void.., to the "Word" that was *with* God.., and the "Word", that *was* God.., *and Yes.., it was especially evident, even there!!...*

But, should I just tell you so easily?.. Should I just tell you the solution to the Zen riddle?., that has plagued and confused Mankind for centuries... Should I unlock the paradox?.. YES!.. I will, and it is my pleasure to do so, but first I must remind you of the words of the Buddha, *(in essence);..* "You must ever be ready to reject a doctrine, even though it be of great antiquity and believed by many people.., in the light of (yogically revealed) Truth"... Thus spake the Buddha... (*)

The "Pure" state, the "Zen" state, the "Natural" state, the "Selfless" state, the "State of Grace".., and the ***"Objective"*** state.., are all the same state!!...

I have identified all of these states of consciousness with the "Objective" state... So you see.., it is not that far away, and it is very attainable... This is the good news...

Many have searched for this state, and were unable to discover it.., because, paradoxically, the more you chase after it, the more it eludes you!.. The more you desire it, the more it recedes from you!.. The more you try to solve the problem, the more paradoxical it becomes!.. The harder you try, the farther away you are!!. It is only when you stop trying, that you are there!!! This is the summary of the writings of the Zen masters, and they are enough to make the most dedicated of students want to pull their hair out by the roots.., and yet the solution is there!., in plain sight...

The shift from Self consciousness to Objective consciousness *is accomplished* by a shift in attention from those thoughts that pertain to self, to those thoughts of an object outside our self (or a subject of contemplation not pertaining to self)... ***Succinctly stated;.. Simple as that!!.*** "You just do it, damn it"!.., and you do it without realizing it.., *effortlessly!!!...*

The "Self" consciousness can only know of the "Objective" consciousness in retrospect... Any effort made by self-consciousness to attain objective consciousness is self defeating!.. You can only "forget yourself" into it by shifting your attention to the "object" (or subject) of your observations... The keenness of your interest (in the object or subject) determines the depth of your "absorption" into the subject matter to the *exclusion* of all other things, *(especially your "self")*... The more keen your interest (in the object or subject), the greater the absorption "into-it", and the more "intuitive" you become... This is the state where it is reported that;.. "The Observer.., and the thing which he observes.., becomes One"... At the first glimmer of self awareness, the Zen-objective state is lost...

To understand the nature of the riddle, you first have to understand the nature of Consciousness, which has a dual nature... It is referred to in the Hindu scriptures as "Shiva-Shakti", or, the "Objective" consciousness (Shiva), and the "Identity" consciousness (Shakti)... Now, you must understand that there are NOT two separate consciousnesses that are involved here, but only ONE consciousness in two separate modes... The Identity consciousness, that knows itself "to be".., and the Objective consciousness that knows the "object" outside of itself, and "other" than itself...

The "shift" of this One Consciousness.., from the Identity mode to the Objective mode, and back again to the Identity mode, is instantaneous, undetectable, absolutely effortless, and spontaneous... So subtle and so effortless, that you do this several times a day, and you never realized it and you never identified the "Objective" State from the "Identity" state...

This is literally; "the sound of one hand clapping"... On the one hand, you have the presence of the "Identity Consciousness" (without any trace of Zen-objectivity).., and on the other hand, you have the "Objective (state of) Consciousness" (without any trace of "Self")... Hence, each hand has a separate function that excludes the other, and never do the two separate hands (modalities) function at the same time, because there is only One hand in an either-or situation... Hence, "the sound of one hand clapping"!.. Riddle solved!.. Shiva Consciousness, and Shakti Consciousness, do not know each other, even though they are one and the same...

The nature of Shiva Consciousness.., or Objective Consciousness, is that it focuses it's attention on the "object" of it's interest, to the exclusion of everything else... It is absorbing information about the "object", and it is absorbed in analyzing the "object", and for that moment, nothing else exists, except that object... and concentration on that object is total, perfect, and effortless... While the analysis of the object is taking place, there is no thought of Self, there is no time, there is no pleasure or pain, there is no desire, there is no emotion.., there is only; the "object"...

The nature of Shakti Consciousness, the Identity Consciousness, more commonly known as "Self Consciousness".., is that it knows itself "to be".., and as such, it has an identity.., and it has desires, emotions, wants, needs, pleasures, pains, and etc...

You can see why the Zen-Objective state of consciousness (the "Selfless" state), is so highly prized over the Self Conscious state, to which the Buddhists attribute every kind of selfish and evil act... *The mistake* is that they try to annihilate the Self Conscious state to achieve the Selfless Zen objective state.., And it cannot be done... This is a philosophical error...

There is no Shiva without Shakti, and there is no Shakti without Shiva... Shakti is absorbed into Shiva in the Objective state, and Shiva is absorbed into Shakti in the Self Conscious state... It is One consciousness, with two separate modalities, and as such, it is already perfect, and it is by this process of "shifting" modalities, that it knows.., that it knows...

So.., the Swami was correct!!, you have to know that you know... And this "One" consciousness, with the interplay of it's two modalities.., that knows that it knows.., *It is none other.., **than the Soul!!!**...*

This is the Irrefutable fact, and it should come as "good news", to the Buddhists, who have heretofore refuted this fact, because this fact confers on them Immortality, where before this "good news", they were looking at "annihilation" of the Self (the Soul) as the remedy for suffering.., and it cannot be done... With this "good news";., "Death, is swallowed up in Victory"!...

Contrast this with the "Triple Gem" of the Hindu Brahman culture, of which Siddhartha Gotama was a practicing member... "Existence-Knowledge-Bliss", is the "Triple Gem".., with "Existence" being the first and foremost Truth of the "Soul".., which is the embodiment of the "Triple Gem"...

Now obviously.., The "Triple Gem" philosophy of the Hindus (Christians, & etc.), and the "Self and Soul" negating philosophy of the Buddhists are diametrically opposed to each other.., with the obvious conclusion that one of these philosophies is correct, and the other is fundamentally flawed and incorrect!.. The "Triple Gem" philosophy is correct, optimistic, life affirming, and true.., and the Buddhist concept is Self negating, pessimistic, fundamentally flawed (leading to gross intellectualism), and simply; untrue... A philosophical error!.. **Somebody** *has to say it!..*

It seems that I have belabored the above facts with redundant repetition, but it seems that these facts are of a very subtle nature and difficult to comprehend, leading to much confusion and misconception, even when spoken of in straight forward language... You can imagine the difficulty of an enlightened teacher trying to transmit this knowledge to a student of base mentality... Misconceptions arise... And you can imagine the misconceptions that arise when this knowledge is transmitted orally from Teacher to student, and that student becomes Teacher to other students of base mentality, who in turn hand this down.., etc,. and etc., over a period of 600 years before it was written down, and even then, it is a misinterpretation of a misconception.., resulting in an idealized "Zen state" that has now become inconceivable and almost unattainable.., at the expense of the "Self" (the Soul) that is denigrated, denied, and to be annihilated... This is the fundamental philosophical error that leads to other errors...

Such is the nature of that "variegated cloak";.., the cloak of words...

Words fail us... Among all the teachings of the Buddha, that of non-soul (Pali; anatta), is considered to be of the utmost importance. But the state of "non-soul" is easily achievable when the "shift" from self consciousness to objective consciousness takes place!.. When the "Shakti" consciousness is "swallowed up" (absorbed) in "Shiva" consciousness...

But, was this the realization that transformed Siddhartha Gotama into the Buddha?.. No, of course not... He had a much more profound experience than that!..

What I have described above, is called the meditation with "seed".., where the objective consciousness is absorbed in the analyses of the object, or subject (seed) of it's enquiry... All profound contemplations start with this "seed" meditation.., but Siddhartha pursued this "seed" meditation to it's ultimate conclusion;., the meditation "without seed"...

Words fail us... How to describe that "event"?.. That moment when "Isolation" is achieved... When the "consciousness principle" is isolated from the self reproductive thought process, and found to be "the observer" of the thought process, and found to be "other" than the thought process... This is called;.. "The first resting place"...

And then, with diligent effort, the thought process is brought to a complete standstill.., and the consciousness principle stands alone... It is at this point that the "train" of self reproductive thought has been broken.., and the next thought to occur is "original".., and not a consequence of preceding thoughts...

It is at this point in the meditation when "phenomena" occurs.., independent and original, and from a source not before tapped into... It is "fifth dimensional" and intuitive... It is vision and revelation... It is knowledge and wisdom... This is the "second resting place"... This is where Siddhartha was tempted by the celestial nymphs of the inner realms of the Deva worlds, but Siddhartha declined the invitation... The Ultimate questions had not yet been answered...

With strong determination, he brought himself back to "Isolation", and to the complete and utter cessation of the thought process and all internal phenomena, to the "final resting place"... To that place of utter and absolute stillness.., to the Void itself... The Realm of Brahma.., the foundation of the Universe...

Siddhartha stood alone in the Great Void, and perceived that he himself was of the nature of voidness, having neither definable location, nor a center, nor a circumference..., He was simply a consciousness principle, devoid of characteristics, standing alone in the Void, and by the natural function of the Shiva-Shakti "shift", he became "One" with the Void.., He became.., "Buddha"... And by the natural function of the "Shakti-Shiva shift", He knew that he knew.., but how to explain it?..

For seven weeks, the Conqueror, Siddhartha Gotama, the Buddha, remained under the shade of the Bo tree, the place of his enlightenment, basking in the glory of his enlightenment, and contemplating the task before him;.. "How to explain it"?.. And should he even try?...

The task was enormous... everything was a paradox... To try and explain the Void alone, was an impossibility (it is, but it isn't).., the "Consciousness principle", (it is, but without substance or any identifying characteristics).., and the consciousness principle ceases to be, when it becomes absorbed into the Void (which isn't.., but this is the reality).., and yet, the consciousness principle that is nothingness, and became absorbed into nothingness, and ceased to be.., returns to tell the story!!. But, to whom?.. A world of mundane and shallow humanity that couldn't comprehend it, and really doesn't care, anyway?... It was futility!..

The Buddha correctly ascertained, that even if he could communicate the enlightenment to his closest disciples, that the teachings would ultimately become corrupted.., by the variegated cloak of words, and by the mundane mind of man... He saw this clearly, and He stated it plainly… (*)

At first, He decided against it.., to try and communicate the incommunicatable.., is futility... *(It is said that the Saints of all the realms, (both inner and outer) wept at this decision)*... But, as the Buddha could now see, with the "inner eye of his Buddha-vision", the desperate plight of a humanity steeped in ignorance, he was overcome.., with Compassion... Because of his great Compassion and love for humanity, he decided to teach... He reasoned, that if all of humankind were blind, and only one person could see, then perhaps all might eventually be led to the light, and see... *(It is said that all the Saints of all the realms rejoiced and celebrated at this decision)*... He had gained the "Ultimate All", and there was nothing else to be gained by any further labor... His only motivation was Compassion, and Compassion.., is the nature.., of a Buddha...

So,.. the "Consciousness Principle", which is composed of nothingness, became absorbed into the Void, which is Absolute nothingness,.. and in the Absolute stillness of "That" Absolute nothingness, the "Consciousness Principle" of Siddhartha Gotama.., ceased to be... And yet He was, and He knew!., and He knew that He knew... And then He returned to tell the story!.. What is this, if it is not evidence of the Soul?.. This is the irrefutable evidence!!... Siddhartha Gotama, the Buddha.., was a "Great Soul"... (Mahatma, Maha-purusa).

And with the "inner eye" of His Buddha-vision, He had distinct recollection of over 500 previous incarnations, and could recall them specifically, by name, place, occupation, and manner of death... What is this, if it be not evidence for the existence and survival of the Soul?.. *Everywhere,* is there evidence and support for the doctrine of Soul...

And yet, He spoke against the doctrine of the Soul,.. *Or Did He??,* or was He really speaking against the "Ego" of self consciousness?.. and how do you differentiate between what is Ego, what is Soul, what is the Mind, and what is the "Self"?.. Were there precise definitions?.. Was there any real understanding?.. We have seen the Zen paradox, where Ego consciousness is "swallowed up" (annihilated?) into Objective Consciousness, and there is no "abstract contemplation" when Ego is present, and what is Ego, but a Soul in ignorance of it's true nature, locked into it's "self centered" mode, as opposed to the "selfless" mode of objective consciousness...

ALL the religious leaders of ALL the religions of ALL the World have spoken against the sinful nature of the Ego centered self consciousness.., and they have ALL extolled the virtues of selflessness...

"Words" have failed us, here... "Words" have failed to communicate... And, although the "words" may have been only slightly different.., the message of the Buddha.., *was the same!!.*

The Buddha rejected as a "vile heresy" the notion that he was teaching a philosophy of his own, thought out by himself... "I have seen, He says, the Ancient way.., the Old Road that was taken by the formerly All-Awakened, and that is the path I follow".., and elsewhere he praises the Brahmans of old, who remembered the Ancient way, that leads to Brahma [3]...

I do not see division, here... I see Unity!.. And, if someone were to ask me what it was that I learned from Buddhism and from Zen, I would have to answer them truthfully;.. I learned about the Soul...

I present this to you, the reader, and to the "Sanga" of the Buddhist community.., NOT as an intellectual argument about a philosophical question.., but as a fact that I have personally verified through my own experience... It was while I was performing a Buddhist meditation technique, that I penetrated into the "fifth dimension" of the Deva realm, and found myself "to be", but without substance.., and without a center or circumference.., and yet.., I was!!. This was NOT a passive observation from an abstract viewpoint.., but rather as an active, awake, alert, self-possessed consciousness, filled with wonder, and asking questions that required answers... As I viewed the reality of the Deva world, in real time, my vision was perfectly clear, because "I" was the "eye".., and my "eye", was "I".., and "I", was astonished!.. After recovering my equilibrium from the astonishment, I tried again to locate "myself"... Sensing that I had the power of infinite expansion and contraction, I "scrunched down" within myself, condensing myself to the smallest infinite point.., and there was NOTHING!., and yet, I was... I had to conclude, that I was.., without substance...

---

[3]   This passage (as well as several others, here) is a condensation from the book: "Hinduism and Buddhism" by; Ananda K. Coomaraswamy.., in which he states that the Buddha is making a direct reference here to the *"Brahmacaria"* (translation: *"Walking with God")* !!, from the Hindu Brahman religious culture that Siddhartha practiced... All of these references are directly translated from the original "Pali Canon".., (100 to 600 A.D.)...

As a further reference, read: "The God of Buddha"..., by Jamshed K. Fozdar (Asia Publishing House, Inc., New York, 1973)...

(There was only; "I think, therefore I am").., and my thinking process (of analyses, deductions, and conclusions) was very clear and exceedingly "quick".., *and I was amazed!!...*

(The concept of "I think, therefore I am.", was never entertained or even considered during this experience. This is the obvious conclusion as viewed in retrospect). Indeed, the thought process is too slow and cumbersome. The quickness of the Self, through analysis to conclusion was almost instantaneous (simply apprehending the obvious and functioning from that knowledge instinctively).., and even quicker than quick, I observed the almost instantaneous process (that bypassed thought), *as it happened!!.,* and I was amazed (at my own "quicker than quick" quickness)!!...

And before this, in the "Iron Owl" experience, I went to another inner realm, and I searched for "myself".., with the exact same result... And I moved (at will) through both of these realms, with "unimpeded motion"... Wherever my attention was focused.., there I was!.. And I could see in the darkness (within the body of the Owl), by my own light...

And before this, as I sat in my living room, listening to the music of the great Masters, I became absorbed in the sound of the music, and to my own great astonishment, I became One with the music, *and I was the sound of the music...* The linear-logical mentality has difficulty conceiving of this, but the Soul (which is non substantive) and the sound (which is also non substantive) had not the slightest difficulty with the absorption and identification into the Oneness of the sound... *I was sound itself!!.*

This is neither conjecture or supposition... This is my experience... I had made three diligent searches for "myself", on these two separate occasions, as well as the third occasion when "I" had been absorbed into non-substantive sound.., *and I am here to testify to the reality of this fact!..*

The Buddha, describing his own attainments, states: "I can remember my former habitations (purva-nivasa; past lives). Having been many, I am one.., being one, I can become many.., I can realize whatever countless powers I will;.. seen or unseen, I can pass through a wall or a mountain as if it were air.., I can sink into the earth and emerge from it as though it were water.., I can walk on the water as though it were solid earth.., I can move through the air like a bird.., I can touch with my hands the Sun and the Moon.., I am a "mover at will", even so far as unto the realm of Brahma" (a.k.a.- the realm of **God!**- (Brahmaloka)...

The Buddha, like other orthodox teachers, forbids the public display of these powers, which are inherent in the Self, or the cultivation of these powers for their own sake.

"I do indeed possess these powers, of movement at will, mind reading, etc., but there is no comparison of these marvels, with the much farther reaching and far more productive marvel of my teaching".., and with His teachings, He set into motion; "The Wheel Of The Law"..., The Holy "Dharma"...

"Thus have I heard".., As the Buddha left the shade of the Bo tree, the place of His enlightenment, He encountered a group of young men who enquired of Him if He had seen a particular woman that had robbed them of their valuables while they slept, and could He help them find her? The Buddha replied;.. "Would it not be better if you were to find the "Self"?". (atmanam gavis)... They answered in the affirmative, were converted, and became the Buddha's disciples... Elsewhere, He gives the admonition; "Make the Self your refuge", and on the occasion preceding His death, He made this pronouncement; (in essence) "Be such as to have the Self (atman) as your lamp, Self as only refuge, and the Law (Darma) as lamp and refuge"...

Could the misunderstanding be as simple as this:.. That the "Eastern School" of thought views the Soul as synonymous with the Ego, while the "Western School" views the Soul as synonymous with the "Self"?.. YES!.. Because, in Truth, what we (of the Western School) call our self consciousness (the Ego), can NEVER approach abstract meditation, and without abstract meditation, there is no transcendence (the trance state of profound meditation, i.e. "Samadii")... The self conscious Ego can NEVER achieve the intuitive states of mind... It is only after the "shift" to the Zen-objective state, (the "selfless-Egoless" state of absorption in the object (or subject) of contemplation) that the profound states of meditation becomes possible... The greater the absorption into the subject (or object) of contemplation, the deeper and more profound becomes the "Samadii", and the more "intuitive" is your meditation.., and the moment that self conscious awareness (the "shift" back to Ego) dawns, in that instant, the "Samadii" is lost...

...And what is this "Consciousness Principle" that is intangible, indefinable, without substance, without circumference or center.., totally vacuous?.. Is it the same Ego that yesterday reveled in the flesh of this "Person"?.. Does this same "Person" even exist, or is he different today than he was yesterday, like a flame, born anew from moment to moment?.. Is he the same, or is he "new"?.. The answer to both of these opposing viewpoints, is "yes"... But if the Soul be identified with the base and tarnished Ego of yesterday, then the Soul be damned!., but if the Soul be identified with the "Self" that has gone through annihilation and rebirth, repeatedly, (the Shiva-Shakti "shift").., and ripened into transparency through knowledge, then the "Self" is immortal.., and nowhere does Buddhism deny the existence of the "Self"...

Indeed, the Mahayana scriptures [4] confirm;..

"When one seeks one's mind in it's true state, it is found to be quite intelligible, although invisible. In it's true state, mind is naked, immaculate, not made of anything, being of the voidness, clear, vacuous, without duality, transparent, timeless, uncompounded, unimpeded, colorless, not realizable as a separate thing, but as a unity of all things, yet not composed of them, of one taste, and transcendent over differentiation".

That is a very good description of the "Self" (found to be "quite intelligible")... But the term; "Self" is not used, in favor of the term; "Mind" for the very purpose that the Ego consciousness be not identified with the term; "Self"!., *(the Buddhists recognized the "variegated cloak" of words)...* While in other scriptures the mind is seen as something that is to be overcome, quieted down to the point of absolute stillness. The (mundane) mind is to be transcended!.. And still other scriptures that speak of the "Universe of Mind", and beyond mind, etc... These "multi-ordinal terms", are just another aspect of the variegated cloak of words: one word with a multitude of meanings (like Love), and one meaning that uses a multitude of interchangeable terms (that may have more than one meaning)... This is ripe ground for misinterpretations...

So how did this great misunderstanding.., this "Great Contradiction" come about???...

"The Compassionate Buddha".., realized that the "Enlightenment" could not be communicated by the variegated cloak of words,.. it could only be ***"experienced"...*** This "experience" is beyond any religious belief system.., in fact, belief systems are an impediment to the dispassionate and quiet state of mind required to achieve the "utter cessation" of the thought process.., *which is to be transcended!..* To this end he established the "monastery system" that was Non-Sectarian in nature, and only guided by rules of conduct, with the primary emphasis on the "technique" of the meditation used to acquire the "quiet" state of mind... He also instituted a monastery system for Women, which prior to this time, had never been done.., for religious reasons!..

It is interesting to note that there was (later on) dissention in the monastery system because of what was perceived as "lack of discipline".., but this was intentionally instituted by the Buddha who Himself had practiced strict discipline and religious conviction, fasting to the point of emaciation, and to the brink of death!!. The Buddha correctly ascertained, that if He had died, as a result of his religious conviction and strict discipline (fasting to the point of emaciation and death), that the Enlightenment would never have happened, and the knowledge He acquired would never have been transmitted!!. He had come to the brink of death, *and failure*, by religious conviction and strict discipline!.. He taught (the parable) of the stringed musical instrument, that if the string is too lax, it is out of tune, and if the string is too tight (strict discipline), it is also out of tune, and the string will break, and the instrument will be ruined... It is only when the string is "just right" that the instrument is capable of beautiful music... Thus was born the doctrine of "The Middle Way".., and the non-sectarian approach of the Buddhist monastery system... But it is difficult to understand how "God" fell out of favor with the monastery system, when prayer and ritual were still a part of the monastic daily life.., but prayer to Whom??. This is the nebulous question... This is the "Great Contradiction"...

Then came the "Intellectual" philosophers.., who made such pronouncements as:.. "If you see

---

[4] This is taken from "The Tibetan Book of the Great Liberation" by: W.Y. Evans-Wentz (Oxford University Press, 1954, page 211).., under the heading; "the seeing of reality", with the document heading: (Mind In It's True State)...

(encounter) the Buddha on the path.., *kill Him"!!!*... The (intellectual) idea here, is that you were not to venerate the Buddha (or God), because this would be an impediment to your ultimate goal, which is to realize that you *are* the Buddha!!. It is impossible *(from the "intellectual" point of view)* to venerate the Buddha and "be" a Buddha at the same time... You cannot become "One" with God (or the Buddha) and "pay homage" at the same time!!!... Only an "Intellectual" ideologue could come up with an absurdity such as this!!! So it is the "intellectuals" that have ripped out the "Heart and Soul" of Buddhism, and have made it (in essence) the first "Secular Humanist" religion.., and it is "I", Iron Owl, that has to ask the question:.. *"Where are all the Buddhas"???...* If it is the promise of Buddhism to accomplish this transformation of common men into Buddhas.., **"Where are all the Buddhas"???...** Where is the "Enlightenment"??... There can be only "slick answers" (intellectual rationalizations) to this question...

There were four "General Councils" that came together over a period of about (approx.) 400 years for the purpose of "reconciling differences of opinion, as well as to present, *reshape*, and *"fix"* the canonical writings" [5]... Each one of these councils was a "disaster" for Buddhism, as the various schools attending the Councils could not agree, resulting in differences of opinion that further divided the Buddhist community with some "schools" refusing to recognize other "schools" and further sub-divisions of schools, resulting in "new" schools, etc. and etc... It was at one of these Council meetings (probably the first or second) that the doctrines concerning "God" and the "Soul" were discussed.., and put to the **"Vote"!!!** By a margin of a little better than 2 to 1 (70% to 30%) the council *"voted"* to eliminate both "God" and the "Soul" from Buddhism, making Buddhism the "first and only" Secular Humanistic and Atheistic religion on earth!!! *And* (of course), the canonical writing had to be *"reshaped and fixed"* to reflect the findings of the council (*of intellectuals*), and anything that pertained to God and the Soul had to be eliminated as "heretical" and not Buddhist!.. An unspeakable tragedy of "Diabolical" proportions has happened here!!...

---

[5] This information is taken (in part) from the very well researched book called: "The Shambhala Dictionary of Buddhism and Zen"... (Shambhala Publications Inc., 1991)...

This is absurd!.. An "Enemy" [6] *has done this!!!* ....And what of the 30% that dissented??. What doctrines were they following?., and what happened to them??? No mention is made of this in the Buddhist records....

For far too long these "Great Contradictions" have gone unchallenged and ignored by the Buddhist community, but eventually, great contradictions will lead to a great confrontation"., and *this* is: *"The Great Confrontation"...* I.., Iron Owl, have proven beyond doubt, by my *first hand direct experience,* the existence of both "God" and the "Soul".., and this book is my testimony... To conceive of "cognizance" without a "cognizer" is an intellectual absurdity.., **and it does not compute!!!** To conceive of annihilation of the "Self" by absorption into the "Vast Ocean" of Nirvanic bliss is **an act of suicide by drowning**, going from a "High" state of awareness, to a "Lesser" state of cognizance devoid of the cognizer, and without purpose or sensibility, which excludes even the awareness of Nirvanic bliss!!. This is a misconception as well as an intellectual absurdity.., **and it does not compute!!!**

Without the concept (and the reality) of a "Higher Consciousness" (**"GOD"**), that is not only "Self" aware, Intelligent and **Super Conscious** to the point of **"Brilliance"** (in every sense of the Word).., **and if this *"Enlightened Super Consciousness"* were not a fact of the Universe.., what is it that Buddhism aspires to???** Could it be that the "Intellectuals" are so smug, self righteous, and clever that they have "outsmarted" and excluded themselves from the ranks of the "Truly" Enlightened??? This would be hilariously funny.., if it weren't so tragic...

*** The Great Confrontation ***

---

[6] This "Enemy" that I speak of here, is most likely that same "Diabolical" entity that is the "Arch Enemy" of God and of Truth.., and his influence is seen here.., But.., there is another enemy that is *specific to Buddhism,* and is the focus element of the human psyche that Buddhism is intent on eradicating!.. It is the "Ego" identity conscious that manifested here as the "Intellectuals"... These "Ego-Intellectuals" were easy prey to the lies of that "Evil One" and through them, he has subverted and separated Buddhism away from God.., and away from the "Mystic Union"... Separated from God.., the "Mystic Union"., doesn't exist!!...

It is perhaps with too broad a brush, that the West paints (interprets) Buddhism as a Godless and Soulless Religion with the primary purpose of putting and end to suffering by achieving extinction...   This is False... Whether this be believed by a Buddhist, or believed about Buddhism by non Buddhists, this is false...

There are too many contradiction within Buddhism for this to be the case... Certainly, the very religious people of the Buddhist community, reciting their prayers, chanting their mantras and spinning their prayer wheels, cannot conceive of a Universe devoid of a Higher Power, which they instinctively bow down to, burn incense, give alms and offer sacrifice... And of the Buddha's, residing in the pleasure realms of the Seventh Heaven, forever and ever, certainly is contradictory to the doctrine of extinction, and implies an eternal Soul... And indeed, what would even be the point of having a religion if there be no God (and consequently no afterlife for a non soul)?.. There is certainly a contradiction between extinction and enlightenment... Liberation from the Sangsara is not by extinction.., on the contrary, the Bodhisattva takes the vow of eternal existence, "Until all sentient beings have achieved Nirvana"...

Indeed!., for the Bodhisattva, having achieved his enlightenment, He renounces the concept of a final absorption (like a drop of water into the Ocean) into Nirvanic bliss, and instead chooses to be an "agent of Universe", motivated by Love and Compassion, assisting a humanity in darkness towards the light... The Sangsara, of the Bodhisattva, has now become his Nirvana... The Sangsara and Nirvana have become One... This is the Ideal of Buddhism...

I have seen this concept of the "final absorption" into the bliss of Nirvana (like a drop of water into the Ocean).., (i.e. extinction).., *and I refute it..,* as Heresy!.. I have seen this concept reiterated in Hinduism, Buddhism, and romanticized religio/philosophical treatises.., *and I refute it* as "fuzzy thinking" and intellectual Heresy!.. This erroneous concept makes about as much sense as (and is quite similar to;).., a lethal overdose of Heroine...

What would be the purpose?.. What would be the purpose, of a Soul that has reincarnated again and again, (perhaps thousands of times) to finally achieve enlightenment, and succumb to the bliss of Nirvana (extinction by absorption)??? Where is the Hero of this story?.. Has "Nirvana" (or the Void?) become greater because of the absorption of our "conquering Hero"?.. Can the stature of "God" (or the Void?) be added to?.. Does Nirvana become more blissful???..

The candidate for enlightenment takes the "Bodhisattva Vow" at the *beginning* of his induction into the "Holy Order", not at the end... The purpose for this is twofold. It would be tragic, if our aspiring candidate for enlightenment "tripped" into a fifth dimensional realm, and decided to stay there.., leaving his teachers with a corpse... (This is very possible)... The second reason is to prevent the even greater tragedy of our aspiring candidate, who has achieved enlightenment, from succumbing to the absorption into the blissful state of Nirvana (extinction), and robbing the world of a Great Saint and Teacher... This would truly be a tragedy... It is the test of Wisdom.., to not go one step too far... It is the test of Wisdom to choose "Life"... Buddhism is a life affirming religion, and the Bodhisattva, is an eternal Soul, on an eternal mission, motivated by love, compassion, and the joy of life!.. **Our Hero lives!!.**
This;.. is Bliss... This;.. is Nirvana...

So.., think not, that I have come here to denigrate or attack Buddhism!.. Quite the contrary... I have embraced Buddhism... I have found great beauty in Buddhism... I have studied the scriptures diligently, taken initiation from a great teacher, and practiced the ancient form of meditation handed down through a long line of teachers that extends back to the Buddha, and I have sat in meditation for thousands of hours… I have made pilgrimage to the Holy places, and I have taken the Sacred Vow of the Bodhisattva; "to bring all beings to the Clear Light of the Ultimate Reality".., and it is in observance of that sacred vow that I now speak… "For I have seen that "Ancient Way".., the Way that was taken by the formerly "All Awakened ", and that is the path I follow"…

Apart from "Union with the Divine".., there is no Buddhahood!!. Apart form "Union with the Divine".., there is no Enlightenment!!. Apart from the Knowledge and *Veneration* of the Divine.., there is no "Communion"... Apart from "Communion" with the Divine.., there is no "Way"... This "Way" is the "Old Way".., the path of the Ancients, and it is the "Way" that always was...   *"Follow the "Way"*

Buddhas, Bodhisattvas, Saints, and the Common Man…

The basic difference between a "Buddha", a "Saint", and the "common man".., is that the "Buddha" has transcended body consciousness (enlightenment), explored the "out-of-body" state and the "Realms" of the "Fifth Dimension", with all of the intuitive insights that pure objectivity can bestow.., has achieved the "Transference of Consciousness", becoming "One" with the Universe.., and has returned to body consciousness to tell the tale... Without accomplishing this last step, of the return to body consciousness.., He would not be a Buddha.., and would be, in fact, in violation of the "Bodhisattva Vow"... The ability to return to body consciousness (The Shiva-Shakti shift) is fundamental to the nature of a Buddha (and the Soul), and without this last step, he would not be a Buddha, but would be "lost in space"...

The "Saint" is one who has realized the expansive nature of his consciousness (either consciously or unconsciously) and is predominantly in the "objective" state of mind, with only the fleeting moments of "subjectivity" necessary to function in his environment... Even in states of deep introspection, his attention is objectively turned to the Divine, and in rare moments, he is in "communion" with the Lord (a revelation-growth-unfoldment process), and there is dialogue... Being primarily in the objective mode of consciousness, he is outwardly aware and almost unaware of himself (ego-less), and as such, his movements and speech become "graceful" and natural, unhindered and uninhibited by self-consciousness... This natural state (of grace) is evident to all who know him... The outstanding characteristic of this "natural" state of consciousness, is the ability to focus his attention, completely, totally, and *effortlessly* (to the point of "absorption"), on the object (or subject) of his observations... Becoming *effortlessly* "absorbed" in the subject of his contemplations, he has intuitive (into-it) insights, and for humanity around him, this intuitive insight manifests as empathy, and compassion... To the outside observer it may appear that the "Saint" is a good man, doing good and humanitarian things, and "his reward will be great in heaven"... But to the "Saint" himself, he has no concept of doing good for heavenly rewards or whatever.., but only in alleviating the pains of a suffering humanity which he feels intimately.., and with which he has "become one", and with whom he identifies... The "Saint".., owing to his level of "purity" of intention, performs his actions without motive, except to do his own will, *with the utmost selfishness* [7].., which is in total harmony with the Divine will, of which he is part and parcel...

And the "Common Man"!.. Ah, yes.., is there anything more uncommon than the common man?.. He is the most diverse and complicated creature on Earth!.. Truly an inspired and magnificent creation!., out of the ordinary!., with ethnic and cultural diversities, abilities to create and destroy, to make love and war, to build and lay waste... Such drama!., such passion!.. Mankind is the "Salt of the Earth", without which the Earth would be flat and tasteless... Kudos to the Lord!.. Halleluiah!..

Now, some would tell you that there is no God, no Creator, no purpose.., "a tale told by an idiot!., full of sound and fury, signifying: *Nothing*"!.. But there is purpose!.. Oh, Yes!., there is definitely purpose.., and it is this:-- the evolution of the common man.., into a Universal, Immortal, and God-like Being!!. This was your destiny from the very beginning!.. And it is not that the Lord picks and chooses.., oh no.., you do that for yourself!.. The Ultimate Cosmic Justice!.. You decide.., whether you are worthy to take your place as a Cosmic Citizen, with God-like powers, in the company of your God-like peers... No assholes allowed here!.. That filtering process is done here on Earth.., and you are in charge of the decisions you make.., and their consequences... So take heed!., because THIS is the testing ground.., and THIS is the Knowledge:-- *YOU* are in charge of your own spiritual evolution... This spiritual journey begins with a conscious decision, usually arrived at by that "moment of truth" cathartic experience commonly known as; being "Born Again"... At that time, a conscious decision is made, and the Western man will undergo a "Baptism", in which he declares to the Lord, to himself, and to all of humanity that he will seek and do "the Good, the Right, and the True", in the service of the Lord... His Eastern counterpart will undergo initiation, taking the "Bodhisattva Vow" to seek enlightenment, not for just himself, but in service to all of humanity... This is the first "expansive step" into *That* much larger Universe...

This "expansive first step", this conscious decision.., puts into motion the "mechanism" by

---

[7] This principle of "utmost selfishness" (a.k.a. "to thine own self be true") is gone into in great detail in the last chapter ("The Preliminary Prerequisite") of this book...

which the evolution of the Soul takes place.., and it has to do with (not surprisingly) the principles of "Zen", and the "Shiva-Shakti shift"!..   With whether you function from the center of your being, focused outward on a suffering humanity (the Zen-objective state of "selfless" consciousness), or functioning from the periphery of your conscious, focused back on yourself (locked into the "subjective-egotistical" self-conscious state)… There is a natural "balance" between these two states, which is predominantly "objective" in the "Saint".., or predominantly "subjective" in the "Egotist"… This "mechanism" is second-nature and instinctive to the Saint, whose focus is outward on a suffering humanity, motivated by compassion... His every action is toward an ever greater expansiveness of consciousness, that eventually, an event will take place in which he identifies so completely (forgetting himself so completely) that a *"transference of consciousness"* will take place (Liberation) into the Humanity (or whatever) that is the object of his compassionate love… Whereas.., by contrast, the "Egotist", is locked into the self-conscious state of mind, where every action is motivated by his own self aggrandizement, which has to be protected at all costs, and he will lie, cheat, steal, and do, whatever is necessary to advance his own cause, at the expense of whomever.., and all the while, he is becoming more and more "entrenched" into his ego-centered world, and is vulnerable to being "hurt".., and there is no stronger and more entrenched ego, than a "wounded" ego, or a "guilty" ego.., which can never even conceive of "Liberation".., unless that traumatic "change of heart" takes place, culminating in that "Born Again" experience, that will change the direction of his life, and put him on the road to "Sainthood"…

To seek "Enlightenment" (Liberation), is the highest purpose on Earth, and it is the essence of "Wisdom".., but to seek it for your self alone, for your own self aggrandizement.., is the greatest folly, and your greatest impediment on the path!..
If you can grasp the seeming contradiction in the above statement, then you have a good understanding of the Zen "riddle" and the "mechanism" involved… But.., even though your seeking may seem "self" motivated, it is in response to a "calling", and the "mechanism" (especially if you understand it) will function in response to your "selfless" (objective) involvements… Consider yourself; "On the Path"…

* * *

"The Pearl of Great Price"

When you read a book (such as this one) you read it to gain knowledge and understanding of a particular subject… In this case, the subject that we are seeking to know and understand, is the most elusive, esoteric, and important subject on earth (or elsewhere)… It is the knowledge of the "essence of our being".., it is the knowledge of the "Soul".., it is the knowledge of the "Self"… It is extremely rare that anyone would even seek it, let alone find it!..

"To many it is not given to hear of the Self.
Many, though they hear of it, do not understand it.
Wonderful is he who speaks of it.
Intelligent is he who learns of it.
Blessed is he who, taught by a good teacher, is able to understand it"...
…..(from the "Upanishads")...

"The Kingdom of Heaven, is likened to a merchant who finds a "Pearl of Great Price", and he will go and sell all that he owns, to possess that Pearl"... *Jesus.*

…. Do you have any idea just how rare this information is?., this knowledge that is presented here.., that I give to you so casually??. The Bible doesn't have it!., neither in the Old testament, or in the New!.. It alludes to it; *"What will a man give in exchange for his Soul"*?., but it conveys no knowledge of it… Buddhism comes close to describing it, in scattered references.., but then it denies it's existence!.. Zen comes close to observing the dual nature of it's functioning (the Yin-Yang shift), but fails to identify it, clothes it in obscure riddles, and even confuses it with the workings of the sub-conscious mind.., and being an off-shoot of Buddhism, denies the Souls existence (the *real* Zen paradox)!.. And Islam!., who knows?.. I have great respect for the Sufi Masters of the ancient tradition.., but as far as I can tell, modern Islam has no knowledge of it, and Mohammad was neither a Sufi, or a Master!.. (enough said)… Only Hinduism comes close.., if you sort through the mass of confusion… They have developed meditation into a science, described the Soul in its essence (Patanjali), and explored the "Herbs of Mysterious Virtue", as well as the Chakra system, and various (altered) states of mind… "Truth", is where you find it.., and you have to give credit where credit is due…

I am espousing no particular religion here… Meditation, as a science is adaptable to all religions, and God, the Creator and the Redeemer, is Universal to all religions that recognize HIM as such… Practice your religion, and seek the Lord in the interior of your heart, in deep introspection and contemplation… The "Way" lies within.., In the process of "Isolating" the "Self" from the thought process, and then focusing on the Lord.., to the exclusion of all other things, and in the "Shiva shift" to pure objective contemplation, a "Transfer of Consciousness" will occur, and you will become "One with the Lord" (the Mystic Union).., and then you will Know…

Herein is contained the essence of the "Mystic Doctrine" (a.k.a. "Upanashads")… "Patanjali" refers to this as; "the easy way"…

Of the millions who seek for the knowledge of the "Way"
Only a handful ever gain that knowledge
Of those who gain that knowledge
Only a few achieve

The admonition of the Saints and Sages; "To Know Thyself", takes on a much more profound meaning… You.., who read these words.., are privy to this most esoteric of all secrets… If I have been a good teacher, you now know what very few people on earth know.., which is the Knowledge of the Soul.., the Pearl of great Price.., which makes you "one in a million".., a very rare person, indeed…

You are one of a rare handful,
May you become one of those few…

* * *   *   * * *

The "Name" of God!!!

(The Prayer To The Root Guru)[8]

Obeisance to all the Conquerors in the One Body of At-one-ment!
O Thou, the True Embodiment of all Protectors,
The Lord of the Great Mystic Faith in it's entirety,
The Holy Lord of all that constituteth my Refuge, now and hereafter,
O Thou, whose graciousness can never be repaid,
Thou knowest, O Thou "Root-Guru" of unsurpassing kindness,
Thou knowest that I pray unto Thee from the very depths of my heart,
That I may speedily attain to perfection on the Profound Path of Consciousness-Transference.
O Thou, in the Akanishta Heaven, the emanation of the Pure Realm of the Dharma-Kaya,
Vouchsafe me Thy "gift-waves", that Self-Knowledge, the Immutable State of the Darma-Kaya may be attained.

This is a Buddhist prayer!.. I, Iron Owl, pray this prayer… A Christian, or a Jew, or a Moslem, or a Hindu, or any one that acknowledges "God" can pray this prayer… This is a Universal Prayer.

The term; "Root-Guru" may, at first glance, seem like a crude translation, but on further analyses, it is a very precise and accurate designation. The "Root-Guru" is the "Teacher" from the very "Root" of creation… "The Teacher from the Source".., "HE", from before the very Beginning. "The Lord of the Great Mystic Faith.., *in it's entirety"*…

This is "HE" of whom I speak… This is "HE" of whom All Religions speak!.. "HE".., The "Ancient One" of Ages.., The Eternal Youth… This is the Central Universal Truth;.. In a Universe of change, "HE" is the one unchanging fact…

"HE", who is beyond Name and Form.., by what Name shall we know HIM?.. What Name can describe HIM ?..

"Patanjali" (the Father of the Yoga system), states:

"The Lord is a "Particular Spirit".., untouched by troubles, works, fruits, or deserts… In HIM does the germ of the omniscient become infinite… HE is the preceptor even of the first, for HE is not limited by time… HIS name (or appellation) is: …
"Glory"!..

And from the Hindu: "Oh Partha! All beings exist in Him and He exists in them as "Antaryamin" (The Indwelling Guide)… (He is also known as the All-Pervading Paramatman)"…
Shrimad Bhagavad Gita, (chapter 8, Q&A 2).

---

[8] From the book: "Tibetan Yoga and Secret Doctrines", by; W.Y. Evans-Wentz, as translated by the late: Lama Kazi Dawa-Samdup… Page 264… (Oxford University Press, 1938 & 1968)…

So.., Who is this "All Pervading Paramatman".?., This "Particular Spirit".?., This "Ancient of Ages", this "Glorious Eternal Youth", This "Indwelling Guide", This "Root Guru"..., of "The Great Mystic Faith in It's Entirety"?..

The Buddhists know this "Indwelling Guide", This "Root Guru".., as the "Adi Buddha"..., The Primordial Lord, Who is without Beginning or End, the Source of all Truth, and the Head of all the Divine Hierarchies…

A Christian might say; "Hey"!., "That description could also apply to "Jesus Christ"!!. By this description, a Jew would recognize "Jehovah"..., A Moslem would recognize "Allah"..., A Hindu would recognize "Brahma"…

All of these religions have their "Divine Hierarchies", and "**HE**".., is Head of them all...

It is on this point (of fact) that All Religions converge... There is no other God, But God.., by whatever multitude of Names **HE** may be known...

Now.., this is a seemingly true and logical statement, except for one thing!!. The religions of the world have not converged!!... As a matter of fact.., they are divided and at war with each other.., and they are divided over the "Name" of God!!!... Is this not the "Ultimate Absurdity"??? And yet each religion claims to have the "exclusive" on the name of God, and they can point to their scriptures and.., "it says right here"..., "and if you don't believe it, well then, God damn you"!!...

So the question arises!., Is there a "Name" that God calls Himself***???...*** Is there "One Name", above all other names, that is the Absolute Name of God***???...*** At the risk of pissing off everyone (again), I will answer that question.., and the answer is; "God only knows"..., but otherwise, the answer is **"NO"**... And the alternative to this answer is;.. **"WAR"!!!...** To wage war in the name of God.., *over* the name of God, is the "Ultimate Absurdity"…

But what about the name; "Yahweh" (often incorrectly spelled "Jehovah") which literally translated means: "HE IS"?..

This;., the "Name of four letters" (called: the "Tetragramaton") is (for all intents and purposes) the "written" generic name for God in the Aramaic language, but it was *NEVER* spoken (as "spelt"), (a great sin!)[9].., not even by Jesus, who always used the term "Lord", or "Father"... It is worth noting, here.., that this name was considered so sacred, that it was never spoken by the common man, but only by the "Sanhedrin" and then only on special occasions, and no one knew the correct pronunciation because there are no "vowels" in the (rather primitive) Hebrew alphabet!! To this day, no one knows the correct pronunciation!!... Furthermore, there was also no numerical system in the (rather primitive) Hebrew culture of that day, so the letters of the alphabet were also used as the numerical system, (very cumbersome), leading to all sorts of "Numerological" absurdities, and is in fact the basis of the bogus pseudo-science of Numerology!!. Furthermore, this "Name of four letters" is considered by many scholars to be an "Acronym"..., in the same way that "NATO" is the acronym for; the "North Atlantic Treaty Organization"..., but the meaning.., like the pronunciation.., has been lost in time...

It is not my intention to cast aspersions on any one of the multitude of names used to address Almighty God.., but only to point out that "no one" has an "exclusive" on the name of God.., or did you think to have some greater power.., access.., or influence.., with God, by using a particular name??. This is the worst kind of **"Vanity"**...

There are in fact, thirty-two (32) officially recognized names for God in the Hebrew tradition, *plus* the Generic (*"Ya"*) !!. There are probably at least three times that number of names used to address Jesus Christ!... (t*he Prince of Peace, the Lamb of God, etc., and etc.)*

But if we are going to use the Bible for reference, I would point you to Exodus 3:13-16, where Moses asks God directly: "Behold, when I come unto the children of Israel, and shall say unto them; The God of your fathers hath sent me unto you; and they shall say to me: What is HIS name?., What shall I say to them"?.. And God said unto Moses: "I AM THAT I AM"; and He said: "Thus shalt thou say unto the children of Israel; "I AM" hath sent me

---

[9] It was considered a violation of Hebrew law, and, in fact, a violation of the "Second Commandment" to utter this name "as spelt", but this fact seems to have escaped the modern televangelists and preachers of today, who utter this name (but with noble intent) to distinguish "The Lord God" from false gods, even though God refers to Himself (in the first person) as Lord and God… (See: Isaiah 45: 5-8, and 18-24)…

unto you"... And God said moreover unto Moses: "Thus shalt thou say unto the children of Israel: The Lord, the God of your fathers, The God of Abraham, the God of Isaac, and the God of Jacob hath sent me unto you; **this is My name for ever, and this is My memorial unto all generations**"...

Now.., before I give you the "Iron Owl" (insightful) translation.., let me point out two things!.. First of all.., When God Almighty is asked a direct question.., you can expect his answer to be the *absolutely succinct bottom line summation!!.., and in the fewest words possible!!...* (i.e. <u>absolutely succinct</u>)... And second.., bear in mind that the entire five books of Moses (the Pentateuch *(Torah)*) were written by Moses in the "third person" format, and that he was probably the most learned scholar in all of Egypt (having a "Genius I.Q., and raised and educated in the house of Pharaoh), and that *as a writer and author,* he incorporates a "literary devise" into this passage *designed to conceal the Sacred from the view of the profane superficial reader, (*who will undoubtedly misinterpret it) *but the intuitive reader will not miss it!!!*

This "literary device", designed to conceal the Sacred from the eyes of the profane, has to do with the simple elimination of punctuation marks, and small case print, where capitalization would usually occur.., and the clue to it being there is that the sentence just "doesn't read right"!.. *(I have run across this literary device on other occasions, while examining "esoteric" documents not meant for public viewing)...*

Before I reveal the correct and accurate translation of this text, I want to point out what this text *does NOT say,* concerning the "Name" of God... **HE** does NOT say; "My name is "Jehovah"... **HE** does NOT say; "My name is "Allah"... **HE** does NOT say; "My name is "Brahma"... **HE** does NOT say; "My name is "Jesus Christ"... **HE** does NOT say; "My name is "Buddha".., or "Krishna".., or "Whatever", etc.!!... **HE specifically does NOT give any specific "Name" at all!!..,** except to say that **HE** is the same <u>**Lord**</u> and <u>**God**</u> of Abraham, Isaac, and Jacob... **HE** specifically uses the "generic" terms: <u>**Lord,**</u> and <u>**God,**</u> to designate "HIMSELF"!!...[10]

---

[10] For those "traditionalists" who insist on a literal confirmation from the Bible, I would refer you to: "Jeremiah 33: 1-3".., and also; "Numbers 6:22-27".., and etc...

What **HE** *does say* (correct punctuation and capitols supplied) is:..

"I AM <u>"*THAT*"</u> ... "*I AM*"!!!..[11]

I don't think that there is anywhere in the Bible a more profound, concise, and succinct statement than this statement made by the Lord God HIMSELF... *Everything* is included in ***"That"*** statement!!. *The Entire Universe!., All **That** is, all **That** was, all **That** will be... All of **THAT!**., **HE** "**IS**"..,* And **HE** emphasizes ***"THAT"*** *by the further pronouncement;* ***"I AM"...***

OUR PROBLEM, is that "WE" are trying to comprehend, "Name", and "Formulate" *Thee* "Absolute Ultimate" Super-Consciousness that is Omniscient, Omnipresent, Infinite, All-Powerful.., and *beyond* any classification of "Name" and "Form".., and in fact, incomprehensible!!... "Our" limitation, is that we can't even realize our limitations!..

Therefore, Moses was correct to conceal this Sacred text from the eyes of the superficial and profane readers, but despite his best efforts there are still those that infer from this passage that the "name" of God is: "I AM".., which is probably acceptable to the Lord, as long as it is well intentioned and sincere.., but *DO NOT* call **HIM;..** "That", because to do so in common speech would infer a base commonality that is disrespectful and Sacrilegious **(a great sin)..,** and this is exactly what Moses was trying to prevent, while at the same time, being *Hist*orically accurate...

> **HE** is the "Lord and God" of all Peoples, of all Nations, of all (true) Religions (that give HIM honor and worship).., and **HE** is known by a multitude of *"Names"* in a multitude of Languages, as well as the generic; "Lord and God"!., and **HE** is head of all the "Divine Hierarchies"..., and of "The

---

[11] Modern day translations (the N.I.V., and modern language King James versions, and etc.) interpret this passage to read: "*I am who I am*" or; "*I am what I am*".., trying to make this passage sound "euphonically correct".., but the "true" translation (from the Masoretic text, as translated by the "Eminent Committee of Jewish Scholars" of the Jewish Publication Society.., as well as by "others".., and etc.) gives the correct translation as "*I am that I am*", which does not sound euphonically correct, giving the clue to the "literary devise" being incorporated here... *Anybody* can say: "I am who I am".., or.., "I am what I am".., but only the Lord God Almighty can say: "*I am "THAT"!.. I AM !.. "*......

Great Mystic Faith" in it's Entirety"...
Hallelujah!!!

* * *   * * *

"The Philosophers Stone"

In that ancient language of Symbolism and Alchemy, there is one key ingredient in the alchemical mixture that is symbolized by a "Rock", or "Stone"... This key ingredient is the "Foundation Stone" on which the whole Alchemical formula is based, and without which it will not work... The purpose of the Alchemical formula is Not to turn base metal into Gold (as you might suppose).., but instead to transform the base "leaden" personality into the pure gold of an enlightened being... This is "Spiritual Alchemy".., and the purpose is "Transformation"...

So.., finding the "Stone" is the chief occupation of the Spiritual Alchemist... Where is this magical "Stone", and of what does it consist?.. What is it that is worthy to be called "The Philosophers Stone".?. How does it bestow Knowledge, Wisdom, and Immortality on he who possesses it.??

Many there are.., who have climbed the proverbial mountain in search of the meaning of the Philosophers Stone, and did not find it... Many have stared it in the face, and did not see it... Many have read of it out loud, and never heard it... Others have heard it, and did not recognize it...

YOU.., have heard it.., and did not recognize it...

"It is on this point (of fact) that all religions converge... There is no other God.., but "GOD"..,
(by whatever multitude of names HE may be known)"... And.., ..."HE"., Speaks to men.!.

"THIS".., point of fact is called: **"The Living Word"...** "THIS".., is the "Stone" of the Wise... This is the "Rock", that is the foundation Stone "of the Great Mystic Faith in it's entirety"... This is the point of contact between God.., and men... This is the philosophical "Rock" of tangible substance... It is the "Living Word".., spoken by the "Living God"., to living men... It is upon this "Rock", that I build my church[12].., and rest my life...

And Elijah was told: (1 Ki 19:11-13): "Go stand on the mountain, and the Lord will pass by"... A great and strong wind came (a hurricane) and smashed even the rocks to pieces.., but the Lord was Not in the wind... And after the wind, there came a great earthquake, and the mountain shook.., but the Lord was Not in the earthquake... And after the earthquake, there came a great fire.., but the Lord was Not in the fire... And after the fire.., there came;.. "a still, small voice"... When Elijah heard the "still, small voice" he wrapped his face in his mantle, went out from his cave, and heard the voice of the Lord: "What doest thou here, Elijah".?, spoke the Lord...

Hidden in plain sight.!. Is it not paradoxical, that the vast majority of the religious community should read these words, and mistake this historical record, of words written on parchment, as the actual "living word".., when the reality of the situation is that Elijah heard directly the true "Living Word", spoken by the true "Living God".?. ...And there was dialogue!..

And what is the significance of Abraham, Isaac, and Jacob?.. The unmistakable significance here, is that they too.., just like Elijah.., were hearers of the Living Word spoken by the Living God.., and there was dialogue!..

So.., there is this abundance of evidence, a record kept of first hand testimony, (which is the entire sum and substance of the Bible) (Old Testament

---

[12] I echo here, the words of Christ (Mt. 16: 15-18) : "Who do you say I am"? Peter answered; "You are the Christ, the Son of the living God"... Jesus replied, "Blessed are you Simon, son of Jonah, *for flesh and blood has not revealed this to thee, but my Father in Heaven*, and I tell you that you are Peter, and *on this rock (the Living Word, spoken by the Living God)*, I will build my church, and the gates of Hell will not prevail against it"... Jesus then (knowing that HE would soon die on the cross) confers upon Peter the Mantle of the Head of His church (i.e. the first Pope)… Now, OBVIOUSLY.., the foundation stone of Christianity was not Peter, but Jesus Himself.., and Peter was a "rock" (a play of words on the meaning of his name) only by virtue of the fact that he had heard the "Living Word spoken by the Living God"… So the tradition of the Popes is that they be "hearers of the Word", (literally), and if they are truly "in dialogue" with the Lord, they are a true Pope, and they are truly infallible (as the Word of the Lord is infallible), and if they do not hear the "the Living Word spoken by the Living God", then they are Pope in name only, and not in the tradition of Peter… The true "Rock" of the Church is not Peter, or the Papacy.., but the "Living Word, spoken by the Living God"…

and New), that presents the Truth about the "Inner Voice".., and the true nature of the "Hearing of the Word"... This is a "Universal Truth".., and it shows up in the scriptures of All the worlds religions...

"Knowledge comes by Hearing.., and Hearing.., by the Word of God"...

I.., Iron Owl.., must testify... Not to what I believe, or to what I think, or to what I have read... But to what I have experienced!.. First hand testimony.., to what I have "Heard".., within the realm of my own being...

I must confess:, because of the subtlety of the "Inner Voice" (the still, small voice).., I did not recognize it for what it was.!. I would venture to say that most people have heard this "still, small voice".., and did not recognize it for what it was... Elsewhere.., within this document.., are described the substance of the "Communions" with the "Inner Voice", but for the moment, we will deal with the general "Nature" of this; the "Philosophical Stone" of tangible substance.., which is the "Cornerstone"...

"Here I am!.. I stand at the door and knock... Anyone hear my voice and open the door, I will come in and sup with him, and he with me"...
(Rev. 3-20)

Do you wait for the second coming.?. What will you do at the second coming.?. Will you crowd around HIM like groupies at a rock concert.?. Will you shout accolades, like fans at a football game.?. Would you ever expect to have a private audience with HIM.?? **... HE IS HERE !!!** ...Where are YOU.?.

The "door", is the door of the "Inner Sanctum".., within the realm of your own Soul... You must block out the external world, and enter the quiet world of introspection, in the pursuit of Knowledge, Wisdom, and answers to those questions that plague your own Soul... The Ego is not welcome here... You must lose yourself into the subject of your enquiry.., into the Zen-objective contemplative state... You must lose yourself in the sincerity of "the Soul that wants to Know"... You must lose yourself in contemplation and become absorbed in your contemplation, *(with the intensity of "a mother who has lost her only child, and can think of nothing else but her lost child")..,* and you will become absorbed in "Communion".., and there will be dialogue...

Generally speaking;.. HE does not speak to the trivial minded, (but HE could)... HE does not speak to the worldly minded, about worldly subjects (but HE might)... HE does not speak to the Ego mentality, (but, on rare occasions, HE has)... Generally speaking; HIS voice is the "still small voice" almost below the level of perception, and is not audible to the outer ear (although it could be)... Generally speaking, HE speaks only to those who seek HIM, in the sanctity and solitude of inner contemplation (but HE might speak to you, as you are walking down the street), etc...
Generally speaking, HIS is the voice of a loving Father, who guides his children in the ways of righteousness (but HE is a stern disciplinarian)...

His Nature is: *"The Will to Good"*...

So.., pay homage to The Root Guru... All Honor, Glory and supplication belong to "HIM"... HE;.. *"THAT"* "still small voice", that stands at the threshold of the Inner Realms.., and speaks to men... Hear HIS voice.!. HE is the Creator and the Redeemer... HE is your Savior... HIS voice is clothed in vision.., and the vision is revelation.., the revelation is Knowledge.., and you will KNOW!., and nothing will be hidden from you...

Knowledge builds upon knowledge, and you will advance in knowledge... Step by step, episode by episode, you will climb the staircase of Knowledge, into the realm of "ALL Knowledge", and the crown.., is "Wisdom"...

I teach nothing new... This "step by step" advancement, up the staircase of Knowledge.., is commonly known as: "The Way"... This is the "Way" that always was...

"For I have seen the "Ancient Way", the Old Road that was taken by the formerly "All-Awakened", and that is the path I follow"...

This is the testimony of Iron Owl, concerning the reality of "the Living Word", spoken by the "Living God" to living men.., which is the voice of HIM, who is the Creator, and this is the "Rock" that is my refuge and my fortress... By whatever multitude of Names HE may be known, HE is the ONE and the Same... HE is the "Indwelling Guide", the "Teacher of teachers".., the Lord of the "Great Mystic Faith in it's Entirety".., and Head of all the Divine Hierarchies... HE is.., the **"LORD"**...

"Hallowed be HIS name".

* * * * *

"Enlightenment"

The Soul, being composed of "Absolutely Nothing", with neither center or circumference, is nevertheless profoundly aware and "Super-conscious" of itself (Shakti mode), and of the object (or subject) of it's observations (Shiva mode) especially in it's "out of body" (Liberated) state… Having achieved the "Mystic Union", (becoming "One" with the Lord) it can exhibit countless powers (which I will not elaborate on, at this time).., But.., One of those powers is: "All Knowledge"…

The term;.. "All Knowledge".., is not a misnomer... Within the realm of secular science, there is a concept of "The Unified Field" in which each branch of science is intimately related to every other branch of science... For instance:.. "color".., is determined not by the eye alone, but by a specific wave length (frequency) of light, and different wave length/frequencies (octaves) yield different colors, some of which are harmonious and some of which "clash"... The field of mathematics can show this by algebraic equations and logarithmic progressions, etc... We can move from the field of "light" to the field of "sound", and the same mathematics apply, with sounds (wave length/frequencies) that are harmonic, and sounds that "clash"... There is a "unified field" relationship here,.. and it will also be found in the field of electricity (that travels at the speed of light), radio, radar, laser beams, etc., (variants of wavelength/frequencies at light speed)... So it seems that everything that we know of is just a variant of this light speed "Energy" functioning at different wave-length/frequencies, from solid matter, to light, heat, sound, color, electronics, etc.., above and below the range of our perceptions (infra-red, ultra violet), up and down the scale of "octaves".., and the same mathematics apply...

The ability to see this relationship (correspondences) between one field of science and other branches of science.., is the key to genius.., and everything.., "relates"...

Everything relates.., and everything has a "cause"... Everything that we see, is an effect of a prior cause, and that prior cause is a result of a prior cause before that, which is an effect of a prior cause before that, etc. and etc.., all the way back to: "The First Cause"...

It is the business and preoccupation of secular science to discover the "First Cause".., but their science is limited only to the field of matter and energy, and they are looking only at the "fourth dimension" of "timeless space", back to the "Big Bang" theory.., which is just another effect of a prior cause.., and all the time, (consciously or unconsciously) they are asking themselves that most esoteric of questions:.. "From whence did we come"?...

But the "First Cause" is not to be found in the fourth dimension of timeless space, because it did not originate there...

The "First Cause" is of the "Fifth Dimension".., which is:.. "The Realm of Mind".., and more specifically: "The Realm of the Mind of God"...

This is a stumbling block to secular science, who make that most presumptuous of assumptions;.. that "existence precedes Essence"... This is the "battle cry" of the "Secular Humanists", the "Evolutionists", the "Behaviorists" and the "Existentialists".., that vast world-wide religion of the "Left", who believe in their heart of hearts, that there is no God...

I could go into mind-numbing detail, of the great "intellectuals" that espouse this religion of the "Left".., Marx, Lenin, Mao, etc. (those dreamers of a Godless "Utopia", who slaughtered millions).., or the father of Existentialism; "J.P. Sarte", ("those who live lives of quiet desperation, waiting to die").., but I won't.., it's too depressing...

It is beyond the realm.., of the linear-logical-material mentality.., to conceive of a Realm.., of "Mind"...

The reality, of a "Fifth Dimensional Universe".., containing Worlds.., populated with living beings.., and etc.., existing simultaneously with this "World of reality" that we know of as planet Earth (floating in the Timeless-Space Continuum of the Fourth Dimension).., and yet cannot be located within the limitless confines of our Universe.., is inconceivable... Even though we enter the "sub-strata" of this Fifth Dimensional Universe in the world of our dreams, this "Universe of Mind" is dismissed as a non-reality.., until we "shuffle off this mortal coil".., and go there...

So, the Fourth Dimension (the timeless-space continuum), and the Fifth Dimension (the mind-space continuum), as well as the Sixth, the Seventh, and the Eighth Dimension.., All exist simultaneously with each other.., as octaves (wavelength-frequencies).., but on a Cosmic scale...

It is said; that in a condition of absolute stillness and quiet, if you listen intently, with the inner ear (the ear of the Soul).., you can hear the sounds of "inner space" (the wavelength-frequencies of each Dimension on the scale of octaves) and if your "samadii" be profound enough, you will become absorbed in that particular wavelength frequency, and enter the world(s) of that dimension... This path (up the scale of the octaves of inner space) is called;.. "The Yoga of the Sound Current" ("Nada Yoga")...

Similarly.., the practitioners of "Kundalini Yoga" seek to awaken that primal Energy force that will adjust their own wavelength-frequency to harmonize with those of the octave-dimension-spectrum.., entering each "Chakra" (dimension-world).., and gaining the Knowledge and experience of these dimensions... These practitioners of the mystical art, are called;.. "Adepts".., and the body.., as a temple.., is far more profoundly mystical and wonderful.., than you know...

The Eighth Dimension.., is (in Essence) the First Dimension (the eighth note of an octave being the first note of the next octave).., is also known as "The Great Void beyond mind".., (the timeless-dimensionless-endless vacuous-space continuum).., also known as; "The Realm of Brahma".., and the "Plane of Creation"...

It is here.., in the Great Void.., the Realm of the Most High.., that the primordial "sound" (wavelength-frequency) was first heard.., and can still be heard...

This primordial "sound" is known as "The First Emanation"... This; "The First Emanation".., which is produced in the Absolute Void, because of the Void, and is a condition of the Void.., which originates from nowhere specific, but is everywhere present and all pervasive.., is the "First Word".., and the "First Cause"...

It is said; (in the Hindu cosmology), that because of this primordial sound (wavelength-frequency-energy emanation) that pervaded the Void, "HE" heard that sound, awoke from the Void, and realized that HE was... and being Formless and Void, HE was the Void and HE was the sound that permeated the Void... And.., since the Void always was, and the sound that permeated the Void always was, "HE".., who heard the sound.., and was that sound.., always was.., and always will be...

"In the beginning was the "Word".., and the "Word" was with God.., and the "Word" was God"...

It is by the articulation of that sound (the manipulation of the wavelength-frequencies), that HE "spoke" the Worlds into being... Within HIS own being, within the realm of HIS boundless imagination.., by the agency of HIS WORD, HE created.., and it was Good*!!.* (Mankind has not an adequate concept of what constitutes; "Glory")...

So creation began within the field of mind.., and THAT field of mind was the mind of the Creator... "Essence".., precedes existence"...

This Primordial Emanation, the First Cause, (the Sound of Silence), is held to be (in the Hindu cosmology) the most Sacred of HIS manifestations.., and is revered as HIS Holy Name, which is;.. "OM" (or "AUM")... The repetition of this Holy Name (consisting of three and a half prosodial moments), and the contemplation of it's Source and meaning is very conducive to the state of abstract meditation...

Using the framework of a "spiders web" as a "model" for the concept of all knowledge, it is seen that all fields of knowledge are inter-related (by their correspondences), and spring from the same Source (the First Cause) in a cause-effect relationship... It therefore follows, that if anyone should ponder (in samadii) a particular field of knowledge, and climb the cause-effect ladder of knowledge back to the First Cause (the center of the web), it would be seen that this First Cause is the cause of All fields of knowledge, and All fields of knowledge can be known (intuitively) from the inside-out, the correspondences can be seen, and the Knowledge becomes self evident... Add to this the "Akashic Records" (the Cosmic memory) that can be intuitively accessed (in Communion with the Divine), and All things will be made known to you, and nothing will be hidden from you... In the course of the development of All knowledge, true "WISDOM" dawns, followed by Compassion and Love.., accompanied by the "Illumination" (enlightenment) of the inner realm of the imagination.., accompanied by the realization of the "Triple Gem"; "Existence-Knowledge-Bliss"!., etc…

"Enlightenment".., has been defined.., but (of necessity), not adequately.., and not completely... All descriptions fall short... "Ye are Gods"... (Thus spoke the Lord)...

The "models", that we have used here, of the "wave-length frequencies", "the octaves" and the "spiders web" are (of necessity), just "devices" to communicate to the linear-logical-material mentality, that which is beyond material conception!.. As far away as the field of "mechanics" is (conceptually) from the field of "quantum physics".., that far away again is the field of the "Inner Realms" of the "Fifth Dimension"... But then again.., the field of the fourth dimension is as near to the fifth dimension.., as the out-side is.., to the in-side...

The only model that is conceptually more accurate is the one that I was "shown":.. "(quote); "It was a cracker crumb, perched on the tip of my index finger.., I looked into the cracker crumb, and saw that it was a world, and on this world there was a being, standing there in a pose, with his finger in the air, with a cracker crumb on his finger tip, and it was a world, and on this world was a man, finger, cracker crumb, world, man.., etc."... (end-quote)...

A Universe, within a Universe, within a Universe, etc... This is not conceptual, and it is a "stumbling block" to the linear-logical-mechanical-(cause-effect) reasoning of the materially based mind... But of the Cosmic Mind.., "it has it's own laws, and nothing is impossible"... And a second "stumbling block" (to the secular mind) to the concept of this multi-dimensional Universe (within a Universe, within a Universe), etc., is the obvious conclusion that must be drawn:., and that is; that there had to be.., a "First"...   ….Or is that an over-simplification??…

* * *   * * *

"The Last Days"

The "Book of Revelation" is probably the most enigmatic book in the Bible, and every theologian has given his personal interpretation of the enigmatic symbols contained therein... Speculations abound, with literally thousands of interpretations.., and there is one author who's speculations have exceeded over 60 *million* books (that was the figure a year ago, probably 70 *million* by now)... This is a phenomenon in the publishing industry, and they are mostly hard cover books priced at 29.95 (+ tax) (how much is that?., 70 *million* times $30.00).., ***and it's all fiction!!...***

But I am neither a theologian nor a Biblical scholar, so you will have to forgive me if I "wonder" out loud about a few things from my simplistic perspective... It seems almost tragic, that the "faithful" have been predicting these "end times" for almost 2000 years, and sadly, they all died without seeing the fruits of their dire predictions becoming manifest!..   Such a disappointment!..

The "signs" of the "last days", are that the *"Four Horsemen of the Apocalypse"* will be unleashed on humanity:.. ***Well!!.., as far as I can tell..,*** These four horsemen have been unleashed and riding roughshod at full gallop from day "One"!!...

A rider on a white horse, bent on conquering all humanity... Gengis Khan??.., Attila the Hun??.., Alexander the Great??.., the Roman Empire??.., Napoleon??.., Hitler??.., Stalin??.., Mao??.., Saddam Hussein??.., ***Etc., and etc.!!...***

A rider on a red horse with the power to take peace from the Earth, and the power to make men slay each other... The dreamers of Utopia:.. Carl Marx and Communism??.., Fascism??.., Socialism??.., Totalitarianism??.., Religionisms??.., Terrorism?? *Religious* Terrorism?? ***Etc., and etc.!!...***

A rider on a black horse holding a pair of scales in his hand, saying; "A quart of wheat for a days wages, and three quarts of Barley for a days wages, and do not damage the oil *(how prophetic!)* and the wine"!.. The Great Depression??.., Inflation??.., Unemployment??.., Poverty??... ***Etc., and etc.!!...***

And a rider on a pale horse, with the rider named "Death"... And they (The four horsemen) were given power over a fourth of the earth to kill by the sword, famine and plague, and by the wild beasts of the Earth... ***This is almost a joke!!!...*** This rider named "Death" has been riding *at full gallop* since the beginning of time.., and over ***"all"*** of the Earth, *and He has overtaken us all*!!, the believers and the unbelievers alike!!...

Death by the sword??, *another joke..,* the sword is obsolete.., not efficient enough.., the sword has been replaced by machine guns, cannons, smart bombs, and nuclear bombs!!... Wars and rumors of wars from day "One", and still in progress!!... ***Etc., and etc.!!...***

And Plagues??.., it is estimated that 300 million people died from the "Small Pox" epidemic that started before the middle ages and ravaged continent after continent, and century after century, up until the latter part of the 20th Century, wiping out entire civilizations (The American Indian population numbered in excess of 75 million when the Spaniards arrived, and due to smallpox, measles, pneumonia, influenza, and etc., they were decimated... The population of Mexico went from more than 30 million to less than 3 million within 50 years... One third of the population of Europe (25 million people) died from the "Bubonic Plague" within three years (after decimating Africa and India).., and the "AIDS" virus is still running rampant throughout the globe, and millions have already succumbed, with millions yet to succumb!!... ***Etc., and etc.!!..***

And "Famines", from Biblical famines, to modern day famines, would require a "book within a book" to record, with as many chapters as there are countries in the world!!... ***Etc., and etc.!!...***

And death by "wild beasts"??!!... ***Another joke!!...*** (is it possible that there be "death by laughter"??)... I'm sorry, but, as far as I'm concerned, the writer of "Revelations" has lost credibility here!.. Compared to war, plague, and famine, death by wild beasts is relatively insignificant... If he had said "death by insects"..., (the mosquito; malaria, West Nile virus, etc.., fleas and tics; that spread the Bubonic plague, etc.., Locusts; that caused famines.., Killer Bees, or the common housefly.., or mention of "Bacteria")..., *now that would have been a revelation!!!..*

And he (the writer of Revelations) spoke of this as a "prophecy", that "must soon take place", "because the time is near"!!!???... (Rev. 1:1-3) **That was 2000 years ago!.,** but I guess just about anything can be rationalized, because; "With the Lord, a thousand years is as one day" (as is *one minute, or the blink of an eye, or one nano-second,* ***ad infinitum!)..,*** and I'm sure that this "near time" has been looked upon as imminent from the first day these words were spoken, just like it is today.., and probably from now on, and perhaps for the next millennium, and etc.!!. I'm sure the victims of the "Black Plague" thought it to be imminent, and the Second World War seemed a fulfillment of the "Four Horsemen" prophesy (**with 50 million dead**).., and that that "near time" had come!!.., with "dooms day" predictors on every street corner...[13]

Am I denying the Apocalypse, or the Rapture, or the great Tribulation??? No.., I am not denying it... In fact, I am affirming it!!! I think that the Apocalypse and the Rapture are the same event!!... Suppose (for instance) that the Earth is hit by an asteroid from outer space (it's happened before!!)... *In a moment,* the tectonic plates of the Earth would buckle, with tidal waves, earthquakes, volcanoes, hurricanes, fire storms, poison gasses, etc., and etc... *In a moment* there would be millions of deaths, and in that moment millions of Souls would be released (the Rapture), and the aftermath of such a catastrophe would be starvation, deprivation, disease, anarchy, (another ice age?).., etc., and etc.., to such an extent that the living (those "left behind" survivors) would envy the dead (the great Tribulation)... Or Armageddon!!. Nuclear War!!... I don't see how it can be avoided...

So.., (among the "true believers"), the question arises?.. Is this the "Truth"?.. The above statements that I have made about the "End Times".., is this the "Truth"??. "***NO", it is not the "Truth".., I don't know the "Truth"!..*** It is just one more speculation.., among the tens of millions of speculations (equal to the number of people who have read "the Book")!..

Now, I am not here to throw stones at the book of Revelations, nor to add to, or take away anything from it.., etc.., but I have to ask the Question: ***"SO WHAT"???*** The book is so enigmatic that no one can decipher it, although everyone tries, and with great debate.., ***but to no avail!!!..*** And the "Great Tribulation"??. *Everyone has tribulations!!. War is tribulation, famine and disease is tribulation, lying in the Cancer ward with tubes sticking out of your body, waiting to die.., is tribulation.., and we all die!.,* ***death is "Death"..,*** *and does it matter if it*

---

[13] I find it interesting to note, (an oversight?), that in all of these prophesies of worldly kingdoms and empires.., the "New World" (North and South America.., 1/3 of the world's land mass).., is not mentioned or even alluded to!., neither symbolically, metaphorically, or actually!...

*be by Atomic Bomb, the "barbarians" coming over the hill, an asteroid from outer space, slipping on a banana peel, **or whatever**, and for all intents and purposes.., when YOU die:, the World Ends!!!.., and you go to meet your Maker!!, (the "Second Coming")?..* There is nothing "new" here!.., this is the way it has always been!!!.

I think I've made my point, but I am always looking for "corroboration".., that is, similarities in other religions that substantiate a "Truth" that is "Universal"!., and I found one, in Buddhism!!!... I found the same "Four Horsemen" (or the same facsimile) spoken of by Buddha, only He described them as:.. **"Old Age"., "Sickness"., "Misery"., and "Death"!!..,** and they are not to happen "soon" (or in the nebulous future).., they are in the process of happening **"Now"!..** The situation is "urgent", and "imminent"!!... **"You are living in a house (the body) that is burning down around you"!!!...**[14] **You must "exit" this house by way of abstract meditation, seeking "Union with the Divine" "Within".,** (in the interior realm of "fifth dimensional consciousness", *where the "Lord" resides*)...

So.., if you are really looking for the "Second Coming", you won't find it in the pages of "Revelation", but you may find it in the interior of your own heart, in the process of contemplation, without "intellectualizing" and with the sincerity of "the Soul that wants to know", and the earnest "desire" for "Communion".., or do you even possess this kind of sincerity.., because.., *you can't fool God!.., even though you may be fooling yourself...*

And So.., (ha ha), I will now give you the "True" signs of the "Last Days"... *How presumptuous!!, how pretentious!!, how audacious!!, how arrogant!!.., etc. and etc...* Yes, I am all of that, as well as sincere.., and I will now give you the "True" signs of the "Last Days"... Are you ready??... The "True" signs of the "Last Days" are: "Your hair turns gray (or white).., Your sight grows dim.., your teeth become loose and fall out.., and of course the very first sign:., *You were Born,* and your death was imminent from day "one"!!., Or you could just slip on a banana peel, and death would over-take you "like a thief in the night"... And when you die.., it's the "End of Your World"...

You can't say that you haven't been warned!... The signs are all there... "Seek ye first the "Kingdom of God" that is within you"... It is a mistake to "wait" for some apocalyptic event...

"REPENT!!!
The Kingdom of God is at hand"!!!...

*** *** ***

The "Truth" of the "Holy Scriptures"

Can the "Bible" (Holy Scriptures) be trusted?., as being the Divinely inspired "word of God"??? Well, that depends, if you are talking about the Hebrew Scriptures.., of the Christian Scriptures.., or the Hindu.., or the Buddhist.., or the Moslem.., or *(Whatever)* etc., and etc... Now, OBVIOUSLY.., each and every one of these different religious "belief systems" believes that their "Holy Scriptures" are the "True and Infallible" inspired "Word of God" and they will go to "HOLY WAR" and slaughter your "Infidel" ass to prove it!!!
What's wrong with this picture???

So.., when I was a young boy.., about the age of 8 or 9 years old, I was going to a Christian school, and I had to learn the intricacies of my religion, and Bible study was an essential part of the curriculum... I walked around in a state of deep contemplation and introspection, weighed down by my own sins and the sins of the world, with an attitude of gloom and doom that was much too serious for my young years... So one day I asked my Father: "Dad.., did you ever read the Bible"?.. "Oh Yeah", he said, "I read the Bible all the way up to the place where Abraham tied his ass to a tree and climbed the mountain"!.. "That was one miracle too many for me", he said, "I slammed the book shut and never read it again"!!. .....I laughed so hard I rolled on the floor!.. I laughed for three days!.. I told all of my classmates at school, and we laughed for three more days...

Now.., I could probably write a 1000 page commentary on this subject.., but I won't... I will leave that task for you to add your own commentary... But I will add another one of those statements that will again piss-off a lot of people, and it is this: Don't let your Bible.., be your God!.. Don't let your Bible.., replace God!.. If your

---

[14] This is the essence of "The Lotus Sutra"., the "parable" delivered by the Buddha.., to an endlessly large throng of "various kinds" of sentient beings on Vultures Peak Mountain...

immediate reaction to this statement is a rebuttal.., you have missed the point!..

But you can be assured of one thing… In those "Last Days".., when the "Anti-Christ" comes.., he will be quoting the Bible forwards and backwards, to make his case!..
Enough said!..

* * *   * * *   * * *

The "Avatars"

Whereas.., The "Bhagavad Gita" is the "Eastern" counterpart of the "Western" Bible, no *true* "Seeker of Truth" will fail to transcend his dogmatic prejudices and see this document in it's true light… While the "Western" Bible deals mainly as an historical record of it's people and their "on again-off again" relationship with God, the "Gita" is (by contrast) a **direct dialogue** between God and man, outlining the principles, the method, and the "Way" for the ultimate purpose and reason for "Life", and that is the "Enlightenment and Union" of God and man into the totally evolved "Super-Being" that it is *man's true destiny* to become…

While the Western Bibliographers were still herding sheep and living in tents, their Eastern counterparts were building magnificent cities and civilizations, excelling in the arts, literature, architecture, music, philosophy, poetry, etc., with their *Superior alphabet.., and esoterically descriptive language,* that; to this day.., "defies" adequate translations into English!!. A "High" civilization and culture so advanced[15] that it eventually succumbed to it's own success.., by overpopulation…

While the relatively "barbaric" Western civilizations were totally ignorant of the existence of their Eastern counterparts.., the Lord God (of course).., was not!.. For Western man *to even imagine* that God would completely ignore, abandon, and disregard his Eastern counterparts is just the *all too clear evidence* of the small minded, self righteous, egotistical, and "holier than thou" mentality of the West!…

To even imagine that your "own" Bible (East or West) is the only valid scripture sanctioned and inspired by God, is to *presume* (a great sin) that God is of the same "small minded" mentality as yourself!.. The literature of India; the Gita, the Upanishads, the Mahabharata, the Rig Veda, and the Yoga Sutras of Patanjali (to name just a few) are the clear *"inspirational"* evidence of the hand of God at work among the Hindu people.., and no mortal author claims credit for these *anonymous* manuscripts.., all predating the Christian era, and some (the Vedas) by thousands of years…

Hear now.., the discourse (Word) of the Lord, as spoken to his chief disciple; the warrior-prince "Arjuna", and recorded in the *inspired* "Song of the Beloved".., (*The Bhagavad Gita*)… The "Blessed One" speaks: (Chapter IV, verses 6 thru 9)…

*(6)… "Though Unborn, Eternal, and Lord of all beings.., yet by establishing Myself in My material nature, **I come into being** by My own power"…*
*(7)… "For whenever there is decline in virtue, and rise in unrighteousness, **then I send forth..,** **Myself**"…*
*(8)… "For the protection of the Good, for the destruction of the wicked, and for the establishment of righteousness, **I am born from age to age**"…*
(9)…Whosoever knows this; My Divine Birth and Actions, is not born again upon leaving the body, but comes directly unto me…

The physical "Incarnation" of the Lord God in human form, is the appearance on Earth of the **"God/Man"..,** (a.k.a.), the **"Avatar"**… Now.., Obviously and without a doubt.., Jesus Christ was an "Avatar".., an "Incarnation of God"… If you want to know the "nature" of God.., study the "nature" of Jesus Christ… But.., of course.., "from age to age".., there have been *"other"* Avatars.., and to say that "my Avatar is better than your Avatar".., **is an absurdity of the first magnitude!!**…

And , (of course), *ALL* of the religions predict that *their* "Avatar" will come again: **The Christians..,** look for the "second coming of *Christ*" (a.k.a. the *Messiah*), and he will come on a white horse, as "King of Kings" and "Lord of Lords" with the double edged sword of his mouth, and a sickle (to reap the earth) in his hand… (symbolism abounds

---

[15] The Hindu culture was the first (15-10 centuries B.C.) to advance the science of (Vedantic) herbal medicine, including advanced techniques of "surgery", and even cosmetic surgery, that are still practiced today, as well as the first metallurgists to produce "carbon steel", and the single digit number system, including the concept of "zero" (which is said to be second only in importance to the discovery of "fire"), as well as advanced techniques in the "Science" of meditation, and "herbs of mysterious virtue"…

here, and this is a composite view)... *The Hindus..,* look for the "Kalki Avatar"... This is the last of the Avatars of the Lord, who will descend as Kalki--- an armed warrior mounted on a white horse furnished with wings, waving over his head with one hand the sword of destruction and holding in his other a "disc" (a space-age weapon to reap the earth)... *The Buddhists..,* look for the coming of "Maitreya", the Buddha of "All Encompassing Love"..., and he comes to usher in the new "Age of Enlightenment"... *The Jews..,* who are still waiting for *their* Messiah...

Etc.., and Etc...

So be prepared!!... The future **"Avatar-Messiah"** *will come!!..,* and HE will satisfy the prophesies of all religions.., and all religions will claim him.., except for (of course) the "Ass-holes".., *whom HE will utterly destroy!!... and HE will not disappoint!!...*

The concept of the "Trinity" (the Father, Son, and Holy Spirit), which all theologians agree is beyond human conception or comprehension, has it's counterpart in the Eastern tradition of**: "God"; the *unmanifested*,** all-pervading , omnipotent, omnipresent, **Spirit,** (which is a "quality" of Consciousness), and the manifestation on Earth of HIS **"Avatar"** Incarnation (a.k.a. the **"Son"** of God.., who **is** God)...

So.., there is no real conflict between the Eastern and Western view of the "Trinity", except for the *concepts,* which all parties agree is beyond conception, and unfathomable to human understanding.., and which is further complicated by the *"Variegated Cloak of Words"...* **Do you see??..,** how easy it is to get tangled up in "Words", and concepts beyond conception.., and dogmatic assertions.., that lead to divisions.., that lead to **Wars!!. Do you see??.** ...And the "True Believer" will leap onto the stage, shouting: "There is no God but God".., and slit your throat because your concepts are different than his!.. **Will this insanity never end??...** And yet.., there are no divisions in the "Truth".., only in your conceptions...

So.., from "Age to Age", the **"Avatars"** have appeared on earth (for the protection of the good, the destruction of the wicked, and for the establishment of righteousness)... India claims to have had at least "Two" Avatars in it's recorded history, and of course, "Jesus" is the Avatar of the Christian era, and "Buddha" is regarded (by some theologians) to have been an Avatar, (as his destiny was foretold from his birth).., which is (of course) "anathema" to those who view Buddhism from the "denial of God and the Soul" viewpoint!.. *The contradictions here are "blatant" and obvious!!,* and must be addressed...

But I prefer to think that "Buddha" was *Not* an Avatar.., but rather that He *achieved* Avatar status!!. *This was a monumental event*!!. In the history of the world.., this was a monumental event... **Here we have a convergence!!,** of all philosophies, of all Religions, and all of Science (even evolution), and the fulfillment of the Divine plan.., that it is man's destiny, to become "One" with his Creator, and a Super-Being in a Galactic Multi-Dimensional Universe!!. **"I have spoken"** says the Lord; **"Ye.., are Gods"!!.** *This* is the potential.., and *This* is the promise.., and this is in harmony with Christian doctrine (as well as all others), that the "Avatar" lives in all of us, as a potential to be realized and re-united with his Creator... *"This"* is the *"Way"*!!.

And it is a tradition of the Avatars.., to refer to **"Themselves"** at times in the "First Person", (as God, the manifested) and at other times referring the people to worship "God the Father" (*the Unmanifested, all-pervading ,"Spirit"*)... **"They"** are (of course) "One" and the same, but **"They"** are making a concession to the people, who are of limited intelligence and not capable of the discernment between God the "Unmanifested", and the physical "Avatar" manifestation they see before them...

Now.., it is not wrong to worship "God" in HIS "Avatar" manifested form, and indeed, this is perhaps the limited capacity of most of the people, but the Avatars themselves encourage the people to worship God in the "Highly Abstract" Universal, Unmanifested, and "Spirit" aspect.., because it is in this unmanifested aspect.., in the "Inner Sanctum" of the Soul, that "Communion" (dialogue) with the "Most High" comes about!.. As Jesus declared: (John 4:23-24): *"Yet a time is coming, and has now come, when the true worshipers will **worship the Father** in Spirit and truth, for they are the kind of worshipers the Father seeks... God is Spirit, and his worshipers must worship in Spirit and truth"*...

The point here; is that the Lord God is active in the affairs of men, and has manifested his "Avatar" presence on planet earth on several occasions.., and more than that, HE has (from time to time) awakened the Avatar that resides in the Soul of "man", and Hero's have arisen and Championed the cause of the Good, the Right, and the True!., and their epic and heroic battles and adventures will be told and retold for millennia…

So, (coming to the point),   When Jesus says: *"I am the way, the Truth, and the Life"..*, and; *"No one comes to the Father but by me"!.,* and.., *"I stand at the door and knock, any one that hears my voice and opens the door, I will come in and sup with him, and he with me"..*, **the question arises!:** Is HE speaking as an entity separate from God.., or is he speaking as God himself, in his manifested "Avatar" form??? **This is the all important question,** and how you answer this question determines whether you separate yourself and your religion from the totality of History (**His-story**), or whether you see your particular "Bible" in the much larger context of "one more chapter" in the vast "Book of Many Chapters" that comprises, constitutes, and co-affirms the never ending and continuous epic battles against the adversary by none-other than the Super-Hero of all time, The "Avatar", who is none other than the Lord God ***Himself!!!…***

So.., (the point being:); ***IT is "I"..,*** (says the Lord).., ***Who AM** the Way, the Truth, and the Life.., and no one comes to Me, but by Me.., and it is **"I"** who stand at that door and knock, and any one hear My voice and answer, **"I"** will come in and sup with him, and he with Me!!!...* **This** is the standing invitation, and it originated with **God the Father,** and it echoes from timeless Eons past, and there are no disagreements here with any of HIS "Avatar-incarnations" who echo this Truth…

So.., (in the final analysis), ***what is it that we are to do??…***   It is probably too much to ask of the common man (nor is it necessary), that he take a World view, researching all the Religions of the world, distilling it all down to a comprehensive "Unified Overview", observing the "footprints" of the Avatars throughout History… but if he were to do this, he would rise above the dogmatic and slavish addiction to any one religion or creed.., he would discover the "Bottom Line" summation of each and every religion to be the same!!, and it is this:

"Seek ye first the Kingdom of God that is within you"…
Love (and seek) the Lord your God, with all your heart, mind, and soul…

Worship the Lord, within the "Inner Sanctum" of your Soul, and listen for His Voice, which is Revelation and Knowledge, because this is "Communion" (dialogue), and herein.., is that *Ancient path..,* known as ***"The Way", and love your neighbor as yourself…***

and.., Do good.., every chance you get…

This.., in it's totality , is the ***"Way"…***
Everything else.., is superfluous!..

✶✶   ✶✶   ✶✶

BOOK X

"Nepal.., and Meetings with Remarkable Minds"

Well.., I had thought to exclude this chapter from this book, because of the enigmatic nature of it, but it presses on my soul, and I find that I must include it after all...

My six month visa for India was almost expired, so I was compelled to leave the Country... My destination; Katmandu, Nepal...

From the border town at Raxall, India, to the mountain city of Katmandu, was a journey of less than 100 miles, but it was over some of the most rugged and magnificently beautiful terrain on the face of the Earth...

First by train, across the "Tarai", a sub-tropical flat land, with rice fields and swampy jungle, known for its outbreaks of deadly malaria, and as the domain of the mighty Bengal Tiger, which is relentlessly hunted by Rajahs, Princes, and great white hunters with high powered rifles, safely seated out of harms way.., on the backs of elephants...

The railway ended at Amlekhganj, where I boarded a rust and mud covered old bus, the roof stacked high with an assortment of baggage, blanket rolls, wicker baskets, crates of chickens, pots, pans, and etc... It was a motley crew of Nepalese, Tibetans, Hindus, Hippies, Buddhist Monks, merchant traders, men and women, children and babies...

The bus traveled ever upwards, along an unpaved road carved out of the edge of heavily forested mountains, with the majestic snow covered Himalayas reaching toward the heavens, and the valleys below, where you could look down.., upon the clouds...

We crested at Chandra-giri pass, at the 8000 foot level, looking down into the Nepalese valley, about 4000 feet below... The lush, emerald green valley, about 12 miles wide and 15 miles long, stretched out below, like a patchwork quilt consisting of an endless array of tiny little squares and rectangles of farmland under cultivation, and terraced rice paddies that made enchanted stairways up the sides of the mountains and down into the valleys...

Legend has it (and geologists confirm) that this was once a great freshwater lake, fed by glaciers, and the great Bodhisattva warrior, "Manjusri", with his mighty sword, cleaved an opening in the mountains and drained the lake, foretelling the birth of the Kingdom of Nepal... Down in the valley off to the right, is the capitol city of Katmandu, with exotic palaces, towers and pagoda temples; their shining roofs covered with sheets of beaten brass, rising up, tier upon golden tier, above the city dwellings…

Off to the right of Katmandu, across the Bagmati river is the sister city of Patan, and about eight miles up river, to the East, is the city of Bhaktapur... These three cities were, at one time, three separate principalities, seemingly in competition with each other, each one trying to outdo the other in the grandeur of it's religious temples, buildings, and of course the central showplace of the city; the palace square; known as "Durbur Square"... Each city has it's own Durbur Square, and the result of this religiously oriented grandeur, is to transport the spectator.., and it does... For centuries, the valley of Nepal, walled in as it was by the impenetrable Himalayas, had been a closed city... Here was the fabled Shangri-la.., where the Celestial meets the terrestrial.., where the religions of Hinduism and Tibetan Buddhism converged and merged.., where the religious art and exotic architecture mimicked the fifth dimensional landscapes of heavenly realms... Here, in this valley of enchantment, is where the rust and mud covered old bus came to a stop, on the cobble stone streets of Katmandu...

We arrived in the crowded square of the "Asan Tol" market place... Free enterprise was not only alive and well here, it was exuberant!.. There was a "joy of life" here that expressed itself in the smiling faces of the people, busy with the business of selling their home grown and hand made wares in this massive flea-market, alive with the red, yellow and green baskets of produce that lined the walkways between the rows of customers making their purchases... This was the meeting place, the ancient cross-roads of the ancient trade route that linked China, Tibet and India with Nepal... "What do you want, Sir?.. Hashish?., Ganja?., Opium?., I can get it for you,.. also I have very fine skins, of tiger and leopard, and look at this Sir.., the very fine pelt of the Snow Leopard!., only two left today"... The square was surrounded by four and five story ancient apartment type buildings, with wooden balconies on every floor, overlooking the market square, and the bottom floor of these apartment buildings consisted of shops that opened out to the market place and contained everything imaginable... There was, of course, the "Hong Kong" shops, with their array of stereos, wrist watches, cassette players, polyester suits, etc.., and the Tibetan shops, loaded with the personal possessions and religious treasures carried out by the thousands of Tibetan refugees that made up part of the citizenry of Nepal.., the Chinese shops, with their fine silks, brocades, glass, ivory, silver and brass.., the Indian "Kashmiri" shops, with garments made of the finest Kashmir wool, religious artifacts, tiger and leopard skins, pots and pans, etc.., and of course, the Nepalese themselves, who were the finest craftsmen, builders of the splendor that was Nepal, renowned for their paintings, stone carvings, intricate wood carvings, detailed brass figurines, hand made carpets, dyed print fabrics, etc... And the "Trekkers" shops, that would outfit you with everything, including the Sherpas that would escort you to the summit of Everest, if that was where you desired to go...

But the finest craftsmanship was reflected in the faces of the people... I recall (not to be forgotten) this young woman; probably in her early twenties, with a basket of produce on her head, stabilized with her left hand, an inquisitive boy child on her right hip, held effortlessly by her strong right arm, dressed in a full length black dress trimmed in red, a red sash around her waist, her glistening jet black hair woven into a bun on top of her head, multiple strings of beads around her neck, beaded earrings that dangled almost to her shoulders, those exotic Asian eyes, high cheekbones, and a smile on her face that would have put the Mona Lisa to shame... The smile was not for me, it was just the joy of life, that emanated from her soul... God, was she beautiful.!. Not only in the classic sense, but in the incomparable beauty that reflected her "Inner" strength, her character, and the nobility of her Spirit.., which was wholesome and Holy... And she was not the exception to the rule, she just exemplified the rule, of this proud and noble people...

I enquired about a hotel, and was escorted by a young boy down a side street into a cafe, and up the steps to the rooms above... I was shown to a room that contained about a dozen beds... "Sorry, Sir,.. no private rooms available, very crowded, many tourists come this time,.. O.K."?.. Yes, I said, o.k., and I placed my backpack on an empty bed among the other beds with backpacks on them... I tipped the young boy.., a smile spread across his face and his eyes lit up like the Milky Way on a dark night... I had a friend for life.!.

The café downstairs had a rough hewn atmosphere, reminiscent of a gold mining camp in the Klondike, with the boisterous chatter of a multi ethnic crowd from everywhere on the globe.., mountain climbers from everywhere mingled with long haired Hippies from all over Europe and America, along with Indian traders, Sherpas, Tibetan refugees, etc... The menu was in English and Nepalese, the food was of simple and robust fare, consisting of a variety of meats and poultry prepared as soups or steaks, along with a variety of vegetables in sauces and casseroles, with heavy bread and black tea sweetened with sugar and thick cream, and the specialty of the house; rice beer.., and fruit pies for desert.!.

I went back to the room, and there were four other occupants there besides myself... We shook hands and introduced ourselves... There was Tom, a medical student on sabbatical from England.., Peter, a blond, long haired, bespectacled and beaded hippie intellectual from Holland.., Knute, a sculptor from Denmark, here to get inspiration.., and Jack, moustache and goatee, from N.Y., on a mission (dope smuggler) to bring Enlightenment to the masses... We fell into conversation as though we had known each other all of our lives... We told stories and laughed till we cried... The chillum[1] was packed with that excellent Nepalese hashish and passed from hand to hand, as great clouds of blue-gray smoke filled the room... Other travelers entered the room, were handed the chillum, took a hit, and you could watch their face light up into a big grin, and they entered the conversation as though they had been there from the beginning... More stories, more laughter, more blue-gray smoke,.. this is why we came, to get High in the Kingdom of HIS Highness, and we got HIGH, and the conversation entered into an elevated level of those things esoteric, those things beyond the ken of

---

[1] A "chillum", is a slender funnel shaped pipe about five or six inches long, used throughout India, Pakistan, Nepal, etc., for smoking hashish. An irregular shaped stone is lodged about ¼ the way down the funnel, the large end is loosely packed with hashish, and the small end is covered with a small piece of dampened porous cloth. It is cupped between the two hands and held upright with the fingers. The smoke is inhaled through the hollow of the hands, and the pipe never touches the lips...

those Priests, Bishops and Rabbis who have never gotten High... Such a tragedy, such a waste, but they will not.!.

The room filled to capacity with travelers, with laughter, and with smoke... At some point we descended to the cafe downstairs for fruit pie and sweet tea... It was a celebration,.. joy and laughter prevailed, and eventually, back to the room for more light conversation and by consensus, the light was turned out.., to deep untroubled sleep...

There is an instant camaraderie that happens among travelers on the road... The one common denominator that united us into a fraternity.., and that was our common search for enlightenment and truth, wherever it may be found... It was the camaraderie of that great adventure of Life.., the adventure of the "open road".., and the incredible improbability that we could all arrive here from our various points on the globe at this exact same time.., which was "Now".!.

I awoke early the next morning, as did we all, and after a light breakfast at the café and a couple of tokes on the hash pipe, I proceeded out into the bright sunlight, into the streets of Katmandu, alive with the hustle and bustle of street traffic, people, kids and animals... My perceptions had changed, instead of being focused on the specific, my perception was now "wide angle", and I was almost overwhelmed with the magnitude and scope of my perceptions that scaled the height and breadth of my surroundings... I marveled at the things that I saw, that had somehow escaped my notice before... It was the hashish.!. Oh yes.!. Halleluiah, Praise the Lord.!. This was "The Kind"... The three, four and five storied buildings had an aged, old, but timeless look about them, as though they had been there forever, with their balconies overlooking the city streets... What I hadn't noticed before was the intricate and ornate designs carved in the wood in the overhead of the balconies.., the delicate colorful streamers that waved in the wind.., the little bells that dangled from overhead, and the flowering vines that climbed up the outside from balcony to balcony, up to the roof, reaching for heaven itself, and heaven rained down sunshine and blessings... At every intersection there was a shrine or a "stupa", that was a work of art and architecture composed of a curvilinear cathedral like geometry that seemed to reach an apex and continue on in a mirror image into the invisible (not easily explainable)...

It's a question of timing... It was 1969 in the fourteenth century,.. or was it the fourteenth century B.C.?. No matter.., it was a timeless time.., a time like no other time before, a unique time, a time that was destined to change.., and not for the better... As I walked down those city streets I considered myself to be blessed, the luckiest of mortal men, caught in this time-warp of timelessness, in the ever present "Now".., the "Now" that always was and always is...

Someone had made the effort of cataloging all of the shrines, the stupas, monuments, pagodas, temples, religious sites, and etc., of Nepal... The number exceeded 3000, and still counting.!. Every day there, was a High adventure of religious exploration, good friends, good times, and a celebration of life, culminating in a feast and festivities in the evening, followed by clouds of blue-gray smoke, laughter, and in-depth conversations into the esoteric mysteries and the meaning and purpose of life, etc., and etc... It was the best of times.., the Highest of times... We together discovered the "Secret"... Perhaps it was The Secret of all secrets, and that was that God was "High"... HE was the "Most High God".!. The Highest of the High,.. and to appreciate that fact, you had to get High yourself, to worship HIM, in HIS High-ness.., and the nature of the Worship consisted of joy, laughter, and a reverence for the mystery of it all... Halleluiah.!.

One of the most prominent religious places in all of Nepal was the temple at "Swayambhu", called Swayambhunath... It was a place of pilgrimage, and devout Buddhists from everywhere on the globe came here to pay their respects... As legend (and History) has it, "Vipasya" (a Buddha from a previous era) observed that in the valley of Nepal, with all of it's natural blessings, it had not the Sacred Lotus flower, and HE set the Sacred Lotus blossom afloat on the great lake that was Nepal, and as the waters receded, and wherever the Sacred Lotus touched earth and bloomed, that was where the temple of Swayambhunath, dedicated to "Swayambhu" (The Ever Existent One), would be built... And just North-West of the city, on a hill that rose 300 feet above the surrounding level plain, was where the Sacred Lotus touched ground and took root...

It was an adventurous climb of 500 steps up the heavily wooded hill, through a tribe of aggressive temple monkeys panhandling for food, to the temple of Swayambhunath at the top... At the top of the steps, in front of the temple, was a large circular stone pedestal with carvings of animals around its exterior, with two life size Celestial stone lions standing guard, one on each side... On top of the pedestal rested the giant "Thunderbolt Dorje" cast in heavy metal, which is the Llamic scepter, signifying dominion and power of both the interior and exterior Realms, and Master of the "Clear Light", of the Ultimate Reality...

The temple itself was not that impressive, having been built about 300 years B.C., but it was impressive because of its history and location, overlooking the city... The modest but ornate temple had a doomed roof on top of which was a cubicle structure (about 6 foot cubed) with the half closed meditative eyes and stylized nose of the Buddha painted on each of the four sides, looking in the four directions... On top of the cubicle, in a graduated tier, rose the 13 gilded disks (representing the 13 realms of the Buddhist cosmology), and at the apex of the (Christmas tree shaped) tier rose the golden (umbrella shaped) canopy, the symbol of Royalty and Divinity... The stone paved and low walled temple grounds contained several shrines as well as other smaller buildings that probably housed an Abbot and several Buddhist monks that resided there and took care of the place as part of their devotional service... It was not permitted that tourists should enter the temple, and it was generally conceded that there wasn't much to see inside the temple anyway, as it was mostly rather empty and dark, the atmosphere most conducive to abstract meditation, which was its purpose... But the temple grounds were themselves a place of peace and tranquility, conducive to meditation, and I came here often for that purpose...

It had been about a year and a half since I had taken my last LSD enhanced meditation.., and I was fearful... I had looked into that forbidden realm.., that most terrifying place of insanity and hopelessness.., that place of damnation called "Hell"... One just doesn't view this unspeakable horror and walk away unscathed... I had been "scathed"... The event had been so traumatic that the memory imposed itself into my everyday waking and sometimes sleeping consciousness and debilitated and impaired my life, and I had to go to India.., and under the tutelage of the good Swami I underwent a concentrated regimen of mental discipline and meditation techniques that successfully repressed and circumvented that debilitating memory/vision... I had successfully pushed back that barrier.., pushed back, but not gone.., never gone...

So, it was with some trepidation that I accepted the capsule, offered by a friend... Is this the real stuff.?, I had asked, reflecting on the bootleg counterfeit that had poisoned my mind on that terrible preceding occasion a year and a half ago... Oh yes, he said.., this is the good.., I've taken it myself, many times... So it had all come together, just like it was supposed to.., the temple location, the magical ingredient, and the vessel...

I had learned a lesson.., that there is a difference between courage and foolhardiness, so if I was to err, it would be on the side of caution... I made no attempt to internalize this experience... No attempt to cross the Bardo to the inner realms... The external reality was, for the moment, spectacular enough, and nature did not disappoint... Vast vistas of clouds rolled in, and it is customary to see pictures in the clouds, but this was incredible!.. There were complete landscape scenes, complete with trees, hills and streams, with people fishing in the streams and gathered around in friendly conversations!.. I am not prone to hallucinations, but I thought, this must be a hallucination... I looked away, and later I looked again, and it was still there!., and complete in every detail!.. There was nothing esoteric or mystical about it.., just this incredibly beautiful nature scene, that remained as long as I cared to look at it... I was filled with awe and wonder, and many insights came to me, and there was gratitude, for all that was...

As I walked around the temple grounds, I chanced upon an unlocked door... The door was closed, but the padlock was lying on the ground. Someone had forgotten to replace it... I pondered at the door, and seized by curiosity, I opened it... I would not violate the sanctity of it by stepping across the threshold, but I had to see... It was a storage room, and in it were stored the traditional musical instruments, used in the traditional religious ceremonies, for the newly born, the newly married, the newly dead, and etc...

There was the traditional Buddhist gong.., made of hammered metal, about 4 or 5 feet in diameter and suspended from a transportable frame.., and also suspended from a transportable frame was this large base drum, that was a drum on the back side and a trumpet in front, and I could only imagine the effect of this "sound cannon"... There were also the traditional trumpets, that were so long (about 12 feet) that they had to rest on the ground, as well as the human thigh bone trumpets, and the double faced drums with the twin clappers that were quickly twisted back and forth to make their staccato beat, the various bells of differing shapes and sizes, stringed instruments, and etc... I observed in silent awe...

Here was the remnants of that ancient space age science.., in storage... From the ancient mystical past came this science, to be resurrected sometime in the far mystical future, but for the present it resided here.., in storage... It is the science of the "Liberation of the Soul".., through sound.!. As I viewed those instruments for the production of their unique sounds, I recalled vividly the time that I sat for meditation.., an LSD enhanced meditation, and from my stereo came the unique sounds.., actually, one specific unique sound that captured my attention so completely that I was instantaneously immersed in the sound.., out of my body and into the sound.!. The Soul.., (being totally non-substantive and devoid of every characteristic) (without center or circumference) WAS the sound!!! I was sound itself, and as it came through the speaker, I could see the speaker vibrate, and observed as the dust danced on the speaker.., and instantaneously, I was back in my body... The experience lasted only a moment, but in that moment, it was a revelation..! There are certain sounds that have the power to capture the Soul, and liberate it from the body.!.

This was the appeal of Buddhism.!. It's approach to the mysteries of "Being and Consciousness" were NOT religious.!, they were scientific and descriptive.!. Christianity doesn't have that.!. Both Buddhism and Hinduism go into profound detail about the Nature and Being of consciousness... Christianity doesn't have that.!. While Christianity acknowledges the Soul, it is almost ignorant of its profound and mystical qualities...

Both Buddhism and Hinduism concur,.. *and have explored and Named*,.. the various dimensions that make up the inner realms of a *multitude* of Heavens and Hells.., Christianity doesn't have that.!. While Christianity acknowledges both Heaven and Hell, it is relatively ignorant and simplistic concerning the vastness of both of these realms... Even the writers of "science fiction" portray "other dimensions".., and even though it is written (Luke 17:21) that "The Kingdom of God is within you".., Christians can't seem to get the concept... Even though "Heaven lies within you".., Christians never go there.!.

Both Buddhism and Hinduism have scientific and esoteric techniques of meditation that are "indispensable" in accessing the inner realms... Christianity doesn't have that.!.

Both Buddhism and Hinduism have that central aim.., of going "within".., to that place of absolute stillness and equanimity, that is the "Stargate".., the entrance to the inner realm, where the Soul is comprehended in its pristine purity and merged into the "Clear Light" of the "Ultimate Reality", and Knowledge is "known".., *Experientially"*... To have this experience is to achieve "Enlightenment".!. Christianity doesn't have that.!. The concepts of "Enlightenment" and "All Knowledge" are unknown to the Christian community!.. The concept of "Illumination" (illumined inner vision).., is (in Christianity).., a halo around your head?!!

The body is a temple... In both Buddhism and Hinduism, the techniques of meditation approach suspended animation, the state of "Samadii", a state of contemplation so deep, that for all intents and purposes, the resident "Soul" of the body loses contact with this dimension, and aided by the profound and mysterious "Kundalini" (psychic energy factor), the consciousness enters into the "Inner Dimension".., and is elevated to profound levels in a step by step orderly progression... "Chakra by Chakra".., the "Soul".., climbs the "Ladder of Knowledge", exploring other dimensions, gaining in knowledge, to finer and finer dimensions, to the ecstatic "Union with the Divine" ("Rapture") in the "Clear Light" of the "Ultimate Reality"... Christianity doesn't have that.!.

The Sacred texts of Buddhism[2] and Hinduism[3] are not so much belief systems, as they are "how to" manuals.., whereas the Sacred texts of Judeo-Christianity are considered to be the unerring "Word of God".., which is the incontrovertible and

---

[2] "Tibetan Yoga and Secret Doctrines",.. "The Tibetan Book of the Great Liberation",.. and "The Tibetan book of the dead",.. as translated by the late "Lama Kazi Dawa-Samdup", and edited by W. Y. Evans-Wentz… Oxford University Press…

[3] "The Yoga Sutras of Patanjali",.. as translated by "Dr. J. R. Ballantyne and Govind Sastri Deva" (Authors note: this is the preferred translation)… "The Upanishads",.. as translated by Swami Prabhavananda and Frederick Manchester (Various translations and Publishers),.. and etc…

uncontestable "bedrock" of the faith... With such a bedrock as the final arbiter, all should be peace and harmony.., all of one mind... All Jews would be Christians, and vice-versa!.. But such is not the case.!. There is in excess of 33,000 different denominations and factions, each one absolutely sure that their understanding of the bedrock Biblical text is the correct one, and denouncing others with a different understanding... Nor are their differences trivial or inconsequential.!. There are deep divisions within the Church (Eastern and Greek Orthodox Vs. Roman Catholic), (Catholic Vs. Protestant), (Baptist Vs. Jehovah's Witness), (Etc. Vs. Etc.), and etc., over whether Jesus Christ be God incarnate, or the Son of God, or both at the same time, or the "Son of Man" that achieved "Godhood" by virtue of the experience of "Rapture" (ecstatic Union with the Divine).., ("The Father is in me, and I in the Father"), Or is it as Jesus stated (John 10:34): that "All men are Gods".., of which Jesus was the "Prime Example" (John 10:36)... But one thing is for certain;... *any man that says he knows.., does not know.!.* He may believe, he may think, he may reason, he may point to the scriptures and pound the Bible,... *but he does not "Know"...* There is only one way to "Know".., and that is to have the experience of the Rapture yourself... Up until that time, this Knowledge is beyond the ken of human understanding... Mere words fail to convey, and controversy is pointless when it is a moot point...

It seems that almost any viewpoint can be supported or opposed by this (alleged) "word of God"... (During the Civil War, Southern Baptist preachers supported slavery with "Biblical" approval)... But it is not for me to point out the inconsistencies and contradictions of the Bible.., there are "enemies of the faith"[4] that are only too happy to do that... I have gone to great lengths to explain the difference between the historical "written word", and the Eternally Ever Present; "Living Word".., but for Christianity in general.., they don't know about this!.. A tragic oversight.., hidden in plain view...

Both Buddhism and Hinduism have their "Sacraments"... Those "Herbs of Mysterious Virtue", that allow Mankind to transcend the every-day mundane level of consciousness, and enter into an "altered state" where "Transcendental" experiences become possible... Buddhism had the "Lotus" flower, (especially the Blue Lotus)[5],.. and Hinduism had their "Soma", (called: the "Drink of Immortality")... In addition to these "Psychedelics", their religious and medical science also incorporated the lesser drugs of Opium, Hashish, Datura, and etc.[6]... Judeo-Christianity doesn't have that.!.

In fact, their absence from any mention at all is conspicuous!!! Surely these "Herbs" were known.!. It is certain that all of these herbs were known in ancient Egypt, including both cocaine and tobacco[7].!. How could they not be known, and why is there no mention of any of these in the Bible.?. Perhaps it was deemed too "Enlightening" for the common man, and kept as a secret of the Rabbinical Priesthood, who committed nothing to writing, lest the secret of their power fall into the hands of the common man... A conspiracy of silence, and then the secret was lost, due to war.., or whatever... Perhaps, perhaps?., but the fact remains that all peoples, on all the continents, were given their "Herbs of Mysterious Virtue".., but Judeo-Christianity doesn't have that...

So.., these were my thoughts, as I stood transfixed, looking through that open monastery door.., looking back in time... I gently closed the door of that ancient repository.., that housed the instruments of that Ancient Secret Science.., and replaced the padlock...

...It was the next day.., and Jack said "Come with me today, I want to get your opinion about something"... He didn't elaborate, and I just assumed it was a religious curiosity, temple site, or other tourist attraction... Always ready to explore new vistas, I said; "Sure,.. Let's go"...

It seemed that we wandered around aimlessly, on the outskirts of the city, engaged in pleasant conversation, and without my realizing it, we entered into a compound of dwellings.., where

---

[4] You may read the writings of "Louis Farrakhan" (called: the prophet of rage),.. and etc., but for a counterbalance you must also read: "Race, Religion, & Racism", by Dr. Fredrick K. Price... (www.faithdome.org)…

[5] Actually, the "Blue Lotus" is more correctly identified as the "Blue Water Lilly"…

[6] See; "The Plants of the Gods",.. by Richard Evans Schultes and Albert Hofmann,.. published 1979 by McGraw-Hill Inc.

[7] Forensic studies done on hair samples of 4000 year old Egyptian mummies positively identified both Cocaine and Tobacco, which leads to the unmistakable conclusion that there was trade with the Americas at least 4000 years before Columbus.!.

"He" resided... I had not the faintest idea of who "He" was.., and I cared less... I wasn't even aware that this was the "something" that Jack was referring to...

He was naked, except for a loin cloth.., and barefoot.!. Just another poor Indian "Sadhu", I thought.., that class of holy men that wander about India, homeless and without possessions, existing on charity... He had long grayish white hair and a beard, and rather light skinned for an Indian, but it had that tanned leathery look, as though having been exposed to the elements.., but His eyes!!; they glistened with the light of intelligence!!, and He was surrounded by about a half dozen disciples, mostly American and European...

We walked up to them, and Jack introduced me to the "Father"... The "Father" looked at me and smiled a "knowing" smile... He bowed from the waist, His long hair dragging on the ground.!. "I am Knowledge", He said, "I am a slave to Understanding"...

Oh, yeah, well.., I said, (totally unprepared for this encounter).., Hey, I'm not looking to become anybody's disciple.., and I have Knowledge myself, I've crossed the Bardo, been to the Deva World, climbed the ladder of Knowledge, etc., and etc., I don't think there is anything "you" can teach "me"...

(I don't recall exactly what I said, but that was the gist of it)... (and there it was again, that hint of arrogance and condescending lack of respect)... His reply.., cut me to the quick.!. If I had catalogued my LSD "trips", and labeled each one with a "key word"...., ...but I had never done that!..

He replied to me, just one sentence.., and in that sentence He incorporated each and every "key word" that triggered the memory of each and every "trip" that I had taken across the Bardo, and the Knowledge/Vision experiences I had received in "Communion" with the Lord.., *as though He had been there!!!*

I stumbled backwards, blown backwards, by the force of His statement, delivered by this unclad, barefoot, old man, with long white hair and beard, that spoke with the voice of authority,.. in perfect English,.. without trace of accent,.. and his speech was beyond articulate,.. it was beyond elegant.!, it was Shakespearian!!,   ...and then He walked away...

I was stunned, and I was speechless!!. I had displayed my arrogant and condescending attitude, and I had been shot down.., "in flames"!!. It was such an incongruity.., to hear this articulate Shakespearian eloquence, coming from this unclothed, barefoot, Indian "Sadhu".., that spoke to me about things He couldn't possibly have known.., *unless He had been there!!. ...A*nd there was something else about Him, something familiar.., Oh, yes, now I knew what it was.., He was the exact image.., of the image.., on the "Shroud of Turin"!!...

I stood there.., stunned, dazed, confused and speechless... I heard laughter... His disciples saw my predicament, and came over to me, with good natured chuckles, they led me and a few other newcomers away into a dwelling where we all sat in a circle on the floor, with one vacant space left in the circle...

We sat there, about a dozen of us, exchanging names, who we were, where we had come from, etc., and eventually the "Father" walked in and sat down in the vacant spot reserved for Him... There was a smile on his face and good natured laughter in his voice... He was handed the prepared chillum by one of his disciples, and cupped it in his hands as his disciple held a flame to the open end of the chillum... The Father inhaled deeply, as fire belched from the open end of the chillum, and huge clouds of blue-gray smoke billowed around his head... His lung capacity was amazing!... The chillum was passed to each one of us in turn, and we each took a long hit on it... The chillum was refilled, and the ritual was repeated... I sat there quietly, still speechless, observing the phenomenon of this scene unfolding here before me, and observing the extraordinary presence of this man; the "Father".., who spoke with the "First Person" commanding authority.., as though He were "God"!... "I am God", He said... This was not said as a grandiose proclamation... He said; "I am God" in the same matter of fact way that someone else might say; "I am Joe"...

Could it be?.. Could it really be??? All the signs seemed to indicate.., that this man had achieved what I had failed to achieve... He had scaled the heights of the inner dimensions, up the ladder of Knowledge (He had spoken to me the "key words" of that experience), and He had reached the level of "Dweller on the Threshold".., *and then He had made that "Leap of Faith" across the Threshold!., into the "Clear Light of the Ultimate Reality"!!...* If

He had done this, He could truly say; "I and the Father,.. are One"!!! If He had done this, He could truly say; (as Christ had said (in essence)) "I am God"... If He had done this, He would have achieved "All Knowledge".., and He would speak with that "First Person" authority (as did Christ)..., *and that's the way He spoke!!!*

Never had I met such a commanding presence.., a man that displayed this total command of the English language.., He had that "Zen" naturalness about Him.., that totally unaffected grace of movement, without trace of self consciousness or self doubt... A totally integrated personality!!.

One of the newcomers to the group voiced an angry protest; "You're not God", he said, "you're just another false prophet claiming to be God... If you are God, then why am I here in your house, exposing you for the heretic that you are"?., etc., and etc.!. His verbal attack was passionate and venomous.!. There was that sense of "déjà vu".., like a Biblical re-enactment...

"You are here because I choose for you to be here", the "Father" stated, "as an example to these others, so that they may decide who is the heretic"...

One of His disciples stood up and announced; "Hey, we have a rule around here", he said.., "you can have any opinion you want, but outside this compound!.. We don't have time for dissenters, here!", and with that he was escorted out the door, still spouting his venomous accusations... (Well, I thought to myself,.. that's one way to win an argument, but I would rather have heard a spirited debate)...

A conversation ensued, that ranged in scope from the philosophical to the metaphysical, and from nuclear physics to astro-physics... There was something in the recent news about the "Van Allen belt", and the "Father" rolled his eyes upward, as though gazing at the inside of His forehead, and gave a scholarly analysis, as though He were viewing the globe of the Earth from a Galactic vantage point!!. I was amazed and enthralled, by this unclothed, barefoot, gray haired old man that had this enormous range of knowledge that would have been the envy of a college professor... He seemed to know all the Philosophers and all of their philosophies, and to have read all the Great Books, and the penetrating insight that delved into the sub-atomic and the Astral-galactic, and He sat here in a circle on an earthen floor amongst a group of Hippies and vagabond travelers, with a chuckle in His voice, a twinkle in His eye, and a chillum loaded with the finest Nepalese hashish in His hand!!.

Again the chillum was fired up, belching fire from the backdraft as He exhaled enormous lungfulls of that blue-gray smoke that billowed around Him, reminiscent of a heavenly personage.., coming in the clouds... His capacity for the magical herb was amazing, and we each partook, as the chillum was passed around the circle of friends, and we got *High!!.*

The conversation resumed at an esoteric level, as we delved into the finer metaphysical mysteries, and at one point He made reference to some peoples "arrogance", and our eyes met for the briefest of moments, and I realized He was referring to me.!. I had been humbled already, and I just sat there in silence, too humiliated to say anything!.. The conversation resumed, and after some time He again made reference to "condescending attitudes", and again He was referring to me... He was intentionally provoking me, and my response just blurted out, unedited; "Forget about that", I said, "just talk"... He had required an apology of me, and I had apologized... One of His disciples chuckled at my concession, and I glared daggers at him, as if to say "So what", "What's it to you"?.. My body language spoke louder than words!.. "What are you laughing at".?, the "Father" spoke to His disciple,.. "He figured it out in five minutes,.. it took you longer than that"... And from that moment on, there was a rapport between us...

(But, I thought to myself, in my analytical way, that if the position had been reversed, I would not have required an apology, but would have overlooked the slight, as though it had never happened.., and I wondered?.; "does He have an Ego"??.)…

The conversation resumed, and drifted into the world of politics... The subject of the president of the United States came up, the most powerful leader in the world at that time; president Nixon... "He would crumble before me within five minutes"!!. The "Father" had spoken these words.., with the steeled voice of authority that made your blood run cold.., and I knew that it was true!!. Genghis Khan would have crumbled before Him!.. He spoke with the absolute authority and conviction of God Himself.., *and that's who He claimed to be!!!*

"The Father"

This was beyond charisma!!. Never before or since have I met anyone.., with such force of personality!!! It wasn't a question of Ego, or of a lust for Power... He had that power!!! The question was, what did He intend to do with it??! And the next question was.., what part was I to play in this scenario??? It seemed to me that I had been singled out.., but why?!!

....I am not one to easily commit myself to discipleship to any man or organization, but here was a man that had Knowledge and Power that was far beyond me, and I would have taken Him as my Teacher.., but just at that moment.., when I was ready to commit myself to discipleship.., He thrust his clenched fist into the air and shouted;.. "Incest is the Way"!!!

Again I was blown back!... "Incest is the Way"!!? Now what in the Hell did He mean by that!?? From what level of consciousness did that come from??? I was completely bewildered... Nor did He explain it!!! Was there some Higher esoteric meaning that I was supposed to grasp??? I didn't know.?. It seemed an incongruity...

But that was the closing statement of the discussion, and we all went outside, into the cold night air... When the Sun goes down in Nepal, it gets uncomfortably cold, but the "Father", being completely unclothed (except for the loin cloth) exhibited no discomfort... He was impervious to the cold!!. We strolled along in light discussion, to the entrance of the compound, where we said our farewells and departed for the night...

Early the next morning, I was back... I wondered if this meeting.., with the "Father".., was mere happenstance, or was it the reason that I came to India in the first place.?. It seemed too much of a coincidence to be just a coincidence.!.

The natural bent of my personality is analytical... I was on a mission.., to discover.., "what"??. I couldn't define it!?. What's it all about?., and what am I doing here?.. The Eternal questions... Did the "Father" have the answers??.

I mingled in with the other followers, busy with their morning chores, preparing breakfast, etc. I engaged them in light conversation, exploring attitudes, getting the "feel" of the place.., Analyzing...

When He saw me, His eyes sparkled, and with a broad smile on his Noble face, He bowed from the waist, His long hair dragging on the ground... "Namestae", I said, bowing my head, with my hands palms together (in prayer mode) in front of my face [8]... He was in the midst of a group of his followers, of which one was a Hippy girl, with that "free love" attitude, and she was displaying wanton glances at the Father, who gave her an affectionate hug,.. with an unspoken promise...

He could see my analytical frame of mind and confided in me... With a chuckle in His voice, He said; "I am God", "I am all things to all people"!.. "She needs me".!. This didn't bother me... Despite his gray hair, He had the physical strength and body of an eighteen year old... There was not an ounce of fat on his lean and supple body, that showed muscle tone and definition beneath his smooth tanned skin... He moved with the quickness and vitality of youth, and obviously, His sexual prowess was not in the least diminished!.. He was impervious.., to the penetrating harshness of the Noon day Sun, shining through a rarified atmosphere, the almost bitter cold of the night, and the sharp stones beneath his bare feet...

He was everything that I had expected an "Enlightened" person would be,.. except celibate!.. But what did I know?.. It was certainly not for me.., to judge Him!!! I was not in a position to cast the first stone.., or any stones!.. No.., no.., He was even more than I expected.., He was a "Law unto Himself"!.. He was dynamic!!!

I found myself caught up in the magnetic aura of His personality, and He spoke to me, personally, of things that no one else would know,.. about the "Threshold".., and Beyond!!.

So I spent the entire day there, in His company, observing.., analyzing... And it was amazing.!. There were entire groups of people that were protesting against the "Father"!!! They would be there on the outskirts of the compound, kept at bay by His disciples, shouting venomous slogans of "false prophet", "blasphemy", etc., and etc.!. I was particularly amazed by the passion and zeal of their venomous attacks!.. What had He done to generate such hatred?., except to claim that He was "God"!!!

---

[8] "Namestae", is the customary greeting in India… It's meaning (in essence) is; "I salute the God within you"…

Almost by osmosis, and analytical observation, I gleaned that there was a dope deal in the works here.!. That didn't bother me... The "High" afforded by this excellent Nepalese hashish was a "boon" to mankind.., an expansion of consciousness with religious fulfillment and objective analysis, that left you with an appreciation of the Grand Mystery of Life, and of all that was... No.., that didn't bother me.., not at all...

The initiator of this operation was not the "Father".., but He was the "Prime Mover" behind it.., and the objective of this endeavor was to fund his transition.., to the U.S.A ... That didn't bother me... So He had an objective.., to go to the United States.., but what was His objective after that??. That concerned me.., but it didn't bother me...

Between the devotees that loved Him, the disciples that served Him, and the hecklers that jeered him.., it had been an interesting day... In the late afternoon we again assembled into the meeting room, seated on the earthen floor in a circle... The chillum was fired up, The "Father" doing the honors, and we all got High... It was a spirited conversation that touched on many subjects, including (as I remember) the subject of sexual gratification, which the Father stated was much more satisfying within the bonds of matrimony than was popularly believed, and much more satisfying than the casual sex promoted by this "free love" generation, etc., and etc... I had to agree with this in principle, at least.., even though the bonds of matrimony had strangled me to near death!.. It was the "free love" syndrome that snared me into it... So much for free love.!.

But just when I was ready to accept this man as my "Spiritual Teacher".., almost on cue!., at the moment of acceptance.., He thrust an angry fist into the air and shouted; "Incest is the way"!!! I was thrown back on myself.!. Thrown into confusion.!. Now that bothered me.!. I had to take a step back from my position of acceptance, and re-evaluate!.. He had shouted this statement almost as a battle cry!!! What did it mean??. He didn't explain it, and nobody questioned it, nor did I... I just sat there, stunned and bewildered.!. The subject abruptly turned to religion;.. "And Christianity".., the Father said.., "I saw through that, too"!!, and with a backwards wave of His hand.., as though brushing away a fly.., He dismissed Christianity!!! Now *that* bothered me...

That really bothered me... I had to take a second step back.., a second look.., at this man that I regarded as the most "Enlightened" man I had ever met... A man that had commanded my respect and loyalty.., that I would have followed!!. The man, that more than any other, had been the most Christ-like man that I had ever met.., that dismissed Christianity.., as though brushing away a fly!!...

The discussion came to a close, and we exited the meeting room into the cool night air... I did the customary "Namestae".., and left the compound, deeply troubled...

I was caught in a quandary... Here was the most enigmatic man that I have ever met, that had exhibited all the signs, exceeding my expectations, and He had just dismissed Christianity!!. "You can't just dismiss Christianity"!!., (I spoke the words to myself), "You can't just dismiss Jesus Christ"!!. "You can't claim to be God.., and dismiss Jesus Christ"!?! No no no!., the Martyrs had died the death, rather than deny Christ, countless Christians had suffered persecution and death rather than deny Christ!.. Were they all wrong??, were they all fools??. What am I supposed to do?, just roll over and go "belly up"?, just acquiesce in submissive silence??? No no no, I can't do that.., I can't make fools of the Martyrs.., I just can't do that!!.

I arrived back at the hotel, downstairs in the restaurant area, amid the rough hewn clientele; the climbers, the Sherpas, the Hippies, Tibetan refugees, and etc., drinking their rice beer and boisterous in their bellicose laughter... I had a cup of "Chai", (black tea, sweetened with thick cream), and a piece of apple pie, and carried it back to an empty table and sat down in the straight backed chair...

I sat there, eating my apple pie, deep in thought, and in a black mood... A tall American with black hair approached my table;.. "You just came from the "Fathers" place, didn't you"?., he said... "So what"?, I answered back, "You writing a book"?.. My attitude was combative... The American walked away...

So.., I had gone from arrogant and condescending, to downright rude and crude, but that was the kind of mood I was in... I finished my apple pie and sat there drinking my tea... The American came by again;.. "How ya doin"?, he said, "my name is Eddie"... I looked up, he was standing there with a broad grin on his face and his hand extended in friendship...   The apple pie had somewhat sweetened my disposition, so I shook his hand and introduced myself... He sat down... "So what do you know about the "Father"?., I queried... "Well, it seems that a lot of people "freak out" around Him... There's one guy that tried to get rid of his Ego identity by burning his passport and all of his identification.!. He's in jail now.., no passport, no visa, no identity papers".!. We laughed...

I noticed that Eddie was missing a couple of fingers!!. Oh, I said.., I've heard about you!!... You're "Eight Fingered Eddie"!., I said... You're supposed to be a "Holy Man" or something.!. Yeah, he said.., I've been accused of that... So how did all of that come about?., I asked... Well.., he said.., "I just got High one day.., really really High.., and I just went over the top"!!! And what did you see??, I asked... (It was a test question)... His eyes rolled back, as though he were looking at the inside of his forehead.., and he said;., "It was absolutely crystal clear", he said.., "and I Knew"!.. If he had said one word more, or one word less, I would have discounted his testimony.., but his answer was precisely precise... "Yeah", I said.., "I saw it too"...

This is a "Universal" experience... In Buddhism it is known as the "Clear Light of the Ultimate Reality".., in Hinduism it is referred to as "Enlightenment".., and in Christianity it is called "the Rapture"... For the most part, this is an "after death" experience... On very rare occasions, it happens among the living... Those rare people.., to whom this experience has occurred, are forever changed!.. It happened to Eddie, and it happened to the Father.., but it hadn't happened to me!.. In my own case, I had scaled the height of the Inner Dimension and peered into the depths of the Clear Light.., and I could see forever and forever... I stood on the threshold, in the bodiless state of Pure Soul, and I intuitively comprehended IT.., but I hadn't merged with IT...

"Eight Fingered Eddie" was kind of an "urban legend"... As the story goes, he had come here to India on a mission, a dope deal, with other peoples money.., the "Family's" money... and as sometimes happens in dope deals, he got ripped off!!, losing the "Family's" money...   The word came down;., "If you return to America.., you're a dead man"... Knowing this to be the truth beyond doubt, Eddie was exiled to India... The story gets kind of vague here, as to circumstances, but he wandered around India for a while and eventually got High, entering into the "Clear Light of the Ultimate Reality", and became "Enlightened"...   The Indian government recognized him as a "Holy Man", and gave him a permanent visa... He has, ever since, just wandered about India, into Nepal in the extreme heat of the summer, and into southern India, mostly the coastal city of Goa, in the winter... He has a following, mostly westerners, that basically just hang out in a loosely knit community around him, receiving his insightful counseling and sage advice...

So Eddie was "Cool"... In his very self composed, laid back sort of way, he was the essence of "cool"...   Here was a contradiction;.. (My interpretation;.. call it: "the varieties of religious experience")... The "Father" had entered the "Clear Light", and having merged with the "Ultimate Reality" He came back and said: "I am God"!!! Eddie had merged with the "Clear Light", and came back and said: "I am God, but so is every body and everything else"!..   (I won't speculate further on this, because the profundity of the "Clear Light" experience is far beyond the comprehension of the mundane mind.., but you can see that how you perceive this experience can shape the remainder of your life)!!! I noted a further contradiction;.. I had spoken to the "Father" in a condescending manner, and he had insisted upon and received an apology... I had practically insulted "Eddie", and he ignored the slight as though it never happened...

So Eddie and I discussed the "Father", but never once did Eddie say anything that could be construed as good or bad concerning Him, only circumstances surrounding Him...   "What does He mean by "Incest is the Way"?., I asked... "I don't know, Eddie said, but He was stoned out of Calcutta, with real stones, supposedly for practicing what He preached"...

I don't know.., I shook my head in puzzlement... Everything seemed a contradiction!.. I was still in a quandary... So people "freaked out" around the "Father"... Yes.., I could testify to that!.. I had spent two days with the Man.., enthralled and captivated.., and then thrown back by the ultimate contradiction...   I witnessed the Power of His personality, the people who loved Him, and the people who hated Him... Controversy surrounded Him.., controversy stampeded through my brain...

Eddie had seen my inner turmoil!.. He picked me out of a crowd to give me counseling!!. That's what Eddie does.., he counsels people!.. He had given me an oversight into the situation, and I couldn't rectify the contradictions, so I made my decision.., to not go back!.. That was their standing rule;.. "they didn't have time for dissent.., you could have any opinion you wanted, but outside the compound"... O.K., that's their rule.., I will keep my dissent out of the compound, and I won't go back!!! End of story!..

So with a cordial handshake, Eddie and I parted company... There was a bond of friendship between us, and our paths would again cross, down the road, at a future time...

I reflected on my decision;.. "What had I been thinking?., Me?!,.. a follower"??! This was not my personality.., how could I have even considered such a thing??? This was an Indian concept;, the Guru as God!!, but it was not a Western concept, no.., it wasn't MY concept... No.., to accept another Man, as God!!, this would be to relinquish free will!., to become a slave to the whims of another!!. (Just contemplating this, I was gripped by fear!., and not an intellectual fear, but the real panic experience of Fear)... Oh my God!., I thought.., this was the way some people felt about Adolf Hitler!!! What if....?, no no no.., I couldn't even think of it... No,.. I won't go back!..

And I didn't go back!.. I spent the next two days just occupying my time with friends, in jovial conversation, with the purpose of distancing myself from the events of the previous few days... Just clearing my mind, and redirecting my thoughts... It was late that evening of the second day, and I was in the café, seated at a long table with six or seven other friends, drinking beverages, telling jokes, laughing hysterically.., and out of the corner of my eye, I noticed two figures standing against the wall, clothed in the burnt-orange garb of Tibetan monks, and they were observing our table.., they were observing Me!!.

I turned and faced them directly, to get a better look.., and it was.., the "Father"!!. He was standing there, accompanied by His disciple!.. I knew immediately that He had come personally, to search for me, to see why I had not returned... I arose from the table and went to greet Him... With the customary "Namestae", I offered Him the hospitality of our table, knowing that He would refuse it... It would have been out of place for Him to accept... I knew that, and He knew that I knew that... He spoke not a word, but just held up his open hand, and shook his head; no... It was obvious

148

that I would not be returning... With a look of wistful sadness, He bowed from the waist, His long hair sweeping the floor... He turned and departed, His disciple by His side, and they were speaking among themselves as they left.., a conversation that I could not hear, but I knew very well the content of their conversation...

So He had come to search for me... Like the good Shepard, that leaves his flock to search for the sheep that is lost, He had come personally, to search for me!.. **Aaauuuwwgghhe!!...** I was screaming inside my head!!. I knew the content of their conversation, because it was the same conversation that was reverberating through my head;.. "An opportunity lost!!. The greatest opportunity ever offered to mortal man, had been offered to me.., and I declined!!. The rare opportunity to be an initiate, studying under a Master who had entered into the "Clear Light" of the Ultimate Reality.., and what is the "Clear Light"?., it is no less than the Mind of God!!, and to enter into the Clear Light is to become "One with God".., it is the ultimate "At-One-Ment";.. the atonement for all sins.., It is the "Rapture"...

I had made my decision to get myself out of a quandary... It was a "damned if you do"-"damned if you don't", kind of quandary, and I had made my decision, and now I was in a "damned if I didn't", quandary!!. Had I missed the greatest opportunity of all time??. Had I failed at my life's objective??, or had I championed the cause of Christianity, and upheld the tradition of the Martyrs??. I didn't know... *I did not Know!..* Why was there all this uncertainty??. The quandary just deepened, and now it incorporated into it a sense of loss, of remorse and doubt... All I knew, was that there was this blank emptiness.., where my heart used to be...

It was time to move on.., but to where?., and for what purpose??. There was no purpose... I was overwhelmed by a sense of purposelessness... I had to escape.., yes, escape.., escape this ever deepening quandary... I was sick.., sick in my mind, my heart, and my Soul.., and on top of that, I was sick in my body...

I had had dysentery for the last two and a half months!!. It was a "controlled" dysentery.., I had taken several different medications for it, including the eating of small amounts of opium to control it, but it persisted... I had no indications of it, except that I continually lost weight, cinching my belt up to the last hole, then punching new holes, cinching them up, and punching new holes again... I had not weighed myself, or looked in a full-length mirror the whole time I was in India/Nepal, but I was emaciated.!. I had lost about 40 pounds from my normal 180 pound frame... I didn't feel ill, but I was becoming weaker all the time!!. It was time to leave...

My visa for Nepal was about to expire, and my visa for India had only three days remaining on it... Three days, just enough time to get from the border town of Raxall to Calcutta, then a plane over Burma to Bangkok, Thailand... I could have waited a few days, and taken a plane directly from Nepal to Thailand, but I just wanted to "get out of town", *Now!*.. The bus was leaving *Now,* and I just wanted to escape, and leave this quandary behind me... I paid my hotel bill, grabbed my back-pack and boarded the bus, up to the high elevation of the Himalayas, and then back down into India, and according to plan into Calcutta and then "touchdown"..., into Bangkok, Thailand... Back to the future.., back to the 20th Century...

* * *   *   * * *

--Introspections in Retrospect--

So, you can see why I was reluctant to include this "enigmatic" chapter in this book... It is painful... The quandary still persists!!. It has lessened in intensity, but it still persists...

I am not skilled enough as a writer, to convey to you the profound impact that this Man, who was called the "Father", had on me... I would imagine it to be similar to a meeting with Jesus, on the streets of Galilee... He spoke with Power and authority, as though He were God, and indeed, that's who He claimed to be... He was dynamic, controversial, enigmatic, and like Jesus.., He was loved and hated...

What would you have done?., if you had walked the streets of Galilee, and this "enigmatic" Man had spoken with eloquence and authority, and said;.. "I Am God"!.. What would you have done??. What would you have done if He had said; "I have seen through your Religion, and it is *pathetic*"!!. What would you have done???

You can say (after the fact);.. Oh, I would have kissed His holy feet, I would have done this, I would have done that, etc., and etc... *"Bull-shit"!!.* You don't know what you would have done in this hypothetical situation.., but it is not hypothetical for me... No,.. I was there!.. In real time, *I was there!!.* Be it the streets of Nepal, or the streets of Galilee, you can see for yourself the decision I made...

That's the thing about making a decision.., you come to a fork in the road, and you can go to the "right", or you can go to the "left"... No matter which road you take, you will never know where the other road would have taken you... You could change the course of your life, by simply crossing the street!!. Many people have crossed the street and been run over by a truck!.. If only they hadn't crossed that street.., where would life have taken them??. But then again, you could save your life by having crossed that street.!. Who Knows??.

But I came to that fork in the road, and I made my decision.., and where that other road would have taken me will always be a mystery... An opportunity lost??. The purpose of my life.., left unfulfilled??. I don't know.., I don't Know.!. I've had a lot of time to think about it, and often I have to reconcile myself to the possibility;., that I made the wrong choice!.. I came to that fork in the road.., and that road that I took did not lead to "enlightenment"...

And often I watch my television set, and I see these "television evangelists", and if you are a believer, you will believe anything.., And what is the essence of the believers belief??: "I don't want to die, and I surely don't want to go to Hell!!. I want to live forever in a Heavenly paradise"!!. (It's the quintessential "bottom line"; the fear of death, and the promise of paradise)... "Well then".., (speaks the tele-evangelist) "all you have to do is believe the way that I believe, and we are both guaranteed entrance into Paradise" (especially the tele-evangelist, because after all, he converted you and saved your Soul!)... "Well golly gosh and gee whiz" (says the believer) "I believe!!, I believe"!., Halleluiah, I believe!!... (and why not?., it's the holy "profit" motive)...

And if you are not a believer, you will see the hollowness of this preacher, who's ministry has eventually become his job, and he spouts endless words, repetitious words, and taken together, they are an avalanche of millions and billions of words, all repeating the same words in an endless variety of ways, endless interpretations, all purporting to be "Thee" word, and it's an endless whirlpool of words, diced, spliced, dissected and translated.., and the true "Living Word" is never heard, and if it is heard, it is not recognized, and it is not spoken about!!. The True "Living Word" has become the "Lost Word"!..

The "service" ends with an impassioned plea for money, and a song that is more often than not; flat and off key... The believer believes.., and the non-believer is confirmed in his unbelief!.. The Atheist is confirmed in his Atheism!.. The Moslem, Jew, Hindu, Buddhist, etc., shake their heads in disbelief, and say: "There.., but for the grace of God.., go I"...

But that's not fair!!, (says the TV evangelist), because Christ said; "I am the Way, the Truth, and the Life".., and "No man comes to the Father, but by Me"... Well, that's True!!.., Jesus, the Christ spoke the Truth, and He pointed the Way to eternal Life, but did they follow the Way, or did they (quoting somebody?) "just suck on Christ's finger"???

And just what is "The Way"?.. The Christ did not waste words;.. It is to; "Love the Lord your God with all your heart, and all your soul and all your mind.., and love your neighbor as yourself"... If the most wretched and primitive of men, follow this Way, with courage, love and compassion as the "native" instinct of their heart, their prayer will be heard by God their Creator!!. Or did you think that Jesus would stand in the way, and say; "Hey!.. No one comes to the Father except by way of Me, and you didn't mention my name!., therefore: "Screw you"!!! Anyone that would think such a thing, obviously, does Not know Jesus Christ... Yet many "Christians" have exactly that attitude...

And there are those "Christians" (the "finger suckers" who follow the "profit" motive) that will chant the name of Jesus: "Yo Jesus, go Jesus, yeah Jeeesus!!! JesusJesusJesusJesusJesusJesusJesus, go-o-oh Jesus"!!.., only to hear those prophetic words, spoken by "Him" who is not deceived:, "Who in the fuck are You??? Be gone from Me, I don't know you"...

So, thinking back, in retrospect, it has occurred to me that the "Father" never said anything at all about Jesus Christ!!.., only about "Christianity"... If Jesus came back to Earth today, would He be a Christian??. I wonder?..

Now, it may seem that I have "slammed" Christianity pretty hard!., but when "push came to shove", I stood with my Christian heritage, and with the Martyrs that died for the cause of Christianity...

I am such a true believer that I would probably stand with Christianity and the Martyrs against Jesus Christ Himself, and in a sense, that may be exactly what I did!!.

So, In retrospect, the fact is that I spent only two days in the company of the "Father"... Perhaps I did not linger long enough at that fork in the road, before making my fateful decision at that crossroad of Life... Perhaps my decision was premature?.. Perhaps, perhaps!?. Who knows??. Perhaps I made the right decision?.. Questions remain... In the face of "not enough information", there will always be these lingering doubts, this lingering quandary...

So.., Who knows??. Somebody out there knows!!. He had several disciples, most of them Americans... What ever happened to the "Father"??? I heard that He made it to America.., to California!.. But I was on the road for over eight years, before I made it back to California... So I am sending out this questionnaire!.. If anybody out there knows, please inform me... Thank You...

* * *　 *　 * * *

"The Bible" (Paraphrased, Simplified, Condensed)

...A Reading from "Between the Lines"...

Well, I was pretty hard on "Christianity" there, and some will say; undeservedly so... Hypocrisy and shallowness of mind are not confined to religionists alone, but are rampant in all walks of life... Let us have a look at the "other side" of this coin...

It was the philosopher, Rene Descartes, who pondered the intangibles of life, and found that everything could be questioned as to the reality of it all, especially as it pertained to the reality of his existence in the mind, as a separate entity apart from the body.., and apart from thinking, the mind itself is substanceless!!. That is to say; the essence of the mind is it's thinking... The only certainty (the bottom line) was: "I think, therefore I am"...

Having found the bottom line of his philosophical enquiry, he conjectured further; "Well, since I have ascertained it to be a fact that I do exist as a reality, even if only in the mind, therefore, it is logical to conclude that consciousness exists in the Universe!, (I am myself proof of that fact) and since I am not alone in the Universe, it is a logical and empirical conclusion;.. that there had to be.., "A First"!!. Descartes had found;.. "God"...

By the process of logical and empirical deduction, Descartes had found first of all the proof of his own existence, and by further logical deduction, the proof of the existence of God.., that is to say; the "First Consciousness", which preceded all others... But we don't have to stop there with our logical progression.., because just as surely as there was a "First".., there also had to be;.. a "Second"!!.

Probably the most enigmatic verse in the entire Bible, is "Genesis 1:26";.. "Then God said;.. "Let *us* make man in *our* image, in *our* likeness".., (etc.)...

"*Us*"??? Who is this "*Us*"??? Well, it is the most logical conclusion on which Christianity is based.[9]... It is God the Father speaking to His first born.., His only begotten Son!!!

So you see.., the biggest problem with Christianity.., is Christians!!. They think of Jesus Christ.., **too small!!**. *(But worse than that.., they think of God the Father as small-minded, and easily manipulated by "praise" and "flattery"... Their self-serving motives are a transparent mockery!!.*

It is the most Heroic and Epic of all stories... It is a tale beyond anything that could be written by Shakespeare, or Homer... It is beyond anything contained in legend!.. It is beyond anything in the Greek, Roman or Egyptian mythologies!.. It is the Epic saga, the greatest story ever told, propounded by God the Father, and carried out on Planet Earth, by the Son of God Himself!!! That which was beyond mythology, became a reality in History!!! (His-story)!!.

Oh, the Majesty and Grandeur of it all!!!... ("It happened a long, long time ago.., in a Galaxy not that far away")... It was on an isolated planetary system suspended in the nether regions of space, in the upper half of the North-West corner of the Eastern quadrant of a relatively small star cluster (just one of many).., known as the "Milky Way"[10]...

It was a beautiful little planet, just the right size,[11] with a moon, that was exactly the correct size,[12] and it rotated on it's axis at exactly the correct speed,[13] and the axis was tilted at just the correct angle,[14] and it circled the Sun, that was proportionately the correct size, in a circular orbit[15] at exactly the correct distance away from the Sun [16].., as the Sun and it's planets hurtled through space.., at exactly the correct speed [17]!!!

---

[9] One of the names of "God", used extensively throughout the Old Testament, is: "Elohim".., which is (interestingly enough), the name of "God" in its **plural** form (translated literally as: "Majesty's")... The singular form is "Eloah", and the "personal" singular (used by Jesus on the cross) would be "Eloi"... Contemplate the significance of this!..

[10] I have exercised some "poetic license" as far as the location of planet "Earth" within the Milky Way Galaxy is concerned,.. but just to give you some perspective, it is estimated that there are 100 *Billion* stars (Suns) in our Galaxy, and it would take 100,000 *Light Years* just to cross it, and it is a relatively small Galaxy (compared to Andromeda, for instance), and it is just one of an estimated 50 *Billion* (countless) Galaxies!!!

[11] If the Earth were just slightly larger, the gravity would be greater, and hydrogen gas would collect, being unable to escape Earths atmosphere, and life could not exist!.. If the Earth were slightly smaller, (lesser gravity) oxygen would escape and the oceans would evaporate...

[12] The Earth and the Moon, because of their exact proportionate size and distance from each other, are locked in a gravitational embrace (called: a "tidal lock"), which stabilizes the Earth, making life possible, and without which the Earth would undergo cataclysmic changes on a daily basis...

[13] If the Earth were to spin slower or faster, there would be extremes of temperature that would make life improbable... Spinning at exactly the correct speed gives us reasonable days and nights, and a moderate temperature...

[14] It is the tilt of the axis of the Earth that gives us the four seasons (a time to plant, and a time to reap), otherwise Equatorial regions would turn into deserts or impenetrable jungles, and Northern and Southern climes would be in constant winter...

[15] Fortunately (or by design), the Earths orbit is relatively circular, which gives a constant and stable temperature range, instead of elliptical, which would give such extremes of temperature that life could not exist...

[16] If Earths orbit were only slightly closer to the Sun, there would have been a catastrophic greenhouse effect that would have wiped out life 4000 *million* years ago, and slightly further away from the Sun would cause the Earth to be encased in glaciers!..

[17] Apparently, a force (the Big Bang ?), strong enough to overcome the gravitational force of the entire Universe (incomprehensible) propelled all the matter in the Universe (inconceivable) away from it's center at the velocity of nearly half the speed of light!!!   Hence; "the Expanding Universe"... This rate of expansion is so

Just one variation in this finely tuned choreography, and Life could not exist!!! The chances of this finely tuned choreography coming together by accident, are one in a hundred million.., to the ^{xxx} *power*!!! (Let the mathematicians do the calculations)[18]...

Even though the unfolding sequence of events would be correct even from the evolutionists point of view (but how would the writer of Genesis know that?), they (the evolutionists) maintain the theory of the "spontaneous generation" of life... Given the right circumstances, they contend, "life" would come into being...

In a highly publicized experiment (early 1950's), scientist Stanley L. Miller brought together all the elements for "life" (called the "pre-biotic soup") in a sealed globular flask, and attempted to spark these elements into life... He succeeded in producing amino acids and even nucleic acids (the building blocks of proteins and DNA), and optimistically announced that;.. "The creation of "life" in a test tube is immanent"!!!

---

finely tuned (according to scientist; Sir Bernard Lovell), that "If the Universe had expanded one million *millionth* part faster, then all the material in the Universe would have dispersed by now, .. and if it had been a million *millionth* part slower, then gravitational forces would have caused the Universe to collapse within the first thousand million years or so of it's existence!!. There would have been no long lived stars,.. and no life"!!!

[18]   We are premature with our calculations, because all of the components of our computation are not yet included.!. For instance,.. the meteorite that smashed into Earth, and wiped out the Dinosaurs (in retrospect, not a bad thing)… The Earth could not survive such bombardments, and it is by a rare stroke of luck (or Design) that the planet "Jupiter" (called; "Earth's Guardian Angel"), which is 1400 times the volume of Earth, and with massive gravitational force(318 times the mass of Earth), has already attracted trillions of comets out of our solar system, and continues to do so.!, (witness: Shoemaker-Levy)… Without a full-size Jupiter, "George Wetherill" estimates, (a planetary scientist at the Carnegie Institute, Wash. D.C.), the bombardment of Earth would be 1000 times greater!!, and Jupiter size planets within planetary systems are a relatively rare occurrence… If Jupiter weren't there, says Wetherill, we wouldn't be here either!!!   (Add this to your computations,.. in addition to;.. etc., etc., and etc.)… (Source: Encarta encyclopedia; 2000)

An army of "Origin of Life" scientists (a specialized field of research) has labored for almost six decades.., thousands of experiments.., and not one bacterium!!!

Professor of Biology; Dr. Dean R. Kenyon, concluded that; "It is fundamentally implausible that unassisted matter and energy organized themselves into living systems"... Even with the assistance of intelligence (the scientists), in optimum conditions, all of their efforts are characterized by "uniform failure"...

Professor of Biology; Lynn Margulis, writes; "To go from a bacterium to people is less of a step, than to go from Stanley Millers mixture of chemicals to that first bacterium"!!.

A noted geneticist from the Polish Academy of Sciences (Institute of Dendrology), Professor Maciej Giertych, states: "We have become aware of the massive information contained in the genes. There is no way known to science as to how that information could arise spontaneously. It requires an intelligence; it cannot arise from chance events. Just mixing letters together does not produce words (*an Encyclopedia!*). For example; the very complex RNA, DNA, protein replicating systems in the cell must have been perfect from the very start. If not, life systems could not exist!.. The only logical explanation is that this vast quantity of information came from an intelligent source"...

In his book; "The Origin of Life", Professor J.D. Bernal states: "By applying the strict canons of scientific method to the subject of spontaneous generation of life, it is possible to demonstrate effectively how **life could Not have arisen,** the improbabilities are too great, the chances of the emergence of life too small"!!!

So in effect, they are saying:., "Scientifically it is correct to state that Life cannot have begun by itself, but by totally ignoring the facts (with **prejudice**), the spontaneous arising of life is the only possibility that we will consider"!!!

So much for the "strict canons of scientific method"... It is painfully obvious, that they have presupposed a conclusion, and are working backwards to support that conclusion by excluding and ignoring the facts that negate their conclusions and bending other hypothetical suppositions to support their conclusions... "The fool sayeth in his heart; *"There is no God"*...

"Genesis" is the simplified condensed version (the "fundamental bottom line").., of a system so vastly more complicated, "than is dreamt of in your philosophy", ("Horatio")... It is apparent that there is more written "between the lines" in Genesis, encompassing a far greater scope, and in the correct sequential order, than the "intellectual" secular humanistic scientist can fathom, because his field of research doesn't include the "Big Picture", but only an increment of that picture"!!!

So "Genesis" is exonerated.., and the same question that was asked of "Job", has to be asked of the proponents of a "random chance" Godless creation, and a mindless evolution:.. "Where were you when the foundations of the Earth were laid"??? The question evokes mirthful laughter, because if random chance were to apply here.., no one would answer!!!

At this point I (the author) must apologize for getting side-tracked into the "Creation Vs. Evolution" debate, and "bogged down" with footnotes, etc., without really giving the subject the proper justice that it deserves, *because I could go on, and on, and on, citing example after example, etc., etc., and etc...* (Books have been written [19], but neither commented on nor disputed by the secular scientists).., when my original intention was simply to explain Jesus Christ to the Christians!!!

So.., back to His-story.!.

The Bible is not clear, as to exactly when and how he showed up in this story, (so this is just speculation), but it seems that there could have been **two** Sons of the Father.., (just speculation).., kind of a "Cain and Able" scenario, even before the creation of Man on Earth... "Sibling rivalry"; (it can happen, even in the best of families), but however it happened,.. it happened!.. It was "Lucifer".., jealous of the "Firstborn" Son of the Father, and jealousy causes an "Ego Identity", and Lucifer became egotistical, and rebellious, and hateful.., and this jealousy and hatred for the Firstborn Son, just seethed and festered within him.., until he became downright "Evil"...

So, the Father, having already established the lush and beautiful Planet "Earth", suspended in the Celestial Heavens under starlit skies, with the Sun in the morning and the Moon at night, etc., and having "tweaked" everything to the exact specifications, He looked down and saw that it was indeed a work of art, and even if He had to say so Himself; "It was Good"!.. So the Father said to His Firstborn Son; "Hey", "Let us make Man.., in our image, and in our likeness".., etc...

Now this really pissed off Lucifer, already seething with rage and envy, and being a very powerful and influential entity, he persuaded about one-third of the angels to follow him down to the Earth that the Lord had made, and for sport, they entered into a herd of goats, and experimented with physical sexuality and entered into bestiality, and did perverted acts on each other in the bodies of the animals that the Lord had created, and Lucifer, being the strongest entity, entered into the body of the lead he-goat, and in a frenzy of perverted lust, he dominated, sodomized, perverted and subjugated them all.., and perversion entered into the world...

The Lord was not amused... "You were a Prince", the Lord shouted at Lucifer, "a Prince of Light.., but now.., because of your great sins of rebellion and perversion.., because of Pride!!, you are now.., the "Prince of Darkness"!.. Your name will be changed to "Satan", and you and your perverted following will be banished from the Paradise Realms, and you will henceforth, as your portion, have dominion over the Realms of that region known as "Hell", and the "goat".., will henceforth be the symbol of your downfall.., the symbol of perverted Satanic Lust (and so it remains to this day)!..

Satan and his followers rebelled, and there was War in Heaven.., but it was a "limp-wristed" rebellion to begin with, and Satan and his followers were outnumbered two to one by the forces led by the mighty Archangel; Michael, and the rebellion was put down.., and Satan and his fallen angels were driven out of Heaven and cast into Hell [20]...

---

[19] The "Truth" is where you find it!.. For a far greater elaboration of these facts, the reader is referred to the book: "Is There a Creator Who cares about You?"... Some of the facts that I have presented here (in condensed form), including the quotes by Profs.: Sir Bernard Lovell, Dean R. Kenyon, Lynn Margulis, Maciej Giertych, J.D. Bernal, etc., are gleaned from this book… (Published 1998 by the Watchtower Bible and Tract Society, Brooklyn, N.Y.)…

[20] The Bible is incomplete (in many instances) in that it does Not contain the record of the "fall" of Lucifer,.. but this account is Not an invention of the author… This account is from an ancient manuscript, contained in a very old book (late 19th or early 20th

"I would rather reign in Hell.., than serve in Heaven", Satan said... "So be it", said the Lord, and so it was done...

So it was done, and the Lord returned to the task at hand... Selecting a fertile valley surrounded by mountains at the headwaters of the Tigres and Euphrates rivers (ancient Mesopotamia)[21], He gathered together all of the finest of the fruits, vegetables, trees, berries, fuzzy creatures, feathered birds, "Herbs of mysterious virtue", and etc., and assembled them in a paradisiacal garden... Then finally.., the Lord created Adam and Eve, and breathing into them the Breath of Life, He said, "multiply and be fruitful", and they did the dance of multiplication at every opportunity...

"Now just one hitch", said the Lord.., Everything in the garden is yours, for your enjoyment, including this special tree here, which I call; "The Tree of Life"... The fruit of this tree has special "consciousness expanding" properties, that will open up the eye of the mind, and allow you to see into the Macro-Cosmic splendors and the Micro-Cosmic wonders, and you will be amazed.., but this other tree, here.., I call this; "The Tree of the Knowledge of Good and Evil"... The fruit of this tree is a "downer".., and it will cause you to be "third eye blind", and you will lose the power of "insight", and you will be restricted to the five senses only, and be trapped into the external world of "harsh reality", the world of "duality", with good and evil at every turn, and eventually.., you will die...

"So don't eat of this tree!., O.K."?.. Both Adam and Eve said "o.k.", and all was well... The Lord looked down on all that He had created, and found it to be good... In fact, even if I have to say so myself, He said, "It is very good"!.. So He dusted off His hands and said; "I think I'll call it a day".., and He rested...

Well, you know the rest of the story... Satan was granted dominion over the "Hellish" worlds, and he reasoned that if he could "raise Hell" on Earth, he would have dominion over the Earth as well, and he would have vengeance against the Lord, and against his adversary; the Firstborn Son.., and furthermore, all the souls that could be recruited from the Earth, would serve him in that final day;.. that day of reckoning.., the battle for the Heavens themselves...

"He doesn't have a chance in Hell", said the Father,.. but let the people of Earth be tested, as to whom they will follow, and by their own free will, let us see the nature of their hearts, be they worthy of Heaven.., ...or of Hell...

And lo, the people of Earth were tested, and found to be worthy of Hell... Satan roamed the Earth, spreading his lies, deceit, trickery and treachery... He corrupted entire cities, infusing them with perverted lust, and unclean practices that resulted in a deadly disease that threatened to consume the Earth!..

"I am beginning to regret having created mankind", said the Lord... "I have a notion to just destroy them all, and drown them like the rats they have turned out to be"... But I will preserve the blood-line of Noah and his family, because they have resisted evil and followed the path of righteousness and *Communion*.., demonstrating both Wisdom and Obedience.., and he shows the promise of a new and regenerated humanity that will repopulate the Earth... And so it was done!..

So the Earth became repopulated with a better class of humanity, but the Lord, having seen the sinful nature of Man born in ignorance, with a predisposition towards errant behavior.., devised a plan for the Salvation of Mankind.., and the "Prophesy of the "Savior", foretold from the beginning, was written in the stars [22]... Abraham

---

century) that I read in my early twenties, and that I have long since forgotten the title of… But the document does indeed exist, and I leave it to my readership to locate that ancient document and inform me of it's source… It is erroneous to assume that every pertinent manuscript, under the authorship of legitimate Seers and Prophets is contained in the Bible (note the discrepancies between the Catholic and Protestant versions, alone), or to assume that there are no Seers and Prophets that have (and will continue) to be forthcoming after the Bible had been codified…

[21] It is interesting to note,.. that the "Evolutionists", completely ignoring the very specific Biblical birthplace of man (and even if the Biblical flood be taken into account),.. have instead selected Africa as mans (logical) birthplace!., and "what" (you may ask) is the basis of their logic?.. Well, Africa,.. is where the monkeys are!… (Ha ha ha, ho ho ho,.. Is this not just too pathetically funny?!. Ha ha ha)…

[22] The "Zodiac".., beginning with Virgo (the virgin birth), chronicles the episodes of struggle and battle between the "Hero-Savior", and the "Evil One" (depicted as the serpent, the scorpion, and the dragon), episode by

and the Patriarchs were tested and found worthy, but the "war" between good and evil endured, and their epic battles became the substance of legend and His-story...

"Woe unto Sodom and Gomorra", said the Lord.., "They have followed the perverted path of the Evil one, and worshiped him with their butt-fucking Satanic rituals and uncleanness, spreading their deadly disease that corrupts even the Soul... I have no choice but to cauterize this festering wound, and to save the Earth from its disease"... And so it was done... With fire and brimstone, the twin plagues of perversion and disease were *obliterated* from the Earth... **"Let this be a lesson to You"**, said the Lord... And so it was, and so it is...

This is an object lesson, a "Hieroglyphic" Knowledge-Picture-Symbol.., for all Peoples and all Nations, and for all time.., Those who have ears to hear, **Let them hear!.,** lest Your name be *obliterated* from the Book of Life!!.

"They will learn from this", said the Firstborn Son... "Yes", said the father, but in time they will forget even this, and by using the "variegated cloak of words".., they will rationalize even this!., especially in the last days...

"But they are ignorant", said the Firstborn Son... "They are third eye blind, and they know not what they do"!.. So the Lord sent down his Commandments, and raised up men of great valor, and Prophets to teach them.., and they stoned the Prophets.., and broke the Commandments!..

"But there are good people down there, Father, and if they are destroyed, then Satan has won, and he can claim the Earth and it's peoples, to their eternal torment!.. I can't let that happen... I will go there myself.., they will listen to me"... "They will kill you!., said the Father, just like they did the prophets"... "Yes, they will".., said the Son, "but then they will repent, and I will forgive them, and they will be changed.., and they will be saved"...

---

episode, around the Zodiac and containing all of the elements: (the cross, the wounding, etc.).., and finally culminating in the triumphant victory (the Second Coming) of the "Lion King" (Leo)… (Source: "The Gospel in the Stars", by Joseph A. Seiss, 1884 & 1979..., and "The Real meaning of the Zodiac". By D.J. Kennedy, Phd., 1989)… Note: This has absolutely nothing to do with astrology.., which is a total corruption of the "Prophesy"…

"My Son, My Son.., I have anticipated the boundless compassion of your heart, and it matches my own... No man on Earth has greater love than this.., So I tested Abraham, and he was willing to sacrifice his only son for my sake.., so how could I do any less for the sake of mankind... I have prepared a way for you, through the blood-line of Heroes, From Abraham through David, and as I have foreseen, and as the prophets have foretold, You will enter the World through the sinless womb of a virgin birth, and through the veil of forgetfulness You will enter the World.., as a man.., and even You, My Son.., will be tested!... So this is not a foregone conclusion, My Son!... You risk everything.., for the sake of mankind!., and not all of mankind is worth saving!.. There are some real assholes down there, and no matter what, they will always choose evil!!.

"I know that, My Father.., but I will teach them.., by my life and by my death.., by example and by parable.., and it is not I who will choose who is to be saved, and who is to be lost, but I will leave it up to the people themselves whom they will serve... By their own free will, they will choose their own fate!!. This is justice... By their own free will, they will take advantage of the Supreme sacrifice that I offer on their behalf, the forgiveness of Sins, and if they will only accept this, and repent of their sins, it will be as though they were "Born Again", and they will follow the way of Truth, Righteousness and Compassion, into Eternal Life, and I will sup with them, and they with Me, and I call all of Mankind to the feast of the Righteous... Halleluiah!., said the Son...

Halleluiah, said the Father, I am with You always, In Spirit, and in Fact... You have my blessings.., Amen...

As it was foretold, so it came to be.., that the Son of God, born of a virgin, in lowly and treacherous circumstances, walked the Earth in human garb, and looked out at the World through the eyes of a man... His mission: ...to save the World!!!

It was to be a battle of epic proportions, The Supremely Good.., Vs.., The Supremely Evil.., With the fate of the World hanging in the balance!..

"You can't win".., said the Devil!.. "The people of Earth are mine!.. They listen to me and they do my bidding"... **"I have seen that there is good in them,** said the Lord, **and I will teach them and they will**

hear my voice and be converted, and I will save them"... "Ha ha ha", said the Devil confidently.., *"You try to save them and they will kill you... I have foreseen it!!, ha ha ha, even those that you call your own will betray you and abandon you... You will see, they will strip you naked and crucify you, and make merriment as you die, and you yourself will curse them!!. You will have failed, and not even the Father will rescue you.., but only call my name, and it is "I" who will save you... You should save yourself the trouble and disappointment.., you should give them to me now, and thank me for taking them...* **"In your dreams"**, **said the Lord...** **"You were a liar from the very beginning, and you are lying now!..** *"Just You wait and see, and remember I told you so, but I don't hold any grudges, just call my name and "I" will save you"...* **"Get screwed"**, said the Lord...

So the battle raged.., at first, in the Celestial regions of "Inner Space".., then to the external realm of life on Earth, where the "Evil one" manipulated his pawns to try and snuff out the life of the infant babe, but by narrow and harrowing maneuvers on the chessboard of life, the babe was saved, and survived... Then into the strategic region of "mind games", and finally, down to the Battlefield of Earth, where the battle became bloody.., and then, finally, the ultimate mind game:... **"Endgame"!.**, said the Devil, *"You see, it is as I told you, you have been betrayed and abandoned by those you sought to save, and now they are going to watch you die!.. ha ha ha, How ironic!.. You have failed in your mission, and even the Father Himself has abandoned you"!..* And indeed!., it seemed that all was lost... *"Admit it*, said the Devil, *none of them are worth saving... The nature of man is evil!.. By this act of betrayal and persecution they have condemned themselves to Hell... Give them to me now, and I will save you from this senseless crucifixion"...* **"I would rather die than give them to you"**, said the Lord... *"Oh yeah, Well, we will see what you have to say when you are hanging on that cross!.. You will change your mind then"!!.*

It was a true test!!. Even Jesus didn't know the outcome, and history records His physical agony, and worse, His mental anguish... Why,.. Why had His Father abandoned Him??. Why was He left totally alone... Had He failed??. Had He really failed??? He was dying!.. The physical agony was unbearable, but the mental anguish was beyond description!.. His dying thought was for Mankind... **"Oh God, don't let my people perish! Don't let this sin be held against them! Forgive them, Father,.. they don't know what they are doing!.. Their sins are against me, and I forgive them all... Let my death be their atonement and their salvation"...** And with that, He commanded His Spirit into his Father's hands, and "faithful unto death", He died!..

It was a Love Story!.. The Greatest Story Ever Told!.. The greatest gamble ever taken,.. The fate of the World hung in the balance, and righteousness prevailed!.. The nature of God had been revealed, and the World of Mankind.., had a true Champion!.. It was Victory!!. A Victory over Life, and a Victory over Death... The prophecies had been fulfilled!..

....And so it was done,.. and so it was written down...

Well.., You can imagine the "absolute outrage" of the Devil!!. His moment of triumph had been snatched away at the very last moment by an act of Love, Benevolence, and Loyalty so profound and yet so innately natural to the "Essential Being" of the Man on the cross.., who proved Himself worthy (by every definition of the word) to be called:, "The Son of God"!!.

The Devil was stunned!!! Not only had his "generous offer" not been taken advantage of, it was not even considered!.. He had not been summoned, but completely ignored!!. By not even being considered, he had been totally rejected!!! Total rejection.., it was a bitter pill to swallow...

"This is War"!., said the Devil... *"You think I was evil before, Well, you just watch my smoke, now"!!.,* he said, as he gathered together his legions of assholes... *"Reject me, will they,.. we will show them, "they", who consider themselves the good and the righteous!!. Yes, we will make war on them, and they won't even know it!.. It won't be a frontal attack, I tried that before, and it is too obvious... No, this will be a subtle warfare... We will infiltrate their ranks, like wolves in sheep's clothing., and with the "variegated cloak of words", we will "baffle them with bullshit" and confuse them to where they will think that good is evil, and evil is good! That which is perverted, we will call: "gay"!, and they will think that "discrimination" (the ability to distinguish between good and evil, right and wrong, smart and stupid, wholesomeness and perversion, etc.),.. is a dirty word!!! They will lose their ability to discriminate!!! Ha ha ha ho ho* *ho hee hee hee,.. Oh yes,.. this is just too easy!., especially among the "intellectuals", who think that there is no God, and Mankind "evolved" from slime, that evil is "cool", perversion is just another "life style", and there is no "Devil"!!! Can you believe it??, "there is no Devil"!!. Ho ho ho hee hee hee!, Oh yes!., these intellectuals, these "secular humanitarians",.., they are my kind of people!., they do my work for me!!. Oh yes, my fellow asshole demons, we don't have to make war on the righteous, because they will make war among themselves.., over who is the more righteous!!. They will slaughter themselves and the "innocent" by the millions, over who is the more righteous!!! Ha ha ha, hee hee hee... I have found weakness even in the priesthood, certain troubled individuals that sought to escape me by joining the priesthood, I will catch them in their moment of weakness, and they will perform Satanic rituals even on children!!. Ha ha ha hee hee hee... This is just too easy.., "there is no Devil"!!. Ho ho ho, ha ha, hee hee hee"...*

So.., the question is:., Can righteousness prevail against this onslaught of evil??. Can we protect our children from the seductive "cool" of the wantonly immoral.., that portray themselves as "Icons" and **"Idols"** of fashion, culture, sexual "liberation", and etc.?? **Can the "ability" to discriminate be re-established among our young people??.** The answer to this question is a matter of Life and Death!!. **Choose Life!!.** For yourself and for your children.., choose ***now*** whom you will follow!!. The battle rages... *Choose your side!..*

***   ***   ***

"The Criteria of Intellectualism"

So..., late in the 20th century, a group of "intellectuals" came together, trying to ascertain "who" was the most brilliant intellectual who had ever lived.., and using the criteria of the relationship of the eloquence of language as an indicator of "I.Q.", they selected William Shakespeare ("The Immortal Bard"), as their intellectual genius of all time!.. And indeed!, having produced 38 plays and 154 sonnets, exploring the breadth and depth of the human psyche, emotions and aspirations of both good and evil, (with profound insights) and in the most eloquent and poetic style.., he is a most excellent choice.., and I could not and would not in any way disagree with their findings... In fact, I would say that he is a prime example of the potential of mankind in general.., although few men live up to their potential...

But with this "criteria" in mind, I would like to point out another work of "brilliance", embodying the breadth, depth and "essence" of the human psyche from a literary standpoint... It is, of course.., the Bible!..

From a literary standpoint, the drama and emotions evoked by the writers of the Biblical "stories" far exceed the scope and grandeur of anything that Shakespeare has written, as these stories were "wrenched" from the Souls of their authors, and have the added prestige of an historically accurate event...   Take for instance; (what Shakespeare would call a "Tragedy") the book of "Lamentations"... Even the title sets the tone of what is to follow, as the author pours out his soul, lamenting *"in poetry and verse"* the destruction of Jerusalem, a city in ruins...

Whereas Shakespeare never failed to put his name to his manuscripts, many of the Biblical manuscripts are anonymous, the authorship ascribed to a "Higher" source!.. So too the book of Lamentations, but it is generally considered to have been written by Jeremiah, because of the previous chapter in which he foretells the destruction of Jerusalem if the inhabitants of that city continued to worship false gods... He was considered a "Prophet of Doom", and ridiculed by the people...

The Babylonians invaded Jerusalem, in a siege that lasted over two years!.. Jeremiah "laments", in poetry and verse the "Death Throes" of the great city!.. All of Her allies had abandoned Her, Her Nobility; princes, elders, priests, and commoners alike, walked the body-littered streets.., homeless, destitute, and aimless... The flower of her citizenry, dragged off into slavery and exile... Starvation so severe that the people resorted to cannibalism, eating even the children that had died from starvation... Solomon's temple had been looted and destroyed, their personal belongings and treasures gone... Utter hopelessness... The King and a remnant fled the city through a hole in the city's wall, only to be hunted down and made to watch as their children were executed before their eyes.., and then their eyes were put out!!, before they were slaughtered in the desert... Etc., and etc...

Now, If this were just a "story", it would be a "Literary Masterpiece"!!. A "parable" with a message for all to see, and for all time.., but it is much more than a story!.. It is History!.. And more than history.., it is an "Historic-parable"...

But what I want you to see.., is the literary "style" of Jeremiah!!. The entire "Book of Lamentations" is poetic verse!!! Each of its five Laments contains 22 verses (the number of letters in the Hebrew alphabet) except the third Lament, which contains 66 verses (3 x 22)... Moreover, the first four poems (1:1; 2:1; 3:1; 4:1) are in an "acrostic" style, following the Hebrew alphabet, one letter for each stanza!!! Although astonished and grief-stricken, his gloom deepening with each passing verse, he never-the-less follows this very precise alphabetical system, indicating that these poems were composed with studied care!..

The "Book of Jeremiah" (preceding "Lamentations") is predominantly poetic in form, although a number of chapters were written mainly in prose (chs. 7,11,16,19, 21,24-29,32-45, and the appendix; ch. 52)... Jeremiah's poetry [23] is as lofty and lyrical as any found anywhere, and he used poetic repetition with particular skill; (*"sword, famine and plague"* found in 15 separate verses)... A creator of beautiful phrases and memorable passages, as well as symbolisms to highlight his message:; (*"a ruined and useless belt", "a smashed clay jar", "a yoke of straps and crossbars", "a large stone in a brick pavement", "etc"*)... Alliteration and assonance were also part of his literary style, and he made use of cryptograms on appropriate occasions...

We have a tendency to think of the Old Testament prophets as "rugged individualists".., "Doomsayers" in sweaty garments made of sackcloth and camels hair.., never thinking them to be learned and refined lyrical poets with the loftiest of thoughts and vision.., but Shakespeare wouldn't make that mistake... No, no.., I have great respect for Mr. Shakespeare.., and I have no doubt that he would recognize in Jeremiah a sophisticated and superior intellect, and lay his trophies and accolades at Jeremiah's feet!..

And before Jeremiah, there was Isaiah!.; Prophet, Poet, and Politician... He has been called; "the Shakespeare of Hebrew literature", and no other Biblical author can match his rich vocabulary and use of imagery. He served as advisor to four Kings, walked the corridors of power, and helped set the course of his nation (740-681 *B.C.!*)... He writes; (of the Lord) *"And He looked for justice, but saw bloodshed; for righteousness, but heard cries of distress"*... In prose and poetry, he denounced those that reveled in power and luxury at the expense of the poor and the fatherless, whose cause he championed, and warned his nation that reliance on military power, or wealth, or any force other than God, would lead to the disaster.., which he prophesied... Etc. and etc...

Shakespeare has the distinct advantage of his classical works being composed in the English language.., whereas the works of the lyrical poets of the Old Testament have to be translated into English, and the poetic rhyme and meter are lost in the translation, even though the power and beauty of the message still shines through...

And consider CONTENT.., *from a Literary point of view,.*; the Epic wonder of the "Creation".., the fall of Adam and Eve in the Garden of Paradise.., Noah, and the Great Flood.., Moses, and the Exodus from Egypt.., the destruction of Sodom and Gomorrah.., The testing and trials of "Job".., the testimonies of Abraham, Isaac, and Jacob.., the beauty of the "Psalms" (songs, set to the music of the harp, the lyre, and the lute).., the Wisdom of "Proverbs".., of David, the warrior king, Goliath, and Bathsheba.., the Song and the Wisdom of Solomon.., or the poignant tale of Joseph, sold into slavery by his brothers, then imprisoned, only to become the ruler of all Egypt, and then the inevitable confrontation with his brothers.., Etc., and etc.., *and with a thread of gold, woven through the tapestry of these Epic stories, is the "Prophesy" of the "Messiah", and it all culminates in*; "The Greatest Story Ever Told"... Do I hear any applause??? Is the Truth not greater (and stranger) than fiction???

The plots and sub-plots of Shakespeare's works are dramas carried out on the "three dimensional" stage of life, involving; *"Tales told by an idiot, full of sound and fury, signifying; Nothing"*!!, (quoting Shakespeare).., whereas the "real life episodes" of the Bible are "Historic Parables" dramatizing the "fifth dimensional" aspects of the "Spiritual Struggles" of man on earth... Shakespeare entertains, and makes you think; *"To be, or not to be"?* (applaudable).., but the Bible *uplifts, inspires..,* AND CHANGES LIVES!!!

Fortunately (for the reader), I am neither a Biblical or Shakespearean scholar, and to continue with this

---

[23] The source of Jeremiah and Isaiah's "literary style" is taken from (and in many cases directly quoted from) Compton's Interactive Bible NIV, 1996-98...

subject would require a "book within a book", which I am not qualified to write.., so I will leave that task to others...

*** *** *** ***

The Proverbial "Philosophical Coin"

Now, having said all of the above, and having seen both sides of this coin, the reader is left with the question;.. just where (and on which side of this coin) do I stand?..

Now, the Religionists would insist that I must stand on one side or the other!., but I cannot!.. I stand directly in the middle... *"Ye must believe"*!!, shout the Religionists.., and although I am *Not* a disbeliever.., *I have not made the Bible my* **"God"**!!!

But that's not fair!!, (shout the Religionists), the Bible is the "Word of God"!!! But I have to ask; is every word of the Bible to be taken literally??, figuratively??, categorically??, symbolically??, allegorically??, metaphorically??, or as a parable??, or to be deciphered by a Kabalistic cryptologist??? And if I was to accept the Bible as the literal and incontrovertible "Word of God", just which one of the 33,830 Christian religious denominations should I align myself with??? [24]

I regard the Bible (with great reverence) as a testimonial.., which is what the Bible calls itself (Old Testimonial.., New Testimonial)... These are the testimonials of men.., Great men, to be sure... They are the Prophets, Seers, Saints, Visionaries, Teachers, and etc., who **heard** the *literal* and **"Living Word"..,** *spoken directly to them..,* and they testified to that fact and followed the directives given to them as "Servants of the Lord"... These Great men had the first-person direct *experience* of **hearing** for themselves the literal **"Living Word"..,** **spoken by the Living God!.,** *and that is the substance of their testimony!!!* .....And to their testimony I add my own.., and that fact is the substance, cause, and motivation of this book!..

---

[24] The 2001 edition of Barrett's <u>World Christian Encyclopedia</u>, identifies 10,000 distinct religions, of which 150 have 1 million or more followers!.. *Within Christianity* (counted as just one religion), *33,830 different denominations are counted*... This would include denominations as large as "Catholicism" and as small as "Shakers"… (Source: www.adherents.com)

You can read the Bible from now until Doomsday.., but if you do not have that first-hand experience of "Communion", your "Faith" lacks substance, and you are just another "one" of the believers of "one" of the more than **10,000 different religions** that make up the mass of humanity…

I strongly advocate this first-person experience, as opposed to the second-hand information of words printed on paper (the Bible)... Your study of the Bible (*which I advocate*) should eventually lead you to this first-hand direct experience of the **"Living Word"**, but in order to **"Hear"** the **"Word"..**, you must clear your mind, and **"Listen"** in silence..., expectantly, respectfully, and *patiently*... This is the real and true meaning of the term: **"Communion"..**, and "Communion" with the Lord is what it (Life) is all about!..

This is *Not* thinking, or day-dreaming... It is an elevated state of mind (an altered state), a state of supreme quiet and clarity, devoted to *listening* intently, until the mind becomes *absorbed, and there is no awareness of the distinction between "I" and "Thou"* (the "Ego" is not welcome here)... The "Key" to entering this state is through *"rapt" contemplation,* where the mind becomes *"absorbed"* in the subject of its enquiry...

The methods to achieve this elevated state of mind have been given in chapter "VII", and as a practical measure (this being the most important single piece of information relevant to your life that you may ever receive), you are urged to review and implement this information... May the Lord be with you...

* * *   * * *   * * *

The Complete **"Body of Knowledge"** *in it's entirety!..*

It may seem that I am "slamming" Christianity and promoting Buddhism and Hinduism... Such is not the case... The objective here is "Truth"... There are no contradictions within the "Body of Truth"!.. There are omissions, but there are no contradictions... What religion is there that can say that they have the complete "Body of Knowledge and Truth" in its entirety.?. There is *None..,* and all of them have errors.!. Where you find contradictions, there you will find errors.., but how will you find omissions.?. You will find omissions by the study of *All* religions... You can only arrive at the complete "Body of Knowledge" if your

"Religion" incorporates *ALL* religions.., and even then, your Knowledge is only superficial, only "book learning", if it doesn't lead you to the **Experience..,** of the Rapture...

With the study of All religions, the revelation comes *Not* with the differences, but with their similarities... The central theme of Buddhism, Hinduism and Christianity, is the same.!, but their sameness is veiled by the "Variegated Cloak of Words"...

In Buddhism, it is called; Immersion in the "Clear Light of the Ultimate Reality"... This is the objective of all of Buddhism.!. To achieve this is to become a Buddha!!!

In Hinduism, it is called "Enlightenment"... It is "Union with the Divine"... It is the end result of the practice of the "Science" of meditation, called; "Yoga".., which means: "Union"... To achieve this is to became a "Saint" (Sat Guru)...

In Christianity, it is called: "The Rapture".. It is the "Ecstatic Union with the Divine", and although many Saints have experienced this throughout the History of the "Church", it is, for the most part, overlooked and misunderstood... In all cases (that I know about) this experience came about during deep *"devotional"* contemplations, characterized by a deep *"yearning"* to Know, a deep *"yearning"* for "Oneness"...

Be it Buddhism, Hinduism, Christianity or whatever.., the method is the same, the result is the same... Forget the labels.., "God", is One...

Prayer, is good! Prayer is talking to God... But meditation and contemplation is better... Prayer is a one way conversation where you do all the talking, and never think to *listen!*.. In meditation and contemplation, you stop the inner chatter (talking) of the mind, and just listen.., intently.!. Pray for HIS counsel, do some abdominal breathing, focusing your attention on the breath to quiet the mind, and just listen.., intently...

This is the "Way of the Owl"... It is the "Way" characterized as the "Combined Multiple Approach", and that is to combine and incorporate anything and everything into your quest, and all of your efforts to the Goal, and to Love the Lord your God with your whole mind, heart and Soul.., and to love your neighbor as yourself.., and do good, every chance you get...

* * * * *

"From out of the Mouths of Babes"

The following statement [25] is from "Ndong Asseko", a native of Africa who had recently been initiated into the "Bwiti" religious sect in the Bwiti chapel at Kwakum, District of Oyem... His new name (upon initiation) is "Onwan Misengue", he is 22 years of age, of the clan "Essabam", not married, works as an "aid-chauffeur", and also plants coffee in his fathers village...

REASONS GIVEN (for joining the Bwiti sect): "I was a Christian but I found no truth in it. Christianity is the religion of the Whites. It is the Whites who have brought us the Cross and the Book. All the things in their religion one hears by the ears. But we "Fang" do not learn that way. We learn by the eyes, and "eboga" is the religion that enables us to actually see"!.. (end quote)... (He then goes on to describe his vision)[26]...

Even though I would not totally concur with his statement, this young man; "Onwan Misengue", has made the point more clearly in one paragraph than I have been able to do in this entire book!!. If you read the Bible, you are a believer (maybe).., but if you have a "vision", then you have become a "Seer" and a "Knower"... Knowledge is transcendent over belief... The vision is the "substance" of which the Bible is just a "testimonial"...

"One picture.., is worth a thousand words"..,
One "Vision".., is worth a thousand Bibles..
One "Communion" with the Divine..,

---

[25] Source: the internet; (key word: "Ibogaine"); "The Ibogaine dossier"... The quote is from the book: "Bwiti": an Ethnography of the Religious Imagination of Africa", by James W. Fernandez.., University Press, 1982

[26] There is a Mitsogho Bwiti legend.., that God gave the Bible and Jesus to the white man for his salvation, but "Iboga" and St. Michael, (as Jesus's brother), to the black man... In Revelation 10, St. Michael gives a scroll (a.k.a.: "book", of pages; a.k.a.: *"leaves"*) to St. John to eat, that will make his belly bitter, but his tongue sweet, and will cause him to utter many prophecies... And again, it is suggested that "Iboga" (or a similar herbal psychedelic) may be a candidate for the Biblical "Tree of Life" that stands on both sides of the river (Revelation 22) yielding fruit, "and the leaves of the tree are for the healing of nations"…

Priceless...

The "eboga" of which the young man speaks is the herbal sacrament of the "Bwiti" Religion (containing the psychoactive alkaloid; "Ibogaine")... The root bark of the Iboga plant is rasped off, powdered, and either eaten directly or drunk as an infusion. It is a powerful psychedelic that transports the initiate to a level of consciousness not attainable by "belief", or by the reading of "words" printed on paper, etc...

"First" of all, let me state here that; first, last, and always.., I am a Christian! Why?., because I am a sinner in need of forgiveness.., not so much for the things that I have done.., but for those things that I have failed to do... Without the hope of forgiveness, I am doomed... And, if you want to know the "Personality" of "God Almighty", examine the Personality of Jesus Christ... **"Secondly"**.., let me state that I agree with the "Testimonials" contained in the Bible, especially as they relate to the experience of "Communion" (*Dialogue*) with the "Living Word", spoken by the "Living God"... **"Thirdly"**.., let me state that I am a Buddhist, because they take a more scientific approach to the experiencing of "fifth dimensional" realities (the Brado, the "After Death" states, etc.) most of which I have personally verified, and because I am at heart.., a Scientist!.. **"Fourthly"**.., let me state here that I am a Hindu, because I recognize the fingerprint of that same "Anonymous Author" (that penned the Biblical scriptures) to also be responsible for *many* of the Hindu Scriptures (the Upanishads, Patanjalie's Yoga Sutra's, etc.)... And **"Fifthly"**.., let me state here that I am also a member of the "Bwiti" sect.., by virtue of the "Ibogaine" experience... **"Etc., etc., and etc."**...

The "*Truth*".., is where you find it!..

My fascination with the herbal sacrament "Ibogaine", had more to do with the fact that it was a "one-shot cure" and a "Godsend" for those poor souls that had become addicted to Heroin, Morphine, Cocaine, Crack, Alcohol, Tobacco, prescription drugs, *and "Whatever"*!!! Imagine!!, THE CURE FOR ADDICTION (along with the accompanying horrendous withdrawal symptoms).., HAD BEEN FOUND!!, *and the Government was not only ignoring it, but actually classifying it as an illegal drug!!!*

Even though I have personally consumed copious and even exorbitant amounts of Hashish, Marijuana, LSD, Mushrooms, Peyote, Cocaine, Amphetamines, Opiates, etc. (and etc.), I have never been addicted to anything (with the exception of tobacco; an insidious addiction that lasted for two years)... So my fascination with "Ibogaine" was in the interest of Science and Humanity...

To the casual observer, this may seem a life of careless abandon, escape, and frivolity, which at times it may have been, but for the most part, each one of these drugs represents a "phase" which included introspection, self analysis, and self awareness, coupled with serious attempts at meditation to observe the effects on the meditative state...

But beyond that (because I am a Scientist), my true field of "Search and Research" is in the field of "Altered States of Consciousness".., and in the laboratory of my own body, I explore the mysteries of my own Heart, Mind, and Soul.., and with the tool of an expanded consciousness, I seek to know the mysteries of the Universe within the mind, the realms of the "fifth dimension", and to "Know" the "First Cause", to understand the Creation, and the Creator... This is neither a frivolous or intellectual exercise... No.!. *I am driven !!!* Far from being an "escape", many of these drugs (especially the Psychedelics) will put you into direct confrontation.., *with Yourself!!*. Are *You* ready for that??. Only the brave should enter here!..

So.., my experiments and experiences with "Ibogaine" were quite significant and memorable (to say the least), and I will tell you about it, but not now... To do so at this juncture would be to interfere with the timeline and sequence of this book, because, as you remember, I had just left Nepal, through India, on my way to Bangkok, Thailand...

* * *   * * *   * * *

BOOK XI

"Thailand.., the Sexual Oasis"

It was like magic!.. A plane ride to Bangkok, Thailand, and it was as though I had been transported into another world... In sharp contrast to the densely overpopulated poverty of India, Bangkok was a mixture of lush tropical beauty, and modern civilization. Department stores and open-air shopping Bazaars, Movie theaters and Buddhist temples, delicious local Ethnic foods and Kentucky fried chicken, banana splits and milkshakes. City streets with Neon lights, and high speed water taxi's with V-8 engines that sped up and down the rivers, in and out of a maze of interconnecting canals, modern hotels and thatched huts.., and everything in between... Everything...

Bangkok served as a "Rest and Relaxation" (R & R) interlude to the American service men, fighting the war in Vietnam. Bangkok was referred to as "Sin City #2", after Siagon, which was "Sin City #1"... A days wages for a Thai citizen might be 50 to 100 Baht... One American Dollar was worth 20 Baht... Bangkok prospered with the influx of American Dollars, and all of the most beautiful girls, from all of the villages, from all over Thailand, descended on Bangkok, with the blessing and encouragement of their families.., for the American Dollar... There was no shame to this, and no taboos against it... It was considered the most natural of things, and they were sincerely joyful and exuberant about it.., and so was I...

Bangkok was a sexual oasis, compared to the sexual desert wasteland that was India... A lush and fertile pasture of beautiful flowers, clamoring in competition to be appreciated.., each one saying; "pick me, pick me.., Oh please.., please pick me"... Let it not be said, that I am without compassion...

I had taken no vows of celibacy... I knew myself better than to do that.., and women.., well, there was mystery there, too... And so I rationalized.., and indulged myself...

The two modes of consciousness;., the one involved in a religious quest, with "high" aspirations.., and the other, the "lust" of the flesh.., are considered incompatible... And indeed, they are... My extensive research into the matter yielded this result:.. I do not think about sex while I am sitting for abstract meditation, and I do not consider abstract concepts while I am having sex... The one would interfere with the other to the detriment of both... And.., there is a "peace and tranquility" state of mind that immediately follows the sex act, that is very conducive to the state of abstract contemplation...

There are two methods to the suppression of sexual desire for the purpose of abstract meditation, unobstructed by sexual fantasy... The one is to take a vow of celibacy, and remove all possibility.., and the other is to remove the desire.., by satisfying the desire...

To remove the desire by satisfying the desire is the way of the "Householder", but even this must be in accordance with the sanctioned traditions of Matrimony... And this, (the Celibates declare); inevitably leads to involvements in home, family, property, physical labor, drudgery, headache and heartache.., and (relatively speaking) the "trivialities" of life.., not at all conducive to the state of abstract meditation, and not the way of "freedom" (from the "Sangsara", and the drudgery of the Householders life)... It is truly far more difficult for the householder, involved in his family life , to achieve a state of tranquility in meditation.., If he could ever find the time.., and if he could clear his mind of the thousand and one problems that beset the family life... Extremely difficult indeed.., but not impossible...

In defense of the Householder, I must quote the words of the Poet-Philosopher; "Rabindranath Tagore", who said:., "I find my Freedom.., in the bonds of a thousand attachments"... He did not consider his family life to be a labor of drudgery, but as a labor of love, which he freely embraced, and he would not be free if he were denied it!.. There is great beauty in this viewpoint... This is Karma Yoga, the Yoga of action, the Yoga of involvement in life, and it carries a great responsibility... It takes a better man than I am, to follow through on this responsibility...

The man that can raise a large family of sons and daughters, and have joy around the dinner table.., this man is my Hero... Providing a good home and education, instructing his children in the path of righteousness, raising them up to be good and true.., this man is my Hero... And the Wife, who shares this burden with her husband, not as a burden, but as a labor of love.., contributing more than her fair share, with a smile on her face and understanding in her heart.., this Woman is a treasure to her husband, and beautiful to the sight of the Lord...

There is fulfillment here... These "laborers in the vineyard", Father and Mother to sons and daughters, Grandfather and Grandmother to the joy of grandchildren, revered Aunt and Uncle.., this is a success story... These are the unsung Heroes.., the backbone of civilization...

Before you make a decision at this crossroad of life, contemplate deeply, and.., "To Thine own Self, be true"... Do not put thy hand to the plow, if you cannot finish the task.., which ever path you choose to follow...

But the Celibates are correct, and Jesus said it best:.. "If you would follow me, you must leave behind Father, Mother, Sister, Brother, etc."... Jesus established the celibate Priesthood, and Buddha started the celibate Monastery tradition... This is a very dedicated path, and the calling to it must be very clear, and although I might aspire to it and pursue it, I don't think I would take the absolute vow.., unless the calling was absolutely and blatantly clear...

And do not think that the Celibate life is easier than the Householders life... No, on the contrary.., beyond the disciplined life of continence and commitment to the art and science of abstract meditation conducted in an atmosphere of secluded isolation, the world is NOT left behind... Indeed, the family of the committed celibate has now grown to include the world itself, and as long as the stomach growls for food, you still must work...

"To be in the World, but not of the World".., is the name of the Game... I am not advocating any particular life style here, especially not my own...

So what did I learn, from my in-depth investigation into the seamy side of life?.. Just this:.. Sex, is a drug... Sex is a mind altering, highly addictive drug... If sex came in a hypodermic syringe, it would surely be banned... Because of its highly addictive nature and its mind altering capabilities, it is responsible for an endless list of crimes... Truly, an endless list of crimes... Sex is "Big Business".., bought and sold (like a drug) in the market place, on the streets and back alleys, over the internet.., turning women into sluts and prostitutes, and men into predators and whore mongers, contracting diseases and spreading diseases.., like "lemmings" racing headlong into the sea.., to their death... If a lingering, miserable sickness unto death (Aids, for example) was the only result of their crimes, that would be fair enough, but the effects of this list of crimes and atrocities outlives the criminal, as the diseases they spread continues to kill others... Victims, (pawns, really) of a force of nature that they have misused and abused to their own detriment... Ignoring the Laws and rules of conduct laid down from the beginnings of time, they will lie about love, seducing the innocent, leaving behind fatherless children to teen age mothers, who are children themselves, doomed to a life of poverty and hardship, raising children who lack guidance, propagating more crime, more pain, more misery.., or they could simply remove the evidence of the crime, by aborting the "fetus".., (premeditated, with motive and opportunity)... Inflicting psychological pain.., and guilt... Rape, perversion, degradation, bestiality, pornography, crimes against children, betrayal, suicide, murder, aberrations.., (etc. and etc.)... What would you do for sex?.. Would you lie.., cheat.., manipulate.., use?.. Such is the power of this drug called; "Sex"...

The list goes on and on... The crimes are unbelievable.., the pain.., the anguish.., is unbearable... This is NOT the path of Wisdom... There is no "enlightenment" to be found here... Even the Angles fear to tread here.., where Fools.., rush in...

Even in a seemingly benign and harmonious situation, (from the view-point of the "Seeker of Truth").., the Ego (which cannot know God, or achieve the Zen-objective levels of abstraction).., is predominant!.. All of the vicissitudes of pleasure-pain, attraction-repulsion, likes-dislikes, wants-needs-abhors, love-hate-anger-jealousy.., etc.., all of the "emotions" (Ego-motions).., be they good or bad, positive or negative.., belong to the Ego!.. And the strongest of Egos, is the emotionally unhappy-unhealthy... (negative Ego-motions)...

"But this is just life"!., you say... Yes it is, and there is nothing at all wrong with involvement in life, especially if it be a good life, with a wife and children, and benevolence toward humanity, etc... The Buddha taught the "Middle Way", and Jesus used the Family model for many of his parables, but you must have your priorities straight. The "Seeker" (of Truth, Knowledge, Wisdom, and God), is a "specialist"... Whether he be a family man, or a Priest, this must be his priority, and this is not dependent on what you think is the better path from an intellectual view-point, but rather on the intensity (or lack of it) of an "inner drive", that springs from the Soul... Search your Self diligently.., and "to Thine own Self, be true"...

As a "specialist".., despite the involvements and commitments to your spouse and family, the inner commitment remains your priority. Even though married, you do not come to the alter of the Lord hand in hand with your spouse... This is a solitary journey, and can only be accomplished in the solitude of meditation and contemplation, and (as my own research indicates), the period of time of "peace and Tranquility" *immediately following sexual intercourse* is very conducive to the state of abstract contemplation... In fact.., this observation (of the "peace and tranquility" following sexual intercourse) is a discovery of major importance in the "art and science" of meditation, and can be even more conducive to meditation than a life of celibacy.., "if ".., you keep your priorities in order, and "if " your family life is balanced and harmonious... This is the ideal, of the "Middle Way".., and the Middle Way.., just might be the better way!..

Saint Paul advocated celibacy.., but the founders of the Faith; Abraham, Isaac, and Jacob.., were family men... Personally.., I might decide to live my life in celibacy.., but I wouldn't be taking any vows... ... Enough said...

* * * * * * * *

(Timeline)... It was several years later.., in the late 1970's.., and I was living in Montreal, Quebec, Canada... There was a "new" drug on the market, called "MDA".., otherwise known as "the love drug"... It was still in the experimental stages, but I managed to procure a single dose... Anxious to try it out, I took the drug and immediately went to see my special lady friend, who lived about 15 minutes away... She saw me coming up the driveway, and anticipating my arrival, by the time I got to her second floor apartment, she opened the door.., standing there, with a big smile on her face.., in all her naked glory!!. She was very happy to see me...

Within a matter of minutes, we were locked together in blissful and frantic love-making.., and when it was all over.., the drug came on!!. My sexual appetite having been appeased, my sexual inclinations were immediately replaced by spiritual inclinations, and my natural inclinations turned to deep introspective meditation, which required seclusion... I explained the situation to her and apologized for my need to go and be alone... She understood completely, and I returned to my own place and sat in meditation... It was a profound meditation...

I noticed immediately the profoundly serene peacefulness of my meditative state, which I observed was the "polar opposite" of the sexually aroused state, and I knew that I had discovered a principle.., a principle that could be utilized for future meditations.., a principle that had seemingly been overlooked by those who advocated sexual abstinence as a prerequisite to meditation...

This profoundly serene and peaceful state of mind is what every meditator strives to achieve, because it is in this "quiet" state of mind that phenomena occurs.., and as I watched, the sky opened up, with billowing white clouds.., and in the distance I could see a Swan winging it's way toward me, it's wings gracefully and majestically flapping in a slow and graceful rhythm, growing larger as it came nearer, and seated on the back of the swan was a person of Royal bearing, and he was accompanied by a complete entourage of men and women clad in brightly colored silks, bearing gifts.., and they were coming to meet with me!!.

Needless to say, I was completely amazed by all of this, and my linear-logical-rational mind kicked in, and I reasoned to myself that: "If I am seeing this with my eyes open (which I was), then what must I be able to see if I close my eyes and view the "inner" landscape of my mind"??.., and I did just that! I closed my eyes and viewed the inner landscape.., and there was nothing there!.. So, after about a minute, I opened my eyes...., and there was nothing there either!!... The vision had vanished!...

I was sick at heart... How could I have been so stupid??. Here was a Royal Personage of another dimension coming to meet with me, complete with entourage, a veritable procession of richly clad bearers, bearing gifts, (or whatever).., and I close my eyes.., breaking the contact... How rude!!., how ungratefully rude.., to do something like

"The Visitation"

that!... I berated myself for days... An opportunity lost!...

I never told anyone about this!.. How could I?.. Who would believe it?.. "You were just having an hallucination".., they would say... and there would be no way I could refute them, because I saw this whole vision-scenario of the sky opening up, and billowing white clouds, with my eyes open...., while seated cross-legged in my bedroom.!., not to mention the utter stupidity of closing my eyes, and breaking the contact...

So, even now.., as I tell this story, those of you who read this account will say: "Yeah, he had an hallucination".., and there is no way to prove otherwise.., and really, I saw this scenario in my bedroom, out of view of the outside sky... So, all of the "evidence" points to the conclusion of hallucination... **But..**, let me point out that this (so-called) "evidence" is from the linear-logical *Secular* viewpoint of the "intuitively deprived" and "third eye blind" *unseeing* common mentality... And furthermore, let me point out that the **assumption** of the common *secular* mentality, that the psychedelically "drugged" state of the participant is somehow a "diminished state", inferior to their own secular non-seeing state.., **is an incorrect assumption**... *(no matter how many times I point this out, it is never heard by the secular mentality)* So, let me further point out that the mental state of the psychedelic participant is an **enhanced state**, with expanded awareness, greater capacity for insights, and with the potential access to alternate dimensions!!. *(something the secular mentality cannot understand!!.)* So, the jury is still out on this one, and the experience was too brief.., but I will always wonder.., what it I hadn't closed my eyes??...

But there were other discoveries that came out of this particular experience!.. First and foremost, was the discovery of the "bounce-back effect", from the sexually oriented state of mind, to the extreme opposite end of the mental spectrum to the spiritually introspective state of mind, most conducive to abstract meditation... And because of the "unique circumstances" leading to this particular experience, I made the personal decision to "Not Experience" sexual intercourse while in the psychedelically enhanced expanded awareness mode of consciousness... My reason being, that to do so would be equivalent to "Marriage", where the two consciousnesses become one.., and I am not ready to do that, especially not on a casual basis...

That would be to take the Sacred down to the level of the profane.., and sex is seductive enough as it is, without adding this extra dimension... So, I know that this has been done on a casual basis by many people, but not by me.., and I don't foresee myself ever doing this... This would be to violate my own personal code of ethics and objectives...

* * * * * * *

"Figuring out Women"!

And what did I learn about Women..? Well, the most important thing I learned about women, I learned from my "Uncle Yody"... My Uncle Yody was probably the most influential teacher in my young teenage life. He didn't believe in God... He had been through the Second World War, and the carnage he witnessed convinced him that there was no God. Through battlefield promotions he rose to the rank of Captain, decorated for bravery and valor. He was a true hero.., and he was my hero... His name was "George", and in the Greek language the name for George is "Yody", and the nick-name stuck, which is interesting because he was a full blooded Italian... He married his high school sweetheart, "Katie Murphy", full blooded Irish... Not exactly a marriage made in heaven, but it endured and prospered with sons, daughter and a multitude of grand children.

I went to live on the farm with my Uncle Yody and Aunt Kate from my 14th through my 17th year. Uncle Yody, (that was his name) was an "arm chair philosopher", with deep insights and practical wisdom. A Godly man, that didn't believe in God.., and I had lots of philosophical and religious questions that we discussed at great length, while we shoveled cow manure, pitched hay, painted the barn, etc.

One day, I asked my Uncle Yody about "Women"... Had he gotten women figured out?.. (Apparently, this was not one of his better days at the experience of connubial bliss)... No.., he said.., "No, I don't have women figured out... I don't think you're supposed to figure them out... Anybody that says they've got women figured out is a God damned liar or an idiot.!. Anybody that tries to figure them out will end up crazier than they are"!!. (end quote), ...as he stormed off to a more secluded area of the farm, away from me and my questions about women...

As irreverent to Women as this sounds, there is a certain truth to it, and I have had many an occasion to ponder Uncle Yody's words... There are people that will tell you (secularists, behaviorists, lesbians) that women are the same as men in their mental makeup, differing only in body and conditioned to be female by directing them to play with dolls instead of guns, as the male children do.., but the difference goes much deeper than mere conditioning. Like two different brand-name computers, they can run a lot of the same programs, but the wiring is fundamentally different. A different species!.. It may well be, that in the Grand Scheme of things, the mystery of women is not meant to be figured out by men... Vive la difference.!. Vive la Grand Scheme... Vive la Mystery...

* * *   * * *   * * *

"Herbs of Mysterious Virtue"

It has been my great good fortune to live in countries where the "Herbs of Mysterious Virtue" are indigenous to the region. Probably the finest product of it's kind, is the "Buddha Grass" of Thailand, called "Thai Sticks" by the general populace because of the unique method of curing and drying the resinous buds of the plant, tied on to slivers of bamboo with Hemp fibers. The great care and craft that goes into the production of this product yields the highest ratio of Delta-9 tetrahydrocannabinol (the THC that gets you "high"), to cannabidol (CBD, that has a sedative effect, and in too high a concentration, has a tendency to make you sleepy)... The result is an exceptionally clear and clean high, without the drowsy side effects. This is a superior state of mind with an exceptional "level of abstraction"...

An exceptional "level of abstraction" (standing back from your Ego), yields an exceptional "level of absorption" (examining Life and all it's phenomena with an un-prejudiced eye), enabling one to "live life larger"... And, if you are very lucky.., you will be able to "lose yourself".., in contemplation... (a Zen state, not as difficult as you may suppose)...

This is a tool.., a tool for the scientist.., whether your analysis be internal (introspection), or external (into nature), or into a book of learning (scholastic), your concentration will be enhanced and your comprehension will be increased. Your academic studies will yield fruit, and you will "relate" this knowledge to the "Unified Field" of knowledge and say..; "Aha"...

Scientists have looked at this plant, trying to determine what purpose the resinous THC content plays in its growth and ecology, and found that it is of no use whatsoever to the plant itself... Since it is unusual (to say the least) for a plant to produce a product for no apparent purpose to the plant itself, the conclusion reached is that the end use of this product is for the benefit of mankind.., to get mankind "high"... There is no other purpose for the THC content of this plant...

Another interesting characteristic of the THC high, is that (unlike other drugs) there is no "tolerance factor"... With most other drugs (opiates, etc.), the body will build up a tolerance, and more and more of the drug is required to get the same "high". Not so with THC... In fact (experienced smokers know), the more experienced that you are with this drug, the less of it is required to get you "high". Two tokes only, will get you as high as you are going to get... Having reached this "plateau", you can smoke as much as you want (but why?) an not get any higher, but you will increase the buildup of CBD (the sedative effect), and eventually fall asleep.., which is a waste of a good "high"... Less, is definitely more... There is neither addiction nor overdose to this drug...

It is also interesting to note, that the sedative effect of the CBD (by intentional design of the intelligence behind the plant), by its relaxing influence, is an enhancement to the high... The genetic quality of the THC and its ratio to CBD is what differentiates (like fine wines) the regional effects and qualities of Cannabis grown at various altitudes and climates. The enhancement of your ability to "relate" new information to previous information (insights) and integrate it into a broader context (the "Unified Field"), is what determines (for you) the superiority of one variety of Cannabis compared to another.

In addition to the "mysterious virtue" quality of the plant, its hemp fibers, woven into rope, have been instrumental in the building of cities and empires, the navigation of ships for commerce and exploration, etc... George Washington, the father of our country, was a hemp (Cannabis) farmer. The Constitution of the U.S. is printed on hemp paper, because of its lasting durability... This plant is as American as "apple pie", and has always been a "Boon" to mankind...

What would you think of a man (a Prince, actually).., who lived in a "Grand Palace" many stories tall, but who lived his life entirely on the ground floor, and only left the ground floor to go to the basement?.. Who never once climbed the "royal staircase" to the rooms on the upper floors, or had the elevated view from the grand balcony?..

And yet, it is just such a person as this, living in his Grand Palace (the body, which is the Temple of God), of base mentality (the ground floor), with sexual and alcoholic appetites (the basement), who will rant and rail against anyone that would climb the royal staircase (get High) and venture into the upper rooms (and altered state) or have the view (the overview) from "on high" (the grand balcony)... Such a person as this lives in a very small and shallow world...

Now.., there are those people who will say I exaggerate, with the "upper rooms", and the "royal staircase", and the view from the "grand balcony"., but those who would say this, have never ventured to look upon the inner landscape, and are instead committed to the "basement" level of mentality... Their view is externalized, material, carnal, and shallow... The determining factor is..; as always; "Intention"... There is a "door" here, but it can only be opened by "intent"... Even so.., that person of base mentality, could receive a "rude awakening"... (stranger things have happened)...

.....(Timeline)... So enamored was I with this plant and it's magical properties, that I decided to share this experience with as many people as possible, for fun and profit... I had discovered the secret of Alchemy... Except that you won't get rich by attempting to turn lead into gold... No, you get rich by doing business, by turning "grass"., into "cash"!..

Over the period of several years that I spent in the Orient, I spent approximately three of those years in and out of Thailand, doing business, and eventually.., one of those three years was spent in ...Prison...

Prison is a very sobering experience... I had had a feeling and an attitude of invincibility... I was naive... I was, after all, engaged in the service of mankind, the very noble act of getting mankind "High"... I believed that then, and I believe that now...

I have no regrets for the experience. Nothing seriously bad happened to me.., although I witnessed many terrible things... Bangkoks "Klong Prem" prison (four months awaiting trial) and another eight months in "Lard Yao" prison (up country from Bangkok) are notoriously evil places, and It would take another book to describe the experience... Space doesn't permit for a "book within a book" here, but other books have been written [1]... Suffice it to say, it was one of those "million dollars experiences".., that I wouldn't take a billion dollars to repeat!!...

....(This "timeline" is out of sequence (having happened several years after the sequential flow of this story), and I mention it only for perspective... So, end of timeline, and back to the story)...

So.., this was my life in Thailand.., enjoying the food, the women, the adventures and intrigues, the Buddhist temples, religion and philosophy, the "Buddha Grass", good books, good times, the friendships of both the local people and that special class of people.., my fellow travelers and seekers of truth and adventure, from all over the world...

A word of advice to my fellow travelers..; If you would travel the world in search of knowledge and adventure.., do it alone... It may seem that there is security (for the insecure) by traveling with a companion, but then you are constantly having to agree on where, when, and how to go.., on where to eat, and where and when to sleep, and I want to go here, and you want to go there, and before you know it, you are disagreeing with each other, and your friendship becomes strained, and what was an adventure turns into an ordeal... If you travel alone, every other traveler that you meet will become your friend, and friendships thus formed will endure the test of time, with no commitments and no restrictions... You have the freedom of the open road, and you will not be lonely...

This is my personal point of view.., a mans point of view... For Women, I would not recommend this... A woman traveling alone in a third world country is not safe...

---

[1] The book; "4,000 Days" written by Warren Fellows, describing; "my life and survival in a Bangkok prison"., and there is also a (true story) movie (the Name escapes me), about an American girl that survived her ordeal in the woman's prison there… Both the book and the movie graphically illustrate the horror and primitive conditions there…

Unfortunately, the "double standard" applies here... "Women's Rights", "Equal Rights" and etc., may be a concept in the West, but don't presume them to have any relevance at all in foreign countries (East or West)... The traditions and customs from time immemorial are not so easily overturned by your "modern" philosophies... I have seen young ladies (girls, actually), come to a Moslem country (Afghanistan), dressed in the equivalent of a sleeveless wet t-shirt.!. The local women of Afghanistan are dressed in "burkas" (a total covering of the body from head to toe, from which they peer out at the world through gauze covered eye holes)... Western women in general (regardless of dress) are considered to be of low moral character, and if indiscreetly dressed can be spat upon at the least, and raped and killed at the worst... Bereaved parents journey to these foreign countries in search of their daughters who have vanished without a trace, offering rewards and passing out pictures. Every Embassy has a picture gallery, a wall of reward posters of missing daughters.., and sons.., of misadventure...

Especially for women..; do not make eye contact.!. In many countries (for men and women alike) it is considered "rude" to look directly into a person's eyes, and for a woman, it is especially suggestive...

The Orient is not nearly as repressive to Women as the "Middle East", but it is still a Mans world, and Women are tolerated, if they behave themselves, but the "double Standard" still applies... Don't go down any "dead end streets" (metaphorically speaking) from which you may have difficulty extricating yourself, and definitely.., not alone...

* * *   * * *   * * *

"Devotional Exercises"

So, after about two months of recuperation and indulgence in the exquisite cuisine of Thai and American food, I had regained my health and most of my weight. I had been an avid student of the martial arts, and I resumed my training in Bangkok at the local Y.M.C.A. under the direction of a Korean Sensai: Mr. Kim... I had previously studied under a Japanese instructor, who was an international champion, and the "best by contest"... I was a good and dedicated student, and although not a black belt, I was very proficient in the art.

As part of the curriculum of the student on the "path" of higher consciousness, a regimen of exercise is required as well as the disciplines of concentration, meditation and contemplation. For most people on the "path", the exercise of tradition has been Yoga... Yoga is good, and it would be remiss to say anything negative about Yoga, and I practiced Yoga for quite some time before getting into Karate... But Yoga (compared to Karate).., is for women...

I had at one time become very cynical about the quest for higher knowledge, and the traditional methods that seemed to be barriers to that quest... It seemed that if a person was qualified for the quest, of sound mind and fit body, with high and noble aspirations, he was coerced and drafted into war, and if he survived that, he was indoctrinated into a specific religion that by the very nature of the "believe it or burn" belief system, precluded any possibility of actual experience... If he still had aspirations, he would be sent to a monastery to recite endlessly repetitious prayers, and he was "locked in" to the system by indoctrination and the consequence of losing his Soul if he should fail to continue.., or he could practice Yoga, and twist his body into a pretzel and stand on his head... But under no circumstances should he ever (never, never ever).., under the pain of insanity, incarceration, death and damnation.., experience the one thing that could give him a glimpse into a greater and more profound universe of Truth..; the "Herbs of Mysterious Virtue".., the psychedelics... You can understand my cynicism...

The art and science of Yoga.., in the esoteric sense (the union of Man with the Divine).., is the ultimate science... There is no science greater than this, no aspiration higher than this, nothing in the world more important than this... This is the Wisdom of the Buddhas.., the "Pranya Paramita".., the Ultimate Wisdom...

The ancient practice of "Hatha Yoga", as a system of physical exercise, is definitely good, and should be incorporated into the "Combined Multiple Approach" (everything that contributes to the union of Man with the Divine)...

The art and philosophy of "Zen" is also aimed at the supreme goal of union with the Divine. The practice of Zen is usually combined into an art form, and it is my personal view-point that if you are going to practice an exercise with the end result being a fit mind in a fit body, it would be to your lasting benefit to learn an art form as well. The art form of Karate (empty handed combat) is superb at bringing the spontaneous Zen objective state down to earth and integrating it into your daily life and your physical stature. The martial arts are especially conducive to bringing about those spontaneous moments of "Purity in Action" that characterize the "integrated personality". The objective here is to harmonize the inner Zen state with the outer expressions of that state. Almost never is the outward expression of that state brought more to the fore.., than in the art of combat…

In a combat situation, where you are fighting for your life, even in mock situations, there isn't time to think about your next move, only to react.., spontaneously… Combining spontaneity with efficiency is the art of survival in a hostile world, and it is the essence of Zen as practiced in conjunction with the martial arts. I would recommend this to every man, woman and child...

The benefits of health, strength, composure, self confidence, gracefulness, and naturalness, becomes evident, and the "bonus" feed-back effect is that these qualities are very conducive to the Zen-objective state required for meditation and contemplation… There is a very definite correlation between "muscle tone" and "mental tone"…

It is up to the individual to decide for himself what form of physical exercise to incorporate into the discipline of the "Supreme and Ultimate Wisdom"..; the science and art of Union with the Divine. But, there are other options to achieve the "muscle tone- mental tone" correlation...

....As I traveled through India, I came to the village of Bodh Gaya, where stands the massive "Bodi Tree" under which Siddhartha Gotama received his enlightenment, and became the Buddha... The Bodi Tree was of course not the same tree of 2500 years ago, but the same tree reproduced from cuttings many generations later. It was a place of pilgrimage, and there were many temples and shrines venerating the Buddha. I walked around to the back-side of the massive tree, and there stood a shrine to the Buddha, and in front of the shrine was a polished wooden floor that resembled a miniature bowling alley... As I watched, the pilgrims, one by one, came to the shrine, knelt down on a kneeling pad, and with a cloth in each hand, slid themselves forward on the polished wooden floor until they lay prostrate in devotion, venerating the Buddha. Then quickly they slid themselves back to the kneeling position and stood up with hands together.., then back down, repeating this devotional exercise in rapid succession about a dozen times each...

The effect was exhilarating... You could see it in their clear bright eyes, their robust good health and their exuberant spirit... Finally, here was a religious devotional ritual that yielded an immediate aerobic "high" and long term benefits.., and there was a healthy glow and cheerfulness that distinguished them from the rest of the crowd.

Not everybody has the time or inclination required to dedicate themselves to the rigorous training involved in the practice of the martial arts or yoga, but the "muscle tone- mental tone" edge can be maintained by practicing a modified version of the above devotional exercise... It takes about 2 or 3 minutes only, and can be performed by anyone who has access to a bath towel and a polished (kitchen) floor.

While kneeling on a knee pad, on a polished floor, and with the hands spread apart a comfortable distance, grasp the towel in both hands, and slide yourself forward a comfortable distance.., and then slide yourself back... You can do a dozen repetitions of this exercise in just a couple of minutes...

The results are dramatic... The chest, abdomen, back, shoulders, arms, thighs, and etc. are toned and strengthened by this exercise, and you can incorporate deep breathing (inhale on the extension, exhale on the retraction) for the aerobic benefits. As you progress in this exercise, you can increase the repetitions, sets, and the length of the extensions. You will be exhilarated with the results, and if you were to also incorporate the devotional aspect into this exercise, you would multiply your blessings... Really...

* * *

Thailand, like most countries, has a restriction on the length of time you can stay there on a tourist visa. Thailand grants a two month tourist visa. When your visa is up, you have to leave the country, go to a neighboring country and reapply for a new visa at the Thai embassy there. I would go to Laos... This was in the late 60's.., before the communist takeover...

* * *

Post Script; Update... Oh Bangkok.., beautiful Bangkok.., that laid-back tropical paradise.., the playground of my youth.., where have you gone?.. Your peaceful villages and exotic architecture have been replaced with high-rise hotels and apartment buildings.., your quiet streets have been replaced with bumper to bumper traffic congestion.., your clean air has been replaced with smog, and that joyful free enterprise sexual abandon has been replaced with big business commercialized sex.., *regarded as an industry!.,* catering to the perverted and carnal lusts of the outside world... The era of unprotected sex is over.., long gone.., replaced with the highest incidences of the Aids virus, and sexually transmitted diseases that laugh at antibiotics... *Fools rush in!.,* and worst of all, even the sexual exploitation of children... The sexual oasis.., has become a cess-pool... In the words of "Thomas Wolf": "You Can't Go Home Again".., because the Home that you knew (late 60's, early 70's).., is no longer there... My heart grieves...

* * *   * * *   * * *

BOOK XII

"Incident in Laos"

The train ride from Bangkok, to the Northern border town of Knong Kai, was a scenic adventure that I looked forward to every time that I had to travel to Laos to renew my tourist visa for Thailand… Through about 500 miles of dense jungle, rice paddies, thatched roofed villages, small towns, teakwood forests.., *and limestone spires!!,* rising up out of a level plain, like skyscrapers in the city.., some 5, 6, and 7 or more stories high, covered with trees and vegetation.., some of the most indescribable natural formations I have ever seen!.. Then, from Knong Kai, by taxi, to the ferry boat that crossed the Mekong River into the city of Vientiane, Laos…

I had made this trip to Laos several times. I loved the city of Vientiane, with it's block long rows of two storied, common walled, open front shops that lined the streets, with Chinese, Indian and Lao merchants that sold all manner of imported and hand made goods, from bolts of silk and cotton cloth, to dry goods, to laundry detergents, to hand carved statues of the Buddha, to transistor radios and cassette players that blared their music out into the streets, to the many small restaurant shops that radiated the tantalizing smells of highly spiced stir-fried foods of ethnic Lao, Chinese, Indian, Thai, and French cuisine. Free enterprise was alive and well. The merchants lived in the apartments above their shops, with open balconies that faced the street, decorated with potted plants, ornaments, and clothing hung out to dry.

The city bustled with traffic, mostly bicycles, bicycle drawn rickshaw taxies, small Japanese cars and trucks, ox carts, buses, and children playing along the streets and sidewalks...

The Lao are a straight-forward people, honest and sincere, with broad smiles, perfect teeth, high cheekbones, and noble features. The women especially, radiate a simple inner beauty that lights up their faces, dressed in colorful ankle-length garb, with silver ornaments, bangles, beads, and earrings that are reminiscent of an age of glory and high civilization that has long since vanished… The price paid for war...

Many were refugees, you could tell from their head-gear, that ranged from the typical straw cone-shaped sunshade, to the various styles of head wraps that distinguished them as belonging to any one of some twenty odd different tribes that had inhabited the remote Northern and Eastern parts of Laos, driven from their homes by the communist North Vietnamese and the Pathet Lao, who were indoctrinated into the communist philosophy, trained as soldiers, given combat uniforms, automatic weapons, and a mission to rid their country of anyone who refused to accept the communist ideology... Refugees by the thousands poured across the Mekong River into neighboring Thailand...

But, for the present anyway, life was peaceful, and the clamor of the city went on as though it were the only place on Earth, and for that moment in time, it was. The local hotel was a long rambling two story wooden structure with an old world, southern plantation kind of charm, that had been built by the French during their long and benevolent colonialization of the area.. I checked in, took a cold shower, changed clothes, and in the company of my fellow travelers that I had met on the train, we ventured into the city, exploring the sights, the sounds, the shops and restaurants. Life was more than just good, it was idyllic…

The following morning, I dropped my passport off at the Thai embassy, had apple pie and sweet tea ("chai") for breakfast, jumped into a bicycle rickshaw, said the magic word "opium" to the driver with the sign language of smoking an opium pipe, and we sped away, down streets and alleys, finally arriving on the outskirts of the city to a small common walled, shack-like dwelling among other shack-like dwellings that hadn't seen a coat of paint, ever...

...This was not a new experience... In the eight or so years that I traveled through the Orient.., in and out of Afghanistan, India, Nepal, Thailand, Laos, Hong Kong, etc., on rare occasions, I smoked opium... It was just part of the experience of these countries, but more importantly, it was the experience of the opium, the exploration into realms of the mind that otherwise lay hidden from the view of pseudo intellectuals... This was more than just an experience.., it was research into the mysteries of consciousness, a key to hidden passage ways... It was the purpose of my life...

I had always imagined an opium den to be a place of opulence, with Persian carpets on the floor, reclining on tasseled silk pillows, a laid back atmosphere, and scantily clad women serving tea and cookies, giving massages and pleasant conversation, etc... The reality was a sharp contrast... All of the opium dens, from Afghanistan to Hong Kong, were in the slum sections of the city, in dimly lit dirty rooms, with men lying on their sides, on newspapers, to keep them off the dirty floor, or newspapers on top of other newspapers, of the bodies that had lain there previously. Instead of a pillow, there was a wooden block on which to lay your head, and tea was served by young boys that earned tips for fetching it from a local vendor. Most surprising of all was the attitude of aggravation that prevailed..; "I paid for the tea last time, it's your turn to pay this time".., spoken in accusatory tones... The only atmosphere of any importance to the opium smoker, was internal...

The rickshaw driver went in with me, and introduced me to the proprietor. I paid the driver his fee plus a good tip, and told him to wait for me.

The proprietor was a man, small of stature, I estimated to be in his mid forties. He wore a light, short-sleeved shirt, open down the front, and shorts and sandals. He was literally skin and bones, with deep set dark eyes and dark skin tightly stretched on his skull-like face, with protruding high cheek bones, protruding collar bones, protruding hip bones, skinny arms and legs, and every rib could be counted. Evidence of years of opium smoking... Other than that, he seemed to be in remarkably good health.

He motioned me over to a wooden bunk, with slats across it with spaces between the slats, and the familiar wooden block for a pillow. Well, at least it's off the floor, I thought. As I looked about the dimly lit room, I saw other bunks, upper and lower, along three walls of the small room, with dark bodies peering at the new arrival. I laid down on the bunk on my right side, head on the wooden block, facing my host, which is the traditional position for smoking opium. A flame burned in the small chimney lamp on the small table next to my bunk. An alcohol lamp is used, because it produces a cleaner and hotter heat source, and the chimney channels the heat. The host prepares the opium.

The opium comes in a small square glass bottle that holds about an ounce of opium in diluted liquid form. The preparer dips a thin steel rod, about a foot long, and about the thickness of a darning needle, into the bottle, coating the rod with about two inches of the black liquid. The rod is then skillfully passed through the heat flow above the chimney lamp, and the liquid is boiled off, leaving a gummy residue of opium on the rod. The rod is dipped again, and the process is repeated about three or four times, until the buildup is sufficient. Then, the tip of the rod containing the tarry opium is rolled against the slightly convex surface of the (tea cup size) bowl of the opium pipe, forming the opium into a tapered cone.

I had seen a lot of opium pipes, but this one was a work of art. It was made from a section of bamboo about 18 inches long, stained a polished black from the saturation of the opium, and fitted with an ivory mouthpiece and end piece that was also stained an amber color streaked with black, from opium use. An offshoot branch from the bamboo body had been cropped and carved into the head of a pig. About two-thirds of the way down the pipe from the mouthpiece was a lily pad, crafted out of nickel-silver, and draped like a saddle over the bamboo body. On top of the lily pad, in bold relief, sat a frog with a blue bead in its mouth, facing the pig. Tadpoles, a centipede, and water bugs, in bass relief, surrounded the frog on the lily pad. Mounted on the back of the frog was a fluted funnel shaped opening that held the tea cupped size bowl. This large bowl had a convex cover over it that served as a working surface for preparing the opium. In the center of the convex lid, that covered the tea-cupped sized bowl, was a small depression, about the size of a collar button, and in the center of the collar button size depression was a hole about the size that a darning needle could fit through.

The preparer then takes the rod containing the tapered cone shaped opium adhering to it, and fits it into the darning needle size hole in the center of the convex lid, scraping off the opium into the collar button size depression made to receive it. There is now a small pellet of opium, about the size of a collar button, shaped like a donut, with a hole in the center. The opium smoker presses his lips to the mouthpiece, as the preparer holds the pipe, tilting the bowl of the pipe into the heat stream of the

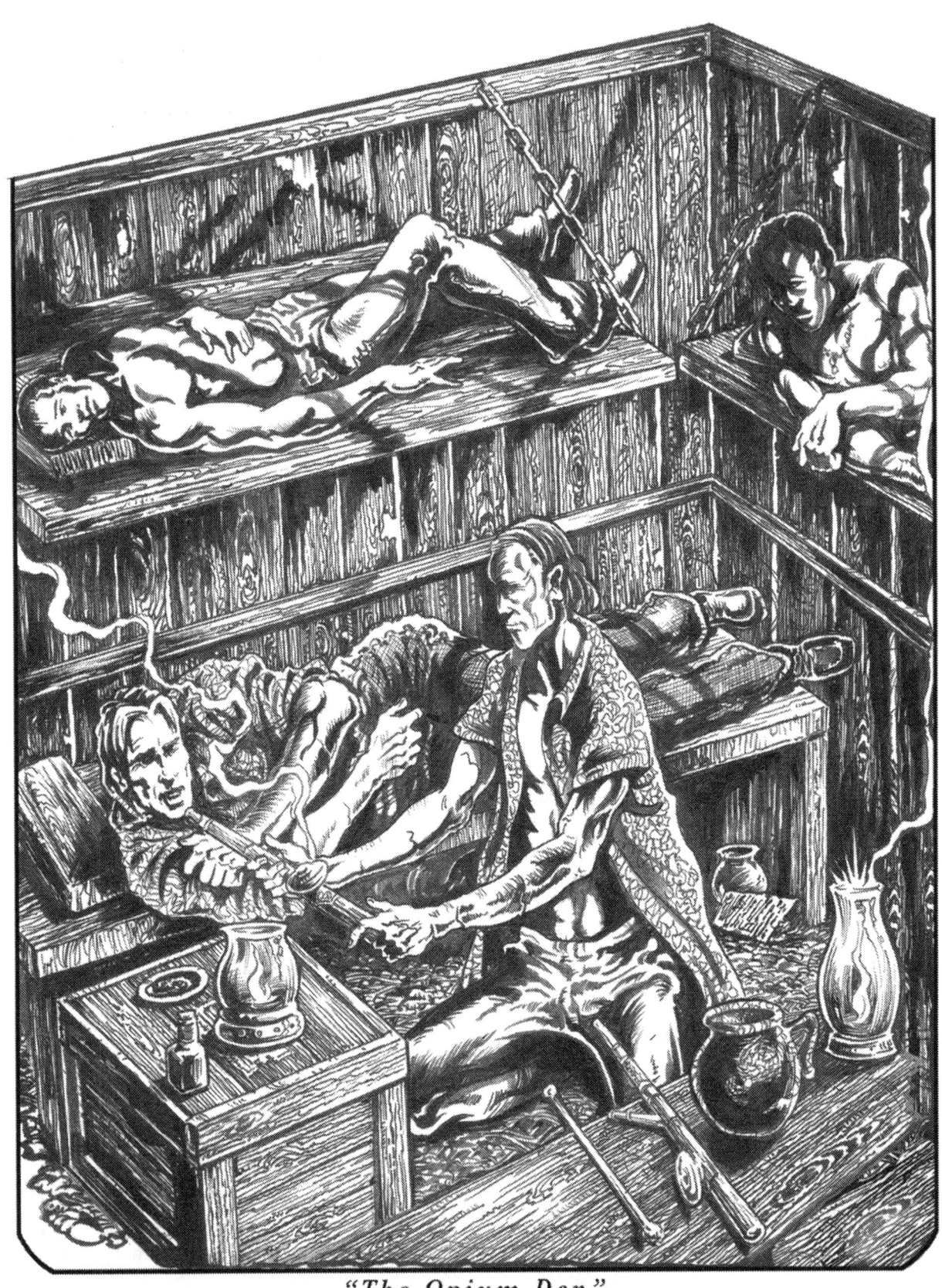
"The Opium Den"

chimney lamp. The opium does not burn, but bubbles and boils as it vaporizes in the heat stream, and the vapor is inhaled through the small hole in the center of the donut. The entire donut of opium is vaporized and inhaled in one breath, lasting about fifteen seconds, and then slowly exhaled, also lasting about fifteen seconds. This constitutes "one pipe" of opium. I was a "lightweight" at opium smoking, so I had only three pipes...

The Poppy is a very sweet smelling flower, and opium is the essence of the Poppy... Smoking opium is like inhaling heavy perfume straight from the bottle... The aroma is overpowering... Its perfume is intensely sweet, sickeningly sweet... The whole time I am smoking the opium, I am suppressing the urge to throw up... After you build up a tolerance for it, it doesn't bother you... I am told that it takes about a month to become addicted to opium, but I wouldn't trust this time-frame. To become addicted, you have to want to become addicted. The most I would smoke was three or four days in a row, on rare occasions...

The little donut of opium is vaporized and inhaled through the small hole, expanding in the large bowl of the pipe, and down the length of the pipe, directly into the lungs. This intensely sweet vaporous perfume permeates throughout your entire body, like billowing smoke expanding in an empty vessel, permeating everything with sensual sweetness... This billowing sweet perfume slowly rolls down your extremities, until all of your body is saturated in sweet sensual perfume.., and that block of wood under your head turns into a feather pillow... Sometimes there are old men, too old for any other use, that earn tips by massaging your arms and legs, facilitating this gradual flow to the extremities. Their tip; another pipe of opium.., and you do not sleep and dream while you are on opium.., you are awake and day dreaming, and there is never a bad dream, they are always good sweet dreams. The opium smoker may appear to be asleep, but his mind is very alert and active.

Opium does not rob you of your faculties, and you can function quite well in the external world, but its power is of the internal world... "How much"? I asked of the proprietor. He quoted me the price, and I handed him the appropriate amount of "kip", which was about $.75 cents in U.S. currency. "How much you want for that pipe?", I asked... He called to his wife in the next room. His wife entered. She was, like her husband, skin and bones.., you could count every bone in her body,

but she had the most beautiful eyes, with a far away look, like a young doe deer, and an enchanting smile. Their bond with each other included their mutual addiction to opium... He conferred with his wife about the sale of the pipe. Soon, he came back, and said; "Hundred Dallah"... A Hundred Dollars?, I said, in mock surprise. (I chuckled a little bit). "No, that's too much", I said, "I'll give you Fifty dollars for it"... "Hundred Dallah, Hundred Dallah", he insisted. "No, I cannot", I said. "O.k." I said. "I'll give you fifty-five", "O.k." I said again, "I'll give you sixty"... "Sixty Dollars, my final offer"... "Hundred Dallah, Hundred Dallah" he repeated again. I walked away to my waiting rickshaw driver, expecting to be called back to the bargaining table. I didn't look back, and he didn't call me back.

We sped away, my bicycle rickshaw driver and I, through the streets and alleys, dodging and zig-zagging in and out of traffic, arriving at my hotel. I handed him a generous amount of kip, and went up the outside staircase and down the long balcony, past the bevy of seductive beauties that called out to me, laughingly soliciting their trade. I smiled and waved back, but went directly to my room... Those who have been seduced by opium, are not much interested in sex...

Almost always, the overpowering, sickeningly sweet, intensely perfumed essence of the poppy, would make me sick, and I would throw up... From experience, I had learned to prepare for this event by eating fruit pies, which tasted good going down, and didn't taste too bad coming back up. If you are going to explore into new frontiers, you cannot be deterred by inconveniences, you just deal with them, and move on.

But this time, I didn't get sick, (dosage is the critical factor)... I lay down on the bed, and waited for the dream reveries to begin.., as I scratched all over my body. You might call this another one of the inconveniences of the exploration into new frontiers, this opium itch, but it felt "Oh so good", to scratch this itch. It was a sensual experience to scratch this itch, and for the next thirty minutes or so, I was intuitively involved (into it) in scratching this sensuous itch, all over my body.

Presently, I turned over on my right side, and turned my gaze inward... It is traditional, when smoking opium, to lay on your right side... Just why this is, I'm not sure, but there are many statues of the "Reclining Buddha" laying on his right side, and it was in this position that the Buddha took his final breath, and died, and this was considered "auspicious"... Did the Buddha smoke opium?.. There is nothing in the Buddhist scriptures that says that he did, but certainly there was an abundance of opium and hashish available to him for the experience... As the dedicated seeker of Truth that He was, and an explorer of the inner sanctum, who studied under many teachers, it is inconceivable to me that He would not have tried them all... I would be disappointed if He had not tried them all. The Buddhas (plural) are associated with "The Blue Lotus", (also called the "Blue Water Lilly", *Nymphaea Caerulea*) which is a powerful psychedelic whose properties are released when the blossom is soaked in an alcoholic drink. The ancient Egyptians also had this flower (as well as cocaine and tobacco)… Also, there was, at the time of the Buddha, the "elixir of immortality"; the "Soma", which (some speculate) has been picked to extinction, but (by the description given in the scriptures) is related to the "Morning Glory" plant…

Now.., I think.., there are different personality types that get involved with opium (or morphine, heroine, etc.), and willpower (or the lack of it) has little to do with it. Intention.., is the critical factor. Intention (or it's lack), has everything to do with it...

With no intentions whatever, the curious person might indulge in opium, just for the sake of curiosity, and get lost in the happy realm of "pipe dreams", eventually falling prey to the super sensual, intensely sweet perfume of the opium Poppy. Words fail to convey this intense super sensual perfumed sweetness... Do not underestimate its power!..

As the billowing clouds of opium smoke inundate and overtake the body (like an empty vessel).., saturating, anesthetizing, and replacing body consciousness with this "around the bend" sensual sweetness that is more addictive than sex, the "consciousness principal" becomes absorbed in this overpowering sweetness, and succumbs to it, drowning itself in the seductive ecstasy of sensual sweetness...

And not only does the "Consciousness Principle" become seduced into this "cosmic quicksand", but the body itself (a separate animal) will crave this sweetness... To pursue this experience "around the bend" more than once, is to become addicted... For some people (the foolhardy, the disdainful of life, the uncaring), one time is already too much... This word to the Wise here will be sufficient... A word to the foolish; "Beware!".., lest you fall...

As for myself.., No thank you... No, It is not my intention to slip into this perfumed quicksand and wallow in and be consumed by overpowering sweetness... NO, No no no... A thousand times, No... I aim at loftier heights than this. This is the difference that intention makes... It is intention that separates the victorious from the victims… Beware, lest you fall victim.., unintentionally...

As I lay on my right side, my body, having been anesthetisized by the opium.., there is a disassociation, a separation.., an isolation of mind from body... I slip in and out of the happy state of "pipe dream" reveries. I have done this many times before, and although this is exceedingly pleasant, it is a repetition of past experiences. I decide to take advantage of the mind-body separation and incorporate a meditation exercise aimed at bringing the production of the dream state reveries to a halt, and further isolate "myself" out from the dreams... This is a lot easier said than done, but after a wrestling match of about an hour of conscientiously applied effort, I am at last at the point where..; "Self, rests in Self alone"...

I had achieved "Isolation"... I had become "centered"... But it was more than just being centered.., I was "Profoundly" centered... This verse came to me from the "Bhagavad-Gita": (VERSE QUOTED HERE) [1]

This profound centeredness.., was a feeling of total power.., a feeling of indominatable will.., a feeling of absolute certainty, without doubt.., a feeling that no-one would dare question my authority.., a feeling that every spoken word would be a command that would instantly be carried out... "Oh yes!".., No doubt about it.., the great "Gengis Khan" had smoked opium, and he had found this place, and every spoken word was a command that was instantly carried out...

And I thought to myself..; with a feeling of absolute power and certainty.., *without a doubt..,* **"I"..,** could rule the World !!!

---

[1] As happens so many times throughout this book, I was unable to find this particular verse.., and it may be elsewhere than in the Bhagavad-Gita.., but it had to do with the Soul becoming "Centered in the Seat of Power"…

...An Inner Voice asked the question;.. *"Do you want to rule the world"?..* I knew for a certainty, that if I chose to, I could and I would... I considered the question in all seriousness... This was "The Question", wasn't it?.. Yes, this was the Question that had been asked by the "Infinite", of Gengis Khan, and he said "Yes".., and picked up the sword... This was the Question that was asked of Alexander the Great, and Alexander replied: "It is better to live a short life of great glory, than a long life in obscurity".., and he conquered the world, ... and died... This was the Question asked of Jesus, the Christ, and he answered; "What does it profit a man to gain the whole world, and lose his Soul"... HE lives forever...

"No"... I answered the unseen Inner Voice... "No… The world is not enough"!, I said...

Then, an amazing thing happened... In my inner vision, I saw in amazing detail... On my left, was the world that I was familiar with, the world that I knew... On my right was a different world, one that I had never seen before.., and "I", was in the middle!.. This was a paradox!.. And I was in the middle, and I had to decide, to the right, into an unknown world, or to the left, into the world that I knew...

Being intrigued by this alternate reality.., but not really trusting it to be real.., I decided to test it... I "reached myself" in to touch it, for substance, *and it was solid!..,* it was a solid reality.., *and I was in!....*

I was exploring this alternate reality at first with amazement, then interacting with people, then totally and completely immersed into the reality of this alternate reality.., to the complete forgetting of that other world, the world on the left, the world that I had previously thought to be so real...

I was totally intrigued with and immersed in this alternate reality, when an amazing thing happened... My body, which had been lying on its side for well over an hour, decided to change positions, and rolled over on its back.., ...shattering the alternate reality and bringing me abruptly back to that other reality, of the world as it was.., ...before I had left it...

I sat up with a start, my eyes staring wide with amazement and the realization..; that I had been deceived!.. This was my first thought; "I had been deceived"!.. I was deceived by this alternate reality, and I had been seduced into it by curiosity. I was intrigued into it, and I had accepted it as absolutely real, and it was absolutely real, down to the last detail... I was shocked with how easily I had forgotten my previous reality and accepted this new reality as the "really real" reality.., only to discover the deception... And I had not been asleep... No, I had been wide awake and alert, and with inner eye wide open, I had gone into it.., and been deceived.., and there was no way out of the deception, no way to see through it, no way to analyze yourself out of it.., and if my body had not rolled over on its back.., I would be there still...

I was shocked by this revelation... I paced the floor, deep in thought about the implication of this experience. I had been awake in this alternate reality, and it was absolutely real in every way, down to the smallest detail, and I had been deceived... Now the question was..; just how deep does this deception go.?. I looked around my surroundings, at the room, out the window to the bustling city that stretched out before me, and I saw that it was real in every detail.., just like in the alternate reality... And now.., I didn't trust *this* reality to be real any more... I was on shaky ground, with the feeling that as I stood here I was being deceived by the world around me, that it was just a phantasm, and at any moment, I would roll over in my bed and discover a previous reality that I had forgotten about...

I left my room and walked out in the street, walking aimlessly, wide eyed, as though seeing the world for the first time, questioning the reality of it, looking for a crack in the buildings walls, that I might squeeze through, and enter into that other alternate reality.., of which this one is but a dream...

I walked on and on, I couldn't sit still, I had to walk... Sometimes observing the world around me, suspiously, looking for a flaw.., and then deep in thought, as though in a trance, not seeing anything, pondering the meaning of it all. What did it all mean.?. Had I had an encounter with "Maya", the Goddess of illusion.?. Had I been tricked.?. Was I susceptible.?. Obviously, the answer was; "Yes"... Or was it just the opium, that I had so successfully challenged the power of, and been victorious.., only to ultimately be deceived.?. And what was the substance of this illusion, that I had tested, and found to be a solid reality.?. And from whence had it come, and to where did it go.?. Was it a product of my own manufacture, my own creation, of my own mind.., and if it was a creation of my own mind, could I create it, and then get lost in it, and be deceived.?. Is this similar to death.?. Is this what happens at death.?; the Soul goes into a happy dream world of his own creation, or, if he be an asshole, a nightmare of his own creation, from which there is no escape.?. No, I answered myself, this is neither Heaven or Hell, this was..; …Limbo…

I asked the question, and I answered it… This was the condition of the "after death" state… The Tibetan Buddhists seem to be the only ones to have researched and explored the after death states, and these texts [2] should be read and contemplated by every explorer. (In essence).., At the moment of death, if the Yogin has been trained, and has the presence of mind, he will recognize the clear light, and be liberated… If not, he goes into the realm of his own mind, and is held captive there, in a dream world of his own creation, from which there is no escape, except to eventually be reincarnated.., or at the final judgment.., or he could be helled there.., for a long, long time…

This "after death" state of the Soul, this "Limbo", is made reference to by Christians as; "Purgatory".., and by the Buddhists as; the "Bardo"… This is another one of those "Universal Truths" that is common to all religions…

…And if this was a creation of my own mind, then the mind itself was a far greater mystery than I had supposed, being able to create an illusion that was perfect down to the very last detail, and independent as to content, and able to mesmerize me with the cleverness of its content, and hold me an unsuspecting captive… And was this my situation at the present moment..?..

…. But wait.!. The trickery was even more clever than that.!. Both of those worlds, the one on the left that I was familiar with, and the one on the right that was new.., both of those worlds were illusion, because neither of those worlds was the external world in which my body lay, in the hotel room, in Vientiane, Laos… I had been deceived from the get-go.., even before I ventured into the world on my right... Had I gone left instead of right, the result would have been the same.!. Oh, thou foul trickster…

The mind.., is considered (by those who Know), to be an organ of the Soul… Even though the words (that variegated cloak); "mind" and "Soul" are often used interchangeably in common parlance, they are not the same… The Soul, is the observer.., and the mind, is the thing observed…

The objective of meditation is to separate the Soul from the mind.., to isolate the Observer from the illusory phenomena that is the creation of the mind, and then bring the mind to a complete standstill… This; is the crack in the wall… This; is the only way out… The mind is an organ of, and subservient to, the Soul.., forming itself into whatever whim that is even slightly contemplated by its master, the Soul… A fascinating mystery, is this mind, having seemingly boundless energy, never stopping its incessant activity, jumping from subject to subject, object to object, forwards and backwards in time.., but never still, not even in sleep… The mind is the willing servant of the Soul, following the slightest direction, when direction is given, but without direction, on its own.., it is the propounder of riddles, the manufacturer of endless illusion… A faithful and necessary servant..,   …a terrible master…

Of the many thousands of times that I had sat for meditation, the number of times that I had accomplished the cessation of the thought process, bringing the mind to a complete standstill, where "Self rests in Self alone".., I could count on one hand… And of those times that I had accomplished it, only once had it been done without the aid of a catalyst.., and I had received a Blessing… Those few precious times.., are the substance of this book…

I walked on and on, deep in thought… I had walked out of the city, to the outskirts, and when I looked around me, I had left the paved streets, and was walking down a dirt road that came to an end in a fenced in compound. The compound was deserted, and there was a wooden building in the center of the compound, that had the typical pagoda style roof that marked it as having religious significance… It was a meditation hall, I thought to myself, or perhaps a one room school house, and no school today, that's why it was deserted… I walked over to the building and sat down on the wooden porch walkway that surrounded the building… I had walked a long way, and I was resting, still lost in thought, still pondering the significance of it all.., still anticipating the moment when I would roll over in my bed…

---

[2] "The Tibetan Book of the Dead", by; W.Y. Evans-Wentz, (a Galaxy Book, Oxford University Press, 1960)

I had sat down on the porch near the corner of the building, and when I got up to go, I turned and looked at the building.., at the corner of the building.., and there it was.!!

It was the ornamental corner brace, that held up the upturned corner of the roof.., and it was the exact replica of the corner brace that I had examined in the Deva realm... Exact in every detail, except that it had been carved out of wood instead of polished gold, as in the Deva realm... Even the angle that I was looking from, and the distance away from where I looked, was the same...

The computer boggled... Some days, there are days like this... Some days, things just get profounder and profounder... I stared at the corner brace... It was a confirmation of the fact that I was not alone in having visited the Realm of the Devas... Other people have been there, and the replication of that corner brace was proof positive... I lamented the fact that I had no camera with me. How trivial I am, I thought...

The thing that amazes me, is the choreography involved in this little dance. The orchestration of it all... It was like the Zen koans, the little riddle meant to shock the initiate into a moment of clarity... I had walked aimlessly, only to arrive at that precise location, and see that precise replica of the Deva world, and view it from the precise angle, from the precise distance, at that precise moment...

At that precise moment, four Universes came together... The Realm of the Devas, the Realm of here and now on planet Earth, the Realm of the alternate reality within my own mind.., and the Realm of the Master Choreographer, who orchestrated this meeting... A confirmation of the fact of an unseen Observer... We are not alone...

I am reminded of the story of Saint (what's his name?), that was walking down the beach, pondering the Infinite, when he saw this little boy carrying buckets of water and dumping them into a hole that he had dug on the beach. "What are you doing?", asked the Saint... "I'm pouring the ocean into this hole", replied the boy... "But that's an absurdity, it can't be done.", replied the Saint. "Nor can your concepts contain the Infinite", replied the boy, and having illustrated the point.., vanished!!. The Saint could not fathom the Infinite, but the Infinite had touched him... The end result of all of this, is.; Humility...

I left the compound, flagged down the first available rickshaw, and was transported back to my hotel. I met my friends for dinner that evening, and reiterated the amazing adventure of my opium induced pipe dream. They listened with rapt attention, as I described how I was seduced by the reality of it, only to awaken to the fact that it was all an illusion... It really was an amazing story...

The next morning I awakened early, and as I lay in bed, recalling the events of the previous day, I was aware that the memory of it was sketchy... I noted that it had the characteristics of a dream, in the manner that it seemed to be fading from my memory...

I wondered..; if an evolutionist smoked opium, and had the experience of an alternate reality, as I had.., would he, while in this alternate reality, attribute all of the detailed phenomena (of the cities, the society, the elaborate architecture, the peoples, animals, fauna, flora, etc.).., would he attribute it all to evolution.?. The concept was laughable... And what would he do, when he rolled over in his bed, and woke up.?. I laughed...

I had been greatly affected by the experience of the "reality" of the alternate reality that was the product of my own mind, so much so, that I seriously doubted the reality of the present "here and now"... So, the question arises; are dreams real.?. One school of thought would argue; "of course they are real, I had one last night"... The other school would argue; "of course not, because when I awoke, it was gone"... So,.. What is the substance of a dream.?. And what is the substance of this dream of reality.?. And what is the substance of the mind itself.?. And do we all exist within the mind and the dream of the Ultimate Dreamer, and within this dream.., did HE plant the opium Poppy.??

Certainly, the "evolutionist" (deluded by his smug certainty), has never considered this question.., but then.., he never smoked opium!..

It would seem that the fantastically potent and mysterious powers of the "mind" and the imagination of the Ultimate Dreamer (God) have far more to do with life on Earth (and Earth itself) than any adaptive modifications of Earth's creatures (mislabeled "evolution")... As far as "reality" is concerned, we are back to "Buddha's Law".., (in essence) "It is all illusion.., but the illusion being the only thing there is, it is therefore reality"... The profundity of this statement.., is an understatement... To conclude from this statement that all phenomena is illusory.., or reality.., is to miss the point...

Certainly, while you are intrinsically involved within the experience of this "reallusion", it is absolutely real, and cannot be proved otherwise. But I would give a further classification to the reality/illusion phenomena..; If the phenomena that I am experiencing be exclusive to myself alone (intra-dimensionally), then I would call it illusory, (and in fact, it faded from my memory)... But, if the experience be common to all of mankind (the Deva realm), and substantiated by corroborating evidence (the decorative corner brace), then I would call this a reality (extra-dimensionally, beyond mind), and in fact, this experience did not fade from my memory...

I had fruit pie for breakfast, and went again to the opium den... This time I had four pipes of opium, upping the dosage...

I discussed again, with the proprietor, about the opium pipe... "Hundred Dallah", he said again... "Too much", I said again, and I upped the offer to $75.oo... "Hundred Dallah, Hundred Dallah" he insisted... I walked away to my awaiting rickshaw, not looking back... He didn't call me back...

Back in my hotel room, I tried to duplicate the experience of the previous day, without success... Opiates are like that, I concluded... That was part of the mystique of the drug.., part of the seduction... Every once in a while, you will have an experience that defies description, and you will say; "Wow", "that was a fantastically Mystical experience",.. and then you try for the rest of your life to duplicate that experience.., and you just get suckered in...

There are many people that go into the opium den, but I see no "Gengis Khans", coming out.., no "Alexanders", no "Jesus Christs", no "Buddhas"... But there are, however, "Samuel T. Coleridge's".., "Thomas De Quincy's".., "Edgar Allen Poe's".., (etc.).., and even in ancient times, it is conceded that "Homer" knew the virtues of opium...

"Samuel T. Coleridge", (who wrote; "Confessions of an Enquiring Spirit").., was addicted to opium, and under the influence, he wrote the poetic masterpiece "Kubla Khan", and the exotic poetry of it tumbled forth from pen to paper, and he tried to complete it the next day, but the magic was gone, and he couldn't get it back... This is typical...

Thomas De Quincy writes: ("Confessions of an English Opium Eater"), of how he at first experienced "music like perfume", and "ecstasies of divine enjoyment", but eventually.., addiction and horror.., living 100 years within the space of one night.., thousands of years in stone coffins.., cancerous kisses from crocodiles.., etc...

All of my experiences with opium had been exceedingly pleasant, but apparently.., it can turn on you...

My body rebelled against the overpowering, sickeningly sweet perfume of the poppy, and I threw up all of my breakfast... Perhaps an over sensitive stomach was a blessing, I thought, as I drifted in and out of my pipe dream reveries, between bouts of nausea...

I wondered if my experience of the previous day was unique to myself, or did every opium addict eventually experience an alternate reality in the same profoundly real way in which I had,.. and I decided..; Yes, they do, eventually.., but it's at the final overdose, at the moment of death... But then again, I can't really answer for the long term addict...

I concluded that my experience was unique to myself, in that it had more to do with the intentional and intense effort of my meditation, in conjunction with the "isolation chamber" effect.., the "sensory deprivation" of the anesthetized-opiated condition of my body, and the determination of intention, as opposed to the usual unintentionality of the victim of the perfumed sensual sweetness... This is the difference that "intention" makes...

I went again the third day to the opium den, and again had four pipes of opium. I didn't bring up the subject of the opium pipe, waiting for the proprietor to bring up the subject... He didn't mention it.

Back in the hotel room, I threw up profusely. It was like a giant hand had grabbed me by the stomach and squeezed, forcibly expelling the contents. Yellow-green liver bile came up, and still I wretched, again and again, throughout the day. Four pipes was one pipe too many, I thought, or perhaps "Someone" was trying to tell me something...

This was reminiscent of the times that I had tried Heroin... Heroin is, just by its very nature, an overdose... Morphine is the derivative of opium (a 10 to 1 concentration), and heroin is two and a half times more powerful than morphine, in concentrated form,.. and it has been chemically altered... To "slam" this over- concentrated power of the Poppy directly into a vein.., is to go from "ground zero" to "off the chart" immediately... The "rush" (you can't imagine) is overwhelming.., and addicting... Sex, doesn't come close. This is an aberration... This is a perversion...

You have to draw the line somewhere, and I draw the line at the needle... I have never stuck a needle in my arm, and I never plan to... I've had many friends go down this road, and I don't like where it leads... If you're not intelligent enough to learn from other people's experiences.., then you condemn yourself to go down that same road yourself.., and it's a dead end.., and it's a waste... Dosage is the critical factor... Don't use the needle...

I am by nature, a research scientist... my field of research is "altered states"... My area of exploration is the realm of my own being.., intra-dimensionally, to the realms within the mind, and extra-dimensionally, to the realms beyond the mind.., and to my "Self".., the observer of this phenomena, and to "HE".., who observes me...

I evaluate the opiates to be a doorway to the intra-dimensional realms, within the realm of mind... In our normal state of awareness, with the externalized senses, eyeballs focused outward, away from the mind.., we live in two dimensions, simultaneously... In this regard, the agency of the body is seen as a God given opportunity.., otherwise, we would simply be held captive within the confines of mind, a Universe unto ourselves.., in "Limbo"... Focused outwardly, the Galactically magnificent creative potential of the mind is "balanced" by the Galactically magnificent Universe that is the outside reality...

In this regard, the body is seen as a God given opportunity... The essence of the "Pranja Paramita" (the Supreme and Ultimate Wisdom), is this..; "Don't waste this Opportunity"... (Having been given this "Supreme and Ultimate Wisdom".., what will you do with it.?.)

To anyone who has experienced the "Galactically Magnificent creative powers of the mind".., and viewed the world of his own mind, "that is perfect down to the last Detail".., it is but a very small leap to realize that we function within the realm of a mind in which a Galaxy.., is only an insignificant part...

Through the agency of the body, we are no longer confined (as an unsuspecting captive) within the realm of our own mind, but we can see both the inner and the outer of it all.., and it is magnificent... But now, the focus of our identity is the body, from which we look "out" from within, and "in" from without.., never really being totally absorbed in either the inner or the outer, and never realizing the full potential of either... So the opportunity lies in mastering the mind (the organ of the Soul).., instead of being deceived by it...

There are basically two ways out of the deception.., and both ways ultimately merge as the same "way".., and that is in the complete and total cessation of the thought process..; i.e., "the stopping of the mind"... When the frenetic activity of the mind has been brought to a complete standstill, only then can it be said, that..; "Self", rests in "Self", alone"...

Of the two ways (that merge into the one way), is First..; "The Way of the Mystic".., which is, the path of devotion...

"Patanjali", (The Father of the Yoga systems) , lists six different approaches, appropriate to six different personality types, and then he mentions the "easy" way, which is the path of devotion, the Way of the Mystic... Simply stated..; "Love the Lord, your God, with all your heart, with all your mind, and all your Soul, and love your neighbor as yourself "... This is the most easy and direct way... This is "Pranja Paramita"...

The Mystic contemplates; and with all his attention focused on some aspect of the Lord, or pondering some question for the Lord.., mind is stilled.., because it is bypassed.!. The focus of "Self", away from "Self", toward the Divine is the automatic achievement of the Zen-objective state of consciousness.., and the focus of attention is one pointed, perfect, and effortless... Ego is non-existent, and mind is not involved... "When the mind is stilled, "Buddhi" wakes up".!. (*) The mind is transcended, and "Communion" is achieved... This Communion is with the "Root Guru", (or by whatever multitude of Names "HE" may be known by).., and there is dialogue.., and the "Inner Voice" speaks, and there is vision, and the vision is revelation, and the revelation is knowledge, and you will Know, and nothing will be hidden from you...   Welcome.., to the region beyond mind...

And the Second way.., is to do battle with the mind... This is not nearly so easy... By constant vigilance, the "Self" is isolated from the mind, and the mind is consciously and deliberately subdued by "chopping the roots" [3].., that is; by constantly interrupting the incessant flow of the self reproductive thought process, and ultimately bringing the mind to a complete stop.., until "Self", rests in "Self" alone... There are a multitude of techniques and variations of techniques aimed at this result... Pick one...

But the first Way, and the second Way, do not have to be mutually exclusive.., and should not be.., because the "Root Guru" stands at the door.., of the region beyond mind, and no one enters, except by "HIM"... So ultimately, the first Way, and the second Way, merge into the same Way... The path of Wisdom here is Self evident, and need not be elaborated on...

Pay homage to the "Root Guru", by whatever Name you may Know HIM... For it is HE, the "ONE", who is beyond all name and form, that stands at that door, and knocks, proclaiming; ...."Any one hear My voice, and open unto Me, I will come unto him, and sup with him, and he with Me".... This is the invitation of the Lord... This is HE, that spoke to Abraham, Isaak, Jacob, and Jesus, and to all the Saints and Seers of all religions, from all ages, and from all times...

So,.. I was evaluating the opiates in general, and Heroin in particular...

Again, dosage is the critical factor, and because of the highly concentrated nature of heroin, dosage is difficult to determine. From experience, I prepared for heroin in the same way as for opium, by eating fruit pies for breakfast... I ingested the heroin by sniffing it up my nose, and found it to be quite similar to opium, but it came on much more quickly and intensely... My body (which was more sensible than I), rebelled against the inundation of the heroin, and I threw-up profusely. I suspect that this had by now become a "conditioned reflex"... After the third day of heroin use, I woke up the following morning and had this sick feeling in the pit of my stomach, and my bones ached, especially in my jaw. I didn't think anything of it, and after a snort of heroin, it was gone... The morning following the fourth day of use I experienced the same sick feeling in the pit of my stomach, and the bone ache in my jaw.., only much more intensely ...

"Holy shit!", I said to myself...   Withdrawal symptoms after the third day, and intensified withdrawal symptoms after the fourth day... No thank you.!. I did NOT get enough from heroin to become addicted to it.!. No thank you...

In the process of trying to figure out what heroin is all about, it can grab hold of you, before you can grab hold of it.!. It did NOT give me the intuitive insights indicative of higher mind functions... It did NOT lead to the realm beyond mind (extra-dimensionally), but only did it lead to the realm within the mind (intra- dimensionally), to the realm of deception.., to Limbo... And I am NOT a sensualist.!. No thank you, to the slippery slope of the perfumed quick-sand of sensually perverted ecstasy, seductive unto death... NO.., Heroin does NOT lead.., to where I want to go...

So I evaluated it, and in this intriguing "Game of Life"..; of good and bad, right and wrong, smart and stupid, life and death, Heaven and Hell.., or Limbo.., I find that heroin is a pit-fall... It doesn't get you "high" in the spiritual sense, but just gets you "sideways" into the Limbo of the intra-dimensional mind, or drowns you in the pit of sensuality, and eventually.., it just brings you "down" into mental, physical, financial, moral, and spiritual ruin... ...End of Game... You lose...

I conducted this experiment while residing in Kabul, Afghanistan (before the Russian occupation), and in a side by side taste test of heroin, opium, and hashish.., my drug of choice was the Hashish... The Afghani hashish is legendary, and it was my great good fortune to partake of this substance that did give spiritual insights, a joy of life, a religious inclination, and a "praise God" kind of "High"... "My Momma didn't raise no fool"... My choice was obvious...

The "science" of Alchemy is in the dosage, and heroin is the incorrect dosage of a chemically altered substance... In the proper dosages, the opiates have been a boon to mankind.

---

[3]   This technique is described in great detail in the book: "Tibetan Yoga and secret doctrines" (by W.Y. Evans-Wentz.., pages 128-129)

I awoke the next morning, of the fourth day, and as I lay there in bed, I tried to recall the experience of the first day.., and I could not.!. It had vanished from my memory without a trace.!. I remembered everything prior to going into it, and of going into it, and that there were people there, and I remembered coming out of it with the realization that I had been deceived, but the dream content itself.., was gone.!. I met my friends for breakfast, and asked them to recall the story of it, as I had told it to them.., and they recalled me telling them the story, but they could not recall what it was about...

As I tell you (the reader) this story now, I regret that the dream content is lost, because it could have been a much more interesting story... And not being able to recall the content, I relegate the experience to the classification of a dream, because it has the characteristics of a dream in that (although it had been intensely vivid) it diminished in intensity from my memory, and finally vanished after three days.., although the psychological impact of the event stayed with me for a long time after that, leaving me on shaky ground, waiting to roll over in my bed... I still have thoughts about it...

I went again to the opium den, and had three pipes of opium... I explained to the proprietor that this was my last day in Vientiane, as I had my visa for Thailand, and the train from Knong Kai was leaving the next morning, and if he wanted to sell that opium pipe, this was his last chance...

"Hundred-TEN-Dallah", he shouted at me... He shouted at me.!! I glared at him through clenched teeth... I was a head taller than him and well over twice the body weight of his 80 pound skeleton frame... He glared back at me with firmly set jaw, and that defiant opium attitude... He had me.!. I really wanted that pipe, and he turned the tables on me, and this was my last chance to get it, and we both knew it. He had me!

Quickly, (before he raised the price again), I reached into my pocket and counted out one hundred and ten dollars, and handed it to him with my right hand, as I grabbed the pipe with my left hand... He didn't let go of the pipe until I let go of the money... He didn't even say "Thank You".., and I didn't say thank you... I turned and walked to the door, and opened it... I thought for a moment, then I turned and said, "thank you"... He nodded... Good enough, I thought...

Well.., I actually admired that little man, that stood his ground and bested me in the fine art of bargaining. He was the Hero of the day, among his little group, and I am sure he told and retold the story of how he out-foxed that smart-ass American. But what he didn't know, was that I would have paid $200.oo for that pipe.., or so I consoled myself...

It wasn't until the next day, on the train ride from Knong Kai, back to Bangkok, as I was showing off my prize to my fellow adventurers, that I realized that he had switched the bowl of the pipe, to a less decorative one. I could only laugh at myself, at how neatly I had been gotten the best of, by that little skeleton of a man...

* * *

The history and politics of opium is, as it has always been, a continuing saga…

Although opium is indigenous to the region, the Laotian society in general does not condone the smoking of opium among it's young people, which is considered a very regrettable and shameful thing.., although the older men will smoke opium occasionally, but not to the point of addiction. Addiction is condoned among the old, the sick, and the dying. Instead of enduring a painful decay, they slip away in a peaceful euphoria…[4]

The French had colonized Laos, as well as Cambodia and Vietnam, and the trade in opium represented 25% of Frances income... The opium was sold in various forms as the medicine of choice throughout all of Europe and elsewhere, for all ailments from diarrhea, vexations of the spirit, and for its pre-eminent use as a pain killer.

This area, of the convergence of Laos, Burma, and Thailand, is known as the "Golden Triangle"... It is from this area, that 20% of the world's illicit traffic in heroin finds it's way to Europe, the Americas, etc... In 1962, President Carter was offered the opportunity of buying the entire inventory of Golden Triangle opium for the sum of $36 million dollars... The offer was declined... Needless to say,

---

[4] Much of the information concerning the history and politics of opium was gleaned from the very fine articles written in "National Geographic Magazine" by Mr. Peter T. White, entitled: "The Poppy" (Feb. 1985, pgs. 143-189), and "Laos Today" (June 1987 pgs. 772-795), and "Report on Laos" (Aug. 1961, pgs. 241-275)…

the heroin found it's way here at 1000% mark up, along with untold misery. Much of it was bought by the North Vietnamese communists and sold to American service men, fighting the war in Vietnam...

This was a fair price, considering that we buy 2/3 of the annual production (hundreds and thousands of tons) of opium from India, converting it into morphine, codeine, etc., for medicinal use in the legitimate market.

It may seem unfair to speculate on "what could have been", but... For a fraction of the cost, we could have eliminated the out-flow of hard currency from the American economy, and into the hands of the forces of evil... We could have eliminated much misery, crime, incarceration, and the expense incurred by this scourge... We could have negotiated with and marshaled the forces in that area, as a buffer against communist incursions, because these are the remnants of the "Koumintang", the fierce anti-communist forces under Chaing-Ki Sheck, that fought and lost the war against the Chinese communists, and retreated to Taiwan and to this Golden Triangle area of Burma. We could have partnered with these people, and brought prosperity to the region, with schools and hospitals, etc. We could have had an enclave, a hot-bed, of free enterprise and capitalism. We could have established trade, and dried up or channeled this outflow into productive channels. We could have saved many Souls... and etc... We could have, but we didn't... And to this day, the opium still flows.., and the heroin still comes... An opportunity.., missed...

The British had colonized or dominated all of the region through Pakistan, India, Burma, Siam, Singapore, Hong Kong, etc., as well as doing a prosperous trade with China... The British merchants got rich transporting tea from China to Europe, for which the Chinese would accept only silver for payment. Soon, The Europeans drank up all the tea, and were depleted of silver. The British countered by transporting opium from India to China, and selling it only for silver. The Merchants and the British Empire got richer... Soon, there were millions of Chinese addicted to opium, and there was a brisk and highly profitable trade. The Chinese government did not like what was happening to its people and banned the British (*and Americans*) from selling the opium... What followed is known as the "Opium Wars" (1840-1842), in which the British were successful in forcing the Chinese to continue accepting the opium in trade, regardless of the detriment to the people... It is estimated that by 1890, there were fifteen million Chinese addicted to opium... There is still to this day bitter resentment among the Chinese people...

I mention this piece of history, because of this question that was asked of Dr. Robert Du Pont (formerly head of N.I.D.A. & the American Council of Drug Education)... The question: "Does this mean that all the anti heroin measures, from aerial poppy surveys to heroin sniffing dogs, etc., are useless?.. That those millions of taxpayer dollars spent here and abroad have been wasted? Wouldn't it make more sense, as quite a few advocate, to simply legalize the stuff"?.. "Not at all", replied the good Dr., "If we didn't have the efforts we make against heroin, we wouldn't have just half a million addicts, we would have 20 million... It's the fight against good and evil... It's part of existence, and it has no end"...

I have to concur with the good Dr... Knowing that opium is much less addictive than heroin, and observing the history of opium in China, it is obvious that he is correct, and I have no quarrel with this battle of good versus evil.., except that it doesn't go far enough...

Simply stated; we must maintain our efforts to eradicate this scourge, and what we cannot eradicate, we must purchase, and divert it to the legitimate market... We must also make it available to "registered" addicts, and at a price below the "black market"... The street value, as well as the source value, will plummet, and the "profit versus risk" factor will not be worth the risk... Any new addicts coming on to the "register" will have to divulge the source of their addiction, and it will be eradicated... The impetus for this scourge to spread, will be eliminated...

The government has attempted to register heroin addicts and to divert their addiction to a synthetic form of heroin called "Methadone", which was partially successful, in that it diverted cash flow away from illicit sources, but the addiction to methadone is even more sinister than the addiction to heroin, and with withdrawal symptoms that are much more severe... If a methadone addict has a change of heart, and wishes to "kick", he must first "step down" from methadone, back to heroin, and then attempt to kick the habit...

And speaking of opportunities (and Souls) lost..; as I write these words, it is the year 2000, and it is with sorrowful amazement that I observe, that the "CURE" for both heroin and methadone addiction, even though it has been available for at least a dozen years.., has not been implemented...

The cure exists in the form of "Ibogaine", a derivative of that "herb of mysterious virtue" known as the "Iboga" plant, native to central West Africa... And not only does this herbal remedy convert the addict away from even the desire for the addictive substance, but totally circumvents and nullifies the withdrawal symptoms!.. And as an added benefit, it gives the (former) addict.., a religious experience!..

This "herb of mysterious virtue", having psychotropic properties, falls under the classification of a "psychedelic".., and as such, it is given a "schedule one" rating, with penalties for the sale or use of this substance in the same category as that of heroin.., if it were available.., but there is no "black market" of this substance, because there is no profit in a drug that not only cancels addictions, but has only a one time use... It seems that the "letter" of the law is strictly enforced, and the "Spirit" of the law.., is dead...

Or perhaps, "They" (the irreligious, secular humanistic, left wing liberal, (God is dead) "powers that be").., object to the "religious experience" aspect of the drug... Furthermore, it must be noted, that not only is Ibogaine instrumental in the cure of heroin, methadone, cocaine, crack, alcohol, tobacco, etc., and other addictions (as well as the withdrawal symptoms), but it is also instrumental in effecting psychological and character changes (such as egocentricity, the lust for power, deep seated neurosis's, and other anti-social behaviors)...

I look forward to the time when the Ibogaine experience will become mandatory for anyone seeking public office... It may well be the dawning of a "new age".., under God, with liberty and justice for all...

And what "if".., Just what "if".., if all the leaders of the world, experienced Ibogaine.., and became of one mind?.. Can you imagine?.. Can you just imagine.?.

Sometimes, The most revolutionary of ideas, are found in the most unlikely of places... And this is not as far-fetched as it sounds, because, after all..,

There is no God but God, and HE is ONE, (by whatever name you may know HIM).., and the TRUTH is ONE, and everyone that KNOWS this TRUTH.., is of one mind... This is the foundation and the cornerstone that will usher in that Millennium of peace on Earth... This is the Truth that is NOT apprehended by belief in doctrine, but rather by direct religious experience... This is beyond belief... This is Knowledge...

So.., (the question presents itself).., Is Ibogain.., or LSD, or the Psilopsybin Mushroom, or the Mescalin, Peyote, or the Ayahuska, or (whatever).., the legendary "Soma" ?., the magical "Elixir of Immortality" ?., by which the "Doors of Perception" may be cleansed ?., by which the TRUTH may be known ?.. The answer is.., "No"... By themselves alone, the answer is; No... By themselves alone, they are just another drug... Very powerful "mind expanding" drugs, to be sure, but the "secret ingredient" is missing.., that would qualify these drugs to be the "Soma"...

So.., (the question presents itself).., What,.. is the secret ingredient..? In the science of Alchemy.., it is the Alchemist himself that is the secret ingredient... He must present himself, a "Purified Vessel", at the font of Knowledge... Purified in heart and mind, in body and Soul, disciplined, without ulterior motives.., an "empty vessel", with noble intentions, with sincerity.., and humility... And not to reign.., but to serve...

Nor is this Knowledge apprehended at one sitting, (like "new wine in an old wine-skin").., but it is gained incrementally.., over time... The faint of heart, the proud, the ambitious, the impure.., need not apply...

But the subject at hand, is opium.., Good, or Evil?..

In a sort of symbiotic relationship, the human body contains receptor sites (in the intestines, the spine, and in the brain) that are specific to the utilization of opiates... The body is even capable of manufacturing its own opiate, called "endorphins", which alleviate pain and gives the body stamina in response to stress. Long distance runners reaching the point of exhaustion, are familiar with this infusion of endorphins by what they call their "second wind"...

Dr. Cicily Saunders.., pioneer of the "Modern Hospice Movement"; a blessed medical innovation for those suffering the excruciating pain and the terrible fear that comes with the ravages of Cancer, Aids, and other terminal illnesses, says; "In these final days, morphine is at the top of the list for pain control. No synthetic analgesic has yet been made that deserves to replace it. It is the mainstay by which all other drugs are compared. It is the drug of choice.., in the right amounts, of course".

The Queen has made Dr. Saunders a "Dame Commander of the Order of the British Empire", and there are those who think she should be made a Saint...

"It is nothing but nonsense.., a myth".., says Dame Cicily, "that you will make junkies out of patients. It makes such a difference, when you take away the pain and the fear. It can save memories. Patients can have friends and grandchildren visit whenever they want, and even their dogs. There can be family reconciliations, a chance to say; "I'm sorry", and "thank you"... Instead of being knocked out, you will see patients free of pain, alert and cheerful with their families... It will be remembered that amid sadness, there was courage and understanding, so that you will remain proud of those last days"...

The Hospice Movement and the Gospel of Dame Cicily has spread to the U.S. and Canada, and has urged Doctors and hospitals to stop the under-utilization of opiate drugs for severe chronic pain and the terminally ill...

So, everything has its use, and its misuse, and the misuse of these drugs carries with it it's own punishment.., while the proper use of the opiates is a boon to mankind.., a gift of God... Let Wisdom prevail...

* * * * *

BOOK XIII

"Incident in Singapore"

I arrived back in Bangkok with my new visa, and the realization that my financial resources were approaching "depleted" status... The American dollar was "King" among the currencies of the world, and my meager savings of about $3,000.oo had lasted me for about a year and a half. I had shunned the tourist routes, and whenever possible I adopted the lifestyles and ate the simple fare of the local people. I had a back-pack and a bed roll, and chose the least expensive accommodations available. I traveled overland, by trains and busses, that were adventures in themselves, and only rarely by airplane. I had lived well, and by my own definition; luxuriously.., but it was coming to an end...

I had made no provisions for return to the U.S., and I wasn't ready to return just yet. I had a mission to accomplish, a …maturity.., to be won, and although I had survived and progressed in one realm of endeavor, it was becoming increasingly evident that I get back down to Earth, if this journey is to continue...

I had regained my health and my body weight, and I would devote the next two months to perfecting myself in the martial art of "Karate".., and getting High.., and enjoying the fine ethnic cuisine.., and the women.., and good friends... And then I would go to Singapore...

There was an oil boom happening all through the area of the South China Sea, Sumatra, Indonesia, etc. and Singapore was the American base of operations in S.E. Asia.., and I knew about oil...

I had left home before my 18th birthday, from an attack of wanderlust, and after three months on the road, and having hitch-hiked across the Country from border to border and coast to coast, I ended up in a "boom town" in the "Four Corners" area of New Mexico... I had grown from a boy to a man, working as a "roughneck" on the drilling rigs... and I knew all aspects of the industry, in its science and in the technology, and I had hands-on experience... I grew up in that boom town, and I could talk the talk, and walk the walk...

I took the train down the long peninsula of Southern Thailand into Malaysia, then down the West coast of the Malay peninsula to George Town, on the island of Penang, just to see what there was to see… George Town was a "Port of Call" for the smugglers of old *(with whom I shared a kindred spirit)..*, and then down to Kuala Lumpur, the capitol, just to see what there was to see.., and then on down to Singapore...

Singapore was the new "boom town"... It was like Las Vegas, without the gambling. Being an island, there was no more room for the population, except straight up, in skyscraper apartment buildings... The oil companies occupied entire floors of office buildings and luxury hotels, with night clubs.., and round faced, slant eyed, grinning Chinese in business suits, cowboy hats, boots, and electric guitars.., on stage.., playing country and western music to the cowboy hatted an booted roughneck oil workers, from Texas, Oklahoma, New Mexico, etc. East meets West... It was bizarre...

Singapore "boomed" even before the discovery of oil... Under the astute leadership of president-for-life; "Lee Quan Yu", the four races of Singapore (Chinese, Indian, Malay, British), and now the Americans, lived in harmony.., and there was no dissent allowed... Designating the Island-Country of Singapore to be a "duty free port" (no taxes), all the shipping companies had a base of operations here, and all the international trading companies, and international banking, and tax-free outlets representing all the high-tech and cottage industry products from all over the world, and a skilled labor force that manned the factories and assembly lines... It was "free enterprise" and "free market" in action.., and it "Boomed" with prosperity and growth... It was the market place to the world, and in addition to this, it was "R & R" to all the Navies of the world, where the sailors took "liberty"... Singapore "rocked", as well as boomed...

I had arrived with less than fifty dollars in my pocket, and as was my modus operandi, I went to the old section of the city, where I felt at home among the cheap hotels, the brothels, the multi-national hippies, the soldiers of fortune down on their luck, and the occasional scents of opium and hashish wafting through the air... This was a step back in time to somewhere in the late 1800's, and there was a vibrancy and color here that was lacking in the modern downtown business district.., and I could live here for about three or four dollars a day...

The old city teemed with life, and bustled with the activity of sidewalk shops and street vendors, selling everything from high-tech electronics, to cameras, wrist watches, shoes, clothing, silks and satins, etc., interspersed with food shops emitting the spicy aromas of Chinese, Malay, and Indian foods. It was a gourmets delight.

And the sounds of the city!.. It was not quiet here. It seemed that among the four races, there was always a wedding, holiday, or funeral to be celebrated by a parade through the streets, with floats, undulating dragon dances and marching bands, accompanied by trumpets, drums, the clashing of symbols, and fireworks.

It wasn't long before I got a job... It was with an oil exploration company, looking for oil in the jungles, tidal swamps, and rain forests of Sumatra... Sumatra lay about 35 miles across the "Straits of Malacca" from Singapore, and was one of the principle island land masses that makes up the country of Indonesia. I would be flown back and forth from Singapore to Sumatra, working for two solid weeks in Sumatra, with a week off, back in Singapore... Two weeks in the jungle, one week in civilization... It was one of the most interesting times of my life...

The search for oil is in itself very fascinating... Teams of geologists study the physical features of the land mass that is Sumatra, drawing grid lines across those areas that they suspect might have oil beneath them, and a lesser amount of grid lines even in areas where they suspect there is no oil, just to be sure... So the entire map of Sumatra is covered with grid lines... Teams of surveyors, working with an army of Indonesian nationals armed with machetes are employed to hack a trail three feet wide and miles and miles long, in a straight line, transferring the grid lines of the map onto the physical terrain. These trail blazers also build single pole bridges with a hand rail on one side, across swamps and small streams, and every three or four miles they will build a camp site, where the North-South grid line will intersect with an East-West grid line... This is next followed by teams of drilling crews, using primitive equipment, drilling 20 foot deep holes, every hundred feet apart.., followed by the dynamite crews, that plant canisters of dynamite in the holes, and string the wires back to a detonator... About a thousand feet back from the dynamite crews, was the "American Team", of seismic equipment and operators, communication equipment, technicians, etc... The seismic sensors are planted at various intervals in the ground, and the dynamite is set off, and the shock-wave is recorded by the seismic equipment... The primary shock wave goes from the dynamite blast across the surface of the ground and the time is recorded on the equipment, and then a secondary shock wave is recorded, bouncing off of the granite layer that lays about a thousand feet below the surface of the earth, and recording its exact depth...

This granite layer.., lays like a carpet beneath the floor of the South China Sea and the Sulu Sea.., and from Borneo through Indonesia, and etc... Exploration Ships traverse the seas, following grid lines, detonating sonic charges, recording the depth of the sea floor and the granite layer beneath it... Mapping this granite layer is what the search for oil is all about... There is oil beneath this granite layer, and where the granite layer "domes up".., chances are good that it is oil pushing up and causing the dome... At the apex of the domes, is where the drilling rigs will be located...

I was flown into Medan.., the largest city in Sumatra, to the regional headquarters and communication center of the Exploration Company, and evaluated as to my background and capabilities, and then transported by Landrover, inland, to one of their many base camps. Base camp was a homogeneous group of "Good Ol Boys", made up of Texans, Okies, Coonasses (from Louisiana), Aussies, Brits, etc., all with their own specialties, in seismology, geology, communications, technicians, mechanics, etc., related to oil... I was the new "drilling supervisor", and I was responsible for the drilling of the holes in which the dynamite was placed and detonated. I had twelve crews of Indonesian nationals under my supervision, 27 men to a crew, and we went wherever the grid lines took us, over tidal swamps, rain forests, and jungles. I co-ordinated the crew boats that ferried us across rivers and to camp sites, and the helicopters that brought in supplies and picked up sling loads of equipment to be transported to new locations.., and ferried me back and forth from the job site to base camp, daily...

If this book were about travelogue, I would tell you of the face-to-face encounters with giant constrictor snakes, deadly river snakes, cobras, etc.., the foot long scorpions, the elephants that wrecked our pole bridges, the "Orang-Utan", the "jungle man" that glided hand over hand through the trees, like poetry.., and the evidence of big cats that left their foot prints, but were never seen...

I would tell you of the helicopter descents into remote thatch-roofed villages, and of the people racing from the fields to the village, to see this Alien space craft, and of being presented with a hand carved replica of the helicopter by a young boy, that bowed with reverence.., and of taking the village elders up for a ride in the sky, seat belted in, and white knuckles holding on for dear life (the doors had been removed for transporting pipe).., as the helicopter dipped and slipped, banking left and right, scaring the elders almost to death, but giving them the experience of a lifetime, and their status was greatly increased with the stories that they could tell...

I would tell you of the intertwining rivers that flowed inland, when the tide came in, and flowed outward when the tide went out, and of water skiing in the bay of a remote native "village on stilts", and the entire village came down to the shore line to watch, and of how I angled my skies sharply into the water and showered the young girls and children with torrents of water as they laughed and giggled, dancing with glee, as the foreigners "flew on the water"...

...And the trip back up the river, by the light of the full moon, stoned on the powerful Sumatran "ganja".., and of the giant bats, with four foot wing spreads.., silhouetted against the full moon.., that descended on us like "Bats out of Hell" in a bad Dracula movie.., as I questioned my sanity, and the condition of my Soul... I had never before seen or even heard of "Fruit Bats", and they had no interest in us, but only in the insects surrounding our boat, stirred up by the outboard motor...

I would tell you of the giant trees that grew in the rainforests, hundreds of years old, taller than the Redwoods and Sequoias, growing taller still, until one day the massive height and weight outgrew the ability of the root structure to support it, and caught by the slightest breeze, they would topple over and come crashing to the ground, flattening the forest beneath it, toppling all the trees around it like a forest of dominoes, and a sound like the Wrath of God, like a thousand locomotives converging on a single spot and exploding with a deafening roar, and the sound filled the air so completely that it could not be determined from which direction the sound was coming.., and it sounded like it was right on top of you... Grown men had been wakened from a sound sleep, and ran screaming naked through the forest in the dead of night, and had to be transported back to civilization for therapy.., not to return...

I would tell you of my 12 crews of Indonesian nationals, 320+ young men, plus boat drivers, guides and translators, that worked ten hours a day, for less than two dollars a day and a tent to sleep in, and all the dried fish, swamp greens and rice they could eat... Their wages were determined by "Pertimina", the Indonesian Oil Co., who shared a 60/40 split with the American oil companies, and to pay the workers any more would upset their economy, and they would be making more money than the mayors, and the chiefs of police, etc.., but they considered themselves prosperous, with wrist watches, transistor radios, blue jeans, printed shirts.., and shoes... And the crew leaders would curry favor with their supervisor by presenting me with small bags of "ganja", saying; "issta-meewa" (very special) and I showed them favor, and they knew they had job security, even though I treated them all equally well...

We drilled the holes by hand.., with a 20 foot joint of pipe , drill bit on one end and swivel attached fire hose connected to a "Briggs & Stratton" powered water pump at the other end... The pipe was twisted into the ground by two men with pipe wrenches at the rate of about 30 RPM, which is a pretty fast and rhythmic pace for two men spinning pipe wrenches around a pipe... After about ten minutes they traded off with two other men, without missing a beat, and etc... I would step in occasionally, and spin wrenches for awhile, and I would be exhausted after ten minutes... They earned their almost two dollars a day... Water was pumped through the pipe under pressure, flushing the cuttings out of the hole. Sometimes there was water nearby, and sometimes it had to be carried long distances in five gallon jerry cans, dumped into a plastic lined reservoir dug in the ground, and recirculated through the drill pipe. After the holes were completed, the entire 10 or 12 crews would load all the equipment on their backs, or slung on poles, and march down the trail to the next location, and begin again...

I became about 30% proficient in the language, which was basically "Malay", and combined with pantomime type sign language I was able to engage in many animated conversations. This language acquisition would serve me well in later travels through Indonesia, Java, Bali, Borneo and Malaysia.

If this were travelogue, I would tell you about base-camp... Base-camp was a psychodrama of nationalities and personality types that included Americans, British, Australians, Texans, Californians, college graduates, specialists, technicians, ramrods, trouble-shooters, and etc.., as colorful and diverse a group as you could imagine, and it was good times, tall tales and laughter, that made for the best of friendships and camaraderie that extended beyond the job to "leave time" in Singapore...

With oil as the common denominator and Singapore as the common meeting ground, my circle of friends grew beyond base-camp. Friendships are the substance of a life experience, and these friendships are the substance of this "incident" in Singapore...

I had two really good friends... "Jeff"..., was a scholar, a geophysicist related to oil, and climbing the corporate ladder, but beyond that, he was the proverbial perpetual student (we had this trait in common). Jeff devoured books and information, and was a fountain of the most obscure facts and information relating to the most bizarre subject matter ever contemplated, and he seemed to know something about everything... I suspected that he sought out my friendship just to pick my brains, but it was mutual in that regard, and we debated, philosophized and dissected a wide range of subject matter, as we drank beer and pounded on the table to make our point, over the noisy background music of the nightclubs that we toured in the course of the evening...

And "Jon"... "Jon" was a few years younger than myself, and lived in the old "low rent" section of Singapore, as I did... Jon was a "hippie" from Switzerland, and exuberantly involved in the adventure of life, and the lure of the open road, with a smile and laughter that lit up the atmosphere around him. There was something special about him, a charm and "charisma" that set him apart from everyone else. He was multi-lingual, in French, German and Italian, but spoke very little English with a peculiar Southern accent. He had a lions mane of long dishwater blond hair, and wore a vest without a shirt, beads, bracelets and an arm band... He looked like a Viking warrior... There was an instant camaraderie between us, and we became the best of friends, like the long lost brother that I never had... If I were to ever be involved in a knock-down, drag-out bar fight, I would have chosen Jon to be guarding my back. That's the kind of friendship we had...

Jon had leadership qualities, and he attracted a following of friends and "ladies" that would hang out at his place, which was a large room on the ground floor of a building converted into a hotel. It was a motley crew that converged there..; hippie type vagabonds of the open road, each from a different place and a different story to tell, and we told our stories and laughed hysterically and got high on ganja and listened to the latest music on the latest stereo equipment. Then we would converge on one of the local pavilion type restaurants, and dine on either Chinese, Malay or Indian cuisine amid uproarious laughter, before going our separate ways with our ladies of the night...

I chose "Sarah"... I had seen her fighting in the street... It was a scratching, biting, kicking, punching, screaming, hair pulling cat-fight, over territory, and she won... "I want You", I said... She grabbed my arm, spat on and cursed her beaten rival, who fled the scene, and we went into the hotel... She was Malay, and had the quality of "fire".., with long straight black hair, golden loop ear rings, and two gold-capped eye teeth that accentuated her savage beauty and lit up her smile, and she was voluptuous... We spent the entire week together, and weeks to come, and she confided to me her secrets... She had murdered.., for money.., with a knife... She was a wild and rebellious girl, and hadn't realized the psychological impact that it would have on her, and horrified by the deed that she had done, she fled Malaysia, embraced her religion, did penance, and was a street prostitute.., her punishment... She loved me, but she was a prostitute, and never mentioned it.., but she served me in the subservient way that is the way of her culture, and asked my permission before doing anything, and catered to my every need before asking a favor, like; "Please, can I buy these shoes?", or whatever, and I didn't refuse her anything.

When I think back.., on the multitude.., I always think of her... She was the pure soul.., and it was I.., who was the prostitute...

....It was just another Saturday night in Singapore, and Jon and I, and three of our fellow vagabond friends were doing the nightclub circuit... Just having fun, getting loud and boisterous, flirting with the waitresses, playfully antagonizing the prostitutes, and laughing ourselves silly, until the bars closed at midnight... Too early!..

After the bars closed, We all proceeded down to "Bugis" Street, (more commonly referred to a "Boogie street")... The big four lane intersection at Bugis street was blocked off to traffic by barriers, and the two dozen or so restaurants that lined the street would set up tables and chairs, with table cloths, menu's, etc., on the street, until the entire intersection was one big open air restaurant, with waiters running back and forth serving food and drinks. It was the perfect conclusion to a night out on the town...

As entertainment, there was a dozen or so female impersonators that paraded themselves in conga-line fashion through the maze of tables, purposely evoking reactions from the boisterous crowd, satiated with food and drink... The reactions ranged from jeers to cat-calls, to laughter and applause, as they flashed their silicone breasts, wiggled their behinds, and batted their fake eyelashes, seeking those whom they could seduce into going with them for the night... Sometimes reactions were bizarre, as a drunk sailor would stand up on the table and strip naked, as the crowd of onlookers laughed and cheered him on... It seemed there was always some poor drunk sailor that was willing to go with them...

The conversation at our table centered around this bizarre scene, as one of our group gave a running commentary on what he knew about "them"... "That one".., he said, pointing to one of the transvestites, "He was a captain in the air force, before he changed.., and that one had the sex change operation.., and they all take the hormone injections, and the silicone implants", etc... "It's difficult to tell the difference from the real women", another one said... "You can tell the difference because they are more beautiful than the real women", another said.., we all laughed... "It just goes to show you how much make-up can do for you if you're willing to spend enough time at it.., any woman can be more beautiful if they spend their whole time at make-up.., and plastic surgery"... We laughed again... "What do you think about it?" I was asked... "It looks pretty queer to me", I said... We laughed... "But live and let live, I always say"... Jon, (always the adventurous one) spoke up; "What do you say we go and check them out"?.. "Not me", I said... "You can go, if you want to, but that's too weird for me"... Jon laughed, as he got up from the table... He turned.., and was gone!..

"Jeeeze!".., I said in amazement.., "I thought we would at least discuss it for awhile".., but Jon was gone!.. We sat and talked for awhile, waiting for Jon to come back, but he didn't come back... eventually, everyone left.., and I waited alone.., until the intersection was deserted, and then I left... The next morning I left for Sumatra, and caught up in my work and responsibilities, never thought about the incident again...

Two weeks later, back in Singapore, I spent the day with Sarah, and in the evening I went over to see Jon... As usual, there was an international crowd of world travelers, hippies, and mutual friends smoking ganja and getting high on the soulful sounds of the "Grateful Dead", "Jimmy Hendricks", the "Moody Blues", etc., and swapping tales of where they had been and where they were going...

English had become the international language of communication, although it wasn't the native language of most of the travelers, and it took a trained ear to understand the "slanguage" (often referred to as "swinglish") of those to whom English was a foreign language, and the subject of language became the topic of conversation... Jon spoke in this broken mixed English, and with an unusually peculiar "Southern drawl" that was as unique as it was colorful, and it was part of the unique charm that was "Jon"... Having been to Switzerland, I knew that there was no such thing as a Swiss language, as in the northern part of Switzerland that borders Germany, they speak German, and along the Western border with France, they speak French, and in the South that borders Italy, they speak Italian... Most Swiss people grow up with these three languages and are naturally multi-lingual.., but English is an acquired language...

I was not at all gifted in languages, but the subject fascinated me, and I wondered aloud at how someone would acquire the English language.., and also acquire a "Southern drawl", and what really piqued my curiosity was that I had heard this unique dialect before.., In Switzerland!.. I wondered if it had something to do with a Southern latitude that naturally contributed to this Southern drawl, and I asked Jon if all Swiss people spoke English with this same Southern drawl accent... He just looked at me with a blank stare, shook his head, and walked away...

....I have a "sixth sense"... It is not that unusual or rare, but the occasions when it is activated are rare... I can "feel" strong emotions in people, especially if they are directed towards me... Once, I had been attending a class, and while in a discussion with another person, this woman walked past me, and I could "feel" the strong magnetic pull of her presence... It was very flattering... She desired me, but I hadn't noticed her before... And another time, I had been playing chess, and I made an incorrect move that gave me an unfair advantage, and without lifting my eyes from the chess board, I could "feel" the anger of my opponent... I reexamined the move, corrected it, and the anger subsided...

Without visual or audible clues or cues, I could feel these strong emotion, just as surely as you can feel heat emanating from a hot furnace.., *and I was feeling it now*.., but it didn't feel like heat.., it felt like; ..."hate"...

I referred to this "sixth sense" as my "Spider" sense, and I could rely on it, and I could feel this malignant emanation approaching me from behind, and I stepped away from it and turned... It was Jon!.. He smiled and said something clever, then he turned and walked away... I must be mistaken, I thought...

There was about a dozen people in the room, and we paired off into groups of about three or four, and stood around having separate conversations.., and again I felt this powerful, negative emanation approaching me from behind... I whirled around, and there was Jon, walking directly toward me... He stopped in mid stride, slightly smiled, then turned to his right and entered into conversation with another group...

There was no mistake... Somehow, I had offended Jon, and his intention had become obvious... I could feel his hatred, and he was intending to vent his anger on me with a mighty "sucker punch", delivered on me when I least expected it.., but now I knew.., and he didn't know that I knew...

I backed my way to the door, not turning my back on anyone, and I stepped backwards out the door onto the sidewalk, and breathed a sigh of relief, wondering what it was that I had said to cause this hatred that I could feel from across the room... O.k. I conceded, it was a dumb question to ask someone about their accent, because no one recognizes their own accent, but to sucker punch me for asking a dumb question just didn't make sense...   ...And then Jon stepped out the door...

"Where ya goin", he asked in a jovial tone of voice, taking a couple of steps toward me, as I took a couple of steps back, maintaining the exact distance between us. "Just getting some fresh air", I replied, as he casually took a few more steps toward me.., and I casually took the same few steps back in synchronized lock-step, as though it was a choreographed ballet... We stood still, under the street light, for a few moments, and I tried to explain about the language thing, but I could see he wasn't hearing me. He continued with casual conversation, as he took a quick, long stride toward me, and as I simultaneously took that same quick, long stride back...   A momentary look of amazement crossed his face as he looked into my eyes and realized.., ...that I knew!..

All pretense was dropped... He clenched his fists and screamed at me.; "You think you are so smart", he began, and advanced towards me mechanically, methodically, step by step, as I retreated in the same manner, maintaining the exact distance between us, and every step he took, his fury became greater and his screaming at me became louder and higher pitched, until we reached the end of the sidewalk, and I stepped off the curb into the empty street... He stood on the curb, elevated above me and screaming obscenities at me...   I stared in stunned disbelief.!.   This was absurd!.. totally absurd.!. I don't deserve this, I thought...   My silent staring at him enraged him even more, and his screaming reached such a high pitch that his voice cracked, and for just a moment.., he sounded.., *like a woman!..*

In that moment.., I knew... In that moment, it all became clear... Immediately I dropped my head, my chin on my chest, giving him the psychological victory.., but my eyes never left him... I peered at him from beneath my eyebrows and I shall never forget that sight... He was standing there on the curb, under the street light.., quiet now, his face turned away in profile, looking upward toward the stars, tears in his eyes, his right hand on his hip, his labored breathing coming in a slight whimper... A look of wounded pride.., and despair...

I turned slowly, head bowed, but observing him from the corner of my eye until the last possible moment, and then my ears straining for the sound of movement, signaling an attack.., that never came... I walked away with my head down, and I didn't turn around until I was a block away... It was a misunderstanding... A complete and total misunderstanding... I was talking about the nuances of language, of accents, and of his peculiar Southern drawl.., and with his very limited understanding of the English language, he had no idea what a Southern drawl was, and he imagined it to be a reference to effeminate speech.., because that's what was on his mind... That.., was what so heavily occupied his mind...

Something had happened to Jon that night on Boogie Street... Something very bad... Something queer.., and it had affected him profoundly...

Had I actually said that?.. "You can go if you want to"... On God, did I actually say that?.. I actually gave him permission... Oh God.., Oh God... He was my best friend... He didn't deserve this... He was just an adventurer.., on the road of life.., experiencing life and filled with wonder... He didn't deserve this... Oh God.., Oh God...

I was filled with guilt, and remorse... Jon was my best friend, like the younger brother that I never had... I saw myself in him and I gloried in his adventures and discoveries of the open road, and now he hated me, and I hated myself... It was like a death in the family... I grieved for my friend...

I couldn't shake off the grief and the guilt... It hung over me like a funeral pall for days... Finally I decided to take a step to overcome this appalling state of mind... Perhaps I could rise above it and clear my mind of it, or get a perspective... I searched through my back pack and recovered a glass bottle that I had stashed there about a year ago... It contained some of the finest hashish that I had ever experienced... Nepalese temple balls.., grown from plants at a mile high altitude, and under the intense unobstructed sunlight of a rarefied atmosphere. The sticky resin adheres to the hands, and as the hands are rubbed together the resin forms itself into little strings about three inches long, fat in the middle and tapered off into nothing at the ends. The strings are rolled together into a little ball, about the size of a golf ball, and resembling a miniature pumpkin, dark brownish black in color... The effect is a spinal rush resulting in an altered state of consciousness.., that is profound...

I shaved some of the hashish into a pipe, took two hits on the pipe, and sat cross legged in a meditation posture... The spinal rush, and the consequent transition phase across the Bardo.., was terrifying... (Many there are, who come to the Bardo, are terrified by it, cannot make the transition.., and never try again)... Finally, I reached a place of equilibrium. I had achieved isolation from the thought process, but the thought process was still active, and I could see the thoughts as they arose, and they were still the gloomy thoughts of my tragically lost friend... I fought and fought against these thoughts, trying to intercept and cancel these thoughts at their inception, and to clear my mind... ...I failed...

…..The Swami had been asked..; "What attitude should I have when I sit for contemplation"?.. The Swami replied..; "Your attitude should be that of a mother who has lost her only child. The mother is totally absorbed on her lost child, she can think of nothing else but her lost child"... I was not a mother who had lost a child... I had lost my best friend...

I fought against these thoughts, but eventually I was overwhelmed, and became absorbed in the thoughts.., and absorbed in the grief... Totally absorbed, I cried out in anguish, and I asked the question..; "Should I have gone with him?.. Is there something to be learned from the homosexual experience?.. Should I also engage in it, just to see what there is to see?...

"No *No* **NO** "... The Inner Voice answered.., with emphasis...

I had heard The Inner Voice before, on many occasions, but I had never objectively noticed it before.., because to hear The Inner Voice, you have to be in the Zen state of absorption, and this is Communion.., and the Communion is total empathy with The Inner Voice, and understanding is complete and comprehensive... But this time.., because of the emphasis of the words, and the "super quick" quickness of the totally empathetic nature of the Communion, I instantly apprehended that The Inner Voice was other than myself, and the attitude conveyed by the emphasis of the words empathetically conveyed to mc the nature of the "Personality" of This Inner Voice...

It was the voice of a Father.., who has this son (myself), whom HE loves dearly.., but the son is not very bright, and the son has just asked his Father the most stupid question that any son could ever ask his Father, and almost in exasperation.., the Father replies to his son; "no No NO" with emphasis and attitude.., and then the Father proceeds to instruct his "not too bright" son.., and as the Father speaks, there is vision, and the vision is revelation, and the revelation is knowledge... And the son, being empathetically absorbed in the vision, comprehends "experientially".., and the knowledge.., becomes known...

…..The "Inner Voice" spoke.., there was vision.., *and I saw!*...

…..*I saw!.,* and comprehended.., that Lucifer.., the Angel of Light, had come down to Earth with his band of angels, his followers, and they entered into the animals that the Lord God had made.., and for sport, they copulated among themselves, through the bodies of the animals.., and it was Lucifer, that had entered into the body of a he-goat, and being the strongest of the he-goats, he dominated them, and mounted them, and butt-fucked them, and he developed an ego, and insatiable lust, and the other goats that had been dominated and degraded lost the natural desire of male for female, and began emulating the Evil one, and proceeded to dominate and degrade each other, and they all developed egos, and the Lord was displeased, and they rebelled against the Lord, and became unacceptable to the Lord, and they were banished from the paradise realms, and made to occupy the Hellish realms... *One-third* of the Angels, *Fell...* Because of this perversion.., ONE-THIRD.., of the **Angels!**., FELL!...

And I saw.., and comprehended.., that the Evil one (now called "Satan").., was the first pervert, and that to this day, the "he-goat" remains the symbol of Satanism, and those who participate in this perversion are emulating the Evil one, degrading and being degraded, and the characteristics and mannerisms of the Evil one (the limp wristed, effeminate swishiness) will become manifested in the participant, and this "limp wristed, effeminate swishiness"..., is the mark.., of the Beast...

Among the beasts of the earth, among the herd animals, it is the one dominant male that will breed with the herd of females... All the other males will be driven off, having been defeated in combat... Occasionally, (it has been observed) that the dominant male will mount the defeated male in "mock" intercourse, adding humiliation to the defeat of the rival male, as a strong warning not to return to the herd... Occasionally, (it has been observed in herds of mountain goats) that the defeated male goat will be allowed to remain within the safety of the herd.., if he serves as female to the dominant male... The rival male has been defeated, humiliated, dominated and emasculated.., losing his natural desire for the females.., and is no threat to the dominant male...

I saw.., and comprehended.., that it is one thing to accept something intellectually, as just another experience, as just another life style.., as live and let live.., but the "psychological impact" of the actual experience of engaging in an act of perversion cannot be intellectually foreseen or comprehended... The intellectual.., simply.., does not know.., that homosexuality.., is "contagious"... And by the intellectual acceptance of homosexuality as an acceptable life-style, he (the intellectual).., and his children.., becomes vulnerable to seduction...

I saw.., and comprehended.., that the acceptance of homosexuality (as an acceptable life style) is a great and grave mistake.., and I saw good people, with good and noble intentions (intellectuals).., marching in parades, carrying banners, proclaiming Liberty, equal rights, and special rights, saying: "it's o.k. to be gay", "It's "normal" to be gay"... and I saw the Leaders of a great nation, saying: "Vote for ME".., and I will advance the cause of your perversion, and I will advance laws, proclaiming your perversions to be normal, and acceptable, and I will force industry to hire you, and I will give you positions as teachers of children, and of our young and impressionable teens, and leaders of the Boy Scouts, and infiltration into Government, and in the Military.., and I will sanctify your unholy unions as "Marriage", and allow you to adopt children... "Vote for Me".., "I am an intellectual".., "Vote for Me".., "Vote for MEEE"... And I saw this contagious disease spread.., *like wildfire*...

I saw.., and comprehended.., that the "psychological impact" (trauma) of engaging in an act of perversion.., is devastating to the personality.., spiritually degrading.., emasculating.., and the consequences of the degrading act of perversion has to be dealt with.., daily.., for the rest of your life... No one.., that crosses the line into perversion, remains unaffected... Too late.., you will discover that what you had accepted intellectually, and experimented with so casually.., has left it's indelible impression on your psyche.., a "psychic injury".., a "trauma" to the Soul.., a "defilement"... It is something for which you can never forgive yourself, and something you can never forget, and it occupies your mind, and you begin thinking queer thoughts, even your dreams will turn against you, and you will go through intellectual and emotional turmoil... "Self doubt", will be your daily companion... "Self doubt", will eat away at your Soul, and you will lose your self confidence, and become painfully self conscious, watching yourself for signs of "swishiness", and to your horror, you will find them... *This,...* is "homophobia"!..

"Homophobia", is a debilitating disease, a crippling dis-ease of the personality.., a contagious disease.., characterized by the terrible and terrifying FEAR.., that you yourself are becoming.., a homosexual... The terrible and terrifying FEAR.., that you are losing your masculinity, becoming effeminate, and that you will become a surrogate female, to be used by men.., (the ultimate humiliation, the ultimate degradation)... And like other contagious diseases, it is transmitted by association... And because this is a mental dis-ease, it can also be transmitted by mental images, by pornography, by dalliance of the imagination, etc.., and by seduction... (They will suck you off.., just to suck you in)... Homophobia, (the terrible FEAR of becoming queer) is the first stage of homosexuality...

The dreaded (and contagious) disease of homophobia comes as an unexpected "shock" to the personality. It is a rude awakening indeed, to realize that you have been deceived by "The Big Lie", (that it is somehow "gay" to be queer).., and that your "integrity" (a spiritual word).., has been "compromised"...

At best.., you will flee from this in terror, and it will remain a deep, dark, soul staining secret, that you will never again repeat... At worst.., you will succumb to this dread disease and become converted (perverted) into a "faggot".., emulating the great sin of your "Leader" (the father of lies).., and incorporating his mannerisms (the limp wristed, effeminate swishiness).., into your own body.., and hanging out on street corners and in restrooms.., seeking those whom you may "devour" (i.e., eat, suck, suck in)... Wolves.., in sheepish clothing.., and they will gobble you up...

The "homosexuals" would have you believe (a deliberate lie), that if you are a heterosexual male, who shuns the company of homosexuals, who sees homosexuality as a perversion, as an abomination.., then it is YOU who are "homophobic"!.., and that homophobia is a heterosexual disease to be shunned by the intellectual!.. This is the intentional mis-use of "the variegated cloak of words".., a deliberate mis-definition.., an intentional lie... If there is one characteristic that is common to the homosexual community.., ***it is that they lie!..*** It is the subtle lie, the lie by innuendo, the implied lie, the lie of omission, the lie of mis-definition, the lie of half truths, and when necessary, the bold-faced lie, and slander, and casting aspersions... They themselves have been deceived by lies (by the father of lies).., and they lie to themselves.., and they will lie to you, with the intention to deceive, and to seduce...

The Inner Voice spoke.., the vision unfolded.., and.., with the "eye of insight".., I saw.., the aftermath...

I saw the faces of a vast multitude.., of those who had been "touched" and contaminated by this dread disease.., recoiling from it in terror, and fighting against the self doubt that eats away at their self confidence, fighting against the profound humiliation of having been seduced and tricked into an act of surrogate femininity, of having engaged in a sexual act.., with another man... I saw the shame.., and I saw the reactions to that shame... I saw the "dis-orientation".., the "non-integration".., the "dis-ease".., of a Soul, living in a body that has been violated and defiled... I saw the confusion of sexual identity, confused emotions, the assault of a pornographic imagination driven by confused lust.., and the final surrender, the capitulation, when he says:;, "I guess I must be one of them, or I wouldn't be having all these confused and perverted thoughts".., and mistakenly, he yields.., becomes seduced.., and perverted.., by the "Dark Side of the Force"..., ...and like an "Alien" presence, it enters into him (through the back door) and it overtakes him, with perverted and confused lust, and he manifests the characteristics of the Evil One.., his speech becomes effeminate and his mannerisms become "limp wristed and swishy".., and out of his mouth comes..; the "double entendre".., words of double meanings, with sexual connotations... I saw the wounded pride, that seeks solace in outrageous behavior and flamboyant attire...

I saw the faces of a thousand young men, dressed in black leather, with silver buckles, belts and chains.., overly "Macho".., overtly "Masculine".., seeking to gain an "Ego boost" by dominating and humiliating weaker males, as a reaction against the humiliating shame of their own submission... I saw this reaction as being the "sickness" of a wounded Ego.., and I saw this disease spread...

I saw the faces of a thousand young men, fleeing from this disease in terror, marrying young women, having children, and later succumbing to the "self doubt" engendered by this disease, and the family is destroyed, and the young woman is in great sadness, having been "used" to combat this sickness.., and the children are without a father, or shamed by their father... I saw that each homosexual was a victim of another homosexual.., and he leaves behind him a trail of victims... His children are victims, his wife is a victim, his Father and his Mother are victims.., saddened by their son (of great promise).., seeing him fall.., into degradation... This is NOT a "victimless crime"... Let no one mistake this for a "victimless crime"... All are victims, and the victims beget other victims, and this contagious disease spreads...

I saw in the faces of a thousand young men, the fear engendered by homophobia, fleeing from it into religion, into the Monastery, taking religious vows, only to meet other young men terrified by the same phobia, and succumbing to the assault of a fevered imagination, even the "holy ground" of the monastery becomes desecrated, and the Priesthood becomes contaminated... Such is the power of this dread disease...

I saw the faces of a thousand young boys, having left home at too early an age, for reasons of child abuse, of broken families, etc., being preyed upon by the faggots, who promise them food, shelter, and a good time.., but leaving them "fucked in the ass", and destitute on the streets, to become "male whores", to be used, abused, degraded and perverted into something less than human... A great crime against our young people... The greatest shame of all Shame...

I saw the faces of a thousand teen-age boys, of great promise.., the pride of their parents.., having been seduced into an homosexual encounter, and then ravaged by the terrible FEAR of homophobia... The guilt, the remorse, the humiliation and the shame are unbearable... The "queer" jokes are a stab into their own hearts... The terrible fear of being found out, and the fear of being identified as one of "those".., (and the "gossip" rumors have already started)... Mental confusion is compounded by sexual confusion, compounded by fear, humiliation, the profound disappointment of parents, the profound disappointment in himself...

All is lost.., all is lost.., unbearable shame.., unbearable despair... The future is lost... No way out...

Our young people (of great promise) are killing themselves.., at an alarming rate... The suicide rate among teen age boys (afflicted by an homosexual encounter) is estimated to be six times greater than for any other reason, but this is inaccurate... The carnage is much greater than that... The accidental deaths, the drunken driving deaths, the "Russian roulette" deaths, the "overdose" deaths, and "accidental" murders.., are largely the result of the emotional impact (trauma) of having been seduced into something so profoundly and uncharacteristically foreign to the nature of the (heretofore) "proud, noble, innocent and naïve" Soul.., who is not equipped to deal with the guilt, the remorse, the rejection, the betrayal, the anger, the humiliation.., and the shame.., that haunts his every waking moment.., self doubt, eating away at his soul... His parents (being intellectuals) might be accepting of him, but he can not accept himself...

The homosexuals would have you believe that the discrimination of society is the reason behind the young mans death, but this again is a "deliberate lie"... It is the young man who cannot accept his "fall from grace", his fall of status from proud "Alpha" male, to surrogate female... The future holds only negative promise... The future is worse than death... He cannot accept this "Alien" presence that is invading his body and perverting his mind... Death.., is preferable...

As it turns out, they (the homosexuals) have been very successful with these lies, because the "sophisticated" intellectual is actually quite naive... (believing that there is no God, that man-kind is an accident of the universe, having evolved from the amoeba, sea-slug, monkey (and whatever), and that "Sodom and Gomorra" is just a "Fairy Tale"... Their "sophisticated" naiveté might be laughable, if the results were not so tragic...

And.., "The Big Lie"..; the "Lie" that it is "gay" to be a homosexual... There is nothing "gay" about being fucked in the ass... There is nothing "gay" about fucking your fellow Man in the ass... There is Nothing "gay" about degrading and being degraded... This is perversion, plain and simple.., and there is nothing "gay" in the consequences of this perversion... Not in the present, and not in the Hereafter... "Gay", is a lie...

I am amazed.., at how easily the "sophisticated intellectuals" have been taken in by this lie... At how easily they have been deceived into not only accepting the mis-definition of a perfectly good word and "perverting" the meaning of the word.., to mis-label a disease of the mind, body and Soul.., that is clearly.., not gay...

I am amazed.., that they (the intellectuals) have not only accepted this lie, but they participate in perpetuating this lie.., totally ignoring the butt-fucking aspect of it.., totally ignoring the "contagious" nature of this most serious of all "contagious" diseases that affects body, mind and Soul, ripping families apart, destroying lives, etc. and etc... Every time the word "gay" is used, a lie of mis-definition and mis-information is repeated and propagated... This is.., *"Propaganda"!...*

I am amazed... at the "intellectual" *gullibility!!...*

I saw.., the various reactions of the "victims", that have been "duped" and "psychically injured" by this dreaded and contagious disease that has the power to harm the Spirit, and pervert the Soul...

I saw that this was a great sin.., a sin against the Spirit.., The "power" of the Alpha male is in the integrity of his spirit, that has never been compromised by defeat or dishonor... Having been "duped".., the spirit is "psychically injured" by the homosexual experience... The Alpha male status is lost, as well as the right to propagate with the females...

I saw the rogue relative, himself having been fucked and twisted by this disease, perverted by Satanic lust.., insinuating himself into the family, and with deception, he betrays the trust of innocent children and destroys their childhood, leaving the parents to deal with their "problem child"... I saw that pedophiles are twisted products of pedophiles, and they destroy lives, and produce more pedophiles, and this "contagious disease", spreads... and I saw, that if I could but lay my hands on the pedophile.., it would be better for him if a millstone had been tied to his neck, and he be dropped into the sea...

The Inner Voice spoke.., the vision continued, and with the empathetic nature of the "eye of insight", I saw...   ....I saw more than I wanted to see...

I saw and I heard the heart-broken, pathetic sobbing, and the whimpering of the "submissives", who had been fucked.., physically, mentally, socially, physiologically, emotionally and Spiritually.., fucked and betrayed, used and abandoned, a hopelessness beyond despair, and dieing of "Aids"... Hell has come, even before death...

And then, in the final vision, **I Saw;**

I saw the Evil one, himself... as in caricature... He was standing at the entrance to an alleyway... He was tall and of slender build, dressed in a single piece, pale blue jump suit, with a plunging neckline and slits up the outer sides of the pant leg, to the calf, with silver buttons (a reprobate tarnished silver) that adorned the neckline and the cuffs, and up the slits of the legs.., his skin was a sickly pale white, with reddish blotches, and his face and head.., was the grinning face and head.., *of the "Joker"* [1]... He was dancing his "swishy" dance, like a "rock & roll" star, and beckoning, with limp wristed hand gestures to follow him, into the alleyway, and it was a one way street, into the alley way... and from out of his red painted lips, he laughed a maniacal laugh, and he spoke in double entendres, and lies of seduction.., and I looked past him, down the alleyway, and it was a winding side street, with night clubs and red neon signs, and loud music, and drunkenness in the streets, and female impersonators soliciting under the street light, and in an alley off the street I could see men in the shadows, butt-fucking and sucking each other, and there was garbage in the street, of liquor bottles and needle syringes.., and trash...

.....I came out of it!.. I had been in samadii I estimated for about 30 or 40 minutes... Absorbed in the vision, my body had sat there, in a posture of military attention, and had not moved an iota!.. ...No effort involved...

---

[1]   Almost no one knows.., the physical appearance of the Devil.., and I would never have made the association, but the "Devil", and the "Joker" (early D.C. comics), (that *resembled* "Liberace").., (see chapter I)., *are one and the same!!...* The same tall slender features, the same prominent chin, the same "pouty" feminine lips, the same "kinky" wavy slicked back hair, parted on the right side, the same "diabolical" grinning face.., etc., and etc... But the question inevitably arises: How could a comic book artist so accurately portray the physical features of the Arch Entity of Evil in the Universe?.. I can only speculate, that the "highly artistic".., are also "highly intuitive"...

"The Face of Evil, Perversion Personified"

Within the space of 30 or 40 minutes, I had reviewed a segment of humanity... I had seen in mass.., a hundred thousand "case histories" pass before my "eye of insight", and I saw the faces of anguish, betrayal, anger, loss.., and I had seen the face of the Evil one himself.., in the guise of the "Joker".., and I heard him laugh his maniacal laugh...

Within the space of thirty or forty minutes my knowledge of "homosexuality" went from practically nothing to practically everything... Much more than I ever wanted to know... I knew more than the homosexuals know.., they can't be objective.., they are too close to the problem... I had the overview...

I had asked the Father; "to see what there was to see", and HE showed me.., and I saw what there was to see... And I saw that the Evil one had been the first pervert, and that this perversion was the first and original sin.., before Adam and Eve, this perversion was the first and original sin... And to those of whom he can corrupt into this sin, are those to whom he can lay claim...

This is Knowledge... This is information and knowledge, for the hetero-sexual, and for the homo-sexual... We are at WAR!!!... Beyond the facade of everyday reality, within the realm of the fifth dimension, within the realm of the inter-galactic mind, there is war, and it is the war for the Souls of Men... It has been a war of stealth.., the "Dark side of the force" has been infiltrating into the ranks of men, slowly, steadily, one by one, first the weak, then the stupid, then the naive, even the curious, have fallen prey... The weapons of war have been lies, deceit, propaganda, and seduction... The unwitting allies of the Dark side have been the Secularists, who say that there is no God, and there is no Devil (ha ha), and homosexuality is just a benign lifestyle that should be accepted (and embraced) by the "modern intellectual".., and as their numbers have grown, the politicians have pandered themselves to the Dark side to win the vote, and are allied to the Dark side... And NOW.., the forces of Evil are marching in the streets, under the banners of Secularism, Humanism, Equal rights, Special rights, God out of the public schools, the acceptance of homosexuality in the public schools, etc...

It is the unthinkable!.. Had our Forefathers known.., that the Constitution of the U.S. would be interpreted to permit this "perversion" of its intent.., they would, to the last man cry; "foul"... Our Forefathers (deeply religious men).., could not have foreseen this possibility because it was unthinkable and unforeseeable.., that such an event could ever take place... The unthinkable.., has taken place...

So.., If the "letter" of the Law be elevated above the "Spirit" of the Law.., then the Constitution of the U.S. has a very serious "flaw".!. Perhaps it is a fatal flaw... Or did you think that "Sodom and Gomorra" was just a fairy tale.?.

The real time event.., the destruction of the twin cities of "Sodom and Gomorra".., is meant to be a graphic "example en toto".., a "Hieroglyph" (a Knowledge-Picture-Symbol), meant to impress upon all people for all time the unequivocal and unambiguous message that this is unacceptable behavior, an abomination, worthy of destruction... The Bible {*} is unequivocal in that message...

* * *   * * *   * * *

BOOK XIV

"Seership and Obligations"

Within the space of thirty of forty minutes, I had acquired more objective knowledge than I could have acquired in a lifetime.., and as I contemplated this knowledge, my memory banks yielded up their store of (heretofore) unrelated events, ancient documents, observations, etc., and I related those past events to this present event, and I saw the relationships, and my understanding deepened, and it all became clear...

I jumped up from my contemplations, and invigorated with newfound knowledge and energy, I had to tell someone what I had seen... I raced downtown to the nightclub circuit, looking for Jeff... I found him, just as the bars were closing for the night. We took a taxi down to Boogie street, and as we sat at the table, I poured out the story of our mutual friend, Jon, and of the events, as they unfolded, from the transvestites, to the tragic confrontation, to the hashish, to the visions, to the conclusion...

I had related the story from beginning to end as though transfixed, and Jeff had listened intently, without interruption, his keen mind taking it all in... Finally he spoke, repeating back to me what I had said; "I saw, I saw, I saw".., what do you mean.., "you saw" .?. He asked the question like a lawyer cross-examining a witness...

I saw it all.., I said.., I saw it in my minds eye.., It was like a documentary.., very much like a documentary... The Inner Voice spoke.., and there was vision.., and I saw things that I had never seen before, never thought of before, things that I had no way of knowing, and it wasn't just information that I had learned, it was knowledge that impressed itself into my Soul.., and there was no doubt...

What do you mean, an "Inner Voice" ?.. What kind of "Inner Voice" ?.. What did it sound like ?., he asked...

I could feel my face breaking into a smile as I looked into the face of my inquisitor, my interrogator, and I said; It was exactly as Christ said.., it was the voice of a loving Father... It was neither commanding nor demanding, but rather like the voice of a Father that is instructing his "not too bright" child, with loving concern and compassion...

What did it sound like?., he repeated the question... I reflected on the question... There was no accent, no dialect, nothing distinguishable.., there was no pitch, no timbre, it was not audible to the ear.., it was a mental voice, and yet it was clear... I might not have even realized it, if there had not been (in this case) the "emphasis and attitude", because the voice is so subtle, and the attention is captured by the vision, with the voice in the background...

So you are a Seer!.. Jeff said, matter-of-factly... It was a statement with a hint of a question.., but it hit me with the impact of an accusation... I was stunned.., that such a word should ever be applied to me... I slid my chair back away from the table, as though the table represented Seership, and I was not qualified to sit at that table.., ...and I immediately went into samadii... I had been in samadii three hours earlier, and I spontaneously went back into it...

I thought about a failed marriage, and I slid my chair.., I thought about my serial love affairs, and I slid my chair.., I thought about the one night stands, and the prostitutes, and I slid my chair.., I thought about the get rich quick schemes, and I slid my chair.., I thought about the outright failures, of tests of character, and I slid my chair... When I came out of it about 60 seconds later, I had slid my chair about 10 feet away from the table, and between two other tables.., and people were looking at me, wondering what I was doing... Jeff was standing up at the table, wondering what I was doing...

I picked up my chair and carried it back to the table and sat down... I had reviewed my whole life within the span of 60 seconds and reached the conclusion that not only was I not worthy to wear the mantle of Seership, but that I had just clumsily fumble-fucked my way through life and was lucky to even be alive... My tombstone should have long ago read; "death by stupidity", and I probably wouldn't be alive, except for some stumble-fucking good luck, good friends, and the grace of God...

No, I said.., I wouldn't call myself a Seer... A Seer has a dedication of Spirit that is constant, not on again - off again, like me... A Seer has a disciplined mind, and I don't have that kind of control... I can't go into samadii at will... I cannot summon the Inner Voice and have HIM speak to me, and reveal to me the secrets of the Universe... No, I couldn't call myself a Seer... I am just a "glimpser"...

Every once in a while.., when the conditions are favorable.., when a situation presents itself.., and even then, only with the aid of a drug.., I would catch a glimpse... Only on rare occasions had I achieved Communion, and heard the "Inner Voice", and there had been dialogue, and revelations... But the incidents were very few, and very far between... Not enough to be called a Seer... Only enough to be called a "glimpser"... That's what I told Jeff...

That's what I told Jeff.., and that's the fact.., but deep in my heart, I knew.., that the glimpses that I had had.., those things that I had seen.., Saints had prayed to see those things, and had not seen them.., Monasteries, filled with Bodhisattvas, Priests, and Rabbis had prayed to see those things, and had not seen them... I felt guilty for having seen them.., and I was very uncomfortable with the terminology...

You should write about this, Jeff said... Ha!., I replied... I don't even write letters!.. I am known for not keeping in touch.., I have a reputation to uphold.., I joked... No, I'm serious.., Jeff replied... You should write about this...

Of all the things in the world to write about, this is the last thing in the world that I would want to write about, I said... I have nothing to do with these.., these.., creatures.., I said, (gesturing toward the transvestites parading themselves through the crowd)... I have nothing to do with this.., this.., this.., sickness!!! I know, Jeff replied... That's why you should write about it!.. ....."It is only the hand without a wound that can safely handle poison"...

I recognized the statement as a quote from the "Dhammapada"... This was "classic" Jeff... You could be discussing the most obscure subject, and Jeff would come up with the most obscure piece of information that he had read about in a book, long, long ago, and far, far away... Only a Buddhist scholar would have known that verse.., only a Buddhist scholar would have recognized it... Only Jeff could come up with that exact appropriate verse at that exact appropriate time... There was a sense of "Déjà vu"...

But I protested... No, I said, to write a book, you have to have the last chapter... I don't have the last chapter... The last chapter is still out there... And besides that..; the homosexual thing.., I learned other things.., other things of far greater importance...

Jeff queried;.. What other things?!, "of far greater importance".?. What other things?., he demanded... I learned about the "Inner Voice", I said...

I had heard the Inner Voice even as a child... I was a particularly devilish child.., and I delighted in pulling tricks on my playmates, like pulling the rug out from under them, and pulling chairs out from under even the grownups, and I terrorized my little sister, and tricked her into eating mud, bugs and etc... The Inner Voice would admonish me, telling me to be good, and do good, and I told the Inner Voice to "go away" because I liked to play mean tricks on the other kids, and I liked to be bad... I can remember that...

It is such a natural thing, the Inner Voice.., and yet it is so subtle as to be heard, but not noticed... The Zen state of absorption is required for this Communion to take place, because.., HE never speaks to the Ego mentality... HE never speaks of menial things or to trivial minds... HE doesn't speak to the "sophisticated intellectual" who believes in his heart of hearts, that there is no God...

There is a protocol, to have Communion with HIM... HE speaks only to the pure of heart, to the sincere and troubled Soul.., and to children... And as you are speaking to Him.., and as HE speaks to you, and as there is vision and understanding, you are absorbed in the moment, and you never ever think to ask; "to whom am I speaking", because only the Ego would ask that question.., and that doesn't happen...

It is only in retrospect, that you will realize that you had a conversation, and it is a quiet conversation... No thunder, no lightning, no commands, no demands, unimposing, and without obligation... HE provides the overview and the understanding.., but your free will.., is still your own.., and you can disobey.., without penalty.., except for the consequences of your actions, and the loss of HIS counsel...

But THIS time.., this time was different... This time.., because of the "emphasis and attitude".., for just the fraction of a moment.., I realized that the "Inner Voice" was other than myself... In that fraction of a moment.., I realized the nature of "THAT".., "Inner Voice".., and HIS nature was love and compassion... It was a revelation within a revelation.., within a fraction of a moment... And I knew!..

You knew what?., Jeff asked... I knew that THIS was the same Voice that Adam had heard in the garden... I knew that this was the same Inner Voice that was heard by Abraham, Isaac, and Jacob.., and all the Saints, Seers and Prophets... This was the same Voice that was the basis for the wisdom of Solomon, the same Voice that was heard on the mountain, by Elijah, and by Moses, and by Christ, when HE said; "As I HEAR, I judge, and my judgment is just"... A thousand times it is repeated in the Bible; "The Lord SPOKE"... this is the continuity of the Bible from the Old Testament through the New... This is what the Bible is all about, from beginning to end... The entire Bible, from beginning to end.., is a testimony to and about; this "Inner Voice"... This is its substance!..

Jeff was wide eyed, but silent.., so I continued... They.., the Religionists.., read the Bible, and proclaim it to be the "Living Word", and it is the living word, in the sense that it will never die, but it is really the "Historical Word".., and as such it is of great benefit, but they have missed the point.!. They have missed the whole entire point.., and the real and true "Living Word", has become the "Lost Word", because nobody thinks to LISTEN... Nobody goes within, to the alter of silence, and just listens... It is only the "Living Word", when you hear it for yourself, in conversation (Communion) with the Living God, and there is vision, and revelation, and you will know.., and there will be no doubt... And., If HE will speak to me, HE will speak to anybody with a sincere heart... All men are Seers.., if only they knew...

Jeff quoted me back, a note of skepticism in his voice; "A revelation within a revelation, within a fraction of a moment"... Yes, I said.., and a deduction...

So what did you deduce from all of this?., Jeff asked... "All Knowledge".., I replied... "All Knowledge"...

This is the "last chapter", I said... All Knowledge... This is what constitutes "Enlightenment"... There is no Enlightenment without all knowledge... There is no Wisdom without all knowledge... Wisdom presupposes all knowledge.., and I "saw" it... I didn't specifically "see" it this time, but this experience confirms it!.. Within the space of 30 or 40 minutes, I learned a lifetime of knowledge, and this knowledge is there, for the asking, and the Akashic records (the Cosmic memory) are there, to be accessed, and I have "seen" this, and I looked into it, and I knew, that all things have their origin in the "First Cause", and all phenomena is just an effect of a prior cause, which was an effect of a prior cause before that, all the way back to the First Cause, and all cause and effect are interrelated, like a spiders web.., and if you trace anything back to the First Cause, you will see the interrelationship between all things, and any subject you care to contemplate.., it will unfold before you, in your mind's eye, and you will see it in context, and you will have learned it.., not from the outside in.., but from the inside out!.. This is the secret of Genius.., and there is no true Genius without apprehending the First Cause.., and guess what!., HE, is the First Cause... HE, the "Inner Voice", is the First Cause...

Jeff looked at me with wide eyes, his lungs filled to the bursting point, like he was about to say something, but he didn't, he just blew it all out in one big exhalation...

....So what you are telling me, he said, is that you won't write about this until you have the last chapter, and the last chapter is "All Knowledge".., the last chapter is "Enlightenment"?!! But what if you don't achieve it?., then the book will never be written!., and what if you do achieve it, then you might have other things to do, more important things, and the book will never be written, and this book needs to be written... No, he said.., you have to write about this... You have been given a certain knowledge about this subject, and you will be derelict in your duty if you don't communicate it...

But I have no talent for writing, I protested... You don't need talent, he said.., you just write a page, and if you like it, you keep it, and if you don't like it, you throw it away, and you rewrite it until you do like it... There are a zillion books out there, and most of them were written by people with no talent... You don't need talent, you just need tenacity... And as you contemplate, the words will come, he said with a chuckle.., exercising his needle sharp, barbed wit... Oh yeah, sure.., I replied... Easy for you to say...

He laughed.., we both laughed... Hey, I've got to go, he said, looking at his watch. I promised Elizabeth I wouldn't be late, and here I am, late again... Oh, did you ever figure out how a Swiss national learns to speak English with a Southern accent?.. Yes, I did, I replied.., I contemplated it, and it came to me... They learn to speak English by watching American movies, and their favorite movies are the cowboy Westerns, and they emulate the idioms and the deliberate slow Texas drawl of the gunfighter, and they practice it down to the dialect... Yeah, that's it, Jeff replied, and he started moving away through the crowd of people and tables, waving his good bye, and as he departed he said ; You should write about this... and he was nodding his head as he said it, as though agreeing with himself...

Early the next morning I was on the flight back to Sumatra for another two weeks in the jungle... Just a 30 or 40 minute flight, and I am gone from the jet age, the go-go dancers, the glittering night clubs, and etc., back to the primitive, back to the dawn of time... It's always a culture shock, making this transition, and it takes about a day to get acclimated, whether from the modern to the primitive, or back again, from the primitive to the modern...

So, this is where I am in life, I thought to myself.., on the far side of the world, the arm-pit of the world, machete-hacking and slashing my way through the jungle... I wasn't supposed to be hacking and slashing... I was the "Tuan", and I had men to do the hacking and slashing for me, and they were distressed that I wouldn't let them do it.., but I was angry.., and I was venting my anger by hacking and slashing...

I was angry because I had lost my best friend... I would have been less angry, if I had lost him to Death, but I had lost him to the faggots (hacking, slashing)... The faggots.., they spoil lives.., they spoil everything... (hacking, slashing)... And Jeff; "write a book", he says.., "I will be derelict in my duty, if I don't".., he says... God didn't tell me to write a book.., only Jeff... (hacking, slashing)... And who's going to believe me anyway, some unknown societal dropout, without academic credentials, on the far side of the world, the arm-pit of the world, hacking his way out of the jungle!.. (hack, slash)... Oh yeah, "write a book", he says... Well, I wouldn't be writing any books anytime soon.., I said defiantly... But for some reason, I felt as though I had incurred a great debt, and I couldn't pay.., and that made me angry... "Those to whom much has been given.., much is required"... Knowledge comes with obligations...

.....And the Devil.., what to do about the Devil.?. Now here.., was a stumbling block...

Most people put the Devil in the same category as Santa Clause and the Tooth Fairy... If someone believes in the Devil, he is looked at with suspicion... If someone says he has seen the Devil, he may be carried off to the mental institution and sedated, etc... To say that I had seen the Devil, not just once, but twice.., is to invite ridicule... To say that I saw him in reality, in my living room, dressed in flamboyant attire, resembling "Liberace"., is to evoke laughter... To say that I saw him a second time, in a vision, and he was in the guise of "The Joker"., is to lose all credibility... To say that he whispered in my ear, and caused me to do wrong.., is self effacing...

It would be much better for me, personally, to omit any mention of the Devil... It is no claim to fame to have seen the Devil, and it can only bring derision.., so you should know with absolute certainty.., that I wouldn't say this if it wasn't absolutely true... The Devil.., is a reality...

Knowing the Devil to be a powerful adversary.., it is not in my best interest to provoke and expose this powerful entity.., to incur his wrath.., and yet.., I must.!. This is one of those "Universal Truths"... This is knowledge and information that is vital for any Seeker on the path... You must know this.., that as you approach the light, there is an adversary that will try to bring you down... His cleverness and deceit is legendary... Take refuge in the Father, and speak no lies, lest you be deceived by lies...

It is not because the scriptures say so, nor is it because of belief, or supposition, or conjecture, that I make this statement.., but it is because of what I Know, because of what I have seen.., as an eye witness.., both with the external eye, and with the "eye of insight"... I had seen him, not just once, but twice.., and although his appearance the second time was a meta-morph of his appearance the first time, there was one characteristic that was unmistakably the same;.. he is a "faggot".!.

This is Knowledge that has been hidden since the beginning of time... This is the hard and harsh reality... The Evil one, Satan himself.., is a faggot!.. he is the "Prince of Faggots"...

"Why me" ?.. I asked, hacking and slashing my way through the jungle... Why is it up to me?.. Why do I have to be the one, to write an exposé on the prince of faggots, and incur his wrath... Who am I, to do battle with the prince of darkness... I will be killed... I can predict my death... I will be murdered... No doubt about it... Every faggot that reads my words will realize this Truth, and will be moved to rage, and they will seek my death, and I will be murdered... First they will ridicule me, and then I will be murdered...

But so what.!. So what if they ridicule me... I am an unknown.., just some poor slob of no consequence, stuck here in the arm pit of the world, hacking and slashing my way through the jungle... To ridicule me would be an exercise in futility... To ridicule the statue of an Owl, a facade made of iron, empty on the inside.., (I laughed) Ha-ha... They might as well ridicule an Aunt Jemima cookie jar, without the cookies.., Ha ha ha,.. Their laughter and ridicule will just reverberate through the emptiness of the Owl, and the echo of that laughter will fall upon them, like condemnation, ... and then they will kill me...

But so what.!. So what if they murder me... It wouldn't be the first time.!. Everybody has got to die!.. One way or another, by fair means or foul.., everybody dies.!. But that void emptiness, within the facade of the Owl.., IS the Owl.., and that voidness is filled with fire!., and it is the fire of Spirit and immortality.., and it is the Owl, that will have the last laugh... Ha ha ha...

Two long weeks.., and 30 or 40 minutes later, the plane touched down, and I was back in Singapore... There were five of us on leave from base-camp, and as usual, we went to the low rent, old section of the city and booked rooms for the week... A night of partying and bar-hopping, until the bars closed, then down to Boogie street for a late night of feasting and drinking amid the laughter and camaraderie of good friends... I had hoped to bump into Jon during the course of the evening, but I didn't see him...

Early the next morning we met for breakfast at the local Chinese restaurant, which was open on three sides, with a kitchen in the back... The equatorial temperature already in the high 80's.., the overhead fans providing a down-draft sufficient to keep the flies away. The five of us were seated at a round table in the corner, deep in discussion about situations back at base-camp.., and Jon walked in...

He didn't see me, and I almost didn't recognize him, his appearance had changed so drastically... His lion's mane of long blondish hair was gone, having been replaced with a conventional hair-cut, neatly parted and combed, and he was growing a mustache... His bare chest and vest were gone, replaced with a printed shirt... The hippie beads and bracelets were gone... The charisma was gone... The laughter that sparkled in his eyes.., was gone... The Viking warrior was gone.., replaced by a non-entity that no one would notice in a crowded room...

He sat down at a table, facing away from the table we were sitting at. The Chinese waiter, dressed only in shorts and sandals, took his order. He sat there, deep in thought. His eyes were staring out at the world, but he saw nothing.., except the movies that were playing in his mind...

Ah.., good!., I thought to myself. I will wait until his food is served, and then I will go over and talk to him... We were the best of friends before, and we can be again... It was only a misunderstanding... I will explain and apologize, and we will laugh about it, and be friends...

I rejoined the conversation at my table, and not a minute had gone by before I again glanced over at Jon's table.., and he was gone!.. I jumped up from my chair and raced to the street. It was early morning, the streets were not yet crowded, and I could see a block in either direction.., he wasn't there... I raced to the nearby intersection and looked a block in both directions.., he wasn't there...

I returned to the restaurant... The only other place he could have gone, was down the narrow alley way between the two buildings. My friend.., had run from me... He had recognized my voice.., and ran away... I grieved for my friend...

That was the last time I ever saw Jon... He disappeared from Singapore, to where, nobody knew... Not all stories on the road have happy endings... But.., I like to think that Jon eventually recovered from this trauma that had afflicted his

Soul... He was, after all, a strong personality.., and he was fighting the good fight... He had removed everything from his person that could have been misconstrued as being effeminate; the long hair, the hippie beads, bracelets, etc., and he was growing a mustache... There was nothing effeminate about Jon... Yes, he would recover from this...

The faggots.., they spoil everything... I grieved for my friend...

I would have liked for this story to end here.., an episode in my life that was over, and on to new adventures, but it was not to be... I had seen the revelation, and with it came a new ability.., a power to see into the hearts of men.., and it was a curse...

Where before.., I had walked down the road of life, smelling the flowers, enjoying the sights and the sounds of foreign lands, laughing faces, good friends.., oblivious... But now.., Now.., I could see... The veil of naiveté had been lifted from my eyes, and I could see into the hearts of men, and what I saw.., was this sickness...

Ugh!.. I don't want to see this... Why do "I" have to see this... This is no special power!.. Every faggot has this ability.., to recognize other faggots!..

Where before.., I had been oblivious, and only the most blatant and obvious were even noticed.., and disregarded as "so what".., "not my business", etc... Now.., now it seemed as though I was surrounded... Everywhere I looked, I could see this sickness... Not only the blatant ones, that were obvious, but now I could see even the ones that sought to conceal themselves. The most distressing of all, were those that had been inadvertently contaminated by this dread disease, and fought daily against the "self doubt" that plagued their Soul, lives in turmoil, strong personalities, Not homosexual.., but rendered submissive by the "taint" of contamination... Followers, that should have been leaders... Tainted Souls.., that were my friends...

Sometimes, they would look at me with searching eyes, questioning eyes.., did I know?., could I see?., what could be done?., did I have any answers?.. I would look away, and pretend I couldn't see... I didn't have any answers.., except the obvious simplistic ones...

That bothered me... I could see this plague, that contaminated the Souls of men, and I could rail against it, and caution people to "not go there".., but what of those Souls that have been injured?.. Could those tainted Souls be restored and made whole again?.. Could the memory of that past "compromising" event be rendered impotent?.. Could the slate be wiped clean, as though it never happened?.. Could a man be "born again"..?

I was convinced that I "knew" more about homosexuality than any man on Earth.., and I could see the effects of this, the most sinister of "contagious" mental dis-eases that was a plague to mankind, with the power to harm the Soul and compromise the Spirit.., and I had "seen" those that had run from this disease in terror, and taken refuge in religion, and in the monastery and in the Priesthood.., only to contaminate both the monastery and the Priesthood.., and I had seen those that had run from this into marriage, and destroyed the marriage and the family.., but I had not "seen" a cure... This bothered me...

What is the point?.. Why should I be able to see the tragic effects of this sinister disease, if there is nothing I can do about it?.. I did have advice to give that "maybe" would help, but I could not say that I "knew" the way out... I could not say that I had "seen" the way out... I could not even say positively that there was a way out.., but I sincerely "believed" that there was a way out... Or was it my mission to say only..; "Don't go there"...

Do not Ever underestimate the power of the "Dark Side of the Force"... Do not Ever underestimate the wiles and wickedness of the "prince of faggots".., or his agents... Do not Ever think that you can "dabble" with this contagious disease and walk away unaffected... Do NOT Ever go there...

* * *   * * *   * * *

"Gratitude In Retrospect"

I consider myself to be among the most fortunate of men, having been raised in an era when children respected their parents, their teachers, their elders, etc., and in an environment relatively free from the blatant sexual bombardment that our children are exposed to today... My childhood of innocence lasted until I was 11 years old, (unheard of today)... We were climbing trees, my friend and I.., and he told a sexual joke... I don't get it, I said... You don't know about sex?!.., my friend asked in disbelief.., and then he proceeded to tell me all about it... "I don't believe that", I said.., "my father would never do anything like that to my mother"!..

I didn't go climbing trees with that kid any more... Where before I had never had a sexual thought, ...now.., I couldn't think of anything else.!. I hated that kid...

At the age of 14, I was sent to live with my "Uncle Yody"... We were giving the old farm house a new coat of white paint, when "Markie" drove up into the yard, and Uncle Yody went to talk to him about some business, or whatever... Presently he came back, and we were slapping paint on the old house, and Uncle Yody remarked; "You've got to watch out for people like Markie.., he's queer, you know"... In what way?., I asked (queer, meaning "odd")... He likes boys.., especially young boys... I was confused... I didn't have a clue... Uncle Yody explained... I was even more confused... What possible pleasure or attraction could there be, for a man, to another male... Uncle Yody explained in detail... It was the most disgusting thing I ever heard of... I was repulsed to the point of nausea...

At the age of 14 years (unheard of today), I learned about homosexuality... It was such a rare thing, back then, that I had never even heard of it... This was the era of the 50's.., nostalgically referred to today as the era of "Happy Days"...

It wasn't two weeks later, I was hitch-hiking back home from my summer job, stocking shelves at the grocery store, when I was picked up by a 19 year old (high school graduate), and the conversation immediately turned to sex, and he feigned amazement that I had never had sex with another male, and he offered to be my friend, and to teach me all about it... You don't know what you are missing, he said.., try it, you'll like it, he said.., etc., and etc... No thank you, I said, this is as far as I am going.., thanks for the ride...

I immediately conferred with Uncle Yody, about this encounter, and we had a long discussion about it, he telling me about the homosexuals he had encountered in the army, in business, in life, etc., and they were all weird stories, and none of them had happy endings...

My best friend in high school.., we used to chase the girls around the roller skating rink, double date, and etc., he eventually was seduced by a faggot, and then tried to recruit me, but I had been informed by my Uncle Yody, and I declined, and we weren't friends any more... He tried to commit suicide three times that I know about, and then his family moved away, and I never heard from him again...

Being an adventurous youth and bored with my circumstances, I left home before my 18th birthday, hitch-hiking my way from Ohio, down the East coast to Florida, then over to Texas, then to California, and back to New Mexico, where I found work on the drilling rigs... Within the space of a little over three months, I had hitch-hiked across the U.S. from border to border and coast to coast, and I had run the gauntlet.., of faggots...

I was a good looking youth of 17 years, and I had run out of money by the end of the first week.., and for the first time in my life, I experienced hunger... For most of the three months on the road, I was hungry. Often I didn't eat for as long as three days in a row, sleeping in bus stations, train stations, park benches, abandoned cars, etc... The faggots would hang out at the bus stations, looking for runaway boys, offering them money, food, a place to stay, etc... Never was I even tempted, I would have starved to death, first.., and I was starving... Never once did a faggot ever offer to even buy me a sandwich...

I would stop in the major cities, looking for work. There wasn't any, except for door to door salesmen... I could always sell magazine subscriptions, and keep the "front money", the few dollars that was my commission, and I would immediately go and eat. It was literally a "hand to mouth" existence. Driven by hunger, I was a good salesman...

Most of the rides that I got, were with faggots... I was amazed at the number!.. It got to be that I could tell the faggots before the car even stopped to pick me up... They would pass me up, going 60 miles an hour, realize that I was a young teenager with a suitcase, slam on the brakes, coming to a screeching halt, and burn rubber in reverse to pick me up.., greeting me with great glee, like I was a long lost rich relative... Normal people don't do that...

They would question me about my circumstances, and I would tell them that I was on the road and hungry, hoping for a hand out (but I would never ask), and they would offer me everything..; wild parties, luxury accommodations, offers of jobs, potentials of movie rolls, with X-rated producers, etc. and etc... Being a salesman, I recognized the polished sales pitch.., and it was all lies.., aimed at seduction... Their motives (and mannerism) were obvious, and I would decline their offer.., and they would let me out at the next intersection... I could see how a young teenager would be taken in by this.., but I was lucky... Uncle Yody had informed me, and I was never even tempted...

Being too proud to beg, I starved... In a land of abundance, I starved... Being offered everything by the faggots, I starved... I slept on the ground, and almost got pneumonia, and a fellow "bum" directed me to the Salvation Army, and they gave me a hot meal, a shower, and a bed for the night... They were my salvation on the road, and I determined that if I ever achieved wealth, I would repay them...

One hundred days on the road, and being propositioned by about ten faggots a day!.. I finally found work in the "grease orchard".., the oil drilling rigs of New Mexico... I had been psychologically affected by hunger, and for the next three months, I ate... My fellow "roughnecks" would crowd around me to watch me eat, as I would consume a full course steak dinner, followed by a couple of hamburgers, triple orders of French-fries, milk shakes, etc., followed by desert... The spell was finally broken when I was taken by my friends to a buffet style "all you can eat" restaurant.., and faced with more food than I could possibly eat.., my appetite returned to normal... But I didn't get fat!.. Working 7 days a week on the drilling rigs, I got strong.., and muscular.., and I graduated into the society of Men.., into Manhood...

Why am I telling you this story?.. I am telling you this story, because my Uncle Yody told me his story, about the faggots that he had encountered in his travels, and there were no happy endings.., and if he hadn't forewarned me.., I would have surely fallen prey to the faggots... Probably most of the young runaways fall prey to the faggots.., who circle around them like vultures, enticing them with lies and empty promises, ruining their lives.., and they don't graduate into Manhood...

I think back to my first encounter, when I was 14 years old, hitch-hiking home from working in the grocery store... "What if".., What if I had not been forewarned by my Uncle Yody.?. What if I had learned about homosexuality from that 19 year old, that wanted to be my friend.?. And there is no predetermined genetic factor here!.. This tragedy could happen to any one!.. Without the intervention and forewarning of my "Uncle Yody"..., this could have been an entirely different story...

Every body should have an "Uncle Yody"... It is with great gratitude to my Uncle Yody, that I tell you this story, because, I.., "Iron Owl the Lucky" (for all intents and purposes) I.., am your.., Uncle Yody!.. Hopefully, I am not too late...

The above story is of only 100 days... There are a lot more stories that I could tell you... The most recent is of my next door neighbor, (true story) an 8 year old boy, fucked in the ass by his 13 year old brother, who is already the most despised creature on Earth.., a child molester... The father beat up the 13 year old, who now lives with his divorced mother, who shows the kid x-rated movies to get him interested in women.., and the 8 year old has stated many times, that he intends to kill his older brother... The question is.., what faggot queered the 13 year old?.. Unfortunately, the 13 year old didn't have an Uncle Yody... Unfortunately, this story is not that uncommon... It's just life in the suburbs...

The intellectual supposition that homosexuality is somehow genetically predetermined is a bold faced, faggot lie.!. There is no hard science to support this... I am constantly amazed at the intellectual gullibility of the secular "apologists" for the homosexual community... They not only accept this lie, without any supporting evidence, but they propagate this supposition as though it were the truth.!, and therefore unavoidably acceptable...

So, You can look around you, at the homosexuals that you have encountered in your travels.., have you seen any happy endings?.. Be sure to tell your children.., before they learn about "sex"..., from the faggots...

* * *   * * *   * * *

At the risk of being "politically incorrect"; (Ha!)... It seems that the "Religion of the Left" (a belief system), more commonly called "Secular Humanism"..., a "Flat Earth" kind of viewpoint in which Mankind evolved from simple fungi, growing on a rock.., there is no God as creator, Man is simply a product of meaningless evolution, with no purpose but our own satisfaction, and when we die.., we are dead...

With this kind of viewpoint there is no moral compass, there is no "Pillar of Truth" on which to set anchor.., everything can be rationalized.., morality has a "sliding scale".., and whoever; (film makers, talk shows hosts, "rap" artists (?), celebrities, etc.).., whoever succeeds in lowering the bar on this sliding scale, achieves instant notoriety.., a sell out.., for money, fame, and the vote.., to the "Dark Side of the Force"... What will you get.., in exchange for your Soul.?.

Behind the facade of everyday tranquility.., an Evil looms... An Evil Force, on the march... Pandora's closet has been opened, and this contagious disease, that is a crime against the Spirit, is permitted free reign among our young people, marching under a banner ("gay").., that is a lie...

They would like to have you "not discriminate"... While it is wrong to discriminate because of race, religion, nationality, etc., you must use this mental faculty to discriminate between good and evil, right and wrong, smart and stupid, and that which nourishes the Spirit, and that which is a contagious disease... Their propaganda suggests that you should abandon this mental faculty completely...

Arguing in the "intellectually abstract".., in terms of Constitutionality.., (as though the Constitution were rigidly adhered to).., (just ask the "Libertarians").., the members of the "Supreme" Court (the designation; "Supreme", being usually restricted to "GOD").., the members of the Supreme court of the U.S. have systematically endeavored to removed God (and any reference to God, the Ten Commandments, worship, etc.) from the government, from the market place, and from the schools... While at the same time, the anti-religion "religion" (a belief system) of "Secular Humanism" (there is no God).., is becoming the law of the land...

Homosexuality (a butt-fucking perversion), has become Constitutionally protected, and pandered to by governmental candidates for office (for the vote), made every-day commonplace by "sit-com" television, (supported by the market place), and become acceptable in our schools and colleges (as an "on-campus" extra-curricular activity)... Our Fore-Fathers (the framers of the Constitution).., would turn over in their graves.., and vomit..!.

I will be called to task for the words that I am using here, as vulgar, and insensitive, etc.., I am very aware of the "Variegated Cloak of Words", and I choose my words very carefully and deliberately... In the "intellectually abstract", the term; "sodomy" doesn't convey a visual picture, and has about as much impact as "waxing the family car" (Simonizing)... Whereas, in the vernacular of the "common people", getting "fucked in the ass" brings the intellectually abstract back down to Earth, down to the level of the common people, down to the level of the highways, the bus stations, the restrooms, the playgrounds, the internet, and the suburbs.., where it can be observed for what it is..; a Pestilence...

I use the term; "faggot".., which some people may object to, (as rude and crude), and I have looked for an alternate word.., but what other word is more appropriate, to describe a class of people who wantonly seek to seduce any and all males, at each and every opportunity, especially the young.., and they hang out at the bus stations, rest rooms, and on the internet, seeking always to satisfy their perverted lust, and they congregate "en mass", in hot tubs and in moving vans, wallowing in degradation, spreading their sexually transmitted diseases.., etc, and etc... The dictionary definition of "faggot" is..: "a bundle of sticks, for burning"... The word is appropriate...

It is interesting to note..; that the "hot tubs" in San Francisco, were not shut down during the height of the "AIDS" crisis, because that would be to "discriminate" against the Constitutionally protected right of "Perversion".., and that was seen to be more objectionable than death by Aids... Is that Not a queer concept.?.

I use the word "homosexual" as distinct from the word "faggot" to describe the more demure "submissive" *victims* of this unfortunate disease, who do not actively seek to seduce, but are content to not display their sexual aberration (in the closet)... Can two neurotic "submissives" find happiness together, in their mutual neurosis.?. Does misery love company.?. In the realm of the intellectually abstract; perhaps.., but I think not... In the realm of the most High;., absolutely Not... Absolutely Not...

If I wanted to be "rude and crude", I would tell you about some of their perverted practices, such as licking each others ass holes.., (is it any wonder that their immune system breaks down).., or the practice of "fisting"... Etc. and etc... Enough said...

But I really don't want to be rude and crude, and some will say that this book is too vulgar and prejudicial, and should be classified as x-rated, and banned.., as though doing it was o.k..., but speaking about it is just too vulgar and obscene... This is a queer rational...

There are many view-points.., but only one "Ultimate" view point... I give you the Ultimate view point, as it was given to me... I know, because I "saw".., and I heard the "Inner Voice".., "and as I hear, I judge, and my judgment is just"... So, I Know.., and You know that I Know.., and you know how it is that I came to Know.., and now You Know....

The Ultimate view-point : The body is the "Temple of the Holy Spirit".., and "sodomy".., is the "desecration of the Temple"... This : the desecration of the Temple.., is a crime against the Spirit!., which is Holy.., and should never be harmed, and compromised, and perverted to the Dark side.., to your everlasting regret... The consequence of this crime is more serious than you can possibly imagine... The bottom line: homo-sex "sucks".., and it is CONTAGIOUS!.. Don't go there... (Pardon me for SHOUTING).!.

You must discriminate... You cannot let this Pestilence enter into your home and into your family... I would not send my children to a public school, today... Where the knowledge of God is not permitted to be taught or even acknowledged... Where the "Ten Commandments" is a forbidden subject.., and the only morality is to "not discriminate"... Where sex education includes graphic examples of "sexual preference", and how to do it.., safely!.. Where the incidence of unwed motherhood has reached epidemic proportions, but can be prevented by abortion.., without parental consent... Where the teachers are assaulted in the class-room, and forbidden to discipline their students, under penalty of incarceration, law suit, and loss of livelihood... Where the high-school graduate can't read his own diploma!??... Etc., and etc...

An education that does not include the Knowledge of God.., is inherently defective in it's approach to Life, and the meaning and purpose of Life... An education that eliminates God, and teaches that homosexuality (sodomy) is just an alternate (and acceptable) lifestyle.., is sabotage!..

There is something very sinister and Evil going on here!.. This is a War!., of super-natural proportions.., and it is time to choose your side...

I will Not send my children to a public school.., to learn what?., a secularly humanistic "Flat Earth", Godless mentality.?, and disrespect.?. I don't think so....

I will Not have my children being taught by homosexual teachers, as role models...

I will Not do my banking at a bank that takes a stand against the "moral straightness" of the Boy Scouts of America, and promotes the inclusion of homosexual boy scout "Leaders"...[1]

I will Not contribute to any "charitable" organization that makes it a point to exclude the Boy Scouts of America from their roster of beneficiaries, because of the Boy Scout oath of loyalty to "God" and Country, and their commitment to "moral straightness", and "reverence"...

I will Not buy any products in the market place that sponsors any pro-homosexual "sit-coms" on television.., or seeks in any way to portray this perversion as "normal"...

I will studiously eliminate all products from my shopping cart from any company that pulls their sponsorship from programs that support moral straightness, against perversion...

I will Not vote for any politician that makes concessions to, panders to, or solicits the homosexual vote.., and I will cast my vote against him... Etc. and etc...

As for me and my house; We will serve the Lord...

* * *

*** The Boy Scouts of America ***

The Scout Oath: "On my Honor.., I will do my best to do my duty to God and my Country, and to obey the Scout law; to help other people at all

---

[1] See the documentary: "The Scoutmaster's Secret", (aired on the "Court TV" program "The System", 2003) which documents the *True Crime* story of the Scout-Master of a small Southern community, who, over a period of 30 years, sodomized over 50 young boys (these are the **known** offenses by residents willing to testify), and easily over 100 cases (not testified to) … He is currently serving a "life" sentence for his crimes…

times, to keep myself physically strong, mentally awake, and morally straight"...

The Scout law calls upon all Scouts to be trustworthy, loyal, helpful, friendly, courteous, kind, obedient, cheerful, thrifty, brave, clean, and reverent...

The Scouts motto: "Be Prepared"...

The Boy Scouts of America is not affiliated with any Military, Political, or Religious organization... Membership requirements include a "belief in God" and to be "Morally Straight"... Excluded from membership are those who do not profess a belief in God (atheists), and those who are not morally straight (homosexuals)...

The Boy Scout oath represents the highest and most noble aspirations of this Country; ("One Nation Under GOD")., and it is the duty of all good Scouts, and all good Americans to stand firm in the face of this "onslaught" of legal battles that seeks to remove the words and precepts of this oath; (namely; God, reverence, and morally straight), as "unconstitutional"... It is hard to believe that in this great country of ours, the Nobility of this oath could ever be questioned, but such is the moral laxity that we have fallen into...

With blatant disregard for God, reverence, and moral straightness.., the Secular Humanists (atheists), and the morally perverted (homosexuals) seeks to undermine the integrity of this oath, with the thinly veiled agenda of giving the term: "scouting for boys" an entirely new and perverted meaning...

All that is required for Evil to prosper.., is that good people do nothing... It's time to take a stand against the forces of Evil, and all those who ally themselves with the Dark Side... The battle has commenced... Choose your side... Stand your ground... Take action.., and "Be Prepared"...

* * *   **"Be Prepared"**   * * *

BOOK XV

"Episode in Singapore"

It may seem that I had gone far afield from my original intentions of "Spiritual Enlightenment".., but not really... It was always first and foremost in my mind, my first thought in the morning, and my last thought as I closed my eyes in sleep... It was my natural preoccupation, and (almost) everything I did was a means to accomplishing that end...

The journeys into "inner space" require a single-minded devotion that leaves the world behind... I didn't have the kind of mental make-up that would permit the total isolation and routine of the monastery... I had tried that, and my mind rebelled in restlessness... Nor did I have the kind of mental make-up that could combine the daily commitments of time and energy required for the "world of work" with the kind of single minded commitment that is required to achieve the spiritual enlightenment that is "beyond this world"...

My "way".., was to alternate between these two extremes, with the "world of work" providing the financial wherewithal to accomplish the monastic regimen, but outside the confines of the monastery...

So I was involved in the "world of work" as a means to this end.., but the world of work is not entirely separate from this end, and does indeed provide for many of "life's lessons"...

Of all the jobs that I have had in my life, I truly did enjoy this job in the jungles of Sumatra, the most of all.., but it just didn't pay enough money to provide for my first priority, which was the resumption of the "quest"...   The "Exploration Company" had four different pay scales, according to the nationality of the employees...   The highest pay scale was the American, in line with American wages, followed by the Australian, in line with Australian wages, followed by the British, in line with wages paid in England.., followed by the Singapore pay scale, paid to the "down on his luck and hired off the street in Singapore" (and probably a temporary employee)...   I was on the Singapore payroll...

There was a demand for experienced "roughnecks" to work on the offshore drilling rigs in the South China Sea. The work was physically hard and dangerous, requiring a skill and awareness that could save your life, or you could lose it, by being in the wrong place at the wrong time.., but they paid American wages, which was about three times as much money as I was currently making, and having been away from America for over 18 months, it was tax free...

Offshore drilling rigs come in several different configurations... This one had the appearance of a ship, but was classified as a drilling barge, because it had no propulsion system of it's own, but was towed into place by sea going tug boats, and maintained in position by twelve giant anchors, strategically placed at twelve locations around the barge... The drilling barge, longer than a football field and almost as wide, was a city unto itself, with a population of about one hundred, and lit up like downtown Las Vegas... It had a helicopter landing pad, as well as high speed motor launches that ferried crew members back and forth, as well as supplies to maintain the operations of the rig... The engine room contained seven massive V-12 electro-motive diesel engines, each one being taller than a man, with a combined length (engine & generator) of about 35 feet... There were three massive "distillation units", that converted salt water into fresh water that supplied the population, as well as centrifuges that purified the diesel fuel, and pumps that shifted diesel fuel from storage tank to storage tank to maintain the equilibrium of the drilling platform... The mess hall.., glistened with stainless steel, and was manned by a half-dozen professional chefs in billowing white hats, supplying the best food in the world; steaks, seafood, pork chops, pastries, fruits and etc., at all hours of the day or night,cooked to order, or ready and waiting cafeteria style... Sleeping quarters resembled small hotel rooms, with upper and lower bunk beds, a writing desk, lockers, table and chairs, television, etc... It was practically a private room, as your roommate worked the alternate shift...

The principle of drilling for oil was the same as it was for drilling holes in the ground in Sumatra.., a length of pipe, with a drill bit on the bottom end, and a fire hose connected to a water pump on the other end, circulating water through the pipe to flush away the cuttings as the pipe is twisted into the ground... The principle was the same, but now everything was of massive proportions, driven by the massive power of electro-motive diesel engines...

The length of pipe, now made of thick-walled tempered alloy steel and joined together in 30 foot sections, could reach a depth of seven or eight thousand feet (experimental wells going much deeper), and the weight indicator for the weight of the "string" of pipe was calibrated in the hundreds and thousands of TONS... The massive weight of the "string" was raised and lowered, and held suspended by a massive "block and tackle" arrangement, suspended within the framework of the derrick, which rose 120 feet into the air, above the drilling platform... The "blocks" were strung with two inch thick steel cable that gave an 8 or 10 times mechanical advantage to the lifting power of the rig, with the cable being neatly spooled onto a massive drum (the "draw-works") that raised and lowered the blocks...

The drill bit consisted of three "roller cones" with teeth that pulverized the rock formation beneath its rotating weight, as the fluid "drilling mud" washed the cuttings away from the bit, and floated them up, out of the hole to be filtered out of the mud, and examined by the geologists for oil bearing content...

To float the gravel cuttings out of the hole from a depth of a mile or more, was a science and industry of its own... The "drilling mud" had to be mixed from special compounds that gave it a "specific gravity" and "viscosity", and caustic chemicals that would keep the mixture from clabbering up and solidifying.., and circulated through the drill pipe by massive "mud pumps", the size of large dump trucks, with piston chambers the size of 25 gallon drums...

As the drill bit pulverized its way through the solid rock sandstone and granite formations, a new joint of pipe would be added to the length of the string, and after about 12 hours of drilling, the bit would wear out and have to be replaced... This required that the entire length of the string of pipe be removed from the ground in 90 foot sections and stood on end within the confines of the derrick, racked into neat rows... The bit would be replaced, and the entire length of pipe was lowered back into the hole, being reconnected in 90 foot sections... This was called a "round trip",.. and "tripping" the pipe was the principal work of the roughneck...

A "crew" consisted of a team of five men..; the "driller", who operated the draw-works, spinning the take-up drum at high speed, reeling in the massive length of the two inch thick steel cable, sending the blocks skyward at high speed, lifting the string of pipe up and out of the hole... There was a "latching" mechanism that hung down from the blocks that would latch on to the drill pipe, holding it securely by the "collar" as it was lifted up through the center of the turn-table in the middle of the floor. Three joints of pipe (90 feet) would be pulled through the floor, and the "slips" would be set, securing the string of pipe to the turn-table floor, preventing it from slipping back into the hole as the three "floor hands" break the connection with the aid of giant power "tongs" that wrench the connection loose, and the turn-table floor is spun, unscrewing the pipe... The 90 foot section of pipe hangs suspended from the blocks, and as it is lowered to the floor it is pushed away from the turn table, and racked off to the side. The moment the pipe touches the floor, it is unlatched from the blocks by the "derrick man", working at the top of the derrick, and with a rope around the pipe he pulls it into place, into the rack at the top of the derrick... The blocks are again lowered to the floor, and latched onto the pipe protruding from the turn table, and the process is repeated until all the pipe is out of the hole, the bit has been replaced, and then back into the hole with the entire string of pipe until the bit is back on the bottom, and drilling is resumed...

I had worked all three positions on the floor, but my specialty was the derrick... I was the "derrick man"... I had no fear of heights, and the view from the top of the derrick was breath-taking... With a safety belt around my waist attached to a two inch thick rope secured to the back side of my perch, I would lean way out into space from the end of the monkey board, nine stories above the floor, thirteen stories above the water line... It was my job to unlatch from the pipe as the blocks descended toward the floor, and the blocks didn't stop on the way down... With precision timing, I would unlatch from the pipe and jerk it clear of the blocks as they descended towards the floor, and then secure the pipe into the rack...

Going back into the hole was a much quicker procedure than coming out of the hole, because the weight of the pipe was going down, instead of being pulled upwards... The latch mechanism hung down about six feet below the blocks, and as the blocks came screaming upwards through the derrick, I would be standing there at the end of the monkey board, holding the pipe in a bear hug in my arms, and at the precise moment, I would start falling forward into open space with the pipe in my arms, and the moment the blocks cleared the top of the pipe, I would thrust the pipe forward into the latch mechanism, grasping the handles, and slamming the latch closed around the pipe as it continued its upward journey, slamming into the collar at the top of the pipe and jerking it off the floor...

On the floor, the choreographed ballet would continue... As the 90 foot length of pipe was jerked off the floor, a roughneck would bear hug the wildly whipping pipe, guiding the threaded end of the pipe into the collar of the preceding pipe, and whipping the "spinning chain" up into position around the pipe, the chain would be pulled by the mechanism of the draw-works, spinning the pipe together at the screw connection and then wrenching it tight with the power tongs... The blocks would be raised, the pipe would be lifted up about a foot, the "slips" would be pulled, and the blocks would descend, screaming downward, pulled by the massive weight of the pipe, and stopping three feet short of hitting the turn-table, the slips would be set, the pipe would be unlatched, and the blocks would be sent screaming skyward, to receive the next pipe that I held in my arms, waiting to throw it into the latch mechanism,.. etc. and etc., until all of the pipe was back in the hole... Then I would remove my safety belt, step out onto the latch mechanism.., and ride the "elevator" back down to the floor.., "trip" completed...

There is a competition between the crews, as to which crew has the fastest time "making the trip" out of, and back into the hole... There is a team spirit and a pride in being good at what you do, and the roughnecks work at high speed efficiency, like a choreographed ballet, "rattling that iron".., and to be out of step could cost you or a team member serious injury, or a life...

"Roughnecks".., are a breed of their own... They are, of necessity, of muscular build, hard fisted, hard working, hard drinking, hard playing, and transient.., drifting from boom town to boom town, and around the world to the next oil field, be it in Alaska, Borneo, Saudi Arabia.., or in the South China Sea...

It was a twelve hour workday, every day, for 14 days, and then seven days off, back in Singapore, and when the rig was towed into the Sulu Sea, leave time was spent in Sandakan, Borneo... I have many good memories of Borneo...

There isn't quite the camaraderie between roughnecks as there is in other trades, because 12 hours a day for 14 days is about all the togetherness you can stand, so when we hit Singapore we all went our separate ways...

Now.., this book is not about the search for oil... Nor is this book about myself, stumble-fucking my way through life.., and it is not about travelogue.., or I would tell you about the magnificent and awe inspiring sunrises and sunsets at sea, and the ferocity and power of the storms at sea, with 40 foot waves crashing onto the deck.., etc., and etc... Nor is this book about the various Cultures, Religions, and belief systems that present the "smoke-screen" that obscures the "Truth"... But where there is smoke, there is fire!., and "We".., are looking for the "Fire" of those Universal "Truths" and fundamental "Principles" that are revealed in the crucible of life's experiences.., and are Universal to all of Humankind...

So.., I was on leave in Singapore, and I stopped by the office headquarters of the drilling company to pick up my paycheck, and then to the bank to cash my check and make a deposit into my savings account.., and the bank was closed... So just for something to do, I stopped in at the local nightclub, thinking to run into some old friends, or whatever.., when I saw..; "Her"...

Somewhere.., locked within the deep recesses of the subconscious mind.., is the blueprint of the "Archetypal" most perfect woman... The most staggeringly beautiful most sensual woman that I have ever seen... She was of Indian descent, but tastefully dressed in Western style, professional business attire, with the deep dark rich tan that all women aspire to, with the high cheekbones of royalty, and she carried herself like royalty, with rich full lips and the thickest, wildest, blackest hair that cascaded down below her shoulders in natural waves, but the most outstanding feature was her eyes, which were almond shaped exotica, and so deeply dark brown that they were almost black.., and they shot fire!., radiating a hot sensual heat...

I stared at her, transfixed... She did not look back, but seemed to be ignoring everybody... The nightclub was filled to capacity, with the music blaring and a haze of smoke that permeated the atmosphere, and nobody was looking at her... I couldn't believe it... Was I the only one that could see her?.. This was an anomaly.., the most outrageously beautiful woman I had ever seen, and no one was looking at her.., except me...

I forced myself not to look at her... It was rude to stare, and I didn't want her to catch me staring at her... You have to know your limitations, and this woman was beyond anything that I could aspire to... She was royalty, and I was just a commoner... I seated myself at a small table and ordered a drink from the scantily clad waitress. I purposely seated myself with my back toward where she was standing, so that I wouldn't stare at this unobtainable archetypal beauty... I sat there staring into my drink, contemplating this mystery.., when she said..; "Hello"...

I was startled out of my wits!.. It was like slapstick comedy, and I was the clown!... I was so startled to see her standing in front of me that I jumped backwards in my chair, and my chair jumped backwards... My lips mouthed the reply "Hello" back to her, but no sound came out, my breath and my words were caught in my throat... I tried again..; "Hello", I said, attempting to regain my composure... She smiled down at me, radiating a humorous charm... "I saw you looking at me", she said.., "Can I talk to you"?.. "Of cccccourse you can", I replied (stuttering and stammering)... She was even more devastatingly beautiful up close, as she smiled at me with her perfect teeth, her perfect smile... She didn't seem to notice my total lack of composure...

She seemed unaware that she was the most beautiful of women... She had no consciousness of self at all, but functioned from her essence with a Zen naturalness that was so rare, as to be supernatural... Her voice was rich and melodic, with a quality of sensuality... I judged her to be in her early thirties, about my age... "So what is a beautiful woman like you doing in a place like this"?, I enquired... She laughed, as though I had told a joke, and then she confided in me, telling of a life of poverty, of being the sole support of her younger siblings, of working in the battery factory for starvation wages, just getting by... "But no more"..., she said... "I have decided"... She had been raised in poverty, and she was tired of poverty, and trying to support her younger siblings in poverty, while the prostitutes made more money in one night than she made in a week at the battery factory... She had decided to trade her virtuosity and her poverty to support her family, and to make as much money as she could.., starting today!.. I stared in disbelief... The most beautiful woman I had ever laid eyes on, with a Royal bearing and a Zen purity... She was a "Sofia".., a diamond in the rough.., and she had not a clue... A Zen anomaly.., and she had decided to become a prostitute!..

I believed every word she said... She had picked me to be her first customer in her new profession, because I had looked upon her with favor, and she could see that I liked her, and I was handsome, and a gentleman... "You want me for all night, or just short time?", she asked... My lips moved, but the words stuck in my throat... I tried again..; "All night", I said... "Good", she replied, obviously pleased... "Is fifty dollars o.k.?" she asked... "Fine", I replied...

Fifty dollars Singapore ($16.66 U.S.), was such a paltry amount.., and proof that she really was a total amateur at her new profession... She could have asked for $500., and I probably would have said "Fine"...

And so it happened.., within 30 minutes of meeting the most beautiful woman in the World, we were on our way, by taxi, to the hotel... I was completely overwhelmed by the rapidity of the unfolding events...

I paid for the taxi and the hotel... She approached her new profession with enthusiasm and childlike anticipation, disrobing completely as soon as we entered the room, anxious to consummate the bargain, and willing to please... Again, I was overwhelmed by her physical beauty, and the purity of her uninhibited personality... I was overwhelmed, and out-classed... I stared at her with open-mouthed awe... I was "star-struck"...

I had never before been confronted by an Archetype, the primordial pattern of voluptuous womanhood, of which all reproductions fall short... No exaggeration... She had an Italian body; with broad shoulders, broad hips, and a slim waist that showed her chiseled abdominals, softly defined beneath the thinnest layer of body fat and dark mahogany skin... Her ample "D" size breasts, perfectly placed and perfectly matched, did not hang, but were self supporting, standing at attention, with large nipples and areolas that were a deep rich chocolate, darker than her complexion, and it was an adornment.., like the frosting on a birthday cake... Her perfectly balanced facial features, with the finely chiseled nose, the high cheekbones, the full lips, and the deepest, darkest exotic almond shaped Asian-Indian eyes.., that glistened with a sensual fire... Her thick jet black hair cascaded down in waves, like from an angry sea.., with pubic hair to match...

This was not the typical, dainty, soft feminine type of beauty... No.., she was large boned and tall, about 5'7", and she carried herself with a poise and dignity that spoke of ancestral Royalty... She moved with the athletic prowess and natural grace of a panther.., so natural, it was Supernatural.., displaying a strength of personality, character and bearing befitting a Queen of the Warrior class... A "Warrior Queen".., with a seductive smile.., I realized at that moment, that she was the rarest creature on Earth..: a true anomaly..; She was an "Alpha" female...

It wasn't love that I felt for this woman.., nor was it lust... It was a primal urge that I had never felt before.., stronger than either love or lust... It was..: "I wanted to have children by this woman"... Here was a "Woman"... Here was a woman that would be the mother of Warriors.., the mother of sons and daughters that would be leaders of men and of nations, the mother of Royalty, and of princes and princesses, and of Kings, that were Warriors!.. Here.., was genetic perfection!..

This was a new experience for me.., being confronted by an "Alpha" female.., with Royal bearing, physical perfection, a spiritual Zen purity and a strength of personality that was superior to my own... I was out-classed, out-Zenned, and insecure... Some people just can't handle prosperity...

She threw herself into her new profession with a lust that was consuming, and I yielded up the prize in less than a minute... Far too soon... Wanting to give her an experience worthy of the esteem in which I perceived her, I tried again, with the same rapid fire result... I was humiliated by my lack of control, and if she was disappointed, she didn't show it, but I was disappointed in my performance... It's that Zen thing..; the harder you try, the farther away you are.., but I will do better in the morning...

She slept the deep sleep of innocence, as I lay awake beside her for hours... Never had I wanted to impress a woman as much as I wanted to impress this one... Finally, approaching day-break, I fell asleep.., and I dreamed... I have vivid dreams... I dreamed about this woman, and as I dreamed about her, I made love to her in my dreams, and I climaxed with orgiastic splendor... Ugh!.. I awoke in horror... I couldn't believe it... Here I am, in bed with the most fascinating woman of my life, and I fall asleep right beside her and dream of her.., and now there is this huge wet spot in the bed... I couldn't believe it... Humiliation on top of humiliation... How could this happen?... This was a Cosmic conspiracy.., a slap-stick comedy.., and I was the clown.., and the entire Universe was laughing at me!..

And now she was disappointed.., that I didn't want to make love to her again... We dressed amid casual conversation, and she asked for her money... A professional would have asked for her money up front, but she wasn't professional... She had instinctively trusted me, because I was a trustworthy kind of guy... I pulled out my wallet, intending to give her a handsome tip as well, only to discover..; I didn't have enough money!.. Oh NO.., Oh my God, No... Further humiliation!.. I had less than $20. dollars Singapore in my wallet... What else could go wrong?.. "I trusted you, and now you are cheating me", she said, convinced that I was somehow not satisfied with her... I apologized profusely, trying to convince her that it wasn't intentional, and it's o.k., because I will just write a check, producing my check book... But her prostitute friends had warned her to never take a check... I wrote out the check as quickly as I could, for twice the agreed upon amount, and I could feel my ears turning a beet red.., as that fire that I had so admired in her eyes was unleashed in a torrent of tongue lashing that ripped into my soul... "The check is good", I protested, handing it to her... She snatched it out of my hand with a fury of unkind words, storming out the door, and slamming it behind her...

I was devastated... I collapsed into a chair... Never had I been so humiliated in my life, and at the hands of the one woman that I had admired more than any other... If the Universe was watching, it was convulsed in uproarious laughter, at this slap-stick comedy.., but for me, It was as though my heart had been cut out with a rusty nail... I had never really experienced rejection before, and it crucified my soul... I was severely wounded.., and as luck (or conspiracy) would have it, my leave time was over, and I left that day to go back to work on the drilling rig...

I had to wonder about the sequence of these events... It couldn't have been just by chance.., there were too many anomalies... It seemed more like a conspiracy.., of retribution.., brought on by my constant overindulgence... I had treated women just like another tourist attraction... You go to a foreign country, and you experience the diversity of the culture, you sample the ethnic foods, taste the wines, sample the drugs indigenous to the region, and sample the women, just like a delicious piece of fruit in the market-place...

I had been guilty of serial love affairs, in which I had genuine affections for my female counterpart, but it would eventually reach the stage where a more serious commitment would be required, and I could never make that commitment, because I already had a previous commitment.., to a higher calling.., and I always knew this, but the attraction to women was strong and intriguing... But the end result was always the same.., sadness...

I was a handsome young man, and women pursued me.., and I was a "pushover"... I had rationalized..; "Well", I am putting myself on the line, and if a certain female can get me to commit, well then she's got me!.. But it was a lie, and I knew it, because of the "higher" commitment... I had caused harm, to the women who had truly loved me... I had inflicted pain, not intentionally, but that was the end result... And I had done it again, and again, and again...

But I am not totally without conscience, and eventually I became aware of my repetitious pattern, and I decided to not do that any more... But the "animal", gets restless...

Asian women were a new experience.., and they were fascinated with Western men, who were bigger, taller, stronger, and had hair on their bodies, like sexual animals... To receive money for sexual favors was the natural state of affairs in Asia, with no disgrace to it, and If they liked you, they may not ask for anything at all, just the pleasure of your company, and to provide a token of appreciation, like food, which they would gladly cook for you.., but if they didn't like you, no amount of money could buy them... (Well, there may be exceptions to that rule!)...

I did not seek them out, but they were everywhere accessible, and so many of them that there was competition for my favor... Such good natured enthusiasm should not go unrewarded, I rationalized, and there were no tangled emotions, no commitments, no promises, and no sadnesses... This was a fair bargain, and great good fun...

It seemed that the world of the flesh, and the inner realms of the spirit had absolutely nothing to do with each other... In fact, it seemed that the realm of the Spirit was more accessible once the flesh had been satisfied, and I would sit for meditation, sometimes immediately after intercourse, and in that calmness and stillness that followed the storm of sexual activity.., there would be clarity...

And so I rationalized.., but I had far exceeded my quota in over indulgence, and I had harmed the women who truly loved me.., and now I had been called to account...

I had been wounded.., seriously wounded... This was not a situation that I had sought out, but this situation had sought me out, and punished me for my serious crimes, of causing harm to the women who had loved me.., and now I had been harmed, and at the hands of a Celestial Warrior-Goddess masquerading as a mortal... This was justice.., this was "Oh, so poetic Justice".., and now it was I who had been spurned.., now it was I that was cast into this empty wasteland.., of rejection...

Words fail to convey.., the dismal, dark, emptiness that pervaded my soul... Now I knew what rejection felt like... Now I knew the extent of my crimes...

Now back on the drilling rig, alone in my room, I observed myself in the mirror... It was a strange feeling.., that pervaded my body... It was as though I was "out of Phase" with my body.., not fully integrated into my body.., kind of "beside myself", in this anxiety ridden emptiness... I looked at my face, and by my own judgment, I looked pathetic... A blank stare, and hollow eyes.., no expression, no life.., pathetic... I looked at my posture.., not standing proud, at attention.., but definitely not "at ease"... My arms hung down, with my fore-arms parallel to the floor.., and my hands.., hung limply down.., from my wrists...

I jumped back from the mirror, horrified by the limp-wristed, pathetic reject that once was myself... Oh No.., Oh God, No... Anything but that... Oh No.., Oh No.., Oh God.., No...

I stared at my hands... they seemed to be alien things, not really a part of me, and they were in the way... It became a problem.., what to do with my hands?.. If my hands were not occupied with doing something, they just hung down, limply... This was an impossible situation... There are no limp wrists on a drilling rig... There is no such thing as a limp-wristed roughneck!.. I became paranoid that someone would see...

When I wasn't working, I kept my hands in my pockets, and when I was working my hands were occupied, and if they weren't, I would carry tools in my hands, and I was always "self conscious"... The very uncomfortable state of being "self conscious" was an ever present condition, and I was "beside myself", as I watched myself do.., everything I did... My integrated personality was gone... My naturalness.., was gone...

Alone in my room, I looked at myself in the mirror, at that pathetic being, and I realized that this "out of sync", "out of phase", disassociated, self conscious emptiness that pervaded my being must be what it feels like to be a homosexual... It was unthinkable, that this condition would become permanent, and that I would eventually become used to it, and it would become my normal state...

Oh God, I had been bested in the game of life by an "Alpha" female, and my Spirit had been broken, and now I was limp-wristed, out of sync, self conscious, and rejected by both God and women...

Anger boiled up in my soul, and I looked at that pathetic being in the mirror, and I shook my fist and growled through clenched teeth..: "If this is the cause, then there must be a cure"... No.., I will never reconcile myself to this fate... "If there is a cause, then there must be a cure"...

"Sha-zam"!... As if by magic.., as though I had uttered the secret words of the "Magical Formula", my Soul.., re-integrated into my body, and I became whole again.., instantly!...

It was such a relief!., to be back in my body... Such a relief, to go from despair, instantly to joy!.. I jumped for joy, I laughed, I danced, I whooped and hollered... I calculated the time; seventy-two hours... I had been out of sync for seventy-two hours, which was probably the normal recovery time for a broken heart, but how was I to know, and now I was back... I laughed uproariously at what a buffoon I had been, at the buffoon that I was... The joke was on me, and it was a very funny joke, indeed.., because it was over...

I burst through the double doors of the mess hall, with my arms in the air.., my hands in the air.., and an ear-to-ear grin on my face, and I shouted to my fellow roughnecks; "The drinks are on me", which was an absurdity, because there is no alcohol on a drilling rig, and all other drinks are free.., and everybody laughed, and accused me of being stoned, and we all laughed and celebrated.., but only I knew why...

So.., This story has a happy ending... I like happy endings... But, at this point, the reader (You), must be saying to himself..; "Well, that's a very interesting and humorous story.., but what's the point".?. What have we learned here, and how does this relate to that great adventure called; "Life".?.

The point of this "Episode in Singapore" story, is that it falls upon the heels of the previous "Incident in Singapore" story, and is a continuation of that story...

You may remember that in the previous episode I had the vision, which gave me an in-depth understanding and insight into the "plague" of homosexuality, and it's deleterious effects on the personality of its victims, harming and crushing the Spirit, leaving its victims limp-wristed, pathetic, out of sync, and ineffective with women... This is more than a human tragedy, it is a Spiritual tragedy, and this emulation of the great sin of the "Evil One" has Spiritual consequences... This is NOT a "happy ending"...

You may remember, that in the previous episode I had gained the ability to "see" into the hearts of those men that had inadvertently and foolishly "stepped over the line".., and had been wounded by this dread dis-ease that crippled their Spirit and their personality, making followers of men that should have been leaders.., but were NOT homosexual.., and they were my friends...

You may remember that I lamented the fact that although I could "see" the effects of these transgressions, and the guilt that these men carried with them on a daily basis.., I had not seen the remedy or the cure.., that would make them "whole" again...

"What is the point" I had asked.., of me being able to see this crippling dis-ease of the Soul and the Spirit, if I had no solution to the problem.?, and was there a solution.?. I had not asked (of the

Father) to see a solution, and I had not "seen" one, and I wasn't sure that there even was one.., but I hoped, for the sake of my friends that there was, and I believed that there was, but the only advice I could give was the obvious "conventional" wisdom.., which is: "Depart from sin, and sin no more"...

But with this latest "Episode in Singapore".., I had been given new information, and perhaps the solution to the problem... I had lamented too loudly.., *and I had been heard.!.*

Although this last episode was specific to myself, and a retribution for my own "high crimes and misdemeanors", it had elements relevant to a Universal problem.., with (hopefully) a Universal solution...

The very first element in the solution to the problem, is:., the utterance of the words of the "Magic Formula"...

This is no simple repetition of words.., No.., this has to be done with "Defiant Anger"..,` and deliberate intent... The "Magic" words.., of the "Magic Formula".., are : ... "NO I WILL NOT" ..

These words are spoken in defiant anger.., through clenched teeth.., and with clenched fist... And you should be angry, for having been tricked.., and used.., and seduced.., by the Dark Side.., having suffered the loss of "Manhood".., having been degraded into something less than "Man"... So this is no pretense of anger... This is genuine defiant anger, and the key word here is..; "Defiant"...

So this is no "slinking away in terror" from a disease that threatens your Soul... This is no simple "New Years resolution" at an "attempt" to change your fate... This is no "pleading for mercy" at your wretchedness.., etc., and etc... "NO"... This is a different attitude altogether... It is the attitude of "defiant anger".., and as you look at your reflection in the mirror, you clench your fist, you set your jaw and you grit your teeth.., and you utter the "Magic Words" that will change your life... You SHOUT the Magic Words that will change your life..: "NO I WILL NOT" succumb to this fate... NO I WILL NOT allow myself to be a victim of this disease of the Soul... NO I WILL NOT be counted a member of the Dark Side... NO I WILL NOT permit myself to wallow in self doubt and guilt... NO I WILL NOT ever engage in an act that will demean my Spirit and my Soul... NO I WILL NOT... NO I WILL NOT... Etc., and etc... And then smash the mirror with your fist.!. Smash the reflection of your past.., and get a new mirror...

So this is a "ritual of initiation", in which a decision is made (a cutting away of the past).., in which you de-side (get off the fence and choose a side).., an act of de-termination (terminate the past and set the terms of the future).., and from which there is no retreat... NO YOU WILL NOT EVER.., retreat from this commitment.., lest you suffer a fate worse than death.., the fate of the faggots...

The breaking of the mirror is an act of defiance... It is a physical act, an external act symbolic of an internal revolution... A revolt against superstition, and a revolt against a mistake... It is an act of defiance that you will always remember as being the turning point.., a memory record that will replace negative memory records, and that you can point to as a "happening"... On such and such a day, of such and such year, this event happened, that gave me back my dignity.., and saved my Soul...

But.., "Be Prepared"... The "Dark Side" does not relinquish Souls so easily... The "sex drive" is a formidable force of nature, and it is the engine that drives the thought process down sexually explicit avenues... To entertain perverted sexual fantasies is almost as damaging as the act itself.., so you must retrain the mind to not go in those directions... (This subject is dealt with at length in Book VIII)... This "technique", utilizing the "Life Breath", is a serious undertaking, and must be practiced diligently... The thought process must be diverted into higher and more noble channels, by reading books of inspiration that satisfy the Soul, and increasing the knowledge base of those subjects that are of academic interest to you... This "technique" of retraining the thought process will yield verifiable and beneficial results within a period of twenty one days.., and forever after...

And.., (as an adjunct to the above process), since it is the sub-conscious *animal* mind, that has been humiliated, it's spirit broken and sodomized, it is the sub-conscious mind that needs to be healed.., and I would suggest you employ the services of a professional hypno-therapist skilled in these matters, to re-program the sub-consciousness back to it's former dignity and self respect…

And as a further supplement to the above process, let me suggest a more pragmatic approach (as a last resort)... Since the sex drive is such a formidable force of nature driving the thought process.., it may be in your best interest to simply diffuse the situation by "getting a grip" on yourself, and releasing the pressure in an unceremonious and anti-climactic sort of way, (discretion being the better part of valor).., utilizing the bounce-back effect to the "opposite polarity"... The "onslaught attack" of disturbing thoughts will immediately cease, followed by a period of clarity, peace and tranquility that should be immediately utilized.., in prayer, supplication, and a reaffirmation of your Noble and determined intentions... You will be successful...

"But Be prepared".., for this "onslaught attack" of disturbing thoughts.., even your dreams will turn against you (you dream about what you fear)... To do battle against this onslaught attack, is to acknowledge its power... The best defense against it is to simply disregard it... You have had a trauma to your soul, and you will be bombarded by thoughts about it, but you must simply ignore them.., dismissing them as a natural consequence to be expected, but not allowing them any power over you... You will defeat them by disregarding them, and by turning your thoughts in more Noble direction...

It goes without saying.., that you must divest yourself of All the "trappings" of your former indiscretions... All the links to the Dark Side must be severed and abandoned... This may include a change of location, residence, job, relationships, clothing, mannerisms, thought processes, etc. and whatever is necessary to affect this transition...

"A house divided against itself, cannot stand"... Having departed from the "house of Evil".., the "Good" must be embraced... Seek always to do good... Go out of your way to do good... Speak only that which is good and truthful... Seek the Lord within you... Serve the Lord...

A trauma has happened to your Soul... Be it wounded by perversity or adversity.., or be it wounded in love... The question is..; how deep is the wound.?..

The deeper the wound, the longer it will take to get over it... With the passage of time and the fading of memory, the impact lessens, and the Spirit (that had been wounded) begins to recover... Full recovery (depending on the severity of the wound) may take as much as three or four years, but You Will recover.., and that crippling episode that harmed your Spirit is now seen in context, and disregarded as having happened in ancient "yesterday".., which has no bearing on "Today"...

And "Work"..; "Work" is your salvation... You can lose yourself in work... Work is an extrovert activity that will divert your attention away from introverted and negative self indulgent, self deprecating, memory based, "soap-operatic" thought patterns, that are so damaging to the Spirit... To replay these soap-operas, is to feel the sting anew, again and again... So Work will divert you out of this repetitious syndrome into the "here and now", and in those "Zen moments" when you "lose yourself" in work.., healing takes place...

The Spirit WILL recover.., "IF".., if you do not dwell on the past.., If you do not continually replay the negative memory records, like a bad soap opera.., if you will guard yourself against the incursion of perverse sexual fantasies.., if you will totally abandon the scene of the crime (the vicinity of temptations), and all links to the past... And if you will utilize the Yogic technique of the "Life Breath" to retrain the mind, diverting it into more noble and productive pursuits (dramatically shortening your recovery time).., and if you will forgive yourself, and those who have trespassed against you, and pray for their redemption.., and if you will work.., and do good every chance you get.., and if you will seek the Lord within you, and serve the Lord...

It is the Spirit that has been harmed.., and it is the Spirit that must rise to the occasion...

So I, Iron Owl, (the intrepid buffoon).., having been rejected in "love" (or whatever), and having had my Spirit broken.., having become limp-wristed and pathetic, having experienced being out-of-sync and self-conscious (a condition that persists and becomes the "norm" for homosexuals).., having experienced this, it was my Spirit that rose up and said: "NO I Will Not"... I recovered immediately!..

But this was not the only time my Spirit had suffered a severe trauma... I had also had the vision of "Hell"... I had been shown down the corridors of Hell.., with my "inner eye" wide open.., as a punishment... My crime had been the sin of "presumption" while in the court of the Most High... My punishment was just and appropriate...

With the "eye of insight" I had "seen", and intuitively experienced.., the terrors of Hell... Word fail to convey... I had seen the pit.., the abyss.., and the demented Souls, the utter hopelessness.., a terror so great, that it left me a quivering, whimpering, terrified, horrified, pathetic, and a wretched "mess" (but Not limp-wristed (?)... The effects of this trauma lasted for over three years, until I learned the "Life-Breath" technique for the training of the mind, under the tutelage of the Swami... Otherwise, the effects would have lasted much longer...

So.., it seems that I was destined to stumble-fuck my way through life, just so that I could document my experiences and present them to you, so that you could profit from my mistakes and utilize the remedial techniques that I had so pains-takingly been shown... And it is my "duty" and my privilege to do this.., (let it not be said that I am derelict in my duty).., because.., I and my "Father", are of one mind concerning this..; "That all Men should be saved (from the terrors of Hell), and come to know the Glories of God, and of themselves.., and none should be lost".., and to present to the Lord.., "gifts".., of Men...

"For as high as the Heaven is above the Earth, so great is HIS mercy toward them that fear HIM"...   "As far as the East is from the West, so far has HE removed our transgressions from us"... (Psalm 103:11-12)...

Now.., there is one other thing that "I" would do.., "IF"... If it were "I", who had fallen victim to the curse of the great sin that destroyed the city of Sodom.., and after I had repented.., and recovered.., and after a sufficient time had elapsed to confirm and solidify my recovery.., THEN.., (and only then).., I would take "Ibogaine" {*} (called: "The Healing Drug").., or one of the other psychedelics.., and present myself to the Lord... That is what "I" would do... But then; "I am the Owl".., in search of Wisdom.., and I will do that anyway...

*   *   *   *   *

Meanwhile.., back on the drilling rig.., two long weeks had gone by... Two weeks of 12 hour days, of hard hats and steel toed boots, of "mud wrestling" and "rattling that iron", and then leave time.., back in Singapore, and back to that same roughneck haven.., the night club...

You could hear the loud music blaring out onto the street...   I entered into the dimly lit, filled to capacity crowd, with the multi-colored strobe lights blinking through the smoke filled haze, everybody laughing and having a good time, yelling to be heard above the din of the music... I surveyed the crowd, as my eyes became accustomed to the dim light... She was there.., and she was with another man...

If she saw me, she didn't let on. I studied the other man; he looked prosperous... Her goal was to get rich at her new profession, and I had no doubt that she would achieve her goal, and probably eventually marry a wealthy man... Well, that would exclude me...

It was still a paradox to me.., an anomaly.., I would have expected all heads to turn, to witness this outstanding beauty.., but no one seemed to notice, not even the guy she was with, and the Zen-anomaly; she seemed to be unconscious of it, herself...   I wondered.., was she really all that beautiful, or was it just me, and my personal archetypal imprinting of what constitutes the perfect woman...   No, I concluded; it wasn't me... She really was this incredibly superior Woman, a Warrior Queen, of unsurpassed beauty...

I didn't look at her again, ignoring her completely... I worked my way through the crowd, meeting old friends, laughing and back-slapping with the other roughnecks that hung out there, and eventually entering into conversation with one of the other "ladies of the night" that tried hard to gain my affections... With mock laughter, I grabbed her by the hand and proceeded to the door, looking back for only the briefest of a moment, to see if my act of bravado was noticed, and in that briefest of moments "She" caught my eye.., and winked!... "Damn".., I said...

She saw my act of bravado for what it was..; an act!.. With that one wink of understanding, my whole facade of braggadocio had been exposed... "Damn", I said... This woman was beyond me... Her physical perfection was beyond me.., her Zen-centeredness was beyond me.., her "Alpha" self confidence was beyond me.., her Royal bearing out-classed me.., and her intuitive perception saw right through me... And looking right through me, what was there for her to see.?, an inept clown?., a buffoon..? "Damn", I said...

I had to do a reality check, here... I could pursue this woman, and make a complete and total fool out of myself, or I could accept the harsh reality... The harsh reality being that in this game of life, sometimes you win, and sometimes you lose.., and I had lost... I had nothing to offer this woman... If I had a kingdom, I could say; come and be my Queen.., but I had no kingdom... A woman such as this would be a full time job for a King!.. The harsh reality was, that she was a Queen, of Royal bearing, and I was just a commoner, a roughneck oil rig worker, gone out to sea two weeks out of three.., an impossible situation... I felt out-classed in her presence... This woman had a power over me.., She could hurt me... She could undo me with a wink!.. ...A man has to know his limitations...

No, I concluded... This was a challenge that I could not win... And even if I did win, what was it that would be my prize.?. A Warrior-Queen that was superior to me.?, an "Alpha" female that was stronger than me.?, a full time job ?.. No, thank you!.. I already had a commitment that was my first priority... Some things never change... .....Funny?., (in retrospect).., I don't remember her name...

It was time for me to leave Singapore... I had been here for the better part of a year, and I had lived a lifetime... I had places to go, things to do, people to see, and lessons to learn... I had replenished my savings and accomplished my purpose... It was time to move on.., and there was a "Holy Man" in Indonesia that I wanted to meet!..

    * * * *   *   * * * *

BOOK XVI

"Scope and Limitations"
(An Overview)

I left Singapore by plane for Djakarta, Indonesia... There was a "Holy Man" that I wanted to see in Indonesia... His name was "Bapak".., he was a Muslim, and the Leader of the "cult" known as "Subud"... The "Subud" movement had spread world wide, and I joined the movement while I was in India... I had spent almost two months in the city of Calcutta, India, for the express purpose of undergoing the initiation into this "cult"...

The city of Calcutta is not on my list of desirable tourist attractions, but the search for "Truth" can lead down many dark and mysterious avenues, and my name can be found on the roster of several of these "cult" organizations. "Truth", is where you find it, and any organization (or cult) that claims hidden or esoteric knowledge, or claims possession of a particular aspect of Truth.., gets my attention...

The initiation is termed a "receiving", and the scene of the receiving is the "Latihan"... The Latihan is held in a spacious room large enough to comfortably contain its occupants, who go into a trance state in which the Spirit descends upon them and controls the movements of their bodies!.. While in this trance state, some participants pace the floor.., some dance, as though in a ballet.., some will sing.., some will shake and gyrate.., some will wave their arms and clap their hands.., etc. and etc., and interestingly enough, they don't seem to bump into each other, although each one of them is in this trance state, seemingly oblivious to each another... After about 30 or 40 minutes of this, they come out of their trance state feeling cleansed an purified, reporting insights, revelations, and etc...

I had become good friends with an Indian member of the organization who was willing to sponsored me into the group, and it was with great anticipation that I arrived for my initiation... About five or six of the "helpers" surrounded me, went into their trance state, prayed and chanted that I be "opened" to receive the Spirit, and then they entered into the Latihan... Nothing happened!!! Nothing!.. I stood there, waiting to be grabbed by the Spirit, or whatever, but nothing happened!.. I must have stood there for about fifteen minutes, waiting for something to happen, watching everyone else go through their gyrations, etc. on the dance floor, and feeling like an idiot!.. My Indian friend came out of his trance momentarily and motioned for me to enter into the Latihan, so I entered onto the dance floor and kind of waltzed around waving my arms and etc., still feeling like an idiot, still waiting for something to happen.., but nothing happened!..

I attended about three more Latihans after that, and I went through the motions out there on the dance floor, still waiting for something profound to happen, and observing the other participants who were obviously truly in a trance state, and I envied them their altered state of consciousness, but for me, nothing happened!..

It seemed obvious to me that the "trance" state of the Subud experience was identical to the state of hypnosis, and the Latihan was group hypnosis... I don't say this to denigrate or belittle the experience, but only to explain it... I have no doubt that the participants were sincere, and the practice was carried out with a "God oriented" motivation, and I only wish that I could have participated more fully into the experience, but alas, I am one of those few people (approximately 10 percent of the population) who cannot be hypnotized!..

As a student of "altered states", the inability to experience the hypnotic state was particularly disappointing to me, and I tried everything, including Sodium Pentathol (a.k.a.: "truth serum") and professional hypnotists, to achieve this state.., but to no avail... Although, the inability to be hypnotized probably saved my life and my sanity!..[1] (Yes, Virginia, there really is a Higher Wisdom)...

That had been about two years previous to this, my journey to Indonesia, that I had undergone my initiation into Subud, and now I was on my way to visit Bapak, personally... Why?., because;.. "Bapak can "open" anyone"!..

---

[1] I am referring here to my encounter with a demon, in the chapter : "The Dark Night of the Soul"... The following sentence; (Yes Virginia) is a parody of that famous answer to that famous question (the Washington Post) asked by a little girl; "Yes Virginia, there really is a Santa Clause"...

I arrived in Tjilandak, Indonesia just in time for the "Fourth Subud World Congress", a celebration, and there were participants from all over Europe, America, Asia, Africa, and etc.., everyone it seems, except "Bapak", who was on tour in America!.. I participated in a few Latihans and socialized with the International clientele, and then it was time to leave!.. It is a story of exploration with an anti-climactic ending...

But this story serves to show that I held no pre-conceived preferences of one religion over another, and that I would go the "extra mile" in my search for "Truth", wherever it may be found, and although it may seem that I have neglected the Moslem (*and also the Jewish*) religion by concentrating more exclusively on the Buddhist-Christian-Hindu religions (that seemed to me to have more of an "esoteric" bent, and to which I could draw parallels and isolate differences), I have actually spent much time in Moslem countries...

Etc., etc., and etc...

Well.., I was going to tell you about my experiences with the Moslem religion, and my encounters with the Moslem peoples in the various Moslem countries (I lived about six months of my life in "Old" Afghanistan, (before the Russian invasion, before the Taliban), and etc.., which would have inevitably led to deep philosophical, moral, political, and historical discussions that go all the way back to Abraham, Isaac, and Ishmael (Abraham's first-born son), and what this has to do with the "Mid-East" crises, September 11th, etc., and etc., and my own Patriotic outrage (*crush the bastards!*), etc., and etc...

And then.., just for balance (*and to make sure that I piss off Everyone equally*).., I would have to tell you about my encounters with the Jewish peoples and their religion, and my studies into the Kabbalah, the "Tree of Life", of numerical codes, gemetria, etc., (*and other non-sense*).., (I attended the "Institute of Kabbalistic Studies", in California, took courses in the Hebrew language, and etc.).., and I would have to tell you of a Jewish scholar that had lost his faith, because; "God parted the Red Sea to save the Jews, but he wouldn't part the railroad tracks that carried six million Jews to the ovens in Auschwitz, and etc.., (and it was true!!. With German efficiency, the trains ran on time, without breakdown or delay.., *and God never raised an eyebrow!!*)... And I studied (*for several years*) under the foremost Kabbalist of his day (by correspondence course)[2].., So you see, for someone who is not of the Jewish lineage or persuasion, I went the "extra mile" to probe the depths of Judaism...

To go into a discussion of the Moslem and Jewish religions would require a "book within a book", and although I have much to say on the subject, there are only so many subjects that can be sandwiched between these pages... So my "limitations" here are of space and of practicality... It seems that if a book has too many pages, people are reluctant to buy it, as it exceeds the attention span and time commitment required to read it...

But more to the point, and I point this out, **because it is a trap!!!** It is a mental "mind-fuck" trap!.. This whole business about the "Mid-East turmoil", etc., and etc., and WHATEVER.., is just a "Huge Distraction" away from the Inner Domain of the Soul, and to search the pages of scripture to make sense of political insanity here on Earth, and who owns what piece of real-estate and why, is to be "deceived by the World"!!! The student of the "Arcane Mysteries" must ever be aware of "The Grand Illusion" of the outside world, and not allow himself to be "sucked in" by these "*Enormous Trivialities*"... "*My Kingdom is not of this world*", spoke Jesus.., *and neither is yours!!!* **Take heed!**.., lest you fall into one of these mental mind-fuck traps (of which there are many), and become "deceived by the World", and distracted from your goal!.. You may rest assured.., the will of the Lord will be made manifest without any interference from you…

* * *

So.., is this a book about Religion??. Well, certainly religion is discussed.., but not "religiously"... No, we are taking an "analytical overview" look at the great Religions of the World to do a comparative analysis with the objective of finding those "Truths" that are Universal and corroborate each other, although perceived and described from different viewpoints.., and also to discern those differences that point to errors or misconceptions.., but the most important observation here is of "omissions"... Yes, it seems that there are certain Truths that are contained in

---

[2] The foremost Kabbalist of his day was the late "Dr. Paul Foster Case", founder of the organization known as "The Builders of the Adytum"… A teacher of the highest order, to whom I will always be indebted.

each religion that are omitted from the others, as though each religion is allotted a *portion* of the whole, and it is only that Explorer that goes the "extra mile" and incorporates "All Religions" (with discernment) into one "Comprehensive Whole", that has any concept of the complete "Body of Knowledge"...

But is it possible to apprehend the complete "Body of Knowledge"?., and if it is.., is it enough??? No.., it is *Not!*.. What does it profit a man, if he be in possession of a treasure map, if he never walks the steps to the treasure?!. He may speak eloquently and persuasively, but it is mere intellectualism!!. And even though he procure the treasure map, and walks the steps to the treasure vault, what is the "Key" that opens the vault, and just what does the "Treasure" consist of!!?

Aha!.. *Aha!!!* Here we have the Question of all questions!.. Most Explorers into the Arcane Mysteries never get far enough to *ask* this Question, let alone answer it!.. Should I just tell you!?, Should I just give the secret away?!! Should I, after having climbed mountain and traversed jungle, suffered pain, disease, imprisonment, hunger and thirst, having circum-navigated the globe several times, explored books and caves, many lands and many religions.., should I just tell you??? Perhaps I shouldn't!..

Perhaps I shouldn't tell you!!. It is written; (Math 7:6) *"Do not give dogs what is sacred; Cast not your pearls before swine; they will trample them underfoot and then turn and tear you to pieces"!..* Well.., I am making the assumption that if you have indulged me enough to have read this book up to this point, then perhaps you really are a seeker of "Truth"... So.., You have to ask yourself at this point; "Do I really, really want of know.., or is this just idle curiosity?.." And if I were to give you the map.., would you follow the steps to the "Treasure".., but most importantly, would you fashion the "Key" that unlocks the vault? Would you possess the Treasure!?? ....So I will answer this; the Question of all questions!., not at this moment, but within this chapter... Stay tuned...

* * *

Is this book a Biography?!! **No**!!, if anything, this book is a "case history", just one of many.., mine.., and yours!.. This is a book about a journey, a Quest that went on and still goes on. It is a quest that is common to all of mankind, and it is your quest, and as you read the pages of this book, it is just part of your quest. The pages of this book cover only about four or five years of this quest, and I was "on the road" (outside the U.S.) for over twelve years, (so you see the "limitations" of this book). In the four to five years covered by this book, I have given you only those selected highlights that point to the deeper and more profound esoteric truths that are universal in nature, and not even all of the highlights! There is much, *much* more that I could have included just within this five year time span, but I am limited by time and space... And although this book is confined to this five year time span, my journeys continued on through Indonesia, to Java, the island of Bali (with it's temples, magic mushrooms, gamelan music, etc.), many stories to tell.., and on to "Borabador" (the mystic ruins of the ancient Buddhist culture that thrived here before the Muslim indoctrination).., and then back to India, (and more meetings with remarkable men).., and back to Afghanistan, and the historic sites of Bamian, and Bandiameir (now destroyed by the Taliban).., back to Thailand, back to Laos, back to Singapore, Hong Kong, the Philippines.., etc., and etc... Many stories to tell, and many lessons learned.., but this would require another book!.. So you see the limitations...

* * *

Is this a book of Adventure, and Travelogue?.! No.., at least not intentionally.., but the search for the Truth, and for the meaning and purpose of Life, *IS* the Adventure of a Lifetime, it is what life is all about, and if there is no adventure in your life, it is because you have missed the point of life!.. Perhaps I am luckier than most people; I think the first word that I spoke as an infant babe was "Why?", and "How?"... Most people don't ask this, the most simple and fundamental of questions, let alone seek to "Know" the answer; there is no purpose to their lives, beyond self gratification!.. But I was born with a "star" to follow, and it was the "Quest" to "Know"... You ask about adventure and travelogue; this quest has taken me, literally, to the far corners of the Earth, from the remotest of primitive villages to the garden spots of the civilized world.., **and beyond!!!** Adventures and intrigues on Earth; I have had many, more than I can tell you about (and some that I can't tell you about, *ha ha*).., but they are not the "substance" of this book... It is the **"and beyond"** that is the subject matter of this book, and it is the plane of "High Adventure"... Compared to this, everything else is a triviality... *"Seek ye first the Kingdom of*

God and His righteousness, and all these other things will be added unto you"... Point made...

* * *

Is this book of "High Adventure" about drugs??. Well, to a certain extent, it is, but there are many books about drugs, written mostly by research professionals "negatively prejudicial" to the subject, *who have never partaken (imbibed)!!!* Their reason for not participating *in* their experiments is; (quote) "We do not want to *compromise* our objectivity" (end quote)!!! So the one thing different about this book, is that I have participated *fully* into these experiments, and without a prejudicial ax to grind... This is a rare book in this regard!..

So.., *"Let's get real"*, with regard to drugs... Now, I am not advocating, nor do I want to see, the wholesale indiscriminate *abuse* (overindulgence) of anything (food, sex, drugs, etc.), but especially drugs... Physical addiction is proof of abuse, proof of stupidity, and tantamount to slavery... I speak out against such things... The biggest addiction of all, is (of course); sex!., and more often than not, the drugs are taken (alcohol, cocaine, crack, etc.,) to accentuate sexual addiction (and mask insecurities, etc.), so this one addiction feeds the others!.. This is a downward spiral leading to degradation, disease, abortion, death, and destruction... *I speak out against such things!..* I don't want to see anyone "blow their mind" or ruin their life because of stupidity, and to overindulge with a mind altering substance (drunkenness) is stupidity... Unfortunately, stupidity is rampant in our society... This message is aimed at "the user" and "the abuser".., *"Dosage is the critical factor"..,* **but the most important factor of all is "INTENTION"!..** Question what your motivations are... Seek maturity, and be around for it... If you are going to use.., don't abuse!.. And don't be stupid...

Although the terminology is constantly used interchangeably (the variegated cloak of words), there is a vast difference between "getting High".., and "getting stoned"... Getting "High", is an enhancement of your faculties and capabilities!.. it is an improvement!!. For instance; "Uppers" (Cocaine, amphetamines, etc.) can *(used in the proper dosage)* enhance your alertness, focus your concentration, increase your endurance, improve physical performance,[3] increase productivity, elevate your mood, and even your I.Q.!!. The "abuse" (overindulgence) of these substances will cause you to become; dependent, anxiety ridden, paranoid, your concentration will be scattered, your health will suffer, sleeplessness, confusion, loss of fortune, high blood pressure, heart attack, stroke, and etc... In other words, the "abuser" went from getting "High", to getting "stoned" (as in; "dumb as a fucking stone")!!.

The same scenario is evident with the "THC" class of drugs (the herbs; Hashish and Marijuana)... In the proper dosage, they enhance the "Soul qualities" of intuitive perception, the appreciation of art and music, they give a Spiritual perspective and a more Religious appreciation for the magnificence and Mystery of Life than you can get from "church"!.. They can alleviate pain by allowing you to rise above it, and communication with a loved one can border on the telepathic!.. But taken to an extreme (overindulgence) the "abuser" depletes his "psychic energy" factor.., and his "enhanced perceptions" are channeled into the senses, resulting in overindulgence of food and drink, sex, entertainment (the "Zen" state of absorption.., into *television*!?!), lethargy, loss of initiative, and etc... Again, (to state the obvious), proper use will get you "High".., and abuse will bring you down... But the down-side of this drug is relatively benign, and can be alleviated with a little self discipline, which includes MODERATION and good quality herbs (high THC and low CBD content)... All in all, the positive aspects outweigh the negative, and it should be legalized, to the replacement of alcohol and tobacco...

And the Opiates!.. To those in great pain, suffering traumatic injury, the terminally ill, wasting away with disease, facing the debilitating fear of impending doom and death.., to these people, the opiates (opium, morphine, codeine, etc.) are a Godsend!.. The U.S. imports *Tons* of opiates for the legitimate use of the medical profession, every year, and no one disputes the fact that they are a veritable Godsend, banishing not only the unbearable pain, but also the terrible *Fear*.., of Death!.. This allows the patient happy association with loved ones, and a death with dignity... This

---

[3] In some futuristic "Brave New World" scenario (the year 2089 A.D.).., which Country (do you suppose) will be the "First" to host the Olympic Games, and *NOT* prohibit the use of performance enhancing drugs???... What kind of records will be set.., and surpassed???...

constitutes the proper "use" of this "God sent" drug... But to many people (the abuser) "Life", is a pain!., with feelings of anxiety, fear, insignificance, insecurity, powerlessness, and etc... The first abuse of this drug, is to concentrate it into the form of heroine, and the second abuse is to put it into a syringe... The "high" comes from the "rush" of this drug, as it is "slammed" directly into the vein and is instantly assimilated into the body!.. The effect is "orgasmic", followed by a sense of well-being and centeredness that is a personality change; from the insecure, timid, and fearful "wimp", to the secure and confident stronger personality... This personality transformation is an almost immediate psychological addiction, and coupled with the physical addiction, the user becomes a slave to this drug... The difference between the fearful and anxiety ridden "wimp" personality and the "fearless" stronger personality is so dramatic that the user doesn't care that he is addicted, as long as his supply doesn't run out!.. He rationalizes that his use of the needle is no different than, say, a diabetic.., but the dosage level keeps escalating, and his use of the needle increases to two, three, and sometimes four times a day, to maintain his "secure and confident" personality, and sometimes he can "maintain" this scenario for years.., but eventually he has poked so many holes in his veins that there are long "tracks" of needle marks that go down each vein, until the vein collapses, and he is running out of places to stick in the needle, and the expense gets into the "exorbitant" category, sometimes hundreds of dollars daily, but with his drug enhanced "confident and persuasive" personality he is able to persuade, coerce, beg, borrow, steal, and "sell".., to support his habit at any cost, because to go without.., is to revert to his insecure and pathetic "wimp" personality.., while going through agonizing withdrawal symptoms.., and sources of supply keep drying up!!. The user is caught in this web of his own making, and travels down that dark road of ruin and despair... Even though he can "kick" the physical addiction, the psychological addiction (strong personality vs. the wimp) will draw him back... At higher dosages he will "nod out" into a fantasy world of lucid dreams, and this is o.k. too, because the dreams are pleasant, and the anxiety world of reality is left behind... At higher dosages still, he will enter the world of dreams, cease to breathe, and die!!. It will be termed an "accidental death" from overdose, but more often than not, it is by choice... A tragic end to a tragic and pathetic life... Stay away from this drug...

And then there are those "assholes", that choose to get "stoned" out of their fucking mind"!!. The psychology of this eludes me!?. Why would anyone want to obliterate their good common sense to the point of drunkenness and stupidity?., but they will do this time after time, and brag about it to their friends!!! They will go to excess and extremes with everything and anything, from alcohol to sniffing glue to smoking concoctions containing embalming fluid (!) and etc... Their lives are destructive to themselves and to whomever they "run into"... I have no advice for these people, except to say: "Find God.., and Get a Life!"...

All of the above having been said, we now have to look at this subject with a different purpose in mind!.. It is a diametrically opposed different purpose!.. Because, that which has been ***"for the downfall of many,*** can be, ***for the edification of the few"***... This message is aimed at the edification of "those few"...

....In what is perhaps the "Oldest Document in the World"[4] *(It's succinct and pithy stanzas committed to memory and handed down by word of mouth from generation to generation in a long line of teachers that extends back before recorded time, long before being put down on parchment, written in Sanskrit)..,* it is stated that; "perfections" (supernatural powers, Enlightenment, etc.) can be attained by: Divine Birth (an incarnation; such as Jesus), by prayer and meditation (over several lifetimes; such as Buddha), and by; "Herbs of Mysterious Virtue"...

So.., the oldest document in the world turns out to be the most advanced document in the world in that it deals with the Nature and "Liberation" of the Soul (the "essence" of mankind)... This (oldest/most advanced) document is the "Missing Link" and "The Holy Grail" combined, in that it contains the Knowledge of the next great "Leap Forward" in the advancement of mankind into the "Enlightened Spiritual Being" that it is his destiny

---

[4] "The Yoga Sutras of Patanjali"... A "timeless" document that deals with the Nature of the Soul and its "Union" (Yoga) with the Divine… It is considered to be the oldest book in the world because it embodies the "Truth" that always was, from the beginning!.. The first translation (into English) was done in the early 1870's by Dr. J.R. Ballantyne and Govind Sastri Deva, and was first published in 1882… While there are several translations of this document, this is the one I recommend… The commentaries are almost cryptic in nature, but yield the greatest insights…

to become!!. The fact that "Herbs of Mysterious Virtue" may be the "Key" that unlocks the vault will come as a shock to a lot of people... To even suggest such a thing.., is going to "piss-off" a lot of people...

To those of you (Jerry and Pat, John and Jack, James an Jimmy, etc., and etc.) who think you have the market cornered on access to God, let "Him" remind you; (Isaiah 55:8-9)... There are children who have greater I.Q.'s than you.., there are teenagers who have had greater religious experiences than you... If you doubt my word, **Taste and see!.,** or is your faith in God so shallow that you would fear to take a step into a larger Universe... The stumbling block is that you cannot imagine *any* intelligence being greater than your own, *let alone your own intelligence being greater than it is now!!. You cannot imagine that an "altered state" could be an "enhanced" state...* **Taste and See,** and bring with you your love of God, your Bible, your religious music, your praise, *and your humility!.,* or are you content to "rant and rail" against something of which you are totally ignorant!!! How is it, that those who have had no experience with an "enhanced" state, are so "rabid" in their opposition to it?., while those who are experienced report that "The Doors of Perception" have been opened??? *....You have been invited!., and your "Window of Opportunity" is swiftly closing!!...*

A word to the Wise here (should be sufficient)... We are talking here *only* about the (consciousness expanding) class of drugs known as "Psychedelics", (and to a lesser degree; "Hashish", and lesser yet; marijuana)... Understand that these *(truly magical)* herbs (or the synthesis thereof) will put you on the "wavelength" (altered state) of "Communion".., *with God!..* So this is a *Religious* ceremony, and you are the "High Priest" and the "Alchemist" of this primordial ceremony, and when you participate in this ceremony.., you are on Holy ground!.. The "Key" is actually the Alchemist himself, and he should present himself as a purified "Vessel", as a servant of the Lord, with sincere and righteous motive.., and the *Magical herb,* is the sacrament... If the Vessel be not pure, with sincere and righteous motive, then you are just another "druggie", and you may even be rejected from this Holy place (a "bad" trip)... So., in the final analysis, it is **You,** who are the Key, (and the "Key" word here is; **Integrity**).., and it is up to you, as the Alchemist, to fashion this key into the image and likeness of the Lord... Amen...

But Wisdom is required here... Now, obviously.., no one can simply take a drug and see God!.. "You cannot put new wine into old wineskins" without serious damage happening.., this is a learning process, a growth process.., and even though the experience may be a revelation, as you see the world with clarity, in all it's magnificence.., you have only entered the courtyard of the potential of what lays ahead!., so tread lightly, and go slowly... Your first experience, awe inspiring as it may be, is just a "get acquainted" experience, to familiarize you with your new terrain, but realize.., you are still looking at the "outside world"... The real "Treasure".., lies "within"...

To make the transition from "without" to "within", is not an easy task!.. Very few people ever make this transition... Of the masses of humanity, only a few make the effort, and of those few that make the effort, only fewer yet ever succeed... If it was easy, everyone would do it!.. So be advised; *No one goes to the Father.., except he who is sanctioned (deemed worthy), by virtue of the sincerity of his quest...*

So it is both Art and Science at the same time! It is the "Holy Science"... It requires; first of all, a "dedicated intent"... It must be your intention to "go within", which further requires..; Solitude!.. And beyond solitude, there is a place of *"sensory deprivation"*... A place of solitude and "quiet" so profound that the senses (taste, touch, smell, hearing, sight, etc.) are withdrawn from the outside world.., and focused within... And then.., you must get beyond the last obstacle, which is..; your own "Mind"!!.

Ah, yes.., the mind!.. That labyrinth!, that propounder of riddles, that "dog" that is forever chasing his own tail.., and you cannot get around the mind by using the mind... You must "Isolate" yourself from the mind, and observe the workings of the mind... As you observe the workings of your mind, you will come to the realization that:.. *You are not your mind!!.* "You" are the "Observer" of your mind, and separate and distinct from it!!. "You" are that "Primordial Essence".., that "Sole Primary Observer".., more commonly known as: "The Soul"...

It is the "Soul" that you seek!.. It is the Soul that is the "I" of your being.., and the "I" is the "eye" of the "sole primary observer" who is in reality, the "Self", and more specifically;., *"Yourself"!..* This "I", which is the "eye".., is the "Treasure" for which you seek!., and it is a treasure like no other in Heaven or on Earth!!.

Shrouded in mystery.., clothed in allegory and symbolism.., it is the stuff of legends and speculations... It is depicted on the "Great Seal" of the U. S. (as the "All Seeing Eye"), It has been called "the Third Eye" (by various "mystery schools"), It has been referred to as the "Higher Mind" (by theologians), It is referred to as the "Self" in the Hindu and Buddhist Scriptures, "Patanjali" refers to it as "the Consciousness Principle", but it is more commonly referred to (by me) as; "The Eye of Insight"...

The "key" word here is "insight", which has two meanings: first of all it is the organ of sight within the inner realms, and second it implies the "intuitive" faculty; the ability to see "into it" and comprehend, which is spontaneous and automatic along with sight, and since the mind (deductive reasoning) has been transcended, conclusions are arrived at *instantly*, because.., *"it is obvious"!!*. And since the "Soul" is "*absolutely*" vacuous, *without form and without substance, having neither center or circumference, and in reality, cannot be found* (the eye cannot see itself)!!, (it can only be ascertained by: "I think, therefore; "I am".)..., since the Soul is "absolutely" substanceless; *it is immortal and indestructible!!!*

Being "absolutely" substanceless and without form, the "Soul" has certain "Superhuman" faculties!.. It has the innate ability to become "absorbed" in the object of it's enquiry (true objectivity; where the observer and the thing observed, become "one"), and to "know", "intimately and intuitively" the history, composition, etc., of the object being observed...

Being "absolutely" substanceless, the Soul has the innate ability of condensing itself into the "infinitely minute", examining the most sub-atomic of particles, etc., and of expanding itself to Galactic proportions and beyond, comprehending the Universe, and etc...

Being "absolutely" substanceless, the Soul has the innate ability of "unimpeded motion" and "quickness", where "whatever and wherever" the Soul chooses to examine (the Sun, the Moon, etc.), it "arrives" there instantly by simply intending to do so!..

Being "absolutely" substanceless, the Soul is not bounded by time, and can insert itself between, and examine; the nano-seconds of a moment, the intervals between vibrations, frequencies, etc...

Being "absolutely" substanceless, and not bounded by time, the "Consciousness Principle" (Soul) is aware of the present (events, etc.) and comprehends their significance.., both past and future...

Being "absolutely" substanceless, and having entered the domain of "Inner Space", the Soul has access to the "Seven Worlds" (that is; the seven Heavenly Realms of "Inner Space", and etc.)...

The Soul (having transcended the limitations of the mundane mind), having seen the inter-relationship of all things from the "absolute" viewpoint, becomes endowed with "All Knowledge".., the consequence of which is *Wisdom,* which begets Love (in it's highest form), which is; *Compassion...*

The Soul.., being endowed with Immortality, Knowledge, Wisdom, *Joy* and *Compassion,* is not without purpose!.. That purpose being (the essence of the "Bodhisattva Vow"): "The emancipation and liberation of all mankind from the bondage of ignorance, and to bring them into the light of Divine Knowledge and Wisdom"... These are called (truly); "The Sons of God"...[5]

....This is the "Truth" about the Soul...

What cannot be communicated here, is the profound sense of "Awe and Mystery", of having entered "The Holy of Holies"... Words fail to convey.., all descriptions fall short.., of the *Magnificence* of this Treasure, which is in reality;., *Yourself...*

* * *

Is this book.., a "Belief System"??. No... Religions are belief systems, and I am not here to start another religion... If I have said it once, I have said it a thousand times; "I do not believe.., *in*

---

[5] Although gender is not manifest in the "unmodified" (formless) state of the Soul, the ability to become manifest (on whichever plane of existence) is one of the "powers" inherent to the Soul... A more complete list of these "powers" (siddies) is contained in Patanjalie's "Yoga Sutras"...

Belief".., and I quote one of my teachers [6], who has also said it a thousand times... In the absence of knowledge, there is belief... To say that you believe is to say that you do not *Know*... Only when you have had first hand *experience*, when you have *seen, heard, smelled, tasted, touched and been touched for yourself..*, only then can you say that you "Know"... I don't invite you to believe.., *I invite you to see, hear, touch and taste for yourself, and to KNOW...*

But I was wrong!.. I have to recant!.. Yes, I believe in belief.., because I see the evidence of belief all around me... I saw the evidence of belief on Sept. 11th, when the twin towers of the World Trade Center fell... I saw the evidence of belief in the Martyrs who were burned alive at the stake and died by the sword, and I saw the believers who burned and slaughtered them... I saw the believers who make war in the name of God, and I saw the believers who prayed to God that their enemies be destroyed... I went through the pages of history, and I saw an endless parade of *Armies of believers*, locked in endless combat, marching to their deaths, believing that God was on their side... And I saw the prophetic and enigmatic writing.., the graffiti.., scribbled on the walls of the Holy Temple.., and it said: "Oh Dear God, Please save us.., *from those that believe in YOU"...*

Whoa!., stop!., (chant the believers)!!, you can't be serious!!; because Christ commands us to believe... Christ said; "Whoever believes and is baptized will be saved", but whoever does not believe will be condemned".., and besides, who can have direct experience of God, except he whom God decides to personally grant such experiences!..

Yes, I will concede this point!.. You can believe Christ, because He wouldn't lie to you.., and belief in God is a prerequisite to having first hand experiences of God in your life!.. It is a simple "open and shut" choice!.. To the believer, the door is **"Open"**, and all things are possible... To the disbeliever, (Secular Humanist, Atheist) the door is **"Closed"**, and the "flat earth" mentality becomes their stark and sterile reality*!!. Simple as that!!.* And Baptism, is the consequence and confirmation of the *heart-felt* "Born Again" experience.., *and I advocate this* **experience** *(as opposed to belief)!!!...*

But beyond this.., when simple belief turns into complicated theology.., when belief becomes a substitute for first-hand **experience..,** when belief becomes dogmatic and fanatic;., *it is Divisive to the point of War!!...* The *"Substance"* is lost, and only dogma remains!!!

....And Christ goes on to say (Mk 17); "These signs will accompany those who believe: In my name they will drive out demons, speak in new tongues, not be harmed by deadly snakes or deadly poisons, they will heal the sick with their hands"[7]... And again; (Jn.14:12) "having faith in Me, you will do *even greater things"* (heal the sick, raise the dead), etc... Who among you has this kind of faith that you can say to this mountain; "Go, throw yourself into the sea" and believing without doubt, it will be done!?? So I ask you, do you really believe, or do you only believe that you believe?.. Perhaps you have only been coerced into belief (by the promise of Heaven and the fear of Hell), or perhaps you just fear death!.. If you were put to the test, (by an enemy of your faith): *"Renounce your faith Now, or be executed, Now"..,* how would you respond??? Be careful how you answer!..

Belief is kind of like "love"; you either do, or you don't!!! You cannot love another person on command, nor can you (in your heart of hearts) believe on command... **But, be not deterred..,** *because miracles do happen!!.* Bone fide, Sanctified, and Certified.., miracles do happen!!. But (generally speaking), they happen to those "Saints" who have had direct **experience** of God, and belief has been replaced by direct **Knowledge,** *and if you "Know"..,* then there is no doubt!!. THIS IS THE DIFFERENCE!!. **So,** *if you have the faith to move mountains, heal the sick, raise the dead, etc. and etc.., you have my respect, and I will sing your praises!..* I only point these things out and ask the question.., it is *You* that must answer the question, for yourself... And what would be the criteria of God, to decide who can have direct experience of Him?.. Perhaps it is granted to those

---

[6] A teacher (philosopher), whom I know only through the many books that he has authored, and with whom I feel a kinship, is "J. Krishnamurti", and it is he that I quote...

[7] It is interesting to note; that this is the verse in the New Testament that is singled out by the enemies of the Christian faith... The Moslem religious leader (a *believer* in Mohammedanism); "Louis Farrakan" (called; "The Prophet of Rage") points to this verse and says; (direct quote) "I see no evidence of these "signs" that will accompany the believers in Christ! You have been bamboozled!"...

that truly seek (*and you will find*), and ask (*and it will be opened up to you*)..

Belief is a very powerful force, and in the face of "not knowing" (ignorance), you will believe!.. Even the Atheist "believes" that there is no God!!. You must be very careful about what you believe... If "belief" were the criteria for entrance into Heaven.., *we are all doomed!..* In a world of approx. 10,000 different Religions.., with *tens of thousands* of different systems, sub-systems, variations, cults, creeds, and etc.., (with Christianity classified as only 1 religion, *with 33,830 different denominations*) [8].., who is it that has the absolutely true (and without error) ultimate belief system??? Is it YOU??? **I don't think so!..**

Remember the story of the "Good Samaritan"?.. The often overlooked point of this story, is that *he was a non believer!!!* But he found favor with the Lord, *because he had a good heart!..* The Lord is not concerned with the truth or fallacy of your beliefs.., because you are a simple (and relatively ignorant) mortal!., because the real "Truth" is in your heart of hearts.., and are you a sincerely good and honorable person with respect and compassion for your fellow man, and do you go out of your way to do good?., and not with the ulterior motive of "buying your way into heaven".., but for the sincere purpose of helping your fellow man, because he needs your help, and your compassion is sincere, without thought of merit or recompense??. Belief, without works, is repugnant to the Lord; it is hypocrisy!.. HE doesn't look at your beliefs, as much as HE looks at your heart... If you are going to "talk the talk".., you had better "walk the walk"...

* * *

Is this a book of Science?.. **YES!!!** Oh Yes!.. *Oh Hell Yes!!.* This is a book of scientific enquiry and of scientific discovery, and I present my findings to the scientific community, and I insist that the men of science (if they truly be "men of science") examine and evaluate my findings!..

This book **opens** with a scientific discovery of monumental proportions and implications!.. It is the discovery (re-discovery) of the *Reality* of the "Fifth Dimension"!., and this is neither conjecture, supposition, or theory.., *I was there!!.*

Just like Columbus traveled the uncharted sea, set foot in the America's, discovered the "New World", proved that the world was round.., and *shattered* the "Flat Earth" mentality.., so too, did I travel to a Realm in the fifth dimension, proving that the linear-logical concept of the timeless space continuum of the fourth dimensional Universe is in reality the modern day version of the "Flat Earth" mentality of those scientists who fail to take into consideration the multi-dimensional aspects of an infinite universe...

The problem here is that we are dealing with a "fact" that is *non-conceptual!!*. To conceive of a fifth dimensional reality within the confines of the fourth dimensional timeless space continuum is an error, and to conceive of a fifth dimensional reality outside of the fourth dimensional timeless space continuum is also an error!.. How can this be?.. This can only be; *in the equally infinite "Realm of the Mind"!!!* To illustrate the point; a dream (for instance), cannot be found either within or without our waking reality, but no one denies it's existence (or the reality of it, by the dreamer while dreaming)... What the secular scientist fails to consider.., is that there may be other dimensions (in the realm of mind), that are *equally as real*, and that **This** fourth dimension reality "of ours" is itself, just another dimension of the "spectrum" of dimensions that makes up the "infinite" Universe.., and we, like the dreamer in the dream, are convinced of it's reality!., although it be just another dimension within the realm of the "Infinite Mind"... And, the "flat Earth" secular mentality will inevitably ask: "Well, then;., is the Universe a physical reality, or is it just mentally conceived"??. The answer: "Of course the Universe is a physical reality, as are all of the Universe-dimensions of the "spectrum" of Universes contained within the mind of God"!!! (In other words; it is a "moot point")[9]!..

But unlike Columbus, I cannot say that I was the first person to traverse the uncharted sea of the "Bardo" and set foot on the shore of an alternate dimensional reality (specifically: the "Diva world")(among others)... No.., documentation of this alternate dimension/reality is abundant, going back into millennium, as is the artwork depicting scenes and peoples (Devas) of this realm, and the replication of the Pagoda style of architecture common to this realm...

---

[8] The source of this amazing statistic is: The 2001 edition of Barret's "World Christian Encyclopedia"...

[9] See references to: "Buddha's Law of Reality", (Book IV, titled "Fifth Dimension", and Book XII: "Laos") …

So I have (within the pages of this book) documented my first-hand experience of this event, and I present it to the world of science as a "Scientific fact" that is "empirical"... That is to say; *"This is a repeatable and verifiable experiment"!!*

Now.., the implications of this Scientific and empirical fact.., are *"enormous"!!*. This changes everything!!! The first thing that it changed, was "myself".., in the fact that it shattered the linear-logical parameters of my own thinking, and my relationship with the *apparent* Universe, which would never be the same again!.. but this is an insignificant insight compared to the world of Science as it perceives (and is perceived) at the present time...

The world of modern Science, with its "flat Earth" and linear-logical secular mentality, is working *feverishly*, on all fronts; with the microscope, exploring the genetic sequences of the DNA code, constructing a "tree of life" as it pertains to the "evolution" of *(All)* life forms as they developed from a primordial *microbe* into ever more complicated life forms, and eventually, after billions of years of trial and error, we are the end result of that microbe!!. (Ain't it all just so wunnerful)?!! While at the same time, other scientist are working at the bottoms of the oceans breaking off pieces of volcanic chimneys, finding life forms that exist at great depths and pressures and at scalding temperatures (in excess of 700 degrees F., living in total darkness, and consuming sulfur, etc.), hoping to find that single primordial microbe that had been "cooked" into life (an extension of Henry Miller's "pre-biotic soup" experiments).., proving that "Life" is a natural occurrence, and with no help from God, thank you... While at the same time, other scientists are working in the frozen Arctic and Antarctic, drilling core samples, miles down into the glacial ice sheet, at sub sub-zero temperatures, searching for that same "grand daddy" microbe that is the "Father" of us all!!... While at the same time, other scientists are sending robotic probes to far distant planets; Mars, the moons of Jupiter, etc., searching for any kind of evidence of any kind of life form that they surmise will eventually (billions of years from now) evolve into an intelligent species that will hunt for their own microbes, and prove conclusively.., that there is no God!!.

Pardon me for being facetious, but absurdity is the basis of all humor, and I am moved to laughter.., except for the tragedy of it all, in that this is an awful lot of effort, time, resources, expense, and the consumption of some of our best "flat Earth" brainiacs!., and to what end?., so that we can say; "Halleluiah, there is no Creator God"!!, there is only this little Great-grand-daddy microbe!.,. Ain't he cute!?. Of course he is a little hermaphroditic at this stage, but give him time, and he will develop into male and female, fuck his little brains out, and produce a whole variety of life forms that will be a wonder to behold!!! Ain't "Life" grand?!!

Meanwhile, back on Planet Earth.., that intrepid "mad" scientist ("Iron Owl, *The Facetious"*); having put the sacramental cup to his lips and drunk the magic potion, he enters into that secret clandestine laboratory located within the depths of his own mind.., he adjusts the focal point of his mind microscope, penetrating into the microcosm, beyond the microbe, beyond the primordial ooze of the "pre-biotic soup", beyond matter itself!., down into the immeasurable realm of the "absolute" *Void!!,* and he finds; "Life"!!! He dances around in the laboratory of his mind, shouting: "It's Alive!, It's Alive!!"[10]... Lo and Behold!!, this mad scientist has penetrated into the absolute Void, and found "Life", and guess what?!..; *It's his own!!*

So.., this mad scientist has "stepped off" the realm of the material world, into the realm of the "absolute Void" and found himself to be of the nature of voidness\, being without substance, having neither center or circumference, nor could he even find, locate, or see himself, because there was absolutely "Nothing" to find, locate, or see!!, and yet he existed, and he knew that he was, because he could think.., *and ever so clearly!!*. In an instant he had comprehended the incomprehensible, and he looked out into the Void, and he could see forever and forever, and he asked; "Why"??, and the Void Itself answered back.., and said: *"Why not"??!...*

Now.., there are some things that are not comprehensible to the mundane mind! For instance; "death"... We think we understand death, but the state of "non-being" cannot really be imagined!.. Likewise, a multidimensional universe.., we understand the meaning of the words, but the concept is so far removed from conception, that it isn't even considered... And likewise, states of mind; the optimist cannot comprehend morbid

---

[10] Still being facetious here; this is a parody of the fictional character: "Dr. Frankenstein"...

depression, nor can the morbidly depressed comprehend optimism, etc... Likewise again, the mystical state of expanded consciousness, brought on by a powerful sacrament of the psychedelic class (LSD, Mushrooms, etc.)... This defies all efforts of the imagination to comprehend, and even though you be a religious leader of the "fire and brimstone" school, and fervent in your beliefs, falling prostrate on your face, this advanced mystical state will elude you!.. Words fail to convey.., and what you do not understand, you will condemn!.. Even though the experience is within their grasp, they prefer to condemn!??... And likewise again.., the "Void"... Absolute nothingness cannot be comprehended.., unless you have been there!..

This mad scientist, having set foot (figuratively speaking) in the absolute Void.., several things became immediately evident!.. First of all.., the erroneous concept of the "Time-Space Continuum", as though "time" and "space" were inextricably linked!!. They are not... The correct terminology would be; the "lightspeed-distance-time factor".., as it (light) proceeds unimpeded through the "Timeless Space Continuum"... So "space" (being absolute nothingness), cannot be touched by either light or time!!, and is absolutely inert and without characteristics... Words betray us here... "Time" belongs to matter, as it goes through changes, etc., but the "Void" (space) is changeless, timeless, and always and forever, the ever present and eternal "Now"!..

Having been at the crux of the ever present and eternal "Now" (you can't really be anywhere else), a second observation became immediately apparent, and that is the erroneous concept of "time travel"... There is no such thing as going "back in time", or "forward in time"!!. It is always "Now" time, and "Now" cannot go forward or backward!!. The concept of time travel makes for great science fiction, but it will always be just that; fiction... You may mess with, bend, and distort light waves and magnetic fields, etc., and etc.., but it is just "a tempest in a teacup" anomaly, with no relevance to the ever present and eternal "Now"!!. You may enter this into the journals of science as an "absolute" axiom: "There is no time travel"...

And a third observation!.. The ultimate achievement of the scientifically intellectual mind!., for which there should be awarded some kind of a "Nobel Prize".., for the all-time ultimate "*Oxymoron*"... And that would be: "Worm holes through space"!!! When scientists think of "space" as "*something*" that can be bent, twisted, and holes bored through it.., it just illustrates how incomprehensible the voidness of space really is... Think about it!.; a hole.., through absolute nothingness!!. The ultimate absurdity...

Having peered into the Void with the "third eye" of insight, I made these three "intuitive" observations... But there is a fourth observation that I made after the fact, in retrospect, and I don't intend for this to be a "law", but only speculation in the realm of theoretical physics... The first law of thermodynamics states: that the "energy/mass" quantum remains constant, and cannot be created or destroyed... Fair enough.., but then I have to look out into the Universe, and I see *two hundred billion galaxies.., each containing a hundred billion stars, suns, planets, black holes, and etc.!!!???* That is just one hell of a lot of "energy/mass quantum" to just "be", for no apparent reason!!! If all of this energy/mass cannot be created, *from "whence" did it come???* Secular science has not even posed the question, let alone speculated on an answer!..

A clue to the answer may be found in the ancient documents of the Hindu religion that point to this one and only characteristic of the Void, and that is; *it's sound!!*. The Hindu's hold this sound *("OM"-mmmmmmmmm>>>", or "Aum")* to be sacred, because it always was, permeating the vastness of the absolute Void, emanating from no specific source, but everywhere present... It is through this sound that the Lord became aware, and knew that HE WAS, and *That* sound was with God, and *That* sound was God (sound familiar?), and through the articulation of this sound (frequency modulation) all things were created, and since the Void always was, and the "sound" always was, so too, God, always was!.. *This is very scientific*!.. This sound.., being a phenomenon of the absolute Void, is a self generating energy source that permeates space!!, and through an energy/matter conversion, "space dust" (or hydrogen gas) is a "fallout" byproduct of this perpetual frequency vibration.., a material condensation from the primordial first cause; the creative "Word/sound" of God!!! From out of nothing (the absolute Void).., came everything!!! The rest is HIStory...

But this is only speculation in the realm of theoretical astrophysics, which points to a convergence of the "physical" with the "metaphysical", which, of course (a foregone conclusion), there just has to be!!.

All of this leads us to a "fifth" scientific observation which by all rights should be logged into the journals of science as an "Absolute "LAW"... Laws should have names; so we will call this law the "Quintessential Law of the Primordial Quintessence"; that is to say: the discovery of the "first essence" of primordial "life"!.. (already, the "Men of Science" are retreating in terror)...

To even suggest that "God" should be entered into the journals of science as a scientific fact is anathema to everything they stand for (and a very unscientific attitude)!.. There are only two possibilities here: either God "is", or He "is not"!!. There could hardly be a more simple and clear cut problem for the scientific mind.., it is either "yes" or "no"... Either the "747" jet airliner was built meticulously according to a preconceived plan, or a whirlwind blew through the junkyard and "accidentally" constructed it... Without even exploring the "yes" possibility, science has presumed, assumed, and embarked on the "accidental" theory, which is not only unscientific, it is downright "Weird"!..

Having searched the primordial ooze, the hydrothermal vents, the glacial ice sheets, the robotic probes to distant planets, etc., and etc., science has failed to find the "recipe" that will "cook" life into being!.. The reason that science has failed is that they have overlooked the first fundamental rule of science, which is: *If you want to find the precursor life form, you have to look where the precursor life form lives!!,* and that would be in the "Fifth Dimensional Realm" of the "Cosmic Mind" (a.k.a., the absolute Void)...

I know this sounds pretentious, But I (Iron Owl, the mad scientist) have succeeded in finding the "precursor" Life Essence, (The Primordial Quintessence), and I tell you this for a fact: HE is alive and well, in the Realm of "Fifth Dimensional Reality" (The Cosmic Mind)... Moreover, I have (superficially) explored the multidimensional levels of this inner realm, and I found an abundance of life forms; animal, vegetable, and Human-like, possessing intelligence and beauty, in cities, that exist on worlds, with mountains and oceans, etc., and etc., *and they all pre-date life on Earth!!.*

It is written; (Jn.20:29) *"More blessed are those who have not seen, yet believed"*... Well.., I cannot claim to be that blessed!!, nor do I even believe in *belief* (for the one-thousand and one[th] time).., nor can I even say that I have seen (The "Formless" form of God).., but I have heard his voice, and we have had conversation.., in the same manner as Abraham, Isaac, and Jacob.., and I am beyond any form of belief!.. I am among the lesser blessed; ***I Know!!.***

I have documented my findings (my first hand experiences) throughout this book, and I have presented my arguments against the "flat earth" intuitively deprived (*Third Eye Blind*), and *shallow* mentality that promotes the "microbial and slime-mold origins" of a "life without meaning" (Godless) evolutionary theory.., and I advanced the counter (scientific and revolutionary) theory of "De-evolution" which explains the sorry state of health (and etc.) that we find ourselves in today...

But will the world of secular science acknowledge my findings??. What do you think?..

But does it really matter?.,(you ask).., because, after all; *we're here*! Whether created, evolved, dropped off by aliens, or shit on a rock and hatched by sunlight.., the end result is the same: *We're Here*!!! **Oh Yes**, *it matters!!!* It matters first of all because only one of the above scenarios is true.., and the rest are lies!.. It matters Historically, it matters Politically, it matters Religiously, it matters Philosophically, it matters Legally, it matters Culturally, it matters Scientifically, and it matters Fundamentally...

Books have been written.., battle lines have been drawn, and the field of battle is the Supreme Court of the U.S.., (as if the Supreme Court was even *capable* of ascertaining truth from lies)... **They are Not!!,** and they are legally bound (a "catch 22" conflict) to *Not* render a decision... But they have (nevertheless) rendered a decision with far reaching consequences... By an unfortunate, misquoted, misinterpreted, misguided, and mistaken misunderstanding of Thomas Jefferson's personal reference to: "the separation of Church and State", the Supreme Court, at the insistence of the secular *Religion*; "Atheism" (a belief system, *hence Religion),* has decided to ban any reference to "God" from every public courthouse, every state and governmental facility, every city and state park, every public school (*Oh where has Wisdom gone?*), our colleges and universities (*of Higher learning?*), the pledge of "allegiance" (*to God and Country*), on our currency ("*In God we Trust*").., etc., and etc.!, while promoting the "*Religion*" of the "Left", which advocates a secular "ignoring" (*ignorance*) of any **Knowledge** of anything having to do with the "*fact*" *of a "Higher Mind" intelligence (Where are you?, Rene Descartes),* while promoting the "abdication" of our faculty of discrimination, to the point where the line between good and bad, right and wrong, gets blurred, and the vocation to military service is banned from campus, and "abominations" (the sodomites) are actually recruited (Harvard, Berkley, etc.) as an "on campus" activity!!.

Thomas Jefferson would turn over in his grave!!, as would Abraham Lincoln, as would all the signers of the Constitution and the Declaration of Independence (our founding Fathers), and George Washington (the "Father" of our country"), etc., and etc... The very "antithesis" of Thomas Jefferson's intentions has been implemented!!! His obvious intention was that government should in "no way" interfere with the "Freedom of Religion" and Religious expression.., but the Supreme Court, at the behest of the "Supreme Assholes" (the **"Religions"** of Atheism, Humanism, and perversion), has "perverted" the intention to imply that expressions of Religious freedom should in "no way" interfere with (and should be "banned") from the workings of an Atheistic, Humanistic, and pro perversion Government!!! *It has become illegal to stand on the courthouse steps and say: "God Bless America" !!!*

Now .., I really don't like to quote the Bible, especially out of context, symbolically, paraphrased, and freely (loosely) interpreted.., because I am *Not* a Biblical scholar, and this is sure to "piss off" everybody; (Left, Right, and Center) (I never pass up an opportunity, *ha ha*)... (Mk.13:14): *"When you see the "Abomination that causes desolation"* (Atheism, Humanism, perversion) *standing where it does not belong—-* (replacing "God" at the "center" of human concerns)—-*let the reader understand—-it's time to get out of town"!!!...* So this "Abomination" (a.k.a. "perversion") not only decimates the body (Aids, etc,) but also perverts and destroys the "Soul", **and it is contagious!!!...** *"So don't look back, forget your coat and possessions, just grab your family and get out of town"...*

So.., In the final analysis, the Supreme Court has elevated one religion above all others (which is unconstitutional and illegal).., and that is the Religion (*belief system*) of "Secular Humanism"... So it is incumbent upon the Supreme Court to see the error of it's ways and decide if this be "One Nation Under God" ***(a generic term, used in the generic sense).., or Not!!,*** and if the Constitution is not a perfect document (a human creation to which 10 amendments[11] have already been made).., **FIX IT!!!... The fact that this really is "One Nation Under God" is the only real "edge" that we have as a World Power...**

So.., in the final analysis.., the "Truth" is the truth, and Science and Religion are *Not* at odds with each other... "Belief" has absolutely nothing to do with anything!.. You can believe in "Santa Clause and eight tiny reindeer" with all your heart, and that doesn't make it true.., or you could disbelieve in gravity,.. or traffic lights and street signs, and suffer the consequences... But the point here is that "God" (The Primordial Quintessence) is a Scientific fact of "Life", as is the reality of a Multi-dimensional Universe (the Fifth Dimension), and the "Clear Light of the Ultimate Reality" (the Cosmic Mind).., *outside of and beyond Religion*!!.

But will the world of secular science acknowledge my findings??. What do you think?..

Post-Script. ... Alack and alas!! I had intended to end this scientific discussion here, at this point.., but I find that I cannot!!! There is one other "scientific fact" that I am obligated to present to the world of science, and I do this out of a sense of **"Duty"**, with great reluctance and foreboding!.. When a scientist presents his findings to his contemporaries, he is often subjected to ridicule and derision, especially if it be a "ground-breaking" pronouncement that cannot be readily substantiated by quantitative analysis... But nevertheless.., and knowing full well the consequences of my actions (the loss of credibility of everything that I have presented here), I am bound by duty to present my findings to the scientific community (from which I will probably be "excommunicated")...

….In the course of my research.., into the Realm of "Fifth Dimensional Reality", I encountered an ***"Entity"*** that was the (literal) *"Personification of Evil"*... He is "real" in the literal and scientific sense, he is immortal, and he is "Evil"...

I know it to be an extremely rare occurrence that anyone would "see" this "entity", and I know of no other person besides myself that has seen him, so the terrible burden of this "exposé" falls to me!.. It is a terrible burden, because I am obligated to tell

---

[11] Correction:.. Actually, (if my information is correct) there has been at least 27 amendments to the Constitution!..

the tale, and very few will believe it!., although there is an abundance of recorded testimony regarding his existence...

He is known by many names; the Devil; Satan; etc.., and I know that it seems like a "Star Wars" science fiction melodrama, of the Supremely Good Vs. the Diabolically Evil.., but "Truth" is even stranger than fiction, and the "war" rages on... The field of battle is the planet "Earth", and the prize to be won or lost.., is the Souls of Mankind... It is the "Epic Struggle" to be recorded in the annals of the "Akashic Records", the memory bank of the Cosmic Mind, and your name will be entered, and your story will be told... It is the "Army of Light" Vs. the "Army of Darkness", and recruitment is underway... Will you be the "Hero" of your life?., or will you be the "Asshole"??. Choose now, to which side you belong, and whom you will serve...

So, I have encountered this "entity" on three separate occasions[12], and I have recorded the circumstances of each encounter and his physical description (which may or may not be relevant due to his ability of "morphing" his appearance) but one thing is certain.., and that is that he is the preeminent "Flaming Faggot" of all time!.. His essential nature is perversion, his method of recruitment is seduction, he seeks to pervert the nature of Mankind, and his army of perverts is on a recruitment drive, by seduction, propaganda, pedophilia, drug rape, lies, and etc... He is the father of lies, deceit and deception, and his articulate cleverness is legendary; don't underestimate him!.. His unwitting allies are the "Secular Humanists", and the "Atheists", who say in their heart of hearts, that; "There is no God", and that good and evil are "relative" viewpoints, perversion is "just another lifestyle", "Life" is an accidental event of no meaning or purpose, and if it feels good; do it.., because there is no "hereafter"., etc., and etc...

Of course I will be ridiculed and laughed at, and I will be accused of everything from homophobia to a hate crime.., and ordinarily my response would be to laugh back, and see who has the last laugh.., but I cannot laugh at criminal stupidity and tragedy in the making... All that I can do is to give a "fair witness" first hand report of my findings...

---

[12] The first encounter: chapter 1, "The Iron Owl Experience"... The second encounter..: (ear whispered lies), also chapter 1... Third encounter (chapter 13) "Incident in Singapore"...

So, I.., Iron Owl, "the **Mad** Scientist".., have walked through the corridors of Hell, and it left a scar on my soul.., and I have personally seen the Evil one.., **and he is a butt-fucking faggot..,** "perversion personified".., and that is the absolute "Truth" (and you can take this to the "bank"), and it is my testimonial; *outside of and beyond the parameters of Religion...* **"Evil exists"** as a scientific fact.., perhaps not as a molecular biological fact, but as a "psychologically malevolent" fact.., and it is a force to be reckoned with...

So I caution you.., if you should enter into the Realm of Fifth Dimensional Reality, and approach the "Clear Light of the Ultimate Reality", you may encounter this "Enemy", who will seek to prevent your entry!..

But will the world of secular science acknowledge my findings?.. What do you think??.

* * *

So.., just what is the "scope" of this book??.

"To solve the riddle of the Universe"!!, "To see the scheme entire"!!, and to bring it all together into one comprehensive whole within the pages of this book!!??.., into the ultimate "Compendium of Knowledge"!!??... Ha ha ha, ho ho ho, (I have to laugh at myself)!!...

No.., the scope is too great.., the ability of this author is too small.., there aren't enough pages in this book.., **But.., I have seen!.,** I have seen the skeletal framework (the *Matrix/Paradigm*) of the process whereby the "Compendium of Knowledge".., ***All Knowledge*** (a.k.a. **"Enlightenment"**).., *can be Known!!,* and I have likened this skeletal framework to a spiders web, in which all of the "spokes" of the web are the various fields of knowledge (the Sciences), *All* having their source at the "God-Head" (the center of the web), and the cross hairs represent the "correspondences" between the sciences (the mathematical equivalents, etc.) which exhibit themselves as relationships...

As "Energy" is to light.., and as light in its various frequencies is transformed into laser-beams, x-rays, radio signals, electricity, sound, color, heat, MASS, and etc.., and as mass begets gravity, polarity, magnetism, and the four constituents of matter: Earth, Wind, Fire, and Water (a.k.a.: solids, gasses, heat (temperature), and liquids).., and "Ether" (devoid of matter; a.k.a.: "space", *between planets, atoms and electrons*)... And as light begets sight, and sound begets hearing, which begets cognition, which begets the *Knower,* which begets philosophy, psychology, religion, *etc., etc., and etc...* Each and every branch of Science and Knowledge radiates from, and has it's source at the Center of the web, and the Center of the web is **"The First Cause"**.., and that "First Cause": **"IS"**... And HE Knows about it all.., *HE Knows*.., He Knows !!!...

Each and every "branch" of Science and Knowledge (in this Matrix/Paradigm) lies next to its "sister Science", and is related by the correspondences, all the way around the web... In short; "Everything relates to Everything"!!... In modern day terminology, this is referred to as; the "Unified Field" theory... This "Unified Field" is indeed the reality!., but it will remain just a theory until the "Mind/ Imagination/Creation" Metaphysics of the Fifth Dimension are incorporated into the totality of Science, without which it is incomplete!!...

Our approach to knowledge (scholastically) is to learn from the "bottom up".., to perceive the apparent, the form, and to investigate what makes the form "tick", and to what use can the form be put... Probing deeper into the form (the particular field of Science), we climb up the web, discovering the cause/effect sequence of events that produced the form... Theoretically, it should be possible to follow this cause/effect sequence of events all the way back to its first emanation at the Center of the web.., but there is a limit to secular understanding... *The "Ego" is not welcome here!!.* No matter how religious you are, the Ego is not welcome here... What is required here is the "Zen" state of absorption.., the "Pure Soul", in "rapt" contemplation!!. The key word here is "absorption".., into the "First Cause".., and "All Knowledge".., becomes Known...

Did you want to know where "Genius" lies??. It lies at the "Center" of the Web.., and all Knowledge becomes Known.., from the "top down", from the "inside out", from the Metaphysical "First Cause" to the final conclusion.., and all the relationships are seen.., and anything that doesn't relate is an error.., or a lie...

All concepts fall short!.. Words fail to convey... **This "Event".,** *is the summation and conclusion of all religion!!...* This is "Enlightenment".., this is the "Ecstatic Union with the Divine".., This is the "Rapture".., this is *Absorption* into the "Clear Light of the Ultimate Reality".., and this is the "Death and Rebirth".., of which the **"Crucifixion and Resurrection"**.., *was a symbolic representation*.., acted out on the stage of Life!!.

Did you think that Heaven was merely a *"place"*??. Far more than that.., *it is a state of Being*!!. This "Event" marks the transition of the Soul born in ignorance.., into the "New Man".., the Enlightened and Immortal Being.., a resident of the "New Heaven" and the "New Earth", *a Champion*.., able to traverse the seven planes of existence...

This.., *is the scope of this book!..*

* * * * *

So.., just what are the "Limitations" in this book??? Well.., the limitations of this book are many.., beginning with the fact that I, as an author.., don't know how to write a book!!. Some people have a natural talent.., I don't!.. Nor do I have the discipline! I have only tenacity.., and a message... I have been writing this book for over *five years* now, and I am still not done!.. This threatens to be the "never-ending" book, because there is always another chapter to write.., and not enough room...

About half way through this book I thought it prudent to read a book about "How to write a book", and sure enough, I did everything wrong!.. You are supposed to "organize" your book by subject headings (chapters) then outline your main topics, then sub topics, etc, summation and conclusion at the end!!., and it emphasized creativity, discipline, etc... Well.., (Such a Joke!), there is no creativity to this book, let alone organization or discipline!., or even continuity!!. First of all, each chapter of this book is an individual entity, or you might say; a book unto itself.., written without regard to any other chapter, and not in a sequential order, as a result of which there are "overlapping themes" (or as some might say: "redundancy"!)... But I justify this because *"It is better to read a good book twice, than to read a multitude of books just once"*.., so, although I repeat myself, it is the same theme (Truth) in a different context and approached from a different angle, thereby proving the axiom!., and it would be a waste if you were to read a "Truth" just once, never proving the axiom.., and never thinking about it again!.. That would be more than just a waste!., that would be a tragedy...

And there is no "creativity" to this book!.. I do *Not* read fiction, and I do *Not* write fiction... This is a book "first and foremost", of *Experiences,* and I relate these experiences to the reader as faithfully as I can, without exaggeration, distortion, or embroidery.., and I am bound by Solemn oath to do this, even though it sometimes portrays me in a bad light, such often being the case... The "experiences" are, for the most part, "out of the ordinary".., and they raise questions; sometimes Religious, sometimes philosophical, sometimes scientific, sometimes political, or ethical, or moral, or legal, etc.., challenging the "status quo" of the way things are, or commonly perceived, but always searching for the "Truth", and not from a relative viewpoint, but from the "Absolute" viewpoint...

So the "organization" of this book is "after the fact", as the chapters (books), written in a non-sequential order, have been shuffled into a semblance of sequential order, and not even that, as what would normally be the first chapter is located at the end, and "this" that I am writing at the moment would probably be more fitting at the introduction, but is well past the middle.., and the summation and conclusion (the attempt to bring it all together into a comprehensive whole) is the purpose of "This" chapter (instead of the last chapter).., and the "organizational outline" (the "Contents"), were put together totally "after the fact"!!!

Add to that the fact that there is no "Editor" involved in the production of this book (probably a mistake)... No "Research Department"!., hence, the bulk of my time is wasted trying to find the reference sources to the facts that I present [13] (I try.., but in which one of the thousand books and documentaries did I glean this or that particular fact)???... No collaboration with an outside source (no feedback)... No "proof-reader" (but my spell-checker is *"smokin'")..,* and (at this point).., No Publisher!!! If this book ever reaches print, we will all be amazed!!!

And I have tried to make this book "timeless" by not identifying with any specific time period, but in the five or six years that I have been writing this book, the world has changed.., and faster than I can keep up with it!!. For instance; all the television documentaries stated that the history of "Human" man (no relation to the Neanderthals) went back about 200,000 years!., and then (without fanfare or announcement) the latest documentaries revised their estimates to 100,000 years.., so I revised my writing to reflect the new estimate.., and then the latest documentary claimed to have found remains (with tools and beadwork) that dated to 120,000 years!!. I didn't revise again... And within the last five or six years of breakthrough scientific discoveries, the "Human Genome" has been mapped, as well as the "Tree of Life" genetic codes of all life forms (plants, animals, insects, bacteria, etc.), as well as our understanding of "Deep Space", and the events of Sept.11th, etc., and etc.., so like it or not, I am stuck in this "time slot"...

Also.., I have also tried to be "Universal" and non-Nationalistic in my approach to the multi-ethnic and multi-cultural peoples of my World-wide audience.., but the fact is, that you have to be from *somewhere..,* and I happen to be an American, from the U.S. of A..., and that is not a bad place to be from, as it represents a multi-ethnic, multi-culture, collection of peoples, and the problems and politics of this nation are at (or near) the forefront of what is happening to the World wide community of Nations, in general.., and in fact "mirrors" these problems to the World wide community of Nations, who, if these problems have not already presented themselves in Your particular Country.., they soon will!.. So.., my message here.., is intended for the World wide audience…

And I have attempted to be very thrifty with my words, to confine myself to the essence of the subject, when my inclination was to elaborate profusely.., and I have "held my tongue" when my inclination was to diverge into several "related" tangents (everything relates)., etc., and etc... These are the limitations…

*   *   *

So.., is this a book of the Mind??... Yes.., This is preeminently a book of the mind.., but it is primarily a book of the Soul!!... Patanjali (the Father of the Yoga system) describes mind as the "organ" of the Soul.., and we will deal with the subject of mind in this context...

---

[13] The reader may have noticed those "asterisks" (*) that occasionally appear throughout this book, signaling a "footnote" that I had intended to include, corroborating a point that I have made.., but to which I was unable to find the "source" of just where such footnote may be found… Perhaps in a second edition.?..

The dictionary definition for "Mind" is: (a) that which thinks, perceives, feels, wills, remembers, and especially reasons... (b) the seat of consciousness... (c) the thinking and perceiving part of consciousness; intellect or intelligence... (d) all of an individuals conscious experiences... (e) the conscious and unconscious together as a unit; psyche... (f) etc., and etc., (on and on!)... Or, as a verb: (a) to remember (b) to attend to closely (c) heed, obey (d) to be concerned about; dislike (e) to be careful, or cautious (f) to take charge of (g) to regard with attention (h) etc., and etc... **Or in Philosophy;** *consciousness is an element in reality..,* contrasted with *"Matter"*...

This is interesting!.. "String theorists" (for example), searching for the most minute building blocks of matter, have dissected the atom (in theory) down to the 11th diminutive power (what they call; "the 11th dimension").., but what is the substance of a thought??... Of what does the imagination consist??... You would think that somewhere down in the 11th dimension there would be a convergence that would explain the whole mystery of matter AND mind.., but then they would be confronted with "The First Thinker".., because after you run out of diminutive powers *(or be locked forever into Zeno's paradox)*, you are confronted with: "The Absolute Void"... Ha Ha Ha!!! (I crack myself up!)!!. *String theorists won't go there!.,* because then they would be confronted with the "Missing Link" between the absence of matter and their "Strings" which would violate the first "Law" of Thermo-dynamics and point to: *(dare I say it?)* **"Creation"!!...** With their "String theory", their massive calculations claim to bridge the gap, and "marry" Quantum Mechanics, Astrophysics, "sub-sub-sub atomics", *and everything else..,* with speculations that go into "parallel universes" ("M" theory), "time travel", etc. and etc.., with no hope *ever* of any experiential confirmation, *ever!.,* and never once do they "marry" any of this to the subject of "Mind", because their endless mathematics cannot bridge the gap *(the "Missing Link")* between the material and the "Spiritual"...

And just what kind of "sound" would this pure energy "string" utter???.., or does the sound.., utter the string??? *AUM-mmmmmmmmmmmmmmm* ... Or, perhaps, *THAT* original Primordial Sound.., *is laughter!!!...* (Ha Ha Ha, and Ho Ho Ho!!.)... But science has (very recently), while looking for the "mysterious force" ("dark matter"?) responsible for the expanding *and accelerating* Universe (that should have *mathematically* been slowing down by now?), has postulated a new theory that they call "Vacuum Energy".., that is; energy *(the primordial sound?)* generated by the vacuum (Void) of space, and the consequent energy/matter conversion and subsequent "fallout" of "space dust" (or energy *"strings"*?) that explains (**"the Iron Owl theory"**) the creation of the Universe!.,.., which can be shown mathematically as: **(0 = (+1)+(-1)), or in other words, out of Absolutely Nothing.., came everything!!!** [14] Which begs the next question: "If a *tree* falls in the Universe, and "No One" hears it.., does it really make a sound?"..??? Well.., apparently (according to the most Ancient Hindu Scriptures), some **"ONE"** did hear it!., which is reiterated (in the New Testament Scriptures) as: "In the beginning was the "Word" (the primordial sound), and the "Word" was *with* God (subjective mode), and the "Word" *was* God" (objective mode)…

What we have here is a *consensus and a convergence,* between the Ancient Hindu Scriptures, Buddhist doctrine, the New Testament Scriptures, Modern Science, and "Mind" Science (the subjective and objective modes of the Primordial Consciousness)… *...And they said it couldn't be done!?!!...*

So what we are looking at here.., is the pre-existing "because" condition (actually, the "Be"-cause) of the *Void produced* "Primordial Energy Emanation" which was both **"heard and identified with"** by; *"Thee* Super-Cognizant Intelligence" that had the *presence of mind* to say: **"I Am"** (subjective mode), and further: **"I Am "THAT""** (objective mode)… And!.; it is not out of place to say here (again) that since the Void always "Was" (the pre-existing condition), the Primordial Emanation that was a consequence of the Void that always was, and the Primordial Sole (Soul) Conscious "Awareness" (a.k.a. **"GOD"**), also, "always was"…

---

[14] The Buddhist doctrine of "Shunyata", that is to say; *"Emptiness"* , is one of the most esoteric and non-conceptual of doctrines, and must therefore be experienced to be comprehended… It is symbolized by the "Diamond" (Vajra), because of it's adamantine, transparent, and indestructible quality, and it stands for "the seeing of the True Reality".., which is "Emptiness"… All things come into being from this Absolute Emptiness (the Void), and all things are therefore (essentially) emptiness… …How interesting.., that this ancient Buddhist doctrine finds it's parallel in the modern day speculations of cutting-edge Science…

So there you have it, folks.., The "Holy Grail" of both Science and Religion!!.., namely; "the "First Cause" (*way* before the "Big Bang"), and the "proof" of all of this is the manifested Universe, and Cognizant Consciousness!.. But what may be the "obscuring factor" here, is that in our multi-dimensional universe, these events may be a product of the "Fifth Dimension" prior to their "Fourth Dimensional" appearance…

But still, Science has not bridged the gap (nor do they try) between matter and "Mind"!.. They are still looking for the "formula" for simple "Life"!.,; (x+y+z = "L").., and therefore; "Life" with consciousness would have to be: (***"w"*** +x+y+z = "LC"), and of course, "Cognitive Consciousness" would have to be: (***"uvw"*** +x+y+z = "LCC")!.. The theory being; the more complex the "Life-form", the more sophisticated the "mind functions"… But ***"Not So.., not so"!.,*** says that Ancient mind scientist; "Patanjali" (the father of the Yoga system).., because: **(and here we come to the "Crux" of the matter.., and the most important and salient point of this discussion and of this book!)..,** because: what the "flat earth" scientists are talking about, and concerned with here is "Brain Mind".., and for all their seemingly educated brilliance, they are functioning from a place of ***"Diminished Capacity",*** and talking to an audience of their peers who are also functioning from that same place of ***"Diminished Capacity"***, and all of the "Bible thumping" preachers are preaching their gospels and etc. from that same self-righteous (but well meaning) place of ***"Diminished Capacity"***, to like-minded congregations of ***"Diminished Capacity"..,*** and the World is enmeshed in wars of nonsense, because we are all functioning from the same place of ***"Diminished Capacity"***, and science is engaged in exploring the "flat earth" Universe with Bodily manned and technically advanced "mechanical" space ships (vehicles), which are all products of the "Brain Mind", while being totally ignorant of the ***"Diminished Capacity"*** from which they (and "we") are functioning!..

So.., take a moment and reflect on the implications of the above paragraph…

But Mankind.., has the potential.., and the promise.., of transcending the "brain-mind" into the "vehicle" of the "Soul-Mind" that knows no barriers of Time or Space, no "Ego" limitations, no Physical limitations, no Light-Speed limitations, no Distance limitations, capable of comprehending, *and experiencing* the Universe and the Atom, and to "Know" his Creator.., and HIS creation… Words fail to convey.., mathematics cannot compute.., and *all* that I have said here.., *is an under-statement!!.*

So.., leaving the realms of Meta-Physics, Astrophysics, Mathematics, Mental Acrobatics, and etc.., and coming back down to the plane of the usable and the workable aspects of what we have learned about the mind.., I would like to think that this book is more than simply a "Book of the Mind", but is in fact a "Handbook of the mind" in that it's information is utilizable and practical…

So "Mind", is one of those multi-ordinal terms.., with a multitude of meanings.., lacking tangible substance… And how do you differentiate between the Mind, the Emotions, the Ego, and the Soul?., and what is the Super-conscious, the Conscious, the Sub-conscious, the unconscious, etc., and etc.??...

Here we are faced with an Enigma!.. A mystery contained in a riddle, contained in a paradox... We are dealing with intangibles, that can only be described inadequately, *by the variegated cloak* of words!!. For instance, the subject of "Space", which, by definition is "Void" of substance, but the word; "Space" is used as a Noun (designating; person, place, or thing)!!. The mind is simply not capable of conceiving of *"Absolutely Nothing",* so we refer to "Space" as "something", and we go even further **in this error** with phrases like: "the *fabric* of space".., and "time-space", etc.!. *This is the Axiom: There is no "Fabric" to space!!, nor is there "Time"...* Both "Space" and the "Void" are absolutely inert and without characteristics.., and can only be described in negative terms: ("It is Not this, It is Not that") (*neti neti*)!!... Even the statement; "It is Not", is a contradiction in terms.., so you see the paradoxical nature of this subject and the "word-trap quagmire" that leads to the complete mis-perception and obscuration of the "Essence"...

I mention this "word-trap quagmire" because it is a phenomena that is responsible for some of the greatest misconceptions and misunderstandings in history, resulting in doctrinal splits within religions, (the Mahayana vs. the Theravada schools of Buddhism).., thousands of books devoted to explaining the "true meanings" of these paradoxical subjects (Zen, and the concept of "no-mind", for instance).., and even wars!, (Buddhism was wiped out in India *(the land of it's birth)* due to the misconceptions relating to God and the Soul)!!. There are panels of judges and batteries of lawyers (for instance), lined up to debate both sides of every sentence in a straight-forward document, like the Constitution of the U.S.!!!...

The question here is: can I supply some kind of an overview that will clarify and dispel this quagmire, or will I *(like everyone else)* simply add to it by trying to explain it??.

Let's start with a subject that I have first hand knowledge and experience of, and that I have "seen clearly" *(Already a paradoxical statement)*; and that is the subject of the "Soul" (which Christianity affirms and Buddhism negates)... I have already documented my "Soul search" into the realm of "Fifth Dimensional Reality" *(another paradox)*, and found "Myself" (the Soul) to be utterly vacuous and transparent, consisting of absolutely "Nothing", totally void of substance, without center or circumference, and I could not even find or locate my "Self".., and yet "I was"!!. So how can I say I have "seen clearly" when there was "absolutely nothing" to see??... (hence the paradoxical statement)... How can I say that the Soul exists, when there is absolutely nothing tangible, no center, no circumference, absolutely void, and cannot be found??? (Hence the Buddhist viewpoint)... And yet, "I was"... It seems that the Buddhists could have benefited from Rene Descartes observation of: "I think, therefore I am"...

But if this was the heart of the paradox, the Buddhists would have seen through it!!. No.., this is just the beginning of the problem, because the real paradox lies in the "Zen" nature of the mind.., and you have to solve the Zen riddle before you can see into the heart of the paradox, and you have to see into the nature of mind before you can solve the riddle (around and around!)... A thousand books have been written purporting to explain what "Zen" is, resulting in highly complex and abstract suppositions (that go round and around!), making the complex; impenetrable and unattainable!!. The more diligently you seek it, the more impenetrable it becomes.., hence, the Zen riddle!!...

Some of the most sophisticated, educated, abstract, brilliant and dedicated thinkers, have sought the solution to the Zen riddle, and came away befuddled!!. But I (Iron Owl, the "Intrepid Riddle Solver")(*ha ha*) have succeeded where they have failed!.. Why?., because I am unsophisticated, rudimentarily educated, non intellectual, and simple minded!!! *You have to appreciate the truly ironic "Zen" nature of this!...* But what is important here, is that **I can communicate it!..**

If there is a "Crowning Achievement" to this book, it is in the fact that I have identified **(named)** the Zen state of mind, as being synonymous with the "Objective" state of mind!!. I have identified the "*dual nature*" of the Soul, as it "shifts" back and forth between the Objective and Subjective modes of functioning (called: "the Siva-Sakti *shift*")... No wonder they couldn't find it!., it is so simple as to be anti-climactic!!, and yet the confusion has prevailed for (literally) *millennia*!...

The "Subjective" mode is the "self aware" mode, identified as the Ego-consciousness, subject to the vicissitudes of pleasure-pain, gain-loss, pride-shame, avarice, lust, anger, etc., and etc. (easily identifiable)... But the Zen-objective mode is characterized by the complete and total loss of self identity, as the consciousness is *temporarily absorbed* ("shifted") into the subject (or object) of it's contemplation.., to the *complete exclusion* of any of the vicissitudes associated with "self" awareness, and the process (the "shift") is completely automatic, undetectable, and effortless!.. Any "effort" to consciously make this "shift" is (by it's very nature) self defeating, and you will *never* be conscious of being in this Zen-objective state, and *you can only be aware of it **in retrospect***... To try to describe this state (to the neophyte) is to use the words: selfless, ego-less, timeless, emotionless, the "natural" state, the state of "no mind", spontaneous, etc., and etc.., all of which creates (in the mind of the neophyte) a "supernatural" advanced state of being that becomes a goal to be achieved, and any effort towards this achievement is totally counter-productive (the paradox)!.., and yet, this "Zen-objective" state truly is an advanced state, characterized by "spontaneous naturalness" that is truly "selfless", and if there are any characteristic by which this state can be identified, they are; *empathy and compassion*...

It remains for the neophyte to contemplate what I have written here and in a previous chapter (chapter 9) and experience for himself these two modes of consciousness, recognizing the difference... This perception and recognition of the dual states of Objectivity and Subjectivity constitutes the knowledge of the Zen state, and it is the beginning (for you) of higher states of meditation!!, and it is *my* "Crowning Achievement" to communicate this knowledge to you...

A further observation in this "Book of the Mind" is to recognize the three states of mind which are; the "Zen-objective", (already explained), the "positive-subjective", and the "negative subjective".., which are pretty much self-explanatory, and were gone into to great length (chapter 8) under the subject heading of; "The Training of the Mind", which is a subject that everyone can benefit from, and can even bring people out of the mental agony of *repetitive* negative-subjective states (sadness, bitterness, anger, etc.) into functional normalcy, releasing them from depression and even from mental institutions!..., into the functional normalcy of the positive-subjective state (an attitude of good will and gladness), with the natural ability to "shift" back and forth between the Zen-objective mode (of scientific enquiry) and the positive-subjective...

Just the ability to observe, recognize, and *"NAME"* these states of mind gives you a certain power over them, and the **"method"** of the training is a priceless gift of knowledge that was given to me, and I give it to you...

We have identified the negative-subjective state of (Ego-consciousness) as a detrimental state (sadness, bitterness, anger, etc.), and a precursor of disease in the body!, and we have to identify it's *causes and effects*... The primary cause is the **Ego**, and the effects of Ego are; "self aggrandizement" (pride, covetousness, lust, anger, greed, envy, and sloth) resulting in **"GUILT"**, which will *"lock you in"* to a downward spiral, resulting in a "wounded Ego" (*the strongest Ego state*), which just amplifies the negativity spiral, *resulting in your physical, mental, and spiritual demise!!*, **Or..,** you could see into the error of the whole Ego generated negativity spiral, naming it, *and abandoning it!!!...* This is equivalent to being "Born Again"!!.

In this; "book of the mind", the "Born Again" experience is of fundamental and primary importance!.. It is a turn around in your life from the secular, "Flat Earth", ego centered, materialistic and Godless mentality, with yourself as victim and victimizer.., into the realization that you are a Spiritual Being with a Spiritual heritage, and a limited time on this Earth, and the potential to be a force for good, and the focus of your life turns outward away from "yourself" as the victim, to the "Selfless" Zen-objective state of compassionate benevolence... Welcome.., to the Kingdom of God!!. *(Jn. 3:3)...* Halleluiah!!.

I have searched the religions of the world, looking for the parallels of experience and knowledge that signify a "Universal Truth".., and here I found a parallel in the concept of Zen enlightenment, and the Christian "Born Again" experience... But where the Zen breakthrough relies on an intellectual apprehension (an "Aha"!!!), and the subsequent meditational exercises to implement it.., the Christian experiences a gut-level catharsis that is a life changing event!., with no knowledge of the intellectual concepts of objectivity and subjectivity that comprise the "Aha" of the Zen breakthrough!..

Having experienced both the Zen "Aha", and the Christian catharsis, it is the "Crowning Achievement" of this book to bring about a convergence to where "East meets West", to the benefit and understanding of both cultures... The West can benefit from the Objective-Subjective understanding of the selfless Zen state, and the East can benefit from the emotional catharsis that solidifies and amplifies this breakthrough... *However..,* having seen the parallels that converge into a Universal Truth.., there are also exposed those elements of doctrine that conflict.., thereby exposing doctrinal errors.., that have to be addressed!..

These "Doctrinal Errors" are brought about by the "variegated cloak of words" that lead to misunderstandings, resulting in erroneous concepts that become unattainable paradoxes!.. For instance; the Buddhists understand the term; "selfless" to mean (literally) no self!.; hence; no soul!.. Their concept of Zen enlightenment is the attainment of total and perpetual Zen-Objectivity without any recourse to Subjectivity, *ever!!!* This is Yin, without Yang!!. This is Siva, without Sakti.., and this is an impossibility... The Christians (on the other hand) are *"blissfully ignorant"* of the whole concept of Objectivity-Subjectivity, Yin-Yang, Siva-Sakti, and etc., with no paradoxical riddles to be solved, and no controversies about no-Soul, or no-mind, etc.., **and no immersion into the contemplative-meditative state!!...**

So.., for this convergence of East and West to take place *(a truly "Crowning Achievement" if it happens!)* two things must happen!... **First**: (for the East) the Zen riddle must be resolved by the realization that the Zen-objective state is not a permanent state (of Yin without Yang), and that the "shift" between objectivity and subjectivity (Yin and Yang) is really **"perfect"** *as it is..,* and does not have to be modified, but only understood (Aha!)!!...

241

The realization is this:., that Yin and Yang are actually two different "modes" of just **"ONE Indivisible Unit"**.., which is identified as: *"Yourself"!!!* (a.k.a.: *"the Soul"*)!!!... And with the realization of the reality of the Soul, it is (by extrapolation) an obvious conclusion that **"THAT"** Primordial "First Cause" Consciousness (God) *IS* the Father of us all... The "Self" identity (the Soul) is therefore not to be *annihilated,* but it is to be **TRANSFORMED*!!!..,*** and this transformation is brought about at the gut-wrenching level of the emotions.., *the Subjective level..,* by the "Born Again" catharsis...

Second: (for the West).., it is *imperative* that the West become aware of the distinction between the "Zen-objective" state (*necessary* for abstract contemplation), and the "Ego-subjective" state (*incapable* of abstract contemplation)!.. The West is (for all intents and purposes) **ignorant..,** of the Art and Science of Meditation!.. Prayer, is man talking to God.., but does God ever talk back??. How would you know??. Do you ever just be still, *and listen??*... Meditation is the realm of **Communion** between God and man, but the *Ego-subjective* is not welcome here!., hence; the art and science of the "shift" to Zen-objectivity, which is **"absorption"** into the contemplative-meditative state.., and the doorway to the Fifth Dimension!!!... Welcome.., (again) to the Kingdom of God!!... *(Jn.3:3)...*

Next.., on our list of "Book of the Mind" breakthrough "Crowning Achievements", we come to the "Treatise on the Sub-conscious Mind"..., which I have identified (and "Named") as being the human "Animal consciousness", separate and distinct from our "Conscious" Human awareness, but subservient to it, like a dog (animal) is subservient to it's Master (Man)... With this knowledge of the "separate and distinct" nature of the sub-conscious mind, it is seen (to our great benefit) that this is an intelligent animal that is our faithful companion and helper, and can be trained in a variety of ways to support and assist our endeavors, be they in the category of habit patterns, work specialties, sport activities, or whatever!..

There are, of course, ***those things and practices*** that are detrimental to our well-being, and especially to the sub-conscious "animal" mind, which being separate and distinct from the Conscious mind (with it's own attitude and demeanor), colors our personality and is foundational to our feelings about ourselves and our attitude toward life... If the human animal is harmed, beaten, rejected, or defeated at the physical level, this defeated attitude colors our personality, effects our life, and may take some time to heal...

Although the perverted and the *"secularly naive"* may not see it this way, it is my "crowning achievement" to point out the fact that homosexuality (sodomy; a.k.a., *being fucked in the ass*) is the most degrading **(literally; demoted to the lesser grade sub-status of surrogate female)** experience of "defeat" that the sub-conscious animal mind has to contend with, and finds himself uncomfortable with, and ostracized from, the company of "Men"... He is forced to seek solace among his own kind, becoming "self conscious" to an uncomfortable degree (homophobic), which prompts him to obscene, bizarre, outrageous, and defiant behavior.., as he rages against the *feelings of rejection* that pervade his every waking moment!!!... He spends a great deal of time in the "negative-subjective" state of mind.., explaining, defending, justifying, rationalizing, and denying the self-conscious sub-status that he cannot help but feel...

If this was a malady of the Conscious mind, it could be dismissed and forgotten about, with no ill after effects, like changing from one political party to another.., but it is of the sub-conscious animal mind, that has been psychologically wounded, degraded, and rendered "submissive"... This is truly a crime against nature and against Man-kind.., ***and it is an abomination!!...*** The after effects are an exaggerated self-consciousness that manifests in limp-wristed and effeminate mannerisms, even the voice changes and becomes effeminate!.. His sexuality becomes very confused, and he seeks to cure his "submissive" inadequacy and wounded Ego by "dominating" another weaker individual (preferably pre-teen, early teen, and even children) by seduction, lies, and even rape.., and it becomes a "sick" game of domination and subjugation, and this malady of the mind and Soul will spread to another individual.., like a contagious disease.., ***as their numbers grow "exponentially"*** into a political force.., which is their unstated goal!!!... The "Queering" of America, and all of Man-kind.., is their goal...

I am a Patriot!!.., ***and we are at War!!...*** The biggest threat to this Nation and to Man-kind is not Communism, Socialism, Terrorism, or Whatever-ism, as much as it is this threat from within.., perpetrated by that Evil Genius himself, and masquerading under the benevolent banner of that

Religion of the Left, known as "Secular Humanism" which denies God, and pretends to be "gooder than God".., and gives free reign and equal rights to those hapless victims of perversion that spread their disease (and diseases)(*with impunity*) to the "secularly naïve", **with deliberate and "seditious" intent**!!... The "secularly naïve" are the unwitting Allies of this "Unholy Movement", but they have been deceived.., and their children will pay the price... **This Nation could fall!!,** like Greece and Rome fell.., like Sodom and Gomorra fell...

The "secularly naïve", with their liberal attitude, are **vulnerable** to the lies and seductions of the perverted (they will "suck you off", just to suck you in), and you will realize "too late" the true meaning of the term: "Homophobia", as you watch in horror.., as your wrists become limp and swishy, as your voice and manner becomes effeminate, and a torrent of unholy and perverted thoughts parade through your mind... "Too late", will you realize that you have been deceived, seduced, and fucked.., check-mated in the game of life!!... To apply the term; "homophobia" to someone that practices "wise discrimination" is a **deliberate lie!!..,** and those that have gone through this dreaded disorder of the mind (and been "turned") know this only too well.., and they sit silent in their shame... Those that have ears to hear.., let them hear: *Get out Now, while you still can... Eternity* depends on it!..

It may seem that I have devoted an excessive amount of time to this subject, but this is a book of the mind AND the Soul, and there is no other ***"disease"*** that attacks both mind and Soul with deliberate and "seditious" intent.., **and it is "Contagious"!!.** So I am obligated; I have no choice!!... Regardless of recriminations, I have to tell what I know!!: **I HAVE SEEN!!.,** (with the "third eye of insight") the "Evil One" himself, the one they call "Satan".., and he is a limp-wristed, butt-fucking, swishy, "faggot"!!... Perversion personified.., **and he is a reality!!...**

Now, this may seem like some sort of religious conviction.., **it is Not!!...** This discussion of the mind would not be complete without a discussion of those two diametrically opposed states of mind, known as the "Secular" and the "Religious" *(*a.k.a.: *Liberal and Conservative;., the Left and the Right;., etc.)*... Religion, without an *experiential* Spiritual confirmation is "Blind Belief"!!, and Secularism is "Blind Unbelief".., a "flat earth" mentality with *no hope of experiential Spiritual confirmation*... I stand at the center of these two opposing viewpoints.., and I find both of them repugnant, and in their extremes; terrifying and dangerous!!... Religion does (in general) abide by a moral code of ethics, (but I wouldn't want the "Ayatollah" dictating dress codes.., or Sharia law!), whereas the Secularists (by contrast) can rationalize **anything** (infanticide *(abortion)* and sodomy is o.k.., but outlaw the death penalty, the ten commandments, and any reference to God)!!... The point is; that the "Truth" (the fact) is independent, outside of, beyond, not beholding to, nor affected by either of these opposing "belief systems" (even "unbelief" is a belief system)... The "Truth" stands alone!!...

So.., When I say that "God" is a fact (the Truth), it is because I have had first-hand experienced of this: I have spoken to the Lord, and HE answered, **and there was dialog,** just like Abraham, Isaac, and Jacob... When I say that the "Fifth Dimension" (The Deva Realm, Heavens, Hells, Purgatory, etc.) is a reality, it is because I have been there, as a first-hand eye-witness, and this book is my testimony... When I say that Hell is a reality, it is because I peered into the great abyss, and walked the corridors of the **hopelessly** insane, and it left a scar on my Soul that I can never forget!!... So.., when I say that the Devil exists as a reality, and that he is a butt-fucking, swishy faggot; the personification of perversion.., it is because I have seen him "face to face".., and I have also seen him in a vision, narrated by the Lord, and in the vision, I saw the devastation, discontent, sorrow, and emptiness.., perpetrated on the citizens of Earth.., in the wake of this "Contagious" disease, known as "Perversion"... ...And when I say that this "enemy within" has infiltrated our ranks, corrupted our laws, deceived our "Leaders" (?) at the highest levels of government.., and poses a greater threat to National Security than does Communism, Terrorism, etc., or *ANY* outside force!!, it is because I have seen the "inner workings" of this Diabolical plot, and it is a "War" waged within the realms of inner space, and acted out on the stage of Life, and "World Domination" is the name of the game.., and the prize to be won is the Soul of Mankind!!... **To Arms!!, To Arms!!,** Snap out of it!.., Wake up!!, your Nation is being attacked, your children are at risk.., ...or am I just a lonely voice, crying in the wilderness??...

If I were to condense the "Essence" of this book into one paragraph.., it would be the above paragraph...

The interplay between the Conscious and sub-conscious is a marvel of unity that is the Crowning Achievement of life on Earth, that separates "Mankind" from the rest of the animal kingdom, and the interplay between Subjectivity and Objectivity makes of Mankind a "Spiritual Being", able to experience life *"in the Mind",* beyond the reach of his physical senses, and beyond the bounds of Earth!!!... Oh, Thou wondrous being, Thou child of God, who art in reality an immortal being, a God amongst Gods, and a "Champion" for good in the Universe.., Awaken to your Divine calling, and be Baptized (immersed) in the Lord... Amen...

You might call this "book of the mind", a course in fundamental logic!.. We have seen that both the Conscious mind and the sub-conscious mind can be trained, *and should be trained* by the "conscious direction" of the "supervising intelligence" that regards the "Mind" as the "Organ" of the Soul... Failure to train and "Master" the sub-conscious, is to fall victim to the animal appetites (food, sex, possessions, aggressions, etc.), and this faithful companion and helper becomes an "unruly cur", if the Master be weak.., and the Conscious mind, left unsupervised, will meander down every avenue ("memory lane") of indiscretion and sorrow, dragging with it its hapless Master into all the vicissitudes of pain and folly, and it's all *"not real"..,* and *"not in the moment"..,* and an unnecessary waste of time and emotional energy.., and if you fail to see through this, these unsupervised thoughts become self fulfilling prophesies that are acted out in real life, and then they have **consequences** *that must be paid for!!...* If you fail to master your mind.., you will be it's servant.., and your life will be; *chaos!!...*

There is a distinction between the mind and the Soul that is not readily describable in words, so I leave it to you to "see" this distinction.., by contemplation... By contemplation, *the mind can be observed,* as it goes from subject to subject, by association, seemingly with a life of it's own, in an unending procession of self generated thought forms... As you observe this process, as you are observing the mind, *it suddenly dawns on you* that "You" are something separate and distinct from your mind**!!!** "You" are the *observer* of your mind!!... (Hallelujah, Oh Happy Day!!) When you realize this; the separation between "You" and your mind, "You" have achieved the exalted state known as "Isolation"!!. "You" have found and "Isolated" (abstracted) your "Self" (the Soul).., from the mind!!!.. Exercising control, You bring the mind to a complete stop!!.. With the mind at complete rest, you have reached the state where; "Self rests in Self alone"... This is known as the "Unmodified State"[15], and at this level of abstraction, the "Zen shift" takes on a whole new dimension (words fail to convey)...

And there are, of course, *those things and practices* that are beneficial and/or detrimental to the mind, and we have gone into long discussions (a book within this book) on the subject of "drugs of virtue" and "drugs of vice".., those things that get you "High", and those things that bring you down.., those things that are for the edification of the few.., and the downfall of many...

Of special interest to this book is the very esoteric subject of *"Spiritual Alchemy",* and those "Herbs of Mysterious Virtue" (*Sacraments*) that can open the "Doors of Perception"... The transition through this "Door" is beyond verbal description (words fail to communicate, *and you have no idea!!)...* **By Tradition;** only the candidate for Higher Knowledge was granted initiation through this doorway, but in this modern era these Herbal Sacraments (or the synthesis thereof) are readily available to one and all... It is the "Tradition" that is lacking, and in this "book of the mind", it is the Tradition that I set before you, so that you may know and understand the seriousness of your actions, and the potential that lays before you... By Tradition; those who seek to enter through this doorway have been singled out for their virtue and character, served an apprenticeship under the guidance of a teacher, and evaluated... It is *with Sincere and Reverent intentions,* that they enter through this doorway, seeking to know the Lord, seeking the Knowledge of the Great Mystery of life,

---

[15] The Soul, in it's pure state, is; without form or substance, having neither center or circumference, or any characteristics by which it can be found or located (hence; "unmodified"), except for the innate knowledge of ; It knows Itself to be… Being without form or substance, it has the innate ability of "absorption" by which it can know the object of it's perception by becoming absorbed in it (where the knower and the thing to be known becomes "one"), and the knower (the Soul) becomes modified by this direct perception (like water becomes modified by the shape of its container) … So too, the Soul becomes modified by the mind, when it becomes absorbed in it, and is subject to all of it's vagaries and vicissitudes… The "Isolation" of the "Self" from the mind is a revelation and a "Liberation" that is in itself a new beginning.., into a much larger Universe…

seeking to know themselves... Only the brave and the dedicated should enter here!!. **Fools beware!!...** To enter through this doorway with less than "Sincere and Reverent intentions" is to court disaster, and to be expelled and rejected at this high level of consciousness is to suffer the psychological pain of rejection that will stay with you a long, long time!!... This is a very "Bad Trip"!.. If your motives are less than honorable, don't go there!!...

But.., apparently.., Teachers of the "Way" are in very short supply, and Candidates for the "Way" are also in short supply, so in this modern day and age, when weapons of mass destruction proliferate the Earth, a sense of urgency prevails, and the tools of the Alchemist (the Sacraments) have been made available to all... Know this; that HE seeks *Not* to expel or reject anyone, but rather to include everyone, and if you take the sacrament, and enter through that door, for a brief time, your "inner eye" may be opened, and a glimmer of light may shine through, and you will be given a new understanding and motivation that you may otherwise never have had, and your life will be changed.., and if you are rejected, it is because you are disrespectful and impervious to the light, and even this is for your own good, as you learn what it means to be rejected by the Lord.., and you can change your ways!!...

The purpose of this book is that you avoid the pitfalls, and be edified, and take that step **beyond belief**.., into the realm of actual experience.., and that can only be done by those that present themselves to the Lord as a "Worthy Candidate", as made evident by the sincerity of your **"intention"**.., and by your adherence to the fundamental laws of Wisdom (a.k.a. the Ten Commandments).., and by your *charity!*.. **Especially by your charity!!... Know This!!:** Entrance into that Holy Order is not granted to yourself alone, for your own self aggrandizement, **NO!!.., (OUT!!, damned Ego)..,** but that you might be a servant to the poor, the downtrodden, a light unto your fellow beings, and to those that are lost... This is known as the "Path".., or the "Way", and it is not traversed in a single day, but over a period of time, and as Wisdom develops, Compassion is a natural consequence... Applications are *Now* being taken.., recruitment is underway... Apply within...

In closing this discussion of the mind, let me say.., that I have seen the workings of the conscious and subconscious mind, identified and named their capacities and functions, and the interplay between them, and I have observed the shift between the Objective and Subjective states of mind, and the self awareness engendered by these states, etc. and etc.., *but there are those moments,* when I sit in a semi-conscious day-dream reverie, and I am presented with *fully formed illustrations,* etched in exquisite perfection to the minutest detail, that if captured on canvas would put the Mona Lisa to shame.., and indeed, if I were to attempt to put such art on canvas, there would be the rough sketch outline, the placement of content, the development of the art, the selection of colors, refinements, etc. and etc.., and I would say; "Look what I have created"!., but contrary to my conscious (and pathetic) act or "creation", the mind has presented to me a fully formed and exquisite masterpiece, perfect in every detail, **instantly..,** and as those experienced in the art of meditation can attest to, as your meditation deepens, bells will ring, and birds will sing!., and I become aware in my reverie and I exclaim; *"WOW", where did that come from"??,* and I realize that this creation / illustration was beyond my personal creative capacity, and it was just presented to me, without any conscious effort on my part.., and I look into my dreams and observe the intricate plots and sub-plots, with a cast of characters perfectly suited to their roles, and all of this is done effortlessly, and for what?., for my casual entertainment!?., and I sit there, amazed and enthralled.., and I realize that I have not fathomed the mind.., and it is a far deeper mystery than I have the ability to fathom or even describe.., let alone say that I understand…

And yet.., those "super intellects", that call themselves "scientists", trying to solve riddles of the universe, absorbed in "the thing observed", and never questioning the far greater Mystery of *"the Observer"* and the far greater riddle and mystery of the instrument of the mind, that they employ in the process of their riddle solving, or of their own creative powers of imagination, visualization, memory , language, communication, etc. and etc… They instinctively ignore "Self" exploration because it is beyond their capacity, which they dismiss with vague theories ("pissing into the wind") of mind somehow evolving out of matter… Such a joke!!…

But one thing is certain, and that is that *the Creative imagination of the "Super Mind" is the "Cornucopia" that is the predecessor of all that has been created…* This is more than Mystery.., **it is "Divine Mystery"…**

Essence precedes existence!..   Amen...

* * *   *   * * *

So, why did I write this book??? What was my motivation?.. Let me start by saying that in the "crap shoot" of life, I have been thrice blessed... Figure the odds; when the dice were rolled, I came out; Male (blessing # 1), White (#2), American (#3)... Freedom!!, in the land of the free, and the home of the brave!., and in a time of prosperity and progress... All of the advantages!.. Say what you want, but on the face of the Earth.., I had won the lottery[16]!.. Furthermore, I had my own personal (peculiar) star to follow (the Soul search), and the undaunted will to pursue it... With a child-like naiveté (in retrospect), and an attitude of invincibility, I conducted my search and research, and the world was my laboratory and my playground, and I went where I pleased and did what I pleased, without regard as to "how"... I just moved through the adventure of life with the careless abandon of an "immortal", and I reached my destinations, not always by the "first class" route, and sometimes suffering hardship, slaying dragons and stepping in shit along the way, but that's what made it an adventure!!. But it never mattered; the hardships, trials, obstacles, etc.., because I was a "rugged individualist" of the Warrior class, and because I knew (in my heart of hearts), that I would never die!!!

So I pursued my quest, wherever it took me, undaunted and without doubt.., and unlike a host of others before me.., *I was Successful!!!* Oh Yes!!. Where the Legions of Orthodoxy; The Priests, Bishops, Rabbi's, Evangelists, Monks, Devotees, and even Popes!., where they had been only mere *believers,* I had "**Seen**"!!! Yes, I (Iron Owl, the Unorthodox) (the "Luckiest" of mortal men), had seen what Saints had aspired to see, and had not seen... I had pierced the veil of the fifth dimension, and traversed the Bardo, the absolute Void of inner space, and I peered in on other dimensions and other Worlds!., places to where astronauts had not gone.., and could not go!!. And I had spoken to the Lord.., Like Abraham, Isaac, and Jacob.., and HE spoke back to me, and there was "Vision", and Knowledge was conveyed.., without doubt... ...And there was something else.., like "love", but even better than love (love is too possessive).., there was *"Friendship"... Friendship with the Lord...*

And then I had these chest pains!.. I drove myself to the hospital, walked in through the emergency door, and they told me I was having a heart attack!!! They opened up my chest and performed a triple by-pass... They pumped six units of blood into me, and six units of blood leaked out!.. They opened up my chest a second time, and plugged up the leak... But Iron Owl (the ever-living).., almost died!!. To my knowledge, I had been in the hospital for three days, but in reality I had been there for about ten days!!! I had almost died!.. I was shocked by this revelation!.. I had come face to face with something I had never conceived of.., never thought possible!!; my mortality!!! I was disillusioned and despondent...

So what did it matter.., that I had climbed mountains and traversed jungles, read libraries of books and ran circles around the globe, even piercing the Veil and assimilating the profoundest Knowledge at the foot of the Lord!!... It had all been a "tempest in a tea cup", a "tale told by an idiot, full of sound and fury, signifying nothing"... The vast knowledge contained in the libraries of Alexandria, all of the science, the technology, the medicine, literature, poetry, etc.., *the entire history of Egypt..,* had all been burned to the ground in a single day!!. ***That*** was my legacy!!! In the final analysis;.. I was a failure...

But, Oh Dear God.., this cannot be!.. How can this be?.. *This must not be!..* I had taken the Bodhisattva Vow!.. Yes, I was "High" when I took the Vow, but I took it in all sincerity, and it is a Solemn Vow; to rescue all beings from the bondage of ignorance, and lead them to the Absolute Freedom of the "Clear Light" of the Ultimate Reality!., and I had done nothing but pursue my own self interests... If I died now, I was an abject failure.., but if I lived.., if I lived I could tell what I know, I could share the knowledge that I had accumulated, and perhaps it could change someone's life!!. Yes, assholes *could* become Hero's, and do good for their fellow men, and feed

---

[16]   At first glance, this statement appears to be chauvinistic, racist, and nationalistic.., but it is a fact of life that does not become evident.., or appreciated.., until you have traveled extensively outside of the U.S.., and seen the plight of women.., and lived in third world countries.., under dictatorial governments.., and it is not so much of how you perceive the World, as it is of how the World.., (*because of your race*).., perceives you!.. It is the World.., that is chauvinistic, racist, and nationalistic!!…

the hungry, and teach the ignorant, and praise the Lord!!, and be "Born Again"!!. YES, that's what it means; to be Born Again.., it is to "turn over a new leaf", it's a change of heart and a change of attitude, it is a "chain of events" triggered by a benevolent act.., as opposed to the thief that "steals his own reward", and triggers his own demise!..

So the purpose of my life, was to find and to Know the "Truth" from the "experiential" viewpoint, and to a great extent, I have accomplished that goal.., but it means nothing, if I fail to bring that Knowledge to You, and not just for your intellectual assimilation, but for you to verify for yourself the truth of my findings, *by your own Experiences,* and that can only be done if you "Keep the Commandments" and seek the company and council of the Lord, and love your neighbor as yourself.., and do good.., every chance you get... Amen...

* * *

BOOK XVII

"Purgatory"

There is one more "Experience" of a "Fifth Dimensional" nature that I want to share with you, and it concerns the drug "Ibogaine"... I had spoken glowingly of this "healing drug" that had the amazing property of curing Heroine addiction, as well as many other addictions, including (possibly) psychological and behavioral addictions... My concern was that the healing potential of this drug was being deliberately ignored and made illegal by those who should have known better, and I suspected sinister motives.., but I had not tried it!.. It is contrary to the integrity of this book for me to write about something of which I do not have first-hand "experience", so it became incumbent upon me to have that experience...

I was fortunate enough to locate someone that was engaged in doing therapeutic work with the drug in it's herbal form, and I made arrangements to take the drug, even though I had no addictions... After fasting for 12 hours, I took the drug in three separate doses, about one hour apart...

This is *not* a "feel-good" drug!., and no one takes this drug for entertainment!!. Most people that take this drug are doing this to be "purged" of an addiction, and believe me.., this is a "Purge"... I threw-up every 20 minutes for 12 hours, mostly liver bile and stomach acid.., I requested an antacid, which slowed down the purging to about 45 minute intervals for the next 24 hours... For 36 hours, I laid on my back on the bed, practically incapacitated, drifting in and out of a reverie that was more like delirium, but never asleep... There has to be someone there in attendance *to make sure that you don't die* (not unknown), and to help you to the bathroom, or whatever, but for the most part, you are alone with your Soul, drifting in and out of a fifth dimensional reality...

The experiences are "Intention Specific"!.. That is to say; that you enter into this "Encounter" with a "Higher Intelligence" for a specific reason, and asking a specific question, and every person gets what he came for.., a specific *experience* appropriate to his specific needs!.. You may not get what you want, but you will get what you need...

In my own case;.. I had survived my brush with death, and I was writing "this" book to pass on my experiences in accordance with the Bodhisattva Vow that I had taken and was committed to, and to add this experience to the sum of knowledge contained in this book.., but my most important question was: "In what capacity could I be the most effective in the fulfillment of my Vow"???

I would liken the experience to the experience of the Prophet; Jeremiah (Jer. 1:11-15).., in that it was a combination of symbols, visions, and the "Spoken Word".., punctuated by bouts of nausea... This was not a pleasant experience...

"I don't like this"!., I said to the attendant, overseeing my reactions to the experience... "No", I said, "This is not a good place", I said, "I don't like this at all"... "What do you see"?., the attendant asked... "I see dead people"!.. "Dead People"!!?, the attendant asked, obviously shocked by the statement... "Is it anyone that you know"?., the question came back at me... "No, there isn't anyone that I know, it is just masses of dead people, but they aren't really dead, they are just here, like Zombies, not really conscious.., they have all died and been traumatized by the death experience, and they are stuck here in this semi-comatose state.., in "Limbo"!!! They can't get out!.. They are in their own dream-reverie state, and they can't get out!.. This is not a happy place.., I don't want to be here"!!!

I threw-up in a bucket, fell back on the bed, and I went again to that dreadful place.., and a crowd of expressionless Zombies stood before me... "Get back", I said defensively, and they all moved back, but there was one that was still too close, and I said; "You"!., "move to the back", and he obediently turned and walked to the back of the crowd, and I realized that I had complete control.., over these masses of dead people!!!

Now I knew where I was!.. I had entered into "The Bardo of the After-Death State"... I had read about this in the "Tibetan Book of the Dead" but I never thought that I would see it, at least not while I was alive!!, and then.., and then.., I heard the Voice of the Lord!.. **"Here is where you will serve"**...

"Oh no, oh no, oh no, oh Dear God, no, I pleaded.., **"and you will stop smoking pot"!..** Oh no, oh no, oh dear God, no, oh no, oh no, oh no.., I pleaded... That was It!.. That was the extent of the conversation!!!

I was devastated!!. I was being punished!., and I knew in my heart of hearts that I deserved this punishment, and it was a bitter punishment... Yes, "I", who had been thrice blessed, given every opportunity and every advantage, having enjoyed the abundance and the bounty of the earth.., was guilty!.. I had been gone far too long.., strayed too far away.., from the company of the Lord... I had taken the Sacred Vow of the Bodhisattva, and then I went my own way!.. I had been seduced by the glitter and glamour of the world, the pursuit of personal wealth, jet airplanes to foreign lands, suitcases full of money, wheeling and dealing, a plethora of women, cocaine, and excitement!.. Even serving a year in the primitive conditions of a foreign prison only served to whet my appetite.., but mostly it was the excitement (I could write a book!)!!. "It was the best of times.., it was the worst of times"...

So.., one just doesn't go to see the Lord, as an afterthought!.. Oh no, it was with fear and trepidation that I undertook this encounter, this meeting with the Lord.., and I knew going in that I was guilty, but I had hoped to redeem myself with the testimony of this book, and to reestablish the connection.., but I had been reprimanded.., severely reprimanded, and now I was in dismal despair... I likened myself to a career military officer who was assigned to perpetual guard duty.., in Siberia!.. Oh no, oh no, oh God no!., and I vomited green bile into the bucket!!.

"And stop smoking pot"!!. What kind of a proclamation was that!?? I didn't want to believe it!!! I questioned it!!. I tried to reason it away, because I knew from experience that not every voice you hear in the Bardo realm is that of the Lord.., but I knew that I was deceiving myself, because I had said it too many times, in the course of too many conversations.., and now I was being put to the test!!! I had said; repeatedly; that "I would never give up smoking pot, not for legal reasons, not for health reasons, not as a condition of employment, for no reason, except only if God Himself told me to".. I had made that statement on many occasions, never ever expecting that such a circumstance would come about.., but the Lord heard my pronouncements.., and now I was being put to the test!!, and my response was: "Oh no, oh no, oh God, no"...

I considered it part of my religion, a sacrament, my drug of choice, which I partook of almost on a daily basis... I did this almost every morning, upon arising, just two or three tokes on my little Meerschaum toke pipe.., that's all that was needed, and I would watch the magnificent sunrise, and think deep and profound thoughts, and my mood was one of congeniality and appreciation towards all of mankind, and I felt sorrow for those people that lived their whole lives on one stratified level of consciousness, never knowing any other, and adamantly opposed to anyone that would dare transcend the boundaries of their own pathetic limitations.., and I was a craftsman, and I did better work under the influence, being absorbed in my work, and I played a better game of chess, and a better game of pool, concentration was dramatically improved; semi-opaque legal documents (for instance) would become comprehensible, music would trigger emotions of awe and inspiration.., and any musician will tell you, that they play better music.., and this is a fact!.. This is the difference between "use", and "abuse".., and I would recommend "use" to anyone and everyone, including my Mother and my adult children!.. The world is much larger and grander than your "stratified level of consciousness" will let you discover... I couldn't live in such confinement!!.

And the Lord had said to me; "Stop smoking pot"!!. It was a bitter pill!.. I threw up bitter green bile into the bucket, mopped the sweat off my face, and collapsed back onto the bed, back into the Bardo, and into a Vision... And I saw myself in the vision, and I was escorting this gray-haired old woman, ravaged by age, and shocked into the zombified state by the death experience, and I escorted her through the "Veil", that shimmered with diffracted light as I brought her through, and as she passed through the veil she was transformed into the young lady of her youth, with wavy yellow blond hair and smiling eyes, and she was beautiful, and I brought her to set foot on the Earth.., *but it wasn't Earth*!!. It looked very similar to Earth in it's architecture and it's people, but it wasn't Earth!..

I wretched and I heaved, mopping the sweat off my body, drifting in and out of that terrible place of the dead, and the dead were looking.., to me!!... *The dead were looking to me!!,* and I wretched and I heaved between glimpses of this place of the living dead, and of this realm that was so similar to Earth, but was not Earth, and I bemoaned my fate and my punishment, and I wretched and I heaved, and finally.., it was over... I was exhausted... I had not eaten or slept for over 48 hours... I ate a small amount of soda crackers, and fell asleep for eight hours...

I awoke the next morning, surprisingly refreshed!.. Not only was I surprisingly refreshed, but I was in high spirits!.. I had gone through an ordeal, but it was a transition of sorts, and there was a sense of gladness in my heart!, but I still hadn't figured it out... It had been a chaotic experience, and the segments of memory, visions and experiences, interrupted by repeated bouts of vomiting, swirled around in my head, as I tried to make sense of it all...

I gained a new respect for the members of the "Bwiti" cult, who undergo this test of endurance and purging, to have direct experience of their religious convictions.., as opposed to their Christian counterparts, who dress up in their Sunday finest and render lip service to the Lord for one hour a week!.. You tell me; who is the more religious in the sight of God; the "Bwiti", or the "Christians"??? I had lost five pounds of body weight, and my stomach muscles and rib cage ached for two days afterwards, from the effort of this purging…

I was contemplating the significance of these events, as I walked along the edge of this alligator swamp (in Florida), and as usual, I had with me the implements of my religion; my little meerschaum toke pipe, a small plastic bag of finely manicured pot, and my lighter, all neatly concealed within the little ostrich-skin leather zippered pouch, in my pocket... I fingered the pouch in my pocket, my faithful companion for more than 35 years, that never failed to lift my spirits and elevate my consciousness.., that I never conceived of abandoning... Thirty five years of use, and no addiction!.. that sounds like a contradiction, or a sarcastic joke, but it is not... I had often gone without, and sometimes for extended periods, with no withdrawal symptoms, except for maybe a little aggravation at being locked in at a lower, stratified level of consciousness... Even my health benefited from it!., as I could be feeling "out of sorts", as though my stomach was doing it's thing, liver doing it's thing, each internal organ independently doing their own thing.., and I could take a toke on my little pipe, and suddenly there was communication between my internal organs, and they harmonized their functions!!. The field of psycho-pharmacology has missed the boat on this important medicine that has the property of integrating the spiritual aspects of mind and body, and at the same time, transcending pain!!. Some might say that I am psychologically addicted!?. Yeah, sure.., like I am also psychologically addicted to "Life, Liberty, and the Pursuit of Happiness"... Get real!.. (Sarcasm intended)...[1]

Now.., some people think.., that when the Lord speaks.., trumpets blare, bass drums boom, and the voice of the Lord bellows like thunder reverberating out from a Celestial echo-chamber!!! Nothing like that!., nothing like that at all... Actually (from my experience), HE is very soft-spoken and mannerly, and speaks like a Father would speak to a son, giving gentle guidance.., and His voice is so gentle and subtle, that if you aren't paying close attention, you could miss it!., and you don't have to accept his guidance!!. No, you can go your own way.., and not be struck by lightening!!. *I Know..,* because I have (in the past) received His guidance.., and went my own way!!! The Lord had spoken to me, in His soft spoken way, and said: *"Don't pursue this woman"!!.* And I, in my lustful state of mind said: "You can't be serious"..! O.K., I thought to myself, I won't pursue this woman, I will let her pursue me (that *must* be what the Lord meant)!!. So I played hard to get, and pursue me she did.., and we did!!.., and she was deadly serious, and I was only poking fun!!... Hell hath no fury!!. Hell hath no fury... She destroyed my reputation among my friends, important friends, (which impacted me financially!)

---

[1] Update: As this book goes to press (2006) Eleven states have defied the U.S. government, and decriminalized the medical use of marijuana… Federal law takes precedence.., but these states will neither enforce the law or prosecute these cases, and it is assumed that the federal government is too busy prosecuting more serious crimes (terrorism, etc.) to bother with prosecuting people trying to eliminate the pain and suffering of Cancer radiation treatments, Multiple Sclerosis, and even Alzheimer's disease… With the discovery of cannabinoid receptors (CB1, and CB2) in the human brain, (a confoundment to both the Evolutionists and the "intelligent design" Creationists (***God laughs!***).., cures and remedies for Alzheimer's (protecting against brain inflammation and cognitive decline), loom on the horizon. (See: "Health breakthroughs 2006", page 5 *(Bottom Line Books)*, quoting from the "Journal of Neuroscience")…
"Sativex" (derived from "cannabis sativa") shows great promise in the treatment of MS… (See: www.drugdevelopment-technology.com/project/sativex/)

and I had to leave town to avoid her wrath and retribution, and to this day I fear this woman, afraid that on some dark night she will jump out from behind a rock, plunge a rusty nail into my chest, and carve my heart out!!! So that's how smart I am!.. I was so clever that I outsmarted myself!!. ***So I know..,*** that you can ignore the council of the Lord and go your own way.., but you will have to suffer the consequences of your actions.., and you will lose the council of the Lord!!. To lose the council of the Lord is a very dear price to pay.., and I paid that price.., for a very long time!!...

So I fingered the little pouch in my pocket, my faithful friend for over thirty five years, that never failed to lift my spirits, and get me "high".., and I thought; "Why"?., Why would the Lord want me to dispense with the practice that I considered to be so essential to my religion??. I could have toked up on my little meerschaum pipe, and the magic would have happened, and I could have dismissed the whole experience as a horrible failure, a distortion caused by a primitive drug... I could just ignore the whole thing, and go my own way!!. Déjà vu.., Déjà vu..! Oh no.., Oh no.., not again.., not again... Oh No.., I will not make that same mistake again!.. If this is a test, let me not fail it!.. If I am to be banished to the farthest reaches of the Netherworld, to the land of the living dead, so be it.., What choice do I have anyway?., it is what I deserve.., but I will not defy the Lord again... And with that, I grabbed my little ostrich skin leather zipper pouch and pitched it into the alligator swamp!.. On the opposite bank, an eight foot long alligator emerged from concealment, raised it's head, and stared at me with unblinking eye...

It didn't happen right away.., but eventually it dawned on me!.. I recalled the vision: "of myself, escorting this gray-haired old woman, ravaged by age, and shocked into the zombified state by the death experience, and I escorted her through the "Veil", that shimmered with diffracted light as I brought her through, and as she passed through the Veil, she was transformed into the young lady of her youth, with wavy yellow blond hair and laughing eyes, and she was beautiful, and I brought her to set foot on the Earth, *but it wasn't Earth*... It looked very similar to Earth, in it's architecture and it's people, but it wasn't Earth".., and I realized that I had seen this place before!!! Yes, I had seen this place before, when I was in Laos, smoking Opium, I had tripped into this place and thought it to be Earth, and that I had been deceived by the Opium, but now I recognized it to be a separate world within the Bardo, a "Twin" to Earth...

With the suddenness of the Sun emerging from behind the clouds.., it dawned on me!!.

Oh my God!., Oh my God!!! It was almost more than I could grasp!.. The Bible had spoken of it, but I had never even thought about it, let alone expect to ever see it.., But I, "Iron Owl the Unworthy", had seen it!..; *It was the **"New Earth"**!!!* I had seen the "New Heaven" and the "New Earth"!!.

It seems that all preachers and theologians had speculated about, conjectured about, and preached about; the "New Heaven" and the "New Earth" (Rev.21:1- Isa.65:17- Isa.66:22- 2Pe.3:13)!.. I had never thought about it in these terms, but the New Earth is a three-dimensional physical reality.., almost identical to Earth.., located within the *infinite* realm of "Inner Space"; ***the "New Heaven"*** (a.k.a.; the "Fifth Dimension")!., and while I confirm and bear eye witness testimony to the fact of the New Heaven and the New Earth, I also have to bear witness to one fact that (some) theologians currently deny.., and that is; "Purgatory"!!.

Call it; "The Bardo of the After Death state", or call it; "Limbo", or call it "the Land of the Living Dead", or call it "Purgatory", (or don't call it Purgatory)!!. Whatever!!. Although the Buddhist religion (among others) goes into great detail about this place ("The Tibetan Book of the Dead").., the Bible makes no mention of this place[2].., hence; some (not all) Christians are either unconcerned with, or disbelieve in an intermediate state between

---

[2] Although this book is commonly called: "the epistle of St. Paul to the Hebrews", the writer of this letter does not identify himself (as Paul always did).., and the style is different… Since the Reformation it has been widely recognized that Paul could not have been the writer… Some scholars attribute the writing to Barnabas.., and other scholars (Martin Luther) attribute the writing to Apollos... Both of these men were close associates of St. Paul… (Source: Compton's Interactive Bible NIV.., Expert introduction to Hebrews) …

And furthermore; (let me point out), that the "true believers" regard *everything* written in the Bible as the absolute unequivocal "word of God", when clearly, it is (for instance) the words of St. Paul, who never intended that *his* words be considered equal to the "word of God", and in this instance, they were not even the words of St. Paul.., and definitely *Not;* "the word of the Lord"… St. Paul would not have approved!..

"From Purgatory to the New Earth"

Heaven and Hell... *I* was unconcerned!!. Furthermore, in the book of Hebrews (author unknown) it is stated that: "...man is destined to die once, and then the judgment" (Heb. 9:27)... This statement is constantly repeated as though it were a "Proclamation by GOD"!!! It is not!!! The topic of this letter was; the Divinity of Christ, and the author was using this "mundane example" to illustrate a much larger point!., and to use this "mundane example" as absolute LAW in the greater context of God's ***judgment!.,*** is to impose a LAW.., on GOD!!! Furthermore, these "Theologians" are making a *presumption* that "judgment" can only be; Heaven or Hell!!. *That's absurd!!.* Even Earthly judges are not bound by such narrow restrictions, and will impose penalties of 30 days, or 30 years, or rehabilitation and probation!!. Are they more merciful than God??. They (the theologians) are guilty of what they accuse everyone else of.., and that is; of taking a quote "out of context", (the mundane example) and attributing to it a much greater scope than what is implied... I tell you this:, that the plans of God, and the journey of the Soul.., is far more intricate and diversified than the simplistic "either *This* or *That*" philosophy that these theologians presume...

Now.., I am not (technically) a theologian, nor am I in theological debate with anyone!.. Nor would I disagree with the assertion that those who die "in Christ" would go directly to heaven.., but there are those people.., good people.., who's faith (a gift) is not all that conclusive.., and Purgatory may not even be a punishment, but may be just the natural consequence of the trauma of death to an unenlightened Soul!... I only know what I see, and what I experience first-hand, and I have faithfully related the details of my first-hand experience.., and I have been to Purgatory.., and I will go back there again.., and again.., and again *ad infinitum*!., if necessary...

Oh Yes, I will go!.. Oh Yes, Dear Lord.., send me!., I will go!!. Who knows the Bardo better than me!?? Send Me!!., *I WILL GO!!!* What greater glory could a Bodhisattva aspire to, than to go into the land of the Dead, and rescue it's inhabitants from their zombified state, locked within the prison of their own minds, waking them to consciousness, and escorting them through the veil of transformation, into their adult prime of life; into *Youth,* and bringing them to set foot on the "New Earth"?... *Oh Yes.., that's why the dead were looking to me!!, because I have the ability to do this!..* Really, what greater good could I aspire to than this??.

This is what happens when you comply with the directives of the Lord... Obedience to the Lord is the height of Wisdom, because HE has your best interest at heart... What I had earlier conceived of as a punishment, and a banishment.., was in reality an honor and a privilege!.. What had appeared to be dismal defeat, was transformed into Victory!.. My base of operations is to be the "New Earth", and I will be doing rescue missions into the Bardo, retrieving those poor Souls locked within the realm of their own minds, locked in Purgatory... *Halleluiah!!.*

So.., it is really quite funny! I don't know what I am going to be doing when I grow up!., but I know what I will be doing in the After Death state!!, and I am ready to go, Lord.., but please.., let me finish this (#%$&#!*) book first!.. Amen...

So.., as an afterthought.., one question remains.., and I have to ask this question of myself, and of the reader... "Obedience to the Lord is the height of Wisdom, because HE has your best interest at heart".., but.., what do you think my fate would have been.., had I *NOT* been obedient??... Something to think about...

* * *   * * *

A year had gone by.., since my previous "Ibogaine" experience.., and I was anxious to repeat the experience.., just to see what there was to see... I had no burning questions to be answered, but just to see if there were any further developments that I should be aware of...

I called to make arrangements for this second encounter, but the "administrator of experiences" was very reluctant to grant me this second encounter because I was admittedly a very strange fellow, having had for one; open heart surgery, and two; entered into the Bardo of the "After Death" state.., which is admittedly a very "spooky" place, and he didn't want to be responsible for, or associated with.., my death!!. But I persisted, and he finally (reluctantly) agreed.., if I would write a suicide note to be found on my body in case I should die!!. I agreed...

It is really "weird" to write a suicide note!., and it goes against every instinct of my personality.., but after many attempts, I put together this statement:

…..(The Letter): …..

(Transcribing): *"To Whom it may concern"*...

…..Let it be known.., That I.., (*Iron Owl*).., being of sound mind and body.., would never, ever, and not in any circumstance.., take my own life in any act even remotely resembling suicide...

That having been said, there are certain elements of risk (called; "the unforeseen event") that are inherent in the adventure of life... All the advancements of science and knowledge contain this element of risk, and it is with this foreknowledge that I undertake this experiment that does indeed put my life at risk... To advance the knowledge and interests of science, and in conjunction with research on the book that I am currently engaged in writing, it is my intention to explore that "borderland" of the edge of Death.., in what has come to be known as: "the Near Death experience"...

Therefore.., let it be known that I undergo this experiment of my own free will, with humility.., with no one else involved, and with no one to be blamed except myself... It is with this purpose in mind that I write this letter...

So.., it is with faith in God that I pray to God, that this letter will be read by no one besides myself... (Signed and dated)... (End of transcription)…

As you can see.., the search for Knowledge is not just a simple "walk in the park"...

Having observed that the taking of antacids did indeed lessen the incidences of nausea and vomiting, as a precursor to this experience I took a long acting acid suppresser as well as having on hand the antacid tablets, and this greatly enhanced the quality of the experience by reducing the incidences of vomiting to about once every hour and a half... A great improvement...

Again I took the capsules containing the powdered herb in three separate doses, about one hour apart... After about the fourth hour, the visions started, as I lay on the bed, unmoving.., as though dead!.. I had become well versed in the universal language of symbols, an Knowledge was being displayed in symbolic form...

"Are you O.K."??, came the question from an outside source!.. My trance state had been interrupted by the "therapist" who was concerned for my life... Yes, I am o.k., I said... "What are you experiencing", he asked, and I described what I was seeing, which was, at that moment the cut-away view of the human head and brain, and the location of the Soul that existed in a plume-like form emanating from the center of the brain.., and he proceeded to question me, engaging me in conversation... Finally, I heard that "Inner Voice", *and HE yelled at me!.,* so I excused myself from the conversation and attempted to reenter the trance state... *Too late*!!. The Zen moment had come and gone! I had missed the most crucial part of the experience... I had missed the "peak" of the experience...

Sometimes.., "shit happens"... I lay there for about another four hours or so, but I was clearly on the down side of the experience, and I had a profound sense of loss... I was being given a profound insight, a gift, perhaps the most important moment of my life, and I missed it, due to a triviality...

Having pretty much eliminated the nausea and vomiting problem by suppressing and neutralizing the production of stomach acid, I was no longer incapacitated and bed ridden, so I got up and sat in a chair, and being clearly out of any danger of dying, the "therapist" excused himself and left... I thought it interesting that the "therapist" had conducted a couple hundred of these sessions, and the nausea and vomiting had always been a major problem, and he used Dramamine to combat it, with only limited success... "Ibogaine" has the unique property of coating the opiate receptors in the body and eliminating the need and craving for the addictive substance, so this excessive "purging" has little or nothing to do with the cure for the addiction...

This experience was unlike my previous experience in that my perceptions were much "cleaner" and crystal clear, uncluttered by the excessive vomiting, etc.., although I didn't go into the Bardo (perhaps because I missed my "peak" experience), but nevertheless, I had a new appreciation for the "quality" of this amazing psychedelic that "came on" in waves of intensity, reaching a "peak" (for about 10 minutes), and then decreasing in waves of intensity over several hours.., but the potential of the drug is made manifest in the reclining position, in the state of introspective reverie... I laid back down on the bed.., and I went to: ; *Sodom and Gomorrah!..*

This was totally unexpected!!. This was not a "Vision", and this was not "time travel"... This was the opening of the "Akashic Records" (the "Cosmic Memory Bank").., and I can only describe it as..; being a spectator.., watching a 3-D movie!!. A documentary, in which I literally "glided" down the streets of Sodom and Gomorrah, as a bodiless spectator, *as sight itself,* unable to touch, but only to see... And I saw.., in graphic detail...

Ugh!.. I don't want to see this!.. Why should "*I*".., be shown "*this*"??. I got up out of the bed and walked around for a while, the effects of the drug were diminishing... I ate some soda crackers and watched a little television.., it was absurdly inane... It had been an exhausting 48 hours... I lay back down on the bed again.., and I immediately went back to Sodom and Gomorrah!..

It was late evening as I "moved" (with unimpeded motion) down the street of Sodom, and I looked in on a pavilion type restaurant, that served food and alcoholic beverages from a large barbeque pit-kitchen located in the corner area to the left of the entrance... the walls of the establishment were about five foot high with wooden posts protruding above the walls to about seven foot, which supported the beams that held up the pavilion roof... The tables were similar to picnic tables that seated about 8 or 10 people, and laid out in orderly rows... The place was crowded, drunken, disorderly and loud!.. Anybody that passed out or was incapacitated from drunkenness was butt-fucked right there at the table, amid the laughter and cheering from the drunken crowd who each succumbed to the drunkenness and debauchery of butt-fucking the incapacitated, until they were themselves incapacitated from drunkenness and butt-fucked repeatedly by whomever, and there were fights, and the losers would be held down and raped, and they all wallowed in this drunkenness and debauchery, driven by rabid, ravenous, and perverted lust!!.

Again, I was driven from my bed by disgust, and I paced the floor, trying to rid my mind of the unholy sights that I had seen, I ate, and took a shower, watched some more television, and finally, I was exhausted, and I lay down to sleep.., and again.., I went to Sodom and Gomorrah!!...

Enough!!, I said... **Three times!!,** three times I had laid down to rest, and three times I had been transported to Sodom and Gomorrah!!!... I had seen enough!.. I didn't want to see any more... Why am I seeing this??, I asked... (No answer) Why??, I asked again.., (No answer)... I had already said everything I intended to say about this subject, and I didn't want to say any more about it... Perhaps I had said too much, already... Perhaps I had said more than was prudent to say, for my own well being... I had no intention of becoming an activist.., or a crusader, or anything like that, and I even included a chapter (over which I deliberated much as to the Wisdom of it) as to a method whereby an individual afflicted with this spiritual sickness might rid himself of it!.. I didn't have to do that!.. I deliberated much about it before I included that chapter... What else could I do??. (No answer)... And I included that chapter, *Not* because I feel any compassion for the "Sodomizers" (because I don't), But because I have seen "Hell".., and it left a scar on my Soul.., and because I have seen Satan.., *and he is a Faggott!!,* and his disciples.., are victims.., and Hell.., is a reality!..

Sometimes.., the Lord will do this!.. He will grant you an insight.., or a revelation.., with no verbal instructions.., with no verbal commandments to do *this,* or do *that*, etc... Because *HE Knows..,* that if specific instructions were to be given.., I would probably screw it up, and be held accountable!.. So HE gives this insight as "background information", to do with as I see fit.., or not!., without obligation... So you see.., without obligation, I am sitting here writing about it!!. (Is the Lord not clever?!!)...

But the truly frightening thing is;., that the things that I saw in Sodom.., are no worse than can be found in our cities today!!. In our cities today.., there is the **"mosh pit"** party-drug scene,[3] where the drug of **choice** is: "GHB" (a.k.a. the "date rape" drug), which is *willingly* (but not always) consumed by the participants to render themselves incapable of resisting any and all types of perversion perpetrated on their bodies by whomever!!, and the "hot tub" bath houses, that are undisguised "wallowing troughs" of communal degradation among "off the street" total strangers.., like lemmings.., racing to their own destruction, driven by the force of perversion.., to their deaths.., and damnation... Take heed, the fate of Sodom!., or did you think it was just a fairy tale?..

---

[3] See the television documentary (Discovery Health Channel); called: "The Price of Ecstasy", which documents the "Party-Drug Scene" in Miami, Fl...

So.., all in all, my second Ibogaine experience was a disappointment!.. I had missed my "peak" experience.., I missed the "gift" that was being given to me (a loss of incalculable proportions).., and I had the grand tour of Sodom and Gomorra.., which, by contrast.., made Purgatory seem desirable!..

And to make matters worse.., the "administrator of the experience" called me on the telephone, enquiring about my well being, after effects, etc., and I told him about how I had missed my "peak" experience due to the interruption of our untimely conversation, and I suggested that he be aware of this so as to not let it happen again with his future clientele, and I didn't tell him about my trip to Sodom and Gomorra, but I had previously said some very unkind things about homosexuals in general, which he took personally, (I had suspected).., and he was into astrology, which I had pooh-poohed as a pseudo-science.., and he took offense!!. I had not intended offense, but that's the way it all came down, and he informed me that there would be no more Ibogaine sessions for me at any price!!. I had lost a friend!., and worse yet, I had lost access to Ibogaine!!...

It was all so depressing... I had missed my peak experience, lost a gift of "incalculable proportions", had a disgusting experience in Sodom and Gomorra, lost a good friend, lost my source of supply for Ibogaine.., and any future experiences that I might have with this remarkable "Herb of Mysterious Virtue"... I was in a state of *Gloom*...

I went to bed that night, in this state of gloom, and I slept.., *and I dreamed*!!. In my dream; I was walking down this long and winding road, when suddenly the road turned to ice!.. Undeterred, I started skating on the ice, with my flat-soled shoes, and with momentum... I skated along, and the road started to incline upwards, and still I skated with momentum, until I reached the vertical wall of an ice faced cliff, and without hesitation and with momentum I scaled the face of the ice cliff, my fingernails biting into the ice, like a cat climbing a tree, and I reached the top, and it was a high plateau, and the road continued on, but the ice had melted, and there were water puddles along the road, and green pastures, with cloud shrouded mountains in the distance, and on my feet, there were these leather lace-up, high-top boots...

This is the classic "psychic dream"[4], and the symbolism is so evident that it doesn't really need to be interpreted, but for those who may not be familiar with psychic dreams *(where the "Super-Conscious" communicates with the "Conscious" via the "Sub-Conscious")..,* I will give the interpretation... The "road" is, of course, the "road of Life" on which we all travel, and it is a spiritual journey (*All* psychic dreams deal with this spiritual journey)... That the road turns to ice, is the natural obstacles on the spiritual journey, of which most people slide off the road, and the road inclines, of which most people "back-slide", but I had momentum, which is the natural "predisposition" of my personality, which is the inborn quest "*to Know*", which takes precedence over *Everything*!.. And the ice covered cliff face; it is the natural limit of human understanding, the barrier of the conscious mind, beyond which the "intellectual" cannot go.., beyond which the "theologian" cannot go.., but I (Iron Owl; "the Impetuous"), without hesitation and with momentum, sought out and consumed the spiritual "elixir", and *transcended* (climbed) this barrier, *transcended* (trance-ascended) the limits of theological intellectualism to the "High Plateau" of "Fifth Dimensional" spiritual *Experience*, to *Knowledge by Experience*, and that road continues on (possibly forever).., and on my feet are these leather lace-up, high-top (calf high) (all-terrain) boots.., which is the symbol of "secure footing" on the journey...

So.., I had reached a "high plateau", and it was a hospitable environment (green pastures), and I had secure footing!.. It was a message of acceptance, and of *comfort*, secure in the *Knowledge* that I was known to God, and HE was aware.., of me!!. **"The Comforter"**.., is one of the Names attributed to the "Holy Spirit"... I had been obedient, and I had received a Blessing... Thank God!..

* * * * *

Well, I had thought to end this chapter here.., and for all intents and purposes, this chapter does end here.., but because of the "dream", I decided to extend a diplomatic olive branch in the form of a letter of apology.., to save a friendship, but more importantly, to save my source of supply of Ibogaine, and to further my experiments into the Inner Realms of Fifth Dimensional experience...

---

[4] For a greater in-depth understanding of the "psychic dream" phenomena, read the book; "The Symbolic and the Real", by Ira Progoff.., (1983)...

"The Arrival"

I am going to reprint the letter here, because it is the longest letter I have ever written.., and because it touches on a subject of Universal Interest.., namely: "Astrology"!., and on other subjects relevant to this book...

I had purposely intended to not include the subject of astrology in this book, because this book branches off on several tangents already, and for the second reason that I had intended to write a second book which would be the "counterpart opposite" of this book (a Book of Truth)... This second "follow-up" book would be entitled: "The Tower Of Babel".., and it would be the counterpart opposite, because it would be; "a Book of Lies" (this has the potential of being *a much larger book*)!!. But who knows?., I may never get around to writing a second book.., so I will include it now...

The purpose of this book is to be a "Handbook", of the "Way"... The "Way" (the road of life) is a perilous journey through life, with many pitfalls, wrong turns, obstructions, barriers, misinformation (The Tower of Babel) and etc., that can cause you endless delays, dead ends, pain, suffering, and even death.., without you ever reaching your goal, or even knowing that there is a goal to be reached!.. Without a handbook, we are "easy prey" to this mountain of misinformation (lies)... To show you the Truth, and to expose the lies.., to give you purpose, and direction.., to show you your destiny and destination, to "streamline" your journey on the adventure of life.., is the purpose of this handbook... Go with God...

…..(The letter transcribed): …..

Dear – (Friend),   June 8, 02

Hey!., Hello again, old friend.., I have been thinking about you!.. I can't help but find it incredibly interesting (fascinating), that you and I.., having walked down that very same long and winding road.., should come up with such incredibly diverse view-points!!! And it isn't as though it is just a difference of opinion.., no.., it is beyond opinion.., it is that one of us is right, and one of us is wrong!.. No middle ground!!! How could this have happened??. The same road.., and opposite conclusions!!.

For instance, you believe in astrology.., but not in God!.. Is that not paradoxical??. It is paradoxical, but it is not new!.. It has happened before!!.

Now.., I know that you are thinking that it is none of my business what you believe, and who am I to say what is the "Truth", and what isn't, except for the fact that these differences of view-point make for very interesting discussions between friends that have walked primarily the same path.., and neither of us has as yet come to the end of that path, really... So the path continues...

I am not ignorant of astrology... In fact I studied it very intently for about a year and a half... Not unusual, considering the fact that for the last 10,000 years (an arbitrary number) every man that contemplated the mystery of the Universe looked at the stars and speculated on their meaning... There had to be a meaning, and in those medieval times, when superstition prevailed, meanings were looked for and meanings were given... A comet flew overhead and a battle was lost, therefore comets were an evil omen.., except for the winning side, that viewed comets as a harbinger of good fortune, etc., and etc., and there were certain anomalies that were mysterious and unexplainable, such as planets that went forward would all of a sudden go retrograde, and of course, that couldn't be good.., it had sinister implications... Everybody freaked out at the eclipse of the Sun and the Moon, the Earth was the center of the Universe, the Sun revolved around the Earth, and the stars formed the "smooth surface" of the "Bowl of the Heavens"... But astrology was the only science in town, and they found that in a rectangular building, if you would drill a hole in the side facing the sunrise, it would project a spot on the back wall, and by marking the progression of that spot daily, after 365 days it would repeat, giving the time sequence of one year, and the equinoxes were discovered (a time to plant and a time to harvest) etc., which was great knowledge for farming and cemented in their minds that astrology was of religious significance... So temples (observatories) were built (Stonehenge and the Druids), and the astrologers became the "High Priests", able to predict future events.., and astrology became their religion... We know that they were an intelligent and industrious race of people, because the massive stones (some weighing 50 tons) were transported from south-western Wales!.. The transportation and placement of these megalithic stones remains one of the most sophisticated engineering achievements of both ancient and modern times!!.

Unfortunately, the religion of astrology failed them completely, and their civilization vanished into dust!!. There is not one artifact.., not one tool.., not one inscription.., no evidence at all.., that they even existed, except for the monument of Stonehenge that gives the clue to their existence and to what they were all about... You see, they didn't believe in God.., they believed in astrology!.. Or, to be more specific;., their *Religion*;., was astrology...

And in my research, I found that the ancient science of astrology very closely paralleled that most ancient of all mythologies, and in fact the mythology was incorporated into, and became an intrinsic part of the astrological landscape... It seemed that the mythology had always been.., even before recorded memory!.. No one knew from whence it came, but it was prevalent everywhere and always... It was the mythology of..; the "Lion-King"...

It is the "Riddle of the Sphinx"... In the temple of Esneh, in Egypt, there is a great painting on the ceiling of the portico, of the Zodiac,.. with all of it's constellations... Between the constellations of Virgo and Leo, there is carved the small figure of a sphinx, with the head of a woman (facing Virgo) and the body of a lion (with the tail pointing to Leo).., telling us that the beginning of the Zodiac is Virgo (the Virgin birth), and the conclusion of the "Myth", is the triumphant "Lion-King" (Leo)... The same sphinx is found in the same place in a number of other paintings of the Zodiac in other parts of the Near East, going back as much as 4000 years, all indicating the true starting place of the Zodiac...

In Virgo, we see the pregnant Virgin, with a branch in one hand, and sheaves of corn in her other hand (symbols of fertility)... In the first decan (10 degrees) of Virgo we see the constellation "Coma", which depicts the Virgin with a young child on her lap, who is the "desired one" (Coma, meaning: the desire of all nations, who shall come)... In the second decan we see the constellation "Centaurus", depicting the Centaur (half man, half beast) that "pierces" with the spear, the "Victim", who is "the despised and rejected of men" (but He is immortal)... And in the third decan, we see the constellation "Bootes" (the Coming One), who comes to subdue, to rule, and to govern... He comes as a great conqueror, and in his head is the star called "Nekkar" (meaning: "the pierced")... He comes forward with a spear in one hand, and a sickle in the other, with which He will harvest the Earth and bring forth men into final judgment... (This symbolism is reminiscent of the symbolism contained in "Revelations")... It seems that Virgo is an "overview" of the story contained in the Zodiac...

In Libra, we see the scales,.. in which men are weighed in the balance!.. The brightest star in the lower scale is called: (in Arabic) "Zuben al Genubi" (the price deficient), and in the upper scale is: "Zuben al Chemeli" (the price which covers), and below the scales is another star called: "Zuben Akrabi" (the price of the conflict)...

In the first decan of Libra, we see the constellation "Crux", which we call the "Southern Cross" (visible in the Southern hemisphere), and it is situated beneath the feet of the Centaur.., and in the darkest part of the sky... The Hebrew name for this decan is "Adom" (which means: "to be cut off"), and indeed, the "Cross" disappeared from view (due to the precession of the equinoxes) at almost exactly the same time as the crucifixion of Christ!., and wasn't seen again until the 16th century, when men sailed into the South Seas, around the Cape of Africa...

The second decan of Libra is called "Victima" (the Victim)... The earliest Arabian figures show the victim as "Sura" (the lamb)... (The lance of the Centaur reaches across from Virgo into Libra to pierce the Victim)...

The third decan of Libra is called; "Corona", or "Corona Borealis" (the Northern Crown)... In Arabic, this constellation is known as "Al Iclil", which means an ornament, or a jewel (a crown of jewels), and the brightest star in this constellation is called; "Al Phecca" (which means: "The Shining")... From the Southern Cross.., to the Northern Crown... The Victim will become the crowned Victor.., the One who has triumphed over death, the cross, Satan, and the grave.., the One who crushes the serpent beneath His heel.., the One who is the great ruling Redeemer of the World...

But wait!!. In the second decan of Scorpio, we see "Serpens" (the Serpent).., attempting to usurp the Crown!!. And in the first decan we see "Orphichus" (the Serpent Holder), wrestling with the giant serpent, and restraining it.., preventing it from usurping the Crown...

This is the constellation of "Scorpio"... In Arabic and Syriac, this constellation is known as: "Al Akrab" (which means: "War", or "the Conflict")... The principal star in this constellation, in the heart of the Scorpion is called "Antares" (meaning: "The Wounding").., and in the tail of the scorpion is another star, called: "Lesath" (meaning: "The Perverse")...

This is the central struggle of the Scriptures, portrayed in the Zodiac!!. We see the "Evil One", portrayed as a giant Scorpion, his left claw grasping at the lower level (the price deficient) of the scale of Libra.., and with his tail he wounds the heel of Orphicus.., as Orphicus with his right heel crushes the head of the scorpion!!. (sound familiar??. It is the *Protoevangelium*: Genesis 3:15)...

Etc., etc., and etc... All the way around the Zodiac, telling the Heroic tale of the Conqueror, who battles his way around the heavens, slaying the entities of evil; the scorpion, the serpent, and the dragon, etc., born of a Virgin and evolving into the God-man (the Lion-King) who will come to rule the Earth...

The myth has stayed remarkably the same, although the characters of the constellations have changed from region to region (no dragons in Egypt, so they substitute a crocodile.., no crocodiles in Mesopotamia, so they substitute a scorpion, etc.), and the serpent is universal, and of course the constellations are given Arabic, Greek, Latin, Hebrew, and English names, according to locality... The Egyptians see "Horus".., The Greeks see "Aesculapius" and "Hercules".., the Romans see (?).., and of course the Christians see the unfolding Biblical epic of Jesus Christ as the prophetic myth turned reality... So.., it wasn't just a myth after all.., It was "Prophesy"!!.

It is also interesting to note that the constellations rarely "look like" what they represent (the "big dipper" looks nothing like a bear *(Ursa Major)*.., etc., so the figures of the mythology (Prophesy) have been superimposed upon the constellations, giving them their meanings, and without which they would be meaningless.., that is to say, the message contained in the constellations.., is the Prophesy...

So.., the "astrologers" project an image onto the stars:.. (say; Libra, the scales).., and then project the qualities of that sign back onto their *believing* subject; *"Oh yes, you are a Libra, therefore you are a very balanced personality, able to see both sides, very diplomatic, good sense of balance, artsy-craftsy, etc., not entirely correct?., well, what's your rising sign? Oh, that explains it!.. And you are a Scorpio,* (the assumption being that at the moment of birth, your brain was somehow imprinted with scorpion characteristics)!., **(Do you really believe that?!!)**, *which means that you are calculating and manipulative... You should be very good in business, or as a policeman... Generally speaking, you are an asshole, but there is Jupiter in the mid-heavens, which sweetens your personality, and what is your rising sign?, oh good!.. And you are a Leo! Well, you have a strong and regal personality, you like to be the center of attention, etc., and you are prone to flattery and praise, you are a natural leader, etc.* (the etc., being more flattery and praise.., sounds like the Lion in the "Wizard of Oz"!..) *and your rising sign is?, Oh wonderful!!.*

Question: Where is the "causal link" between the image projected onto the stars, and the characteristics of that image (sign) being projected back onto the "believer"??. **Answer: *There is no causal link!!!***...

What is at work here is the power of suggestion, rendered potent by belief!!. (the elements of hypnosis: the post hypnotic suggestion, and the self fulfilling prophesy)... Everything that coincides (or wished for) is accepted as validation and proof,.. and anything that doesn't coincide is explained away as influences of your rising sign, or the moon, or your environmental upbringing, etc., and because.., after all.., "the stars don't compel, they only impel".?!

Nothing can be nailed down as specific, everything is generalizations, and the generalizations are open to interpretation... And the real irony, is that the astrologer is even more deluded than her/his subject!!. Those things that really do have an influence on your person/personality (your genetic, ethnic, racial, environmental, experiential, economic, linguistic, scholastic, political, social, nationalistic, and Religious inheritance.., as well as what you ate for breakfast).., ...are not even considered!!.

The process of "characterizing" your personality, is very similar to the process of "handicapping" horses at a horse race (except that the relevant information about horses is more concrete)!.. And what is the results of this astrological handicapping?.; people are "pigeonholed" and "profiled" with an unjustified prejudice (pre-judging) (positively or negatively, but incorrectly)... I have seen marriages that could have been saved, fall apart because of this astrological profiling (*"I'm a fire sign, and he's a water sign, therefore we are astrologically incompatible"*), etc., and etc... How many tragedies have occurred.., by the erroneous introduction of an erroneous logic.., that does not apply??.

So now we come to the **Big** question… Just how (and why) did the original intent and prophetic message of the zodiac get so skewed (screwed) up??!... **Who**.., changed the original starting point of the zodiac from Virgo to Aries (?).., thereby rendering the prophetic message contained in the zodiac into incoherent **"babble"** ???   **Who**.., is responsible for this deliberate act of sabotage??. The answer: (It doesn't take a rocket scientist).., **an Enemy has done this!!.**   That very enemy portrayed in the Zodiac has done this!, (or did you think that this "Enemy" was only a myth??.)... By changing the outcome of the prophesy, the "evil one" seeks to render the prophesy "null and void"... To the extent that in the minds of those people who are not aware of the prophesy, but have embraced astrology.., *he has been successful!!.*   He has screwed with your mind, introduced a logic system that doesn't compute, and turned you away from reliance on God (the God of Abraham, Isaac, and Jacob).., to reliance on astrology!!! *You have been deceived!!.*

The God of Abraham, Isaac, and Jacob, is the God that *speaks* to men... (This is the most important fact in the Bible, and the most overlooked)!.. It is a "phenomenon" more commonly known as; "The Inner Voice"... Abraham, Isaac, and Jacob (as well as all the other Seers, Saints, and Prophets) testified to the reality of this "Inner Voice", that gave them direction and guidance... The entire Bible, from beginning to end, is a testimony to the reality of "The Inner Voice"... But if you are looking for guidance and direction from "astrology" (how pathetic!).., you will never hear the "Inner Voice"...

This "phenomenon".., of the "Inner Voice".., is a universal constant... It can be found in all religions and doctrines from the most arcane to the most primitive.., and yet the most sophisticated can read the Bible (for instance) and miss it completely!!. It remains hidden from the "externally oriented".., from the sophisticated intellectual.., from the secular humanists.., from atheists.., from evolutionists.., from the profane, the perverse, the wicked.., and from astrologers (etc., and etc.)... And now you know...

Consider this;.. that the astrologers studied the stars for 10,000 (or 100,000) years.., and didn't know that the Earth rotated on it's axis.., or that the Earth traveled around the Sun.., or that the Sun was the center of our Solar system.., or that there was a Solar system, that contained *nine* planets instead of only five... They didn't know about Super Novas and Black Holes!.. They didn't know that the "blanket" of stars that they saw were actually light years removed from each other, and from the Earth (one light year = five and a half *trillion* miles)... They didn't know!!. And they are going to predict your future??!...

So the "Tower of Babel".., is a metaphor... If you were to take all of the books written about astrology.., and stacked them up into one pile.., what would you have??. It would be a "tower" reaching to the stars.., dedicated to the stars.., and it would be a tower of **babble...** Utter nonsense!!. So the construction of this tower of "babble" is not a construction of bricks and mortar, as much as it is a construction of nonsensical ideas that subverted the original intent of the "Prophesy", and diverted the attention of the practitioners of this "babble" away from the "True" Religion of the "People of God".., which was the reliance on the "Inner Voice" (the literal "Word Of God")...

Well..! (to paraphrase)... You can just imagine how pissed off the Lord was at this turn of events!!. His people had been deceived and seduced away from the true "Fountain of Knowledge" (within), and the "Prophesy" written in the stars had been reduced to babble!!. So He confused their tongues into different languages (perceived as babble by each other) and dispersed them (the "Diaspora") throughout the world... More metaphor??? Probably.., but it makes the point...

But.., it seems that in these confused times, "babble" reigns supreme!!. Babble Rules!!. By radio, by television, newspapers, magazines, and beamed to Earth by satellite, we are bombarded by babble!!, and every nation of all languages (still ignorant of the Prophesy contained in the zodiac).., has sought to resurrect the "Tower of Babel" of astrology!!! Uncontested and unopposed.., as though they had good sense...

So.., my friend.., you have inspired me!!. I had not intended to include any discussions of astrology in my forthcoming book, but due to our discussions on the subject (diametrically opposed).., I perceived the need!..

"The Tower of Babble"

And.., as I have invested a lot of time and research [5] into the above (incomplete) compilation intended for publication.., consider it to be copyrighted (©) by me as of the above date.., although you may distribute it to any of your astrologer acquaintances for their consideration... Feedback would be welcomed...

"Somebody" has to say *"Something"*!!!...

But will one lone voice have any effect upon the "believers" of this misbegotten *"religion"*??? Probably not!.. I am reminded of the time when I went to see "Sai Baba"[6] in India, and my Indian friend showed up on crutches!.. Gupta!, I said, what happened?!.. "Oh, I fell down the steps and broke my leg", he said, "but Sai Baba saved me"!!. But your leg is broken, I said.., how did Sai Baba save you??. "Well, if it wasn't for Sai Baba, I would have surely broken my neck"!!... How can you argue against that kind of logic??.

So.., (to wax philosophical here, for a moment).., we are, all of us, on that same long and winding road... Destination: "Enlightenment"... This road.., is the path of "Trial and Error"!.. Many trials.., and many errors... But hopefully, we can learn from our errors, retrace our steps, and continue on; *(oops!., wrong road!., dead end!., back up, turn around, Right face, go Straight)*... If we were to follow the advice of our Enlightened predecessors, we would follow the path of the "Straight and Narrow" (emphasis on "Straight"), but who, in this "enlightened" age (sarcasm intended) follows their advice?.. That path (simply stated) is: "To love the Lord above all things ("Communion" with.., and reliance upon.., the "Inner Voice").., and to love your neighbor as yourself" (do good.., every chance you get).., and that is really a very exciting path to follow!!.

To "deviate" from that path is to go down long and winding roads that are detrimental to body, mind, and Soul.., and where will these roads lead you?., to the "Shunyatta"??? [7] *An Enemy has done this!!...* Is this your enlightenment???..; that there is no God?., and consequently no Devil?., and the only truth is that there is no truth?., that all who have gone before you were fools??!.. *An Enemy has done this!!*

Sodom and Gomorra.., is not the wave of the future... Perhaps it is history repeating itself!.. There could hardly be a more diametrically opposed point of view, and I don't expect that either one of us could ever sway the viewpoint of the other... So why bother?.. I have pondered the response to my effort, and all that I can foresee.., is contempt!.. So why bother?.. *Because I don't abandon my friends so easily!..* If there is no God.., then nothing matters!!. But if there is.., *then it matters!!.*

Consider; "Descartes"... After a lengthy philosophical enquiry into the nature of his own being, the only thing that he could really ascertain for sure (the bottom line) was;.. "I think, therefore I am"... By the process of logical deduction, he concluded that "he was" in fact, a reality!.. But his philosophical enquiry didn't end there... He further concluded that if he did indeed exist as a reality, then (obviously) "consciousness".., in fact; "intelligent consciousness", exists in the Universe!!. He was himself "proof" of that fact!.. And since he was not alone in the universe, nor did he come into being by his own intention, nor was he even the "most intelligent" of intelligent beings.., he further

---

[5] My research into this subject is principally gleaned from the book entitled: "The Real Meaning of the Zodiac" by Dr. D. J. Kennedy, Ph.D. .., with further references to: "The Heavens Declare" by William D. Banks.., "Witness of the Stars" by E. W. Bullinger.., "The Hieroglyphics of the Heavens" by Bertha Carr-Davis.., etc., and etc…

[6] It was during my second trip to India that I encountered this (so called) Hindu "saint" that bills himself as: "The Living God".., and I perceived him to be a "Liar and a Charlatan" who has deceived his followers by claiming to be the reincarnation of a previous well known Saint, and by performing simple "slight of hand" magic tricks… I further discovered him to be a homosexual pervert (he "came on" to me), and I wouldn't trust him around children (for corroboration see the book: "Theologia Mystica", by; Bhagwan Shree Rajneesh.., page 70)… It was especially distressing to see Westerners (Americans, Europeans, Australians, etc.).,, bowing down before this "fraud".., believing this lie…

[7] The "Shunyatta" is probably the most misunderstood ancient philosophical doctrine ever put down in print!.. It states (condensed version) that since everything was created out of Absolute Nothingness, therefore Nothingness is the (hidden) reality of everything!.. The (intellectual) "Secular Humanists" of Buddha's day interpreted this doctrine to mean that the ultimate reality is Nothingness!., hence, there is no God, no Heaven, no Hell, no afterlife.., and that the only "Truth".., is that there is no "Truth"!.. But this is a total ("Flat Earth" mentality) misunderstanding and corruption of the philosophy…

concluded (by logical deduction) that in this chain of events; there had to be;.. a "First"!!.   By the process of logical deduction, Descartes observed that all of nature exhibited the "proof" of a "First Cause" intelligent consciousness that was in fact; "Genius"!!!... Descartes had found "God"...

That was by simple logical deduction!.. Add to that the multitude of eye witness (and "ear" witness) testimonials.., of paranormal events.., and the case is conclusive.., to all but the most determined (grossly materialistic) skeptics... I am sure you could supply a few testimonials of your own...

But speaking of paranormal events;.. you may recall that on my first "excursion", I entered the Bardo of the "After Death" state (Purgatory??!).., and I viewed the "living dead" as they existed in their "zombiefied" state, having been traumatized by the death experience... (Not a pleasant experience)... It was at this point that the "Inner Voice" spoke to me (rather harshly) and told me that this was where I was to "serve"!.., to which I replied: "Oh no, oh no, oh God, no".., then "He" further instructed me that I was to "stop smoking pot" (!!.).., to which I replied: "Oh no, oh no, oh God, no"... It seemed to me a punishment!.. So I threw up, and lay back down to further visions.., and I perceived myself in the Bardo, escorting these traumatized souls through the "veil" (a "stargate"), and into a beautiful realm, similar to Earth, but not Earth, and as they entered through the veil, they resumed their awake, alive, and youthful appearance!.. So I accepted the assignment (as if I had a choice), reluctantly at first, and then enthusiastically, and I complied with the directives...

So.., a year later.., my second "excursion" into the "twilight zone".., amid fear for my life, but having complied with the directives, I was received much more cordially by the "Lord of the Bwiti" (for want of a better name?) [8], and (it seemed) that after several hours of gradual escalation I reached the "peak" of the experience.., but I didn't realize it!!. I was being given a "gift" of a certain type of knowledge.., and observing the cut-away view of the human head and brain, and the location of the Soul within the brain which was shaped like a feathered "plume".., and where the brain was animal and mechanical, the feathered plume (of the Soul) was the real "consciousness principal" and the "intelligence factor" that separates "Man" from the rest of the animal kingdom... It was at this point that you enquired about the state of my well-being, and I proceeded to tell you about the "cut-away view" that I was seeing at that moment, not realizing that I was interrupting the sequence of the vision.., and I didn't realize it.., until "He" yelled at me!!!... *"He" yelled at me!!!...* Being yelled at got my attention, and I focused in on what was happening, but it was mostly too late!.. The "Zen moment" had passed, and all that I got was the knowledge of the location of the Soul.., and it resides within the brain... But even this.., is valuable knowledge!..

This second excursion.., although it was nothing like the first, it was indeed the logical extension of the first!.. There was a "closer" communication, and even a "camaraderie" with the "Bwiti" (Intelligence)... It was a "cleaner" high.., and of longer duration.., and there were subsequent revelations of a personal nature which I choose not to disclose at this time... But the similarities.., in terms of format.., and the nature of the "communion" with the Lord have made me comfortable with the experience...

Then we had our phone conversation, in which you informed me that you wished to be no longer involved in "my" excursions, and I couldn't afford your services at any price, etc., and etc... I think (in retrospect), that I might have conveyed the impression that I blamed you for the interruption at the "peak" of the experience.., and of course.., *I don't* !!... Hey!!, shit happens!!, what can I say??, nobody's fault!!. I should have recognized where I was at.., but I didn't... You were only conscientiously doing your part, and if I gave any impression to the contrary.., you have my most humble apologies!!!

But that night.., I went to bed.., and I dreamed!!! It was one of those "psychic dreams" (in which the "Super-conscious" communicates to the "Conscious" via the "Sub-conscious")... The characteristics of this type of dream is that you wake up immediately and remember it clearly, and it doesn't fade from memory... So I dreamed;.., that I was walking down this (long and winding) road, and the road turned to ice!.., but no problem, and I began skating on the ice, and the road started to incline upwards, but I was skating along with momentum, and I was skating up the incline until it

---

[8] I use the term: "Lord of the Bwiti" here, synonymously as one of the (many) names of God! There are (for instance) 32 names for God in the Hebrew religion alone, plus the generic form; "Ya"… There is only "One" God.., but his names are many!..

went vertical!., and still I climbed up, my fingernails biting into the ice, like a cat climbing up a tree, and I was standing on level ground (a plateau), and the ice had melted into water puddles along the road, and on my feet were "leather lace up" "Red Wing" (brand name) boots!...

Translation:.., I had reached a high plateau, on safe and level ground, with secure footing... It was an invitation by the "Lord"..., as I am an accepted member of the "Bwiti" "cult"!., and whomever the Bwiti accepts, should *Not* be rejected by the "Gatekeeper"!!... To do so, would be to incur *"extreme bad luck"*!!... So, my good friend (and you have been a *good* friend), I certainly do not wish you any bad luck on my account, and I pray to the Lord that you be absolved from "His" displeasure, whatever decision you make on this matter.., but I do think that you should "reconsider"... It would not be good to be at "cross-purposes" with the "Bwiti"..., whom you represent...

Furthermore.., you should consider me to be an ally.., and an investment.., because we are both on the same team, representing the "Bwiti", and "Ibogaine"..., and with the publication of my book, (not only nationwide, but worldwide) your "clientele" will multiply exponentially.., and how many "initiates" into the Bwiti cult do you know of that would be willing to follow in your footsteps, assisting you in your expanded enterprise??, (as I am doing, here)… I admire the work that you do.., and I am still your biggest fan...

I did explore the internet, looking for an alternate source of supply, so as not to be a burden to you.., but of course.., I found nothing that was readily or conveniently available... I know that you would prefer to "maximize" your profits.., and I would not dream of diverting a life saving medication away from someone in dire need for my own less urgent need.., but I don't think that this is really the case!.. This would be true only "IF" you had a fixed number (say 50) of doses, and an equally fixed number (say 50) of clients... But you do not have a fixed number of clients, and you have a renewable source of supply.., so you should never run out of supply and no one will be denied treatment (except me, ha ha)... So my "nominal fee" (paltry though it is), will always be; "in addition to".., and not.., "in place of".., your final total profit!.. But there are some things in life that are more important than "profit".., and.., if I may humbly suggest;.. "it is time"..., it is time for you to address the "Bwiti"... You have issues that need to be reconciled.., (*but don't we all*)!..

So.., enclosed you will find the paltry sum (the "nominal fee") which I know is not much to you, but it is a real effort for me, toward the purchase of the "magical elixir"..., and if this is insufficient, consider the balance due and payable upon publication of my book...

Well.., I hope that you have found the contents of this letter at least entertaining, if not informative... I wish you well in all of your endeavors, and I look forward to seeing you again in the future... May the Lord be with you always...

Highest Regards,   (I.O.)

*   (End of transcription)   *

Well.., that was the letter!.. As you can see, we had a difference of opinion on many things, and my attempt at diplomacy was a failure.., but I had to try...

He replied promptly, telling me that I didn't know the first thing about astrology, and my references to the "Evil One" were weird, and that he did indeed believe in God (a complete reversal from his previous "Shunyatta" philosophy, *which shows growth and promise),* that he does not and never did represent the "Bwiti", that he didn't believe in "bad luck", that he didn't need any "fans", and that in his "business" no one in need was turned away, except for me, which he wouldn't accept at any price, and he returned my "nominal fee", telling me that I could try Canada, or Amsterdam!!... **Ouch!!.** The only thing that he didn't reply to was the reference to the "Straight and Narrow" (emphasis on "Straight")!., which is probably (no doubt) the underlying personality conflict (disapproval, rejection) that he felt!..

What can I say?.. Diplomacy is not my strong point.., but I had to try!..

..* (End of story.., temporarily) * * *

"Artwork and the Tarot"

As history and legend tells the story, the "Tarot" dates back to a time-period "era" (probably 13th century A.D.) following the destruction of the "Great Library of Alexandria" (a tragedy of such proportions that it is second only to the "Great

Flood" of Noa)… As the story unfolds, it seems that a group of "intellectually sophisticated" learned "wise men" of the day, congregated in the city of "Fez", in Morocco, which boasted a University of higher learning that was considered to be the successor to Alexandria… They collaborated and conspired to encompass all of the known "knowledge and principles" of life and the world into one book.., and "relate" all of this knowledge by its "correspondences"… It would have taken another Alexandria type library to do this, so they decided to incorporate each "knowledge-principle" into a symbol, thereby condensing all of the knowledge (both esoteric and secular) into a book of pictures and symbols… It was postulated, that anyone who had an understanding of the pictures and symbols, could go to a desert island, meditate and contemplate on the pictures and symbols, and eventually arrive at "All Knowledge"!..

The concept was no less than **"Brilliant"**!.. This was possibly the first attempt at a "Unified Field" theory, encompassing both the metaphysical and the physical universe, with the objective of: *"To See the Scheme Entire"!...*

They chose as their layout "matrix" for this system of pictures and symbols, the 22 letters of the Hebrew alphabet (hence; 22 picture cards), incorporating the astrological symbols and planets as correspondences, and the numerical system (based largely on the Hebrew letters), corresponding to the letters, and relating the pictures and symbols to the letters, numbers, planets, etc…

The Tarot, having been created in the era of (relatively speaking) the "Dark Ages" of superstition and pseudo-mysticism, has undergone many changes, *evolving* into its (relatively speaking) present form, the most popular being the many variations of the "Waite" deck (by: A.E. Waite)… The story that these cards tell, by the pictures and by the symbols, is intriguing.., to say the least.., but to understand the message and the principles requires a knowledge of the meanings behind the symbolisms… For instance; the male figure, throughout the Tarot deck, always represents the *conscious* mind.., and the female figure always represents the *sub-conscious* mind… This interplay between conscious, sub-conscious, *and the Super-Conscious..,* is the "esoteric knowledge" that the Tarot was originally designed to convey… Now you have just an "inkling" of what the Tarot is all about.., and it was *never* intended for fortune telling…

As I said, the concept was "Brilliant".., but unfortunately.., this was **not** "The age of Enlightenment"… The Hebrew letters, and their subsequent attributions to "gematria", random sequence letter "codes", letters to numbers; "numerology", etc., is in **"total disrepute"**… Astrology.., a "bogus pseudo-science" is also in **"total disrepute"**… "Numbers".., once considered a mysterious and esoteric science available only to the "privileged" (numbers that could not be divided by 2 were considered "odd" and unlucky, etc..).., is now an advanced science understood even by children… And the "Tarot" itself has been replicated into *"Hundreds"* of different variations, degenerated into "Fortune Telling" and is the parent of today's card games, used for gambling, etc… So the "Tarot itself, is in **"total disrepute"**.., and rightly so.., but the original concept.., is still "Brilliant"…

But there is a certain "Magic" to the Tarot.., and that is in its ability to "evoke thought"… The "root word" behind "magic" is "image", hence "imagination"… By contemplating the universal language of pictures and symbols, the mind automatically busies itself in the analytical process of deciphering the meanings of the pictures and symbols, going into a reverie of imagination.., Analysis by imagination!.. An everyday process, that if we could but appreciate it.., is truly "magical"…

So I have attempted to incorporate this element of magic into the illustrations of this book, in that it contains many elements (symbols and pictures) that "evoke" thought in the mind.., that deserves to be elaborated on by further contemplation, and to be entered into the comprehensive whole of the "Unified Field" of the "Great Mystic Faith in its Entirety"…

I mention this because, although most of the illustration in this book are depictions of actual events, at least four of the illustrations contained herein are based on the Tarot.., but in an "evolved" format…

So I was a student of the Tarot… A dedicated, serious, and intent student, over a period of several years!.., and I owe much to the Tarot, and to my teacher, from whom I benefited greatly… The man that I call my teacher of the Tarot, I have never met.., He passed away during my youth, and I know him only through his writings, which spoke to me, eloquently and clearly… But there was a line (a prejudice) that my teacher would not cross.., and I crossed that line… The line that I crossed, was into the science of "Alchemy".., with the implementation of "Herbs of Mysterious Virtue"…

In a sense.., I surpassed my teacher.., which is a humbling experience… But I think he would have been proud!.. I saw farther, by standing on his shoulders… Hopefully, you who read this book will see farther than I… Hopefully, this book will be a stepping stone to greater heights of Spiritual achievement, in your service to the Lord.., which would be your crowning achievement.., and I will be proud!.. So with the aid of my expanded consciousness, I looked deeper, and I saw farther, and I discovered "errors" in the Tarot system.., and I also discovered a "Truth" that I will share with you, now…

That "Truth" is this:.. No matter how brilliant you are.., no matter how high your I.Q. .., no matter how well educated.., no matter the depth of your dedication and commitment.., the conscious mind is still *Not Capable* of "seeing" the "Absolute Truth" in its pristine purity… It is still the "surface consciousness", locked into its linear-logical-material frame of reference, and is just not capable of "seeing" and comprehending the depth of the Absolute and Arcane "Truth"… ***Therefore.., it follows:*** that: "However logical a series of deductions may be.., they are worth ***nothing,*** unless the original premise be correct"…

….Think about it!.. (case in point): There are (for instance) any number of dedicated men.., scholars.., searching the "Bible" for the "Truth".., all believing the Bible to be the "bedrock" "Word of God", and each Christian denomination has at its head one of these dedicated scholars.., *and there are 33,860 denominations of Christianity alone,* each claiming to be the "Truth".., and there are 10,000 other religions besides Christianity, each purporting to be the "Truth", and not one of them "Knows", because the Conscious mind is just not capable of it… **Point Made! …** So too, with the multitudes of versions of Tarot!..

The ability to see this "Truth" is reserved for the "Liberated Soul" that has transcended the boundaries of the Ego consciousness, and exists in its "unmodified state", as "Sight" alone.., which is referred to as the fabled "Third Eye".., which is the "Eye" of "Insight".., The "Eye" of the Soul… This "Trance-ascendance" to the state of the "Liberated Soul Consciousness" may be facilitated by "Herbs of Mysterious Virtue", or by the activation and raising of the Kundalini psychic energy factor.., or both!..

So the conscious mind, *unaided..,* is capable only of a superficial, "intellectual" understanding.., which falls short!.. With the introduction of a psychedelic (consciousness expanding) drug, *coupled* with an in-depth and disciplined technique of meditation, the level of consciousness is elevated, and the intuitive faculty is brought into play, relationships and correspondences are "seen" and assimilated, with profound understanding…

So with my newly discovered "Expanded Consciousness", I delved again into the arcane symbolism of the Tarot, and the symbolisms "pregnant with meaning" gave birth and expounded their knowledge before my inner eye… The symbolisms worked their magic, and my imagination came to life, and I delved ever deeper, relating information, seeing the correspondences, and for the first time.., I was "Seeing the Scheme Entire"!..

The most important card (and concept) of the Tarot, is card number 5; the "Hierophant" [9], and in *both* earlier and later versions, was called: the "Pope"… The distinguishing characteristic by which a "Pope" is known, and by which he receives his authority, is his faculty of "Inner Hearing".., that is to say; he hears directly the **"Living Word"..,** spoken by **"The Living God"…** There is no other fact of life, no other concept, no other doctrine, no other knowledge, of any esoteric fact.., that even compares to this "experience".., that is the goal and desire of every true aspirant on the "Path".., and it is a goal that is not necessarily attainable by merit, but is a "gift" granted at the Lords discretion.., *if* you make it a point to "listen"…

To assign to the "Living Word".., a "number".., a "letter".., a "planet".., and an "astrological sign".., is to mix the "Sacred" with the profane!.. In a time

---

[9] "Hierophant"; (from the Greek) : The High Priest, who was the expounder of the (Sacred) Eleusinian Mysteries…

long gone by.., in the dark ages of ignorance and superstition.., these were considered to be: the "Mystic Arts"!.. It is a tragedy, that they were ever integrated into the same system of the Truth of the "Living Word".., and the further tragedy is that the Truth of the "Living Word" has been all but forgotten, and the fallacious superstitions of the so-called "Mystic Arts" has survived, and are still being taught to a foolish generation!..

We owe much to those pioneers and explorers that have gone before us.., blazing trails and drawing the maps that future generations could follow, and avoid the treacherous terrains, the dead-ends, the poisonous jungles, the quick-sand, and the quagmires, etc., lest we lose our way.., and get "lost"… So too, "I" (Iron Owl, the intrepid explorer) have gone down these many roads of ignorance and superstition, wasting my time, losing my "way", and then finding the "Way"… **"Been There, Done That"..,** and you can either learn from my mistakes.., or you can repeat them… These are the choices we make, on this "Journey" through Life…

To abandon the "Living Word", the **True** "Fountain of Knowledge and Wisdom".., and lose your "way", and your valuable "time" (the "substance" of your life), wandering through this quagmire-maze of superstition and ignorance.., into dead-end misconceptions.., is to "lose".., at: that most intriguing game of all.., **"The Game of Life"!..**

* * *

The "Tower", is the structure of error and ignorance, which is struck by the "Lightning Flash" of a spiritual *"Awakening"*… It is interesting, that the originators of Tarot would use this symbolism to convey essentially the same meaning that I am using it to convey here!.. The "Sun", from which the "Lightening Flash" of "Awakening" occurs, is the symbolic representation of "Super Consciousness"… The male and female figures falling from the tower represent the conscious and subconscious mind, and they are falling to their destruction… Through this structure of error and ignorance, the mind has been subverted away from the true Knowledge of the "Living Word", and diverted into pseudo-magical systems that are essentially "Babble"… The greatest of tragedies… The Lightening flash of the "Awakening", knocks off the false crown of this false religion…

Unfortunately, this "Tower of Babble" is a very pervasive, hard and harsh "living reality"!.. By consulting an "on-line" book-seller, I was able to list 40 titles of this "babble" within the space of 20 minutes, and these are the titles that appear on the "Tower", and they are available today, at your local book-store…

* * *

Tarot card number "1" (for instance), is called: "The Magician"… In this illustration, we see the male figure, the Magician, standing in his garden (the "field" of his environment, under cultivation), with his right hand raised above his head, holding a "wand" (symbolizing a "scepter" of authority).., and with his left hand, he is pointing to "Earth"… The meaning is; that the Magician is the "intermediary" (conscious participant) between the "Heavenly Power" above, and directing it into the field of his environment, to do "work" on "Earth"!.. …A very Noble concept… In the "field" of this picture, the Magician stands before a table (his work-bench) upon which are the implements of his craft: a wand, the cup, the sword, and the coin-pentacle, symbolizing the constituents of matter (in the ancient tradition) of: Fire, Water, Air, and Earth, or (in the modern tradition); Heat (radiant energy), liquids, gases, and solids.., and later devolving to the playing cards: spades, clubs, hearts, and diamonds….

In this "evolved" scenario, the Magician has now become the "Alchemist"… He holds in his right hand the "Vajra-Dorje".., which is the "Llamic scepter", which signifies mastery of both the inner and outer realms of being… It is made from a diamond, signifying the crystal clarity and the adamantine indestructibility of the "First Cause", which is the "Absolute" in the Pristine Purity of His "formless form" aspect, which is "Nothingness" in its Absolute Essence!.. (*Not*-conceptual)… From out of Nothingness, came Everything!., $\{0 = (+1) + (-1)\}$… This is the most ancient of doctrines, and the most modern (cutting-edge and controversial) concept of astro-physics…

He stands before the table of "Intention", the implements of his craft being displayed there-on… The unleavened bread and wine, (symbolizing his dedication and commitment).., his research materials (the Book of the Mind, Patanjalie's yoga).., The "Sword of Truth" (discriminating wisely).., The "mortar and pestle" (symbol of

Alchemy)..., The vase (containing the Magical Herbs, "of Mysterious Virtue")..., The Bible, opened to Revelations 22:2.., (describing the "Holy City", the "Tree of Life", and the "herbal remedy" that is for the "healing of Nations")... In his garden, grows the "Peyote Cactus", the "Sacred Mushrooms", the "Morning Glory", etc.., and below.., in the region of "Hell"..., are those unfortunate souls.., who have failed at the "Game of Life"..., those who have "failed to discriminate"...

"One Picture.., is Worth a Thousand Words"...

* * *

The Tarot card depicting the beginning of the Soul's "Journey" through life is called: "The Fool".., denoting the naive innocence of the pure soul as it leaves the heights of an elevated realm of consciousness into the material world of manifestation... The dog at his side represents a lower form of consciousness, which in the material world would be sub-consciousness, but in the elevated realms of consciousness is: the intellect!.. In earlier forms of Tarot, the dog was shown as an antagonist, chewing at the ankles of its master (which is the case with most intellectuals) but in the later versions was given a more positive "spin" to show a more amicable relationship... With the Sun (representing Super-Consciousness) at his back, and the red rose (of desire) in his left hand, he leaves the mountains (representing abstract concepts, etc.) on his search into the adventure of Life...

The "Return" of the "Fool" to the heights of this elevated consciousness, is the hope and desire of every aspirant on the "Path"... It is a depiction of the "Triumphant and Eternal Intelligence", in that he has experienced the "Communion and Union" with "Super-Consciousness", and has realized that he is an "Immortal Soul" on an eternal mission (an Agent of Universe)... He faces into the East (background), toward Super-Consciousness, with the staff (representing the "scepter" of dominion and free will) in his right hand, the Lotus flower (a psychedelic) in his left hand, and his faithful dog (also looking east) at his side (representing an enlightened intellect, with fifth dimensional reasoning)... The "Logo" on his back represents the Triune God Consciousness, the bag on his shoulder representing the accumulation of memories and experiences of his journey, the architecture of the bell housing, represents the Deva worlds of fifth dimensional manifestations, his belt; the charkas, and the Bell, representing *That* primordial sound-vibration that echoes throughout the Universe... His path leads on through the mountains.., an eternal adventure...

* * *

Those of you who are familiar with the Tarot will recognize the central figure of this next piece (Titled: "The New Earth") as having been taken from the final card of the Tarot deck, called: "The World"... The wreath is a symbol of attainment, and in this case it serves as the "Stargate" transition point between two dimensions, namely; "Purgatory", and the "New Earth"... The "New Earth" (as I saw it), is very similar to "The World" that we know, except it is located within the realm of the "Fifth Dimension"... The principle difference between "The World" and the "New Earth", is that all of the population is composed of "Good People"!.. *No assholes!..* No slums, no poverty, no disease, etc...

My personal encounter with this realm was very brief, so I don't know a lot about it, except that it is an "after death" state that worthy departed souls go to, and also those souls that have spent time in the temporary state of "Purgatory", imprisoned within the bleak comatose nether-world of their own minds... The "awakening" from Purgatory to the New Earth, is a spectacular event, and don't confuse this "Fifth Dimensional" event as simply "mental phenomena", because I can assure you, the "New Earth" is a "Tangibly Real" Reality!..

* * *

Now.., if someone had told me that the artwork contained in this book would take almost two years to complete.., I would have run screaming from the building!.. This far exceeds the parameters of my patience.., but I didn't know this when I first conceived of these illustrations... Fortunately for me, my artist and friend; "Raz" (the Illustrious Illustrator) is not only a very fine artist, he is also blessed with the gift of "patience"... I would make a very rough conceptual drawing, from which he would produce a rough draft, I would critique and correct the rough draft, to produce an "evolved" second rough draft, then a third, and a fourth, etc., evolving and refining until we were both satisfied with the final result... He would then "ink" the rough draft, and then I would make some final corrections (much to his dismay) (ha ha)!..

The original artwork was done on poster size art paper, embellished with much intricate detail that is somewhat obscured when shrunk down to page size, and is produced here in "black-and-white" to keep this book in the affordable price range.., but to appreciate the fine detail, you may want to view this art with the aid of a good magnifying glass.., but the full "poster size" artwork is so artistically compelling and intricately detailed, that I have decided to make the poster sized, fully colored, original renditions available to whomever wants them, at a nominal price, and in a variety of sizes (yet to be determined)…

* * *   * * *   * * *

BOOK XVIII

"The Preliminary Prerequisite"

So.., every book has a last chapter... at this point I had been on the road for about five years, and my journeys, on the road, away from my native country, would ultimately go on for twelve years, with far too many experiences to fit between the pages of a single book... So this is not the final chapter of my travels, but it is the last chapter of this book...

Since this book is still ongoing.., as are my travels on this journey called "life".., and since this book is not necessarily in chronological order, I will end this book with what would ordinarily be.., the First Chapter...

In chronological order, this was my first experience of a Metaphysical nature. All journeys begin with a first step. This was my first step.

This first step.., is a prerequisite.

Suffice it to say, that in almost all respects I am your common, everyday, 20th century man. I speak in the vernacular of the common man, because that is what suits me.

At the age of about 25 years, I was already a family man. I worked hard as a craftsman, about 10 hours a day, six days a week, plus occasional side jobs. I really worked too hard, but there was a mortgage, and bills to pay, and, like everybody, I was trying to get ahead. But my heart wasn't really in it. It seemed to me that I was the pawn in somebody else's game. I had let myself be painted into a corner. My game, the inner quest, the prime directive of my soul, had to be put aside, so that I could provide for every body else's game. I was a martyr to goodness, doing the right thing, even though I felt that I had been manipulated into this position. I was too good for my own good, but that's the way I was raised, to do the right thing. Because of this tendency, my reactions were predictable, and I was vulnerable to being imposed upon, and I was... My spirit yearned to be free, but I was ensnared in a web.., of trivialities.., that consumed my time, my energy, and my purpose.

.....I think I hated that little old man.... I didn't know him. I had never met him... He was an older man, probably a veteran of the last world war. His legs were amputated well above the knees, almost to the crotch, and you had to wonder just how extensive his amputations were... And there he sat.., day after day, every day, on his little 2 x 2 ft. square platform, with the caster wheels.., and worn out gloves on his hands that he used to propel himself down the sidewalk... He was a tragedy... A tragic sight, the corners of his mouth turned downward in a sorrowful frown, a dilapidated hat on his head, shielding his eyes from the harsh sunlight, a three day growth of beard, an alcoholics reddish bulbous nose, a bunch of pencils.., and a tin cup... He positioned himself in front of the local drugstore.

Every time I went to the drugstore I had to walk by this tragic sight, and I would feel guilty, because I had two good legs to walk with. Reluctantly, out of some sense of duty, without even looking at the man, I would drop some spare change into his tin cup. And just as reluctantly, he received my meager donation. The sorrowful frown on his face remained unchanged.

.....I was an avid reader. I read everything that presented itself to my view, but non-fiction only. I have had many great teachers.., the Authors, of many great books...

In my world of martyrdom and self sacrifice, as I was browsing through the bookstore, I happen on a book with an intriguing title;., "The Art of Selfishness"... I thumbed through the book;.. Oh yes!.. The book dealt with the simple philosophy of "To thine own self be true", selfishly true, and those people who would impose upon you will have to rely on themselves, and everything works out for the best... I fit the profile of the one imposed upon, and I was looking for a philosophically righteous reason to tell everybody to "turn blue and drop dead"... Yes, I needed to adopt this philosophy of selfishness.., in self defense...

In this moment of selfishness, I bought this book, and regarded it as a treasure... I was determined to be self righteously selfish... "No more Mr. Nice Guy"!..

With the zeal of a convert, I practiced the utmost selfishness. I searched my Soul for more ways to exercise this "Art of Selfishness". I analyzed every situation to determine my most selfish motive, then acted out my most justifiable selfishness... I gloried in the freedom of my new-found selfishness...

It was at this point that I had to make a purchase at the local drug store.., and there he sat.., that tragic sight.., that little old, sorrowful, legless man.., "Well, not this time".., I said to myself with selfish determination... No more will I allow this little man to manipulate me into giving him my hard earned money. No more will I be fooled by his facade of sorrowfulness. He's probably wealthy from the donations he receives... He probably has a chauffeured limousine, that drops him off at this location, and the chauffeur is probably a "busty blond babe", and he's laughing all the way to the bank... He's probably even more selfish than I am!..

With an attitude of haughty indifference, I walked past him, ignoring him completely, and feeling justified by doing so... I made my purchase, and started to leave the store. I'll leave by the side door, I thought, and not even walk by this manipulative "con man", thereby expressing my utter contempt for him...

I left the store by the side door, and was walking across the parking lot to my car, when suddenly I was hit by a "twinge of conscience"!.. I stopped dead in my tracks... How could this be?.. How could this possibly be?.. How could I feel a "twinge of conscience" when I had resolved to not have a conscience?.. With my new-found philosophy of self-righteous selfishness, I shouldn't be bothered with "twinges of conscience"!.. Perhaps I still wasn't selfish enough... I plumbed the depths of my Soul to bring forth my utmost selfishness... What did "I", in my utmost selfishness, want to do in this situation?.. I analyzed this "twinge of conscience", against my philosophy of selfishness, and I came up with my most selfish inclination... I took a couple of bills from my wallet, and put them in my shirt pocket... I walked around to the front of the store. I stood right in front of this little man, towering over him, looking down on him...

"How ya doin"?., I asked. "Oh, not so bad", he said, "How's yourself"?.. I dropped down on one knee, my elbow resting on my other knee, looking him straight in the face... We started talking... There was a transformation!.. His round face lit up like a Halloween Jack-O-lantern!.. He had the largest mouth I had ever seen!.. His gap-toothed smile reached from ear to ear!., and that dilapidated hat on his head.., that red bulbous nose!.., He was a clown!!.., the *Ultimate* clown!!... He radiated joy!.. We were talking.., then we were joking.., then we were laughing.!. I unobtrusively took the bills from my shirt pocket and put them in his tin cup, from which I took two pencils. He bellowed with laughter.., his legless body was convulsed with laughter.., and so was I... We shook hands, and bid each other farewell, waving good by, and still chuckling, as we parted company...

"What happened"?.. I asked myself... This was something new that just happened, something different... I analyzed the situation.., I had pushed myself to my most selfish moment.., and in that moment of utmost selfishness, I was..; ...benevolent!.. This was a revelation!..

In one sense, nothing had changed... I had walked by this little old man, just like I always did, and given him my meager donation, as I always did, and he received it, as he always did... I had given my donation reluctantly, and he had received it reluctantly.., but this time.., this time, I had given my donation willingly.., and NOT for the benefit of that little old man!.. No, let there be no mistake.., my motive was much more selfish than that... There was no self sacrifice involved in this... It was pure selfishness!..

Pure selfishness... That's why I did it... It made "ME" feel good... It gave "ME" pleasure to do this... It was "I" who benefited from this act of doing what "I" wanted to do... This was my most selfish motive.., my most selfish moment.., *ever*!.. And for the very first time.., I made my donation willingly, because it pleased ME to do so, and for the very first time, that little old man received my donation.., with joy!..

Outwardly, nothing had changed... It was the same act, the same donation... But inwardly, everything had changed... My motive had changed... I understood, for the first time.., that there are NO unselfish acts! There is always a motive...

But, what had been my motive, previously?., my hidden motive.., my hidden ulterior motive?.. I analyzed the situation... Was it because it had made me feel good? No, that wasn't the reason. It hadn't make me feel good.., I resented it!.. I resented that little old man... He made me feel guilty for being healthy... It was extortion!.. I had given him

"The Gift"

money to ward off my feelings of guilt!.. I gave him money because I was the martyr... I gave him money for the self aggrandizement of my own soul.., to say..; "Look at me Lord".., this self sacrificing martyr, giving my hard earned money to this cripple that I don't even like!..   And now.., now I knew the Truth... I had given him money for all the wrong reasons.., and they were secret selfish reasons... Oh, Thou Fool!.. Thou pitiful selfish fool...

I had read the book, but I had missed the point!.. The point had been driven home to me by that little old man... I had achieved total selfishness.., and my most selfish act was benevolent... It was a paradox... There could be only one solution to this paradox... My essential nature must be..; "Good"!.. I hadn't known this about myself! This was a surprise!., a revelation!.. When I was my most selfish, I was the most sincere, and true to my own nature, which was essentially..; "Good"... I derived selfish pleasure out of doing Good...   I must therefore be..; "Good"!!.

This was a personality change. I had been unsure of myself before, but now.., I knew about myself... I trusted myself and my instincts, because I knew myself to be good... I had a new self confidence!.. I did what I wanted to do with a sincerity that came from my most selfish motives.., and it was Good! There were people who liked me before, that didn't like me now.., and there were people who didn't like me before, that liked me now!.. My attitude had changed... No longer did I want to be the guest at the party who would indulge himself with food and drink because it was free.., No.., I was much more selfish than that.., I wanted to be the Host of the party, and I would say:., "Indulge yourself, because it pleases me"...

I reviewed my life of self sacrificing martyrdom, and found it to be a sham, and a tragedy, not only to myself, but to people around me. There was always an ulterior motive, based on reason, and the reasons were;., shallow.., and even though I considered myself a martyr.., I always did what "I" wanted to do... It was always my own decision!.. But now.., now I was doing those very same things that I felt that I had been forced to do before, except now.., now my motives were totally selfish.., and my burdens.., *had become light*!..

I had given that little old man a pittance.., and I had received a treasure.., and two pencils!..   I look upon this incident as the very best day.., of my entire life!!. It was some time before I went back to the drugstore again.., and he wasn't there!!... I enquired about him, but could find no one who even remembered him being there... Somehow, I knew that this would be the case... I never saw him again...

I made a leap of faith, here... I reasoned that if my most selfish instincts were essentially good, then this must also be true for everyone. I evangelized about this book that had brought about such a radical transformation in my personality and my life. I purchased and gave away as gifts several copies of this book to anyone who showed an interest.., or a need...

But, I guess the point of the book is subtle, and difficult to grasp.., kind of a "Zen" thing... Not everyone can get beyond the shallow selfishness, down to the "nitty-gritty" True selfishness. It seemed that everyone benefited from the book in some way, but some of them got to be more selfish than others, which causes me to question my first assumption.., that everyone is basically Good... Perhaps some people really are assholes!..

But I prefer to think not... I prefer to think that it just takes some people longer than others, but the Goodness is still there, somewhere, and eventually, a purely selfish act of goodness will emerge.., and change the course of your life!!.

And something has to be said.., about Love!.. When you sacrifice of yourself to the benefit of another, there is a reward involved, be it a psychological indebtedness, or the currying of favor, or whatever shallow reason... Your supposed unselfish act carries an unspoken price... This is not an act of true love, but is instead the act of a self seeking manipulator disguised as a martyr...

True Love.., When your personal selfishness extends to and includes "your neighbor as yourself", that's true love... Without attachment, without recompense... Regardless of the effort, no sacrifice involved... My motive?;, to see you benefit!.. That's what "I" want... It Pleases "ME".., and my reward is;., self gratification...

This is in praise of selfishness... Selfishness is good!.. It doesn't matter if your selfishness be of the "shallow" kind, or of the "deep" kind.., as long as you know the Truth about it.., as long as you are not deceiving yourself or someone else about it... It's a question of seeing through yourself and into yourself, and of being honest with yourself about what your motives really are, and we already know, and have to acknowledge.., our motives are selfish!., and selfishness, shows a profit!., and profit is good...

It was Adam Smith, that observed the results of true selfishness, when he wrote his book;.. "The Wealth of Nations".., that became the cornerstone of the American system of free enterprise, and the private ownership of property, and the prosperity engendered by the True selfishness of working for your own self interests, that translated into the wealth of this nation, and every other nation that followed this principle... This theme was further elaborated on by "Ayn Rand", in her book entitled: "The Virtue of Selfishness"...

Contrast this philosophy with the fate of those countries that view the ownership of private property as selfish, and therefore immoral... Contrast this philosophy with the fate of those countries that say that free enterprise is selfish and immoral, and all profit should go to the State.., for the benefit of the masses... Their ideal of unselfish equality results in lack of incentive, conformity, stagnation, and Communism.., and they are all equal in their blandness, and in their relative poverty... Etc...

In praise of selfishness, The Art of Selfishness, The Virtue of Selfishness?.. Yes, But.., What about those people that cheat, and steal, that take more than their fair share, and profit at their neighbors expense?.. Yes, this is also selfishness, but it is the superficial, shallow selfishness of the "asshole", and he is also being true to his self, or is he?.. Does he even know himself?.. Does he even have a chance of finding himself?.. or is he really just an asshole?., that says in his heart of hearts that there is no God.., and "fuck you"!..

So where does the essence of YOUR selfishness lay?.. This is what you have to find out. This is the question that you must answer for yourself. There are two roads out there, and with the utmost selfishness you must pick one...

.....Pick one!.. This is the preliminary prerequisite, and to thine own self.., be True!., and be not false to any man.., ...or woman...

* * * * *

So.., choose the road that you will travel, and if you are Truly selfish, you will choose the road that leads to Enlightenment.., in the service of.., and in Communion with.., The Lord.., "Of the Great Mystic Faith in it's Entirety".., and you will endeavor to live your life in truth and sincerity, and love your neighbor as yourself...

This is a decision.., this "fork in the road"... This is a dramatic "change of heart", that some people might call; being "Born Again"... It is the call..; to the Spirit of the Lord, that dwells within the Soul of Man... It is the "*Thee* within Me", that in a moment of recognition, a moment of clarity, decides..: to stop playing the "asshole", and instead, become the "Hero" of your own life, and the Hero to your family.., doing good, every chance that you get, with gratitude for the opportunity...

This "change of heart".., is the most significant event of your life!!. Be it a reasoned conclusion, or triggered by an external event, or by an internal realization.., it is the most significant event of your life, and you should solidify this most significant internal event with an equally significant "external event".., (lest this most significant event pass away, and you revert to "asshole" status)...

This most significant "external event" is called: "Baptism"... It is the most important external event of your life.., more important than your birth, more important than your wedding day, more important than the birth of your first born child.., it is your rebirth.., into the brotherhood of the family of the Lord...

Baptism is different than any other religious event... It is NOT something that you do as a routine procedure, such as joining a church, or for the purpose of marrying into a different faith, or in conformity with your peers, or as an infant babe that has no concept of what is happening, etc... (This is just a dedication ceremony).., a Baptism of water, only...

NO, No, *No*.., Baptism is the consequence of that "Internal Event", that "change of heart".., that motivates you, to go to the servant of the Lord, and ASK to be Baptized... This is the Tradition!., You must ASK to be Baptized... You must speak the words: "Please, Baptize me"... Even Jesus followed this Tradition, and asked to be Baptized...

This is the "Baptism of Fire"... This is the Event that declares to God, to all men, and to yourself, that you have taken this step into the Brotherhood of the family of God!., deliberately and intentionally, motivated by the "fire" and passion of the Spirit, dedicating your self to that which is the Good, the Right, and the True... A "New" vessel...

This is the event that you can point to, the day and the year of your commitment.., and remember it as the turning point of your life... Even though the fire of passion may fade, the memory of that event will keep you on the straight and true path...

So.., If you would be a serious student of "The Great Mystic Faith in it's Entirety".., Your first step, is the "Baptism of Fire"... *You must ask to be Baptized...* The ceremony is called:., "The Baptism of Fire and Water"...

To Thine own Self, be True.

* * * * * * *

The Game Of Life

In an effort to make this book of Universal appeal.., I have endeavored to show the Universality of God and the Universality of Truth, with no partiality to any religion in particular... Even this most important event of Baptism has it's equivalent in every religion... It is not your particular religion that is important here.., it is your relationship with the "Most High God".., (by whatever name HE may be known).., that is of the most paramount importance...

Now.., What if?., What if "Life".., was just a Game.?. Not just any game.., but the "Ultimate Game"... The Ultimate Game, propounded by the "Ultimate Gamesman".., and the first element of the game.., was that you didn't know it was a game!!.

This is the Game of games... You passed through the veil of forgetfulness to enter into this game, a "clean slate", without any preconceived notions, in complete ignorance of the game... This makes it a very serious game.., This makes the game; "Real"...

The second element of the game, is that it is a "crapshoot"... It is just a roll of the dice.., the luck of the draw.., whether you were born rich or poor, black or white, slave or free, male or female, Oriental or Occidental, Northern hemisphere or Southern, this or that genetic inheritance, this religion or that.., or no religion at all... Or will you be aborted from the game at the get-go?..

The third element of the game, is "free will"... What will you do.?. What will you be.?. What role will you play in this Game of games.?. Will you be; "butcher, baker, or candle-stick maker", will you be a warrior or a farmer, will you be the "Hero".., or will you be the villain?., will you choose the Good, or will you choose Evil.?.

The fourth element of the game?., the rewards of the game..; success or failure, wealth or poverty, health or sickness, friends or enemies, laughter or sorrow, life or death.., Heaven.., or Hell... This is a very serious game...

The obstacles in the game..; the "Tower of Babble"... That mountain of mis-information, mis-direction, superstition, errors and lies... The pitfalls..; "pride, covetousness, lust, gluttony, anger, envy and sloth"... The snares..; the liars, the thieves, the cheats, the money changers, the false Gods, the false prophets, the pimps, the pushers, and the faggots...

The objectives of the game..; to navigate through this obstacle course, avoiding the pitfalls, avoiding the snares, seeing through the Tower of Babble, separating the Truth from the lies, choosing the good and the True.., and to realize.., the nature of the Game.., the nature of the Master Gamesman.., and the nature of your eternal Self...

Now.., "What if"?.. What if this "Game of Life" is based upon your personal and individual "Search" for the Truth (the Ultimate "scavenger hunt").., and what if ALL of the Truth was not contained in just one religion, but each and every religion contained a portion of the Truth (as well as errors).., and the Truth was far more Glorious in It's dimensions and aspects than just one religion could contain.., and the grand prize went to those individuals that had transcended the confines of one particular religion, but instead saw the Universality of ALL religions, and recognizing the similarities of Truth in All religions, could also discern the errors... And what of those Truths that lay outside of religion, in Nature, and in Life's experiences.., only to discover that this was religion too...

Each of these religions.., developed independently.., in regions of the Earth isolated from one another.., but each one seeking to know their Creator...

"The Game of Life"

Of course they would develop differently, with different Patriarchs (their men of vision), with a variety of religious experiences (the landscapes of the fifth dimension being so vast and so varied)... Of course they would have different Saints and Holy Men, with different Heroes and legends... Of course their portion (of the Truth) would be different, as is their approach, and the questions they would ask in the context of their quest... Of course they would have a different history, a different culture, and different Divine Hierarchies.., and each one of these independent Religions would arrive at similar "Truths".., and also discover a portion of the Truth.., that the others had not found...

Who among You?., would seek to See and to Know the scheme entire.?. Who among you would discover the hidden secrets of;.. "The Great Mystic Faith in its Entirety".?. Who among you would encounter "HIM".., who is the Lord of, and the Head of *ALL* the Divine Hierarchies...

Each one of these Religions.., is just a part of the whole... All of them taken together, constitute "The Great Mystic Faith in its Entirety"... Each one of them separately is a way unto itself, and they all concur.., that the way out of the Game.., lies within...

Or did you suppose.., that your particular belief system was the one and only Truth, and that the one and only God Almighty came for only you and your particular denomination, and that all other religions and their religious folk were doomed to perdition.?. Did you suppose that only you and yours were God's "chosen people".., or the "master race".., or that you yourself were somehow unique and special.?. Only in your absurd imagination...

The Truth is where you find it.., and all external Truth is (relatively speaking) superficial... "HE".., is no respecter of persons, or religions, or peoples, or races.., and the only "chosen people" are those that choose to Know "HIM"... Only those.., who come to "HIM", in the "Inner Sanctum", of the "Holy of Holies".., only these.., are HIS people... Only these who go "within".., are the Masters of the Game...

Heaven lies within you...

** *The End* ??? ***

It is most appropriate that the "end" of this book should conclude with the chapter that is in reality the beginning of the "Great Adventure"!., because there is no end to the Great Adventure of Life!!. Even "Death" is not the end!.. Death has been called the "Grand Illusion"... Surprise, surprise!., there is no death!!! *The Joke is on you!..* Just think.., if the great adventure were to end!., what then?.. boredom?, stagnation?.. No no **No!**., there is always more and more to see.., and to learn.., and to do.., and *You* are the "Hero" of this Grand Adventure, and as long as there is ignorance, hatred, sorrow, stupidity, and *Evil* in **any** of the planes of existence (inner and outer).., you have a purpose, and work to do!..

So start now!.. Hopefully, this little book will be a starting place for you.., like that legless old man was for me, and you will find the true nature of your soul *(the prerequisite),* and realize, with the utmost selfishness, that the essence of your nature is "Good", and you have opportunities to do much good yet in this life.., *and Not to "earn" your eternal reward, but because* **you already have it!!,** (immortality as a child of God)!!, and you will Champion the cause of good and righteousness with the utmost selfishness, because it is your honor, pleasure, and privilege to do this!!! This total selfishness translates into the purity of heart recognized as "Sincerity", which manifests itself as the **"Will to Good"**, which is motivated by that even deeper deep-seated driving force by which God is known..; It is called: "Love".

Hallelujah!.. Go with God!..

*** Amen ***

Well.., that was to be the closing statement of this book... So the question arises.., why am I still writing??. Because this is the "Never Ending Book".., and I have asked myself and the Lord this same question: "Oh Lord, will this book never end"??., will I ever be finished??... Perhaps not!!... But I have one more story to tell you.., one more experience…

Just when you think you know it all!!.

Several years later (back in the States), I was on a "mission" (classified), driving through central Florida on my way to Miami... It was a typical hot and humid day, and my air conditioner wasn't working, so I stopped off at a roadside tavern to have a sandwich and something to drink... It was lunch time, and a boisterous labor class crowd filled the place... I sat at the bar eating my sandwich and drinking a cold beer, and I was turned around on the bar stool, watching the pool table in the center of the floor, and the contest between the two players...

Pool is my game!.. I don't play golf, and I don't care for baseball, etc., but I enjoy a good game of pool... So I was sitting there, intently watching the game, and two bar stools down from me sat (what was referred to at that time, as;) a "Mongoloid Idiot"[1] seemingly fascinated by me and my interest in this game!!. I don't normally speak to Mongoloid Idiots, but his curiosity with me, and my intent interest in this game of pool, for some reason, fascinated his "simple" mind!.. *"You like this game"?.,* he asked, in his simple, thick tongued, way... I looked at him, and he was shaped like a blimp, with an oriental slant eyed moon face, that looked like a Chinese version of a "Happy face", but with the innocence of a new-born babe!..

"Yes", I answered, "I like this game"... I never really had a conversation with a Mongoloid before, but being a student of human nature, I engaged him in conversation, and found out that his name was "Jocko" and he had a job as a janitor at a car dealership (probably a relative), and this job was the most important thing in his life!.. He wasn't here alone, but with other personnel from the car dealership that were keeping an eye on him...

"You want to play pool?" he asked me, with his thick tongued, slurred speech... "With you?!!", I asked... "Yes", he said... I was momentarily stunned!.. I was being asked to play pool with a Mongoloid Idiot!!! I looked at him intently.., he was young, 21 at the very most, very neatly dressed, and his fine blond hair was neatly parted and combed... Obviously, he had a mother who loved him!., and the expression on his face was that of a Cherub angel, with the joyous innocence and anticipation of a young child... I looked at the table, and the previous players (as if on cue) finished their game and walked away from the table!.. I couldn't say; "No"...

"Sure", I said, "Come on".., and I proceeded to the table, put a couple of quarters into the slot, and racked the balls... I picked out a cue stick for him, being absolutely positive that he had never played the game before... "I will break the balls", I said, "and then we can take turns shooting the balls, o.k."?.. "O.k., o.k., o.k.".., he said, nodding his head in joyous anticipation...

I broke the balls in the conventional manner, and they scattered over the table, but nothing went in... I had intended to pick out the easiest shots for him, giving him the satisfaction of making a few balls, but there was not an easy shot on the table... There was only one long shot on the 14 ball, and it involved a critical 45 degree angle to make it in the corner pocked... I explained to him that he had to hit the cue ball with his stick and hit the 14 ball with the cue ball, and make the 14 ball in the corner pocket... O.k. o.k. o.k. he said...

He held the cue stick across his waist, parallel to the floor, and he grasped it with a double overhand grip, like he was going to paddle a kayak!!. He approached the table almost backwards, with his left buttock facing the table, and looking over his left shoulder, he twisted his body around and echoed a mighty "Huh", as he took a vicious arcing round-house slash at the cue ball.., missing it completely!!!

Oh Lord, what have I gotten myself into?, I thought to myself.., I will be lucky if he doesn't rip the felt cloth cover of the table... "Huh", he echoed again, like a Karate master breaking bricks, and another vicious arcing slash at the cue ball, and again missing it completely...

Oh Lord, I prayed to myself, this is impossible!!. If he ever does hit the cue ball, it will probably go through the window!!. So I went to the table and explained meticulously how the cue ball was supposed to travel in a straight line to the 14 ball, and the 14 ball was to go into the corner pocket, and I drew an imaginary line in the air with my index finger above the balls, from the cue ball to the 14 ball, and into the corner pocket, and I held my index finger pointing into the corner pocket.. O.k. o.k. o.k., he said, and with a mighty "Huah", he twisted his body into that vicious arching slash at the cue ball!!!

It was a blur!!! The cue ball streaked across the table like it had been shot out of a cannon, straight

---

[1] I have been informed that the "Politically Correct" term for this unfortunate mental condition is called: "Downs Syndrome", and I do apologize to anyone offended by my seeming lack of sensitivity… The term; "Downs Syndrome" was not in use at the time of my very "common" upbringing…

into the 14 ball, which slammed into the corner pocket with such "sledge hammer" force that I'm surprised the table held together!!, missing my index finger by the merest fraction of an inch!!!. Instinctively, I leaped backwards away from the table, grasping my right index finger with my left hand, in a delayed reaction to protect my finger from being smashed to a pulp... The cue ball rolled around and hit one other ball, that also raced to find a pocket!!!

My mouth dropped open like a trap door, and I stood there for a moment in disbelief!!. This had to be a fluke!., no one could possibly make a shot like that on purpose, with the cue stick across his waist, held like a paddle from a kayak, and twisting his body into the cue ball!!! It couldn't be done!!!

O.k., I said, that was a good shot!.. Now try this one, and again I drew the imaginary line in the air, from the cue ball to the object ball, and into the pocket, and this was also not an easy shot, involving a critical angle.., but I didn't stand behind the pocket this time...

"Huh", he said, slashing at the cue ball with that vicious circular round-house arc.., and missing it completely... "Huh" he said again, and again missed the cue ball completely... "Huah" he said the third time, and he connected with the cue ball, and it streaked across the table into the object ball which slammed into the pocket, and the cue ball careened into two other balls that also raced into pockets!!!

I still couldn't believe it!.. It had to be just dumb luck... "O.k." I said, "Now try this one", I said, drawing the imaginary line in the air...

"Huh", "Huh", "Huah", he said, slashing at the cue ball three times in rapid succession *(He was learning!!!)*... Two misses and a hit, sending the cue ball careening across the table into the object ball and into the pocket, with the cue ball racing around the table like a crazy electronic pinball machine which sent balls scattering around in all directions, colliding, bouncing off rails and colliding again, and racing for pockets!!! It was more like bowling!!! The cue ball finally came to rest in the middle of the table and sat there, spinning!!! There were three balls left on the table!.. Three balls that despite the mass collisions on the table, hadn't moved!!! Any balls that moved, had gone into pockets.. I counted the balls... He had made seven balls, with that last shot!!.

Again I stood there with my mouth hanging open, disbelieving what I had just seen... *"Time to go, Jocko"*, someone yelled from across the room... *"Gotta go, gotta go, time to go, Jocko gotta go"*, he said, almost in a panic, and he scurried out the door, with his fellow caretakers, to his job, which was the most important thing in his life!..

I left the tavern, talking to myself, mumbling... What the Hell had just happened here??, *and Why??*. I was totally confused... Usually, when something like this happens *(and this seemed to be one of those "orchestrated" events)*, there is a message in it!!. Something I am supposed to "get".., but I didn't get it, and I still don't get it!!. Had I just had an encounter with an "Idiot Savant"?., one of those rare "imbecilic Geniuses" that exhibit an extraordinary gift of God that somehow compensates for their imbecilic state?., or was it the uncomplicated workings of the sub-conscious mind, uninhibited by any interference from the Conscious mind?., or was it Conscious?., or was it the "Super-Conscious"?., or was it "unconscious"?..., or was it just a fluke?!, an accident of chance?!, just dumb luck.., *three times in a row?!!?..*

I continued my journey on down the road... I had things to do, and people to see, but I would be back!., Oh yes, I would be back.., and I would find that idiot kid and take him on the road!!! With his special talent and me as his promoter we would both get rich!!! *Oh Yes!!...*

....It was three years later when I finally got back there, to that tavern.., and of course, nobody.., not the bartenders, not the clientele, nobody.., had any recollection of ever seeing a Mongoloid, ever!., not in this tavern, not in this city, nowhere!!! Somehow.., I knew this would be the case!...

So what is the moral to this story?.. I don't know!.. I didn't get it then.., and I don't get it now.., and maybe that's the lesson here!.. I had set out on a mission, to solve the "Riddle of the Universe"*.*., to find the ultimate religious philosophy, the "TRUTH", and put it all together into one comprehensive whole.., to see the "Scheme Entire"!!. No less than this was my goal.., and just when I thought I had it pretty much figured out.., the Lord sent me a Mongoloid Idiot to let me know that I didn't know *"Jack* ("Jocko") *Shit"!!!*...

The Lord has a sense of humor!!. The Universe laughs...

* * * * *

So.., in conclusion (again, ha ha).., Understand that "This Book".., is unique, and distinct, in this one very important "Way", in the fact that it is "Confrontational", and not just passively confrontational, but "in your face" confrontational, and it will not lie quietly on the book shelf and disappear quietly into the night... It demands to be answered!!! You have decisions to make!..

* * *

It is my hope that this book has benefited you in some way, and hopefully, in a profound way... But whatever, I would like to hear from you, with your comments and criticisms, and hopefully, you can contribute some corroborating information to add to the footnotes that I was unable to find.., because even though we have come to the end of this (never ending) book, it is only the first edition, and with your help and suggestions.., a second edition will contain a more complete and succinct "updated" version...

You can contact me at my web site: www.ironowl.com , or at my e-mail address: ironowl777@aol.com , or by writing to me c/o the publisher...

...I Thank You... *Iron Owl...*

* * *

~ADDENDUM~

(This post-script is an addendum written after this book had been completed)...

"The Devils Advocate"

D.A. ... (Publisher-Critic);.. "I can't publish this".!. "It's too strong.., too inflammatory.!. It takes away from the rest of the book.!. People will not remember you for your explorations into the "fifth dimension".., they will only remember you for this, they will only remember you for your stand against homosexuality... This subject dominates and overshadows the rest of the book".!.

I.O. ... (Iron Owl);.. "What would you have me do".?.

D.A. ... "Tone it down, or better yet, eliminate it completely"... "If this book is to be a commercial success, you have to stick to the main subject... This book is about "spiritual things", stick to this main topic, and it will be a success"...

I.O. ... "As far as "spiritual things" are concerned, it is just as important to see the way NOT to go... No, it is even much more important to see the way not to go... "An ounce of prevention is worth a lifetime of cure"... I don't think you understand.., this was a revelation, a vision from God, and the whole "Incident in Singapore" happened just exactly as described... I cannot eliminate this chapter or even tone it down.., I can't change one word... I can't add or subtract even one word".!.

D.A. ... "But you use such words as "faggot", and "queer", these words are inflammatory, and you will be condemned for your language"...

I.O. ... "I am a student of words.., I know about the "variegated cloak of words".., I choose my words carefully, as does my "Adversary"... What words would you rather I use.., Pervert?, Deviant?, Sodomite.?. No matter what words I use, they will make a pretence of being offended, but the reality is that they hide behind polite replacement words, to conceal their shame, and they are offended because they are exposed!., and I make a distinction between the "faggots"..; driven by lust, seeking as many casual encounters as possible, indiscriminately, without "Love", motivated only by lust, and the perverted desire to dominate, subjugate, and "initiate by sodomy", as many hapless victims as possible.., ***Especially The Young!.,*** ....*as* **distinct** *from the "homosexual"*, who has been the victim of seduction, rendered "submissive" by having been dominated and "fucked", degraded (*literally*) to the status of "surrogate female", excluded from the company of "Men".., and he spends the rest of his life trying to understand, justify, and adjust to the "loss of dignity" that is his ever-present condition... ***You are being lied to,*** with polite "replacement words"... This butt-fucking perversion is now called; "an alternate life style".!. This sickness of the Soul is now called; "gay".?? These are outright Lies!.. Snap out of it!.. Wake up!.. Your children are in danger... It is these LIES that are "inflammatory" to anyone who values TRUTH...

....And as far as being a commercial success is concerned, I am concerned only with the success of the "reader", if he reads my book and implements the knowledge and information contained therein... The "reader" cannot be a success if he is seduced into perversion... The "Adversary".., is a reality!.. There is an unseen WAR raging in the domain of the Spirit.., and to lose a Soul to the "Dark Side".., is inflammatory.!.

D.A. ... But if the book is not a commercial success, your message will fall by the wayside.., about the "Reality of the Fifth Dimension".., the knowledge of the "Inner Voice".., the Knowledge of the Soul.., the proper and ceremonial use of the Sacraments (the "Herbs of Mysterious Virtue").., the meditation technique of "The Life Breath".., etc., and etc...

I.O. ... I have personally verified these things, and it would be a tragedy if this knowledge fell by the wayside.., if this book were not a commercial success... But you failed to mention the "Knowledge of the

Reality of the Adversary" (Satan), which I have also personally verified.., and I would be "derelict in my duty" if I failed to expose this fact... The "Body of Knowledge" is not complete without this fact!..

....And if this book is a commercial success, it will be a success only for the publisher and the printer.., Not for the Author... Any profits generated from the sale of this book will be returned to the printer to print additional books that will be given "free gratis" to those who might otherwise never get this information... It will be distributed "free gratis" into prisons.., to those prison inmates who have the "time" on their hands to contemplate a "New Philosophy".., and perhaps change their lives...

I will distribute it "free gratis" to the members of Congress who pass the laws in conformity with the Freedoms guaranteed in the Constitution...

I will distribute it "free gratis" to the members of the Supreme Court, who have passed laws that infringe on the "Freedom of Religion" as it applies to the herbal "Sacrament" (Peyote) of the Native American Indians.., and who (in their lack of Wisdom) seek to ban God from the classroom and the government.., and with their blanket assumptions; (the prohibition against getting "High", which has religious as well as recreational significance) that are an affront to the Constitutional doctrine of "Life, Liberty, and the Pursuit of Happiness" (those "God" given "Inalienable Rights").., while perversion runs rampant in the street, Constitutionally protected... Etc., and etc... (It is interesting to note that alcohol and tobacco are excluded from their blanket prohibitions)...

I will put this book in the hands of those good people who selflessly work at the task of rehabilitating drug addicts, but who lack the tools (Ibogaine) and the
"Philosophy"...

I will put this book in the hands of those Religious leaders who are passionate about the "Book learning".., but have never heard the real "Living Word"...

I will put this book in the hands of those "true believers".., who have the courage to cleanse the "Doors of Perception" and to EXPERIENCE for themselves, and to replace their belief with Knowledge...

I will put this book in the hands of the "drug culture", of those who use and abuse drugs, only because they lack maturity and purpose... I will give them the Knowledge, the information and the direction... They will gain maturity and purpose...

I will put this book into High Schools and Universities, to give Knowledge and direction to those who are embarking on the great adventure of life, that the Truth will be sought after, and their lives may be examples of Integrity...

I will put this book into the hands of those Professors, those teachers of "Comparative Religion" and of "Philosophy", that they may see the Universal Truths that are common to all religions and philosophies, as well as the individual truths that are unique to each, and replace their "intellectualism" with first hand experience and synthesis...

....And I will put this book into the hands of those who would barter their Soul for fame and fortune... Those "celebrities".., who achieve instant notoriety by lowering the bar of the non acceptable.., the movie and television producers of pornographic and perverted movies and sit-coms, making common place and acceptable that which is expressly forbidden... The talk show hosts, the movie stars, the rap artists (?), the purveyor of indecency, etc., and etc... ....They won't be able to say: "I didn't know"...

D.A. ... Yeah, well.., that's all well and good, if you can get them to read the book in the first place, which is doubtful, even supposing that the book is a commercial success in the first place, which is also doubtful.., especially if there is negative publicity against it because of the inflammatory nature of your stand against the homosexual lifestyle, which has now been largely accepted as a relatively normal thing in our society...

I.O. ... Yes, well that's their strategy, isn't it?., to make this perversion so common place and acceptable that it will eventually come to be considered "normal"... But no matter how common place it may become, it will never be "normal", and it will always be perversion... The problem is, that it is expanding exponentially, just like any other contagious disease... Each faggot recruits (by seduction) an "x" number (a dozen or a hundred) of our young people, who in turn become faggots, each seducing an "x" number, etc. Each child molester fucks up the life of "x" number of children, who in turn become child molesters, faggots, etc...

The fact that this is a contagious disease of a psychological nature, **with physiological consequences that manifest in physical changes..,** is overlooked!! The limp wrist, the "swishy" movement, the effeminate voice, the demure submissiveness, the double entendres, etc.., this is overlooked.!! *What is overlooked here, is that these characteristics are an emulation of the Evil One himself.!!* I have seen him face to face, and he is a faggot, and these were his characteristics...

D.A... So you have seen the Devil "face to face".., and he is a faggot!.. Do you realize how fanatic that sounds?..

I.O... Yes.., but sometimes, the "Truth" is stranger than fiction, and when I call the Devil a faggot, it is really an inadequate choice of words... Let me rephrase that... "The Devil is a God-damned, limp-wristed, swishy, butt-fucking "flaming" faggot.., bent on the humiliation , degradation, perversion, subversion, destruction, and sodomization of Man-kind.., into the effeminate likeness of himself"!.. This is the "Truth" from the "Absolute" view-point, as seen through the eyes of a "Seer".., and "Yes", I do realize how fanatical that sounds.., but the polite and "politically correct" world at large just doesn't see it, as the agenda of the "Evil One" is politically advanced in Country after Country... I have to speak out.!! I have to testify about what I Know because of what I have Seen... and (improbable as it may seem) the burden of this expose falls to me.., because I have seen.., and I know.., and I cannot keep silent!.. I have to say *something*.!! **SOMEBODY has to say SOMETHING!..**

D.A. ... So you see yourself as the Savior of Man-kind, saving Man-kind from the "plague" of homosexuality?..

I.O. ... "Savior" is a pretty strong word.., but if I can prevent some one from falling into this trap of degradation, and being physically, mentally, psychologically and Spiritually degraded.., and of going through the mental anguish of "true" homophobia (the terrible fear of becoming queer).., and of observing in himself the terrifying physiological changes brought about in himself as a result of an immoral act from which he cannot forgive himself.., then "Yes".., I will do everything in my power to do that... And if it means suffering the "slings and arrows of outrageous Fortune".., which is the fate of a Savior, then;.. "So be it"!!., and as far as a "plague" is concerned.., Yes!., It has the characteristics of a plague.., in the fact that it spreads exponentially, by physical contact with those that are infected..

But from a Spiritual perspective.., I see it more as an invasion by a Demonic force bent of the destruction of "Man-kind".., a battle waged within the interior realm of the fifth dimension, and played out on Earth.., and it is a battle for the Souls of Men... It is a stealthy invasion.., by seducing and degrading their hapless conquests, converting (perverting) their hapless conquests into the enemy camp.., growing in numbers, into a political force.., infiltrating into positions of power and influence... It is a "propaganda" war.., the main weapons of which are **lies** of seduction, utilizing the "variegated cloak of words" and the naiveté of a "polite society" that doesn't want to offend anyone by utilizing their God-given faculty of discrimination.., to the detriment of their own children...

As a "polite" and well meaning society, we have championed the principles of fair play, equality and non-discrimination as it applies to the races of mankind, their ethnic heritage, their religious (or not) inclinations, their economic status, their gender, and etc... These are all noble and well meaning sentiments, and the hallmark of an advanced and civilized society.., but have we (with our good and noble intentions).., painted ourselves into a corner?!! Have we (with our good and noble intentions) played into the hands of the Adversary?!! If we fail to discriminate between that which is good and noble, and that which is perverted and degrading.., then we will have definitely played into the hands of the Adversary.., and we will have failed as an advanced and civilized society.., as other advanced civilization have failed, falling to outside forces because of this internal weakness...

Are we bound (by our good and noble intentions) to give the homosexual community (a "minority" in no other respect than their perverted lifestyle) the same recognition that we give to lesser advantaged minorities?.. "No".., we are not bound to do this.., and we should not do this.., but we have!.. We have done more than this!.. We have given them and their "contagious" perverted lifestyle "special" privileges... With simple polite "replacement words", We have been deceived by the Adversary!!! We are guilty of "aiding and abetting" in a plot to seduce our Youth to the Dark Side of the Force... We have been gullible to the point of criminality!..

"Common Sense" would seem to dictate that a "contagious" disease should be isolated and quarantined, and that a "cure" should be sought after.., but common sense is a very uncommon thing, these days...

D.A... So you see the homosexual community as being engaged in a conscious conspiracy, as knowing agents of the "Adversary".., the "Dark Side" of the Force.?.

I.O... No, they are not "knowing" agents of a "conscious" conspiracy... They are "Dupes"..! They are Victims..! They have been literally, figuratively, psychologically and Spiritually "fucked"!.. Whether by seduction, immorality, curiosity, and even rape, they have been tricked.., fucked and degraded.., into a "surrogate femininity"... The "Temple of God" (the body) has been violated, desecrated, and defiled!.. "Too late".., too late do they realize that there is a price to be paid for their indiscretions... Too late do they realize what it means to be degraded.., to be less than Man.., as they experience the loss of Spiritual "Integrity".., the loss of an integrated personality, as they begin to function, not from the center of their personality, but from the periphery of it, watching themselves (self consciously) as the insidious disease of "Homophobia" overtakes them.., and they watch in terror, as the physiological changes become evident in their personality.., as a torrent of perverted thoughts invade their minds.., as "self doubt" becomes their ever present companion.., and eats away at their Soul...

These are the victims of the Adversary.., and they go through horrendous mental turmoil.., as they are "turned"... Many do not survive this "turning" (especially the young), and they commit suicide, or engage in suicidal behavior, and accomplish an "accidental" suicide... A few.., the "truly strong" personalities.., might (maybe) resist this "turning", but the self doubt will linger for years as they conceal this deep dark secret indiscretion.., and even so, they may eventually be turned... Those that survive the horrendous mental anguish of the "turning" will eventually forget what it feels like to be an "integrated personality", and the "self conscious" mode will come to be their "norm"... This is not mental health.!. This is not what you want for your children...

D.A. ... You seem to know an awful lot about the psychological make-up of the homosexual? It might even be said that "Thou protesteth too much"... It might be said that you yourself are "homophobic"...

I.O. ... Yes, of course they will say that!.. That is their first and standard response to any criticism of their perverted life style... They try to nullify any criticism about their perversions by casting aspersions (slander by insinuation) on anyone who points out the fact that their lifestyle consists of butt-fucking and degrading each other and everyone else that they can seduce into bending over...

But being "phobic" (fearful) of homosexuals.., is a mis-definition of the word.., and a deliberate lie.!. I (personally) see homosexuality as a contagious social disease that debases Mankind, negatively affects the personality and is a "cancer" to the Soul... But I am not "homophobic".!. I (personally) will shun the company of homosexuals (fools rush in).., but I am not "homophobic".!. There are many diseases that destroy the body, but the disease of "homophobia" destroys the Soul.!. I (personally) do not have this disease... I am not "homophobic"... You (and the "Intellectual" community in general) have been mislead (lied to) into believing this mis-conception of what "homophobia" is all about... Only the homosexuals truly know what homophobia is.., the heterosexuals are (blissfully) ignorant of what it is, and are therefore easily deceived.!.

"True" homophobia.., is a true mental disorder, a true "phobia".., characterized by the terrible fear, to the point of panic.., that you are (yourself).., "turning".., becoming a homosexual... With terrible guilt and self loathing, you watch in terror for the "signs".., the effeminate mannerisms that are characteristic of becoming "queer".., and to your great horror, you will find them... These "signs".., in your head and on your hands.., this is *"the mark of the Beast"..,* and it's on **You !!.** ...***This,*** is homophobia.!.

D.A. ... But these people say they didn't choose to become homosexual, they just "are" that way and they can't help it, and maybe they were just born that way!.. What say you?., were they born that way, or was it a choice??.

I.O. ... This is a commonly asked question, and it illustrates just how "Ignorant" the general public really is about this disease of the Soul... It is a stupid question because it presupposes a "this" or "that" answer, when the answer is; "neither"... They were definitely not born that way, nor did they choose to become that way... Each and every one of them entered into homosexuality as a result of seduction by another homosexual... The only thing that makes you a homosexual, is engaging in a homosexual act! The act itself is a crushing defeat of the "Spirit" of each individual, resulting in self doubt, self loathing, and a submissive posture as a result of having "submitted" to an act that causes a "loss of dignity", unbecoming to a "Man"... This "loss of dignity" is not felt at the intellectual level, but at the sub-conscious emotional level, and it eats away at the Soul, as it causes the classic "homophobic" symptoms of self-loathing and effeminate submissiveness... Even those people that consciously chose to become (enter into) the homosexual life style, could not have imagined the psychological consequences of such a decision.., *they were deceived!!.* But having entered into it, they spend the rest of their lives trying to justify it, rationalize it, make excuses for it, and adjust to it.., but the "Soul" (which is a spiritual entity) never does become comfortable in it...

Unfortunately, the "intellectual" acceptance of homosexuality (by non homosexual *liberals*) as "just another life style" ***is an error and a lie*** *that contributes to the seduction process...* Many are deceived by this lie!!.

Now, there are some people that "*seem*" to have a predisposition towards homosexuality, but this is a misconception... There are those people that have been psychologically injured, damaged.., by "parental rejection" (for instance) at an early age, sometimes too early in life to remember, but the psychological scar remains.., or rejected in "love", or even physically defeated ("beaten", with severe injuries) in combat, or even a severe accident could cause a "feeling of defeat", that is similar in nature to the "loss of dignity", which is a severe blow to the "Spirit" (and the Ego) of the individual, and is felt at the sub-conscious emotional level, with symptoms that mimic those of homosexuality... It is unfortunate that the individual that has been psychologically injured by "a crushing defeat, a humiliating indignity, or rejected in love, etc." in his life would question his own feelings of inadequacy with "self doubt", and arrive at the *mistaken conclusion* that he was somehow less than a "Whole" Man, and therefore; homosexual... ***And you can be sure,*** that the "Faggot Seducers" can recognize the psychologically damaged individuals, and exploit the situation... But again I must emphasize the point that the only thing that makes you a homosexual, is "submitting" to a homosexual act as a result of seduction... **This is "Knowledge"!!.** So now you know the consequences of being seduced by these "lies" of seduction... To be fore-warned, is to be fore-armed!!. This Knowledge is a "shield" against the "Adversary"...

D.A. ... How is it that you know so much about this??. Could it be that you have an ax to grind?., that this disease has affected you in some personal way.?.

I.O. ... An ax to grind?., Yes, I have an ax to grind... I have lost two of my best friends to this insidious disease... I value my friends.., and I don't like the Spiritual defeat of losing my best friends to the Adversary... I take this very personally... But contrary to your accusation of "grinding my ax", *Who else* is there (besides myself) that has actually proposed a remedy (Book XV) whereby those people that have fallen victim to this most devastating disease of the soul, might be redeemed??. My purpose is not simply to condemn, but to prevent and redeem!!.

I have documented (in this book) the chain of events that led me to the understanding of this "malady" that effects so much of humanity... ***I have the overview!!.*** I know more about homosexuality than the homosexuals do... I asked of the Father, and I was shown, in a vision.., and I saw.!. With the "third eye" of insight.., I saw.!. With the third eye of insight I walked the streets of Sodom and Gomorra, and I saw more than I wanted to see... I walked the streets of Bangkok, Singapore, and San Francisco, and I saw more than I wanted to see!!... I wish I hadn't seen, because it confers upon me a responsibility to speak out, when I would rather be blissfully ignorant, but I cannot un-see what I have seen, and I cannot un-know what I know.., and I cannot be silent as I watch the advance of the Adversary making conquest after conquest, as the Supreme Court and a naïve and "liberal" society acquiesce to *spiritual defeat,* while political candidates for High Office vie for the pervert vote and make concessions to them...

In defiance of the will of **"We The People",** the Supreme Court of the United States has banned the Ten Commandments from public viewing (the Judge Roy Moore case), and legalized sodomy (the Texas decision)!!. In other words, the Ten Commandments have been relegated to the closet!., and the perverts are out of the closet!!!... This is legalized Anarchy!!... This is the antithesis of the vision of our Founding Fathers!!... This is the destruction of the moral fiber underpinnings of this Nation!!... **This is sabotage!!!...** ***I call for the overthrow of the "Oligarchy" of the Supreme Court!!!...*** In our system of "checks and balances", the Supreme Court is without a check, and is out of balance... The Supreme court has become "packed" and politicized with left wing liberal judges "railroaded" into place by a left wing liberal faction of Congress utilizing the undemocratic avenue of filibuster, and in effect, legislating Supreme Court decisions from the floor of Congress!!!... ***There is a flaw in the system!!...*** The Supreme Court is legislating the "Religion" of "Secular Humanism".., and this is blatantly "Unconstitutional"...

D. A. ... That is a very political statement!!...

I.O. ... Yes, I guess it is.., But the Adversary has taken the political high ground, and if good people do nothing, Evil wins!!...

D.A. ... You're too late.., They have already succeeded politically and socially, being accepted into churches, sit-coms on television, legalization of marriages, even the adoption of children, etc., and etc... You are one man, standing on a lonely shore, fighting a tidal wave!!...

I.O. ... So, the question is.., can one man make a difference??. God, I hope so!., but I am not alone!.. There is a silent majority out there who are observing all this, but they don't have an overview, and their misgivings haven't been formulated into words.., and in fact, they have been deceived by words, because they lack the "big picture" overview...

D.A. ... But what does it matter?., if two homosexuals, or same sex couples want to get married, if they love each other... What is the harm?.. Many newspapers, like the New York Times (for instance), are recognizing these "unions" and listing them in the "Marriages" section...

I.O. ... If there is no God.., then it doesn't matter!.. If there is no God, then nothing matters!.. If there is no God, then there is no right and wrong, there is no such thing as perversion, so in the Godless religion of "secular humanism", all things are permissible... So the question is; can two neurotics, suffering from the same perversion find happiness together, fucking each other in the ass, and of these two "submissives" which one is the more submissive, and "Who's the Daddy"??... At it's best, this is a neurotic, sick, and dependent relationship, and it requires a new category listing in the newspaper.., under "Abominations"...

Excuse me for being so graphic, but if I don't make explicit the true picture here, the common folk will be deceived by the simple substitute "word-lies" (like; "Gay"), and the fact of the matter is; that there really is a God, and it really does matter, and there really is a Devil, and he is the "Prince of Faggots", and there really is a clear cut distinction between right and wrong, good and evil, that which is wholesome and uplifting and that which is unwholesome and degrading.., and the relative viewpoint doesn't apply here, because this distinction is from the ***"Absolute"*** viewpoint.., and you ask: "What is the harm??!".., the harm is incalculable!!, and it really, really matters!!...

D.A. ... But who are you to dictate what a person believes, or thinks, or feels, or does, for that matter!.. It is, after all, a free country...

I.O. ... Yes, but freedom only works if you choose the right, the good, and the true.., and not from the secular viewpoint, but from the "Absolute" viewpoint!.. Marriage is more than just a legal contract!., it is "Holy Matrimony"; a consecrated union of a Man and a Woman for the purpose of procreation.., as opposed to the **"unholy union"** of two sodomites for the purpose of justifying their emotionally neurotic, dominant/submissive, perverted behavior... For two sodomites to actually stand at the alter of God, and ask *HIM* to "bless" the *abomination* of their "unholy union"!.., **is not simply Blasphemy.., it is a "Sacrilege"!!... You ask What is the harm??...** For a Nation.., *This Nation..,* to accept and sanction **"Blasphemy and Sacrilege"** as the common practice and the "Law" of the land??.., *the harm is beyond anything you can imagine.., **the harm is incalculable!!...***

But the legalization of "marriage" for sodomites has far broader implications than the act itself!.. **First** of all, it signals to **"We the People"** of this country *(and to the World!)* that our "Leaders" have taken us irretrievably down the road of "secular humanism" *(the "Religion" of the "Left")*, far from the roots of "righteousness" that has made this country great, and diametrically opposed to the vision of our Founding Fathers...

And **Secondly,** this "legalization" of Sodomite "marriage" opens up *(literally) a* "whole new can of **worms**"!!. The next logical step in the progression of this "unholy union" ("aberration"), is that they will demand to be able to adopt children!!.... *This is every parents worst nightmare!;, that their children might fall into the hands of perverts!!!...* And yet.., several *States* have already acquiesced to this demand!.. Somehow.., the accusation of "discrimination" seems (to some "legislators") to be a greater offense than **the pandering and procuring of children** into the hands of sexual deviants !!!...

"Failure to Discriminate"; is their crime*.., and it is a crime of the first magnitude!!!...* Of such (legislators) as these, it is written: *(Mt 18:6-7) "If anyone causes one of these little ones to sin, it would be better for him to have a large millstone hung around his neck and be drowned in the depths of the sea"...* (and): *"Woe to the man through whom (such things) come"!..*

D.A. ... You seem to be very passionate about this!..

I.O. ... You have no idea!., *No idea!!...* If it were up to me, I would carry out the sentence prescribed above.., but it's not up to me, so I can only wish them an untimely and violent death!!. I want to see a list published of every legislator of every state and government office that has signed their name to any document in favor of this "Deviant" procurement of adopted children, for every voter to see.., and this list should be hung in the post office, next to the "Wanted" posters of other criminals...

D.A. ... But still.., wouldn't adoption into a "loving" home be preferable to the poverty of an orphanage?..

I.O. ... Into a *Good* home, Yes.., but into the house of perversion; *Absolutely Not!!...* The orphanage is a thousand times more preferable.., *Infinitely* more preferable!., than putting a child into the clutches of perversion with no chance of escape, no recourse, showered with affection into an emotional bonding.., a totally compromising situation.., that culminates in seduction.., and the perverts will say; "but it was by his own choice"., and the child will confirm this...!!, but really, what choice did the child have???

And the orphanage isn't poverty!., it is an escape from poverty, with a roof over their head, food in their belly, the camaraderie of their peers, and good people looking after them.., guardians and role models, and they are given an education and guidance... And if the truth be told; the orphanage is often preferable to the upbringing a child receives by parents who are derelicts themselves, or in one parent "broken" homes with little or no parental supervision, etc... Presidents and high achievers have gotten their start in orphanages, and they make good parents to their own children... I support the orphanage system.., I contribute to orphanages...

D.A. ... What orphanages??.

I.O. ... I contribute on a (more or less) regular basis to such organizations as "Father Flanagan's boys and girls home".., "St. Josephs American Indian school".., the "American Indian scholarship program".., the "American Indian relief Council".., "Food for children".., etc...

D.A. ... Your donations seem to lean heavily towards the American Indians...

I.O. ... Yes, they do... The American Indians have been badly mistreated by this Nation, and I have had the "dream-vision"!!... I am "Iron Owl", and I have a spiritual connection with these people... But I also make donations to other organizations, such as "Feed the Children", the "Salvation Army", and local "Missions" engaged in feeding the hungry, and basically to anyone that asks.., as the Spirit moves me!!., and I also contribute to those activist organizations that are engaged in legal battles against the "A.C.L.U." and etc...

Let it be known, that anyone that buys this book is not only advancing his own cause, but is also involved in feeding the hungry, the homeless, the destitute, etc., and is also involved in promoting "Truth" and "Knowledge"... Hopefully, the reader will become enlisted in the Army of God, a citizen soldier, choosing the good, the right, and the true.., opposing the adversary, a ray of light and a beacon of hope in a world that is mired in lies and ignorance.., and doing good, every chance he gets... **This** is the "calling"!..

D.A. ... So you're not making a profit from this book?..

I.O. ... No, not personally.., just my overhead and my daily bread, which isn't much!.. I eat only two meals a day, I own no property, have no assets, except for my 17 year old pick-up truck... My savings account is zilch, and my checking account is in the low four figures... I have always lived in the moment and for the moment, unencumbered by property or possessions, free to travel, and I have never ever made provisions for my old age!!. I don't expect much change in my life style, regardless of cash flow... My profit is in the dissemination of the Truth and the Knowledge that I have personally verified, and in the good that I can do for my fellow man...

D.A. ... So what is your beef against the A.C.L.U. ??.

I.O. ... If the Devil has an Advocate (and he does), it would be an *organization of Lawyers!!*. **The Devils Advocate is the A.C.L.U. !..** The first lie is in their name; (American Civil Liberties Union), because they are the most "Un-American" of organizations, and in fact Communist in their origin, being founded and staffed by Communist ideologues, and their "civil liberties" are for the advancement *(and promotion)* primarily of homosexuality in all it's forms;.: same sex "marriage", the legalization of sodomy, the adoption of children by same sex perverts, promoting homosexuality in the schools as sex education, *even advocating the "North American Man-Boy Love Association"* ("NAMBLA", *a criminal pedophile organization),with the undisguised intention of sodemizing children under the age of eight, with their slogan being:* **"after eight is too late")!.,** while promoting pornography, abortion, and etc... But the "civil liberties" are denied to Christians and the people of God, to the extent of the elimination of any reference to God or the Ten Commandments from every vestige of public property, the school system (where evolution is taught as "truth" and creationism is banned as religion), the National Anthem, etc., and etc.!!

You have to wonder about an organization that battles against the good and God.., and promotes the religion of secular Atheism and perversion!!, and you also have to wonder about those who contribute to their blasphemous cause!!; those successful businesses, companies, wealthy individuals and etc., who contribute millions of dollars to promote this anti-God organization of *Lawyers (Advocates)!!* *It is time to take an activist stance against the organized forces of Evil... I want to see a list published of every contributor and contribution to this organization, and* **I call for a "Boycott" against these companies, businesses, and individuals!!.** *You have to know with whom you are doing business, and* **refuse your business, and refuse the Vote!!,** to anyone who aligns themselves with this anti-God religion of the Left!!... **Get this list!.. Publish and distribute this list!!...** *It is time to take a stand!!... It is time to Stand Up and be counted..*

D.A. ... But you must know that there is one area where you and the A.C.L.U. are in agreement.., and that is in the area of the legalization of drugs...

I.O. ... Appearances to the contrary, there is a great distinction between my position and that of the A.C.L.U... I have gone into great detail about the distinction between "Drugs of Virtue and Drugs of Vice".., making the point that if the drugs of virtue are made legal and available, and the drugs of vice (the highly addictive and anti-social ones) being severely criminalized (to the point of "caning"), then the user will choose to get "high" (elevated in an intelligent and even *Spiritual* sense) rather than to get debased, debouched, drunk, stupid, and addicted.., with "Evil" drugs that carry a high penalty!.. Given the **Choice** between the legal (High and Recreational) and the illegal (down and dirty), the user will choose the legal.., and law enforcement can focus their attention on the ever diminishing (economically starved out of business) illegal drug trade... Drug war over.., **and Won!!**.

This gives the greatest degree of Freedom and Liberty (guaranteed in the Constitution) to the people, and at the same time frees up the Court systems, prisons, and law enforcement, at tremendous savings to the tax payers.., and can actually reverse this expense *(Billions)* with positive tax flow and economic prosperity!!. ***Everybody Wins!!...***

This book will probably not make the "New York Times" "best seller list", because it's purpose is *Not* entertainment!!. The target audience for this book is: "the drug culture"!.. This is destined to be an "Underground Book".., because these are my people!., the people with whom I relate, and with whom I have much in common!!. These are the people of independent mind that have gone beyond the limits of the conventional three-dimensional mentality and discovered the reality of "Altered States"... These people at least have the hope of achieving "Higher" states of mind, if they know the potential.., if they have the information and the "Intention".. Whereas the conventional mind *("locked" within their belief systems and their three dimensional mentality)* have no idea about "Altered States" and cannot fathom them!.. Their only hope in achieving "Higher" mental states, is "after death", *(hopefully)*...

It has been further pointed out that "drugs" (in general) are for the downfall of many and the edification of the few, but with the determining factor being; *"Intention"..*, this trend can be reversed, ***to the edification of the Many!!.*** It is my purpose and the purpose of this book, to reverse this trend!!...

D.A. ... So you are advocating and promoting the use of drugs?..

I.O. ... The drugs are already out there and available, without any promoting by me... If anything, I am promoting the intelligent "use" (as opposed to the unintelligent "abuse") of drugs to those who already have access... But primarily, I am advocating "The Journey Within", into the realm of the Soul.., and the doorway within is closed to the general public, regardless of your religious fervor, if you don't have the specific "intention" of blocking out the external world and entering into the solitude of your own being!!... This is (by definition), an "Altered State", and this is what I am advocating and promoting... It is almost laughable (a Cosmic joke), that the drug user (if he be a good person) has a greater likelihood of having a religious experience than does his Bible-pounding, church-going (holier than thou) counterpart!.. It is a fact of History (*Ancient* History), that that doorway within has been traditionally accessed with the ritualized use of "Herbs of Mysterious Virtue"... It is this "Ritual of the Ancients" that I am promoting...

D.A. ... But how do you "know" that what you are seeing is true??. You are, after all, under the influence of an "hallucinogenic" drug!.. How do you know that it isn't all just an hallucination???.

I.O. ... Well.., finally we arrive at a confrontation.., where the "Variegated Cloak of Words" is intentionally utilized to promote a "propaganda viewpoint… The strategy is this:, by simply *"labeling"* something, we can promote a viewpoint!.. (For instance):., whether we call a military force a "Liberation Army", or an "Occupation".., dictates a viewpoint!.. Whether we call them "Insurgents" or "Patriots", dictates a viewpoint!.. And by ***mis-labeling*** something (such as "Perversion") by calling it "Gay" (when clearly, it is not!), *dictates a mis-leading (propaganda) viewpoint!, that is clearly a **Lie!..*** ...And whether we label a substance as "Mind Expanding", of "Hallucinogenic", dictates a viewpoint... But the fact remains, that (from a higher viewpoint), one is the "Truth", and the other is a "Lie"...

The *single* greatest achievement of the 20th Century was the **Re-Discovery** of the "Herbs of Mysterious Virtue", and their synthesis (LSD, MDA, Mescaline, Psilocybin, etc.).., and the *second* greatest discovery of the 20th Century was made by the Nobel Prize winning father of modern genetics; "Francis Crick".., who was under the "Mind Expanding" influence of LSD when he deduced the double-helix structure of DNA nearly 50 years ago (1962)... Now, *obviously*.., they do not award you the Nobel Prize for having an hallucination!.. The *Lie* is exposed...

This is one of those "stumbling block" *intellectual* questions that can never be resolved intellectually!!., but what should be immediately obvious (even to the intellectual) is the fact that *the ones who absolutely don't know.., are the ones who have never had the experience!!,* and these are the ones who are making the rules, and the Laws, operating from the vacuum of total ignorance and no experience, with the mistaken assumption that they are of superior intellect because of their "drug free" lack of experience, and can therefore dictate to the masses their "denial of experience" and lack of vision!.. But the fact remains, that they are the ones who do not **"know"**, cannot **"know"**, and really; ***don't have a clue!!...***

But understand, that the person who is having the experience, is *Not* operating with diminished capacity (as would be the case with alcoholic drunkenness, or under hypnosis), but quite to the contrary, this is an ***expanded state of awareness*** in which the "critical faculty" is in no way impaired, and is in fact more acute!!., so when the "experiencer" sees something that is not visible to his "third eye blind" counterparts, he immediately judges for himself whether this is a distortion of vision with no significance, or whether he has tapped into an intelligence beyond his own that is relaying a message of significance relative to himself personally.., and as is usually the case, it is a "vision/scenario" with profound implication for his life, which can be dramatically changed from that moment on!!!...

Only the person having the experience is capable of judging whether it be "true" or not, and if his life be changed as a result of that event, then obviously he has had an encounter of a spiritual nature, and there really is a "Higher Power"!.. This is assuming that he has the proper reverence and "intention"... But even so, those recreationally oriented "dabblers" may have profound insights which will have an influence on their life, which they may otherwise never have had, and for which they will be grateful, or, if they are acting irreverently they may have a "bad trip", experiencing visions of a horrifying nature, but this is also an "object lesson" of a spiritual nature coming from that same "Higher Power" but with a chastising effect.., but it is always the "experiencer" who ascertains for himself the "truth" (or not) of the things that he has "seen".., and it is always the "third eye blind"/"flat earth mentality" that will ask the question.., and never "know", never have a clue, make the laws.., and preach condemnation!!...

....And he (the "Flat Earther") will use the word "hallucination" and in effect; explain away everything!!. With this one word he can explain away; Visions, Miracles, Healings, Paranormal Events, the entire Old and New Testaments, etc., and etc.!, but the one thing (among many) that he cannot explain, is "hallucination" itself!!... Just what are the "mechanics" of an hallucination?., from whence does it originate?., where does the "vision" take place?., of what is it's substance?., or the mystery of imagination, or of "mind" itself.., or of even a single thought??. These questions are never asked, because to answer them might give a clue to the understanding of "Creation" itself.., but the "Flat Earther" has no interest in that.., but only in negating that which he has not experienced and of which he cannot conceive...

D.A. ... It still sounds like you are saying: "Drugs are the way"!., and your target audience is the "underground drug sub-culture"..., and if your book appeals only to the underground drug sub-culture, what is it that you are hoping to accomplish?..

I.O. ... "Drugs", in and of themselves, are definitely NOT the Way... The "Way" that I am advocating is known as the Science of "Alchemy", of which only that "God-given" class of natural substances, known historically as the "Herbs of Mysterious Virtue" ("psychedelics") are an integral part... Knowledge of the

"Way" is an integral part.., but the "Spiritual Integrity and Intention" of the Alchemist is the most important part… It is the "Key" ingredient of the Alchemical formula… And it is not that I am targeting the "underground drug sub-culture" specifically, **but only as a starting point!..** It is they, who will be the first (*"the last will be first"*) to realize the significance of the relationship between Alchemy and Metaphysics.., and the ability to enhance their level of consciousness in a Metaphysical and God oriented direction…

It seems that I am continually being asked this same question, and I am continually repeating myself, but it just seems to go over everybody's heads as to what my mission is, here?.. Simply stated, it is this: (again): (*quote*)**:** "I am trying to give the "Underground sub-culture" the direction and the zeal of the "Evangelicals" (<-used as an adjective).., and I am trying to introduce to the "Evangelicals" (the "Men of the cloth" of whatever *God oriented* religion) to the "Chemical Key" (or; *the Alchemical Key*) of the Underground sub-culture!!! It is a paradox!!. The one has the Key, but not the direction.., and the other has the direction, but not the Key!!! I am trying to bring about a **"Convergence"** of these two cultures!.. Can you imagine the results of such a convergence!?. Can you??. *The World would be Transformed!!.*, and that is **Really** what I am trying to do, here… I am trying to transform the World.., one person at a time.., beginning with YOU.., and not just for You yourself alone.., but exponentially, to others through you"… (*end quote*)!..

D.A. … Well, those are noble, if unrealistic, sentiments.., and just how do you see all of this unfolding…

I.O. … This book will strike a resonant chord, first, with the underground drug sub-culture, and also with those individuals of a decidedly "metaphysical bent" to their personalities.., who are by inclination "true seekers", and open to those Universal Truths, wherever they may be found… These two categories of individuals are closely aligned already, and their ranks "overlap" into each other, with a further significant "overlap" (probably 50 %) into our Colleges and Universities, which are made up of the truly bright and open-minded students who are searching for knowledge, for their own identity, and philosophy of life… This book will become a "must read" on campus, and will be discussed in classes on Comparative Religion, Philosophy, and the Sciences.., and it will "overlap" into the intellectual community and on into the "Intelligencia".., and "overlap" again into Organized Religion, where it will be hotly debated.., and because of the controversial nature of the subject matter, it will peak the interest of the News Media.., and controversies will rage.., and it will be debated by Law Enforcement and by those who make the Laws.., and it will go into the Monasteries, from which will emerge a "New Class" of Spiritual Emissaries.., and they will be "both" the future religious and political Leaders of a much more "Enlightened" age.., and it will Transform Religion from mere dogmatic belief systems into systems of Enlightenment!., and this is only the beginning!., a "New" beginning.., and It is a phenomenon that will engulf and transform the World!..

In the final analysis, I am just another "Evangelist" on a Sacred Mission… There are 10,000 monasteries out there, (an arbitrary number) filled with "Hundreds of Thousands" of worthy Souls, as well as the "lay" individual seekers.., seeking to know themselves and their Creator.., seeking the "Ultimate Truth"… This "Ultimate Truth", is out there.., and it is attainable.., but there is only one "gifted" Soul in an "x" number of thousands that has the capacity and the tenacity to make the "breakthrough" into the esoteric realms, and have that "first person" direct experience whereby he can say; "*I Know,* because I have heard HIS voice, and I have seen"!.. Such a person as this will pick up the "Torch of Truth" and become an evangelist (adjective) and a beacon to his fellow man.., and his effect will be multiplied exponentially…

But these few (very few) "gifted" Souls do not need this book!.. They have tapped into *"That"* Higher Source, and picked up the Torch!.. But there is a shortage of gifted Souls and scarce few torchbearers to make World Transformation a reality!.. It is that vast majority of Souls.., worthy Souls.., diligently seeking their Creator.., seeking to know themselves, and to know the "Truth", but they are locked into a belief system that precludes any possibility of them having "*That*" first hand direct experience of "Communion" and the Knowledge of their potential… This is my "real" target audience!.. It is to them, that I present this manuscript, which contains the "Secret of Secrets" (meditation, combined with the catalyst of "Herbs of Mysterious Virtue"), which is (in essence) the Knowledge of the "Alchemical Formula", whereby they can transcend the limitations of their belief systems and acquire the Knowledge of the Devine… It is to this Vast Army of the "common man" that I give the Knowledge of the True Meaning of the "Philosophers Stone" which is the "Communion" with the "Inner Voice", which is the Voice of the Lord, and the "Source" of vision and revelation… It is to this Vast Army of the "common man" that I give the insights into the mystery of the Soul, and of that "Fabled Third eye" (of insight and intuition), and of the enigma of Zen (the "objective" and "subjective" states), and of the ever-present helpmate of the subconscious mind, (that can be programmed, reprogrammed, and "trained")… It is that Vast Army of the Common Man, that I would enlist into the Army of Righteousness, armed with Vision, Insight, and Knowledge, that having seen and traveled "The Way", will pick up the Torch, and be a bearer of the Light, enlisting his fellow man, ***exponentially*** elevating the consciousness of Mankind, and changing the World… End result:

World Enlightenment, and World Peace…

Etc., and etc…

(The debate goes on).., (the debate never ends)…

* * *   *   * * *

www.ingramcontent.com/pod-product-compliance
Lightning Source LLC
Chambersburg PA
CBHW080532170426
43195CB00016B/2536